DICTIONARY
of CANINE TERMS

Frank Jackson

The Crowood Press

First published in 1995 by
The Crowood Press Ltd
Ramsbury, Marlborough
Wiltshire SN8 2HR

British Library Cataloguing in Publication Data

A catalogue record for this book is available from the British Library.

ISBN 1 85223 795 3

Line-drawings by Annette Findlay

Typeset by Phoenix Typesetting, Ilkley, West Yorkshire
Printed by Redwood Books, Trowbridge, Wiltshire.

Contents

Preface

It amuses me to talk to animals in a sort of jargon I have invented for them; and it seems
to me that it amuses them to be talked to, and that they respond to the tone of the conver-
sation, though its intellectual content may to some extent escape them.

George Bernard Shaw, *Killing for Sport*

With the possible exception of the ubiquitous flea, dogs have had a longer and closer association with man than has any other creature. The association has given rise to a range of richly
varied activities, none of which could reasonably expect to be generally regarded as respectable
until it had produced a jargon which conveyed precise meanings to insiders and obscured that
meaning from outsiders, as is the purpose of all jargon. 'Every jargon,' says Philip Howard in
The State of the Language, 'in a greater or lesser proportion, is a mixture of hard technical terms
that are useful codes for the cognoscenti, and gobbledygook that is used to sound grand and
blind the eyes of the ignorant.'

The use of jargon in an effort to impress is nothing new. A telling illustration of the desire
to create a complex jargon around dogs and the activities in which they are involved is to be
found in an anonymous Middle English poem, which lists no less than seventy-eight names by
which hunters might have referred to a hare. Even this list does not contain all the names used
by sportsmen to refer to hares. Similar lists could be made of the names which refer to other
hunted animals, in whole or in part. Sportsmen appear to have a very strongly developed liking
for jargon. Pepys noted the tendency when he recorded in his diary on 22 November 1663 that
'most of their discourse was about hunting, in a dialect I understand very little'. There are even
specific terms used to refer to the excrement of hunted animals. Oliver Goldsmith, in his elo-
quent *History of the Natural World* [151c], touches on the subject.

Those who hunt this animal [the stag] have their peculiar terms for the different objects of
their pursuit. The professors in every art take a pleasure in thus employing a language
known only to themselves, and thus accumulate words which to the ignorant have the
appearance of knowledge. To this manner, the stag is called the first year, a calf, or hind
calf; the second year, a knobbler; the third, a brock; the fourth, staggard; the fifth, a stag;
the sixth, a hart. The female is called a hind; the first year she is a calf; the second, a hearse;
the third, a hind. This animal is said to harbour in the place where he resides. When he
cries he is said to bell; the print of his hoof is called the slot; his tail is called the single;
his excrement the fewmet; his horns are called his head; when simple, the first year, they
are called broches; the third year, spears; the fourth year, that part which bears the antlers
is called the beam, and the little impressions upon its surface glitters; that which rise from
the crust of the beam are called pearls.

As a consequence of the varied activities which dogs support and in which they are involved,
several vocabularies of jargon now exist, each catering for the needs of some particular canine
interest. Some make use of words that are already used in a less specialized way, and of these
there are some that are used to convey a completely different meaning to that which the word
usually carries. Conversely, words coined for a specific purpose are sometimes pressed into more
general service. Philip Howard's *Weasel Words* [179] provides an apposite example:

The new sciences are prolific at pupping litters of new words, and soon replacing them
with others.

Philip Howard extends a line of authors who have made good use of terms which have their origins in canine activities. The line began with Chaucer and continued through Shakespeare. The bibliography to this dictionary gives only a brief glimpse of the way in which it has spread through literature. A great many authors have made use of their knowledge of dogs or of activities in which dogs are involved in order to illustrate particular points. From Chaucer, through Shakespeare to the Brontës, many authors and poets have provided evidence of their interest in and knowledge of dogs. Such interest and knowledge is generally less apparent among more recent writers. Perhaps dogs are no longer such an integral part of the everyday life of authors as was once the case.

Thus our enjoyment and certainly our detailed understanding of literature, particularly literature written before the turn of the century, may be marred if we fail to appreciate the meaning of canine terms, some of which have now fallen into obsolescence. Shakespeare, whose familiarity with coursing, poaching, hunting and bear-baiting is apparent throughout his work, makes frequent use of such terms: *alow, babbling, baited, bandog, brach, canker, counter, cry, cub-drawn, curtail, doubt, drawer, embossed, fallow, feeder, flews, gaze, longtail, mouth, music, peat, recheat, shough, tarre, trammel, trash, uncape, unkennel, warrener, water-rug, whelp,* and more are all used by him both to carry their precise canine meaning and to support and embellish a more general meaning.

Some words and uses, having served their purpose, are now largely forgotten. Many have never achieved more than local currency, others have travelled far afield. New words continue to appear in response to new needs, out of a desire for novelty or to enable their users to appear more knowledgeable. In all these respects the world of dogs (nowadays usually and conveniently, if to the chagrin of pedant lexicographers, referred to as *dogdom*), is no different from any other of man's activities.

Dogdom may, however, be different in that a need to communicate a precise meaning may occur between people who share a general interest in dogs but whose specialist interests differ. The vocabularies used by breeders, behaviourists, coursers, dog-fighters, exhibitors, geneticists, hunters, racing enthusiasts, shooters, veterinary surgeons, and so on, may each differ from the rest. Over the years all manner of canine interests have developed vocabularies which are precise, extensive and, in some ways, exclusive, often deliberately so. Yet each group of people may, from time to time, need to communicate with the others.

The problem is exacerbated by the existence of many words which, though they are in use in most areas of canine interest, mean something different to each. *Breaking* has a very different meaning to a show person, to one engaged in shooting, to one with a particular interest in racing and to one interested in dog-fighting. Exhibitors and judges must choose between two meanings for *put down*; veterinary surgeons are accustomed to one which differs from both, and hunting people might add yet another. *Entry* conveys one meaning when applied to a show dog, quite another when applied to a working hound or terrier, and yet another when it refers to a hunted stag. All these meanings to some extent differ from those which the words usually carry in day-to-day life.

Confusion may also arise when a word carries different meanings on each side of the Atlantic. When a bitch is *bred* in the United States, she has been mated; in the UK she has not been bred (from) until she has given birth. Still more confusing, the word may also be used to enquire into parentage. Thus a simple query may, depending on which side of the Atlantic the question is asked, give rise to at least three answers, only one of which would convey the desired information.

Vets and geneticists have need of a highly specialized and precise vocabulary, and the emergent profession of canine psychology is already making a bid for respectability by producing its own jargon. Their jargons may be unintelligible to anyone who has not enjoyed a course of special training. And it is not difficult to understand why, as a result, breeders prefer to apply the simple but graphic, precise and unequivocal term *wobblers* to puppies affected with what veterinary surgeons variously refer to as cervical spondylolithesis, cervical spondylopathy and cervical vertebral instability, and the term *rubber jaw* to renal secondary osteodystrophia fibrosa. They can also be excused for referring to keratoconjunctivitis sicca as *dry eye*, a term which has the merit of being simple, memorable, descriptive and accurate. On the other hand there is little to explain why vets and breeders should not choose between *flat puppy syndrome* and *swimmers*. The professions and their clients need to communicate with one another and may have their ability to do so reduced by unnecessary reliance on specialized jargon with a surfeit of synonyms.

Similar complications arise out of the classification of breeds whose origins are outside the English-speaking world and of efforts, often irrational, to anglicize their original names: if it is not necessary for the Dachshund to be anglicized into Badgerdog, why should the Wachtelhund be turned into a German Spaniel?

Robert Surtees' Cockney Master of Foxhounds, John Jorrocks, claimed to have 'measured a yard and a half of downright hard printing on the word 'oss.' Were he to carry out the same exercise in respect of the word *dawg* he would need a lengthy tape-measure rather than a yard-stick.

The fertile proliferation of canine terms and the way in which they have provided general enrichment for the English language helps to underline the important part which dogs have played and continue to play in our society. Not only do they themselves provide us with interest, enjoyment, companionship, competition, security, service, sport, a reason for pride, a means to improved health, even a culinary delicacy, and much more, but also through them our ability to express ourselves is enhanced. No one can examine the way in which dogs and dog activities have influenced our language without realizing just how important dogs have been and are to the society in which we live.

I am not a trained lexicographer, that will doubtless be apparent, perhaps glaringly so, especially to those with professional expertise. I am merely someone with an enthusiasm for dogs and for words. This book is a product of those enthusiasms and of an effort to meet a perceived need. It began as no more than an idea that a more comprehensive glossary than those which existed might be useful, and it has grown into a task which has occupied some years, has required that new skills be learned, and has taken me down unfamiliar but fascinating by-ways. Had I realized how long and difficult the journey would be I might have hesitated prior to embarking upon it, but to have avoided it would have denied me a great deal of enjoyment. John Marston's *A Scholar and his Dog* [248] revealed that the difficulties I have experienced and doubts I still harbour are not new:

I staggered, knew not which was firmer part;
But thought, quoted, read, observed, and pried,
Stuffed noting-books: and still my spaniel slept.
At length he waked, and yawned; and by yon sky
For aught I know, he knew as much as I!

Many sources have been consulted during the making of this dictionary. The bibliography lists over 500 from which information or quotations have been taken; at least as many others have also been referred to, and I am grateful to all the authors, whether named or not. Making this dictionary has been a task which could not have been accomplished without the generous help of family and friends who share my enthusiasm. By thanking any I risk failing to thank some, but it would be churlish not to take that risk. I am particularly indebted to unidentified experts at the Oxford University Press who offered constructive and valuable criticism of early, fumbling efforts. Lori Athey Coulsen, Fiona Gibson, Terry Giles, Peggy Grayson, Mona Hedman, Peter Larkin, Desmond Morris, Teresa Slowik, Eric Smethurst, Ian Southwick, Bertha and Brin Sullivan, Hellmuth Wachtel, John Williams, have all helped in various valuable ways. I am indebted to my editor at Crowood, Elizabeth Mallard-Shaw, who has guided, goaded or curbed according to what was appropriate at the time, and whose attention to detail has been above and beyond the call of duty. Steve Parkinson and my daughter, Elspeth, have sought, with only partial success, to convince me that a micro-chip is an obedient amanuensis. I am, as ever, particularly indebted to my wife, Jean, who has restrained her impatience when I might have been doing something of more immediate use and has helped unravel many Gordian knots of taxonomy, derivation and meaning. Without her support I doubt if I would ever have embarked on the task and am certain that I would never have got it to its present state. I hope that our joint efforts have produced a book which will be a useful tool as well as a pleasant and, perhaps, occasionally even an amusing pasture in which to browse.

This is not the first book to examine canine terminology; indeed the very first book devoted exclusively to dogs to be published in English, Abraham Fleming's *Of Englishe Dogges* [139] provides *A Supplement or Addition containing a demonstration of Dogs names how they had their origins included*. Many glossaries, which define some of the terms used in some aspects of dogdom, exist, both as independent publications and as part of larger works. None, as far as I am aware, has had the conceit to attempt to encompass all aspects of interest in dogs. Undoubtedly this book defines more words than any previous canine glossary or dictionary, and to that small extent it may break new ground. For that reason, if for no other, this work is unlikely to be without omissions, or to be such that no one could argue with some of the definitions. It therefore seems appropriate that the sentence with which James Halliwell opened the introduction to his *Dictionary of Archaic Words* [150] should close this.

> The difficulties proverbially attending the first essay in a literary design of any magnitude constitute one of the very few apologies the public are generally willing to concede an author for the imperfect execution of his undertaking.

If what follows requires such an indulgence I hope it will be forthcoming.

Frank Jackson, 1994

GUIDE TO THE USE OF THE DICTIONARY

Structure and Arrangement of Entries

Words defined, whether main or sub-entries, are given in bold type.

All headwords, whether single words or phrases, abbreviations, acronyms or contractions, are listed in strict alphabetical order. So, for example, entries that consist of more than one word are treated as though they were a single word: *stake out* is listed after *staked*, and not after *stake*. Proper nouns are entered independently of other words with the same spelling.

Sub-entries are indented after the primary headword, so *puppy clip* and *puppy farm* are indented after *puppy*.

In cases where more than one definition of a word exists, the individual definitions are numbered, e.g.

> **layback**   1. the receding profile of brachycephalic breeds.   2. angle which the scapula makes with the upper arm.

Cross-referenced words appear in small capitals. In cases where more than one definition of such a cross-referenced word exists, the number of the appropriate definition is given in brackets after it. Where there is no bracketed number following a cross-reference, the first, or only, definition of the word is implied.

Where a word is illustrated, [*illus.*] follows the definition. If the word is illustrated, but not in its own right, the word under which the illustration can be found is indicated within the square brackets, so:

> **tarsus**   hock-joint. [*illus.* SKELETON]

Classification

While the taxonomy of wild canids is subject to rapid, and sometimes apparently pointless, change, the taxonomy of domestic breeds is even less systematic and more confusing. In this work, popular names of wild canids are cross-referenced to a primary entry, which is the name used by Corbet and Hill in their *World List of Mammalian Species* [96]. In the absence of any similar authoritative guide to the taxonomy of domestic breeds, all breeds are listed under the name that is in customary rather than official use, thus, *Cocker Spaniel* is preferred to *Spaniel (Cocker)*, and *Miniature Bull Terrier* to *Bull Terrier (Miniature)*. Colloquial names for breeds are included and cross-referenced to the primary entry, so,

> **Finkie**   (colloq.) FINNISH SPITZ.

The primary entry for breeds recognized by an English-speaking kennel club registry appear under the anglicized name. Unofficial anglicized names, the name/s by which a breed is known in its country of origin, the name by which it is recognized by the Federation Cynologique Internationale (FCI), and diminutive, colloquial, or obsolete variations of the name, are cross-referenced to this primary entry. Where different anglicized names for one breed are used by different kennel club registries, the main description of the breed is under the name by which it is recognized by the Kennel Club.

Where a name is in official use, and so recognized by one or more kennel clubs, this is indicated in square brackets immediately after the entry.

As a general rule, and in keeping with apparent convention, accents have been omitted from non-English names that are in common or official use in English, such as *Bichon Frise*. They are retained in names that are not in common or official use, such as *Jugoslovenski Posavski Gonič*.

Confusion of a somewhat lower order exists with regard to veterinary and anatomical terms.

Once more, variations are cross-referenced to a primary entry which, in this case, relies on the authority of Blood and Studdert's *Baillière's Comprehensive Veterinary Dictionary* [54].

This work departs from usual dictionary conventions in that where a definitive statement in support of a definition has not been found, definitions from earlier authorities are sometimes included in order to illuminate the possible nuances of meaning or interpretation. In such cases, the source is always indicated.

Notes on the Bibliography

Many sources have been consulted during the making of this dictionary. Some are ancient texts, many of which are accessible only in part and only via contemporary anthologies. As a consequence, it has not always been possible to provide full bibliographical information on every original text.

However, every effort has been made to provide the reader with sufficient information to facilitate further study or investigation. To this end, the bibliography to this work is arranged in order of original author, followed by the original title of the text and the date of first publication in square brackets. (The original publisher of the work is not given, except in cases where the original edition of a work has been consulted.) The anthology or other work from which the text has been sourced is given afterwards, following a colon, and is arranged thus: [from] author/editor; title of anthology; publisher, place and date of the edition consulted. Where no author/editor of the secondary text is given, the author of the original text is implied. So, the poem *Rex* by D.H. Lawrence, which was first published in *The Dial*, a book of his poems, in 1921, is treated thus: Lawrence, D.H. *Rex*, in *The Dial*, Laurence Pollinger (London, 1921).

Each author has been allocated a number, which appears in square brackets following any quote given in the main part of the dictionary. A bibliographical reference number may follow the definition of a word, thus indicating the source from which the definition has been gleaned even though no direct quote has been taken.

Abbreviations Used

abbr.	abbreviation	Ger.	German
AKC	American Kennel Club	Gk	Greek
Ang.	Anglicization	Ital.	Italian
Am.	American	Jap.	Japanese
Aus.	Austrian	joc.	jocular
Aust.	Australian	KC	Kennel Club [UK]
Brit.	British	L.	Latin
Can.	Canadian	lit.	literary
cent.	century	NZ	New Zealand
colloq.	colloquial	obs.	obsolete
contrac.	contraction	OE	Old English
der.	derivative; derived from	orig.	originally
derog.	derogatory	pl.	plural
dim.	diminutive of	pref.	prefix
Eng.	English	prep.	preposition
esp.	especially	Scot.	Scottish
euph.	euphemism	sing.	singular
FCI	Federation Cynologique Internationale	Span.	Spanish
		syn.	synonymous with
fig.	figurative	var.	variant; variation of
Fr.	French		

A

A gene symbol for solid colour agouti (dominant black). [395]

a gene symbol for agouti (recessive black). [395]

a^s gene symbol for saddle pattern agouti. [395]

a^t gene symbol for bicolour agouti. [395]

a^w gene symbol for grey agouti. [395]

a^y gene symbol for golden agouti. [395]

AAD abbr. ADVANCED AGILITY DOG.

abandoned patient veterinary patient whose owner cannot be found or has deserted the animal.

abasia inability to walk.

abatement reduction in pain level.

abaxial at a distance from the axis of the body or limb.

abbay 1. (obs.) bay or bark. [159] 2. (obs.) HOLD AT BAY. [159]

abdomen that part of the body, between diaphragm and pelvis, which contains the viscera.

Aberdeen dim. ABERDEEN TERRIER.

> Welcomed by barks from an elderly Aberdeen. [309]

Aberdeen Terrier (obs.) SCOTTISH TERRIER.

> A name which is erroneously applied to the hard-haired Scottish terrier. . . . The Granite City, however, possesses no claim to a monopoly of the breed, which is distributed all over Scotland. [320]

Aberdeenshire Terrier variant of ABERDEEN TERRIER.

> This breed of dog is considered by many competent judges to be merely a sub-variety of the prick-eared Skye. It is, to our mind, clear that the Aberdeenshire Terrier and the Scottish Terrier are identical animals, possessed of but very slight structural differences. [320a]

abiotrophy (PNA) inherited condition causing premature loss of vitality in tissues, organs and nervous system. (Mode of inheritance, recessive.)

ablactation process of weaning.

ablastin serum antibodies which prevent or reduce the reproduction of protozoa.

ablate remove, esp. by surgical means.

ablatiotinae detachment of the retina.

ablepharia congenital condition which produces deformed or absent eyelids.

ablepsia blindness.

abort cause or undergo abortion.

abortifacient a substance used to induce abortion.

abortion premature birth, natural or induced, of a foetus too young to survive.

abortus dead foetus, the product of abortion.

abrachia congenital absence of the forelimbs.

abrachiocephalia congenital absence of the forelimbs and head.

abrasion shallow wound caused by friction.

Abyssinian Sand Dog unrecognized and probably extinct hairless breed from western Africa. Glover [150] suggests that the breed may have been the progenitor of all domestic hairless breeds; this is very unlikely. Probably the same as the AFRICAN SAND DOG.

Abyssinian Sand Terrier ABYSSINIAN SAND DOG.

Abyssinian Wild Dog CANIS SIMENSIS.

Abyssinian Wolf CANIS SIMENSIS.

acalasia inherited defect producing a pocket that obstructs the oesophagus and prevents food from reaching the stomach; successful treatment is problematical. (Mode of inheritance, uncertain.)

acanthosis nigricans skin disease characterized by hair loss, and thickening, darkening and hardening of the skin.

acariasis skin irritation caused by mite (ACARID).

acaricide any substance that destroys ticks and mites.

acarid tick or mite of order Acadia.

acarus TYROGLYPHUS.

account for know the fate of a quarry, usually either to kill or run quarry to EARTH.

accretion 1. growth of a part additional to that which is usually regarded as normal. 2. the growing together of parts that are normally separate, such as webbed toes in breeds in which they are abnormal.

acetabulum hip-socket; cup-like depression at the junction of the ilium, ischium and pubis in the pelvic girdle, which receives the head of the femur to form the hip-joint. [*illus.* SKELETON]

achalasia constriction.

Achilles tendon hamstring; large tendon joining the rear of the femur with the os calcis.

Achondroplastic limbs.

achondroplasia inherited condition in which bone growth failure leads to dwarfism. (Mode of inheritance, recessive.) [*illus.*]

achromotrichia loss of hair pigment resulting from nutritional deficiency, freezing or injury.

acid milk milk with an abnormally low pH value, causing sickness and death in unweaned puppies.

acid units group of taste receptors in the mouth stimulated by acid substances.

Acores CÃO DE FILA DE SAN MIGUEL.

acquill (obs.) FIND. [159]

acquired immunity FIELD IMMUNITY.

acquired inheritance discredited belief that acquired characteristics, as distinct from the ability to acquire them, can be inherited.

acquired megacolon enlargement of the colon caused by chronic constipation.

acral lick dermatitis localized skin disorder caused by excessive licking.

acral lick granuloma ACRAL LICK DERMATITIS.

acral mutilation syndrome HEREDITARY SENSORY NEUROPATHY.

acrodermatitis inflammation of the extremities of the body.

acrodermatitis enteropathic opathica ENTEROPATHIC ACRODERMATITIS.

acromegaly abnormal enlargement of the bones (especially in the feet and head) produced by an excess of pituitary hormones, and causing unusual bulkiness in a dog. The condition is regarded as normal in the MASTIFF breeds.

acromegalic of, or relating to, ACROMEGALY.

acromicia abnormal smallness of the bones, especially of the feet and head, resulting from a development defect.

acropruritic granuloma ACRAL LICK GRANULOMA.

ACTH abbr. ADRENOCORTICOTROPHIC HORMONE.

actinomycosis bacterial infection, most often resulting from a deep wound.

action the way in which a dog moves.

acute sharp or severe; intense.

acute dermatitis severe, nonspecific skin ailment with several probable causes.

acute gastric dilation rapid abdominal distension caused by fluid or gas.

acute gastritis severe inflammation of the stomach caused by eating contaminated or putrid food.

acute haemorrhagic pancreatitis severe and progressive abdominal pain, bleeding, shock, diarrhoea and vomiting, leading to diabetes and not uncommonly to death.

acute hepatitis severe inflammation of the liver, of viral origin.

acute metritis severe inflammation of the uterus, often produced by retained foetal membranes.

acute moist dermatitis severe nonspecific skin ailment characterized by watery discharge. There are several probable causes.

acute pancreatic necrosis ACUTE HAEMORRHAGIC PANCREATITIS.

acute pancreatitis intense abdominal pain followed by rapid death; most common in obese or sick dogs, and often following a large, fatty meal.

acute renal failure sudden onset of kidney failure.

AD abbr. AGILITY DOG.

adaptation measure of ability to become suitable for a particular purpose.

Adare Irish BEAGLE pack formed in 1952 to hunt a COUNTRY in County Limerick.

Addison's disease ADRENAL HYPOADRENOCORTICISM.

additive traits cumulative effect of multiple genes influencing certain polygenically inherited characteristics.

adduction pull, of a muscle, towards the central axis of the body.

adenocarcinoma cancer of the glands.

adenoma benign glandular tumour.

ADH ANTIDIURETIC HORMONE.

adhesion the joining of two tissues, most often in the abdominal cavity and as a consequence of surgery or injury.

admonitor WARNER. [139]

adrenal associated with the kidneys.

adrenal glands ductless glands above kidneys, from which adrenalin is secreted.

adrenal hyperadrenocorticism Cushing's syndrome: condition caused by excessive secretion of adrenocorticotrophic hormone resulting in excessive thirst and urination.

adrenal hypoadrenocorticism Addison's disease: deficiency of cortisol and aldosterone, resulting in loss of appetite, vomiting, diarrhoea and weight loss.

adrenocorticotrophic hormone hormone secreted by the pituitary gland cortex.

Advanced Agility Dog American second title, awarded in AGILITY competitions.

Aelianus, Claudius Aelian of Praeneste, Roman author of *On the Characteristics of Animals*, which is largely a collection of myths and tall stories.

Affenpinscher [AKC, FCI, KC] breed of old, German origin. Its comical expression and TERRIER-like liveliness has earned it the names Monkey Terrier and Monkey Dog. At one time the breed may also have had a larger size, the extinct Deutscher Rauhhaariger Pinscher, but this is by no means certain.

The proportionately small head is round and DOMED, covered with shaggy hair; the MUZZLE short, the eyes round and very dark, the ears small and high set. The neck is short and clean, the forelimbs straight, the back short, the ribs WELL SPRUNG and the outline square. Hindquarters are not excessively ANGULATED. The coat is fairly long, harsh and wiry, usually black but black and tan, red or grey are also acceptable. Height 24–28cm (9½–11in); weight 3–4kg (6½–9lb).

Affie dim. (colloq.) AFGHAN HOUND.

affix name exclusive to the use of a particular KENNEL(4); exclusivity is protected by the KENNEL CLUB, with whom the affix must be registered.

afftype KENNEL TYPE.

Afghan   dim. AFGHAN HOUND.
Afghan Greyhound   (obs.) AFGHAN HOUND. [123]
Afghan Hound   [AKC, KC] striking and justifiably popular SIGHTHOUND with origins in northern India where it exists in a number of variant forms. It is principally used to COURSE deer, foxes and wolves. The luxuriant coat is a distinctive feature whose glamour should not be allowed to obscure the breed's genuine effectiveness as a sighthound.

The skull is long with a prominent OCCIPUT, the jaws punishing; triangular eyes are preferably dark; silky-coated ears are set low; the neck is long. The forequarters are long and sloping, with straight, well-boned forelimbs; the level back is well-muscled, with a broad, rather short LOIN and prominent hip-bones; hindquarters are powerful with long PASTERNS. The tail is set and carried low with a characteristic TERMINAL RING. The coat is long and of fine texture and may be of any colour. Height 63–74cm (24½–29in).

> The tazis, now universally called Afghan Hounds, were referred to by early historians as greyhounds, Persian Greyhounds, Afghan Greyhounds and the Afghan Hound – also known as the Kurran Valley (Hound), Kabuli (Hound) and the Barukzy Hound after the ruling families in those districts. [265]

Afghan leukodystrophy   HEREDITARY MYELOPATHY.
Afghanischer Windhund   [FCI] AFGHAN HOUND.
afield   in the FIELD.
> Afield he is a swift-moving hunter. [6, IRISH SETTER]

Afonwy   FOXHOUND pack, founded in 1907 and recognized in 1962, hunting a steep and rugged COUNTRY with some woodland in the Radnorshire part of Powys.
African Bull-Dog   (obs.) RHODESIAN RIDGEBACK.
> In the year 1874 Mr Theodore Bassett . . . astonished the Bull-dog world by importing an 'African' Bull-dog . . . and though superior to the latter in every Bull-dog characteristic, was very soon after his first appearance relegated . . . to the foreign dog class. [320a]

African Bush Dog   name under which the BASENJI was first shown in Britain, at the 1937 CRUFTS show.
African Hairless Dog   AFRICAN SAND DOG.
African Hunting Dog   *LYCAON PICTUS.*
African Lion Dog   RHODESIAN RIDGEBACK.
African Lion Hound   RHODESIAN RIDGEBACK.
African Sand Dog   hairless breed, now probably extinct:
> The skin should be bluish in colour, resembling in this respect the colour of an elephant's hide, although it is frequently mottled, which, however, should not be the case. These Terriers are apple-headed, with large bat ears, and vary in size from about 10lb up to 20lb or 25lb. They are very symmetrical. . . . Care should be taken by an intending purchaser to satisfy himself that he is buying a genuine Hairless Dog, and not a Terrier without hair. In the dogs that have been exhibited as African Sand-dogs this crest appears to be shorter and much harsher than in the Chinese dogs. [123]

African Wild Dog   *LYCAON PICTUS.*
> His modern name is the deab. He is of considerable size, with a round muzzle, large head, small erect ears, and a long and hairy tail, spotted with black, white, and yellow, and having a fierce wolfish aspect. [406]

afterbirth   placenta and attached membranes expelled by the bitch after a puppy has been born and through which the puppy received nourishment during gestation.
agalactia   absence of milk in a nursing bitch.
agasaeus   AGASSES.
> There is, besides, an excellent kind of scenting dog, though small, yet worthy of estimation. They are fed by the fierce nation of painted Britons, who call them agasaei. In size they resemble worthless greedy house-dogs that gape under tables. They are crooked, lean, coarse-haired, and heavy-eyed, but armed with powerful claws and deadly teeth. The agasaeus is of good nose and most excellent in following scent. [276]

Agasses   small, rough-coated, TERRIER-like dogs noted for their ferocity, said by John Whitaker to have inhabited Britain prior to the Roman conquest. (der. L. *agaso,* an awkward servant.)
> Train'd by the tribes on Britain's wildest shore,
> Thence they their title of Agasses bore. [384]

Agassoei   ancient type of dog, AGASSES; on the evidence of a misunderstood translation from the *Venatiae Novantiqua,* DRURY suggests that they are BEAGLES:
> They are very slender and small, and being much like the hare, hunt them out in the burrows where they dwell . . . They are bred so that one hand may encompass the whole of their body. [123]

age   dogs are independent of their parents by the time they are five weeks old, fully grown and sexually mature at six months or soon after, and might live for fifteen or more years, though the average life span, and the point at which full maturity is reached, varies considerably from breed to breed. Thus, the popular method of comparing a dog's age with our own by multiplying its age by seven is very unreliable.
agene process   former method of bleaching flour for human consumption which produced hysteria in dogs fed on products of the flour.
Agility Dog   first title awarded in American agility trials.
agonistic behaviour   aggressive attitude.
agouti   coat pattern produced by individual hairs banded in different colours – the normal hair coloration of most mammals, the basic coat colour phenotype.
  agouti series   alleles that influence SABLE and GRIZZLE coat coloration.
Agrippa, Cornelius   (1486–1535) author of the three-volume *Occult Philosophy*; said to have sold his soul to the devil and henceforth to have been constantly accompanied by a malignant familiar in the form of a black HOUND.

Aguara wild dog.
> ... bearing a strong resemblance to a smooth or a
> half-rough Collie with prick ears. [123]

Ahascragh Setter strain of rare, and now extinct,
wholly red IRISH SETTERS kept by Ross Mahon of
Galway from about 1838. [221]

Ahk-Tas-Eet KIRGHIZ GREYHOUND.

AI abbr. ARTIFICIAL INSEMINATION.

Aichi old Japanese SPITZ-type breed, probably
extinct.

Aidi [FCI] Moroccan pastoral GUARD, which may
also be used as a hunter in support of SIGHTHOUNDS.
The breed's lean body is well-muscled. The coat is
coarse and resistant to extremes of weather; white is
the preferred colour but black, tawny, tan or PIED are
permitted. Height 53–64cm (20¾–25in); weight 25kg
(55lb). The breed is also known as the Chien de
l'Atlas, the Atlas Sheep Dog and the Dorar Dog.

AIHA abbr. AUTO-IMMUNE HAEMOLYTIC ANAEMIA.

Aiken (US) AMERICAN FOXHOUND pack formed in
1914 to hunt 1,600 acres of woodland and 18 miles
of DRAGLINES in South Carolina.

Ainou HOKKAIDO.

Ainu HOKKAIDO.

Ainu Dog HOKKAIDO.

Ainu Ken HOKKAIDO.

Airedale 1. dim. AIREDALE TERRIER. 2. 15in
smooth-coated BEAGLE pack founded in 1891 to hunt
a COUNTRY in Yorkshire.

Airedale Terrier [AKC, FCI, KC] largest of the
TERRIERS and for that reason sometimes referred to
by its admirers as the 'King of Terriers'. The breed
has its origins in the Aire Valley and surrounding districts of Yorkshire as a CROSS between OTTERHOUNDS
and the native rough-coated BLACK-AND-TAN
TERRIERS. Airedales, being far too big to GO TO
GROUND, were originally used to seek out and
despatch surface game and vermin.

The skull is long, not too broad and flat, with no
apparent STOP and a strong MUZZLE; the small eyes
are dark; ears are V-shaped, folded slightly above the
level of the skull. The neck is clean and muscular, the
forequarters long and WELL LAID. The body is short,
the TOPLINE level and the short LOINS muscular; ribs
are WELL SPRUNG. Hindquarters are powerful with
long thighs, well-bent STIFLES and low HOCKS. Feet
are small, round and compact. The tail is carried
GAILY and is traditionally DOCKED. The coat, always
black and tan, is hard, dense and wiry. Height
56–61cm (22–24in).

> Personally, I have been astonished at the number of
> Airedale Terriers I have seen in the south of England
> and in the suburbs of the metropolis; after the Fox
> Terrier, who comes first in numbers, he certainly
> appears to divide favouritism with the Irish Terrier.
> This is, perhaps, because he is a sensible sort of dog,
> and too big for the dog stealer to pick up and hide
> away in the pockets of his greatcoat. [221]

aitchbone hip-bone.

aitches upper points of the hip-bones.

Whole body should be strong and level with no sign
of waistiness from aitches to hips. [203, former
SUSSEX SPANIEL]

Akbash ANATOLIAN SHEPHERD DOG.

Akbash Dog ANATOLIAN SHEPHERD DOG.

AKC abbr. AMERICAN KENNEL CLUB.

Akita [AKC, FCI] JAPANESE AKITA.

Akita Inu JAPANESE AKITA.

Alain (var. spelling) ALAUNT.

Alan (var. spelling) ALAUNT.
> Skins of animals slain in the chase were stretched on
> the ground and upon a heap of these lay three alans,
> as they were called, i.e. wolf greyhounds of the
> largest size. [314e]

Aland (var. spelling) ALAUNT. [159]

Alangu hunting dog and DOMESTIC GUARD from the
Thanjavor and central Tamil Nadu districts of India,
the short, DOUBLE COAT may be any shade of red or
fawn with black MASK, or solid black. Height about
68cm (26¾in).

alanine transminase liver enzyme.

Alano SPANISH MASTIFF.

Alapaha Blue Blood Bulldog unrecognized breed
developed on the plantations of Georgia, principally
by the Lane family. The appearance is closer to that
of a MASTIFF than to a modern BULLDOG. The head
and body are broad and strong, the coat smooth and
either patched or MARBLED with black, blue, buff or
brown on a white GROUND. Height 61cm (24in),
weight 34–47kg (75–103½lb).

Alaria arisaemoides parasitic fluke of the bronchial
and intestinal tracts.

alariasis *ALARIA ARISAEMOIDES* infestation.

alarm-dog dog that gives warning by barking.

Alaskan Malamute [AKC, FCI, KC] a superlative
SLED-DOG with origins among the Mahelmut Indians
of north-western America. The breed's appearance
is strongly supportive of the theory that there is a
recent relationship with the wolf; others argue that
dogs crossed the Bering Straits with early settlers and
so share ancestry with the SIBERIAN HUSKY.

The breed's strong and compact build is indicative of its legendary stamina and power: the head is
strongly wolf-like, the tail long and thick and less
curled than in most SPITZ breeds. The DOUBLE COAT
has an outer layer of grey or black on a white
GROUND. Height 58–71cm (22¾–28in); weight
38–56kg (84–123lb).

alatrate (obs.) growl or bark. [159]
> Let Cerberus, the dog of hell, alatrate what he liste
> to the contrary. [342]

Alaunt large, extinct MASTIFF, said to have been
introduced into Britain by the Alani, a Caucasian
tribe which invaded Western Europe in the 4th century.
> Aboute his char ther wenten whyte Alaunts,
> Twenty and mo, as grete as any steer,
> To hunten at the leoun or the deer,
> And folwed him, with mosel faste ybounde,
> Colers of gold, and torets fyled round. [86]

Alaunte (var. spelling) ALAUNT.

Alauntz (var. spelling) ALAUNT.
Also comonly alauntz ben stordy of here owyn nature, and have not so good witte as many other houndes have. [125]

alay introduce fresh dogs to the hunt. [159]
With greyhounds, according to my ladyes bidding, I made the alay to the deere. [283]

Albanian Dog extinct type of MASTIFF.
Can be traced to a very remote period of history. Some of the old authors speak of it as the dog which in times of ancient mythology Diana presented to Procris. [406]
Said to stand about 27 or 28 inches high, with a long pointed muzzle, powerful body, strong and muscular limbs, and a long bushy tail, carried like that of the Newfoundland dog. His hair is very fine and close, being of a silky texture, and a fawn colour, variously clouded with brown. He is used for hunting the wild boar and wolf. [338]

Albanian Wolfdog possible ancestor of the GERMAN SHEPHERD DOG.
It is interesting to consider other dogs of similar type which existed long before the present Alsation was bred. By similar type it must be understood dogs typically wolf. [185]

albinism rare hereditary condition caused by a deficiency of colour pigment in the skin, coat, nails and eyes, producing white coat, pink skin and eyes. (Mode of inheritance, any one of several mutant alleles.)

albino individual suffering from ALBINISM.

Albrighton FOXHOUND pack, founded in 1830, hunting a grass and arable COUNTRY in Staffordshire.

Albrighton Woodland FOXHOUND pack, founded as a division of the ALBRIGHTON in 1908, hunting a hill and woodland COUNTRY in Shropshire, Staffordshire and Worcestershire.

albuminurea presence in the urine of the protein albumin.

Alco South American wild dog with pendulous ears, a short tail and HOG BACK. [338]
The native dog of Central and South America. Fernandez describes two breeds, one of which is called the Alco or Michuacaneus, and by the natives Ytzcuinte Porzotli. [380]

Aldenham HARRIER pack established in 1878 to hunt a COUNTRY in Hertfordshire and Buckinghamshire.

Aldershot Command Beagles 15in BEAGLE pack formed in 1882 by the officers of the Aldershot Command to hunt a COUNTRY in Hampshire.

aldosterone mineralocorticoid hormone secretion of the adrenal gland, which controls the kidney's reabsorption of salt and water.

Aldrovandus, Ulisse Aldrovandi (1522–1605) Italian naturalist who wrote extensively about dogs.

Alentejo Herder RAFEIRO DE ALENTEJO.

Alicant Dog ANDALUSIAN DOG. [406]

all-age HOUNDs of any age.

All-Alaska Sweepstakes oldest of the premier SLED–DOG races.

Allan archetypal MASTIFF.

Kind of big, strong, thicke headed, short-snouted dog, the brood whereof came first out of Albania. [98]

Allan de Boucherie formerly a MASTIFF-like butcher's dog. [98]

Allan Gentil formerly a type of GREYHOUND.
Is like a Grayhound in all properties and parts, his thick and short head excepted. [98]

Allan Vautre formerly a type of MASTIFF.
A great and ugly cur of that kind, having a big head, hanging lips, and slouching ears, kept only to bait the Beare and wild Boare. [98]

all-breed show show at which any breed can be exhibited, provided an appropriate class is available.

all-meat syndrome metabolic stress produced by a diet deficient in fibre.

all on every HOUND in the pack present or accounted for.

all-rounder judge with experience of several breeds but not of owning the one in question.

allantois inner membrane that surrounds alleles.

allele each of those genes that influence the same characteristics, but in different ways.

allelic pertaining to ALLELE.
allelic genes genes that occupy the same locus in a pair of chromosomes.
allelic series sequence of mutations to a normal gene.

allelomorph (obs.) ALLELE.

allergen substance that produces allergy.

allergic relating to ALLERGY.
allergic bronchitis bronchial condition produced by an allergic response.
allergic contact dermatitis skin condition caused by an allergic response.
allergic reaction the symptoms of an allergy.

allergy sensitivity to substances that are usually harmless.

allometry relationship, in terms of size, between a part of the body and the body as a whole.

allopatric theory of speciation the theory which holds that species arise within specific areas and become unable to interbreed in geographically separate regions.

almond eyes tissue surrounding the eye forming an opening shaped like a shelled almond nut. [311]

alopecia 1. inherited condition producing total absence of hair, regarded as normal in hairless breeds but occasionally found in some others. (Mode of inheritance, recessive). 2. chronic loss of hair. 3. (obs.) MANGE, esp. in foxes.

Alopex galopus CANIS LAGOPUS.

Alopex lagopus CANIS LAGOPUS.

alow (obs.) HALLOO. [319h]

Alpendog name proposed in 1828 for what is now called the ST BERNARD.

Alpenländische Dachsbracke [FCI] a short-legged HOUND principally used for finding game or for trailing wounded game. The head is broad and strong, the ears pendulous but not over large; the body is strongly made and the legs, though short, are straight. Height 33–43cm (13–17in); weight 15–18kg (33–39½lb).

alpha dog natural pack leader; a dog with strong characteristics.

alphachloralose chloralose: anaesthetic.

Alpine Basset Hound ALPENLÄNDISCHE DACHS-BRACKE.

Alpine Dachsbracke ALPENLÄNDISCHE DACHS-BRACKE.

Alpine Dog ALPINE MASTIFF.

Alpine Mastiff 1. extinct ancestor of several continental MASTIFF breeds. 2. (obs.) ST BERNARD.
> The Alpine Mastiff is the St Bernard dog imported into England about 1825. [185]
> Hark! Alpine mastiffs at the Convent gate
> Summon the brethren from their slumbering state.
> Attended by the pious monks they tread
> The frozen paths, if but to find the dead.
> So pass the lives of Bernard's dogs, till years
> Behold them buried 'midst their masters' tears. [403]

Alpine Spaniel former name for the ST BERNARD.
> A breed almost peculiar to the Alps. [406]
> The name Alpine Spaniel has been given to the St Bernard dog and also to a variety of Spaniel said to have existed, at one time, in the area of the Alps, and said by some to be the originator of the present day Clumber Spaniel. [185]

Alriche ancient name popularly bestowed upon a dog. [159]

Alsatian GERMAN SHEPHERD DOG (ALSATIAN).
> He was my first Alsatian, and the memory of his cheerfulness and courage and fidelity is so vivid that I am not likely soon to have another. The truth of the saying that Alsatians are one-man or one-owner dogs was proved by him every minute of the day and night. [237]

Alsatian Hound ALSATIAN. [185]

Alsatian Wolf-dog former Anglicized name for what is now the GERMAN SHEPHERD DOG.
> That certain strains of Alsatians do contain wolf blood can be taken for granted, if only on the authority of such a great expert on the breed as Monsieur Otto Rahm, of Wohlen, Switzerland, who has told us that the great-granddam of the well-known 'Hector von Wohlen' was the product of a mating between a dog wolf and an Alsatian bitch. [108]

Altamira site of cave paintings dating from about 12,000 BC which depict hunting scenes in which dogs are involved.

Altcar Lancashire COURSING ground on which competition for the WATERLOO CUP and associated trophies are held.

Altcar Club society formed in 1825 now responsible for organizing the WATERLOO TROPHY competitions.

alter (Am. euph.) castrate.

alternative inheritance MENDELIAN INHERITANCE.

altruism biological reference to the phenomenon in which one entity or individual promotes the welfare of another at its own expense.

Alunk hairless TOY breed used principally as a

DOMESTIC GUARD, and which originates from the south-eastern Indian region of Tamil Nadu (especially Thanjavur). The breed closely resembles other hairless breeds found in other countries.

amaurosis (obs.) blindness without apparent cause. [406]

amaurotic idiocy inherited disease which causes excitability and inability to accept training. (Mode of inheritance, recessive.)

amble fast rolling walk having an irregular four-beat tempo, intermediate between a true walk and pacing.
> Powerful, driving, free and easy [movement]; ambling permitted but not desirable. [203, BOUVIER DES FLANDRES]
> The gait has a typical roll when ambling or walking. [203, OLD ENGLISH SHEEPDOG]

ambler a dog that habitually AMBLES.

amblyopia poor eyesight caused by organic or refractive defects.

ambulance dog (obs.) dog used to search for wounded soldiers, esp. during the Second World War.

American Black and Tan Coonhound BLACK AND TAN COONHOUND.

American Blue Gascon Hound new world version of the BLEU DE GASCOGNE, which it resembles both in appearance and in the quality and size of its voice. Used principally for hunting racoon. The smooth white coat is usually heavily TICKED or ROANED with any colour. Height 81cm (31¾in); weight 50kg (110lb).

American-bred [AKC] show class confined to dogs born in America.

American Bulldog result of efforts to preserve and improve upon BULLDOGS imported into America during the early days of the 19th century. The breed remains capable of all the uses to which Bulldogs were put in earlier days but is now legitimately used as a DOMESTIC GUARD and in weight-pulling competitions.

The head is large and powerful, the ears small and high set, when not CROPPED; the neck is powerful, and the shoulders are very broad and strongly muscled. The coat is smooth, with red being favoured among the BRINDLES but white, red, fawn or PARTI-COLOURED dogs being acceptable. Height 45–64cm (17¾–25in); weight 30–48kg (66–105½lb).

American Bull Terrier former name for the BOSTON TERRIER.

American Cocker Spaniel [FCI, KC] Known in the USA as the Cocker Spaniel, the breed significantly differs from the British COCKER SPANIEL in head, which is less strong, in coat, which is more profuse, and in size, being smaller.

The head is strongly MODELLED with distinct MEDIAN LINE, deep STOP and distinct chiselling around the eyes; the ears are long, lobular and luxuriously coated. The neck is long, rises strongly and with a slight arch from deep, clean-cut shoulders. The body is square and deep, the COUPLINGS (1) short. The abundant coat is any solid colour, including black, with tan markings limited to certain defined areas and not exceeding 10 per cent of the whole. Height 33.75–38.75cm (13¼–15¼in).

American dog tick DERMACENTOR VARIABILIS.

American Duck Retriever NOVA SCOTIA DUCK TROLLING RETRIEVER.

American Eskimo ESKIMO DOG.

American Foxhound [AKC, FCI] imports of old world FOXHOUNDS during the 17th century formed the basis of the American breed. Very similar in appearance to the foxhound, particularly the more lightly boned hounds of the northern packs.

The head is long and DOMED, the square MUZZLE long and the ears, which are often rounded, rather long. The shoulders are CLEAN and WELL-LAID BACK, the LOIN is slightly arched and the TUCK-UP apparent. The STERN is carried GAILY and is slightly FEATHERED. The Breed Standard does not specify coat colour but TRICOLOUR is the most common. Height 53–64cm (20¾–25in).

American Hairless Terrier recent mutant of the unrecognized RAT TERRIER. Unlike other hairless breeds the characteristic is said to be autosomal recessive rather than semi-lethal. A well-muscled, deep-chested dog standing on strong legs. The ears are customarily erect. The skin may be pink, black, grey, red or tan. Height 23–36cm (9–14in); weight 7–14kg (15½–30¾lb).

American Hound AMERICAN FOXHOUND.

> The supreme merit of pure-bred American hounds
> is their fitness for their business. [329]

American Kennel Club organization governing American breeding and showing, established in 1884.

American Mastiff unrecognized breed which seeks to reproduce the old English BANDOG, apparently often with much the same purpose in mind. Weight about 58kg (127½lb).

American Pit Bull AMERICAN PIT BULL TERRIER.

American Pit Bull Terrier breed developed during the later years of the 19th century, principally in the southern states of America, for dog fighting. It quickly evolved into a superlative fighting dog which has almost totally replaced older breeds for this illicit but still widely practised 'sport'. In spite of contrary claims the Pit Bull is carefully bred with PEDIGREES that are at least as pure as those of officially recognized breeds.

A formidably strong dog with a broad and strongly muscled head; the DROP EARS are CROPPED both for fighting and for reasons of fashion. The head is carried on a powerful neck set in a deep, WELL-SPRUNG chest. The back is rather long, with thick LOINS and powerful quarters, whence comes the dog's attacking drive. All colours, with or without markings, are acceptable. Height 46–56cm (18–22in); weight 16–36kg (35–79lb).

American Staffordshire Terrier [AKC] American version of the British STAFFORDSHIRE BULL TERRIER from which it differs principally in its greater size, weight and substance. The breed is powerfully made, with a strong head furnished with well-developed cheek muscles. The coat is short and glossy and may be of any colour or combination of colours. Height 43–48cm (17–18¾in); weight 18–23kg (39½–50½lb).

American trypanosomiasis CHAGAS' DISEASE.

American Water Spaniel [AKC, FCI] biddable and enthusiastic worker, the breed was developed from various imported WATER SPANIELS and carries the coat and colour which many of these breeds share.

The skull is broad, the jaws strong, the body rather long and set on powerful legs. The coat, solid liver or chocolate, is curled and resistant to extremes of weather. Height 36–46cm (14–18in); weight 11–20kg (24–44lb).

Amertoy American miniature version of the SMOOTH FOX TERRIER, created by crosses with the CHIHUAHUA and ENGLISH TOY TERRIER. The breed should resemble a small Fox Terrier except that the ears should be pricked and the colour preferably TRI-COLOUR, although white (with or without tan) or black are also acceptable. Height 25cm (9¾in); weight 1.5–3.5kg (3¼–7¾lb).

Amnicola limosa porosa species of snail which acts as the intermediate host of the liver fluke METORCHIS CONJUNCTUS.

amnion outer membrane surrounding a foetus.

amniotic of, or relating to, AMNION.

 amniotic fluid fluid contained in the amniotic sac.

 amniotic sac membrane containing the foetus.

amoebic dysentery acute form of dysentery caused by *ENTAMOEBA HISTOLYTICA*, which appears spontaneously but rarely in dogs, more frequently in man.

amoxycillin penicillin analogue used in the treatment of gastric illness.

amphetamines drug used in the treatment of some behavioural disorders and as a performance stimulus in some sporting dogs.

Amphicyon extinct ancestor of both dogs and bears.

Ampleforth College Beagles BEAGLE pack formed in 1915 by members of the College to hunt a COUNTRY in Yorkshire.

anaemia blood condition resulting in a reduced ability to carry oxygen.

anal appertaining to the anus.

 anal abscess acute infection most often found in the ANAL SACS.

 anal canal that part of the intestinal tract between the rectum and the anus.

 anal furunculosis PERIANAL FISTULA.

 anal gland the gland contained in each of the two ANAL SACS, and which has ducts leading to the anus. The sacs store apocrine and sebaceous cell secretions. [*illus.*]

 anal sac sac within the anal cavity, and con-

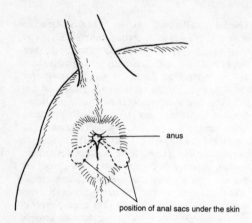

anus

position of anal sacs under the skin

Anal glands.

taining the anal gland which secretes a substance associated with territorial marking. [*illus.*]

analgesia insensitivity to pain.

analgesic substance producing ANALGESIA.

anaphase the phase or phases of cell division during which the paired chromosomes separate.

anaphrodisia loss of sexual urge.

anaphylactic of, or relating to, ANAPHYLAXIS.

anaphylaxis extreme allergic reaction to antigens.

anascara subcutaneous oedema: swollen tissue beneath the skin. [406]

Anatolian Karabash Dog ANATOLIAN SHEPHERD DOG.

Anatolian Shepherd Dog [FCI, KC] PASTORAL GUARD with origins in Turkey. The breed is tall, powerful, shows both speed and stamina, and is adapted for work in extreme temperature. The skull is broad with a slight MEDIAN FURROW, the STOP slight, the lips pendulous. The eyes are rather light and small; the ears are of medium size and carried flat to the skull. The body is deep and powerfully muscled, the hindquarters noticeably lighter than the forequarters. The coat is short and dense with a thick undercoat and may be of any, preferably whole, colour with black MASK and ears. Height 71–81cm (28–31¾in); weight 41–64kg (90–141lb).

anchor hound (Am.) BEAGLE that marks a CHECK when hunting rabbit.

Ancient Danish Gundog GAMMEL DANSK HONSE-HUND.

Ancylostoma brasiliense tropical species of HOOK-WORM which affects dogs and cats. Its larvae can infect humans.

Ancylostoma caninum common canine HOOKWORM.

Ancylostoma ceylanicum Asiatic HOOKWORM species.

Ancylostomatidae HOOKWORM.

ancylostomiasis HOOKWORM infestation.

Andalusian Dog extinct breed described by YOUATT.

Has the short muzzle of the pug with the long hair of the spaniel. [406]

androgen male sex hormone.

aneurism swelling caused by internal bleeding; a blood-blister.

angiohaemophilia Von Willebrand's disease: inherited disease caused by clotting factor VIII and its antigen. (Mode of inheritance, uncertain.)

angiosarcoma HAEMANGIOSARCOMA.

Angiostrongylus vasorum LUNGWORM found in dogs and foxes.

angle-closure glaucoma primary glaucoma which inhibits filtration as a consequence of the iris reducing the angle.

Anglesea Setter formerly a localized type of SETTER. Did not spring, as might be supposed, from the island of that name, but from Beaudesert, the residence of the Marquis of Anglesea. . . . They were in character a light, active, very narrow breed of dog, with no chest, though deep in ribs. They were rather leggy, and possessed the habit of standing with their forelegs and feet close together. This breed of dog was constitutionally delicate, but as long as they stayed, showed great pace in the field. In colour they were mostly black-white-and-tan, though not so smooth and flat as a modern Setter. [320a]

Anglesey former HARRIER pack dating from 1744.

Anglo-Français Blanc et Noir black and white variety of the Anglo-French HOUNDS.

Anglo-Français Blanc et Orange rich tan and white variety of the Anglo-French HOUNDS.

Anglo-Français de Moyenne Venerie [FCI] product of crosses between HARRIERS imported from Britain and native French HOUNDS. Height 51cm (20in); weight 22.5–25kg (49½–55lb).

Anglo-Français de Petite Venerie [FCI] product of crosses between BEAGLES imported from Britain and native French HOUNDS. Height 40–45cm (15¾–17¾in); weight 16–20kg (35–44lb).

Anglo-Français Grand [FCI] crosses between FOX-HOUNDS imported from Britain and native French HOUNDS produced the Blanc et Orange, one of a small group of Anglo-French pack hound breeds and principally used for larger game. The breed is less strongly built than the foxhound but in other respects the two are very similar, even to the occasional appearance of rough-coated individuals. Two colour varieties, the BLANC ET ORANGE and the TRICOLORE, are recognized. Height 61–69cm (24–27in); weight 30–32kg (66–70½lb).

Anglo-Français Tricolore TRICOLOUR variety of the three Anglo-French HOUNDS.

Anglo-French Black and White ANGLO-FRANÇAIS BLANC ET NOIR.

Anglo-French Tricolour ANGLO-FRANÇAIS TRI-COLORE.

Anglo-French White and Orange ANGLO-FRANÇAIS BLANC ET ORANGE.

Anglo-Spanish Greyhound GALGO ESPAÑOL crossed with a GREYHOUND CROSS-BRED HOUND.

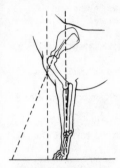

Angulated shoulder.

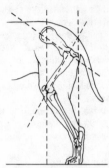

Angulated stifle.

angulated apparent or pronounced ANGULATION. [*illus.*] *See also* WELL ANGULATED.

angulation geometrical relationship between various adjacent long bones, especially of the limbs and quarters.

Hindquarters, very muscular, stifles well angulated. [203, SAMOYED]

anisogamy system of sexual reproduction involving union between large female and small male gametes.

ANKC abbr. AUSTRALIAN NATIONAL KENNEL COUNCIL.

ankle HOCK.

ankle bone proximal tarsus bone; TALUS. [*illus.* SKELETON]

ankle joint hock-joint: TARSUS. [*illus.* SKELETON]

ankylosis abnormal adhesion of bones forming a joint; stiffening of the joint.

Annual Specials competitions which run throughout a year at AKC shows.

anoestrus part of the OESTROUS CYCLE, the interval between seasons. [*illus.* OESTRUS]

anoplura sub-order of PHTHIRAPTERA.

anorchia total absence of testicles.

anorchidism inherited condition in which there is absence of testes. (Mode of inheritance, uncertain.)

anorexia absence of appetite for food, usually resulting in progressive weight loss.

anoxia oxygen deficiency in tissues.

Antarctic Wolf *CANIS LUPUS ANTARTICUS.*

antenatal before birth.

anterior terminal hemimelia inherited condition resulting in the absence of forelimb bones. (Mode of inheritance, probably recessive.)

anthelmintic vermifuge: drug used to destroy parasitic worms.

anti (pref.) opposing; against.

antibiotic substance derived from micro-organisms which inhibits the growth or life of other micro-organisms.

antibodies protein molecules that counter the effect of invasive antigens.

anticoagulant that which prevents the clotting of blood.

antidiuretic hormone hormone which inhibits the production of urine.

antidote that which counteracts the effects of a poison.

antifungal substance that inhibits the growth of fungus.

antigen foreign protein molecule which threatens the body, provoking the production of antibodies.

antihistamine drug that counters the effects of histamine.

anti-inflammatory drug drug that reduces inflammation.

antimicrobial that which acts against microbial infections.

antipyretic drug that relieves or prevents fever.

antiseptic substance, usually chemically based, which destroys micro-organisms on living tissue without destroying the tissue itself.

antiserum substance rich in antibodies, usually derived from an immune source, which counteracts the effects of micro-organisms or their toxins.

antisialic agent which reduces the flow of saliva.

antisocial behaviour exhibiting a tendency to attack.

antitoxin antiserum that acts specifically against toxins.

Anubis Egyptian deity, sacred to the setting sun, whose task was to take the souls of the dead before his father Osiris, the judge. Anubis is represented with a human body and the head of a jackal.

anury inherited absence of caudal vertebrae, regarded as normal in some breeds. (Mode of inheritance, recessive.)

anury lacking a tail.

anus external opening to the rectum.

anvil INCUS.

Anwn's Dogs CWN ANWN.

Any Solid Colour Other than Black show classification used principally for AMERICAN COCKER SPANIELS.

Any Variety class open to all breeds for which the show caters.

Any Variety Not Separately Classified show class for breeds that are not provided with their own breed class at that particular show.

aorta large artery which carries blood from the heart.

aortic pertaining to the AORTA.

aortic aneurysm dilation of the aortic walls caused by the larvae of *SPIROCERA LUPI.*

aortic subvalvular stenosis inherited condition in which there is constriction of the aorta leading to congestive heart failure. (Mode of inheritance, threshold.)

aoutat *TROMBICULA AUTUMNALE.*

apex highest point, esp. of the head; the OCCIPUT.

aphacia inherited absence of eye-lens. (Mode of inheritance, probably recessive.)

aphis dog trained dog used by the US Department of Agriculture's Animal and Plant Health Inspections Service (APHIS) to search tourists and other visitors for food items that it is illegal to import into the USA.

aphrodisia condition, usually of male dogs, in which the sexual act is simulated on inappropriate objects.

apish having monkey-like features or expression.

apnoea temporary cessation of breathing.

apocrine cystic dilation common skin condition associated with hyperplasia.

apocrine tumour cystic and papillary tumour.

Appenzell Cattle Dog APPENZELLER SENNENHUND.

Appenzell Mountain Dog APPENZELLER SENNEN-HUND.

Appenzeller APPENZELLER SENNENHUND.

Appenzeller Sennenhund multi-purpose Swiss breed used as a GUARD, as a draught dog and as a cattle-herder. Strongly built with a rather long body, a deep and powerful chest, and well-boned, well-muscled limbs. The head is broad, and the MUZZLE strong; the ears drop forward. The short and smooth coat is dense and always in the classical TRICOLOUR pattern. Height 48–60cm (18¾–23½in); weight 23–25kg (50½–55lb).

Apple dome.

apple dome APPLE HEAD. [*illus.*]
A well-rounded 'apple dome' skull, with or without molera. [6, CHIHUAHUA]

apple head smoothly DOMED upper skull, desirable in some breeds but not in others.
Head large, round, not apple-headed, with no indentation of skull. [203, PUG]

applications preparations for external treatment.

appointment 1. time and place of a MEET. 2. invitation to judge accepted and terms agreed.

apricot (of coat) rich, orange-coloured.

apron profuse coat on the neck and chest.
Where Lassie's coat was rich tawny gold, this dog's coat had ugly patches of black; and where Lassie's apron was a billowing stretch of snow-white, this dog had puddles of off-colour blue-merle mixture. [211]

Apso dim. LHASA APSO.

Aquarius WATER DRAWER. [139]

Aquaticus sevinquisitor WATER SPANIEL. [139]

aqueous humour watery fluid produced by the ciliary PROCESS of the eye to nourish the lens and cornea and balance pressure.

aquiline nose hooked nose, in which the line from STOP to nose is convex.

Arabian Cur fierce breed which 'are said to have their generation of the violent lion'. [139]

Arabian dog ARABIAN CUR.

Arabian dogge (var. spelling) ARABIAN DOG.

Arabian Greyhound SLOUGHI.

arachnid member of the order Arachnida, which includes mites and ticks.

arachnoid spinal cord web of membrane serving the spine.

Arapahoe (US) ENGLISH FOXHOUND pack formed in 1929 to hunt plain and timber COUNTRY in Colorado.

arched curved.

Arched loins.

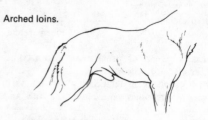

arched loin having a slight rise in the TOPLINE over the LOIN; ROACH. [*illus.*]
Slightly arched loin. [203, DACHSHUND.]

arched neck curved from OCCIPUT to WITHERS.

arched over the loin ARCHED LOIN.

arched skull a skull in which the curve is either lateral or transverse but not, as in a DOMEd skull, curved in both directions.

arched toes KNUCKLED UP.

Arctic Fox *CANIS LAGOPUS.*

Arctic Husky SIBERIAN HUSKY.

Ardennes Bouvier BOUVIER D' ARDENNES.

Ardennes Cattle Dog BOUVIER D' ARDENNES.

Ardrossan (US) BEAGLE pack formed in 1961 to hunt Kansas Jack and cottontail rabbit over a rolling farmland COUNTRY in Pennsylvania.

arecoline extracted oil of the *Areca catechu* nut, formerly used to treat CESTODES.

arecoline hydrobromide substance that acts as a laxative in dogs.

arere (obs.) (of HARE HOUNDS) LOOSE. [159]
That all maye hym here, he sahll say arere. [50]

argentaffinoma carcinoma of the argentaffin cells, the cells within the digestive tract which secrete serotonin.

Argentine grey fox *DUSICYON GRISEUS.*

Argentinian Mastiff DOGO ARGENTINO.

Ariége Hound ARIÉGEOIS.

Ariége Pointer BRAQUE DE L'ARIÉGE.

Ariégeois [FCI] French pack HOUND used for hunting hare and other small game, developed early this century from crosses between native French hounds. A hound of great elegance, finely built and slender, with a long, ARISTOCRATIC head and unusually long, FOLDED ears. The coat is short, black patched on a white GROUND which itself is heavily TICKED. Height 56–61cm (22–24in); weight 30kg (66lb).

aristocratic (usually of head or gait) fine; elegant; unworkmanlike.

Arle Court former HARRIER pack which hunted a COUNTRY in Gloucestershire.

arm forelimb: humerus and attached muscles.

  arm bone HUMERUS.

  armpit axilla.

Armagh and District Irish 15½in BEAGLE pack formed in 1916 to hunt a COUNTRY in Armagh.

Armagh Harriers TYNAN AND ARMAGH.

Armant Egyptian herding dog of variable size and type, squarely built, with a shaggy and woolly grey, black or black-and-tan coat. Height 56cm (22in); weight 22.5–27.5kg (49½–60½lb).

Arnold-Chiari malformation congenital deformity resulting in spina bifida and hydrocephalus.

arre (obs.) snarl. [159] (der. the sound of the letter R.)

> They arre and bark at night against the moon,
> For fetching in fresh tides to cleanse the streets. [343]

Arrian, Flavius (AD 94–175) author of *A Seminal Treatise on Greyhounds*; born in Nicomedia, Bithynia, he enjoyed dual Athenian and Roman citizenship.

Art de Venerie, L', oldest known book devoted entirely to hunting, dating from c1328, and written by William Twici, huntsman to Edward II.

arteriole small branch of an artery.

arteriosclerosis group of diseases characterized by thickening and hardening of the walls of the arteries.

Artesian Norman Basset BASSET ARTESIAN NORMAND.

arthropathy disease of the joints.

arthrosis progressive disease of the joints.

articular pertaining to a joint.

articulation relationship between bones on either side of a joint.

artificial unnatural; man-made.

  artificial bone prosthesis.

  artificial earth man-made underground refuge intended to attract foxes to a particular area by providing a desirable residence.

> Artificial earths in coverts encourage foxes to go from one place to another in the hope of finding an unstopped sanctuary [235]

  artificial insemination (AI) effecting conception by taking semen from a donor male and inserting it by artificial means into a receptive female.

  artificial selection selective breeding; human intervention in the selection of breeding partners, in which the survival of animals and their ability to produce are not the only criteria to determine the choice.

> We have the dog so constantly with us; the grand result of centuries of artificial selection and training is so patent to every one, that we actually come to look upon this animal as by nature superior in mental endowment, genial qualities, and general adaptiveness to all others. [182b]

  artificial vagina receptacle in which semen is collected for inspection or use in artificial insemination.

Artois Dog former TOY breed from Northern France.

> With his short, flat muzzle, is a produce of the shock-dog and the pug. He has nothing peculiar to recommend him. [406]

Artois Hound CHIEN D'ARTOIS.

Aryan Molossus MOLOSSAN breed from northern India and Afghanistan, used as a PASTORAL GUARD and as a fighting dog. The breed may now be extinct in its pure form.

ascariasis ROUNDWORM infestation.

ascarid ROUNDWORMS including *Ascaris, Parascaris, Toxocara* and *Toxascaris*.

ascites abnormal accumulation of serous fluid in the abdominal cavity.

ASCOB abbr. ANY SOLID COLOUR OTHER THAN BLACK.

asepsis process of cleansing prior to surgery.

aseptic free from septic matter.

  aseptic necrosis of the femoral head LEGG CALVÉ PERTHES DISEASE.

asexualization the process of neutering.

asexualize neuter.

ashen light-grey coat colour.

Ashford Valley FOXHOUND pack, founded as a harrier pack in 1873 but exclusively hunting fox since 1922. The COUNTRY is largely grassland.

Ashland (US) BASSET pack formed in 1960 to hunt cottontail rabbit over a COUNTRY in Virginia.

Asian Wolf CANIS LUPUS PALLIPES.

asiform protruding bony point of the carpus. [*illus.* SKELETON]

Askham EAMONT.

ASPCA abbr. American Society for Prevention of Cruelty to Animals.

aspecific without a specific cause.

aspergillosis congenital fungal infection of the foetus leading to abortion or dermatitis.

aspermatogenia inability to produce sperm.

asphyxia respiration failure.

Aspull and Pendle Forest former HARRIER pack formed in 1850 to hunt a moorland COUNTRY in Lancashire. From 1884 to 1890 the pack was known as the Garswood.

assay 1. determine the purity of. 2. test the condition of deer by exposing fat on the brisket. [159]

Asse Fox CANIS CHANIA.

assistance dogs dogs trained to serve the needs of disabled people.

associative learning PAVLOVIAN CONDITIONING.

assortive matings unlike-to-unlike mating: the practice, positive or negative, of mating individuals that are dissimilar in appearance.

assortment of genes random combination of genes producing the gametes.

asthenospermia lack of viable sperm.

asymptomatic lacking apparent symptoms.

asyntaxia abnormal foetal development.
atactic ATAXIC.
atavism REVERSION.
ataxia inherited condition in which there is lack of muscular co-ordination, often associated with odd vocalization. (Mode of inheritance, recessive.)
ataxic of, or relating to, ATAXIA.
　ataxic demyelination inherited condition in which there is progressive lack of muscular co-ordination. (Mode of inheritance, recessive.)
Atelocynus microtis DUSICYON MICROTIS.
atelectiasis collapsed lung.
at fault of HOUNDS that have lost the scent.
Atherstone FOXHOUND pack, founded in 1804, and hunting a mixed COUNTRY in Leicestershire, Warwickshire, Staffordshire and Derbyshire.
atavism quality that produces offspring resembling some distant ancestor; throw-back; REVERSION.
　The inheritance of characters from remote, but not from the immediate ancestors. [185]
atlas first vertebrae in the neck which supports the skull. (der. Atlas, a Titan in Greek mythology, who supported the world on his neck.) [*illus.* SKELETON]
Atlas Dog AIDI.
Atlas Sheep Dog AIDI.
atopic 1. of, or relating to, ATOPY. 2. of a body structure, displaced from its normal position.
　atopic dermatitis CANINE ATOPY.
atlas vertebra ATLAS.
atopy allergic, sometimes seasonal, skin hypersensitivity producing secondary pyoderma.
atresia congenital condition resulting in the incomplete closure of a normal body structure opening.
atrial septal defect congenital heart defect caused by the failure of the Ostium primum or Ostium secundum valves to close.
atrophy loss of body mass resulting from illness.
atrium cavity or chamber within the body.
attack-dog any dog trained to attack people.
attern (obs.) fierce, snarling. [159]
attitude run short training run made under ideal conditions and used as a means to restore enthusiasm to a SLED-DOG team and to discover the way in which the team works together.
attrition erosion; reduction caused by wear, as in dental attrition.
at walk of dog being reared or trained by – and therefore boarded with – someone other than its owner.
Aucupium hunting dogs. [139]
Aucupatorij hunting dogs used for birds. [139]
aural of, or received by, the ear.
　aural resection surgery to open up the external ear canal to facilitate treatment of the inner ear.
auricular pertaining to the ear.
　auricular haematoma external thickening, and sometimes bleeding, caused by damage to the ear; a thick cauliflower ear.
　auricular mange OTODECTIC MANGE.

auricle PINNA.
Aussie dim. (colloq.) AUSTRALIAN TERRIER.
Australian Barb AUSTRALIAN KELPIE.
Australian Cattle Dog [FCI, KC] developed from a number of CROSSes between assorted imported and native breeds, this versatile cattle-herder is particularly well adapted for the strenuous life in the Australian outback. A strong-headed, PRICK-EAREd dog, with broad chest and quarters, the latter being well muscled. The tail is set low and well coated with coarse hair to form a 'good BRUSH'. The DOUBLE COAT is smooth, hard, straight and weather-resistant; in blue dogs it may be blue, BLUE-MOTTLEd, or SPECK-LED with black, blue or tan on the head only. Red-speckled dogs have an even speckle all over. Height 43–51cm (17–20in).
Australian Dog DINGO.
Australasian Dog DINGO.
Australian Greyhound the result of CROSSes between various imported SIGHTHOUNDs, developed in order to produce a dog capable of tackling kangaroo. Thus, it was necessary to combine speed with strength and intelligence. Since the kangaroo became protected, what had been well on the way to becoming a well-established breed of stabilized type has become very much less easy to find.
　The head is long and narrow, the ROSE EARS unusually small, the body exceptionally deep and the legs very well muscled. The coat is hard and dense, but smooth and of any colour. Height 68–76cm (26¾–30in); weight 36kg (79lb).
Australian Kelpie [FCI, KC] developed from imported British COLLIES, with some likelihood of CROSSes to the DINGO, in order to produce a stronger dog capable of herding a variety of livestock in inhospitable country.
　The slightly rounded head has a short and strong MUZZLE with pricked ears; the neck is arched and of moderate length. The shoulders are WELL LAID BACK and muscular, the ribs WELL SPRUNG and deep. The coat is short, harsh and dense, and may be blue, chocolate, black or red, the last two with or without tan. Height 43–51cm (17–20in); weight 11.5kg–20.5kg (25½–45lb).
Australian National Kennel Council (ANKC) Australia's KENNEL CLUB, founded in 1958.
Australian Native Dog DINGO.
Australian Queensland Heeler AUSTRALIAN CATTLE DOG.
Australian Sheep Dog AUSTRALIAN KELPIE.
Australian Shepherd [AKC, KC] breed developed and vigorously promoted in America. According to some authorities the breed survived the disappearance of Atlantis. In fact a conglomeration of several pastoral breeds from various parts of the world. The head is long and lean, the DROP EARS rather small and the eyes brown, blue, or WALL-EYEd. The strong neck fits snugly into broad shoulders and a deep

chest. The tail is BOBBED naturally or DOCKED. Coat is abundant but not unduly long and may be of any shade of MERLE, black, liver or red with or without tan. Height 46–58.5cm (18–23in); weight 16–32kg (35–70½lb).

Australian Silky AUSTRALIAN SILKY TERRIER.

Australian Silky Terrier [AKC, FCI, KC] the strong influence of the YORKSHIRE TERRIER remains apparent in this TOY terrier's silken blue-and-tan coat. First shown in Australia in 1907, the breed had to wait until 1930 for recognition in Britain, and until 1959 for recognition in America.

The breed is refined and lightly built, the flat skull contributing to a wedge-shaped head, the body rather long and low, and the well-muscled limbs WELL ANGULATED; the ears are small and pricked. The coat is straight, fine and glossy, blue or grey-blue and tan. Height 23cm (9in); weight 4kg (9lb).

Australian Terrier [AKC, FCI, KC] a combination of imported TERRIERS has produced two slightly similar terrier breeds, this and the more glamorous AUSTRALIAN SILKY TERRIER. The differences are such that the Australian terrier appeals more to terrier people than to those who prefer TOY dogs. The flat-skulled head is long, the MUZZLE strong and the small, pricked or DROP EARS set high. The neck is rather long, the body long and low set. The coat is harsh, straight, and dense and may be blue and tan or sandy. Height 25.4cm (10in); weight 6.34kg (14lb).

Austrian Black and Tan Hound BRANDLBRACKE.

Austrian Brandlbracke OSTERREICHISCHER GLAT-TAARIGE BRACKE.

Austrian Short-haired Pinscher OSTERREICHISCHER KURZHAARIGER BRACKE.

Austrian Smooth-Haired Hound OSTERREICHISCHER GLATTAARIGE BRACKE.

Austrian Hound BRANDLBRACKE.

Austrian Pinscher AUSTRIAN SHORT-HAIRED PIN-SCHER.

Austrian Short-haired Pinscher heavy-bodied WATCH-DOG with a red, black, brown, fawn or black-and-tan short coat. Height 51cm (20in).

Austrian Smooth-coated Hound BRANDLBRACKE.

autogenous vaccine vaccine prepared from a culture derived from the patient.

auto-immune of antibodies, produced by the body, that attack part of the body's own tissues.

auto-immune disease condition caused by the response of the body's own cells or antibodies.

auto-immune haemolytic anaemia condition which causes the immune system to attack red blood cor-puscles.

autonomic nervous system that part of the nervous system which operates without conscious control, vital to the function of heart, lungs, digestive tract, glands and skin reflexes.

autopsy post-mortem examination to ascertain the cause of death.

autosomal of, or relating to, AUTOSOME.

autosomal chromosome AUTOSOMAL GENE.

autosomal gene genes that are not sex-linked; pairs of genes, other than the sex chromosomes. Domestic dogs have 38 pairs of non-sex-linked genes.

autosomal inheritance inheritance controlled by genes located on the autosome.

autosome any chromosome other than those that determine sex.

Auvergne Pointer BRAQUE D'AUVERGNE.

AV abbr. ANY VARIETY.

avauntlay position LEASHED HOUNDS where the quarry is thought likely to pass. [159]

AVMA abbr. American Veterinary Medical Association.

AVNSC ANY VARIETY NOT SEPARATELY CLASSIFIED.

Avon Vale this Wiltshire COUNTRY was hunted as Captain Spicer's from 1895 to 1899, when it was returned to the DUKE OF BEAUFORT. Since 1912 it has been hunted as the Avon Vale. The country is largely pasture with some plough and woodland.

Avondhu Harriers AVONDHU HUNT CLUB.

Avondhu Hunt Club formerly known as the Avondhu Harriers, the pack has concentrated on fox since 1961 and hunts a COUNTRY in County Cork.

awards prizes won by merit.

away 1. advice to a GUNDOG that the object of his search has departed.

> That 'Away' (or 'Gone' or 'Flown') is an indica-tion that the thing for which he is hunting, and of which he smells that taint, is no longer there. [184]

2. GONE AWAY. 3. AWAY HERE.

away here verbal command to send a WORKING SHEEP DOG to the right.

away to me AWAY HERE.

Axe Vale FOXHOUND pack founded by J.D. Lang in 1879 as the Sid Vale Harriers. The pack hunts a banked COUNTRY in east Devon.

axial skeleton pertaining to bones of the head and spine.

axilla inside top of the forelimb at the point where it joins the body.

axis 1. imaginary line or plane through the body. 2. second vertical vertebra adjacent to the atlas. [*illus.* SKELETON]

Azara's Dog *DUSICYON THOUS.*

Azara's Fox *DUSICYON THOUS.*

Azawakh [FCI] one of several SIGHTHOUND breeds with origins in northern Africa, the Azawakh has not become established as a SHOW-DOG.

An important characteristic of the slender, pear-shaped, finely chiselled head is that it should be enhanced by five 'warts' and carry white markings. The body is that of a typical sighthound, the SABLE and white coat is soft and short. Height 58–74cm (22¾–29in); weight 17–25kg (37½–55lb).

Azores Cattle Dog CÃO DE FILA DE SAN MIGUEL.

azoturia CANINE HYPOXIC RHABDOMYOLYSIS.

B

B gene symbol for black. [395]
b gene symbol for liver. [395]
b. abbr. BITCH.
B12 malabsorption inherited condition in which there is inefficient absorption of the vitamin B12, resulting in poor appetite, lethargy, and anaemia. (Mode of inheritance, recessive.)
Baastrup's disease bony growth between lumbar vertebrae, found in man and in some large breeds of dog.
babble GIVE TONGUE without cause, hence babbling.
> Of babbling curs disgrace they broken pack. [328]
> Whilst the babbling echo mocks the hounds,
> Replying shrilly to the well-tun'd horns. [319t]
> Ringwood, a dog of little fame,
> Young, pert, and ignorant of game,
> At once displays his babbling throat. [145e]

babbler HOUND that GIVES TONGUE when it is not on the scent.
> The chien de chemin should inspire complete confidence and therefore must not be a babbler nor speak falsely. A babbler upsets the whole pack but they quickly discover that he deceives them and do not listen to the liar. [369]

babbling *see* BABBLE.
Babès-Ernst granules small nodules found in the brain of rabid animals.
Babesia canis pyriform protozoa transmitted by ticks, the cause of babesiosis.
babesiosis group of diseases caused by the protozoan *Babesia* and transmitted by blood-sucking ticks. Symptoms include anaemia and jaundice.
babiche rawhide strips used to make strong but flexible joints between the parts of a sled.
Babinski reflex test for abnormal responses in the cerebral cortex. An upward stroke of the metacarpal and metacarpus bones induces flexion of the toes: extension is suggestive of brain damage.
baboon dog individual suffering from an inherited condition resulting in a very short, distorted spine.
BAC (Am.) Beagle Advisory Committee.
Bacille Calmette-Guérin test method of diagnosing tuberculosis in dogs.
bacillus rod-shaped bacterium that causes disease in body tissue.
back 1. upper part of the body, especially that part between WITHERS and CROUP. 2. (esp. of GUNDOGS and HOUNDS) give support to the actions of another dog.
> How long ago it was discovered that a dog would 'back' the point of his kennel companion it would be hard to say, but at the present time no dog is considered thoroughly broken unless he will acknowledge the point of his fellow-worker, and become cataleptic directly the other dog draws up to game. [186]
> To complete his education he must be made staunch to 'bird, dog and gun' – to back his partner, to quarter his ground thoroughly and honestly – to know his place. [4]

back, types of ARCHED, CAMEL, LEVEL, OVERBUILT, ROACH, SADDLE, SWAY, WHEEL.
back arched over the loins ARCHED LOINS.
back blood term formerly used to describe the influences that produce ATIVISM.
> The term applied to the hereditary trait which exists in a family of dogs, and which is liable to influence the conformation, constitution, and temper of its members. [320]

backbone LUMBAR VERTEBRAE. [*illus.* SKELETON]
backcast cause HOUNDS to retrace their steps in order the rediscover the scent.
backcross mating to one or other of a dog's parents, most often to a parent carrying a desirable recessive gene; mating between a heterozygote and a homozygote.
back dropping through withers TOPLINE falling over the WITHERS.
backflow abnormal regurgitation.
backing 1. supportive work by GUNDOGS whereby one imitates the reactions of another.
> Backing, backsetting or backstanding, synonymous terms, is that act of stopping and standing performed by one dog when he sees another point, the attitude assumed by the backing dog being generally much the same as that which he assumes when pointing. [378]

2. highly specialized behaviour of some, particularly Australian, SHEEP DOGS, which run over the backs of densely crowded sheep. [204]

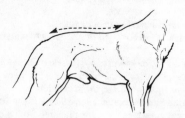

Backline.

backline profile of the back from WITHERS to CROUP. [*illus.*]
backsetting BACKING.
backskull that part of the skull behind the OCCIPUT.
backstopping BACKING.
backtrack follow the line of a scent against the direction in which it was laid.
bacteria microscopic organism; germ; microbe.
bacteria overgrowth cause of recurrent diarrhoea resulting from malabsorption due to the prevalence of *Clostridium* and other bacteria in the colon.
bacterial skin disease PYODERMA.

baculum   OS PENIS.

bad doer   dog that fails to respond to good care.
> A bad-doer is a dog which, although it may feed greedily, entirely fails to fill out or look a credit to its owner. [185]

badger   1. largest of the Musselidae (weasel family). (der. *badge* from the white facial stripe). 2. coat colour consisting of a mixture of black, brown, grey and white hairs.
> Mainly white with patches of badger, wolf-grey or pale yellow. [203, PYRENEAN MOUNTAIN DOG]

badger-baiting   barbaric sport in which dogs are encouraged to attack captive and often previously maimed badgers.

badger-digging   removing badgers from their setts using TERRIERS and spades.

badger-drawing   using TERRIERS to pull captive badgers from barrels or boxes.

badger-hunting   formerly a legitimate sport for which packs of TERRIERS were usually employed to remove badgers from their setts. Hunting took place at night.

badger-pied   (of coat colour) consisting of BADGER(2) and white patches.

badger-pye   BADGER-PIED.

Badger Dog   DACHSHUND.
> Dachshund means 'badger dog' and is a title fairly and squarely earned in his native Germany. [225]

badgering   BADGER-DIGGING.

bad shower   dog that does not enjoy shows and so does not look its best in the ring.

Badsworth   oldest Yorkshire FOXHOUND pack, founded in 1720 by Thomas Bright, hunting a plough and pasture COUNTRY.

Baermann technique   method of separating parasites from a faeces sample.

baffer   1. type of SPANIEL, which gave tongue and was adapted for hawking. It is mentioned in *The Master of Game* (1406–13), by Edward Duke of York. [221]. 2. a barker. [159]
> He says they should be great 'baffers' or barkers, which, in my opinion, is a great mistake, and detracts considerably from the value of any Spaniel. [186]

baffyn   BARK. [159]

bag   1. product of a day's shooting.
> My father never went out to kill a heavy bag. Such things were never boasted of in those times as now, when a man who shoots, say, one hundred brace in a day is looked up to as quite a hero. [241]
> My bag was three pheasants, two rabbits and one jack snipe. [166a]

2. dim. BAGMAN.
> The use of the bag in any shape or form destroys all the romance and spirit of Fox-hunting . . . Yet the curious thing is that the bag was once used quite seriously in the west country by two masters of Foxhounds whose names stand very high in the lists of sportsmen. Sir Walter Carew and Rev. John Russell both hunted bag foxes. [396]

3. shoot; catch.

bagged   shot or caught; brought to BAG.
> I sprung from my horse, a la Ducrow, without stop-

ping, and bagged one with the first, and two with the second barrel. [166a]

Baganda Hunting Dog   primitive African pack HOUND, with a short, fawn, brown or black-and-white coat, PRICK EARS and a characteristic RING TAIL. Height 50cm (19½in).

bag-fox   BAGMAN.
> Turn out bag-foxes to your young hounds, but never to your old ones. [47]
> He spent a small fortune on bag-foxes which were supplied by a London dealer and we are not told how many got away because of the unpredictable behaviour of his hounds. [175]

Bagirmi Dog   sharp-featured, short-coated, medium-sized primitive AFRICAN HUNTING DOG. Probably extinct in its pure form.

bagman   captive fox which is released from its bag in front of hounds.
> 'Certainly,' replied Proudlock, with an emphasis – 'certainly,' repeated he, as though he had never shot a fox in his life, or turned down a bag-man either. [344c]
> During the hunt they changed on to the 'real thing' in the form of a wild fox and, having killed the bagman, they went on with their new quarry, hunting him for twenty-six miles when he eventually went on board ship at Sunderland quayside where he was rescued by the crew! [101]

bait   1. attract a dog's attention, especially in the show ring, by means of titbits. 2. harass, persecute unfairly; to set dogs against each other or another animal in unequal combat.
> Like a wylde bull, that, being at a bay,
> Is bayted of a mastiffe and a hound
> And a curre-dog [333a]

baiting   *see* BAIT.

Bakhund   GAMMEL DANSK HONSEHUND.

Bakmull   type of AFGHAN HOUND that has long hair on the entire body, including the ears.

balance   quality in which all parts contribute to a harmonious whole.
> Length of tail in balance with body. [203, CAVALIER KING CHARLES SPANIEL]

balance and feel   measure of a dog's ability to maintain a distance between itself and sheep which will enable it to exert control over them; the distance varies with the type and temperament of both sheep and dog.

balance examination   palpation of muscles on both sides of a GREYHOUND's body in order to locate areas of abnormality.

balanced   having the quality of BALANCE.

balanced head   head in which the STOP occurs midway between nose and OCCIPUT.
> The skull balanced with the foreface. [6, AFGHAN HOUND]

balancing   ability of a WORKING SHEEP DOG to maintain a distance between itself and sheep which will keep them bunched and moving at a controlled pace.

balanitis   inflammation of the glans penis.

balanoposthitis   inflammation of the mucous membranes of the penis.

bald mask facial MASK in which white extends behind the ears and brow to form a roughly circular pattern, especially in SIBERIAN HUSKIES.

bald thigh syndrome tendency of some GREYHOUNDS to develop localized alopecia in the early stages of a training programme.

Baldwin/Waddington effect process by which natural selection can make it seem that acquired characteristics are being inherited. The effect may also be seen in a modified form among domestic animals subject to artificial selection.

Balearic Greyhound PHARAOH HOUND.

Balearic Hound IBIZAN HOUND.

Balloch Setters formerly a localized breed of SETTER. LEE speculates that the strain, which is now extinct was freely used by LAVERACK.

> Long, low dogs, with great bone; they had nicely-shaped, but rather short, heads; their peculiarity lay in having a thick coat of, so to say, 'fur', almost wool, at the roots of the ordinary jacket – an undercoat, in fact, like a good collie should possess. [221]

Ballymacad 1. FOXHOUND pack founded in 1946 to hunt a COUNTRY in County Galway and South Mayo. 2. former Irish HARRIER pack formed in 1797 to hunt a COUNTRY in County Meath.

Balkan Harrier BALKANSKI GONIČ.

Balkan Hound BALKANSKI GONIČ.

Balkanski Gonič [FCI] PACKHOUND with origins in Yugoslavia. The DOMED head is broad and long, the ears of medium length, the TOPLINE falls from WITHERS to CROUP and the limbs are strong and WELL ANGULATED. The short, hard and dense coat ranges in colour from red to tan, always with a black SADDLE. Height 43–53cm (17–20¾in); weight 20kg (44lb).

Balkh Greyhound AFGHAN HOUND.

Baluchi Hound AFGHAN HOUND.

Bakhmull type of AFGHAN HOUND.

> There are three types of this breed. 'Bakhmull' which means velvet because it has long hair on the entire body as well as the ears. The second is called 'Luchak' or short-haired and the 'Kalagh' which has long silky hair on the ears and legs but is otherwise short haired.[265]

BANAA abbr. British Animal Nursing Auxiliaries Association.

band (of chromosome) a segment of a chromosome, differentiated from adjacent bands during examination for abnormalities by their differing acceptance of stain.

banded (of coat hair) striped, so that the colour at the root of the hair contrasts with that at the tip.

banded chromosome chromosome subjected to a technique by which the number, position and intensity of its BANDS are made visible.

Bandog 1. MASTIFF. [139] 2. any large dog that is tied or chained by day but, in order to deter malefactors, allowed to roam at night.

> The names Tie-dog and Bandog intimate that the Mastiff was commonly kept for guard. [225]

Lighter, smaller, more active and vigilant than the Mastiff, but not so powerful. . . . It attacks with eagerness, and its bite is keen and dangerous. [51]
Boling: The time when screech-owls cry, and bandogs howl,
And spirits walk, and ghosts break up their graves. [319g]

Bandogge (obs.) BANDOG.

bandy outwardly bowed fore- or hind limbs.

bandy-hewitt small, crook-legged dog; a TURNSPIT. [159]

Bangara Mastiff northern Indian version of the TIBETAN MASTIFF. The coarse coat is black and tan. Height about 58–64cm (22¾–25in).

bangled (of ears) pendulous.

Banjara Greyhound Indian SIGHTHOUND, sturdily built with a broad and muscular back, long head and neck, and a shaggy, silky coat of black or dappled grey. Ears, legs and tail, heavily FEATHERED. Height 68–74cm (26¾–29in); weight 23–30kg (50½–66lb).

bank country hunting COUNTRY in which obstacles consist largely of earth banks. Common in Ireland.

Bankside Elizabethan London bear-pit situated next to the Globe theatre.

Banstead Drag MID-SURREY FARMERS' DRAG HOUNDS.

Bantu Dog Zulu version of the more popular BASENJI, used principally for hunting small game and as a DOMESTIC GUARD. A small and slender dog with foxy head, PRICK EARS and a curled tail.

Banwen Miners FOXHOUND pack founded in 1963 and hunting a COUNTRY in Dyfed.

BAOS abbr. BRACHYCEPHALIC AIRWAY OBSTRUCTION SYNDROME.

bar 1. (Aust.) HUMERUS or upper arm. 2. ready-made FLAG(3).

barak any Yugoslavian HOUND.

Barakzai AFGHAN HOUND. [185]

Barb 1. AUSTRALIAN KELPIE. 2. dim. BARBET.

Barbary Dog type of dog supposedly found in north Africa.

> According to Cuvier, has a very thick and round head, the ears erect at the base, large and moveable, and carried horizontally; the skin nearly naked, and black or dark-flesh colour, with large patches of brown. A sub-variety has a kind of mane behind the head, formed of long stiff hairs. [406]

Barbet [FCI] the breed's age and general characteristics put it forward as a possible ancestor of both the POODLE and several of the breeds of WATER SPANIEL. The breed has a typically SPANIEL head, the body is rather long and deep, the legs strong and the feet unusually large. The distinctive coat is slightly CORDED and resistant to adverse weather, it may be black, shades of chestnut, tan or grey, or white and is commonly of mixed colours. Height 56cm (22in); weight 16–25kg (35–55lb).

> The Barbet is a small poodle, the production of some unknown and disadvantageous cross with the true poodle. [406]

In France, it is stated, the breed [Poodles] had been kept pure, and were so often used when shooting duck as to be known as 'caniche' or 'chien canne', or as a 'barbet', the diminutive of barboteur, a dog paddling in mud. [37]

Barbone　POODLE.

bare pastern　(in AFGHAN HOUND) PASTERN with short hair, while the rest of the body is long-haired.

Barge-dog　SCHIPPERKE.

The Schipperke at one time had no more aristocratic owners than the Belgian barge and canal-boat men, or it may be of drivers of coaches, carts, and other vehicles. [123]

Barguest　goblin that often assumes the form of a dog.

bark　loud noise made by domestic dogs (wild dogs do not bark).

What delite can there be and not rather dyspleasure in hearynge the barkynge and howlynge of dogges? [259]

The dogs did bark, the children screamed,
Up flew the windows all;
And every soul bawled out, Well done!
As loud as he could bawl. [102]

While he was pausing in amaze
At London's famous sights to gaze,
And barking, which he deemed his duty
At the ill deeds of Punch and Judy,
Amidst the bustle, crowd, and rattle,
He lost the farmer and the cattle. [339]

barker　dog given to barking.

Barkless Dog　(colloq.) BASENJI.

Barlow　FOXHOUND pack hunting a grass and moorland COUNTRY in north-eastern Derbyshire which runs into Yorkshire. Founded in the late 17th century as a TRENCHER-FED pack to hunt hare and fox.

Barlow's disease　HYPERTROPHIC OSTEODYSTROPHY.

barrel　ribcage, esp. one that is rounded.

Barrel hocks.

barrel hocks　HOCKS that turn outwards creating a rounded space between the hind legs. [*illus.*]

barrel leg　BARREL HOCKS.

barrelled　(of ribcage) rounded.

barrelled vent　protuberant anal sphincter.

barrow　badger sett. [249]

Barry Hound　name given, in certain parts of Switzerland, to dogs from the St Bernard Hospice. The name is derived from a famous individual dog.

Barukhy Hound　Indian SIGHTHOUND, a possible ancestor of the AFGHAN HOUND.

Barukhzy Greyhound　(obs.) AFGHAN HOUND.

Being chiefly used by the sporting sirdars of the royal Barukhzy family. [123]

Barukhzy Hound　BARUKHZY GREYHOUND.

Barzoï　(obs.) BORZOI.

Basanski Ostrodlaki Gonič-barak　profusely coated, Yugoslavian tracking HOUND.

Basenji　[AKC, FCI, KC] small dog used by the natives of Zaire as a vermin hunter. The breed's SPITZ-like type has encouraged some authorities to claim descent from the similar breeds depicted in Egyptian wall paintings and even from earlier rock paintings.

In common with most other primitive breeds, and all wild canids, oestrus occurs only annually, and usually in autumn, though domestication in the west appears now to be making seasons less regular and twice-yearly.

The breed is lightly and cleanly built, and graceful in movement. The head is flat and well-chiselled, tapering through a slight STOP to a pointed MUZZLE. The neck is slightly crested and strong, the shoulders WELL-LAID, the short back level. The tail is set high and curled close to the back. The coat is short and glossy, and may be red, black or BRINDLE, with white confined to legs, BLAZE and COLLAR; or TRICOLOUR with tan MELON PIPS and MASK. Height 40–43cm (15¾–17in); weight 9.5–11kg (21–24lb).

Bashkir Laika　one of five Siberian LAIKA breeds identified in 1896 by Prince Andrew Shirinsky Shihmatoff. [380]

bashyal　BASIHYOID BONE.

basihyoid bone　part of the hyoid bone found at the root of the tongue.

basihyoideum　BASIHYOID BONE.

basioccipial　bone that forms the base of the skull.

basisphenoid　one of the bones on the floor of the skull.

basket　that part of a dog sled in which cargo or passengers are carried.

Basketmaker Dog　extinct native American breed.

Basque Shepherd　recent variation of the AUSTRALIAN SHEPHERD from which it varies principally by having a tail. The name is derived from claims that some of the Australian Shepherd's ancestors originate from the Basque region of France and Spain.

bas rouge　particular colour pattern comprising tan and black.

Colors – Bas Rouge (bicolor): black and fawn [269]

Bas Rouge　BEAUCERON.

basset　1. an EARTH DOG. [159]　2. (Fr.) any short-legged HOUND.

Basset　dim. BASSET HOUND.

There are now several packs of Bassets kept in England, and they show very fair sport after hares; but it is not their natural vocation, and their massive build is against the possibility of their becoming popular as harriers. [225]

Basset Artesian Normand　[FCI] short-, but straight-legged French pack HOUND with characteristic large, cone-shaped, pendulous ears, ARISTOCRATIC head and expression, and long, finely chiselled MUZZLE.

The throat carries a moderate amount of DEWLAP. The TRICOLOUR or orange-and-white coat is short. Height 25–36cm (9¾–14in); weight 15kg (33lb).

Basset Bleu de Gascogne [FCI] one of the four breeds that form the BLEU DE GASCOGNE group of SCENTHOUNDS. Short-legged but in other respects typical of the group. Height 30–36cm (12–14in); weight 16–18kg (35–39½lb).

Basset Fauve de Bretagne [FCI, KC] HOUND which has its origins in Brittany and might be regarded as a shorter-legged version of the GRIFFON FAUVE DE BRETAGNE. The head is long, the pendulous ears of medium length, and the neck muscular and rather short. The chest is wide and deep and the forelegs either straight or only slightly crooked. The LOINS and hindquarters are strong. The tail is set high and carried like a sickle. The harsh, dense coat may be red-WHEATEN or fawn, preferably without white markings. Height 32–38cm.

Basset Griffon Vendéen [FCI] GRIFFON VENDEEN.

Basset Griffon Vendéen, Petit [FCI] GRIFFON VENDEEN.

Basset Hound [AKC, FCI, KC] short-legged, heavily built pack HOUND, placid and affectionate, with a characteristic deep melodious voice. Used principally for hunting the hare it was developed in Britain from hounds imported from France during the mid-1860s.

The head is DOMED with a prominent OCCIPUT and some STOP, the MUZZLE is rather long, the skin on the skull moderately wrinkled and the FLEWS substantially overlapping the lower lips. The lozenge-shaped eyes are dark (to mid-brown in lighter-coloured hounds); the fine, velvety ears are low set, long and narrow and curling inwards along their length. The arched, fairly long neck is muscular, the shoulders are WELL-LAID BACK, the short forelegs powerful and heavily boned with the upper forearm inclined slightly inwards. The body is long and deep, with well-rounded ribs and prominent breast-bone, the LOINS are slightly arched and the hindquarters muscular, with well-bent STIFLES and WELL-LET-DOWN HOCKS. The skin on the fore- and hind limbs is wrinkled. The feet are massive and WELL-KNUCKLED UP, the STERN rather long, carried SABRE fashion. Movement must be true, free and powerful. The coat is smooth and short, most frequently TRICOLOUR or lemon and white, but all hound colours are acceptable. Height 33–38cm.

Basted former 14½in BEAGLE pack formed in 1919 to hunt a COUNTRY in West Kent; the pack was disbanded in 1925 and re-formed as the Bolebroke.

Batak Spitz unrecognized African DOMESTIC GUARD and hunting dog, of medium size, thick-coated and long in the leg. Height 30–46cm (12–18in).

Bâtard (Fr.) 1. CROSS-BREED. 2. [Bâtards] GROUP of six HOUND breeds, which prior to 1957 were differentiated by the addition of the name of their place of origin to that which signified their cross-bred status, e.g. Bâtards du Haut-Poitou, Bâtards Anglo-Gascon-Saintongeois.

batch kind of NORTHERN HOUND. [159]

Bat-eared Fox *OTOCYON MEGALOTIS*.

Bat ears.

bat ear large, forward-facing, erect ear, wide at the base and rounded on top. [*illus.*]

Bat ears, of medium size, wide at base, rounded at top. [203, FRENCH BULLDOG]

Battak Sumatra has produced this unrecognized breed, which unusually combines the instincts of a PACKHOUND with those of a DOMESTIC GUARD. The breed is also regarded as a culinary delicacy among the natives of Indonesia.

The breed is small but strongly made, with a vulpine head, the tail is curled and well covered with coarse hair. The coat is harsh and thick, colour red, though shades of tan to WHEATEN, brown or grey with or without black BRINDLING are common. Height 30–46cm (12–18in).

Battle Creek (US) AMERICAN FOXHOUND pack formed in 1929 to hunt a hilly woodland COUNTRY in Michigan.

battue arrangement by which BEATERS and dogs drive gamebirds towards a line of waiting guns.

bausyn (obs.) badger.

> That beest a Bausyn hight, a Brok or a Gray;
> Thes iii namys he hath, the sooth for to say,
> And this the cause theof. [50]

Baux Hound type of hunting dog. [159]

Bavarian Mountain Hound [KC] SCENTHOUND principally used for trailing wounded deer. Shorter in leg and more lightly built than other BLOODHOUNDS and lacking their exaggerated FLEWS and wrinkle. The red and BRINDLE coat is short and glossy. Weight 25–35kg (55–77lb).

Bavarian Schweisshund BAVARIAN MOUNTAIN HOUND.

bawl (of hounds) speak when not on the scent. [159]

bawler HOUND whose cry is long and drawn out.

bawty (regional Eng.) a white-faced dog.

bay 1. prolonged cry of a hunting HOUND.

> A little way below I could hear a confined baying of hounds among the trees. [309]
> He was feeling a little like some Eliza who, crossing the ice, heard the baying of the pursuing bloodhounds. [400]

2. howl mournfully.

> The deep mouth'd Mastiff bays the troubled night. [385]

3. the sound a hunted animal makes when he is bereft of any means or route to escape hounds. [151c]

Here was thou bay'd, brave hart;
Here did'st thou fall. [319e]
He stands at bay against yon knotty trunk
That covers well his rear; his front presents
An host of foes. [328]

4. the barking of a terrier when marking underground.

Let Terriers small be bred, and taught to bay,
When Foxes find an unstopt Badjers earthe. [244]

see also HOLD AT BAY; BRING TO BAY.

bayen 1. bark. [159] 2. BAIT(2). [159]

Bayerischer Gebirgsschweisshund [FCI] BAVARIAN MOUNTAIN HOUND.

bayet BAY. [159]

B-B shot pulse WATER HAMMER PULSE.

BC abbr. BACKCROSS.

BCG test abbr. BACILLE CALMETTE-GUÉRIN TEST.

beady (of eyes) small, dark and deep set, with intense expression.

Beagle smallest of the hounds and probably one of the oldest of the PACKHOUNDS. Queen Elizabeth I took several diminutive Beagles with her in order to relieve the tedium during her various 'progresses' round her kingdom. Principally used for hunting the hare, and followed on foot. The breed's small size and ability to live happily together also made it the dog favoured as a laboratory animal. Only during the late 1950s did the breed begin to enjoy popularity in Britain as a companion animal.

The breed is small but powerful, amiable and alert, showing neither aggression nor timidity. The slightly DOMED head is strong without being coarse, the ears are long and fine in texture, the neck relatively long and slightly arched; the forequarters are WELL LAID BACK and clean, with short PASTERNS. The TOPLINE is level and the COUPLINGS short. Hindquarters are muscular and WELL BENT. The STERN is high-set and carried proudly. The coat is short and dense and may be of any recognized HOUND COLOUR other than liver. Minimum height 33cm (13in), desirable height 40cm (15¾in).

Now almost entirely displaced by dwarf specimens of the foxhound, or by crosses with it in varying proportions. [338]
A good beagle is slow but sure; he dwells on a cold line until he puzzles it out, and, throwing his musically smart voice, calls the remainder of his fellows to him and away they dart, crawling through fences or topping stone walls, on the scent of poor puss. [221]
The beagle is smaller and therefore eats less. It is followed quite a long way off by persons of maturity acting under medical advice. [379]

Beagle Field Trials (Am.) organized TRIALS intended to test the ability of BEAGLES to follow the scent of cotton-tail rabbits, their enthusiasm and voice.

Beagle Harrier TRICOLOUR French PACKHOUND of relatively recent origin, used for hunting hare and deer. Essentially a large BEAGLE or small HARRIER. Height 38–48cm (15–18¾in); weight 20kg (44lb).

beagling hunting hares with a pack of BEAGLES.

bean-bag fabric pillow-like container filled with small particles of foam plastic used as a dog bed.

bear-baiting former barbaric sport in which a captive bear was attacked by relays of dogs.

The Puritan hated bear-baiting, not because it gave pain to the bear, but because it gave pleasure to the spectators. [240]

bear coat long, coarse and upstanding coat.

beard growth of hair under the chin.

Head and skull in proportion to build and stature, general impression of massiveness, accentuated by beard and moustache. [203, BOUVIER DES FLANDRES]

Bearded Collie as with most old breeds, attempts to trace the origins of the Bearded Collie rely most often on conjecture and imagination. In the mid-18th century Gainsborough painted a portrait of the Duke of Buccleuch with what is undoubtedly a Bearded Collie, a breed doubtless used for some years to control sheep on the Duke's Scottish estates.

The Bearded Collie is a lean and active rather LONG-CAST dog, with a broad, flat skull flanked by medium-sized pendulous ears, and with a strong MUZZLE. The forequarters slope well back into WELL-SPRUNG ribs affording plenty of heart room. The hindquarters are WELL ANGULATED and the HOCKS low. The tail is low set and carried in an upward swirl. The profuse untrimmed flat harsh and straight topcoat lies over a soft, furry undercoat. The colour is slate grey, reddish-fawn, grey, sandy or black, with or without white markings on chest, legs and feet. Height 51–56cm (20–22in).

Over the Borders were to be seen many shaggy-haired, large-headed, large eyed, big nostrilled sheepdogs, bung-tailed, tousy looking; they were 'tikes', as one authority described them. They had coats like untidy doormats. These dogs, now termed Bearded Collies, may or may not have had Deerhound blood in their veins. [37c]

Beardie dim. (colloq.) BEARDED COLLIE.

bear ear small, erect and rounded ear.

Ears strong and thick, erect, triangular and slightly rounded at the tips; they should not be large or pointed, nor should they be small and 'bear-eared'. [6a, SAMOYED]

bearing female genital tract.

bearing retainer appliance used to retain a vaginal prolapse.

bear-like bite PINCER BITE.

Teeth should meet in a bearlike bite; however, a scissors bite is acceptable. [6a CHINOOK]

bear-pit an enclosure used to contain a bear for the purpose of baiting. *See* BEAR-BAITING.

beastings colostrum-rich first milk secreted after birth.

beasts of the chase 1. animals regarded as second-rate quarry but still capable of providing sport.

But there ben other bestes five of the chase;
The buck the first, the seconde is the do;
The fox the third, which hath ever hand grace;
The for the martyn, and the last the roe. [366]

2. any legitimate quarry for HOUNDS.

beasts of venery animals regarded in the first rank among quarry.

beat move noisily, creating an ordered disturbance, to encourage game to run or fly.

> After we had rid about a mile from home, we came upon a large Heath, and the Sports-men began to beat. [2]

beat the water drive an otter from its holt into the water.

beater person or dog whose purpose it is to BEAT during a shoot.

beating *See* BEAT.

Beauceron [AKC, KC] originally used as a hunting dog – principally for wild boar – the Beauceron is now almost entirely used as a PASTORAL GUARD. Apart from the breed's short coat, it has much in common with the BRIARD, both having origins in the Brie region of northern France. A strong, intelligent and highly biddable dog, muscular and agile, with limitless stamina.

The head is lupine, the neck thick and strong, the chest deep and the TOPLINE arched over the CROUP. The black, black-and-tan or HARLEQUIN coat is short and dense. The characteristic tan legs give rise to the breed's alternative name of Bas Rouge. Height 63–71cm (24¾–28in); weight 30–38.5kg (66–84½lb).

Beauce Shepherd (colloq.) BEAUCERON.

Beaufort American and crossbred FOXHOUND pack formed in 1929 to hunt a grass and woodland COUNTRY in Pennsylvania.

beauty spot lozenge or spot of coloured hair within a white BLAZE on the skull.

beaver (of coat coloration) BADGER(2).

Bedale formed as an offshoot to the RABY HUNT in 1832, the hunt occupies a COUNTRY in north Yorkshire.

Bedford County (US) American, English and cross-bred FOXHOUND pack formed in 1961 to hunt a hilly woodland COUNTRY in Virginia.

Bedlington Terrier [AKC, FCI, KC] one of three related TERRIER breeds developed in the north-eastern Border region of England and of south-west Scotland. Originally known as the Rothbury Terrier and briefly as the Northern Counties Fox Terrier the Bedlington is very different from any other terrier breed. Originally used for COURSING ground game but also expected to GO TO GROUND(2). A graceful and lithe breed with distinctive pear-shaped head and deep-chested, arched-backed body reminiscent of a SIGHTHOUND. The blue, liver or sandy, twisted coat is thick and LINTY. Height 41cm (16in); weight about 8.2–10.4kg (18–23lb).

> A mason named Joseph Aynsley has the credit for giving the name 'Bedlington' to this terrier in 1825. It was previously known as the Rothbury Terrier, or the Northern Counties Fox Terrier. [225]

Bedouin Shepherd Dog an unrecognized breed of varied type, used in the northern African deserts for herding goats and camels.

beefy (esp. of the hindquarters) coarse, heavy and muscular.

beestings BEASTINGS.

bee-sting tail short, thin, straight and pointed tail.

beghis (obs.) BITCH or bitches. [159]

behavioural period each of four periods – neonatal, transitional, socialization and juvenile – during which canine behaviour conforms to a particular pattern.

behaviour therapy those methods which arise from LEARNING THEORY, and are used in the treatment of canine psychological disorders.

Belgian Barge Dog (colloq. Ang.) KEESHOND.

Belgian Cattle Dog (colloq. Ang.) BOUVIER DES FLANDRES.

Belgian Congo Dog (colloq. Ang.) BASENJI.

Belgian Draught Dog (colloq. Ang.) CHIEN DE TRAIT BELGE.

> The favourite breed is a descendant of the old Flemish Mâtin often crossed with a dog of Great Dane type. Apart from the Mâtin, any tall and muscular breed may be employed. [225]

Belgian Griffon (colloq. Ang.) GRIFFON BELGE.

Belgian Mastiff (colloq. Ang.) CHIEN DE TRAIT BELGE.

Belgian Pointer (colloq. Ang.) BRAQUE BELGE.

Belgian Sheep Dog group of four Belgian pastoral breeds – Groenendael, Laekenois, Malinois and Tervueren – each with origins in different parts of Belgium, and distinguished from each other by coat type. All have a close relationship to other lupine herders developed in the surrounding countries.

Medium-sized dogs with finely chiselled, proudly carried heads, triangular, pricked ears, rather long necks, long, oblique shoulders with prominent WITHERS, and well-boned forelimbs with strong PASTERNS. The body is elegant but powerful, with a straight TOPLINE, deep chest and a slightly sloping CROUP. The hindquarters are well muscled, the forefeet round and the hind feet slightly oval, with well-arched toes. The tail is of medium length, and the tip may be carried above the TOPLINE. The Groenendael has a medium-length black coat; the Laekenois has a shaggy fawn to mahogany coat; the Malinois has a short fawn to mahogany coat; and the Tervueren has a rough fawn to mahogany coat. Height 56–66cm (22–26in).

Belgian Shepherd Dog BELGISCHER SCHAFERHUND.

Belgian Shepherd [Groenendael] [KC] GROENENDAEL.

Belgian Shepherd [Laekenois] [KC] LAEKENOIS.

Belgian Shepherd [Malinois] [KC] MALINOIS.

Belgian Shepherd [Tervueren] [KC] TERVUEREN.

Belgian Short-haired Pointer (colloq. Ang.) BRAQUE BELGE.

Belgian Tervueren (colloq.) one of the four types of BELGIAN SHEEP DOG.

Belgischer Schäferhund group of four closely related but individually distinctive Belgian pastoral breeds; which consists of the Groenendael,

Laekenois, Malinois and Tervueren. *See* BELGIAN SHEEP DOG.

Belgium Mastiff (colloq. Ang.) CHIEN DE TRAIT BELGE.

bell ear LEATHER shaped like a bell.

Belle Hollow (US) AMERICAN FOXHOUND pack formed in 1961 to hunt a hilly woodland COUNTRY in New York State.

Bellinter Harriers TARA.

Bellmount former Irish 12–13in BEAGLE pack formed in 1897 to hunt a COUNTRY in County Cork.

belly underside of the LOINS.

belton (of coat) white flecked with another colour.
> Black and white [blue belton], orange and white [orange belton], lemon and white [lemon belton], liver and white [liver belton] . . . flecked [belton] all over preferred. [203, ENGLISH SETTER]

Belvoir FOXHOUND pack, founded by the Duke of Rutland in 1750, which has hunted fox exclusively since 1762. Hunts a Lincolnshire and Leicester COUNTRY extending westward from Melton Mowbray. Former huntsmen include Will Goodall (1842–59) and Frank Gillard (1870–96).

Belvoir Fox Terrier TERRIERS of a particular type formerly used with the BELVOIR FOXHOUNDS.

bench 1. raised cubicle on which a dog is exhibited for public view at some shows.
> Many of our best dogs on the bench are capital workers, and only ignorance would hold the whole of our exhibition dogs are useless for sporting purposes. [242]

2. raised platform on which dogs, especially sporting dogs, sleep.

benched show show at which BENCHES are provided.

bend peninsula of land formed by a winding river across which a hunted otter may run in order to save time or avoid strong currents.

Bengalese Harrier (obs.) DALMATIAN.
> The claim to be a Bengalese Harrier seems to rest on the single fact that a spotted dog, resembling our modern Dalmatian, was once brought from Bengal to Spain. [123]

Bengal Fox *VULPES BENGALENSIS.*

Bengal Harrier (obs.) DALMATIAN.
> I have joined the common harrier to the Dalmatian dog, or harrier of Bengal, because they differ only in having more or fewer spots on their coat. [72]

benign (of tumour) unlikely to recur or spread.

Bercelettus BRACHETIS. [186]

Bergamaschi CANE DA PASTORE BERGAMASCO.

Bergamaschi Herder CANE DA PASTORE BERGAMASCO.

Bergamasco (colloq. Ang.) CANE DA PASTORE BERGAMASCO.

Bergamese Herder (colloq. Ang.) CANE DA PASTORE BERGAMASCO.

Bergamese Shepherd (colloq. Ang.) CANE DA PASTORE BERGAMASCO.

Berge Polonais de Vallée POLISH LOWLAND SHEEP-DOG.

Berger (Fr.) SHEEP DOG. generic reference to sheep dogs of French origin; includes a number of breeds.

Berger a Face Rasee BERGER DE PYRENEES A FACE RASE.

Berger da Castro Laboreiro CÃO DE CASTRO LABOREIRO.

Berger da Serra de Estrela ESTRELA MOUNTAIN DOG.

Berger de Beauce [FCI] BEAUCERON.

Berger de Brie BRIARD.

Berger de Picard rough, heavy-coated French herder, grey and fawn in all shades. Height 53–65cm (21–25½in).

Berger de Savoy heavily muscled French herding breed with strong head, developed for use on sheep and cattle. The coat is thick and often patched with blue or brown on a grey GROUND. Height 46–56cm (18–22in); weight 20.5–25kg (45–55lb).

Berger des Pyrenees herding dogs with origins in the Pyrenees, which are also the birthplace of a number of other pastoral breeds. The Berger itself has three varieties: the smooth-faced variety, the BERGER DE PYRENEES A FACE RASE; and the goat-haired and long-haired varieties. All three varieties are agile, quick and biddable.

The skull is strong, the ears high-set, the strong neck is long as is the deep-chested body. The coat varies in colour from black, through BRINDLE and blue, to pale grey with white POINTS(4). Height 38–56cm (15–22in); weight 8–14.5kg (17½–32lb).

Berger des Pyrenees a Face Rase smooth-MUZZLED version of the BERGER DES PYRENEES.

Berger du Languedoc with origins in the Toulouse area of France, this group of five PASTORAL GUARDS – Camargue, Carrigue, Farou, Grau and Lazao – are almost indistinguishable from one another. All may now be extinct in their pure form. All the breeds had DOUBLE COATS, either dark or light fawn. Height 40–56cm (15¾–22in).

Berger Picard CHIEN DE BERGER PICARD.

Berger Polonais de Valais POLISH LOWLAND SHEEP DOG.

Berger Polonais de Vallée POLISH LOWLAND SHEEP DOG.

Berghund former type of HERDER.
> Was a large dog fabricated in Waldheim as a rival to the Leonberg. [225]
> Means mountain dog, and although various rough-haired dogs have been described as the Berghund, to-day each variety of these mountain dogs has some special name by which it is known. [185]

berkar one who barks. [159]

Berkeley in the late 16th century the Lord Berkeley hunted fox over a huge COUNTRY from north and west of London extending as far as Bristol. The country is now confined to plough and woodland in Gloucestershire. A former huntsman was Will Rawle (1887–1905), who had formerly hunted PARSON JACK RUSSELL's hounds.

Berkenhout, John author of *An Essay on the Bite of a Mad Dog* (1783).

Berkhamstead 1. former STAGHOUND pack formed in the late 19th century to hunt a COUNTRY in Hertfordshire. 2. former 14in BEAGLE pack formed in 1890 to hunt a country in Berkshire and Hertfordshire.

berkin barking. [159]

Berkshire and Buckinghamshire Farmers' former STAGHOUND pack formed in 1901 when the ROYAL BUCKHOUNDS were abolished.

Bernardine Dog (colloq.) ALPINE MASTIFF. [406]

Berner Laufhund [FCI] Switzerland has produced a number of SCENTHOUNDS, which includes the Berner Laufhund itself and the BERNER NEIDERLAUFHUND. The Laufhund is a tall, lightly built HOUND, with characteristic long, pendulous ears, a long, lean head, deep BRISKET and pronounced TUCK-UP. The coat is soft and short, invariably black and white, with or without TICKING, but with obligatory tan markings to the head. Height 46–59cm (18–23¼in); weight 15.5–20kg (34–44lb).

Berner Neiderlaufhund [FCI] shorter-legged version of the BERNER LAUFHUND. A long and lightly bodied HOUND that also differs from the Berner Laufhound in that it is wire-coated. Height 33–43cm (13–17in); weight 13.5–18kg (29½–39½lb).

Berners, Dame Juliana alleged author of the *Boke of St Albans*, written in rhyme and published in 1486 which deals with hawking, hunting and heraldry.

Berner Sennenhund [FCI] BERNESE MOUNTAIN DOG.

Bernese Cattle Dog (colloq.) BERNESE MOUNTAIN DOG.

Bernese Hound (colloq.) BERNER LAUFHUND.

Bernese Laufhund (colloq.) BERNER LAUFHUND.

Bernese Mountain Dog [KC] Swiss draught breed of MOLOSSON extraction. Strong and compact, with a broad chest, a level TOPLINE and rounded well-muscled rump. The head is strong and flat, with a slight FURROW and well-defined STOP; the triangular ears drop close to the head. The tail is bushy reaching to just below the HOCKS. The soft, shiny, black-and-tan coat has white on the MUZZLE, chest and, sometimes, feet. Height 59–70cm (23¼–27½in); weight 40–44kg (88–97lb).

Bernese Scenthound (colloq.) BERNER LAUFHUND.

Bertiella genus of TAPEWORM.

bertielliasis *Bertiella* infestation.

Bertillon racing dog's certification of its breeding, age, sex and identification.

Best in Group (BIG) BEST OF BREED winner adjudged best in its particular group.

Best in Show (BIS) award made to the dog that is unbeaten by any other at the show.

Best Linear Unbiased Prediction mathematically based technique used to evaluate the propensity of a dog, or other animal, to transmit particular characteristics.

Best of Breed (BOB) award made to the best dog from classes for a particular breed.

Best of Winners (BOW) American equivalent to BEST OF BREED.

Best Opposite Sex (BOS) award made to the dog that has been beaten only by BEST IN SHOW or BEST OF BREED winner.

beta-haemolytic streptococci (BHS) uterine bacteria possibly implicated in FADING PUPPY SYNDROME.

Bewcastle former TRENCHER-FED pack of FOX-HOUNDS hunting a COUNTRY on the English/Scottish border.

Bewick, Thomas (1753–1828) incomparable wood-engraver and author of *A General History of Quadrupeds* (1790).

Berwickshire FOXHOUND pack that has been in existence since before 1740 and has since, at various times, been known as the Northumberland and Berwickshire.

Bhotia HIMALAYAN SHEEP DOG.

BHS abbr. BETA-HAEMOLYTIC STREPTOCOCCI.

Bhuteer Terrier (obs.) LHASA APSO.
   Lhassa Terrier, an interesting little breed formerly found under the inappropriate name of Bhuteer Terrier. [123]

bibarhunt archetypal TERRIER.

Bicester and Warden Hill FOXHOUND pack hunted by John Warde until 1778 when Sir Thomas Mostyn took over until 1829. The COUNTRY lies in Warwickshire and Oxfordshire and is largely pasture and ploughland.

Bichon type of TOY dog originating from various Mediterranean islands and spreading to various other islands in which different types were developed.

Bichon à Poil Frisé [FCI] BICHON FRISE.

Bichon Bolognese BOLOGNESE.

Bichon Frise [AKC, KC] pure white, silky, profusely coated TOY breed with origins in the Canary Islands. Under the coat, which is the breed's most striking characteristic, is a well-made, unexaggerated, small dog with a rounded skull, pendulous ears, arched neck, sturdy body and well-muscled quarters. The PLUMED tail curves gracefully over the back. Height 23–28cm (9–11in).

Bichon Havanais [FCI] typically BICHON in appearance and probably originating in the Iberian peninsula, from whence it was taken to the islands around Havana. Differs from the BICHON FRISE principally in its colour variation, which includes cream, gold, silver, blue and black. Height 20–28cm (8–11in); weight 3–5.5kg (6½–12lb).

Bichon Maltiase MALTESE.

Bichon Tenerife BICHON FRISE.

bicolour two-coloured; having a coat composed of two distinct colours.

biestings var. BEASTINGS.

BIG abbr. BEST IN GROUP.

big dog (colloq.) FOXHOUND.

Big-Dog-Little-Dog Syndrome injuries to the cervical vertebrae caused by a large dog attacking a smaller one, picking it up and shaking it violently.

Big-eared Fox BAT-EARED FOX.

bigenic characteristic determined by two genes.

Big 'n Blue AMERICAN BLUE GASCON HOUND.

bilateral cryptorchid having neither testicle descended into the scrotum.

biliary fever BABESIOSIS.

bilious vomiting syndrome tendency of some dogs to vomit early in the morning, thought to be the consequence of the counterflow of bile during sleep.

bilirubin component of liver secretions. Excess amounts produce jaundice.

Billy 1. one of relatively few breeds which owe their existence to the efforts of an individual breeder, in this case M. G. Hublot du Rivault, who named the breed he produced after a town in the region that surrounds Poitiers in France. The Billy is a HOUND that combines elegance with superlative hunting qualities. The head is lean, the pendulous ears slightly curled, and the voice, which is an important characteristic of the breed, is very musical. The short, smooth coat is white, spotted with lemon or orange. Height 58–66cm (23–26in); weight 25–30kg (55–66lb). 2. (colloq.) badger.

Bilsdale said to be the earliest pack of FOXHOUNDS in England. Hunted by the Duke of Buckingham from 1670, the COUNTRY lies in north Yorkshire and consists of moorland and pasture.

Bilton Beagles CLARO.

Bingley Terrier former name for the AIREDALE TERRIER.

> Mr. Dalziel suggested that the name Bingley Terrier would be more distinctive and applicable, inasmuch as Bingley seemed to be the district around which this Terrier was to be met with in the greatest numbers. . . . Sundry newspaper correspondence had taken place about this dog, when some of his admirers called him the Bingley Terrier . . . but a consensus decided that he be called the Airedale Terrier. [221]

binocular vision degree to which vision in each eye overlaps to produce a single image. Wolves have 15 to 25 degrees of binocular vision, DINGOS about 70 degrees, SPANIELS and GREYHOUNDS about 80 degrees.

biochemical screening tests which make it possible to assess the propensity of individuals to transmit some hereditary conditions.

biometry use of mathematical methods to study biological principles.

biopsy surgical removal of tissue for analysis or examination. (der. Gk *opsis*, appearance.)

biotin vitamin H, found in offal, egg-yolk, and legumes, and used in the metabolism of fats and amino acids. Deficiency causes various skin diseases.

Birchwood (NZ) hunt formed in 1886 as the Wallace County to hunt DRAG(2) and hare over open sheep COUNTRY in Invercargill.

bird dog (Am.) dog used by those who shoot birds.

Bird Dog Field Trials (Am.) competitive American tests of the ability of dogs used to find game birds. First organized in Memphis, Tennessee, in 1874.

bird-of-prey eyes round, yellow and staring eyes.

> Light yellow (Bird of Prey) eyes are not desirable and are a fault. [6, GERMAN SHORT-HAIRED POINTER]

bird tongue inherited lethal condition in which the tongue is folded laterally so preventing the puppy from suckling or swallowing. (Mode of inheritance, recessive.)

bird work (Am.) activities of a BIRD DOG.

birdy (Am.) (of a BIRD DOG) conscientious.

birth defects congenital defects.

birth order sequence in which puppies are born. This is significant – along with the interval between births – in the identification of the cause of problems such as still birth.

birth weight weight of a newborn infant. Significant for its effect on the chance of survival.

BIS abbr. BEST IN SHOW.

Bisben fierce and strong Himalayan MASTIFF with a thick coat and long, bushy tail.

biscuit 1. hard-baked cereal product used as part of a dog's diet. 2. (of coat) pale tan colour.

Bisley hunted from about 1793 as the Ripley and Knapp Hill Harriers, re-established as Fulton's Harriers in 1851.

Bisley and Sandhurst FOXHOUND pack hunting a heathland COUNTRY in Surrey and Hampshire. It was formed by the amalgamation of the BISLEY and the SANDHURST in 1963.

bitch female dog.

> Ashamed himself to see the wretches,
> He mutters, glowrin' at the bitches [73a]
> When I come to die,
> We go together in love, my bitch and I.
> Or, if you fear to let such love return,
> Go to, and shut your gates. Sweeter to burn. [387a]

bitchy having the attributes of a bitch; effeminate.

bite 1. injury caused by the teeth. 2. to inflict injury with the teeth. 3. relative position of the upper and lower teeth when the jaws are closed.

bites, types of BEAR-LIKE, EVEN, LEVEL, OVERSHOT, PINCER, SCISSOR, UNDERSHOT, WRY.

Bithoratic ectronelia inherited condition resulting in the absence of forelimbs. (Mode of inheritance, recessive.)

Bjeras leukodystrophy inherited condition characterized by ataxia, paralysis and blindness. (Mode of inheritance, recessive.)

black and fallow (obs.) black and tan. [245]

Black-and-Fawn Russian Hound Russian PACKHOUNDS derived from CROSSES between native and imported FOXHOUNDS. A rather thick-set dog, with wedge-shaped head and blunt MUZZLE, the ribs are WELL SPRUNG, the body rather long. The long tail is carried SABRE fashion. The coat is short and always black and fawn. Height 53–61cm (20¾–24in); weight 25–30kg (55–66lb).

Black-and-Tan Coonhound [AKC] first of the

American COONHOUNDS to be accorded official, AKC recognition. Used principally to hunt racoon, the breed has also occasionally been employed on larger GAME. A solid and muscular dog. A medium STOP separates the oval skull from the strong MUZZLE; the large ears are pendulous. The TOPLINE is level, the ribs rounded, the limbs well-boned and muscular. The head and chest carry a degree of loosely fitting skin. Height 58–69cm (23–27in); weight 25–34kg (55–75lb).

Black-and-Tan Setter GORDON SETTER.
> Whether the dog under consideration should be called the Black-and-Tan or the Gordon Setter is a subject open to controversy. [123]

Black and Tan Terrier 1. archetypal TERRIER formerly found in Britain.
> The old style of Black-and-Tan Terrier was stronger than, but not so elegantly built as, his modern representative, and the stouter-limbed, broader-chested, thicker-headed, and coarser-coated dog that illustrates the original form from which our show dog has sprung is occasionally still to be met with. [123]

2. [AKC] MANCHESTER TERRIER.

Black-and-Tan Toy Terrier ENGLISH TOY TERRIER (BLACK AND TAN).

Black-backed jackal *CANIS MESOMELAS.*

Black Bobtail extinct breed of Australian HERDER.
> The original Cattle dogs brought to Australia were Black Bobtails, a breed quite unknown in this country today. The Black Bob-tail was the first dog used for cattle in Australia; he was a big, rough-coated, square-bodied dog, with a head like a wedge, a white frill round the neck, and saddle-flap ears. He got over the ground like a native-bear. Faithful enough, handy and sensible; but he couldn't stand the heat and long trips; besides, he bit like an alligator and barked like a consumptive. [160]

Black Combe and District BEAGLE pack formed in 1959 in succession to the WEST CUMBERLAND BEAGLES.

Black Elkhound (colloq. Ang.) SVART NORSK ÄLGHUND.

Black Fell Terrier FELL TERRIER.

Black Field Spaniel FIELD SPANIEL.
> There can be no doubt that this variety of spaniel, which is comparatively speaking a modern production, has been crossed with the Sussex by some breeders to the detriment of the latter's purity; nor is there any difference as regards its shape and make from other varieties of field spaniels, from which it is divided only by colour. [320]

Black Forest Hound (colloq. Ang.) SLOVENSKY KOPOV.

black hair follicle dysplasia inherited condition in which there is thinning and dullness of the black coat in PIEBALD animals. (Mode of inheritance, recessive.)

black mange former name for follicular mange: DEMODECTIC MANGE. [46]

Blackmont Terrier early, localized SCOTTISH TERRIER from Perthshire.

Blackmore Vale FOXHOUND pack hunting a COUNTRY in Dorset and Somerset, which dates from 1826 when it was hunted by the notorious Rev. Harry Farr YEATMAN.

Blackmore Vale (Miss Guest's) private FOXHOUND pack which hunted the Blackmore Vale's eastern COUNTRY from 1914 to 1954, when the two packs were reunited.

Black Mountain (US) BEAGLE pack formed in 1959 to hunt cottontail, jack rabbit and DRAG(2) over a hilly COUNTRY in California.

Black Mouth Cur SOUTHERN CUR.

Black Norwegian Elkhound SVART NORSK ÄLGHUND.

Black Poodle spectral dog said to haunt the grave of priests who have broken their vows.

Black Russian Terrier (colloq. Ang.) TCHIORNY TERRIER.

Black Spaniel variety of SPANIEL formerly found in Britain.

Black St Hubert JURA LAUFHUND TYPE ST HUBERT.
> I have seen some black-tanned Hounds, of a breed which puzzles me, called by their owner the Black St. Hubert breed, and they are certainly very grand specimens of the dog. [186]

black tongue symptom of niacin deficiency; colloq. name for niacin deficiency.

Blackwater former OTTERHOUND pack formed in 1961 to hunt the Boyne and the Blackwater and their tributaries in Ireland.

bladder internal organ in which urine is collected prior to discharge.

blade SCAPULA.
> Long in blade with upper arm of equal length placing legs well under body. [203, GOLDEN RETRIEVER]
> Long blades, well laid back with only slight space between the shoulder blades at the withers, [6, AUSTRALIAN TERRIER]

blade bone SCAPULA.

blain (obs.) HAEMATOMA. [406]

blaireau (Am.) of a PYRENEAN MOUNTAIN DOG with a correctly patched coat.

Blanford's Fox *VULPES CANA.*

blank a DRAW which fails to discover the quarry; BLANK DAY.

blank day day during which HOUNDS fail to find their quarry.
> The hounds drew all day without finding a fox. This was my first experience of a blank day. [309]

blanket (of coat) dark marking covering the upper back and flanks.

blanket finish describes the end of a race in which several dogs finish so closely together that a blanket would cover them all.

Blankey FOXHOUND pack dating from 1871 when the Old Burton COUNTRY in Lincolnshire and Nottinghamshire was divided.

blastocyst the foetus at the stage which follows the morula, and during which the foetus has not yet become attached to the uterine wall.

blastogenesis early stage in the development of cells following conception.

blaze   white stripe running centrally down the forehead and between the eyes.

Blazers, The   COUNTY GALWAY.

Blean   13½in BEAGLE pack formed in 1853 as a farmers' pack to hunt a COUNTRY in Kent.

Bleasdale   BEAGLE pack formed in 1920 as the Oakenclough Beagles to hunt a COUNTRY in Lancashire, Westmorland and west Yorkshire.

bleeder   (colloq.) haemophiliac.

Blencathra   Cumbrian FOXHOUND pack hunting a demanding fell COUNTRY on foot. Former huntsmen include John Peel, whose famous 'coat so grey' remains part of the hunt uniform.

blending inheritance   where the inherited characteristics of an individual are intermediate between those of its parents.

Blenheim Spaniel   red-and-white CAVALIER KING CHARLES SPANIEL.

> Cannot be traced as far back as the King Charles, but it is believed to have been first imported from Spain in the reign of Charles II by John Churchill, the first Duke of Marlborough. [123]
> A breed cultivated by one of the Dukes of Marlborough . . . from its beauty, and occasional gaiety, it is oftener an inhabitant of the drawing-room than the field. [406]

blenheim   (of coat) rich chestnut markings on a white GROUND.

   blenheim spot   THUMB MARK.

blepharitis   inflammation of, and discharge from, the eyelids.

Bleu d'Auvergne   BRAQUE D'AUVERGNE.

Bleu de Gascogne   group of four SCENTHOUNDS, which includes the GRANDE BLEU DE GASCOGNE, BASSET BLEU DE GASCOGNE, PETIT BLEU DE GASCOGNE and the PETIT GRIFFON BLEU DE GASCOGNE.

blind retrieve   a retrieve in which the dog has not first had the opportunity to see where the bird fell.

blind search   a search in which neither handler nor dog have seen where objects have been hidden.

blind track   track laid without the dog or handler being present.

blink   (esp. of GUNDOG) to pass over game.

blinker   GUNDOG which indecisively indicates the position of birds.

blinking   see BLINK.

blister   former supposed remedy for several ailments which involved the application of an irritant poultice which raised a blister on the dog's skin.

bloat   GASTRIC DILATION-VOLVULUS.

blocky   (esp. of a head) square and solid.

> Fault: Blocky or chunky in appearance. [6, BOSTON TERRIER]

blood   1. of the STRAIN, so-called because blood was thought to be the means by which characteristics were inherited.

> Judicious crossing makes the good dog, and one should go as far as possible for fresh blood, for strength is lost by inbreeding. [229]

2. (esp. of HOUNDS) the kill; hounds that have recently killed are said to be 'in blood'.

> There was never a truer saying in connection with foxhounds than 'Let them begin regular hunting with blood up to their eyes'. [316]
> Do not set too high a value on blood, unless it has been well earned by your hounds. [266b]

3. induce HOUND or TERRIER to work; also ritual induction of a hunt-follower.

> I must also tell you, that, as foxes are plentiful in this cover, the principal earth is not stopped; and the foxes are checked back, or some of them let in, as may suit the purpose of blooding. [47]

Bloodhound   [AKC, KC] archetypal TRACKER, possibly the biggest of the HOUND breeds. The deep, sonorous voice is an important characteristic of the breed, as is its superlative ability to follow even the coldest trail.

The head is rather narrow and deep with a pronounced OCCIPUT. The long, thin, low-set, pendulous ears, the heavy FLEWS and loose skin about the head contribute to the breed's dignified, almost judicial, expression. The long neck carries a generous DEWLAP. The body is deep, with a strong back and slightly ARCHED LOINS. Hindquarters are very muscular, the HOCKS WELL LET DOWN. The STERN is long, thick and carried like a scimitar. The short, smooth coat is black, or liver and tan, or red. Height 61–66cm (24–26in); weight 41–50kg (90–110lb).

> The greater sort which serve to hunt, having lips of a large size and ears of no small length, do not only chase the beast while it lives . . . but being dead also by any manner of casualty, make recourse to the place where it lies, having in this point an assured and infallible guide, namely, the scent and savour of the blood sprinkled here and there upon the ground. [139]
> And hark! and hark! the deep-mouthed bay
> Come nigher still and nigher;
> Bursts on the path a dark bloodhound,
> His tawny muscle tracked the ground,
> And his red eye shot fire. [314b]
> He comes from a town down in Georgia where his uncle is the high sheriff, and one of the bloodhounds' name is Nip, and the other Tuck, and they are both trained from infancy to track down guys such as lags who escape from the county pokey. [306]

blooding   1. hunting ritual whereby noviciates have their faces daubed with the blood of the quarry after witnessing their first kill. 2. (esp. of HOUNDS or TERRIERs) introducing dogs to work, allowing them to come to grips with or taste the blood of their quarry.

blood-line   related dogs carrying the same BLOOD derived from a common ancestor; a STRAIN.

blood sports   An emotive term, used by opponents of field sports, to describe such.

bloom   (esp. of coat) in good condition.

Bloomfield Open   (US) AMERICAN FOXHOUND pack formed in 1917 to hunt a pasture, plough and woodland COUNTRY in Michigan.

blotch   (obs.) ECZEMA.

blousy   (of coat) soft and woolly.

> Faults . . . Open coats, blousy coats, too short or dead coats. [6, CAIRN TERRIER]

blow-in client who attends a veterinary surgery without prior appointment.

blown 1. out of breath; tired. 2. (of coat) well past its best; describes a coat that has an abundance of long, dead hairs.

blown coat *see* BLOWN(2).

blue slate coat colour produced by dilute black or by a mixture of white and black hairs.

blue belton white coat flecked with blue. Blue or black flecked or TICKED with white.

> 'Blue Beltons', as Mr Laverack was the first to call them, taking this name from the village or hamlet in Northumberland. [221]

blue eye *keratitis profunda*. Condition sometimes resulting from the use of certain forms of live egg-culture canine hepatitis vaccines, or from the disease itself.

blue merle blue and grey mixed in a MARBLED(2) pattern.

blue mottle (of HOUND's coat colour) blue TICKING on a white GROUND.

> The Staghound is of the prevailing Hound colours, including every marking except blue mottle, which is a hue now excluded from almost every Foxhound pack as being indicative of Harrier blood. [186]

blue pill formerly used as a purgative, its principal ingredients were mercury and liquorice. [185]

blue speckle (of coat) TICKED with blue on a lighter GROUND.

> Blue, blue-mottled or blue-speckled with or without other markings. [203, AUSTRALIAN CATTLE DOG]

blue tongue characteristic of some SPITZ breeds.

Blue-and-Tan Terrier BLUE PAUL.

> The Blue [also kown as the Blue Paul] and the Blue-and-tan are often by enthusiasts dignified as distinct varieties, but they are not entitled thereto. They are mere colour 'sports' and generally, as far as type is concerned, inferior to the Black-and-tan. [123]

Blue Dobermann Syndrome BLUE DOG SYNDROME.

Blue Dog Syndrome inherited condition characterized by thin, poor quality coat, hair loss and scaly skin. (Mode of inheritance, familial.)

Blue Fox species of Arctic Fox with a grey coat.

Blue Gascony Basset BASSET BLEU DE GASCOGNE.

Blue Heeler AUSTRALIAN CATTLE DOG.

Blue Lacy American herding breed developed in Kentucky. Sturdy yet lean in appearance, the smooth, sleek coat is typically a gunmetal grey but may also be tan, black and tan, or shades of yellow, usually solid but PARTICOLOURS and TRICOLOURS are also seen. Weight 18–23kg (39½–50½lb).

Blue Paul extinct fighting dog formerly found in and around Glasgow.

> A dog about forty-five pounds, weight bred at Kirkintilloch, which has come and gone within the last century and a half. [320a]
> Some writers have endeavoured to introduce to the public as a distinct variety a creature they called a 'Blue Paul'. This, we believe, had its birth in Scotland, but was only a coarse bull-terrier, which nature, for once negligent, had allowed to come into the world with a skin more like that of a Berkshire

pig than of a respectable member of the canine race. [221]

> An old breed of blue-coloured dog of the bull-mastiff type which has become practically extinct . . . The Blue Pauls being cultivated by the patrons of dog-fighting. [320a]

Blue Paul Terrier BLUE PAUL. [123]

Blue Peter localized type of TERRIER formerly found in southern England.

> The blue peter was once popular in London. [383]

Blue Picardy ÉPAGNEUL BLEU DE PICARDIE.

Blue Picardy Spaniel ÉPAGNEUL BLEU DE PICARDIE.

Blue Riband of the Heather the award bestowed upon the Supreme Champion, winner of the ISDS International Sheep Dog Trials.

Blue Ridge (US) English and crossbred FOXHOUND pack formed in 1888 to hunt blue-grass pasture farmland in Virginia.

Blue Shag Sheep Dog type of rough-coated SHEEP DOG, possibly an ancestor of the OLD ENGLISH [SHEEP DOG], formerly to be found in the west of England.

> A good terrier, like a good horse, cannot be of a bad colour, but blue on a rough dog generally means a long silky coat, the mark being derived originally from the blue shag sheep-dog, an animal very common in the counties of both Dorset and Devon. [318]

Blue Terrier dim. BLUE-AND-TAN TERRIER. [123]

Blue Tick dim. BLUETICK COONHOUND.

Bluetick Coonhound [AKC] American HOUND whose colour probably derives from imported GASCONY HOUNDS. A medium-sized hound, rather lightly boned and on the leg. The medium length, smooth coat is typically white, finally TICKED with blue, which may form patches on the head and ears where tan markings are also required. Height 51–69cm (20–27in); weight 20–36kg (44–79lb).

Bluey (colloq. Aust.) AUSTRALIAN CATTLE DOG.

> The Australian Cattle Dog – affectionately known as 'Bluey' throughout the length and breadth of the continent – is a 'made-up' dog. [160]

bluie (esp. of CORGIS) dog with blue coat, light, sometimes blue, eyes and blue pigmentation of nose, lips and eye rims.

> Bluies: Colored portions of the coat have a distinct bluish or smoky cast. [6, PEMBROKE WELSH CORGI]

blunt (of MUZZLE) short, broad and square ended.

Blunt-tipped ears.

blunt-tipped (of ears) narrow to a point but rounded at the apex.

BLUP abbr. BEST LINEAR UNBIASED PREDICTION.

board   take care of another's dogs, esp. for a fee; to be accommodated on a temporary basis.

boarding kennel   place in which dogs are provided with temporary accommodation.

Boarhound   GREAT DANE. [123]

boat foot   SLIPPER FOOT.

BOB   abbr. BEST OF BREED.

bobbed   (of tail) very short, whether DOCKED or naturally so.

bobbery pack   ill-assorted collection of HOUNDS.

Bobby   GREYFRIAR'S BOBBY.

bobtail   without a tail, whether naturally so or DOCKED.
> The sheep-dogs of different countries differ most essentially from each other. Take, for example, the dogs used for this purpose in Scotland, called the Colly, and compare them with the bob-tailed curs which are known in England. [358]
> Tail . . . natural bobtail or docked. [6, AUSTRALIAN SHEPHERD.

Bobtail   (colloq.) OLD ENGLISH SHEEPDOG.

Bobtailed Sheep Dog   (colloq.) OLD ENGLISH SHEEP-DOG.

body   1. that part which lies between the shoulders and hindquarters.   2. 'in good body', in good condition; BODY UP.

body length   distance from WITHERS to base of tail.

body loosely strung   of a body that appears to be suspended, almost hammock-like, between the fore- and hindquarters, usually also lacking muscular tone and fitness.

body up   acquire substance and muscle as a consequence of feeding, exercise or maturity, hence bodied up.

Bohemian Griffon   ČESKÝ FOUSEK.

Bohemian Terrier   ČESKÝ TERRIER.

bold in eye   of dog with round or protruding eye.

Bolebroke   BASTED.

Bolognese   [FCI, KC] typical, squarely built, and surprisingly solid little BICHON developed in northern Italy. Height 25–31cm (10–12¼in); weight 3.5–4kg (7½–9lb).

bolt   1. eject a quarry from its place of refuge.
> From the very commencement of fox hunting in this country, small terriers were kept at each of the various kennels, for the purpose of bolting the fox from his earth when run to ground by the hounds. [338]

2. (of a GUNDOG) run away from the handler.

bolting eye   full and prominent eye.

Bolton Greys   formerly a popular type of Scottish SETTER (poss. misspelling of BELTON).
> Now the fancy is strong for the black-speckled Setter, known as Bolton Greys – 'the hue [as a Scotch keeper told me] of a Scotch mist'. [186]

Bolventor   HARRIER pack formed in 1949 to hunt a COUNTRY in Cornwall.

bonding   process by which animals become emotionally attached to each other.
> Must have the calm, quiet, steady temperament needed to establish proper 'bonding' with the sheep. [6, AKBASH DOG]

bone   relative skeletal development, esp. of the leg bones.

bone-crusher   (colloq.) fierce dog. [280]

bone marrow dyscrasia   condition in which there is abnormal production of cells within the bone marrow.

booster   BOOSTER VACCINATION.

booster vaccination   repeat vaccination given at regular intervals in order to maintain protection.

Bordeaux Bulldog   DOGUE DE BORDEAUX.

Bordeaux Dog   DOGUE DE BORDEAUX.

Bordeaux Mastiff   DOGUE DE BORDEAUX.

Border   FOXHOUND pack hunting a hill and moorland COUNTRY in Northumberland and Roxburghshire. Founded in the 1830s by the amalgamation of private packs hunted by the Dodd and Robson families, it is still in the hands of these same families. Jacob Robson hunted the pack from 1879–1933.

Border Collie   [AKC, FCI, KC] the first-choice sheep-herding breed of shepherds all over the world (by whom it is most commonly known as the WORKING SHEEP DOG), as well as the root from which several other herding breeds have been developed. An ancient working dog, it was recognized by the KC in 1976. Speed combined with stamina, intelligence and a biddable nature are essentials.

The skull is fairly broad, the tapered MUZZLE fairly short with a distinct STOP; the eyes are wide set with a mild yet alert expression; ears may be erect or semi-erect. The body is athletic, with deep chest, broad and deep LOINS, the hindquarters muscular and sloping to strong, low HOCKS. The tail reaches the hock and is carried with an upward swirl at the end. Movement is smooth and tireless. The coat may be moderately long or smooth, but always dense and weather-resistant; a variety of colours, which must always dominate any white, are acceptable, although black and white is the most popular. Height about 53cm (20¾in).

Border Counties, North Wales   former OTTERHOUND pack formed in 1906, following an amalgamation between the Border Otterhound Hunt, itself formed in 1903, and the Ceriog. The pack hunted the Rivers Severn, Dovey, Tanat, Banw, Vrnwy, Dee, Dysynni, Ledr, Conway, Llugwy, Dane, Alyn, Peover and Weaver.

Border Otterhound Hunt   BORDER COUNTIES, NORTH WALES.

Border Terrier   [AKC, FCI, KC] superlative working TERRIER developed by the hunts which occupy the countries on the borders of England and Scotland. The breed's otter-like head is an important characteristic but not more so than the soundness, agility and resourcefulness to follow a horse across hunting COUNTRY.

The outline is RACY, the body fairly long and narrow, the hindquarters well muscled. The PELT is thick to provide protection against cold weather; the

DOUBLE COAT comprises a soft undercoat and harsh, close, weather-resistant topcoat of red, WHEATEN, GRIZZLE, or blue and tan. Weight 5.1–7.1kg (11–15½lb).

Bordetella bronchiseptica a small bacillus, one of the causes of KENNEL COUGH.

bordetellosis diseases caused by *Bordetella bronchiseptica*, including bronchitis, bronchopneumonia and infectious tracheobronchitis.

bore out (of a dog) force another to run wide during a race.

borken BARKing. [159]

Borrelia burgdorferi spirochete transmitted by *Ixodes dammini* and the cause of LYME DISEASE.

Borzoi [AKC, FCI, KC] one of several Russian SIGHTHOUNDS originally used for COURSING wolves but now developed into an elegant, glamorous SHOW-DOG and companion without sacrificing the strength and speed demanded by its former occupation.

The head is long, lean and finely chiselled, the skull DOMED with imperceptible STOP, the ears small, set high and usually folded back along the neck; the neck is strong and slightly arched. The forequarters are clean and sloping; the chest is of great depth and narrow, the TOPLINE distinctly arched, the LOINS broad and powerful. The long tail is low set and carried like a sickle. The silky coat may be flat or wavy; any colour or combination of colours is acceptable. Height greater than 68cm (26¾in) for bitches; 74cm (29in) for dogs.

BOS abbr. (Am.) BEST OPPOSITE SEX.

Bosanski Barak BOSANSKI OSTRODLAKI GONIČ-BARAK.

Bosanski Ostrodlaki Gonič-Barak [FCI] Yugoslavian hound which combines the qualities of SIGHT- and SCENTHOUNDS and used on a variety of QUARRY. A rough-coated, yellow, grey, PART-COLOURed or TRICOLOURed dog. Height 46–56cm (18–22in); weight 16–24kg (35–53lb).

Bosnian Brack BOSANSKI OSTRODLAKI GONIČ-BARAK.

> Wire-haired, and about the size of a Collie, generally red or brown, or white with yellow or red patches.[225]

Bosnian Coarse-haired Hound BOSANSKI OSTRODLAKI GONIČ-BARAK.

Bosnian Hound BOSANSKI OSTRODLAKI GONIČ-BARAK.

Bosnian Rough-coated Hound BOSANSKI OSTRODLAKI GONIČ-BARAK.

Bosnian Rough-haired Hound BOSANSKI OSTRODLAKI GONIČ-BARAK.

bossy (of shoulders and upper arm) heavily muscled.

Boston Terrier [AKC, FCI, KC] the original Boston Terrier, which appeared just before the turn of the century, was bred from an assortment of gladiatorial breeds; it weighed as much as 27kg (59½lb) and was a formidable animal.

Since then the breed has been miniaturized to produce a lively breed with a characteristic relatively large, ROUND HEAD, a short and sturdy, compact, deep-chested body on strong legs, the hind legs being WELL ANGULATED. The coat is SMOOTH and short, black or BRINDLE with white markings ideally confined to MUZZLE, BLAZE, COLLAR, chest and lower legs. Weight: lightweights under 6.8kg (15lb); middleweights under 9.1kg (20lb); heavyweights under 11.4kg (25lb).

> The history of the Boston terrier goes back to the early bulldogs and bull-terriers, for it is from old British stock that the breed has been evolved, and that in America the history started when Mr Robert C. Hooper, of Boston, purchased the dark brindle with the blazed face. [37]
> He could discuss Confucianism with a Pekinese, And address the Boston terrier on Beacon Hill in purest Beaconese. [262]

Bottolo formerly a type of Italian TOY dog.

> Nowadays they have found another breede of little dogs in all nations besides the Melitaean dogs, either made so by art as inclosing their bodies in the earth when they are whelped so as they cannot grow great by reason of the place, or lessening and impayring their growth by some kind of meat or nourishment. These are called in Germany, Brachen, Schoshundle and Gutschen Hundle and in Italian, Bottolo. [359]

bottom stickle STICKLE.

Bouldogue du Mida massive MOLOSSAN found principally in southern France.

Bouledogue Français [FCI] FRENCH BULLDOG.

Boulet GRIFFON À POIL LAINEUX.

bouncer (Am.) someone employed to act as a BEATER to BEAGLES.

Bourbonnais Pointer BRAQUE DU BOURBONNAIS.

boutonneuse fever ricket disease caused by the tick *Rickettsia conorii*. Dogs, especially in Mediterranean countries, may be infected and provide a reservoir for the disease.

bouvier (Fr.) breed developed to herd cattle.

Bouvier dim. BOUVIER DES FLANDRES.

Bouvier Bernois BERNESE MOUNTAIN DOG.

Bouvier d'Appenzell APPENZELLER SENNENHUND.

Bouvier des Ardennes Grande herding dog originally developed for herding pigs, which task called for a dog of substance and mettle. The head is large and characteristically whiskered, the ears are pricked, the coat coarse and of any colour. Height greater than 60cm (23½in).

Bouvier des Ardennes Petite smaller version of the BOUVIER DES ARDENNES GRANDE. Height under 60cm (23½in).

Bouvier des Flandres [FCI, KC] ancient cattle DROVER with origins in Belgium, which has undertaken a new career as an intelligent and lively DOMESTIC GUARD and companion.

The large size of the head is accentuated by the characteristic BEARD and MOUSTACHE which imparts a forbidding expression. The skull is flat, the MUZZLE fairly short, broad and powerful. The oval eyes must be as dark as possible, neither protruding nor sunken and showing no HAW. The triangular ears are high set and traditionally CROPPED. The strong and muscular neck is slightly arched; DEWLAPS are discouraged. The straight forelegs are very strong, with long muscular shoulders; the body is short, deep and broad with little TUCK-UP, the CROUP continuing the line of the back. Hindquarters are well muscled with powerful thighs and WELL LET DOWN HOCKS; feet are round and compact. The tail is traditionally DOCKED but some dogs are born tail-less. The abundant coat is coarse and thick with a tendency to mat, a characteristic which provides added protection. Colours range from fawn to black; white or pale colours are objectionable. Height 59–68cm (23¼–26¾in); weight 27–40kg (59½–88lb).

BOW abbr. BEST OF WINNERS.

Bowden Harriers SOUTH POOL.

bowed bent outwards (esp. of the forelegs).

  bowed front legs bent outwards.

bow hocks BARREL HOCKS.

bow-legged outwardly curved legs.

Bowood (Aust.) pack formed in 1955 to hunt kangaroo over coastal plain and wooded hills in Tasmania.

bow-wow 1. childish term for a dog. 2. childish imitation of a BARK, hence (1) above.

bow-wow mutton (18th cent. Brit.) dog flesh.

box STARTING BOX.

  box broken (Am.) a dog that has been trained to start from a STARTING-BOX.

  box buster (Am.) a racing dog that starts unusually quickly.

Boxer [AKC, KC] developed from the old German BULLENBEISER, this breed is now a popular GUARD and companion.

  The head is an important feature of the breed to which the STANDARD devotes much detailed attention. The skull and MUZZLE are balanced, the powerful muzzle broad and deep, the eyes forward-looking, the ears, traditionally CROPPED, thin and of moderate size. The arched, clean and muscular neck rests on long, sloping shoulders. The forelimbs are straight and strongly boned. The body is square in outline, with a deep chest, short back and LOIN and a pronounced TUCK-UP. The hindquarters are powerfully muscled and WELL ANGULATED. Feet are small and catlike. The tail is traditionally DOCKED and set high. The short and glossy coat may be fawn or BRINDLE, with or without white markings which must not exceed one-third of the body area. Height 53–63cm (20¾–24¾in); weight 55–70kg (121–154lb).

Boxer cardiomyopathy inherited heart disease characterized by slow heartbeat, weakness, arrhythmia and heart failure. (Mode of inheritance, uncertain).

Boykin Spaniel liver, wavy-coated American WATER SPANIEL. Height 38–46cm (15–18in); weight 14–17kg (31–37½lb).

Brabaçon former name for the TOY type of GRIFFON.

Brabanter smaller version of the BULLENBEISER.
  The small Bullenbeiser or Brabanter had been bred and trained to hold in check the most fiery bull and to obtain a grip on the nose which he held, regardless of the animal's efforts. When social conditions eliminated his function in the court hunts, the transition to a cattle dealer's dog must have been easy. [115]

bracco (Ital.) POINTERS.

Bracco Italiano [FCI, KC] POINTER of Italian origin. A squarely built, clean-limbed dog, with a DOMED skull, and characteristically folded, pendulous ears. The short white coat may have orange or chestnut markings, whether in patches or in the form of ROANing; black is unacceptable. Height 56–66cm (22–26in); weight 25–40kg (44–88lb).

Bracco Navarone PERDIGUERO NAVARRO.

Bracco Carlos VIII BRACO NAVARRO.

Bracco Navarro old Spanish POINTER, formerly very popular but now probably extinct as a pure breed.

braccoid of animal with BRACHYCEPHALIC characteristics.

brace two dogs, esp. of similar appearance, shown or worked together.

  brace-mate each of a BRACE.

  brace work employment of two dogs, as with SHEEPDOGS.

bracelet long hair shaped into a round on the pastern of a show-trimmed POODLE.

brach (obs.) any hunting dog.
  A term of general application to all hunting dogs. In old English and old French it is spelt Brache, and in modern German Brack, and it is applied to dogs that hunt by scent. [123]

brache 1. (Eng.) female of a type of BLOODHOUND. [139] 2. small HOUND.

brachell (obs.) SCENTHOUND. [191]

Brachen BOTTOLO. [359]

Bracheta dim. (obs.) BRACHE(2).

Brachetis dim. (obs.) BRACHE(2).

brachy pref. short.

Brachycephalic head.

brachycephalic rounded skull form typified by broad MUZZLE, defined STOP, pendulous ears and full lips; skull that gives a CEPHALIC INDEX of about 85–90. [*illus.*]

brachycephalic airway obstruction syndrome (BAOS) gross distortion of the nostril, soft palate and larynx, causing respiratory difficulty.

brachydactyly inherited condition characterized by abnormally short limbs. (Mode of inheritance, probably recessive.)

brachygnathia having an abnormally short mandible; OVERSHOT BITE.

brachygnathic of, or relating to BRACHYGNATHIA.

brachyury inherited condition resulting in an abnormally short tail. (Mode of inheritance, recessive.)

bracke German SCENTHOUND.

braco (obs. spelling) BRACCO.
> The Spanish Braco is flat-nosed, from the usually blunt, square nose of dogs that hunt by scent. [123]

braconier person employed to hold LEASHED HOUNDs until they are required by the hunt. [159]

bradytocia unusual slowness in giving birth.

Braes of Derwent Northumberland and Durham FOXHOUND pack formed in 1854 from Mr Humble's private pack, which itself had become the Prudhoe and Derwent in 1837 with some of the largely woodland and moor COUNTRY going to the Slaley Hounds.

brag-bag (colloq.) show sponsor's gift, commonly a bag or holdall, which advertises an exhibitor's previous wins.

braggled BRINDLEd. [159]

brain room skull capacity sufficient to suggest that the brain is easily accommodated; capacious skull, especially one that is not long and narrow. The implication that dogs with long narrow skulls lack brain or intelligence is erroneous.
> Head deep rather than broad, but broader than muzzle, showing brain room. [203, GORDON SETTER]

brake 1. dim. (obs.) a car adapted for carrying shooters and their dogs in the field. 2. metal fork used to retard the motion of a sled.

Bramham Moor west Yorkshire FOXHOUND pack, dating from about 1740, hunting a woodland and plough COUNTRY.

Branchwater (US) American and crossbred FOXHOUND pack formed in 1950 to hunt a hilly grassland COUNTRY in Alabama.

branding method of making an indelible identification mark, often using a red-hot iron, formerly used esp. on HOUNDS.
> If you mark the whelps in the side (which is called branding them) when they are first put out . . . it may prevent their being stolen. [47]

Brandlbracke [FCI] silent, hunting, short-coated, black-and-tan Austrian HOUND, used principally to bring game to BAY(5). Height 46–58cm (18–23in); weight 23kg (50½lb).

Brandywine (US) AMERICAN FOXHOUND pack formed in 1892 to hunt undulating pasture in Pennsylvania.

braque 1. BRACH. [123] 2. group of French GUNDOGs principally used as POINTERS.

The name signifies a Pointer, and has been given to a number of dogs, of a variety of types, which can hardly claim to be, in every case, a distinct variety, for the differences are very slight, and often only such differences as one might expect to find in a single breed. [185]

Braque Belge BELGIAN SHORT-HAIRED POINTER.

Braque Charles X BRAQUE SAINT GERMAIN.
> Although a coarse, inelegant dog to look upon, is remarkable for his keen scent and his steadiness on point . . . a smooth-coated, liver-and-white dog. [225]

Braque d'Auvergne [FCI] smooth-coated POINTER of French origin. The breed is powerful and imposing but does not lack elegance. The head and pendulous ears are always SELF-COLOURED with the bold eyes brown; the coat is white TICKED or ROANed with blue or black. Height 56–64cm (22–25in).

Braque de l'Ariège [FCI] possibly the oldest of the French BRAQUE (2) breeds and closest to the ancestral type. A powerful but elegant breed, an indomitable and steady hunter intended for work in rough country. The rolled pendulous ears, dished MUZZLE and slight DEWLAP are all characteristic. The coat is short and fine, invariably white, with orange or chestnut TICKING. Height 58–68cm (23–26¾in); weight 25–30kg (55–66lb).

Braque Toulouse BRAQUE DE L' ARIÈGE.

Braque du Bourbonnais [FCI] multi-purpose, muscular GUNDOG, long-necked and deep-chested. The pear-shaped head is furnished with pendulous, medium-sized triangular ears; the jaw is slightly OVERSHOT, the tail sometimes absent. The white coat is short and smooth with liver, brown or orange TICKING. Height 56cm (22in); weight 18–26kg (39½–57lb).

Braque Dupuy [FCI] unusually tall and fast GUNDOG, preserved after the French Revolution in the Abbey of Argensolis. The head is narrow, with slight STOP, and a slightly convex MUZZLE. The chest is deep, the LOINS narrow with strong TUCK-UP. The coat is sleek and smooth with chestnut TICKS(2) and patches on a white GROUND.

Braque Français [FCI] BRAQUE FRANÇAIS DE GRANDE TAILLE and BRAQUE FRANÇAIS DE PETIT TAILLE.

Braque Français de Grande Taille GUNDOG with origins in the Pyrenees which, as with others, has been saved from the brink of extinction. The body is lean and elegant, suggestive of stamina. The head is broad and the MUZZLE slightly dished. The coat is short and dense, usually white with extensive dull chestnut patches and TICKING. Height 56–68cm (22–26¾in); weight 20–32kg (44–70½lb).

Braque Français de Petit Taille slightly smaller version of the BRAQUE FRANÇAIS DE GRANDE TAILLE. Height 48–58cm (18¾–23in); weight 17–25kg (37½–55lb).

Braque Saint Germain [FCI] originally developed during the reign of Charles X, hence its alternative name. The breed is now slightly modified to produce a combination of elegance, speed and stamina.

The skull is DOMED, the STOP not pronounced, the ears rather low set and the MUZZLE slightly rounded. The chest is deep and the LOINS and hindquarters strong. The white, short, smooth coat is FLECKED with orange, which may form patches on the head and ears. Height 51–61cm (20–24in); weight 18–26kg (39½–57lb).

Bray Irish HARRIER pack formed in 1900 to hunt a COUNTRY in County Dublin.

Brazilian Fila FILA BRASILIERO.

Brazilian Greyhound VEADEIRO CATARINENSE.

Brazilian Mastiff FILA BRASILIERO.

Brazilian Molosser FILA BRASILIERO.

Brazilian Terrier TERRIER BRASILIERO.

Brazilian Tracker RASTREADOR BRASILIERO.

bread DOG BREAD.

break 1. (of GUNDOG or HOUND) train: BREAK IN. 2. leave; depart: BREAK COVER; BREAK FENCE. 3. change: BREAK COLOUR. 4. BREAK UP. 5. point at which a SEMI-PRICK EAR bends. [*illus* SEMI-PRICK EAR]

> The ears are in proportion to the size of the head, and, if they are carried properly and unquestionably break naturally, are seldom too small. [6 COLLIE]

6. (of a GUNDOG or SHEEP DOG) act before the command to do so has been given. 7. (of fighting dogs) separate. *See also* BREAKING STICK. 8. (of racing dogs) set off from the TRAP.

break colour (of coat) assume adult coloration. Puppies are often born with a coat that is darker than it will be when they are older.

break cover quit a hiding place, orig. of a fox or other quarry.

break fence (of a GUNDOG) leave the enclosure occupied by his HANDLER.

> You will not let your pupil 'break fence', or get out of your sight. [184]

break in (esp. of GUNDOG or HOUND) train.

> However, Shot, who was, as a matter of fact, quite unbroken, tore after them, and soon returned with a fine young black-cock in his mouth. [241]
>
> Let it be observed, however, that all the perfection to which we have brought both the breeding and breaking of these animals, we are not always sufficiently particular. [166a]
>
> The cruelties that are perpetrated on puppies during the course of the education or breaking-in, are sometimes infamous. [406]

break of ear BREAK(3).

break up (of HOUNDS) eat the quarry.

> Hounds who don't break up foxes usually fail to do so either because they are fat and blown and too gross, or because they have not been encouraged in the right manner and have got into this slack habit. [235]

breaker one who breaks or trains GUNDOGS.

> The chief requisites in a breaker are – firstly command of temper, . . . secondly, consistency . . . and, lastly, the exercise of a little reflection, to enable him to judge what meaning an unreasoning animal is likely to attach to every word or sign. [184]

breaking stick lever used to prise open the mouths of fighting dogs.

> He always carried a wedge-shaped breaking stick, whittled from a piece of Grandfather Purse's hickory cane, in his belt just in case the dog latched on to someone and he had to pry his jaws loose. [131]

breastbone STERNUM.

breast-high scent scent that hangs above the ground enabling HOUNDS to run with their heads up.

> The scent most favourable to the hound is when the effluvium is kept by the gravity of the air at the height of the breast. This is what is meant when the scent is said to be 'breast-high'. It is then not above his reach, nor does he need to stoop for it. [393]

Brecon founded as the Brecon Harriers in 1871, the pack has hunted fox since 1906. The COUNTRY in Powys is largely hill and moor.

Brecon Harriers BRECON.

bred by exhibitor 1. of a dog whose DAM was owned by the exhibitor at the time of its birth. 2. [AKC] show class, self explanatory.

bred in the purple of a dog whose parents were champions at the time of its birth.

breech 1. inner surface of the thigh, adjacent to the anus.

> The breech musculation should also be strongly developed [203, former BOXER]

2. (of birth presentation) feet or hindquarters first.

breech birth BREECH(2).

breech presentation BREECH(2).

Breeches.

breeches profuse growth of hair on the rear legs. [*illus.*]

> There should be abundant coat to form a mane, breeching and brush. [6, BORDER COLLIE]

breeching 1. long hair forming BREECHES. 2. tan-coloured hair on the inside of the thighs.

> Tan outside hind legs, commonly called breeching, is undesirable. [203, MANCHESTER TERRIER]

breed 1. dogs that look alike and are the product of parents with a similar appearance and which, when mated together, reproduce their kind.

> Men are generally more careful of the breed of their horses and dogs than of their children. [282]

2. select mates for the purpose of producing puppies. 3. (Am.) MATE.

breed club association formed to promote and protect a certain breed.

Breed Standard detailed description of a breed's characteristics intended as a guide for breeders and judges.

Breed Council [KC] federation of breed clubs in the UK.

breeder 1. owner of the bitch at the time she gives birth. 2. (Am.) bitch used for BREEDING(3).

breeder's class FCI show class for a group of four dogs of the same breed or variety that have been bred – but not necessarily owned – by the same breeder.

breeding 1. parentage.
> Her lineage and breeding were no less
> Than of a Persian royally descended. [86]

2. having an aristocratic PEDIGREE.
> (For true good breeding's so polite,
> 'Twould call the very Devil white). [231]

3. The practice of selecting a STUD-DOG and BROOD-BITCH for the purpose of mating.

breeding programme carefully thought out sequence of matings intended to produce a particular result.

breeding stock animals used for BREEDING(3).

breeding terms arrangements whereby a former owner retains rights to STUD-WORK from a dog, or more frequently, to all or some of the offspring of a bitch.

brennage (obs.) a tax levied on the coarse BREAD formerly fed to dogs. (der. probably from the fact that the main constituent of the bread was bren or bran.)

Breton Spaniel BRITTANY. [184]

Briard [KC] rugged French herding breed of ancient origin.

The slightly DOMED skull and strong square MUZZLE, with characteristic black lips, are of equal length; the large eyes have an expression which is both gentle and intelligent. The short ears are high set and fall close to the head. The neck is of good length and the shoulders WELL LAID BACK. The TOPLINE is level to a slightly sloping CROUP; the chest is broad and deep. The hindquarters are muscular and WELL ANGULATED, feet are strong, slightly rounded and with firm pads. The tail is long and carried low with a terminal upward hook. The long, dry, slightly wavy coat is either SELF-COLOURED or shaded in black, fawn or slate grey. Height 56–69cm (22–27in).

brick-shaped head long, rectangular head, in which the skull and MUZZLE are of similar width.

Bride Valley Irish BEAGLE pack formed in 1960 to hunt a COUNTRY in County Cork.

bridge topline of the MUZZLE, as seen in profile.

bridle 1. (of an IN-SEASON bitch) demonstrate sexual arousal. 2. lines which run under a sled and attach to the gangline ring.

Bridlespur (US) 1. American, English and crossbred FOXHOUND pack formed in 1927 to hunt a COUNTRY in the foothills of the Ozark Mountains in Missouri. 2. (US) BASSET pack formed to hunt a COUNTRY in Missouri.

Brighton Coach-dog (obs.) name given to the DAL-MATIAN as a result of the fame of a particular dog.
> For a long period a Dalmatian dog accompanied the only coach which, in 1851, ran between Brighton and London. He belonged to the ostler at the Newcastle Place stables, Edgeware Road. [123]

Bright's disease acute or chronic inflammation of the kidneys.

Brighton Foot former 15½in BEAGLE pack formed in 1891 to hunt a COUNTRY in Sussex. A rabies scare resulted in the entire pack being destroyed in 1897; a new pack was formed in the following year. In 1941 the pack was amalgamated with the Storrington, formed in 1926 and the name changed to Brighton and Storrington.

Brighton and Storrington BRIGHTON FOOT.

brindle randomly striped pattern formed by black hairs on a lighter, but not white, GROUND to create an overall effect which may be light or dark.
> She was a lovely creature – the purest brindle without a speck of white, and free from the unbalanced look of most dogs of her breed. [143a]

brindling BRINDLE markings.

bring to bay pursue quarry into a situation where its further flight or escape is prevented.

brinke 1. (of coat) coloured patch. [159] 2. var. BRINDLE.
> One patch of brown brinkle on the left eye and left ear. [356*]

briquet French HAREHOUND.

Briquet CHIEN D'ARTOIS.

Briquet Griffon Vendéen [FCI] one of the four varieties of GRIFFON VENDÉEN.

brisket line formed by the sternum; the lower line of the chest between the forelegs. [*illus.* POINTS]
> How coolly he takes it! – and how he will suffer himself to be dragged, shaken, and rattled, till his opponent is tired! – and then how he goes to work! and eats his way from leg to leg, and finishes at the brisket! [32]
> Chest, wide and with good depth of brisket. [203, LARGE MÜNSTERLÄNDER]

bristle (of coat) short, stiff.
> Coat . . . Short and bristly; harsh to touch. [203, SHAR PEI].

Bristol and Clifton Harriers CLIFTON FOOT.

Britannia former 16in CROSS-BRED BEAGLE pack formed in 1878 by officers of the Royal Navy College to hunt a COUNTRY in Devon.

British Bulldog BULLDOG.

British dog tick *IXODES CANISUGA.*

Brittany [KC] the breed's SPANIEL-like appearance formerly resulted in its being regarded as a spaniel outside its French homeland but, in fact, the Brittany is basically a SETTER which, in common with many European GUNDOG breeds, is also a versatile POINTER and RETRIEVER.

The head is of medium length, slightly rounded and with slight MEDIAN LINE. The STOP is well defined and the MUZZLE tapered but not SNIPY. The pendulous ears are described as vine-shaped. The chest is deep and the LOINS short and strong. The tail may be naturally short. The coat is fairly fine, but dense, with orange, liver, black or TRICOLOUR on a white GROUND. Height 47–50cm (18½–19½in); weight 13–15kg (28½–33lb).

Brittany Spaniel BRITTANY.

broad jump one of the obstacles in OBEDIENCE TRI-ALS, a test of ability to jump a distance.

brock 1. BADGER.
> Driv'st hence the wolf, the tod, the brock,
> And other vermin from the flock. [199a]

2. a three-year-old stag.

Brocklesby the hunt dates from about 1714 and hunts fox in a wold and arable COUNTRY in Lincolnshire.

Broholmer [FCI] MASTIFF breed with origins in Denmark. It was established during the last century and rescued from the brink of extinction during the 1970s.

  A large and powerful breed, with an impressive head with broad, flat skull, strong MUZZLE and FLEWED lips. The chest is broad and deep, the back rather long with strong LOINS and a sloping CROUP. The short, harsh coat is shades of yellow or brown, with dark POINTS(4); some white is allowed on the chest. Height 70–75cm (27½–29½in); weight 52–63kg (114½–138½lb).

broken 1. uneven, not uniform; damaged. 2. of a GUNDOG trained to its intended purpose.

broken coat interim between WIRE and SMOOTH coat.

broken colour 1. (of coat) solid colour interspersed by hairs of another colour. 2. white patches on an otherwise dark coat. [185]

broken down 1. (colloq.) IN SEASON. 2. (of racing dog) injured.

broken ear deformed ear.

broken hock fracture of the scaphoid bone. A common injury to racing GREYHOUNDS.

broken pasterns DOWN IN THE PASTERNS.

broken up face face in which a receding nose, LAY-BACK, deep STOP and exaggerated WRINKLE(2) 'break up' the smooth lines of a normal face.

Broken-Haired Terrier AIREDALE TERRIER. [123]

bronchioles branched tubes within the lungs which carry air to the alveoli.

bronchus large passageways which convey air to the lungs.

bronze dark bluish-brown with a metallic sheen.

Bronwydd former 15½in BEAGLE pack formed in 1845 to hunt a moorland COUNTRY in Dyfed.

bronzing (of coat) tan coloration undesirably inter-mingled with black hairs.
> When tan-coloured hairs appear amongst the black ones. [320]

brooch bone FIBULA.

brood-bitch bitch used for BREEDING(3).

brought to their noses (of HOUNDS) obliged to resume hunting by scent after losing sight of the quarry.

brown dog tick RHIPICEPHALUS SANGUINEUS.

brown lick stain stain on the upper lip of some dogs caused by persistent licking of vulvar discharge.

brown mouth syn. BROWN LICK STAIN. Stain seen on the upper lips of dogs which lick an excessive vulvar discharge.

brown nose nose which is not black, either through fading, resulting from dietary deficiency, or as a desirable or undesirable inherited characteristic.
> Nose solid brown or black depending on coat colour. [203, GERMAN SHORT-HAIRED POINTER]

brows superciliary arches formed by the frontal bone above the eyes.
> Skull broad, slightly rounded at top, with fairly prominent brow. [203, ST BERNARD]

Bruce-Lowe system (obs.) discredited breeding system invented by Rev. Rosslyn Bruce. See SATURATION.

Brucella canis a species of gran-negative rod [54]; an infectious cause of abortion. See BRUCELLOSIS.

brucellosis disease caused by *Brucella*. (der. Sir David Bruce, bacteriologist who identified *Brucella* in 1931.)

Bruno de Jura Swiss SCENTHOUND used to find and disturb game. A dog with a strong resemblance to a lightly built BLOODHOUND to which the breed is closely related. Height 43–59cm (17–23¼in); weight 15–20kg (33–44lb).

Bruno Jura Laufhund BRUNO DE JURA.

brush 1. tail of a fox.

2. any tail that resembles that of a fox.
> Tail. Well furred of round fox brush shape. [203, SIBERIAN HUSKY]

brushbow the curved prow of a sled.

brushing moving so close behind that the legs touch.

Brussels Griffon [AKC] GRIFFON BRUXELLOIS.
> Partakes of the Yorkshire Terrier, though much smaller in the skull and shorter in the face than is associated with that breed; added to which he has a protruding chin, a very harsh coat, and an altogether quaint expression. [123]

Búansú wild dog inhabitant of northern India.
> The wild dog of Nepal, the Búansú, . . . is more or less prevailing through the whole of Northern India, and even southwards of the coast of Coromandel, he [Hodgson] thought that he had discovered the primitive race of dog. This is a point that can never be decided. [406]

buck 1. male hare or rabbit. 2. male fallow deer. [151c] 3. (Am.) an object used to teach dogs to retrieve.

bucket muzzle MUZZLE(2) made of sheet material with apertures to admit air.

buckhound (obs.) STAGHOUND.

Buckinghamshire former OTTERHOUND pack formed in 1890 to hunt the rivers Ouse, Nene, Welland, Lovatt, Glen, Gwash, Cherwell, Granta, Arrow, Evenlode, Ivel, Towe, Avon, Sowe, Leam, Bain, Wreake, Awn, Thame, Stour, Anker, Blythe, Windrush, Colne, Isis, Ray, Idle and Dove, and their various tributaries.

Buckland Beagles WORCESTER PARK AND BUCK-
LAND.

Buckram (US) BEAGLE pack formed in 1934 to hunt
hare and cottontail rabbit over a rolling, open,
plough and woodland COUNTRY in New York State.

budding iron SEARING IRON.

> We determined to try the cautery to its full extent.
> We chained him up in the morning, and penetrated
> through the skin with the budding iron. The spasms
> were dreadfully violent, and he was scarcely able to
> walk or to stand. [406]

bufe (17th cent. Eng.) dog.

bufe's nob dog's head.

buffer dog. [280]

buffer lurking dog stealing. [280]

buffer nabber dog thief. [280]

buffer napper dog thief. [280]

buffer's nab dog's head. [280]

Buffon, George Louis Leclere Comte de Buffon,
1707–1788, French naturalist who produced *Histoire
Naturelle* (1749–1789) and *Epoques de la Nature*
(1777). He was among the first to attempt to classify
dog breeds.

bugher dog. [280]

Buhund Norwegian house-dog.

bulbus glandis bulb midway along a dog's penis
which enlarges greatly during mating and facilitiates
the TIE.

bull and terrier formerly descriptive of CROSSES
between old BULLDOGS and various TERRIERS
intended either for fighting or BAITING smaller
animals.

bull-baiting the practice of using dogs to torment a
tethered bull.

> The practice of bull-baiting is not merely permitted,
> it is even enjoined by the municipal law in some
> places. [330]

bull-biter BULLENBEISER.

bull neck thick, muscular, bull-like neck.

Bull Run (US) AMERICAN FOXHOUND pack formed
in 1911 to hunt undulating pasture in Virginia.

Bull Terrier [AKC, FCI, KC] James Hinks of
Birmingham produced the bull terrier from earlier
BULL AND TERRIER CROSSES, which – despite dog
fighting having been made illegal in Britain in 1835
– continued to be tested against their former purpose
at least until the early years of the 20th century.

The breed's characteristic smooth, egg-shaped
head, small, deep eyes, and small PRICK EARS are distinctive. The body is powerful, rounded and short
and the well-boned limbs heavily muscled. The coat
is short, harsh and close, either entirely white over a
white skin (colour being permitted on the head), or
coloured, preferably BRINDLE, but reds, fawns
and TRICOLOURS are permitted; blue and liver are
unacceptable. Of size the BREED STANDARD says
only that there are neither weight nor height limits,
but that there should be the impression of maximum
substance for the size of the dog.

> I used to think, should e'er mishap
> Betide my crumple-visaged Ti,
> In shape of prowling thief, or trap,
> Or coarse bull-terrier – I should die. [80]

> And those pups, what do you think I'm to do with
> 'em, when they're twice as big as you? – for I'm
> pretty sure the father was that hulking bull-terrier of
> Will Baker's – wasn't he now, eh, you sly hussy?
> [128]

> The stone parapets bordering the Thames became,
> as a consequence, the sauntering ground of
> Argentinian women and their bull-terriers. [147]

Bull Terrier, Miniature miniature version of BULL
TERRIER. Height under 35cm (13¾in).

bulla osteotomy aural surgery to enlarge infected
canals.

Bulldog [FCI, KC] although the breed was developed from the old gladiatorial breeds, the Bulldog
had become more massive, larger-headed and
shorter-limbed even before its former activity was
outlawed in Britain. The modern breed is thick set,
low slung, powerful and compact.

The head is massive, the face short and the MUZZLE
broad. The body is short, well muscled, and the
TOPLINE ascends towards the hindquarters. The
hindquarters are lightly made in comparison with the
massive forequarters. The coat is fine and short,
whether whole coloured, BRINDLE, red, fawn,
FALLOW, white or PIED. Weight 22.7–25kg (50–55lb).

> Taylor, who praised everything of his own to excess,
> in short, whose geese were all swans, as the proverb
> says, expatiated on the excellence of his bull-dog
> which, he told us, was perfectly well shaped.
> Johnson, after examining the animal attentively, thus
> repressed the vain-glory of our host: 'No, Sir, he is
> not well shaped; for there is not the quick transition
> from the thickness of the fore part, to the tenuity –
> the thin part – behind, which a bull-dog ought to
> have.' This tenuity was the only hard word which I
> heard him use during this interview, and it will be
> observed, he instantly put another expression in its
> place. Taylor said, a small Bulldog was as good as
> a large one. Johnson: 'No, Sir, for, in proportion to
> his size, he has strength: and your argument would
> prove, that a good Bulldog may be as small as a
> mouse.' It was amazing how he entered with per-
> spicacity and keenness upon everything that
> occurred in conversation. Most men, whom I know,
> would no more think of discussing a question about
> a Bulldog than of attacking a bull. [58]

> When bull-baiting and dog-fighting ended, the
> [Bull]dog was bred for 'fancy', and characteristics
> desired at earlier times for fighting and baiting pur-
> poses were exaggerated, so that the unfortunate dog
> became unhappily abnormal. In this transition stage
> huge, broad ungainly heads were obtained, legs
> widely bowed were developed, and frequently the
> dog was a cripple. [37]

Bullenbeiser German MOLOSSAN used for hunting
wild bulls, literally the bull-biter.

> The larger type of Baren or Bullenbeiser with his
> tremendous strength and courage and ancient lin-
> eage, was gradually replaced by the faster and more
> elegant Englische Dogge. [115]

Bullet Head (colloq.) former name for the BOSTON TERRIER.

Bullmastiff [FCI, KC] archetypal Gamekeeper's Nightdog (as the breed was formerly known) used to deter or apprehend poachers. A powerful, yet active dog with a large, square skull; the short MUZZLE, with FLEWS(1) of moderate length, is always black. The neck is well arched and the chest wide and deep, the body short and compact. The hindquarters are wide and muscular, the tail set high. The coat is short and hard, of any shade of BRINDLE, fawn or red; white is permitted on the chest. Height 61–68.5cm (24–27in); weight 41–59kg (90–130lb).

Bullous pemphigoid one cause of non-infectious auto-immune disease of the skin and oral mucosa, characterized by blisters or ulcers.

bullring 1. metal ring to which bulls were tethered for BAITing (2) 2. enclosure within which bulls were baited.

bully having bull-like physical characteristics: short, heavy, thick-set.

bumping (Am.) prematurely FLUSHing a bird.

bumpy (of cheeks) protuberant; having protuberant cheeks.

bung-tailed (obs.) having a naturally short tail.
No attempt was made to keep the bung-tailed breed free from outside crosses, and by interbreeding with long-tailed dogs the variety, if it was a genuine one, was lost. [37c]

bunny-hopping abnormal gait in which the hind legs move in unison, as with the gait of the rabbit. Often a symptom of spinal dystraphism.

Burdizzo emasculatome instrument designed for bloodless castration, but also illicitly used to alter ear carriage in dogs.

Burgos Pointer PERDIGUERO DE BURGOS.

Burmese Wild Dog
closely resembles the Malay Wild Dog, but is more strongly built. . . . The Burmese Wild Dog was found in Upper Burma. [185]

burr fleshy protuberance in the external ear canal.
'Rose ear' correct, i.e. folding inwards and back, upper or front inner edge curving outwards and backwards, showing part of inside of burr. [203, BULLDOG]

bursa membrane enclosing an internal organ or structure.

burst short and unusually fast run; or that part of a run in which HOUNDs move unusually quickly.

Burton FOXHOUND pack formed in 1774 to hunt fox in a heavy-plough COUNTRY in Lincolnshire; it was hunted by Squire Osbaldeston from 1809–1813.

Burton Constable Beagles HUNSLEY BEACON.

bury rabbit's burrow. [159]

Bush Dog *ICTICYON VENATICUS.*

Bushey Heath former 14in BEAGLE pack formed in 1890 to hunt a COUNTRY in Hertfordshire.

Butcher Hound BUTCHER'S DOG.

Butcher's Dog variety of the KEEPER(2).
So called for the necessity of his use, for his service affords great benefit to the Butcher as well as in following as in taking his cattle when need constrains, urges, and requires. [139]

Butcher's Hounde BUTCHER'S DOG. [139]

butterfly dog (obs. colloq.) PAPILLON.

butterfly nose PARTI-COLOURED nose.
A slight butterfly nose is permissible. [203, OTTER-HOUND]
The nose is black; butterfly or pink noses in any color are disqualifying. [6, SHIBA INU]
Flesh colored ('Dudley noses') or spotted ('butterfly noses') are undesirable. [6, ENGLISH SPRINGER SPANIEL]

Butterfly Spaniel (obs. colloq.) PAPILLON.

buttocks fleshy part of the rump or hips. [*illus.* POINTS]

Button ears.

button ear short ears which fold forward, with the tip close to the skull. [*illus.*]
The tip of the leather points downwards, so that the entrance to the ear is practically concealed. [46]
'Button ear' – ear flap folding forward, tip lying close to skull to cover opening. [120d, PUG]

buying the board (Am., of a gambler) placing wagers on several dogs in the same race.

Bwllfa Hounds LLANGEINOR.

bye qualification to move into another round of a competition without the need to compete.

bye-dog dog that receives a BYE.

Byelorussian Ovtcharka Russian herding breed with many similarities to a more than usually sturdy GERMAN SHEPHERD, from which it is probably descended. Height 61–74cm (24–29in); weight 35–48kg (77–105½lb).

by sired by; signifies that a dog is sired by the dog subsequently named.
'Marmion was by Sir Bellingham Graham's Marmion, you know; and Marcia was by Lord Lonsdale's Monarch out of Modish'; and so he went on through his entry. [344a]

C

c gene symbol for albino. [395]

c^b gene symbol for blue-eyed white. [395]

c^ch gene symbol for chinchilla. [395]

c^d gene symbol for dark-eyed white. [395]

ca Spanish dog.

cabin cur Irish MONGREL house-dog.
> In some cabins you will now and then find a nice little terrier, or a small spaniel, but the generality are what people call cabin curs, most of them very ugly dogs with large heads and long rat-like tails. [195]

cabriole front CHIPPENDALE FRONT.

Cabul Dog (obs.) AFGHAN HOUND. [123]

CAC CERTIFICATE D'APTITUDE AU CHAMPIONSHIP.

cacao poisoning consequence of over-indulgence in chocolate, the theobromine in which is poisonous to dogs.

cachere hunter. [159]

cachexia weakness produced by illness or injury.

CACIB CERTIFICATE D'APTITUDE AU CHAMPIONSHIP INTERNATIONALE DE BEAUTÉ DE LA FCI.

CACIT CERTIFICATE D'APTITUDE AU CHAMPIONSHIP INTERNATIONALE DE TRAVAIL DE LA FCI.

cacomelia congenital limb deformity.

Ca de Bestiar [FCI] PERRO DE PASTOR MALLORQUIN.

Ca de Bou PERRO DE PRESA MALLORQUIN.

caecitis inflammation of the caecum, often caused by WHIPWORM infestation.

caecocele hernia of the caecum.

caecum 1. first part of the large intestine, in dogs a small coiled organ.
2. pocket of tissue.

Ca Eivissencs IBIZAN HOUND.

caesar dim. CAESARIAN SECTION.

Caesarean section surgical removal of puppies via the abdomen. (der. Julius Caesar, reputed to have been so born.)

caesarotomy CAESARIAN SECTION.

Cairn Terrier [AKC, FCI, KC] one of the TERRIER breeds indigenous to Scotland, and originally used to control vermin. The breed is alert and workmanlike, with an air of confidence.

The head is noticeably small in relation to the body, the skull broad and the STOP pronounced, the eyes are slightly sunk and protected by bushy eyebrows, the ears are small, pricked and pointed. The forelimbs are straight, the TOPLINE level and the chest deep and WELL SPRUNG, the LOINS strong and supple. The hindquarters are strongly muscled with HOCKS WELL LET DOWN. Forefeet are larger than the hind feet. The tail is naturally short and carried GAILY. The DOUBLE COAT is weather-resistant with a soft, short undercoat and a harsh, profuse but not open topcoat; the colour may be cream, WHEATEN, red, grey, whether BRINDLED or not. Height 28–31cm (11–12¼in); weight 6–7.5kg (13–16½lb).

> So the only people who liked him were the owners of a Cairn,
> Which frequently bit him, thus reassuring them that its heart was not hisn but theirn. [262]

Caius, Dr Johannes (1510–1573) author of *De Canis Anglicas*, intended as a contribution for Conrad Gesners's encyclopedia but translated into English by Abraham Flemming in 1576. Caius was the physician to three monarchs. Gonville Hall, Oxford, had originally been founded in 1348; Caius elevated it to the status of a college – Gonville and Caius – in 1558.

Cajun Rules rules used to govern organized dog fighting, especially in the southern states of America.

calcaneus rear tarsal bone, to which is attached the muscles and tendons that flex the HOCK-JOINT. [*illus.* SKELETON]

calcaemia condition characterized by excessive levels of calcium in the blood.

calcibilia condition characterized by the presence of calcium in the urine.

calcifying sponeurotic fibroma development of nodular masses esp. on the ZYGOMATIC ARCH.

calcinosis circumscripta CALCIUM GOUT.

calcinosis cutis lesions in a thin skin caused by hyperadrenocorticism.

calcium dietary mineral essential to the growth and maintenance of bone.

calcium carbonate insoluble salt occurring naturally in bones; necessary to skeletal development.

calcium gout inherited condition resulting in the development of calcium nodules in subcutaneous tissue. (Mode of inheritance, familial.)

calf One-year-old stag or hind. [151c]

calf knee sloping PASTERN.

Californian disease COCCIDIOIDOMYCOSIS.

Callaby Hounds WEST PERCY.

calling 1. (euph.) IN SEASON, more often of cats which tend to be very vocal at this time. 2. the art of attracting game by means of imitative sounds.
> A Jack Hare can be called in March and April if the weather is suitable. [165]

callus horny growth, esp. over joints, formed as a result of pressure or friction.

Calvé-Perthes disease LEGG CALVÉ PERTHES DISEASE.

Camargo (US) American, English and crossbred FOXHOUND pack formed in 1925 to hunt a post-and-rail COUNTRY in Ohio.

Herder BERGER DU LANGUEDOC.

cambra dog. [280]

cambrel (obs.) HOCK. [159]
> His cambrels crooked. [245a]

Cambridge University DRAGHOUND pack formed in 1855 to hunt carted deer; converted to draghounds in 1910.

Cambridgeshire 1. FOXHOUND pack dating from the mid 18th century and hunting a COUNTRY in Cambridgeshire, Huntingdonshire and Bedfordshire. 2. HARRIER pack which originated in 1745 and was re-established in 1891.

Camden (US) American and crossbred FOXHOUND pack formed in 1926 to hunt a flat woodland, pasture and riverside COUNTRY in South Carolina.

Camel back.

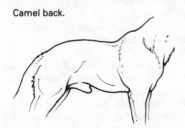

camel back a TOPLINE that dips behind the WITHERS, rises to a hump and then falls to the rump. [*illus.*]

Cameroons Dog long-legged, PRICK-EARed, short-coated, medium-sized primitive African hunting dog. Either pied or variegated; unrecognized breed.

Campylobacter fetus jejuni bacteria which can cause abortion.

Camus breed of dog which warned William, Prince of Orange of an attack by the Duke of Alva's men.

> For troth, ever since, untill the Prince's dying day, he kept one of that dogges' race; as did many friends and followers. The most or all of these dogges were white little hounds, with crooked noses, called Camuses. [394]

Canaan Dog [FCI, KC] breed which has probably been domesticated since biblical times but which has also existed as a PARIAH. Type remains variable and the breed has an equally variable range of use, from DOMESTIC GUARD, to HERDER and hunter.

The head is typically vulpine, with a slightly rounded skull, dark, slightly slanted eyes, and low set PRICK EARS. The neck is arched and set into well-laid shoulders, with straight forelegs. The TOPLINE slopes from WITHERS to CROUP, with a deep BRISKET and pronounced TUCK-UP. Hindquarters are strongly muscled and broad. The bushy tail is set high and carried curled over the back. The coat is straight and harsh, sandy to red brown, white or black, with or without white on body and legs. The MASK may be dark or light. Height 51–61cm (20–24in); weight 18–25kg (39½–55lb).

Canadian Eskimo Dog ESKIMO DOG.

Canadian Kennel Club organization responsible for the administration of canine affairs in Canada; founded in 1888.

Canal-boat Dog SCHIPPERKE.

Canarian Warren Hound PORTUGUESE WARREN HOUND.

Canarian Warren Dog PODENCO CANARIO.

Canary Dog PERRO DE PRESA CANARIO.

cancer inherited tendency to produce malignant tumours. (Mode of inheritance, polygenic.)

candida fungal infection.

candle-flame ear ears narrower at the base than in mid-section, then curving to a sharp point.

> Ears. Candle-flame shape, slightly pointed tips. [203, ENGLISH TOY TERRIER (BLACK AND TAN)]

cane (Ital.) dog.

Cane Corso re-creation of extinct Sicilian drover; typically MOLOSSAN.

The head is broad and strong with a powerful MUZZLE and usually CROPPED ears; the neck is muscular and the rather long body powerful; the legs are well boned and muscular; the tail is traditionally DOCKED. The coat is short and harsh, with black or BRINDLE being popular colours. Height 51–56cm (20–22in).

Canecutter's disease LEPTOSPIROSIS.

Cane da Pastore Bergamasco [FCI] PASTORAL GUARD and HERDER from northern Italy, the breed has much in common with herding breeds from France and Poland and its heavy corded coat suggests a strong relationship with the breeds of Hungarian origin.

The skull and MUZZLE are strong and broad, the STOP well defined. The body is athletically muscled, the chest deep with good spring of rib, the back strong and the limbs well boned. The tail is POT HOOK carried low. The wiry coat is corded except over the quarters where a woolly texture is usual. Colour may be grey or PEPPER AND SALT. Height 56–61cm (22–24in); weight 26–38kg (57–83½lb).

Cane da Pastore dell'Italia Centrale MAREMMA SHEEP DOG.

Cane da Pastore Maremmano Abruzzese [FCI] MAREMMA SHEEP DOG.

Cane de Quirinale VOLPINO ITALIANO.

Cane de Quirnale VOLPINO ITALIANO.

Cane di Macellaio CANE CORSO.

Canes aucupatorij land and water SPANIELS. [139]

Canes bellicosi Roman dogs used in war or in the arena.

Canes defensores defending dogs. [139]

Canes nares sagaces Roman dogs which hunt by scent.

Canes pastorales pecurarii Roman shepherd dogs.

Canes pugnaces Roman dogs used in war or the arena.

Canes rustici coarse dogs such as the SHEPHERD'S DOG and MASTIFF which Fleming further subdivides, according to their use, into KEEPER or WATCHMAN, BUTCHER'S DOG, MESSENGER or CARRIER, MOONER, WATER DRAWER, TINKER'S CUR and FENCER, as well as WAPPS or WARNERS, TURNSPITS and DANCERS.

Canes venatici hunting dogs. [139]

Canes villatici Roman HOUSE-DOGS.

Caniche POODLE.

Caniche de grande taille [FCI] STANDARD POODLE.

Caniche nain MINIATURE POODLE.

Caniche toy TOY POODLE.

Canicola fever LEPTOSPIROSIS.
Canidae family of mammals which includes thirty-five species of dog, wolf, fox and jackal, distributed throughout Eurasia, the Americas, Africa and Australasia.
canine appertaining to dogs.
> 'Well, old boy,' said Romford, laying his heavy hand on Jonathan Lotherington's shoulder, 'I've come to see these 'ere canine dogs. [344c]

canine CANINE TOOTH.
canine adenovirus Type 1 infection INFECTIOUS CANINE HEPATITIS.
canine adenovirus 2 one of several viruses implicated in KENNEL COUGH.
canine appetite (of man) huge appetite.
canine atopy inherited seasonal allergic response resulting in pruritus and self-trauma. (Mode of inheritance, unknown.)
canine babesiosis blood disorder caused by *Babesia canis* or *Baesia gibsoni* infestation.
canine brucellosis disease caused by *Brucellosis canis* and resulting in late abortion, infertility in females and scrotal dermatitis in males.
canine coronavirus infection one cause of acute gastroenteritis esp. in young puppies.
canine Cushing's Syndrome CUSHING'S SYNDROME.
canine cyclic haematopoiesis inherited condition which reduces ability to resist infection as a result of the fluctuating numbers of circulating neutrophils.
canine distemper (CD) DISTEMPER.
canine ehrlichiosis tick-born disease transmitted by the tick *RHIPCEPHALUS SANGUINEUS*.
canine eosinophilic granuloma EOSINOPHILIC GRANULOMA.
canine haemorrhagic fever CANINE EHRLICHIOSIS.
canine haemorrhagic gastroenteritis condition causing acute vomiting and blood-infused diarrhoea and leading to dehydration.
canine hepatitis Infectious Canine HEPATITIS.
canine hereditary hypotrichosis BLACK HAIR FOLLICLE DYSPLASIA.
canine herpesvirus infection viral infection producing respiratory disease and genital lesions; a subsidiary cause of KENNEL COUGH.
canine hip dysplasia HIP DYSPLASIA.
canine hypertrophic osteodystrophy disease resulting in painfully swollen limbs, lameness, fever, lethargy and weight loss. Most commonly found in rapidly growing juveniles of very large and giant breeds.
canine hypoxic rhabdomyolysis collapse following strenuous or unaccustomed exercise, often associated with a diet high in carbohydrate. Occurs esp. in SIGHTHOUNDS. Also called azoturia, Monday morning disease and tying-up syndrome.
canine hysteria condition characterized by frenzied movement and convulsions, and brought about by exposure to agene (the agent used formerly to whiten flour). Since the use of agene was discontinued, the condition has disappeared.
canine infectious tracheobronchitis inflammation of the bronchia and trachea; KENNEL COUGH.
canine juvenile osteodystrophy OSTEODYSTROPHIA FIBROSA.
canine letter R. (der. its growling sound.)
canine malignant lymphoma malignant tumours of the lymphatic system.
canine nasal mites PNEUMONYSSUS CANINUM.
canine parainfluenzavirus major cause of KENNEL COUGH.
canine parvovirus infection recently mutated viral infection which attacks the lymphoid tissues resulting in severe dysentery dehydration and, if untreated, collapse and death.
canine parvovirus type 1 (CPV-1) parvovirus infection not associated with clinical symptoms.
canine parvovirus type 2 (CPV-2) parvovirus infection characterized by blood-infused, foul-smelling diarrhoea, enteritis, rapid dehydration, and probable death within 24 hours of the onset of symptoms. Puppies that survive may develop PARVOVIRUS MYOCARDITIS.
canine piroplasmosis BABESIOSIS.
canine reovirus widespread virus which causes respiratory disease in dogs.
canine respiratory disease DISTEMPER; KENNEL COUGH.
canine rickettsiosis CANINE EHRLICHIOSIS.
canine secretory alloantigen (CSA) inherited susceptibility to allergic responses.
canine tick typhus CANINE EHRLICHIOSIS.
canine tooth each of the two upper and two lower fang-like teeth just behind the incisors. [*illus,* Denture]
canine transmittable venereal tumour tumorous growth of the male and female genitalia, most frequently found among roaming dogs.
canine tropical pancytopenia CANINE EHRLICHIOSIS.
canine typhus 1. STUTTGART DISEASE [185] (obs.) CANINE DISTEMPER. 2. CANINE EHRLICHIOSIS.
canine viral hepatitis viral disease which affects the kidneys. Infection is carried in the urine of infected animals, esp. rats.
canine viral papillomatosis multiple warts especially on the lips, tongue and mouth parts, occasionally in the eyes and on the skin. Regression may be spontaneous.
canine viral rhinotracheitis KENNEL COUGH.
canine wobbler syndrome WOBBLER SYNDROME.
Canis one genus of the family CANIDAE.
Canis adustrus side-striped Jackal. A long-headed inhabitant of the area around Kilimanjaro.
Canis adustus CANIS ADUSTRUS.
Canis anthus North African Jackal. A larger variation of the European and Indian Jackals.

Canis aquaticus major Great Water-Dog, which has long, curled hair like the fleece of a sheep, which about the ears is longer and hangs downwards. [72a]

Canis aquaticus minor Lesser Water-Dog, small variety of CANIS AQUATICUS MAJOR. [72a]

Canis aureus Golden Jackal. Found throughout India, Ceylon, Burma and Tegu, it is a hunter of small animals and a scavenger.

Canis azarae Azara's dog. Range extends over most of South America east of the Andes. Responds to domestication.

Canis bengalensis Bengal Fox. Common throughout India and easily domesticated, it is a slender-limbed, elegant fox with no strong odour; they are used as a quarry for local breeds of SIGHTHOUNDS.

Canis brecipilis Pyrame. Dog with a small, rounded head, short snout, and a tail turned up on the back. [72a]

Canis cancrivorus Carasissi or Crab-eating Dog. Range extends from the Orinoco to La Plata. It much resembles a rather powerful fox, but it has a short tail, and it varies considerably in size. Although it usually subsists off small mammals, it has a tendency to catch and eat crayfish, hence its popular name.

Canis canus Hoary Fox. Very small fox from south-west Asia.

Canis cauda [sinistrorsum] recurva breed which curls its tail to the left. Classified by LINNAEUS.

Canis chania Asse Fox. Short-MUZZLEd, long-eared fox from East and West Africa.

Canis corsac Corsac Fox. Inhabitant of central Asia, smaller than the COMMON FOX and with rounder eyes and a different scent.

Canis cove (obs., colloq.) dog-fancier, thief or dealer. [280]

Canis cultos (obs.) KEEPER. [128]

Canis dingo DINGO.

Canis domesticus SHEPHERD'S DOG. [72a]

Canis duckhunensis 'Colonel Sykes, . . . writing in 1831, described the variety named by him *Canis duckhunensis*, which he said was the wild dog of Dukhun, or Deccan.'

> Its head is compressed and elongated, its nose not very sharp. The eyes are oblique, the pupils round, the irises light-brown. The expression is that of a coarse, ill-natured Persian greyhound, without any resemblance to the jackal, the fox, or the wolf; . . . Ears long, erect, and somewhat rounded at the top, without any replication of the tragus. Limbs remarkably large and strong in relation to the bulk of the animal, its size being intermediate between the wolf and the jackal. [380]

Canis etruscus primitive Pleistocene Wolf.

Canis eurostictis Striped-tail Dog. A Brazilian wild dog with unusually large first upper molars.

Canis extrarius SPANIEL. [72a]

Canis famelicus Ruppel's Fennec. A small inhabitant of the Nubian Desert.

Canis familiaris domestic dog; 'faithful dog' [49a]

Canis familiaris cauda [sinistrorsum] recurvata class of dogs, identified by Linnaeus, which have tails curved to the left. [338]

Canis familiaris inastronzewi Mesolithic and Neolithic dogs found in northern Europe.

Canis familiaris matris-optimae Neolithic SHEEPDOG found in the Rhine valley.

Canis familiaris palustris primitive domestic dog dating from about 4000 BC, found in Neolithic Swiss lake dwellings, thought to be the ancestor of the smaller SPITZ breeds, TERRIERS, SCHNAUZERS and PINSCHERS. [312]

Canis familiaris poutiatini Neolithic dog found near Moscow.

Canis ferrilatus Tibetan Fox, probably a short-eared version of the Corsac Fox.

Canis fricator Pug-dog. [72a]

Canis fricatrix Rubbing or Cold Dog. [*227]

Canis furax Thievish Dog. [128]

Canis graius GREYHOUND. [*227]

Canis hallstromi New Guinea Singing Dog. An eponymous PARIAH dog now rare in the wild but safe from extinction in zoos and kennels. The head is wedge-shaped, the ears pricked, the body long and short-coated, usually in shades of red, with or without white markings. Height 35.5–38cm (14–15in); weight 9kg (20lb). The popular name derives from its unique musical howl.

Canis hybridus Bastard Pug-dog. [72a]

Canis islandicus Iceland Dog. [72a]

Canis jubatus Maned Wolf, the largest wild canine in South America which inhabits parts of Paraguay and surrounding areas; it is characterized by its exceptionally long limbs, large ears and bright coloration.

Canis lagopus Arctic Fox. A distinct species characterized by its dense blue or grey fur which turns white in winter and is much sought after as a fashion accessory. Unlike most foxes the species is gregarious, and has no unpleasant odour.

Canis laniarius FRENCH MATIN. [406]

Canis lantarium BUTCHER'S DOG. [128]

Canis latrans Prairie Wolf or Coyote. Found in the southern states of America and southwards to Costa Rica, its intense and eerie vocalization induces unreasonable fear of it.

Canis leucopus Desert Fox. A native of the Indian plains and resembling the Corsac Fox. Much used as quarry for HOUNDS brought from Britain.

Canis lunarius MOONER. [128]

Canis lupus Northern Wolf. Species that was formerly widespread throughout Europe, but now inhabits only remote parts of the continent.

Canis lupus antarcticus Antarctic Wolf. Small subspecies now confined to the Falkland Islands.

Canis lupus arabis small Desert Wolf of Arabia.

Canis lupus chanco Tibetan Wolf. A variation of the Northern Wolf (*CANIS LUPUS*), its short MUZZLE suggests that it is the most likely ancestor of the MASTIFF breeds.

Canis lupus hodophylax Japanese Wolf. A shorter-legged, shorter-MUZZLEd version of the Northern Wolf (*CANIS LUPUS*).

Canis lupus pallipes Asian Wolf. Smaller, lighter and with a shorter coat than the Northern Wolf (*CANIS LUPUS*), it is now confined to plains south of the Himalayas, formerly found as far west as Syria and Palestine.

Canis magellanicus Magellanic Dog or Colpeo. Inhabitant of area extending from northern Chile to Tierra del Fuego, it has a long MUZZLE and prominent OCCIPUT; unusually for a wild dog it barks, if only weakly.

Canis major (astronomy) Southern hemisphere constellation containing Sirius, the Dog Star.

Canis mandatarius CARRIER. [128]

Canis mastinus MASTIFF; 'great dog'. [*227]

Canis matris optimae early SHEEP DOG found in the Rhine valley.

Canis melitacus SHOCK DOG. [72a]

Canis melitaeus Maltese or pet dog. (Linnaeus)

Canis mesomelas Black-backed Jackal. A native of southern African savannah.

Canis microtis Small-eared Dog. Little-known native of the Amazon basin, it stands about 36cm (14in) high, and has a pointed nose, short, dark grey fur, and small ears.

Canis minor (astrology) constellation in the Northern hemisphere.

Canis mustelinus Weasel-coloured Dog. (Linnaeus)

Canis niger seu rufus Texan Red Wolf. A dark red or black subspecies of the Coyote (*CANIS LATRANS*).

Canis oegyptius Egyptian Dog. (Linnaeus)

Canis pallidus Pale Fox. A long-eared South African fox which much resembles a large FENNEC.

Canis parvidens Small-toothed Dog. An inhabitant of Brazil, remarkable for the small size of its CARNASSIAL TEETH.

Canis pastoralis SHEPHERD'S DOG. [128]

Canis piscator FISHER. [128]

Canis pomeranus POMERANIAN. [72a]

Canis primaevus Mrs Hodgson gave the name *Canis primaevus* to the BÚANSÚ of Nepal. [380]

Canis procyonoides Racoon-like Dog. Inhabitant of Japan and parts of China, where its flesh is regarded as a delicacy; they are more omnivorous than other foxes and may also hibernate.

Canis rufus Red Wolf. Native of south-east Texas and surrounding area.

Canis sarcinarius TINKER'S CUR. [128]

Canis sibiricus Siberian Dog. [72b]

Canis simensis Abyssinian Wolf. A small, lightly built variety now confined to Ethiopian uplands.

Canis sumatrensis a small, fox-like dog with smaller ears and a reddish colour. [380]

Canis variegatus LITTLE DANISH DOG. [72a]

Canis velox Kit Fox. A native of the plains of Saskatchewan and Missouri, a small and elegant fox subspecies.

Canis virginianus Colishé, Grey Fox or Virginian Fox. Range throughout Virginia, Texas, Guatemala, Honduras and Costa Rica. A popular quarry for HOUNDS, and one that has a tendency to climb trees in order to escape.

Canis vulpes Common Fox. With a more extensive range than any other Canidae, it is the familiar archetypal fox with red coat and brush tail.

Canis zerdab *VULPES ZERDA.*

canker nonspecific infection of the external ear canal.

> It was his business to take them out every day for walks, to pull thorns out of their feet, keep cankers out of their ears. [387b]

cannonball (of dogs) to increase pace dramatically towards the end of a race.

cannon bone METATARSAL BONE.

canophile someone with an inordinate interest in and liking for dogs.

canophilist CANOPHILE.

> The dog-worshippers, or canophilists as they are sometimes called, a people weak in their intellectuals, and as a rule unveracious, although probably not consciously so. [182c]

Cantab Terrier archetypal TERRIER breed said to have been developed by Doggy Lawrence during the late 19th century, and kept by students at Cambridge University; an ancestor of the NORFOLK and NORWICH TERRIERS.

canter gait intermediate between the trot and the gallop and with a three-beat tempo. The two hind legs and one foreleg move in unison, the other (independent) foreleg – either right or left – being referred to as the leading leg. (der. *Canterbury Trot*, supposedly the pace at which pilgrims travelled to Canterbury.)

canthus meeting point of upper and lower eyelids.

Cão breeds with Portuguese origins.

Cão da Serra de Aires [FCI] pastoral HERDER and GUARD with origins in southern Portugal. The breed is agile and quick, with a broad skull, slightly tapered MUZZLE and high-set, pendulous ears. The back is fairly long with a rounded CROUP and strong hindquarters. The coat is long and wavy, fawn, brown, yellow, WOLF, grey or black, but not white. Height 40.5–56cm (16–22in).

Cão de Agua CÃO DE AGUA PORTUGUÊS.

Cão de Agua de Pelo Encaradolado curly-coated variety of the CÃO DE AGUA PORTUGUÊS.

Cão de Agua de Pelo Ondulado long-haired version of the CÃO DE AGUA PORTUGUÊS.

Cão de Agua Português PORTUGUESE WATER DOG.

Cão de Castro Laboreiro [FCI] cattle HERDER and GUARD with origins in Portugal. The breed is characterized by a melodic, rather high-pitched voice. A very muscular and strong, long-bodied breed, with apparent affinity with the MOLOSSAN breeds. The short, harsh coat is often strongly BRINDLED in grey and brown. Height 53–63.5cm (20¾–25in); weight 23–34kg (50½–75lb).

Cão de Fila FILA BRASILIERO.

Cão de Fila de San Miguel Portuguese HERDER recently created in the islands of the Azores.

The head is massive and MASTIFF-like, the chest deep and strong, the body of fair length and the legs well-boned and muscular. Ears are traditionally CROPPED and the tail DOCKED. Height 48–60cm (18¾–23½in).

Cão da Serra da Estrela [FCI] ESTRELA MOUNTAIN DOG.

Cão da Serra de Aires Portuguese HERDER with long coarse coat in shades of yellow, brown or grey. Height 40–52cm (15¾–20½in); weight 12–18kg (26½–39½lb).

cap 1. collection, frequently of a predetermined amount per person, taken at a MEET to defray the hunt's expenses.

> Capping, or collecting for the huntsman after he has made his kill, also led to many abuses, for when scent was poor hounds might be laid on to a hare or rabbit in the hopes that when the field rode up the creature would be killed and eaten and so passed off as a fox. [175]

2. direct HOUNDS using hand signals.

> Never cap your hounds, with halloos, to a bad scent; it makes them wild and eager. [266b]
> 'Who the hell are you, sir?' exclaimed his grace coming on an unfortunate wight, hat in hand, capping the hounds. [344e]

3. (of coat colour) distinct darker marking on the top of the skull, giving the impression of a cap.

> Combination of cap and mask not unusual. [203, ALASKAN MALAMUTE]

cape growth of longer and, usually, harsher coat over the shoulders.

> The coat should be most abundant on the frill, neck, mane and cape, with long feathering on the chest and hind legs above the hocks. [41]

Cape Fox *VULPES CHAMA.*

Cape Hunting Dog *LYCAON PICTUS.*

capillaries small, hair-like blood vessels.

capped hock BURSITIS.

capped mask facial MASK in which the white arches over the eyes but the dark of the skull extends down and between the eyes, especially in SIBERIAN HUSKIES.

capsule medicinal preparation for internal use enclosed in a soluble envelope.

Captain Nugent Hope's Hound GOLDEN VALLEY.

Captain Spicer's AVON VALE.

Carasissi Dog *CANIS CANCRIVORUS.*

Carbery dating from 1764 when the hunt was known as the Cashelmore Hounds, the present name being adopted in 1787 when John Beamish took over the mastership. The largely pasture COUNTRY lies in County Cork.

carcinogenic cancer-producing.

carcinoma malignant form of cancer.

cardiac appertaining to the heart.

Cardigan Corgi WELSH CORGI (CARDIGAN).

Cardigan Welsh Corgi WELSH CORGI (CARDIGAN).

cardiomyopathy inherited condition producing frequently lethal pulmonary oedema and dilation of heart chambers. (Mode of inheritance, uncertain.)

cardiovascular disease inherited assorted heart and vein defects. (Mode of inheritance, polygenic.)

card dim. PRIZE CARD.

care advice to a GUNDOG that he is close to that for which he is searching.

> That 'Care' means that he is near to that for which he is hunting. . . . You will use it when your young dog is racing too fast among turnips or potatoes. [184]

carenated keel-shaped, especially of the BRISKET.

Carinthian Brandlbracke AUSTRIAN BRANDL-BRACKE.

Carlecotes LONGENDALE.

Carlin 1. PUG.

> 'For some time on the Continent, in France especially, Pugs went by the name of Carlins, owing to the black mask on their faces, which is a characteristic of the breed. The analogy between Carlins and masks lay in the fact that formerly there was a famous and very popular harlequin in France whose name was Carlin. [320a]

Carlin à Poil Long extinct long-haired version of the PUG.

Carlisle former OTTERHOUND pack formed in 1863 to hunt the rivers Cairn, Caldew, Eamont, Eden, Esk, Gelt, Irthing, Liddle, Louther, Lyne, Petteril, Wampool, Waver and their tributaries.

Carlow hunting a COUNTRY in County Kildare, the Carlow dates from 1810 when it was known as the Tullow Hunt; the present country was formed in 1853 when that formerly hunted by the Carlow and Island was added.

Carlow and Island CARLOW.

Carmarthenshire FOXHOUND pack formed in the early 19th century to hunt fox in a COUNTRY in Dyfed, Wales.

carnassial teeth fourth premolars; the strongest teeth in the jaw. [*illus.* DENTITION].

carol dogs, esp. hounds, howling in unison, apparently out of enjoyment of their own vocal efforts.

> They carol loud, and in grand chorus join'd
> Salute the new-born day. [328]

Carolina Dog yellow short-coated native American dog with very large, usually erect, ears, developed from stock kept by southern tribes of Indians; very similar in type to some of the dogs recovered by archaeologists in the southern states of America. The breed is distinctly PARIAH in appearance and lifestyle but efforts are being made to bring it into closer domestication.

A long-bodied, rangy breed with vulpine head, arched neck, deep chest and long legs. The coat is short and dense and usually of a rich golden yellow, hence its popular name, Old Yaller. Height 56cm (22in); weight 13.5–18kg (29–39½lb).

carpal subluxation inherited condition resulting in dislocation of the CARPAL JOINT; associated with HAEMOPHILIA A. (Mode of inheritance, familial.)

carp back ROACH BACK.

carpals small bones which form the PASTERN joint.
 carpal joint wrist or PASTERN joint. [*illus.* SKELE-
TON]
 carpal pad small pad just below carpal joint; also
called the stopper pad. [*illus.* DIGITAL PAD]
 carpal torus CARPAL PAD.

Carpathian Sheepdog RUMANIAN SHEEP DOG.

Carpet Spaniel Small SPANIEL.
 Very delicate and small dogs, have exquisite noses,
 and will hunt truly and pleasantly, but are neither
 fit for a long day nor a thorny covert. [239]

Carre's Disease DISTEMPER.

Carriage Dog DALMATIAN. [123]

Carrick Harriers KILMOGANNY.

carrier 1. dog used to carry small packages and
messages.
 He carries letters from place to place, wrapped up
 cunningly in his leather collar, fastened there-to, or
 sewed close therein. [128]
2. dog which is capable of transmitting an inherited
condition but which does not itself show its characteristics.

Carrigues Herder BERGER DE LANGUEDOC.

Carrot tail.

carrot tail short, straight tail which is thick at the
root but tapers to the point. [*illus.*]

carry 1. (of a pervasive scent) to travel, and thus be
identifiable at some distance from where it was laid.
2. to take sheep to be used in a trial from a flock and
drive them to the point at which the trial will begin.
[204]
 carry a line stick closely to the line of the scent.
carry a good head (of HOUNDS) hunt well on a wide
front.
carry the horn to be in charge of the pack while
hunting; act as the huntsman.
carted deer captive deer released, hunted, and then
recaptured unharmed.
cartilage pad of gristle between moving bones.
cart training training SLED-DOGS using a wheeled
vehicle.

Casanova (US) American and crossbred FOXHOUND
pack formed in 1909 to hunt a grass and woodland
COUNTRY in Virginia.

case (obs.) dismember a fox or hare before HOUNDS.

Cashelmore Hounds CARBERY.

cast 1. encourage HOUNDS to fan out or move across
the likely line in order to find the scent.
 In casting for a fox make your casts so that they will
 be sure to 'cross' any line which a fox would make.

 A long straight cast is no use as you may be casting all the time parallel with where the fox has gone.
 [235]
2. send a GUNDOG in search of game.

cast back encourage HOUNDS to return along a scent
or the line of a DRAG(2).
 I have observed how they followed all the hare's
 doubles, and with the true Harrier instinct, cast back
 when in perplexity, never babbling, skirting, or puz-
 zled by other stains. [186]

cast off release LEASHED HOUNDS so that they can
begin hunting.

cast out (of a SHEEP DOG) run to the far side of a
flock of sheep without disturbing them prior to LIFT-
ING.

Castleton BEAGLE pack formed in 1940 to hunt a
COUNTRY in south Wales.

Castor-dog mentioned by Xenophon as used for
hunting hare.
 The first are so called because castor, whose chief
 delight was hunting, kept them. [404]

castrate emasculate; surgically remove testicles.

Castro Laboreiro Sheep Dog CÃO DE CASTRO
LABOREIRO.

Catahoula Cur CATAHOULA LEOPARD DOG.

Catahoula Hog Dog CATAHOULA LEOPARD DOG.

Catahoula Leopard Dog PASTORAL GUARD and
HERDER developed in the southern states of America
and principally in Louisiana.
 A tough and hardy breed, with a large, strong head
and exceptionally strong MUZZLE. The chest is
deep, the TOPLINE level and long. The limbs are well
boned and strongly muscled. The POT HOOK TAIL is
high set. The MERLE or black and tan coat is short
and dense. Height 51–66cm (20–26in); weight
18–23kg (39½–50½lb).

Catalan Herder CATALAN SHEEP DOG.

Catalan Sheep Dog fawn, BRINDLE or GRIZZLE, long
wavy-coated Spanish HERDER. Height 46–51cm
(18–20in); weight 18kg (39½lb).

Catalan Shepherd CATALAN SHEEPDOG.

catalogue publication giving details of competitors
at a show, etc.

Catalonian Sheepdog GOS D'ATURA.

catalyst substance that accelerates a chemical reaction without causing other change.

cataract inherited tendency to opacity of the eye
lens, which may affect either juveniles or have a later
onset to affect only adults. (Mode of inheritance,
dominant or recessive.)

catchweight organized fight arranged between dogs
weighing over 24kg.

catchy scent fitful or intermittent scent.
 He taught them to hunt on a catchy scent without
 looking for help. [309]
 When scent varies a good deal from one field to the
 next it is said to be 'catchy' [95]

Catelli Roman pet dogs.

cat foot small, rounded foot with arched toes. [*illus.*]

Cat foot.

> Cat-like feet are much insisted on, and this point has
> been so much attended to that some breeds have
> been produced remarkable for having their feet even
> more round than those of a cat. [338]

Cathenarius MASTIFF. [128]

catheter instrument passed through the penis or
vagina to remove urine from the bladder.

catmill implement used to train fighting dogs, consisting of a long pole across a hub with a caged cat
at one end and the fighting dog at the other. The dog
then runs in a vain effort to reach the cat.

> The catmill with its long weighted arm and cage, in
> which Dexter kept a Halloween mask of a goblin as
> a lure instead of a cat, was empty. [131]

Catterick BEAGLE pack formed in 1930 to hunt a
COUNTRY in north Yorkshire.

Cattistock dating from the end of the 18th century,
this hunt was founded by the Rev. W. Phelps of
Cattistock Lodge to hunt fox in a COUNTRY which
principally lies in Dorset.

cattle dog dog which is used to protect and herd
cattle.

cattle-herder CATTLE DOG.

cattle tender CATTLE DOG.

Caucasian Ovtcharka KAVKASKAIA OVTCHARKA.

Caucasian Sheep Dog KAVKASKAIA OVTCHARKA.

cauda tail.

  cauda equina neuritis inflammation of nerves
  within the spinal cord producing paralysis of the
  tail, anus and rectum, and leading to incontinence.

caudal close to the tail.

  caudal vertebrae bones of the tail.

caudectomy surgery to DOCK tail.

cautery destruction of tissue to stem bleeding or
destroy infection.

Cav. abbr. CAVALIER KING CHARLES SPANIEL.

Cav-1 Infectious Canine HEPATITIS.

Cavalier dim. CAVALIER KING CHARLES SPANIEL.

Cavalier King Charles Spaniel [FCI, KC] in its present form the breed owes its existence to the initia-
tive of an American, Roswell Eldridge, who gave a
prize at CRUFTS in order to encourage British breeders to return to breeding what he described as
'Blenheim Spaniels of the Old Type', by which he
meant TOY spaniels with longer noses than the
increasingly BRACHYCEPHALIC KING CHARLES
SPANIELS. What quickly came to be regarded as a separate breed achieved its own register in 1944.

The breed is active, bold and gentle with a broad,
flat skull, shallow STOP, large, dark eyes, long, high-
set pendulous ears, and a well-filled MUZZLE. The
SHORT-COUPLED body stands on straight forelimbs
and well-turned hindquarters; the tail, of which
DOCKing was traditionally optional, is carried gaily
but not above the level of the TOPLINE. The long,
preferably straight, silky coat may be black and tan,
TRICOLOUR, RUBY or BLENHEIM. Weight 5.4–8kg
(12–17½lb).

cavitating leukodystrophy inherited disease in which
there is progressive inability to co-ordinate movement, and blindness from an early age. (Mode of
inheritance, recessive.)

Cavvy dim. (colloq.) CAVALIER KING CHARLES
SPANIEL.

cawing away (obs. colloq.) of a dog driving sheep
away from its master. [103a]

Caygotte native domestic dog of the Mexican
Indians.

> . . . being the Mexican Spaniards' name for the
> Indian's dog. [380]

CBC complete blood cell count.

CC abbr. CHALLENGE CERTIFICATE.

C colour series that series of genes which give rise
to rich coloration, to chincilla coat patterns or to
albinism.

CCS abbr. Canine CUSHING'S SYNDROME.

CD abbr. 1. canine DISTEMPER. 2. curative dose.

CD virus abbr. canine DISTEMPER virus.

CD suffix which signifies that a dog has won the
AKC title of COMPANION DOG.

CDRM abbr. Chronic degenerative radiculomyelopathy.

CDX suffix which indicates that a dog has won the
title of COMPANION DOG EXCELLENT.

CEA COLLIE EYE ANOMALY.

Cedarcroft (US) BEAGLE bitch pack formed in 1958,
on the basis of the Vernon-Somerset pack and
Beagles imported from England, to hunt cottontail
rabbit over a COUNTRY in Pennsylvania.

cell division MITOSIS and MEIOSIS.

cell mediated instigated by activity of the cells.

cellulitis inflammation of facial tissue leading to
permanent scarring.

Celtic Dog SEGUSIAN.

Central Asian Ovtcharka SREDNEASIATSKAIA
OVTCHARKA.

Central Asian Shepherd Dog SREDNEASIATSKAIA
OVTCHARKA.

centralized Progressive Retinal Atrophy PROGRES-
SIVE RETINAL ATROPHY.

central peripheral neuropathy PROGRESSIVE
AXONOPATHY.

cephalic index ratio between the widest part of a
dog's head and the length from nose to OCCIPUT,
which determines whether the skull is DOLICHO-
CEPHALIC, BRACHYCEPHALIC or MESATICEPHALIC:
breadth × 100 ÷ length = cephalic index.

cerebellar of the lower posterior part of the brain, which is responsible for movement control and the maintenance of balance.

cerebellar ataxia inherited tendency to unco-ordinated and exaggerated movement resulting from progressive brain damage. (Mode of inheritance, recessive.)

cerebellar ataxia hydrocephalus inherited condition resulting in enlarged cranium and associated with muscular inco-ordination. (Mode of inheritance, recessive.)

cerebellar cortex atrophy inherited tendency to prancing gait and progressive ataxia. (Mode of inheritance, recessive.)

cerebellar cortical abiotrophy inherited condition producing lack of muscular co-ordination. (Mode of inheritance, recessive.)

cerebellar degeneration inherited muscular inco-ordination. (Mode of inheritance, recessive.)

cerebellar hydroplasia inherited cerebellum cell deficiency. (Mode of inheritance, uncertain.)

cerebellar neurozonal dystrophy rare inherited degenerative disease found in New Zealand and Australia resulting in unco-ordinated movement.

Ceredocyon thous DUSICYON THOUS.

Ceriog BORDER COUNTIES NORTH WALES.

Céris extinct French SCENTHOUND, one of the ancestors of the BILLY.

Ceroid lipofuscinosis inherited brain atrophy resulting in blindness, mental dullness and abnormal behaviour. (Mode of inheritance, familial.)

Certificat d'Aptitude au Championship (CAC) an FCI award bestowing the title of National Champion.

Certificat d'Aptitude au Championship Internationale de Beauté de la FCI (CACIB) an FCI award bestowing the show title of International Champion.

Certificat d'Aptitude au Championship Internationale de Travail de la FCI (CACIT) an FCI award bestowing the title of International Working Champion.

cervical appertaining to the neck.

cervical ankylosis immobility of the intra-cervical joints.

cervical spondylosis inherited hind limb muscular inco-ordination, progressing to paralysis.

cervical vertebrae neck bones, typically seven in number.

cervical vertebral deformity muscular inco-ordination progressing to paralysis.

cervix neck of the uterus.

Ceskoslovenský Vlcák [FCI] Czechoslovakian Wolf Hound

Ceský dim. ČESKY TERRIER.

Ceský Fousek [FCI] breed which appears to have been created during the 19th century, fallen into decline, and then been revived during the 1930s as a versatile GUNDOG.

The narrow head is long and proudly carried, the skull slightly rounded and the STOP fairly pronounced; the dark amber eyes are deep set and almond-shaped; the slightly rounded, pendulous ears are set unusually high. The neck is muscular and of moderate length; the forequarters are strongly muscled, with short, slightly sloping PASTERNS. The body is short, with WELL-SPRUNG ribs carried well back, the BRISKET dropping below the elbows. The LOIN is short, broad and slightly arched, with only moderate TUCK-UP. The hindquarters are well-muscled with moderate ANGULATION commensurate with a short HOCK. The coat is usually hard, rough and close-fitting, forming characteristic moustache and coarse FEATHERING to legs, underside and traditionally DOCKED tail. Off-white, with or without brown markings and ROANing, brown with honey colour to chest and limbs, or solid brown are all acceptable colours. Height 58–64cm (23–25in); weight 22–34kg (48½–75lb).

Ceský Terrier [FCI, KC] TERRIER created soon after the Second World War by Franta Horak of Klanice. A long cylindrically bodied, short-legged dog built rather like a SEALYHAM but with a distinct resemblance to the KERRY BLUE TERRIER. The resemblance is further enhanced by the style of trimming and by the breed's pale, almost pastel, blue or brown coat. Weight 7–8kg (15½–17½lb).

cestode intestinal worm that has flattened body (eg. TAPEWORM).

Cevennes Shepherd BERGER DU LANGUEDOC.

Ch. abbr. CHAMPION.

chace (obs.) chase. [328]

Chagas' disease frequently fatal disease caused by infestation with *Trypanosoma cruzi.*

Chagrin Valley English FOXHOUND pack formed in 1908 to hunt pasture and woodland in Ohio.

chain trail of air bubbles which ascend from an otter's coat when it is swimming underwater.

> When he goes no splash will be visible, and the only sign to the eye will be a small 'chain' of bubbles, known as 'the chain'. [238a]

chain weight weight of a fighting dog prior to training for a contest.

chair leg (esp. of GREAT DANES) undesirable bend in the foreleg above the PASTERN. [*illus.*]

chalk ingredient of DUSTING POWDER used to improve the appearance of a dog's (esp. white) coat.

challenge 1. competition among unbeaten dogs usually for one of the CHALLENGE CERTIFICATES. 2. the first HOUND to speak on a scent is voicing a challenge.

Chair leg.

And the joy of the far-flung challenge sounds
Till it shivers against the blue. [272f]

Challenge Certificate major Kennel Club breed award for each sex at British CHAMPIONSHIP SHOWS; three of which, won under different judges, and at least one having been won after the dog has passed its first birthday, entitle a dog to the title of CHAMPION in Britain.

Chambray larger version of the BILLY.

chamois (esp. of skin or ear) thin and soft.

champers HOUNDS. [159]

Champion dog which has won those awards that qualify him for this title.

Champion class FCI show class for national or international CHAMPIONS only.

Championship BEST IN SHOW or BEST OF BREED at working TERRIER shows.

Championship Points [AKC] breed award at CHAMPIONSHIP SHOWS; 15 points must be accumulated in order to qualify for the title of Champion.

Championship Show event at which awards that count towards the title of CHAMPION are to be won.

chancer (colloq.) judge whose knowledge is more apparent than real.

chang (regional Eng.) cry of hunting HOUNDS.
'An a' the grove, wi' gladsome chang. [334]

change (of HOUNDS) leave or lose the scent of a hunted animal in favour of a fresh one.
Changing from the hunted fox to a fresh one, is as bad an accident as can happen to a pack of fox-hounds. [47]

chant 1. advertise a reward for a lost or stolen dog.
. . . their agent of the district, who is always on the look-out for 'chants', will either go or send to you with the joyful tidings of your favourite. [166a]
2. dogs howling in unison.
It is on such nights that the dogs lift up their voices and join in a chant which disturbs the most restful sleepers. [313]

chap heavy, drooping jowl.

character general demeanour regarded as typical of the breed in question.

Charles James (colloq.) CHARLIE.

Charlie fox. (der. Charles James Fox, who had a reputation for cunning, even among his fellow politicians.)
Some people will wipe a little aniseed round the edges of the tube, so when Charlie is bolted he will carry a very high scent. [244]

Charnique extinct Spanish COURSING hound. [150]
There is a hound very similar to the Podengo peculiar to the Balearic Isles . . . a lean, ungainly dog, with a long muzzle, and long erect ears, and stilty legs, it gives one the impression that it is masquerading as a Greyhound or an overgrown Whippet. [225]

Chart Polski [FCI] Polish SIGHTHOUND very similar in many respects to an unusually strongly made GREYHOUND.
The head is strong, the skull flat, the MUZZLE arched, the dark eyes have a piercing expression. The forepart of the TOPLINE is level, but is arched over

the LOINS. The chest is deep and the TUCK-UP pronounced. The hind limbs are muscular and WELL-ANGULATED. The coat is hard, with some coarse FEATHERING to tail and hindquarters. All colours are permitted. Height 68–80cm (26¾–31½in).

chase 1. enclosed deer park or forest protected by Forest Laws. 2. the act of hunting.

chasing one's tail (fig.) exhibiting great activity without making progress. (der. the tendency of dogs to chase their own tails.)

chaste trained, as applied to HOUNDS or dogs. [159]

Chawston former BEAGLE pack formed in 1889 to hunt a COUNTRY in Huntingdon.

check 1. interruption during the course of a hunt, caused by hounds losing the scent.
Ha! a check. Now for a moment's patience. [47]
2. restrain or curb a dog's progress by jerking the LEAD. *See also* CHECK CHAIN. 3. hold hunting HOUNDS back in order to prevent them from overrunning the DRAG.

check-chain syn. choke chain: metal-link running noose forming a collar that tightens around the neck when jerked by the handler.

check-collar CHECK-CHAIN; leather or material version of the CHECK-CHAIN.

check cord CHECK LINE.
The cord may be from ten to twenty-five yards long, according to the animal's disposition, and may be gradually shortened as he gets more and more under command. . . . In thick stubble, especially if cut with a sickle, the drag will be greater, far greater than when the cord glides over heather. [184]

check line cord used to control GUNDOGS during breaking or training.
A long line, with a running noose at one end, used by dog-breakers to teach their pupils to come to heel. [320]

cheek fleshy part of the side of the head below the eyes.

cheekbone ZYGOMATIC ARCH.

cheekbumps well-developed masseter muscles.

cheeky having well-developed, rounded cheeks.
Well-developed chewing muscles, but not so much that 'cheekiness' disturbs the rectangular head form. [6, STANDARD SCHNAUZER]

cheer vocal encouragement to hunting HOUNDS.

cheiloschisis HARE LIP.

chemotherapy treatment of disease by means of chemicals.

chenil (Fr.) KENNEL.

Chepstow Harriers CURRE.

Cheremiss Laika one of six European RUSSIAN LAIKA breeds identified in 1896 by Prince Andrew Shirinsky Shihmatoff. [380]

Cheriton former OTTERHOUND pack formed in 1850 by William Cheriton who hunted hare and otter with the same pack. Former masters include Arthur Heineman, 1902–1904. The COUNTRY lies in Devon.

cherry eye an eye in which the inner surface of the third eyelid is exposed.

cherry hog (Brit. rhyming slang) dog, especially racing greyhound. [142]

cherry nose unpigmented nose.

Chertsey Beagles HORSELL.

Chesapeake Bay Dog CHESAPEAKE BAY RETRIEVER. [225]

Chesapeake Bay Retriever [AKC, KC] one of several breeds which are said to owe their existence to the unlikely circumstances surrounding a shipwreck. In 1807 two dogs, a dark-red male and a black female swam ashore in Chesapeake Bay, Canada from the foundering ship *Canton*. They are said to have interbred with the indigenous RETRIEVER population to give rise to the Chesapeake Bay Retriever.

The breed is amiable, robust, intelligent and tough. The skull is broad and rounded, with medium STOP; the yellow or amber eyes are wide set, the ears are small and fairly high set. The neck is strongly muscled, the chest deep and wide, flanks are well TUCKED UP and the hindquarters high and muscular. The coat is short and thick, DEAD GRASS, sedge or brown of any shade. Height 53.3–66cm (21–26in).

Cheshire 1. dating from 1763 the hunt occupies a bank and ditch COUNTRY in Cheshire. 2. former 15in BEAGLE pack formed in 1854, as the Scratch Beagle Club, to hunt a COUNTRY in Cheshire. The original name was changed to Chester Beagles and then to the Cheshire Beagle Hunt.

Cheshire Forest dating from the mid-19th century, the hunt occupies a COUNTRY in the Wirral.

Cheshire Terrier extinct, localized type of TERRIER formerly to be found in north-west England,
closely allied to the Bull-terrier. [238]

Chester Beagles CHESHIRE.

Chessy dim. CHESAPEAKE BAY RETRIEVER.
The 'Chessy', once king of the field-trial-circuit, is a big, rough-and-tumble animal capable of withstanding terrible hardships of weather and work. [93]

chest that part of the body which encloses the lungs.
chest founder (obs.) paralysis of the forelimbs. [406]

chestnut rich red colour, esp. on BLENHEIM CAVALIER KING CHARLES SPANIEL.

Chestnut Ridge (US) AMERICAN FOXHOUND pack formed in 1905 to hunt a pasture and woodland COUNTRY in Pennsylvania.

Cheyletiella genus of rabbit fur mite; small ectoparasite which causes a mild form of dermatitis, most especially on the nape of the neck and along the back.
Cheyletiella parasitivorax mite that infests dogs, cats, foxes, rabbits and hares.
Cheyletiella yasguri dog-specific rabbit fur mite.
cheyletiellosis rabbit fur mite infestation.

chiasma process by which segments are exchanged between pairs of chromosomes during meiosis.

chiasmata (sing.) CHIASMA.

Chiddingfold hunt found in 1863 by Mr T. Sadler; amalgamated with LORD LECONFIELD's in 1942.

Chiddingfold Farmers hunt formed in 1943 to hunt fox in a Surrey downland COUNTRY.

Chiddingfold and Leconfield amalgamation between the Chiddingfold and Lord Leconfield's hunts, which took place in 1942. The COUNTRY is mainly woodland and pasture in Sussex and Surrey.

chiding (obs.) cry of a pack of HOUNDS. [314c]

Chien Canne POODLE.

chien courant (Fr.) HOUND.

Chien Courant de Bosnie à Poil Dur KELTSKI GONIČ.

Chien Courant de Jura BRUNO DE JURA.

Chien d'Artois [FCI] the Briquet, one of the oldest of the French SCENTHOUNDS, it was recreated by Levair and Therouanne, and is now principally used on hare.

A broad-skulled HOUND, with a serious expression, and long pendulous ears. The body has a rectangular outline, with well-boned straight forelimbs and WELL-ANGULATED, strongly muscled quarters. The TRICOLOUR coat is smooth and dense. Height 51–59cm (20–23¼in); weight 18–24kg (39½–53lb).

Chien de Berger Allemagne GERMAN SHEPHERD DOG.

Chien de Berger Belges BELGIAN SHEEP DOG.

Chien de Berger de Beauce [FCI] BEAUCERON.

Chien de Berger de Brie [FCI] BRIARD.

Chien de Berger de Picardie an ancient herding breed with origins in northern France, and which has only fairly recently been rescued from the point of extinction.

A strong-headed dog with small, narrow, pricked ears and a long MUZZLE. The back is long, the chest deep and capacious; the legs are quite long and well boned; the long tail is carried SABRE fashion. The tousled coat is rough and may be grey or fawn. Height 53–66cm (20¾–26in); weight 23–31kg (50½–68lb).

Chien de Brie variant of the BEAUCERON.
Has a shorter head than the Beauce variety. [225b]

Chien de Franche-comté PORCELAINE.
Often called the Porcelaine. [225b]

Chien de Gascogne unrecognized French HOUND.
Generally useful hound . . . weighing about 62lb, but he is strong and of great endurance. He, too, has something of the St. Hubert in his inheritance, which is visible in his occipital peak, his very long and much-folded ears, his wrinkled visage and deep flews. His coat is hard on the body, but soft and silky about the head. In colour he is blue, or white with many black spots, blue mottled, with slight pale tan markings. [225b]

Chien de l'Atlas AIDI.

Chien de Montagne des Pyrenees PYRENEAN MOUNTAIN DOG.

Chien de Normandie unrecognized French HOUND.
Appears to have been introduced in the time of Louis XIV, is adapted for the pursuit of all kinds of the larger game in the French forests. He is a heavy, strong dog, somewhat coarse in bone, in shape approaching the Bloodhound rather than our Foxhound. [225b]

Chien de Pays GRIFFON NIVERNAIS.

Chien des Garrigues extinct form of French HERDER and PASTORAL GUARD.

Chien de St Hubert [FCI] BLOODHOUND.

Chien de Trait Belge BELGIAN MASTIFF. Probably extinct in its pure form, it was formerly a valuable DOMESTIC GUARD and draught dog.

A strongly muscled active and heavily boned MOLOSSAN breed. The head was massive, the MUZZLE broad and blunt, the neck short and muscular and the body powerful. The short coat was usually shaded fawn or tan with dark POINTS(4). Height 69–78cm (27–30¾in); weight 45–50kg (99–110lb).

Chien d'ours de Tahltan TAHLTAN BEAR DOG.

Chien Français Blanc et Noir TRICOLOUR French pack HOUND, tan being confined to eyebrow, cheek and ear spots. Height 66–74cm (26–29in); weight 28–30kg (61½–66lb).

Chien Français Blanc et Orange orange-and-white French pack HOUND. Height 66–74cm (26–29in); weight 28–30kg (61½–66lb).

Chien Français Tricolore French TRICOLOURed pack HOUND. Height 63–71cm (24¾–28in); weight 27kg (59½lb).

Chien Gris de St Louis former name for the GRIFFON NIVERNAIS.

Chien Loup KEESHOND.

chien plongeur dog used in France to rescue people from water.
> Swimming dogs, attached to the river police, on the banks of the Seine in Paris. . . . In addition to tracking down malefactors infesting the river banks, these dogs are taught to rescue persons who have accidentally fallen or intentionally thrown themselves into the water from bridge or quay. [225b]

chigger mite HARVEST MITE.

Chihuahua breed of Mexican origin said to have been kept in large numbers by unnamed Aztec nobility who fed their dogs on the testicles of castrated virgin boys. The smallest of the domestic breeds, but an alert, brisk and forceful creature.

The head is well-rounded with a pronounced APPLE SKULL; the eyes are large, round, set wide apart and forward facing; the ears are large and angled at about 45 degrees to the skull. The neck is slightly arched, the shoulders WELL LAID BACK and the forelimbs straight. The TOPLINE is level, the ribs WELL SPRUNG, the BRISKET deep and the body slightly longer than high. The SICKLE TAIL is of medium length and carried proudly over the back. Coats may be either smooth, soft-textured, close and glossy, or long, soft-textured, flat or wavy, with FEATHERING on ears, feet and legs. All colours or mixtures of colours are permitted. Weight up to 2.7kg (5½lb), ideally 1–1.8kg (2¼–4¼lb).

Chilmark BEAGLE pack founded in 1950 to hunt a COUNTRY in Wiltshire.

chime confident cry of hunting HOUNDS.
> When a lifted cap for sign
> Sets a sixteen-couple chorus
> Chiming loudly on his line. [272g]

Chin Chin JAPANESE.

china eye clear blue eye; WALL EYE.
> An impression prevails in some localities that the vision of these 'wall' or 'china' eyes is stronger and more powerful than in the eyes of ordinary colour, and that they never contract cataract or ophthalmia. [221]
> China or walleyes are to be disqualified [6, GERMAN SHORT-HAIRED POINTER]

Chinchilla Hound unidentified, allegedly Russian, HOUND used for small game.
> Grey, with black-points, kept upon the Oxus for many years. They are a decorative race, much dependant on man's society, yet for myself I would prefer to see them employed on their proper avocation, not paraded in the streets of London on the end of a string. [367]

Chinese Crested Dog [FCI, KC] one of the few hairless breeds. The first Chinese Crested appeared at a show in the United States in 1885, allegedly having been brought from China.

The breed is small, active and graceful, a deer type being more finely boned than the larger cobby type. The elongated skull is slightly rounded, the STOP moderate and the MUZZLE tapering but not pointed. The entire head is cleanly chiselled. The wide set eyes are very dark, showing little or no white, the ears are low set, large and erect, with or without a FRINGE of hair. DROP EARS are permissible in POWDER PUFFS. The neck is lean, long, arched and carried high, the forequarters clean, narrow and WELL LAID, the forelimbs straight and finely boned. The body is of medium length, the chest broad and deep, but not BARRELLED; TUCK-UP is moderate. The long, tapering tail is set high, elevated when the dog moves but falling at rest; a sparse plume of hair is acceptable. The skin is fine-grained, smooth, unusually warm to the touch and may be of any colour or combination of colours. Height 23–33cm (9–13in); weight not more than 5.5kg (12lb).
> There can be no doubt that these dogs are the same as the African Sanddog and Hairless Dogs of Mexico and Japan [123]

Chinese Crested [Powderpuff] coated version of the CHINESE CRESTED which varies only in that it has an undercoat covered by a characteristic soft veil of long hair. The reason for the existence of a coated version is that the gene for hairlessness is dominant and lethal as a homozygote. Thus some puppies are born with hair.

Chinese Edible Dog (obs.) CHOW CHOW. [123]
> a visitor to Canton, China in 1878 stated that he counted no fewer than twenty restaurants in that city, which specialized in the meat of the chow. [200]

Chinese eye ALMOND EYE.

Chinese Fighting Dog SHAR PEI.

Chinese Greyhound breed which comes in two sizes with large, erect ears, short, smooth, fawn, cream or brown coat with white blaze, and FRINGED TAIL.

Chinese Hairless Dog CHINESE CRESTED.

Chinese Hound said to be descended from the

BÚÁNSÚ, a medium-sized, long-bodied dog with a coarse, red coat, pricked, rounded ears, broad, domed skull, and long, bushy tail.

Chinese Shar Pei SHAR PEI.

Chinese Spaniel (obs.) PEKINGESE.

> There does not seem to be any valid reason why the first-named variety [Chinese (Pekinese) Spaniels] should be called Pekinese. A far more appropriate name would be Chinese Spaniels [123]

Chinese Spitz CHOW CHOW.

chino PELON. [221]

Chinook created as an improved type of draught dog by Arthur Walden in the United States during the early years of the 20th century from various CROSSES. The breed was used by Admiral Richard Byrd during his 1929 polar expedition.

The breed is rectangular in outline, muscular and compact with immense stamina and strength. The head is typically SPITZ. The chest is deep and the ribs carried well back to a strong LOIN. The tawny coat is short, dense and close-fitting. Height 53–66cm (20¾–26in); weight 29–40kg (64–88lb).

Chippendale   front
front with exaggerated bow to the legs and splayed feet. [*illus.*]

Chippiperai THAMBAI.

chiselled of head with clean outline.

> Foreface not dished or falling away quickly between the eyes, delicately chiselled. [203, IRISH TERRIER]

Chippendale front.

chitterlings (obs.) loose flesh on the throat; DEWLAP.

> The exuberances of flesh and rough hair on the lower side of it, called, by kennel men, 'chitterlings', or 'ruffles,' the hound having them being termed throaty. [266b]

Choban Kopeyi (Turkish) ANATOLIAN SHEPHERD DOG.

chocolate dark brown.

choke-chain CHECK-CHAIN.

choke-collar CHECK-COLLAR.

choking method of separating fighting dogs by restricting their intake of air.

Chomar (obs.) ANATOLIAN SHEPHERD DOG.

chondrodysplasia inherited abnormal development of the cartilage especially in the spinal column, associated with dwarfism. (Mode of inheritance, ??)

chondrodystrophia suffering from CHONDRODYSPLASIA.

Chondrodystrophia fetalis EPIPHYSEAL DYSPLASIA.

chondrodystrophoid breeds those breeds which tend to have spinal cartilage defects.

chondrodystrophy CHONDRODYSPLASIA.

chondrosteoma inherited cartilage malformation.

Chootch Laika one of five Siberian LAIKA breeds identified in 1896 by Prince Andrew Shirinsky Shihmatoff. [380]

chop 1. bite while on the run. 2. kill quarry before it has had an opportunity to run.

> You are in danger of chopping your fox. [266b]

3. foreface of BULLDOG: CHOPS.

> The upper lip, called the 'chop', or flews, should be thick, broad, pendant and very deep. [225]

chops (of BULLDOG) FLEWS.

> Flews [chops] thick, broad, pendant and very deep. [203, BULLDOG]

chop mouth CHOPPER.

chopper HOUND with a staccato cry.

chordectomy debarking by surgical means.

chorea involuntary, uncontrolled, irregular muscular movement; St Vitus's Dance.

chorion outer layer of foetal membranes.

chorioptic mites species of mite which causes MANGE on the legs.

Chornyi TCHIORNY TERRIER.

choroid that part of the eye between the sclera and retina which contains the main blood supply vessels.

choroidal hypoplasia inherited eye defect characterized by scleral ectasia, coloboma of the optic disc, and microthalmia. (Mode of inheritance, recessive.)

choriocapillaris blood supply vessels within the choroid.

chorioretinopathy inflammation of the retina, a symptom of DISTEMPER.

Chornyi TCHIORNY TERRIER.

Chortaj Russian SIGHTHOUND.

The head is long, the skull narrow with strong OCCIPUT and imperceptible STOP flowing into a long, arched MUZZLE. The chest is very deep which accentuates the degree of TUCK-UP. The coat, usually of shaded tan, is close and dense. Height 63–66cm (24¾–26in).

chortle sound made by BASENJIS.

> Barkless but not mute, its own special noise a mixture of a chortle and a yodel. [203, BASENJI]

Chow Kow CHOW CHOW.

> The Chinese word for dog is kow. The chow is known in China as the chow kow, that is, eatable dog. Chow is a somewhat slang Chinese word meaning eatable. [200]

Chow Chow [AKC, FCI, KC] an aloof and dignified dog with a distinctly leonine appearance.

The skull is flat, broad with moderate STOP, small, deep set ALMOND EYES and small thick PRICK EARS. The tongue and FLEWS are characteristically blue-black. The neck is strong and slightly arched, the body broad and deep, short and compact. The forequarters are muscular and sloping, the hindquarters muscular, with characteristic straight HOCKS which give a short striding, stilted movement also characteristic of the breed. The tail is high set and carried well over the back. The coat is abundant, dense and STAND-OFF with a soft woolly undercoat and may be either rough or, less usually, smooth. Colours are black, red, blue, fawn, cream or white, always self-coloured but some shading is permitted. Height 46–56cm (18–22in).

CHR abbr. CANINE HYPOXIC RHABDOMYOLYSIS.

Christ Church former private 15½in BEAGLE pack formed prior to 1852 to hunt a COUNTRY in Oxfordshire. The pack was converted to HARRIERS in 1865 and hunting ceased from 1872 to 1875. A Beagle pack was reformed in 1875 but, with the exception of a solitary bitch and puppies AT WALK, these were destroyed in 1887 by rabies.

Christ Church and New College BEAGLE pack formed in 1950 by the amalgamation of the Christ Church and New College packs.

Christmas disease HAEMOPHILIA B.

chromatid half chromosome formed during the process of meiosis.

chromosomes those parts of a cell which convey genetic information.

  chromosome complement number of chromosomes normally carried by a particular species. Domestic dogs have 78, half inherited from each parent.

  chromosome number CHROMOSOME COMPLEMENT.

  chromosome set CHROMOSOME COMPLEMENT.

chronic (esp. of disease) lingering.

chronic degenerative radiculomyelopathy (CDRM) inherited condition in which there is degeneration of the nerve roots and spinal cord. (Mode of inheritance, genetically predisposed.)

Chrysanthemum Dog SHIH TZU.

Chrysanthemum tail.

chrysanthemum tail (of a Pekingese) tail incorrectly formed and held so that it forms a 'wheel' on one side. [*illus.*]

Chryseus scylex DHOLE. [406]

Chrysocyon brachyurus Maned Wolf, found in the grasslands of eastern Brazil and northern Argentina.

chthonophagia habit of eating soil or earth.

chunky head short, thick head.

chur (regional Eng.) subdued growl.

chute area immediately behind the starting line of a SLED-DOG race.

cingulum fibrous band in the female genital tract, the contraction of which around an enlarged glans penis facilitates the TIE.

circuit several shows held consecutively in the same area.

Cirnego dell'Etna SICILIAN HOUND. [312]

cilia hair-like structures which aid the flow of blood through hollow organs.

Circassian Orloff Wolfhound former type of BORZOI with a flat coat. It is faster, with longer legs, shorter head and, according to Drury, more intelligent.
  A cousin of the Siberian Borzoi, but it has a few special characteristics that show it to be a distinct variety. [123]

circle (of quarry or scent) to return to starting place.

circular eye having a round aperture formed by the lids.
  Eyes. Dark, small and rather deeply set, as near as possible circular in shape. [203, SMOOTH FOX TERRIER]

circular foot rounded foot.
  Feet. Circular, well padded, well feathered between toes. [203, former SUSSEX SPANIEL]

third generation

second generation

first generation

Circular mating.

circular mating breeding system in which equal-sized groups of males and females are mated, each female being mated twice (to different males). A male and female offspring from each resulting litter are then mated as with the previous generation. [*illus.*]

Cirneco dell'Etna [FCI] Sicilian GREYHOUND probably taken by Phoenician traders from northern Africa and still very similar to other SIGHTHOUND breeds from the region.

The head is long and lean surmounted by large, high set PRICK EARS; the oval eyes are deep set and of medium size. The neck is long and elegant but well-muscled, the forequarters, long lean and very free; the outline of the body is square, the chest WELL LET DOWN but not greatly sprung, LOINS are well filled, the CROUP flat and the tail carried PUMP-HANDLE fashion. The hind limbs are WELL ANGULATED with low-set HOCKS. The coat is very short, smooth and close-lying. Solid white or orange, or shaded fawn with white markings (other than a white COLLAR(2)) are permitted. Height about 48cm (18¾in).

cistron method of defining a particular gene or a length of chromosome.

clap on to put HOUNDs on the scent.

> The moderns flog bushes and halloo to the hunts-man to clap on his Harriers. [186]

Clare former Irish HARRIER pack formed in 1892 to hunt a COUNTRY in County Clare.

Claro BEAGLE pack formed in 1928 as the Bilton Beagles to hunt a COUNTRY in east Yorkshire. The present name was adopted in 1937.

class 1. having quality and refinement. 2. sub-competition within a larger event.

classical conditioning those methods used to educate a dog to respond in a way which the situation would not normally produce. Pavlov's experiments, in which he taught dogs to salivate when they heard a bell ringing (the bell being associated with the imminent provision of food) is a good example.

classification arrangement of classes at a show.

classification of breeds the way in which show classes are defined in order to facilitate competition. Thus there may be classes for Cairn Terriers, or these may be catered for in a class for Terriers of Scottish origin, or for Terriers of British origin or, as in Scandinavia in classes for short-legged Terriers. The particular arrangement will depend on the size and status of the show.

claudication limping.

clavicular intersection small band of tendon in the brachiocephalic muscle; a vestigial collar bone.

claw horny growth at the end of the toes.

> The whole claws should be dark, but the claws of all vary in shade according to the colour of the dog's body. [203, former DANDIE DINMONT TERRIER]

clean 1. (of anatomy) smooth, fine. 2. of human hunting trail.

clean boot a hunting trail created by a RUNNER. Two stakes were provided, the one of the 'clean boot', the other for the 'not clean boot'. The latter in this instance meant that the shoe soles of the man acting as quarry had been rubbed with horse-flesh, the only material at hand for the purpose. [221]

clean cut lacking LUMBER.

clean eye of an eye which has tight, well-fitting lids and is neither weepy nor runny.

Clean head.

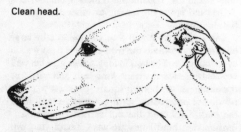

clean head of head without excessive muscular or fleshy development. [*illus.*]

clean hound faultless.

clean in cheeks of cheeks that are without excessive muscular or fleshy development.

clean neck of neck that is without excessive skin or flesh.

clean shoe CLEAN BOOT.

> The bloodhound requires nothing but the so-called 'clean shoe', and, once lay him on the track, he hunts it as a foxhound would the fox, or the harrier or beagle the hare. [221]

clean shoulders well-constructed forequarters; without BOSSINESS.

> On shoulders clean, upright and firm he stands. [328]

cleanin' (regional Eng.) AFTERBIRTH.

cleaning (regional Eng.) AFTERBIRTH.

cleansing (regional Eng.) AFTERBIRTH.

clear season OESTRUS in which the vaginal discharge is seen not to be infused with blood.

cleavage initial cell division in a fertilized egg.

clecking (obs.) of a fox in OESTRUS.

cleft palate inherited fissure of the hard or soft palates. (Mode of inheritance, recessive.)

cleft palate with hair lip inherited fissure of palate and lip. (Mode of inheritance, familial.)

cleft lip congenital condition of the upper lip in which the left and right halves are not joined, leaving a fissure. Common in BRACHYCEPHALIC breeds, it is a fault that may be congenital, inherited or developed. (Mode of inheritance, recessive.)

Cleveland North Yorkshire FOXHOUND pack formed in 1827 as the trencher-fed Roxby and Cleveland hunt by Tommy Page.

click of a mating which achieves the desired result; the partners of such a mating are said 'to click'.

clicket CLECKING. [159]

Clifton former foot 16½in HARRIER pack formed in 1884 to hunt a COUNTRY in Gloucester and Somerset.

Clifton Foot HARRIER pack hunting on foot over a north Somerset COUNTRY; formed in 1888 as the Bristol and Clifton Harriers.

Clifton-on-Teme FOXHOUND pack hunting a COUNTRY in Herefordshire and Worcestershire loaned from adjacent hunts.

clinker (usu. of hunting dog) dog of exceptional merit.

> I remember one hound in the New Forest Deerhound Pack, about 1910, who was very head-strong, but once he got on with the job he was a clinker. [238a]

clints (regional Eng.) testicles.

clip 1. style in which the coat is trimmed. 2. the act of trimming the coat.

> Clipping is an art which is quite beyond the capacity of an amateur, and therefore it is fortunate that, with the exception of poodles, no breed of dog is subjected to the practice in this country. [320]

3. strike the forelegs with the hind legs when moving, resulting in a crab-like action. 4. (Am.) CROP.

> In clipping the ear is almost completely amputated to the point where it forms a nearly equilateral tri-angle. [6, NEAPOLITAN MASTIFF]

clipped 1. (esp. of movement) shortened, truncated. 2. (Am.) CROPPED.

 clipped keel used principally with reference to DACHSHUNDS to describe an abnormally short sternum.

clippers cutting instruments for coat or nails.

cloddy low, thick set and heavy; lacking quality or elegance.
> Defects . . . a thick, short, cloddy neck. [6, BEAGLE]
> The Irish Terrier must neither be 'cobby' nor 'cloddy'. [6, IRISH TERRIER]

clone one of a number of individuals derived from a single cell and therefore genetically identical to all others derived from the same cell.

Clongill Hunt MEATH.

Clonmel Irish HARRIER pack formed in 1922 to hunt a COUNTRY in County Tipperary.

close 1. command, esp. when at HEEL, to encourage a dog to stay in the heel position. 2. of gait, either in front or behind in which the legs closely pass but do not cross each other.

close-coupled 1. short from last rib to hip; short in LOIN. 2. fastened together on a short COUPLE(2).
> A-strain on your leashes, close-coupled together. [272k]

close-cupped foot CAT FOOT.

close hound one that can be relied upon to stick to the scent in difficult conditions.

close season time when hunting cannot take place.

closed stud self-sufficient BREEDING establishment.

closely set ears DROP EARS that lie close to the head.

Clostridium tetani bacteria responsible for causing TETANUS.

cloverleaf mask facial MASK in which the junction between white and dark forms an arch over each eye and has a small rounded finger of white extending up and between the eyes, esp. in SIBERIAN HUSKY.

clown face head which is one colour on one side and another colour on the other side.

Cloyne former Irish HARRIER pack formed in 1911 to hunt a COUNTRY in County Cork.

Clumber Spaniel [AKC, FCI, KC] a distinctive GUNDOG developed in Nottinghamshire on the Clumber estate of the Dukes of Newcastle. The breed was developed from SPANIELS imported towards the end of the 18th century from the kennels of the Duc de Noailles in France. The breed was originally used in teams to act as BEATERS.
A heavily boned, massive yet active gundog. The head is square, broad, heavy browed and massive, with clean, dark amber eyes, large, vine-shaped pendulous ears and strong jaws. The neck is fairly long and thick, the forequarters strong, muscular and the limbs short, strong and straight. The body is long, heavy and low to the ground, the chest deep and the ribs WELL SPRUNG; the back is broad and long with a straight TOPLINE. The hindquarters are very powerful and muscular, with low HOCKS and WELL-BENT STIFLES. The tail is low set and well FEATHERED. The coat is abundant, silky and straight and may be wholly white or with lemon or orange patches. Weight ideally 29.5–36kg (65–79lb).

Clydesdale Terrier Former soft-coated version of the SKYE TERRIER.
> This is one of the most beautiful breeds of dog in existence . . . a silky-haired, prick-eared Skye terrier, and probably the beauty of its glorious steel-grey jacket is attributable to a Yorkshire terrier cross. Owing to the profusion of his silken jacket the Clydesdale terrier is not adapted for rough work. [320a]
> Was also known as the Paisley terrier until the Kennel Club in 1888 adopted the name. [221]

CN dilution genetic effect which turns black pigment to a dull grey and yellow pigment to light beige or off-white.

Coach Dog DALMATIAN.
> Everything he sees is peculiar: the silent roll and easy motion of the London built carriage – the style of the coachman; it is hard to determine which shines brightest, the lace on their clothes, their own round faces, or their flaxen wigs; the pipe-clayed reins – pipe clayed lest they should soil the clean white gloves; the gigantic young fellows, in huge cocked-hats bedaubed with lace, in laced silk stockings, new kid gloves, and with gold-headed canes, who tower above 'Mr Coachman's' head; not forgetting the spotted coach-dog, which has just been washed for the occasion. [266c]

Coaly species of CUR famous for its sagacity. [159]

Coally Dog formerly a type of northern English herding dog.
> The Cur Dog is a trusty and useful servant to the farmer and grazier; and although it is not taken notice of by naturalists as a distinct race, yet it is now so generally used, expecially in the north of England, and such great effort is paid in breeding it, that we cannot help considering it as a permanent kind. In the north of England, this and the foregoing [The Shepherd's Dog] are called Coally Dogs. [51]

coarse 1. (of dog) lacking quality and refinement. 2. (of coat) harsh in texture.

Coarse-haired Dutch Shepherd HOLLANDSE HERDERSHOND.

coat 1. growth of hair which covers the skin. 2. protective jacket for warmth or protection, designed for dogs. 3. COTE.

cobby compact, squarely built, short-bodied.
> Decidedly square and cobby. [203, PUG]

COCA CONFEDERATION CANINA AMERICANA.

coccidia parasitic sporozoa found in the intestines, liver and other organs.

 coccidial of, or caused by, COCCIDIA.

 coccidiosis enteric disease caused by COCCIDIA.

coccidium (sing.) COCCIDIA.

coccidiodal granuloma lung, bone and skin lesions characteristic of COCCIDIOIDOMYCOSIS.

Coccidiodes immitis coccidium species causing COCCIDIOIDOMYCOSIS.

coccidioidomycosis respiratory fungal disease transmitted by rats, especially in hot dry climates, and caused by COCCIDIODES IMMITIS.

coccygeal vertebrae   tail bones. [*illus.* SKELETON]

coccygectomy   DOCKING.

coccygotomy   incision made in the tail, sometimes illegally undertaken in order to alter the carriage of the tail.

cochlea   spiral tube forming the inner ear.

 cochletis   inflammation of the COCHLEA.

cock his leg   (of dog) to urinate. (der. from the dog's position when urinating.) Not to be confused with 'cock a leg', which refers to the act of getting astride a horse.

cock tail   tail carried gaily, as with a cockerel.
> And the Bagman resolved upon bringing him up,
> To eat of his bread and drink of his cup,
> He was such a dear little cock-tailed pup! [43]

cocked   (of ears) pricked; held in an attentive state, usually higher than their natural position.
> Ears, small, cocked, sharply pointed. [203, FINNISH SPITZ]

 cocked up   (of tail) COCK TAIL.

Cocker   dim. COCKER SPANIEL.

Cocker Spaniel   1. [FCI, KC] developed during the 17th century from the broader family of SPANIELS, with the intention of producing a dog for FLUSHing game, especially woodcock, from which the breed's name is derived. Recognized by the KENNEL CLUB(2) as a separate breed in 1892.

A merry, sporting and sturdy dog, compact, active and well balanced. The skull is well developed, the STOP pronounced and the MUZZLE square. The brown or dark brown eyes are full but not prominent, the rims are tight. The pendulous ears extend to the tip of the nose and are well FEATHERED. The neck is of moderate length and muscular, the shoulders well laid, and the forelimbs straight. The body is strong and compact, with deep BRISKET, WELL SPRUNG ribs, short LOIN and well-rounded hindquarters with good bend of STIFLE. The tail is traditionally DOCKED and is in constant merry movement. The flat, silky coat should not be too profuse but sufficiently so to produce FEATHERING to limbs, and the underside of the body. The KC STANDARD describes colours as 'various'. Height 38–41cm (15–16in); weight 13–14.5kg (28½–32lb).

2. [AKC] AMERICAN COCKER SPANIEL.

Cockermouth   former 16in BEAGLE pack formed in 1857 to hunt a fell COUNTRY in Cumbria.

Coquetdale Hunt   WEST PERCY.

codominance   the expression of both alleles in the heterozygote.

coefficient of inbreeding   mathematical expression of the precise degree of INBREEDING between a dog and any individual in its pedigree.

coefficient of relationship   measure of the relationship between individuals.

Coenurus cerebalis   larval form of *TAENIA MULTI-CEPS.*

Coenurus serialis   larval form of *TAENIA SERIALIS.*

coffin head   long head with narrow BACKSKULL and MUZZLE but broader across the eyes.

coin tail   tightly curled tail.

coital crouch   lordosis: the characteristic attitude assumed by a sexually receptive bitch.

coitus   copulation.

cold line   COLD SCENT.

cold nose   1. said to be a sign of health in a dog. (said to derive from the theory that a dog plugged a leak in the Arc with his nose.)   2. (Am.) ability to follow a COLD SCENT, hence cold-nosed.

cold scent   scent that has deteriorated due to age, ground or weather conditions; scent that has been laid some time prior to HOUNDs being set on.
> They possess greater patience in working out a cold line, and are perfect in making casts on their own account. [221]

Coldstream   (US) BASSET pack formed in 1962 to hunt cottontail rabbit.

coliform pyometra   severe form of pyometra with purulent vaginal discharge and blood poisoning.

Colishé   *CANIS VIRGINIANUS.*

colitis   inflammation of the colon or large intestine.

Coll   (obs.) COLLIE.
> It has been suggested that Coll and Collie may be from the same root as collar, and the name given to the dog because of the white collar round the neck. [123]

collar   1. restraint that fits round a dog's neck, used for the purposes of control and/or to facilitate identification by the attachment of an identity tag or disc. 2. markings, usually white, round a dog's neck.
> White legs, blaze and white collar optional. [203, BASENJI]
3. means of identification for COURSING GREY-HOUNDS: red for the dog on the left of the SLIP, white for the dog on the right.

 collar harness   type of padded leather harness used on some SLED-DOGS.

collarette   growth of coat around the neck.
> Especially long and abundant hair, like a collarette, around the neck. [6, BELGIAN SHEEP DOG]

collected gallop   fast CANTER.

College Valley   Northumbrian FOXHOUND pack formed in 1924.

collie   herding dog.

collie eye anomaly   CHOROIDAL HYPOPLASIA.

collie nose   form of dermatitis on the nose, lips and round the eyes, stimulated by sunlight.

Colne Valley   1. former HARRIER pack formed in 1919 to hunt a Yorkshire moorland COUNTRY.   2. pack formed in 1850 as the Slaithwaite and Golcar foot harriers; the name was changed in 1900 and in 1951 the pack was converted to BEAGLES.

colon   that part of the large intestine which lies between the caecum and the rectum.

Colonel R. P. Croft's   former private STAGHOUND pack formed in 1885 to hunt a COUNTRY in Hertfordshire.

colonic impaction chronic constipation.

colony group of dogs kept for experimental purposes.

colostrum ingredient in the first flow of a bitch's milk, which contains antibodies, thus imparting immunity.

colour breaking (of coat) changing from juvenile to adult; BREAK COLOUR.

colour clearing the process in which coat coloration becomes more defined as the dog matures.

colour mutant alopecia BLUE DOG SYNDROME.

coloured said of water which has been muddied by HOUNDS, hunt servants or followers, or by flood.

coloured working terrier show classification which excludes predominantly white breeds.

Colpeo Fox DUSICYON CULPAEUS.

comb 1. toothed grooming instrument. 2. (esp. in SETTERS) fringe of hair hanging from the underside of the tail.

> **comb fringe** fringe of straight hair.
> It should be what the usual term applied to the stern of the Setter implies – a comb fringe. [186]

come by verbal command to send a working SHEEP-DOG to the left.

Comforter SPANIEL GENTLE. [139]
> Is a most elegant little animal, and is generally kept by the ladies as an attendant of the toilette or the drawing-room. It is very snappish, ill-natured, and noisy; and does not readily admit the familiarity of strangers. [51]

coming on improving.

commended minor show class award: seventh place.

commensal living in or with another species, either in mutual harmlessness or with benefit to one or both species. Literally, sharing the same table.

commisures points at which upper and lower lips meet.

common lacking refinement and type; COARSE.

Common Fox CANIS VULPES.

common hunt dispensation which, during the 13th century, allowed certain Scottish peasants to hunt over common land.

Common Zorro DUSICYON THOUS.

communal pad large pad at the rear of each foot; the metatarsal pad. [illus. DIGITAL PAD]

compact closely knit construction.
> Elegant and aristocratic, smart, compact with profuse coat. [203, JAPANESE CHIN]

compact coat coat which lies close to the body.

compact feet feet in which the toes fit closely together, not to be confused with the CAT FOOT.

compaction whelping complication in which two foetuses are simultaneously engaged within the pelvis.

Companion Dog (CD) (AKC) title won in Novice Obedience stakes.

Companion Dog Excellent (CDX) (AKC) title awarded to a dog that has attained a certain level of success in OPEN CLASSES at AKC OBEDIENCE TRIALS.

compensatory mating breeding method intended to correct faults by going to the other extreme, i.e. mating very small dogs to very large ones with the intention of producing medium-sized puppies.

Compiègne Pointer BRAQUE SAINT GERMAIN.

complement 3 deficiency inherited deficiency in which there is increased susceptibility to bacterial infection. (Mode of inheritance, recessive.)

complementary genes independent genes which operate together.

conception moment at which sperm enters the ovum.

conceptus product of conception: foetus.

condition quality of health evident in coat, muscle, vitality and general demeanour.

conditioned reflex involuntary response to a CON-DITIONED STIMULUS.

conditioned response voluntary reaction to a CON-DITIONED STIMULUS.

conditioned stimulus stimulus from which dogs learn to respond in a particular manner.

conditioning process of getting into top condition.

cone-shaped head CONICAL HEAD.

coney (obs.) rabbit.

Coney Dog small type of LURCHER principally intended for hunting rabbit and other small game, often a CROSS between a WHIPPET and a BORDER TERRIER or BEDLINGTON TERRIER.

Confederate Hunt TANATSIDE.

Confederation Canina Americana (COCA) federation of South and Central American KENNEL CLUBS.

conformation make and shape: the natural form of the body.

congenital of a condition present at birth, whether inherited or a result of developmental abnormality.

congenital lymphoedema inherited lymph drainage deficiency resulting in oedema of the limbs and hindquarters. High mortality occurs.

congenital nystagmus eye defect characterized by involuntary movement of the eyeballs, associated with albinism.

congenital pyloric hypertrophy PYLORIC STENOSIS.

congenital seborrhoea scaling of the skin in young puppies. The condition gets progressively worse and has no known cause.

Congo Bush Dog BASENJI.

Congo Dog BASENJI.

Congo Hunting Terrier BASENJI.

Congo Pygmies' Bush Dog unrecognized primitive African hunting dog: medium-sized, with short, yellowish fawn coat, a long head and PRICK EARS. [312]

Congo Terrier BASENJI.
> A couple of Congo Terriers were exhibited at Cruft's some ten years ago as Lagos Bush dogs. They were red and white, with white on the neck, rather dingo-headed, and decidedly breedy-looking. [225]

conical head head that is circular in section and tapers uniformly from skull to nose.

Coniston North Lancashire and Westmorland FOX-

HOUND pack dating from 1825 and formed by Mr Gaskgarth and Mr Jackson as a TRENCHER-FED pack to hunt fox, hare and mart. The COUNTRY is mainly fell and moorland.

conjunctiva   delicate mucous membrane which covers the eyeball.

conjunctivitis   inflammation of the conjunctiva.

connective tissue dysplasia   EHLERS DANLOS SYNDROME.

constipation   irregular or difficult production of excrement.

contagious   disease which can be transmitted by physical contact. (Not to be confused with INFECTIOUS.)

Continental clip   one of the traditional CLIPs used on POODLES.

> In the 'Continental' clip the face, throat, and base of the tail are shaved. The hindquarters are shaved with pompoms (optional) on the hips. The legs are shaved leaving bracelets on the hind legs and puffs on the forelegs. There is a pompom on the end of the tail. The entire shaven foot and a portion of the shaven foreleg above the puff are visible. The rest of the body is left in full coat but may be shaped in order to ensure overall balance. [6, POODLE]

Continental Landseer   black and white NEWFOUNDLAND.

Continental Toy Spaniel, Papillon   PAPILLON.

Continental Toy Spaniel, Phalene   PHALENE.

contrast venography   a method of facilitating the radiographic examination of veins, involving the use of a water-soluble contrast medium slowly inserted into one of the veins via a catheter. The technique began to be used on dogs in mid-1994.

control   1. ability to direct behaviour.   2. instance used as comparison with an experiment in order to measure or verify change.

convention   several organized dog fights taking place at a single venue.

Coollattin   FOXHOUND pack founded by the 6th Earl Fitzwilliam in 1853 to hunt a COUNTRY in County Wicklow.

cool-out shelter   covered area in which racing dogs can be cooled down after exercise or a race.

Coon Dog   dim. (colloq.) COONHOUND.

> Suddenly, from here, there and everywhere, occurred a rush of persons from beneath the Paddock trees, from underneath the grandstand and out of the recesses of the Racing Administrative Building, all towards the trackside rail, all in answer to the thrilling alarum, 'They're off'. Like a red coon dog catching high scent, the Secretary broke into a run and was gone. [224]

coon-footed   taking the weight of the body on the heels.

> Faults: cat-footed (up on tip toes); coon-footed (standing on heels). [6, LOUISIANA CATAHOULA LEOPARD DOG]

Coonhound   any one of several American HOUND breeds developed principally for hunting racoon but also used on a variety of both large and small game. Breeds include the AMERICAN BLACK AND TAN, BLUETICK, ENGLISH, REDBONE, TREEING WALKER, TENNESSEE, and their variants.

Cope's Rule   rule which holds that evolution tends to produce animals with larger body size. The effect is evident among domestic animals.

copper toxicosis   inherited copper storage malfunction leading to liver degeneration. (Mode of inheritance, recessive.)

coprolith   mass of hardened faecal material in the intestine.

coprophagy   depraved appetite, esp. eating excrement.

copulating lock   TIE.

Coquetdale Terrier   BEDLINGTON TERRIER.

> The Bedlington might appropriately have been named the Coquetdale Terrier. [123]

copulation   act of mating.

corded   of a coat which is allowed or encouraged to grow into ringlets or dreadlocks.

> The coat, which we have mentioned earlier, commencing in a woolly condition, gradually grows, twisting itself into cords, the newer hair clinging and twisting round the cords, and constantly increasing in length, gradually forming ropes; and to prevent the cords becoming soiled and entangled, as when neglected the coat becomes somewhat offensive, the cords are often cut back and thus kept under control; or if long cords are desired, they can be gathered up [when the dog is not being exhibited] and tied in a bundle on its back, to allow the dog freedom of movement. The cords may become several inches longer than the height of the animal, so as to make its life unhappy. [37]

Corded Poodle   variety of POODLE in which the coat is CORDED.

Corgi   cattle-herding dog of Welsh origin. (der. CURTAILED, a dog which, naturally or as a consequence of surgery, has a short tail; or, the Welsh cor [dwarf] and ci [dog]); WELSH CORGI.

Cori's disease   GLYCOGENOSIS TYPE.

corker   lively and eye-catching individual of exceptional quality.

corkscrew tail   spirally curled tail.

corky   compact and alert.

Corn Dog   spirit dog said in some European countries to inhabit fields of ripe corn.

cornea   transparent membrane which covers the iris.

corneal dystrophy   inherited condition leading to oedema and ulceration. (Mode of inheritance, recessive.)

Cornish Greyhound   extinct localized type of GREYHOUND.

corny feet   hard and calloused pads.

coronoid process   FCP.

corpulmonale   chronic heart disease resulting from vascular disease in the lungs.

corpuscles   minute bodies that form a major part of a blood vessel.

corpus luteum   uterine bodies which excrete progesterone.

corrective mating   matings between individuals with

different desirable qualities in the hope that these will be combined in the offspring.

Corrigan's pulse WATER HAMMER PULSE.

cortex outer covering of an organ or structure.

corticosteroids hormone secreted by the adrenal glands.

cote (obs.) COURSING term for when one GREY-HOUND outran another and made a TURN or WRENCH.
> A cote is when a greyhound goes endways by his fel-low, and gives the hare a turn. A cote served for two turns, and two trippings or jerkins for a cote; if the hare did not turn quite about she only wrenched, and two wrenches stand for a turn. [383]

Cotley 1. private FOXHOUND pack founded in 1797 by Mr T. Eames and owned by the family. The stiff bank COUNTRY lies in Devon, Somerset and Dorset.   2. former HARRIER pack formed in 1796 to hunt a COUNTRY in Devon, Somerset and Dorset.

Coton de Tulear [FCI] TOY breed with origins in Madagascar and probably derived from Maltese dogs imported during the 17th century. The breed is characterized by its fluffy, cotton-like SINGLE COAT which is long and fine, usually white, though cham-pagne and black markings are not discouraged. Height 25–31cm (10–12¼in); weight 5.5–7kg (12–15½lb).

Cotswold FOXHOUND pack dating from 1858, when Lord Fitzharding gave up part of his hill and vale COUNTRY.

Cotswold Vale Farmer's FOXHOUND pack estab-lished in 1947 to hunt a COUNTRY centred on Cheltenham and Gloucester.

Cottesmore hunt dating from prior to 1666 when Viscount Lowther took HOUNDS from the KENNEL in Westmorland to hunt fox in the Leicestershire, Rutland and Lincolnshire COUNTRY.

cottontail variety of American rabbit hunted instead of hare.

coucher dog used to drive gamebirds into nets.
> We are also told by Edmond de Langley that they should be 'coucher', by which I understand him to mean that they should drop to the bird to take quail and partridge. [186]

cough spasm of the throat produced by an irritant and creating a rasping sound; usually in reference to KENNEL COUGH.

counter (obs.) to hunt against the direction of scent.
> A hound that runs counter and yet draws dry foot well,
> One that, before judgement, carries poor souls to hell. [319a]

country area within which a particular pack of hounds operates.

County Clare Irish HARRIER pack formed in 1923.

County Down Irish STAGHOUND pack formed in 1881 to hunt a COUNTRY in County Down.

County Galway known as The Blazers, the hunt dates from the early 19th century.

County Longford Irish HARRIER pack formed in 1860 as a private STAGHOUND pack.

County Sligo Irish HARRIER pack.

couple 1. copulate. 2. two sporting dogs.
> When the Ringwell-bred puppies came in from walk, he began the season with no less than thirty-seven couple of unentered hounds. [309]

couple boy formerly, a person employed to carry COUPLES(2) taken from HOUNDS.
> He hired a youth called Mark Buck to go with Harry the huntsman and hounds, the same being, as Mr Heavyside noted, 'capital when settled to their fox, but rather mettlesome before,' most likely very riotous, and Buck was to be whipper-in under the inferior title of couple-boy. [344c]

coupled joined with another dog to form a COUPLE(2).
> So have I seen ill-coupled hounds,
> Drag different ways in miry grounds. [346]

couples 1. (of HOUNDS) more than one COUPLE(2).
> Sixty-five couples of hounds in full work will con-sume the carcases of three horses in one week, or five in a fortnight. [406]

2. equipment with which two dogs can be fastened together for exercise or training; COUPLINGS [illus. COUPLINGS]
> That your young dog may not hereafter resist the couples, yoke him occasionally to a stronger dog, and for the sake of peace, and in the name of all that is gallant, let it be to the one of the other sex who appears to be the greatest favourite. [184]

coupling union of two alleles from different loci.

couplings 1. LOINS.
> The body must be of fair length in the couplings, with ribs well sprung. [41]

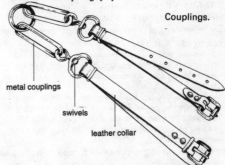

Couplings.

metal couplings

swivels

leather collar

2. leash for holding two dogs; COUPLES. [illus.]
> Let Hares and Hounds in coupling straps unite,
> The clocking Hen make Friendship with the Kite. [145g]

Couriers of the Air CWN ANWN.

course 1. hunt or chase with SIGHTHOUNDS.
> He who shoots a hare in a good open coursing country must expect reproaches from 'the still small voice of conscience' [226]

2. one round of an organized coursing meeting.

3. (obs.) period during which an animal is BAITed.

courser one who indulges in COURSING.
> And let the Courser and the Huntsman share
> Their just and proper Title of the Hare. [246]

coursing see COURSE.

Coursing Greyhound HOUND bred esp. for COURSING.

courtesy scratch if an organized dog fight is ended because one of the opponents is outclassed or seriously injured both owners may, before formally ending the fight, return their dogs to scratch in order to demonstrate that the dogs themselves are willing to continue hostilities, thus demonstrating that their dogs do not lack courage.

Couteulx Hound one of three divisions of BASSETs existing in England: the Couteulx, or Fino de Paris; the Masson, or Termino; and the Lane. [123]

Courtenay Tracy, The former OTTERHOUND pack formed in 1887 by Mr Courtenay Tracy to hunt the Wey and Till in Surrey, the Meon and Itchen in the New Forest, the Wylye, Avon and Nadder in Wiltshire and the Stour and its Dorset tributaries.

Coventry, Francis author of *The History of Pompey the Little, or the Life of a Lap-dog* (London, 1751).

cover 1. COVERT.
2. (of stud-dog) to mate.

cover hair GUARD HAIR.

covering ground 1. economical movement which achieves maximum forward propulsion.

> Co-ordinated, smooth and effortless [movement], covering ground well. [203, AMERICAN COCKER SPANIEL]
> Covers ground effortlessly with good drive behind. [203, GLEN OF IMAAL TERRIER]

2. standing with rear limbs extended behind the body.

covert woodland or thicket which provides shelter for game.

> Seek'st thou for hounds to climb the rocky steep,
> And brush th' entangled covert. [328]

Covert Hound type of HOUND formerly employed to drive quarry out of cover in order that they could be taken by other means.

> Anyone who shall put out the eye, or cut off the tail of the king's covert-hound, is to pay twenty-four pence to the king, for every cow that the dog may be rated at in value.
> There is one animal which rises in value from fourpence to a pound in one day; a covert hound: if it belong to a taecog in the morning its worth will be four pence, and if it be given to the king, its value is one pound. [12]

cow action moving with HOCKS turned inwards and hind feet outwards.

cowardice collective noun for a group of CURS or MONGRELS.

Cowdray FOXHOUND pack established in 1922 to hunt a down and woodland COUNTRY in West Sussex. The country was hunted from 1679 by the Old Charlton Hunt and then by the Goodwood hounds.

cow hocks HOCKS turned inwards causing hind feet to turn outwards. (der. the normal stance of cows.) [*illus.*]

> 'Cowhocks' – that is, the hocks turned in and the feet turned out – are intolerable. [6, IRISH TERRIER]

Cow hocks.

Cowley Terrier strain of TERRIER first produced by John Cowley during the last few years of the 19th century but which is now totally extinct.

> There is the Cowley strain kept by the Cowleys of Callipers, near Kings Langley. These are white wire-haired dogs marked like the Fox-terrier and exceedingly game. [225]
> A more modern strain [than the Sealyham] . . . is the extremely varmint looking, short-legged, wire-haired terrier, which Mr Cowley has taken – and is still taking – such pains to cultivate. [221]

cowlick hair on the nose which grows contrary to the direction of the rest. (der. the formation of hair resulting from a cow licking itself.)

Cowper's gland gland which secretes a lubricant to ease the passage of semen during mating.

coxarthrosis disease of the hip-joint.

coxofemoral articulation joint between the femur and pelvis.

Coy Dog 1. LURCHER. 2. dim. DIDYCOY DOG. [383] 3. naturally occurring CROSS between a coyote and a dog.

Coyote *CANIS LATRANS.*

CPRA Centralized PROGRESSIVE RETINAL ATROPHY.

CPV-1 CANINE PARVOVIRUS TYPE 1.

CPV-2 CANINE PARVOVIRUS TYPE 2.

crab move with the body inclined at an angle to the direction of travel.

Crab-eating Dog *DUSICYON THOUS.*

> Very similar in appearance to the Azara's Dog . . . and is found in an area roughly described from Guano to La Plata. [185]

Crab-eating Fox *DUSICYON THOUS.*

crack (esp. of a pack of HOUNDS) of the very best quality.

> Look at even the first flight, with a crack pack of hounds. [388b]

Cranbourne WILTON.

craniomandibular hyperostosis CRANIOMANDIBULAR OSTEOPATHY.

craniomandibular osteopathy abnormal enlargement of the jaw, occipital and temporal bones.

cranioschisis CRANIUM BIFIDUM.

cranium bifidum inherited failure of the cranial bones to close. (Mode of inheritance, recessive.)

crank sharp bend, esp. in a tail.

crank tail desirably bent tail, as in the BULLDOG; when the crank is undesirable it is customarily described as a kink.

crash HOUNDS giving tongue simultaneously.

> A crash of rare music – Oh, sweetest of sounds
> To the man on the stayer, alone with the hounds? [272]

Craven Farmers pack formed in 1739 by the 4th Lord Craven to hunt fox in a Berkshire, Hampshire and Wiltshire downland COUNTRY. From 1814 to 1825 hounds were hunted by John Warde.

Crawley and Horsham pack formed in the early 19th century to hunt fox in a Surrey and Sussex pasture COUNTRY. From 1951 until 1961 the country was hunted, jointly with a committee, or in her own right, by Mrs H. G. Gregson.

creaseless free from wrinkles.
> Head. . . . Flat, creaseless forehead. [203, SCHNAU-ZER]

crepitus sound caused by movement of a fractured bone.

Cresselly Hunt SOUTH PEMBROKESHIRE.

Crested neck.

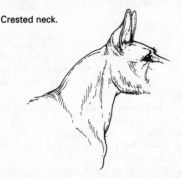

crest arched TOPLINE of the neck. [*illus.*]
> Pronounced crest blends with back of skull. [203, JAPANESE AKITA, interim Breed Standard]
> Close to their master's side they press'd,
> With drooping tail and humbled crest. [314c]

crested neck *see* CREST.

crinkly coat coat forming tight waves.

Croatian Ovcar HRVATSKI OVČAR.

Croatian Sheep Dog HRVATSKI OVČAR.

Crockford Harriers ISLE OF WIGHT.

crompyng (obs.) curve of a dog's tail. [159]

crook (esp. of tail or limbs) not following the normal direction. [*illus.* ACHONDROPLASTIC]
> Forelegs straight, a slight crook is acceptable; thick and well boned. [203, PETIT BASSET GRIFFON VENDÉEN]

crook tail CRANK TAIL. [46]

crooked front bowed forelimbs.

crooked mouth upper and lower jaws laterally displaced.

Croom Irish HARRIER pack formed in 1921.

Croome from 1600 to 1719, HOUNDS were kept at Croome. There have since been some blank periods and the present pack dates from 1874; until 1882 the pack was hunted as the Lord Coventry Hunt. The COUNTRY is largely pasture, plough and woodland and lies in Worcestershire, Warwickshire and Gloucestershire.

crop to remove surgically part of the ear flap.
> Cropping is an infliction of too much torture for the gratification of a nonsensical fancy; and, after all, in the opinion of many, and of those, too, who are fondest of dogs, the animal looks far better in his natural state than when we have exercised all our cruel art upon him. [406]
> Fly-away, Houndish, or cropped ears are to be penalized. [6, LOUISIANA CATAHOULA LEOPARD DOG]

crop ear ear that has been CROPPED.

cropped *see* CROP.

cropping clamps metal devices which are used both to hold ears that are to be CROPPED, and to act as a template to guide the cut.

cross 1. dog with parents of two different breeds or from two different strains of the same breed.
2. BREED(2) from animals of dissimilar STRAINS or BREEDS.
> It requires three years to find out of the results of any cross. [266b]
3. symmetrical white chest marking esp. on BERNESE MOUNTAIN DOGS.
> Slight to medium sized symmetrical white head marking (blaze) and white chest marking (cross) are essential. [203, BERNESE MOUNTAIN DOG]

crossbred descriptive of CROSS.

crossbreed CROSS (1) and (2).

cross-drive to drive sheep across the front of the handler.

Cross Fox type of fox inhabiting northern Europe.
> Inhabits the coldest parts of Europe, Asia, and North America. . . . It derives its name from the black mark which passes over its back across the shoulders, and another along the back to the tail. [51]

cross-track scent which passes over that which is being followed.

crossing (of gait) movement in which the front feet cross over one another; WEAVING.

crossing over 1. WEAVING. 2. the passage of genes, during meiosis, between chromosomes.

crouch exaggerated angulation of the hind limbs.

croup upper part of the back immediately in front of the tail. [*illus.* POINTS]
> Back short with loin short and strong with slight slope of croup to hindquarters. [203, BRITTANY, Interim Breed Standard]
> A sunken or slanted croup is a serious fault. [6, BOUVIER DES FLANDRES]

Crowhurst former OTTERHOUND pack formed in 1902 to hunt the Cuckmere, Ouse, Adur, Arun, Medway, Eden, Darenth, Stour, Rover, Rother, Dudwell, and their tributaries.

crown 1. highest point of the skull.
> Median line distinctly to rather more than half-way up crown. [203, AMERICAN COCKER SPANIEL]
2. achieve the final qualification for the title of champion. 3. ridge of upstanding coat.

cruciate ligaments ligaments arranged in the form of a cross which provide stability to the STIFLE-joint.

cruciate ligament rupture inherited tendency to rupture of the STIFLE ligament. (Mode of inheritance, uncertain.)

Cruft, Charles *see* CRUFTS.

Crufts Crufts Dog Show, the KENNEL CLUB's own Championship Show founded in 1891 by Charles Cruft.

crupper CROUP.

crusty (of the nose) hard and dry.

cry 1. sound made by hunting HOUNDS.
> What these want in speed, he endeavours to make amends for by the deepness of their mouths and the variety of their notes, which are suited in such

manner to each other, that the whole cry makes up a complete concert. [2]

2. (esp. of HOUNDS) group or pack.

3. collective noun for CURS.

> Cor. You common cry of curs! whose breath I hate
> As reek o' the rotten fens. [319b]

cryosurgery surgical technique which makes use of the destructive effect of extreme cold on tissue.

cryptorchidism inherited condition in which the testes fail to descend into the scrotum. (Mode of inheritance, familial.)

crystalline corneal dystrophy inherited developmental condition producing crystalline granules leading to corneal oedema and ulceration. (Mode of inheritance, recessive.)

CSA CANINE SECRETORY ALLOANTIGEN.

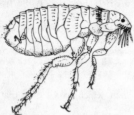

Ctenocephalites canis: common dog flea.

Ctenocephalites canis Dog flea. External parasite that causes acute irritation to the dog. The intermediate host of the *DIPYLIDIUM CANINUM* tapeworm. [*illus.*]

cub juvenile fox or otter.

cub-drawn (obs.) (of vixen) in poor condition after suckling young.

cub-hunting CUBBING.

Cuban Bloodhound type of GUARD formerly found in Cuba and surrounding islands.

> It is doubtful whether the Cuban ever attained any fixity of type, and as far as it is possible to ascertain it resembled a bad Great Dane, more than anything else, and was undoubtedly a savage brute. [123]

Cuban Mastiff muscular gladiatorial breed formerly found in Cuba (extinct).

> He was not a native of Cuba, but imported into the country. [406]
> Strong and well covered with muscle, they were used for bull-fights. The head was broad, and the muzzle short. The lips were heavily developed. The ears were drop-ears, and the coat was short and close. [185]

Cuban Shock Dog (obs) HAVANA BICHON.

> Poor little Nero, the dog, must have come this winter. The railway guard brought him in one evening late. A little Cuban shock, mostly white – a most affectionate, lively little dog, otherwise of small merit, and little or no training. [82]

cubbing cub-hunting; informal hunting prior to the start of the season intended to disperse cubs or reduce their number.

> I find that I can usually wake up for shooting or cubbing without a watch. [387]

cuff area of short hair on the PASTERNS.

cull 1. destroy substandard puppies; eliminate

unwanted dogs. 2. (Am.) a substandard puppy which is likely to be culled.

> When an occasional 'cull' appears in a litter, it should be given away or destroyed, never registered and never used in breeding. [84]

Culmstock former OTTERHOUND pack formed in 1790 by Jewell Collier to hunt all the rivers flowing into the Bristol Channel from Bristol to Lynton.

culottes hair or FEATHERS on the back of the thighs; BREECHES.

Culpeo South American fox.

Cumberland established in 1825 to hunt a Cumbrian grassland COUNTRY. Originally hunted by John Peel. At various times it has been split into the Cumberland, Cumberland Farmers and the Cumberland West.

Cumberland Brampton former HARRIER pack formed to hunt a Cumberland COUNTRY in 1853.

Cumberland Farmers CUMBERLAND.

Cumberland Sheep Dog extinct form of SHEEP DOG formerly found in northern England. More strongly made, broader in skull and with a thicker coat than the BORDER COLLIE, but otherwise similar to that breed.

Cumberland West CUMBERLAND.

Cuon alpinus Dhole or Red Dog: a widely distributed wild dog found in the mountains of Siberia, Mongolia and Tadzik, as well as in the forests of Java. Resembling a small wolf, it has a red coat and a luxurious fox-like BRUSH(2). Height 43–51cm (17–20in); weight 10–18kg (22–39½lb).

cur 1. formerly a SHEEP DOG but now applied to any dog of unknown parentage; a MONGREL.

> The term Cur has no more reference to a docked dog than to any other, and even curtail has nothing to do with tail, but is, says Skeat, a corruption of the older form curtal [verb, to dock]. [123]
> His colour was a blend of yellow and red,
> His ears and tail were tipped with sable fur
> Unlike the rest; he was a russet cur. [86]
> So, by some hedge, the gen'rous steed deceas'd,
> For half-starv'd snarling curs a dainty feast;
> By toil and famine worn to skin and bone,
> Lies, senseless of each tugging bitch's son. [73c]

2. any dog, other than a HOUND, met while hunting.

3. group of hound breeds of American origin: Black Mouth, Mountain and Leopard Cur.

curative dose (CD) single dose to cure ailment or disease.

cur dog 1. (obs.) SHEEP DOG.

2. any MONGREL dog; CUR.

Cur Fox urban fox.

> Is the least, but the most common, and approaches nearest to the habitations of mankind. [51]

Curly-Coated Retriever [AKC, FCI, KC] a tireless GUNDOG well adapted for work in water.

The head is long, with a flat skull, strong jaws, large but not prominent dark eyes, and small, low-set ears which lie close to the head. The neck is of moderate length, the forequarters deep and muscular, the ribs are WELL SPRUNG and the BRISKET deep.

There should be little TUCK-UP. The hindquarters are strong, with low, well-bent HOCKS. The tail is moderately short, never carried GAILY or curled. The black or liver coat is a mass of small, crisp curls, which also cover the tail. Height 63.5–68.5cm (24–27in).

Curly Poodle reference to the POODLE with curly coat, one of several coat types formerly found in the breed.

> Toys [Poodles] have come more into vogue of late years, and with them may be found all the variations of coat named – Corded, Curly and Fluffy; but, as with their larger brethren, the last two are far more numerous than the first named. [123]

Curragh Irish BEAGLE pack formed in 1954 to hunt a COUNTRY in County Kildare.

Curraghmore, The WATERFORD.

currant jellyer (colloq.) one who follows BEAGLES. (der. hares are traditionally eaten with currant jelly.)

curre (obs. spelling) CUR. [19]

Curre prior to 1847 the COUNTRY was hunted by Lady Curre's Chepstow Harriers; from 1854 to 1867 the pack was known as the Itton. The country is in Monmouthshire and consists largely of plough and moorland.

curtail 1. dog which has had its tail DOCKED. 2. DOCK.

> Other admirers of the race say that they can tell a natural bob-tailed dog from one that has been 'curtailed', by the manner in which the former 'wags his hind-quarters' when pleased. He has no tail to wag, so he wags his buttocks say they. [221]

curtail dog originally a dog owned by someone who was not allowed to hunt in the forest and was obliged to have his dog's tail amputated to mark the fact; subsequently any low-bred dog or dog not meant for sport. [159]

curtain fringe of hair which hangs over the eyes.

Curtal Dog DOCKED dog, especially an OLD ENGLISH SHEEPDOG.

curtall CURTAIL DOG. [319j]

curve of normal distribution GAUSSIAN CURVE.

Cury a HARRIER pack formed in 1860 to hunt a COUNTRY in Cornwall.

Cushing's Syndrome hyperadrenocorticism: excessive producton of cortisol by the adrenal glands.

cushion 1. (esp. of BULLDOGS, MASTIFFS, etc.) thick parts of upper lips giving the appearance of fullness.

> On the thickness of the 'chop' depends the amount of 'cushion'. [221]

2. exceptionally thick foot pad.

cut 1. carry out surgery, most often to castrate or DOCK.

> It is a common trick among low farmers and poachers who keep a wire-haired greyhound, or a Lurcher, to cut his tail, and pass him off for a sheep-dog. [166a]

2. remove certain sheep from a flock; SHED(2).

cut back (of a FIELD-TRIAL dog) move towards the handler after a CAST(3).

cut-up steeply arched belly; TUCK-UP.

The loins should be arched very high, when the dog is said to have a good 'cut-up'. [225]

cut up of loin degree to which the belly is arched.

cutaneous appertaining to the skin.

cutaneous asthenia EHLERS DANLOS SYNDROME.

cutaneous lymphoma lymphatic disease producing raised skin nodules.

cutis hyperelplasia EHLERS DANLOS SYNDROME.

Cutts hyperelastica EHLERS DANLOS SYNDROME.

Cwn Anwn Anwn's Dogs or Couriers of the Air: fabled dogs whose nocturnal cries are said to presage death.

cwoley (regional Eng.) SHEEP DOG. (der. COLLIE.)

cyanosis blue or purple discoloration of the skin usually resulting from a deficiency of oxygen.

cyclic haematopoiesis inherited lethal fluctuation in the number of circulating neutrophils, and characterized by grey coat coloration. (Mode of inheritance, recessive.)

cyclic neutropenia CYCLIC HAEMATOPOIESIS.

cyno (pref.) appertaining to dogs.

cynocephalus fabled dog-headed man.

cynophile one who studies dogs or matters appertaining to dogs.

cynophobia unreasonable fear or dislike of dogs.

cynosure something which attracts notice; a guide. (der. L. *Cynosura*, the constellation of Ursa Minor in which the brightest star, Sirius (the Dog Star), acted as a guide to travellers.)

Cyon one genus of the CANIDIAE family, containing the DHOLEs, which are wild dogs with a characteristic fetid odour. All Dholes are untameable.

Cyon albinus (obs.) northern subspecies of CUON ALPINUS.

Cyon javanicus (obs.) southern subspecies of CUON ALPINUS.

Cyprus Greyhound GREYHOUND originating from Cyprus, which was formerly celebrated for the breed. [406]

cyst 1. bladder, or other hollow organ, from which liquid is secreted. 2. swelling or sac containing diseased or unwholesome fluid.

cystic of, or relating to, CYST.

Cystericerus ovis larval form of *TAENIA OVIS*.

Cystericerus pisiformis larval form of *TAENIA PISIFORMIS*.

Cystericerus tarandi larval form of *TAENIA KRABBEI*.

Cystericerus tenuicollis larval form of *TAENIA HYDATIGENA*.

cystine uriliths inherited tendency to produce calculi caused by secretion of high levels of cystine. (Mode of inheritance, uncertain.)

cystinuria CYSTINE URILITHS.

cystitis inflammation of the bladder.

cytology study of cells and their development.

cytoplasm contents of a cell, other than the nucleus.

Czech Coarse-haired Pointer ČESKÝ FOUSEK.

Czech Coarse-haired Setter ČESKÝ FOUSEK.

Czech Terrier ČESKÝ TERRIER.

D

D gene symbol for no dilution. [395]

d gene symbol for dilution. [395]

d. abbr. dog.

Dachs dim. DACHSHUND. [35]

Dachsbracke (obs.) originally developed in Germany as a hunter of small game, the breed is now also used to follow the blood-trails of larger, wounded game. The two varieties consist of the ALPINE DACHSBRACKE and the WESTPHALIAN DACHSBRACKE.

The skull is slightly rounded, the MUZZLE strong. The round eyes reflect the colour of the coat, the pendulous ears are of medium length, set high and quite far back on the skull. The fairly long neck is muscular, the TOPLINE falling from WITHERS to a rounded CROUP. The ribs are WELL SPRUNG and the TUCK-UP is pronounced. Forequarters are well muscled and the forelimbs sometimes slightly bent at the wrist. The coat is hard, short and dense and may be black or brown with tan, red, or, in the Westphalian Dachsbracke white with red. Height: (Alpine) 34–42cm (13½–16½in); (Westphalian) 30–35cm (12–13¾in).

Is a Dachshund with longer legs and was at one time very well-known amongst sporting men in Germany. [185]

Dachs Bracken (obs.) DACHSBRACKE. [123]

Dachshound formerly a common Anglicized misspelling of DACHSHUND. [36]

Dachshund group of three breeds, each divided into standard and miniature forms, separated only by the texture of their coats: smooth, wire or long. A HOUND of German origin used to hunt badger (Ger. *dachs*, hence the breed's name), and other ground game which may also be followed to GROUND. The breed is also used to follow the blood-trails of larger wounded game. The miniature version known as Kaninteckel, are too small to face badger and are used principally to hunt rabbit (Ger. *kanin*). A divergence of type between the German, which is appreciated throughout mainland Europe, and the British, which is shorter-legged, longer-bodied and heavier, and favoured in America and Australia, as well as in Europe, has in effect split the breed into two, although increasing interbreeding offers some hope that the dichotomy may eventually be repaired or at least reduced.

The breed is long, low and level, but never to the point at which the ability to hunt is impeded. The conical head is long, with a slightly arched skull, high-set pendulous ears and medium-sized almond-shaped eyes, which may be WALL EYES in DAPPLES. The slightly arched neck is long, clean and muscular. The body is long and well muscled with a well-developed KEEL and short, strong LOIN. The forelimbs are short and strong in bone without bend or knuckling over. The hindquarters are strong and WELL ANGULATED. The forefeet are noticeably larger than the hind feet. The tail is long, slightly curved, not carried too high. All colours, other than white, are allowed. Height 9-12kg (20–26½lb).

Persons unfamiliar with the sporting properties of this long-bodied breed are apt to refer smilingly to the Dachshund as 'the dog that is sold by the yard'. [225]

Dachsie dim. (colloq.) DACHSHUND.

DAG abbr. DIETARY ANION GAP.

Dakhun wild dog wild dog from southern Nepal. Its head is compressed and elongated, but its muzzle not very sharp. The eyes are oblique, the pupils round, and the irises light brown. The expression of the countenance is that of a coarse ill-natured Persian greyhound without any resemblance to the jackal, the fox or the wolf. The size is intermediate between the wolf and the jackal. The neck is long, the body elongated and the entire dog a red-brown colour. [406]

Dalby Hall Basset former BASSET pack formed in 1906 to hunt a COUNTRY in Leicestershire.

Dallam Tower Basset former private BASSET pack formed by Sir Maurice Bromley-Wilson in 1898 to hunt a COUNTRY in Westmorland. It has been recorded that the pack 'contains many noted prize-winners'.

Dallie dim. (colloq.) DALMATIAN.

Dalmatian [AKC, KC] spotted dogs have been known and highly prized since the days of ancient Egypt but precisely where the modern Dalmatian has its origins remains a matter for inconclusive debate. Traditionally the Dalmatian is associated with stables, carriages and horses, with which it often appears to have an unusual affinity.

A strong, muscular, active and friendly dog, capable of both speed and endurance. The head is of fair length, with a flat, reasonably broad skull and long, powerful MUZZLE. The high-set rounded ears are pendulous, the eyes round and bright. The forequarters are clean and muscular, PASTERNS slightly SPRUNG; the body is deep and capacious without being too wide, the LOIN is strong and slightly arched. The hindquarters are rounded with strong second thigh and good ANGULATION. Movement is smooth, powerful and rhythmic. The short, hard, white coat is decorated with evenly spaced black or liver spots. Height 55.9–61cm (21¾–24in).

Has been erroneously called the Danish Dog; and by M. Buffon, the Harrier of Bengal. [51]

The plum-pudding dog, Bengal harrier, Dalmatian, or, as it is better known perhaps, 'the carriage dog', is an old variety. Its name, 'Dalmatian', is a mystery. In 1253, in a Dutch account of a visit to Dalmatia, we find a description of dogs kept there, of so large a size and of such considerable strength

that they fought successfully against bulls, and even, according to this account, overcame lions. But their use to the people of that country was their great power to pull along the carts, just like their oxen. Unfortunately, no mention is made of the colour of these great dogs, nor in any way is it suggested that they had black or brown spots. [37]
She'd a crest to mark her station,
And a motto en cartouche,
And she'd Daniel the Dalmatian
Trotting under the barouche. [85]

Dalmatian spotting evenly spaced and sized black or liver spots on a white GROUND.

Dalmatinac [FCI] DALMATIAN.

dam female parent. (first used 1330.)
Try to buy direct from the breeder. See the Mother (dam) as this is a good indication as to how the puppy will develop. [203a]

dancer MONGREL which has been taught to dance or to perform tricks.
There be also dogs among us of a mongrel kind which are taught and exercised to dance in measure at the musical sound of an instrument, . . . as to stand bolt upright, to lie flat upon the ground, to turn round in a ring holding their tails in their teeth, to beg for their meat . . . to move men to laughter for a little lucre. [139]

Dandie dim. DANDIE DINMONT TERRIER.
The grey man eyed him with grim unwelcoming stare.
'What is he?' he asked.
'A Dandie, of course,' said the lady. 'Isn't he a duck?'
'I've seen uglier,' allowed the Laird. [274]

Dandie Dinmont Terrier [AKC, FCI, KC] the breed, probably formerly known simply as the Dandie, from which Sir Walter Scott derived the name of his character Dandie Dinmont in *Guy Mannering*, the surname being borrowed from a notorious Border reiver. The Dandie is one of three TERRIERS that have their origins in the Border region, the other two being the BEDLINGTON and the BORDER TERRIER itself. In spite of very obvious differences, the three share subtle similarities which suggest that all three derived from the same distant root stock.
The Dandie Dinmont has a distinctive, unusually large head crowned with a silky topknot; the rich hazel eyes are large and round, the low-set ears pendulous and feathered; the teeth are of extraordinary size. The body is long, low and flexible, with a TOPLINE that falls from the WITHERS before arching over the LOIN and then sloping to the scimitar tail. The forelegs are heavily boned and muscled, set wide, the muscular, well-angulated hindquarters slightly longer than the forelimbs. The DOUBLE COAT has a soft LINTY undercoat and crisp topcoat. Colour may be either PEPPER or MUSTARD. Weight 8–11kg (17½–24lb).

dandy brush grooming brush with very stiff bristles.

Dane dim. GREAT DANE.
The grand figure, bold muscular action, and elegant carriage of the Dane, would recommend him to notice, had he no useful properties. [127]

Danish Broholmer BROHOLMER.

Danish Dachsbracke STRELLUFSTÖVER.

Danish Dog formerly a smaller variety of the DALMATIAN [338]; other authorities, including LEE, do not differentiate between it and the Dalmatian.
'Is smaller than the Dalmatian; but, being spotted in the same way and characterized by the same fondness for horses, they are generally confounded under the term 'Coach Dog'. [338]

Danish Farm Dog DANSK SVENSK GARDSHUND.

Danish Swedish Guard Dog DANSK SVENSK GARDSHUND.

Dan Russel (obs.) FOX.
Daun Russel, the fox, stert up at oones,
And by the garget hente Chaunteclere
And on his bak toward the wood him bere. [86]

dansers dancing dogs. [159]

Dansk Svensk Gardshund Originating in Denmark, and recently revived, short-coated, medium-sized domestic GUARD, with a strong resemblance to the JACK RUSSELL TERRIER.

dapple (of eyes or coat) evenly distributed dark markings on a lighter GROUND.
The white hound runs with our dappled pack
Far out behind him strung. [272j]

Dare Devil IRISH TERRIER.
There is a heedless, reckless pluck about the Irish Terrier which is characteristic, and coupled with the headlong dash, blind to all consequences, with which he rushes at his adversary, has earned for the breed the proud epithet of 'the Dare Devils'. [203, IRISH TERRIER]

Darlington former private 18in HARRIER pack formed by Captain G. F. Lucas to hunt a COUNTRY in Durham and Yorkshire.

Dartmoor 1. FOXHOUND pack formed in 1827 by John Bulteel, a schoolboy friend of the Rev. Jack Russell, to hunt fox over a moorland, pasture and plough COUNTRY in Devon. 2. former OTTERHOUND pack formed by John Pode in 1825 as an adjunct to the Dartmoor Foxhounds, which continued the association until 1884. The pack hunted the Dart, Harbourne, Avon, Erme, Yealm, Plym, Tavy, Lynher, Fowey, and their tributaries.

Dartmoor Terriers type of FOX TERRIER formerly to be found in the south-west counties of Britain and one of the ancestors of the PARSON and JACK RUSSELL TERRIERS.
I can well remember Rubie's and Ton French's Dartmoor Terriers, and have myself owned some of that sort worth their weight in gold. [113]

Dart Vale DART VALE AND HALDON.

Dart Vale and Haldon HARRIER pack formed in 1947 by the amalgamation of the Dart Vale and the Haldon to hunt a COUNTRY in Devon. The two original packs date from 1759.

Darwinian Theory Charles Darwin's theory of natural selection, which holds that species evolve and thus adapt to their habitat or environment through the survival of those individuals most suited to it and the demise of those that are unsuited. The theory formed part of his *Origin of Species* published in 1859.

Darwinism appertaining to Darwin's theory of evolution. *See* DARWINIAN THEORY.

dauncer FLEMING's spelling of dancer, a mongrel which had an aptitude for dancing. [139]

David Davies FOXHOUND pack formed in 1905 by Lord Davies to hunt fox in a Montgomeryshire hill COUNTRY. HOUNDS were originally light-coloured, BROKEN-COATED Welsh hounds.

dawg (lit.) phonetic spelling of dog.
> Nothing like blood, sir, in hosses, dawgs and men. [352]

Daxel DACHSHUND. [123, possibly a misspelling of TECKEL.]

day blindness HEMERALOPIA.

daylight refers to the distance from BRISKET to ground. A dog showing plenty of daylight is HIGH ON THE LEG.

Deab (obs.) AFRICAN WILD DOG.

dead 1. instruction to a GUNDOG to await the order to seek nearby shot game.
> 'Dead' (which it would be well to accompany with the signal to 'Heel') means that there is something not far off, which he would have great satisfaction in finding. [184]

2. (of ears) that do not move in response to attraction.

dead game quality of extreme, reckless courage, esp. in a TERRIER, originally a literal reference to a fighting dog that died while still fighting.
> Alligator was supposed to die still fighting, and that would make him worth at least double the value at stud among men who spoke the words 'dead game' to one another as if it were some sort of incantation or holy password. [131]

deadgrass shade of fawn.
> Colour dead grass (straw to bracken), sedge (red gold), or any shade of brown. [203] CHESAPEAKE BAY RETRIEVER Interim Breed Standard].
> Deadgrass takes in any shade of deadgrass, varying from a tan to a dull straw color. [6, CHESAPEAKE BAY RETRIEVER]

deafness partial or complete inability to hear sometimes associated with white and MERLE dogs. (Mode of inheritance, familial.)

dealer one who buys and sells dogs bred by others.
> I endeavoured to obtain possession of a lame dog, but failed. A one-eyed dealer in Seven Dials, to whom, as a last resource, I applied, offered to lame one for me for an extra five shillings, but this suggestion I declined. [194a]

death ritual when hunted quarry is caught by HOUNDS. Followers who have kept pace with hounds are said to be 'in at the death'.

debarking surgery that destroys a dog's ability to bark.

Debutante [KC] minor show class.

Deccan WILD DOG OF DAKHUN. [406]

deep brisket a BRISKET that reaches to or below the elbows.

deep chest DEEP BRISKET.

deep ribs DEEP BRISKET.

Deep Run (US) American and English FOXHOUND pack formed in 1887 to hunt a pasture and woodland COUNTRY in Virginia.

deep through the heart DEEP BRISKET.

Deerhound [FCI, KC] basically a rough-coated GREYHOUND developed for pulling down wounded deer. A quietly dignified breed as befits its long history.

The head is long, with a flat skull, aquiline nose, dark eyes and high-set ears that are clothed with mouse-like coat, and generally carried folded back, although they may be raised at moments of excitement. The neck is strong and muscular, the forequarters WELL LAID, with a broad forearm and straight forelimbs. The body is deep rather than broad, the LOIN is arched and the long tail carried drooping. The hindquarters are broad, powerful, drooping and wide set. The shaggy coat is thick and close lying, harsh and wiry on the upper surfaces of the body, slightly softer on the belly, breast and head. White is permitted only on chest and the tip of the tail; colours include dark blue-grey, grey, BRINDLE, yellow, sandy-red and red-fawn with black points. Height of dogs not less than 76cm (30in), weight about 45.5kg (100lb); bitches may be 6cm (2½in) smaller and 9kg (20lb) lighter.

deffete cut up the kill. [159]

de Fouilloux, Jacques author of *La Venerie* (1561), a book dedicated to Charles IX of France and which describes the process of stag, hare and boar hunting and the HOUNDS used.

degenerative myelopathy inherited condition in which there is progressive paralysis, initially of the hind limbs but then of the forelimbs. (Mode of inheritance, recessive.)

degenerative pannus inherited condition in which there is cellular infiltration, vascularization and pigmentation of the cornea. (Mode of inheritance, uncertain.)

Delande's Fox *OTOCYON MEGALOTIS*.

deleterious gene gene with undesirable or harmful effect; a LETHAL GENE.

demodectic of, or relating to, the *DEMODEX* mite.

demodectic mange parasitic skin disease, produced by infestation with the DEMODECTIC MITE, also called red mange and follicular mange. Acquired congenitally, it is not contagious.

demodectic mite *DEMODEX CANIS; DEMODEX FOLLICULORUM*.

demodectic pododermatitis DEMODECTIC MANGE.

Demodex canis parasitic mite causing DEMODECTIC MANGE. [*illus.*]

Demodex canis: demodetic mange mite.

Demodex folliculorum   parasitic mite, considered to be identical to *DEMODEX CANIS*.

demyelinating myelopathy   inherited condition in which there is progressive muscular weakness, leading to paralysis first of the hind limbs then of the forelimbs. (Mode of inheritance, recessive.)

dental defects   additional, absent or crowded teeth. Such defects are inherited. (Mode of inheritance, familial.)

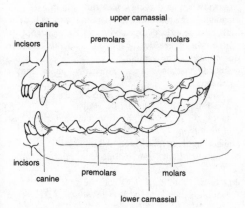

Dentition.

dentition   arrangement of the teeth. [*illus.*]

deoxyribonucleic acid   protein component of the chromosome DNA.

depigmentation   loss of colour.

Derby   major competition, as Greyhound Derby. (der. The Derby for 3-year-old colts at Epsom.)

Dermacentor occidentalis   Pacific Coast tick found on various domestic animals, including the dog. Occurs in western North America.

Dermacentor reticulatus   Tick that attacks ruminants, dogs and horses. Common in Europe. Transmits canine babesiosis.

Dermacentor variabilis   dog tick, found only in North America.

Dermacentor venestus   Tick found on various mammals, including dogs. Occurs in North America. Transmits canine babesiosis and is the cause of American tick paralysis.

dermatitis   nonspecific inflammation of the skin.

dermatomysitis   inherited acute skin and muscle condition characterized by inflammation of the skin and subcutaneous tissue, and necrosis of the muscle fibres. (Mode of inheritance, dominant.)

dermatosis   any skin disease.

dermis   layer of the skin which lies between the epidermis and the subcutaneous layer.

dermoid cysts   fibrous cysts lined with hair follicles which occur in subcutaneous sites. Inherited. (Mode of inheritance, probably recessive.)

dermoid sinus   inherited abnormal sinus running from the skin to the spine; the anterior opening of the sinus is surrounded by a tuft of hair. (Mode of inheritance, recessive.)

Derry   former Irish HARRIER pack formed in 1790 to hunt a COUNTRY in Derry, Donegal and Tyrone.

Derrygallon   Irish HARRIER pack formed in 1930 to hunt a COUNTRY in County Cork.

Derry Harriers   STRABANE(2).

Derwent   hunt, which in its present form dates from 1808 and hunts a north Yorkshire moorland, woodland, pasture and plough COUNTRY.

Derwent Valley   BEAGLE pack formed in 1947, and known as the Huby Beagles until it changed its name in 1953. The COUNTRY is split between part of Dumfries and an area around York.

Desert Fox   CANIS LEUCOPUS.

Deutsche Bracke   [FCI] smooth-coated TRICOLOUR German HOUND, 40–53cm (15¾–20¾in).

Deutsche Dogge   [FCI] GREAT DANE.

Deutsche Langhaar   GERMAN LONG-HAIRED POINTER. [312]

Deutsche Sauerlandbracke   DEUTSCHE BRACKE.

Deutsche Schäferhund   GERMAN SHEPHERD DOG.

Deutscher Drahaariger Vorstehhund   [FCI] GERMAN WIRE-HAIRED POINTER.

Deutscher Glatthaariger Pinscher   [FCI] the smooth-haired variety of PINSCHER.

Deutscher Grosspitz   [FCI] one of five typically SPITZ breeds of German origin which differ principally in size. Height 41cm (16in).

Deutscher Jagterrier   [FCI] German breed which, in all probability, was created from imported British TERRIER breeds. A top-quality and willing, if unusually hard, working terrier capable of facing almost any game above or below ground.

The skull is flat and broad tapering to a minimum STOP and powerful MUZZLE equipped with unusually large, strong teeth. The eyes are small and deep set with close-fitting eyelids; the V-shaped, high-set ears fall close to the head. The neck is powerful and slightly arched, the forequarters long, sloping and well muscled, the forelimbs robustly boned and straight. The chest is deep and WELL SPRUNG, the TOPLINE level and the LOINS and CROUP well muscled. The muscular hindquarters are long and WELL ANGULATED. The coat is smooth, close and hard, and may be black, black flecked with grey, or brown with or without tan PATTERNing. Weight 7.5–10kg (16½–22lb).

Deutscher Kleinspitz   small GERMAN SPITZ.

Deutscher Kurzhaariger Vorstehhund   [FCI] GERMAN SHORT-HAIRED POINTER.

Deutscher Langhaariger Vorstehhund   [FCI] GERMAN LONG-HAIRED POINTER.

Deutscher Mittelspitz   Standard GERMAN SPITZ.

Deutscher Rauhaariger Pinscher   AFFENPINSCHER.

Deutscher Schäferhund   GERMAN SHEPHERD DOG. (Alsatian).

Deutscher Spitz [FCI] GERMAN SPITZ (KLEIN).
Deutscher Stichelhaariger Vorstehhund [FCI] GERMAN WIRE-HAIRED POINTER.
Deutscher Wachelhund liver-coated German spaniel, height 40–51cm (15¾–20in); weight 20–30kg (44–66lb).
Deutscher Zwergspitz POMERANIAN.
devil dog emotive term much used by tabloid journalists during the early 1990s to refer to the ROTTWEILER, probably as a result of the breed's being featured in the film *Damien*.
Devon and Somerset STAGHOUND pack formed prior to 1775 to hunt a COUNTRY consisting of the Exmoor Royal Forest.
Devonshire Cocker type of GUNDOG formerly to be found in Devon. According to Stonehenge it closely resembles the Welsh Cocker, both being of a deep liver colour.
> Although the Devonshire Cocker has little or nothing to do with the show specimens of today, no article dealing with the smaller varieties of land spaniels would be complete without some mention of the breed, which was well-known and appreciated many years since for its sterling worth and working qualities. [285]

Devonshire Pointer former localized type of GUNDOG.
> No other country can lay claim to older pointer blood than that which is found in Devonshire. . . . Long before dog shows and field trials became fashionable, Devon pointers were distinguished for their high quality, for their total freedom from anything approaching a hound cross, and for their natural working characteristics, such as staunchness on point, range, and readiness to back. [221, quoting Norrish]

Devonshire Spaniel DEVONSHIRE COCKER.
> I scramble over a gap in the bank, smearing myself all over with a greasy yellow clay in the process, and, knowing the wild ways of the Devonshire spaniel, hasten forward alongside the spinney. [140]

Devonshire Terrier breed of working FOX TERRIER native to Devon which became absorbed by PARSON JACK RUSSELL's breed.
dew-claw rudimentary first digit normally found only on the forelimbs, sometimes abnormally found on the rear limbs and in some breeds occurs in a double form; regarded as normal in some pastoral guarding breeds. [*illus.* DIGITAL PAD]
dewlap pendulous skin on the underside of the throat.
> Neck sufficiently long to enable the hound to come down easily to scent, slightly arched and showing little dewlap. [203, BEAGLE]
> He is old, grey, brindled; as big as a little Highland bull, and has the Shakespearian dewlaps shaking as he goes. [65]

Dkohi Apso TIBETAN TERRIER.
Dhole 1. *CYON ALBINUS*. 2. *CYON JAVANICUS*.
> The native wild dog of India . . . resembles the dingo, in all but the tail, which, though hairy, is not at all bushy. [338]

diabetes insipidus a hormone condition in which excessive amounts of dilute urine are produced, and resulting from changes in the production of vasopressin by the hypothalamus.
diabetes mellitus inherited insulin imbalance resulting from pancreas malfunction. (Mode of inheritance, recessive.)
diabetic 1. one who suffers from diabetes. 2. of, or relating to, diabetes.
 diabetic neuropathy disease of the nervous system associated with diabetes; seen rarely in dogs.
diagonals the relationship between the front foot or limb on one side of the body and the rear foot or limb on the other side: the diagonals operate together during normal movement.
diamond THUMB MARK, especially on a PUG's forehead.
> Muzzle or mask, ears, moles on cheeks, thumb mark or diamond on forehead. [203, PUG]

diaphragm muscular partition between the chest and abdomen.
diaphragmatic hernia inherited intestinal protrusion through the diaphragm. (Mode of inheritance, familial.)
diarrhoea condition in which the fluid content of the stools is increased to the point at which they verge on being liquid.
diathesis predisposition to a certain disease.
Didycoy Dog LURCHER.
Diehard (obs.) popular name for SCOTTISH TERRIER.
> A name applied to the hard-haired Scottish terriers by their admirers. [320]

dietary anion gap a beneficial balance of ion concentrations, particularly of sodium, potassium and chloride, in a dog's diet.
differentiation process by which individual cells combine to form a more complex organism.
digit toe.
digital of a toe.
 digital hyperatosis increased thickness and hardness of the pads, whether as a consequence of injury or an after-effect of DISTEMPER.
 digital pad pad associated with a particular digit, not the communal pad. [*illus.*]
digoneutic having two breeding cycles each year.
dig out unearth a badger. [159]
dilution colours coat colours which occur in a range of lighter shades.
dimples depressions on either side of the sternum.
Dingo dog imported into Australia by early aboriginal settlers which has returned to a feral or even

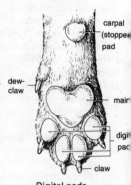

Digital pads.

wild state. During the early 1990s it moved from being classed as vermin to be exterminated by any means, to recognition as Australia's national dog. The breed is typically vulpine in appearance, with a broad, wedge-shaped head, pricked rather rounded ears, and a long, bushy tail. The usual colour is sandy or fawn but other colours, perhaps originating in recent crosses with domestic dogs, are not uncommon. Height 48–58cm (18¾–23in); weight 23–32kg (50½–70½lb).

Dinocyon extinct ancestor of the CANIDAE.

dioestrus period of the oestrous cycle when sexual activity is dormant, oestrogen levels high and progesterone levels low.

dip back DIPPED BACK.

diploid chromosome number number of individual chromosomes carried by a particular species. Since chromosomes are paired it is customary to refer to the number of pairs – the HAPLOID number.

dipped back TOPLINE that is concave between WITHERS and CROUP.

Dipylidium caninum tapeworm.

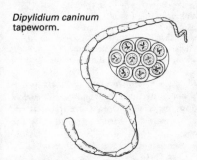

Dipylidium caninum TAPEWORM, growing up to 50cm (20in) long. [*illus.*]

Dirofilaria immitis heartworm: nematode parasite transmitted by mosquitoes and found in the blood vessels, esp. those of the heart.

Dirofilaria repens nematode parasite transmitted by mosquitoes and found in subcutaneous tissue.

dirty puppy syndrome CONGENITAL SEBORRHOEA.

discontinuous variation descriptive of those characteristics that are subject to sharply defined changes without any intermediate variation.

dish-faced concave from STOP to nose.
    The hollowness in the line of the nose from nostrils to the eye, giving the nose the appearance of being higher at the nostrils than at the stop. [46]
    Skull, flat and moderately broad with a slight stop between eyes, in no way accentuated, avoiding a down or dish-faced appearance. [203, FLAT-COATED RETRIEVER]

dishing moving the forefeet in an outward arc.

displacement activity instinctive behaviour which is an appropriate response to the stimulus: faced with certain quandaries a dog may scratch or yawn.

disqualify official decision to deprive a dog of an award.

disassortative mating unlike to unlike mating.

distemper highly infectious viral disease, usually fatal, formerly thought to arise out of an imbalance of morbid humours, and resulting in encephalitis and myelitis. Symptoms include vomiting, coughing, and eye and nasal discharge. The disease can result in permanent paresis, paralysis and ataxia. (der. L. *distemperare*, to mix wrongly.)

distemper teeth teeth which have been discoloured and deformed either as a result of DISTEMPER or by some nutritional deficiency or traumatic experience.

distichiasis inherited double rows of eyelashes. (Mode of inheritance, familial.) [*illus.*]

Distichiasis.

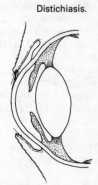

diuretic that which promotes the flow of urine.

divergent hocks spread or BARREL HOCKS.

division when unbeaten GREYHOUNDS remaining in a STAKE mutually agree or are obliged to share honours.

DNA deoxyribonucleic acid.

Dobe dim. (colloq.) DOBERMANN.

Dobermann [FCI, KC] an eponymous breed which carries the name of its originator, Kart Friedrich Louis Dobermann, who appears to have combined the duties of DOG-CATCHER, court official, taxation officer, butcher and night watchman in the town of Niederrossia, Apolda, in Thuringia, central Germany, with a considerable interest in dogs. Herr Dobermann began a breeding programme in 1870 which was intended to produce a top-quality guard dog.

A medium-sized, muscular and elegant dog, compact and tough, intelligent and obedient. The head is long, CLEAN CUT, in profile resembling a blunt wedge. The almond-shaped eyes are deep set, the ears are small, neat, high set and may be pricked or dropped. The lean neck is fairly long and slightly arched. The forelimbs are straight, parallel and well boned, the body is square with deep, WELL-SPRUNG ribs, short back and marked TUCK-UP. The CROUP is well filled and the hindquarters muscular with a long, well-turned stifle. The tail is traditionally DOCKED. The coat is smooth, short and hard, black, brown, BLUE or fawn, with rich tan markings. Height 65–69cm (25½–27in).
    About 1870, Dietsch, at that time owner of a gravel pit at Apolda, had a blue-grey bitch, a sort of Pinscher, which he mated with a black butcher's dog. This sire already had characteristic tan markings and was a cross between sheepdog and butcher's dog. Dobermann, the carcase cutter, who unfortunately dies prematurely, crossed the issue of these two dogs, which became good guard dogs, with German Pinschers. That is the origin of today's Doberman. [391]

Dobermann cardiomyopathy inherited heart disease characterized by acute pulmonary oedema, cardiogenic shock and occasionally sudden death. (Mode of inheritance, unknown.)

Dobermann eye anomaly inherited condition in which there is opaque cornea, prominent THIRD EYELID, and retinal detachment. (Mode of inheritance, recessive.)

Dobermann, Kart Friedrich Louis originator of the DOBERMANN.

Doberman Pinscher 1. [AKC] DOBERMANN. 2. Common misnomer for the DOBERMANN. 'PINSCHER' means TERRIER and, in Germany, was dropped from the Dobermann's name in 1949. 'Pinscher' continued to be used in the United States coupled with a misspelling (Doberman) of the name of the breed's originator.

Dobson, William (of Eden Hall, Cumberland) author of *The Kunopoedia, A Practical Essay on Breaking or Training the English Spaniel or Pointer with Instruction for Attaining the Art of Shooting Flying*. Published in 1814 this was the first book devoted entirely to the training of SETTERS and POINTERS.

dock 1. to surgically shorten a tail.

> Columnelle writeth, that when a whelp is just fortie daies old, if his taile be bitten off at the nethermost joint, and the sinew or string that cometh after, be likewise taken away, neither the taille will grow any more, nor the dog ever to bee mad. [286]

> But then another tragedy loomed. He must be docked. His floating puppy-tail must be docked short. This time my father was the enemy. My mother agreed with us that it was an unnecessary cruelty. But my father was adamant. 'The dog'll look a fool all his life, if he's not docked.' And there was no getting away from it. To add to the horror, poor Rex's tail must be bitten off. [219]

Docked tail.

2. dog's tail, especially after having been DOCKED. [*illus.*]

dockan DOCKED tail [159]

docked (of tail) *see* DOCK.

dodge dog. [159]

doe female deer, rabbit or hare.

dog 1. member of the CANIDAE family. (der. Indo-European *k'uon* from which are also derived Armenian *shun*, Old Chinese *k'iuan*, modern Chinese *k'ou*, East African *kunano*, Erse *shuan*, Siberian-Ostiak *canac*, old Greek *kyon* and Latin *Canis*. The last two give rise to French *chien*, Italian *cane*, Rumanian *caine*, Portuguese *cão* and Old Spanish

cau. Sumerian *nug*, Tamil *nay*, and Japanese *inu* have an obvious relationship, as have Old Egyptian *uhor* and Basque *hor*. The Germanic languages, German, Dutch and some of the Scandinavian languages use derivations of *hund* or *hond* to refer to all dogs, although the word *hound* has, in English come to refer only to hunting dogs. Interestingly enough the English word *dog*, which derives from the Old English *docga* (first recorded in 1050), has made the converse journey in that it originally referred only to hounds but has now come to refer to all dogs.

> 'What a lot of dogs!' She was corrected. 'Those are hounds, darling!' She again studied the pack, and then said, controversially, 'Well, they're very like dogs.' [329]

2. male of the dog family.

dog bed place where dogs sleep.

dog biscuit hard-baked cereal product intended for feeding dogs.

> Previous to his return, I had given The O'Shannon a biscuit. The O'Shannon had been insulted; he did not want a dog biscuit; if he could not have a grilled kidney he did not want anything. [194]

> 'I was thinking of dog biscuits, of dog biscuits, of . . . er . . . in short . . . dog biscuits, I wonder,' said Lord Emsworth, striking while the iron was hot, 'if I could interest you in a good dog biscuit?'
> The blonde at the wheel weighed the question.
> 'Not me,' she said, 'I never touch 'em.' [400]

dog box 1. case in which small dogs are transported or secured, particularly at shows. 2. vehicle in which dogs, especially HOUNDS, are transported.

dog bread poor-quality bread intended only for feeding dogs.

> The *Panis caninus* [dog-bread] of Juvenal occurs in the Middle Age. [141]

> The Kings of France surpassed all others in their day for the splendour of their hunting establishments. That of Philip the Good consisted of one Grand Veneur, or great huntsman, with twenty-four attendant huntsmen, a clerk, and twenty-four valets; one hundred and twenty liverymen, six pages of the hounds, six pages of the greyhounds, twelve underpages of the hounds, six superintendents of the servants of the kennels, six valets of limers, six of greyhounds, twelve of running hounds, six of spaniels, six of small dogs, six of English dogs (mastiffs), six of Artois dogs (matins), twelve bakers of dog's bread, a great wolf-hunter, and four wolf-hunters. [393]

dog buffer (18th cent. Brit.) dog thief who, at a price, returned the dogs to their owners, or who killed them and sold the skins, feeding the remainder to others. [157]

dog cage container in which dogs are transported or restrained, especially at shows.

dog carriage 1. specially designed vehicle in which dogs were formerly transported by rail. 2. DOG CART. [344b]

dog cart 1. two-wheeled horse-drawn carriage with seats arranged back to back under which is space to carry dogs.

> Dog carts bore milk-white terriers and greyhounds

whose sheets carried embroidered records of the matches they had won. [267]

2. wheeled vehicle drawn by a dog or dogs.

dog-catcher person employed to catch stray dogs.

dog churn churn designed to be turned by a dog. In various parts of America, a churn is worked by a dog, and called, in consequence, the dog churn. A pretty large circular wheel is placed not quite horizontally, but inclining obliquely at a moderate angle. The dog is made to walk the outer circle of this wheel, so that, on the principle of the treadmill, his weight sets it in motion; and his position upon the wheel is such that as it moves from under him, he finds it necessary to continue walking up the inclined plane. [393]

dog collar COLLAR.

dog day 1. appointed day for rounding up stray dogs.

One summer day – a dog day – when all dogs found straying were hauled away to the police-office, and killed off in twenties with strychnine. [65]

2. the period when the DOGSTAR rises and sets with the sun (usually 3 July – 11 August), and spuriously thought to be the time when dogs are susceptible to hydrophobia. 3. *See* Dog's Day.

dog dealer one who buys and sells dogs bred by others.

A dog-dealer told me that he hardly knew what made many gentlemen so fond of bull-dogs, and they were 'the fonder on 'em the more blackguarder and varmint-looking the creatures was,' although now they were useless for sport. [250]
The thief kept the dog perhaps for a day or two at some public house, and he then took it to a dog-dealer with whom he was connected in the way of business. These dealers carried on a trade in 'honest dogs,' as one of the witnesses styled them (meaning dogs honestly acquired), but some of them dealt principally with the dog-stealers. [250]

dog do (euph.) dog excrement.

dogdom summation of all activities which result from an interest in dogs.

Nature, who made you rough and grey and meek,
Reft you of dogdom's silent power to speak;
Cut off your tribal customary flag,
And left you nothing you could wave or flag. [222]

dog draw (obs.) offence committed by a person trailing a wounded deer.

An apparent deprehension of an offender against venison in the forest. Dog-draw is where any man hath stricken or wounded a wild beast by shooting with a cross-bow, or long-bow, or otherwise, and is found with a hound or other dog drawing after him to receive the same. [100]

dog erythrocyte antigens ERYTHROCYTE ANTIGENS.

dog fancier one who is involved in or pursues canine activities.

These robberies [dog stealing] are generally committed by dog-fanciers and others who confine their attention to this class of felonies. They are persons of a low class, dressed variously, and are frequently followed by women. [250]

dog farrier (obs.) person who makes shoes for draught dogs employed in transport.

dog fight battle between two dogs, either spontaneously or as an organized event. *See also* DOG FIGHTER.

dog fighter person who organizes a DOG FIGHT, or owns a dog used for organized fighting.

dog finder (obs. euph.) DOG STEALER.

dog flea *CTENOCEPHALIDES CANIS*.

dog fox male fox.

Up he comes with a great ruddy dog-fox in his hand, whooping and holloaing as hard as he could shout. [344c]

dog gauge measure formerly used to assess the size of dogs for licensing or control.

doghouse (Am.) KENNEL.

dog kennel KENNEL.

dog killer person employed to kill dogs during hot weather as a precaution against the spread of rabies. [159]

dog lead LEAD.

dog leech (19th cent. Brit.) unqualified person who treats dog ailments.

dog letter CANINE LETTER.

dog leucocyte antigen complex LEUKOCYTE ANTIGEN COMPLEX.

dog licence LICENCE.

dog louse *MALLOPHAGA*.

dog man person with a liking for and affinity with dogs.

When dangled prizes, medals, cups
The dog-man's keen ambition train,
Be sure the donor will have the honour
Of winning them back again. [136]

dog match 1. organized dog fight.

Until within these twelve years, indeed, dog-matches were not infrequent in London, and the favourite time for the regalement was on Sunday mornings. [250]

2. type of show in which one dog competes against another on a knock-out basis.

dog meal small-sized kibbled biscuit fed to dogs.

dog measure 1. DOG GAUGE. 2. implement used to measure the height of some breeds at shows.

dog meat any flesh – traditionally esp. of horses – used in the manufacture of dog food.

dog merde (euph.) dog's excrement. (Ostensibly Elizabethan term coined by Anthony Burgess, making unacknowledged use of the old word merd, meaning excrement.) [159]

dog nipper DOG THIEF. [280]

dog otter adult male otter.

dog pit PIT.

dog run enclosure, usually open air, in which dogs are confined.

Dog's Day Kashmiri holiday, *Khich Mavas*, and Nepalese holiday, *Swana Boli*, during which dogs wear flower garlands and the red spot of Hindu holiness and are given choice food in recognition that they are worthy fellow beings.

dog shelf   the floor, where dogs are supposed to sit.

dog show   competition at which the perceived relative merits of dogs are compared and the best rewarded.

> A great deal has been said for and against dog shows, I consider them a step in the right direction, if honestly and honourably carried out, without favouritism (which I think it is by the majority), and the judges competent. [218]
>
> The numerous dog-shows in various parts of the country have done much to educate the public eye. [186]

dog-skin   leather made from the skin of a dog, esp. for use in making gloves.

dog sled   (Am.) sleigh drawn by dogs.

dog sledge   (Brit.) sleigh drawn by dogs.

Dog Star   (astronomy) Sirius, of the constellation CANIS MAJOR. See also DOG DAY(2).

dog stealer   one who steals dogs.

> The return shows that 151 ladies and gentlemen had been the victims of the dog stealers or dog finders, for in this business the words were, and still are to a degree, synonyms, and of these 62 had been victimized in 1843 and in the six months of 1884, from January to July. [250]

dog tax   (obs.) taxation formerly imposed on dog ownership in the UK.

> Lord Mahon rose to inform the House, that a petition had been put into his hand, figured by a respectable number of inhabitants of Durham and the town of Berwick, stating that the breeds of dog had greatly increased, and praying, that a tax might be laid upon dogs of all descriptions. [26]

dog thief   DOG STEALER.

dog tick   tick that especially affects dogs. There are various species, each of which tend to be more common in or even exclusive to a country or part of the world: Australia, *IXODES HOLOCYCLUS*; Britain *IXODES CANISUGA*; Europe, *RHIPICEPHALUS SANGUINEUS*; USA, *DERMACENTOR VARIABILIS*.

dog track   arena in which GREYHOUND racing takes place.

dog trot   deliberate and economical pace.

dog turd   dog excrement.

dog-walker's elbow   occupational hazard faced by those who habitually exercise several undisciplined dogs.

dog warden   person employed to enforce dog control legislation.

dog whipper   person employed to evict dogs from places to which they are not welcome, most often churches and churchyards.

> The dog-whipper's instrument consisted of a long ash stick to which was fastened a thong of leather three feet long. But he often combined with this duty that of sluggard-waking, and for that purpose was armed with a rousing-stick. Not a few people in bygone ages felt it a duty to leave part of their worldly wealth to pay dog-whippers and sluggard-wakers. [195]

dog whipping day   appointed day for rounding up stray dogs. Usually St Luke's Day, 18 October, because a dog was said to have eaten the consecrated wafer in York Minster on that day.

dog whistle   whistle with a high pitch which can be heard by dogs but not by people.

dog wolf   adult male wolf.

doggess   (facetious) BITCH.

doggery   collective noun for dogs.

dogging   shooting with dogs.

doggish   dog-like.

doggy   1. childish name for a dog.   2. of one who has a liking for or interest in dogs.   3. like a dog, usually referring to smell.

doggy bag   receptacle in which a customer takes uneaten food, ostensibly to feed the dog, from a restaurant.

Doggy Lawrence   originator of the CANTAB TERRIER.

Dogo Argentino   [FCI] produced in the 1920s by Dr Antonio Nores Martinez, the Dogo Argentino was bred as a pack animal to hunt wild boar, jaguar and cougar.

The breed is agile, strong and tireless. The skull is broad, the STOP sharp and the MUZZLE short and immensely strong. Ears are traditionally CROPPED. The neck is well muscle, and the body rectangular in outline. The forelimbs are strong, well boned and straight, the hindquarters fairly long and well muscled. The tail is carried to reach the HOCKS. The coat is always white, short, smooth, thick and glossy. Height 60–65cm (23½–25½in); weight 37–43 (81½–94½lb).

Dogue de Bordeaux   [FCI] an impressive archetypal MOLOSSAN. The breed was originally used for BAITING and fighting sports (the different sizes – the Dogue being the larger and the Doquin the smaller, being used as appropriate).

Typically ACROMEGALIC in appearance with a huge, immensely impressive, heavily wrinkled head, with short, broad skull, deep MEDIAN FURROW, abrupt STOP, short, square jaw, UNDERSHOT mouth, wide set, oval eyes, and small, pendulous ears. The neck is exceptionally strong, the forequarters well sloped and the limbs heavy, muscular and straight. The chest is broad and deep, the back broad and muscular; the hindquarters are long and muscular and slightly narrower than the forequarters. The tail is carried low to reach the HOCKS. The coat is fine, short and smooth and may be mahogany fawn, golden or black BRINDLE. Male Dogues over 45kg (99lb), females over 40kg (88lb); Doquins between 35kg (77lb) and 45kg (99lb); height about 61cm (24in).

Doguin   former name for the PUG or Carlin.

> Prior to Carlin's popularity they had been known as doguins or roquets, but afterwards they obtained the commoner, if less euphonious, name of pugs. [221]

dolichocephalic   having a long, narrow skull; skull that gives a CEPHALIC INDEX of about 50–55. [*illus.*]

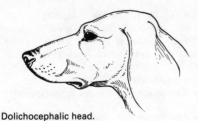

Dolichocephalic head.

domed (of the upper part of the skull) pronounced roundedness.
> Head and skull well developed and rounded, neither flat nor domed. [203, AMERICAN COCKER SPANIEL]

domestic guard guard dog used to protect property, as distinct from the pastoral guard which protects livestock.

dominance propensity of one allele to mask the effect of another.

dominant 1. demonstrate superiority behaviourally; behaviour in keeping with that of an alpha dog. 2. (of genes) allele that has the ability to mask the effect of another.

domino light MASK on a darker GROUND.

Dongolah Dog PARIAH dog formerly said by Loisel to have been found in Twelfth Dynasty Egypt.

donkey stripe TRACE.

Doquin smaller variety of the DOGUE DE BORDEAUX.

dorsal of the upper surface of the back.
  dorsal vertebrae thirteen vertebrae which form the withers and back, and from which the ribs spring.

Douar AIDI.

Douar Dog Kabyle dog. [312] AIDI.

double 1. (esp. of hunted animals) return along the route just traversed.
> She doubles, to mislead the hound,
> And measures back her mazy round;
> 'Till, fainting, in the publick way,
> Half dead with fear she gasping lay. [145a]

2. the winning of both CCs in a breed at a show.

double coat having an undercoat (usually soft) and a topcoat (usually harsher).

double curled of tail that is curled twice, as exhibited by the PUG.

double handling practice of attracting a show dog's attention from outside the ring in order to make it more alert, hence the dog has two handlers.

double lead SLED-DOGS harnessed side by side at the head of a team.

double mongrel (obs.) first CROSS; the offspring resulting from a mating between parents of pure breed.
> The Maltese, or lap-dog, is a double mongrel, produced between the small spaniel and the little water dog. [72]

double-nose nose with a distinct vertical cleavage down the centre.
> There is a circumstance worthy of notice in Pointers, that some of them have a deep fissure in the centre of the nose, which completely divides the nostrils.

Such are termed double-nosed, and supposed to possess the power of scenting better than others. [127]
> In certain quarters we are aware of the existence of a lingering superstition to the effect that a 'double-nosed' Pointer has superior scenting powers, but for our own part we cannot agree with the theory, and have never seen it proved in practice. [320a]

double up when the same dog or bitch appears on both the sire's and dam's half of the pedigree, the offspring is said to be 'doubled up' to that individual.

doubt CHECK during the progress of a hunt.
> The hot scent-snuffling hounds are driven to doubt,
> Ceasing their clamorous cry till they have singled
> With much ado the cold fault cleanly out. [319x]

Douge d'Argentine DOGO ARGENTINO.

Dover's Powder compound of ipecacuana, opium and sulphate of potash formerly used to treat DISTEMPER, catarrh and diarrhoea. [184]

Dove Valley former HARRIER pack formed in about 1850 to hunt a COUNTRY in Staffordshire and Derbyshire.

down 1. lie flat; a command to a dog to do so; thus stopping its forward progress. Also used as a verb: 'to down a dog'. 2. collective noun for hares.

down-charge 1. of a GUNDOG which runs into another's birds. [184]
> When you get the dog to drop well to the word, it is easy to teach him to do so at wing, or fur; to down charge, to come close to heel, and ware fence is nothing to teach. [218]
> I almost always used him single-handed for every purpose, as he would of his own accord 'down-charge' and bring the game when told. [166]

2. formerly synonymous with DOWN(2).

down face MUZZLE that makes an obtuse angle with the skull.
> If the upper and lower jaws are level, and the muzzle is not turned upwards the dog is said to be 'down-faced'. [225]

downfaced having a profile that shows DOWN FACE.

Downham Foxhounds WEST NORFOLK.

Downham Harriers WEST NORFOLK.

down in pastern of dog whose faulty action or construction produces PASTERNs which, standing or in movement, are not vertical.

DR (of COURSING) abbr. DRAW(2).

draft 1. HOUND surplus to the pack's requirements and made available to others.
> I have accepted draft-hounds myself, and they have been very good; but they were the gift of the friend mentioned by me in a former letter. [47]
> If you determine on forming a pack by drafts from different kennels don't fail purchasing twice as many as you may require, for, depend on it, one half of them will be useless. [266b]

2. dispose of surplus HOUNDS.
> During the forty-five years the Lambtons had these hounds they were very carefully bred and drafted. [101]

3. remove certain HOUNDS from the pack in order to achieve uniformity of pace in the remainder.

drag 1. scent laid by hunted quarry.

> There is infinite pleasure in hearing a fox well found.
> When you get up to his kennel with a good drag, the
> chorus increasing as you go, it inspires a joy, more
> easy to be felt than described. [47]

2. artificial scent trail.

> It is hardly necessary to say that Dr. Hickey also had
> been convinced by the way the hounds ran that it
> was a drag. [329a]

draghound HOUND used to hunt artificial scent trails.

drag hunting 1. hunting an artificial trail.
2. HUNTING THE CLEAN BOOT.

dragging DRAG HUNTING.

dragline DRAG(2).

drapes VEIL.

draught 1. type of HOUND. [159]

draught dog dog used to carry or pull burdens.

Draughthound BLOODHOUND.

> To find out the Hart or Stag, where his harbour or
> Lare is, you must be provided with a Bloodhound,
> Draughthound, or Sluithound, which must be led in
> a Liam; and, for the quickening his scent, it is good
> to rub his nose with vinegar. [53]

draw 1. use HOUNDS to search cover for their intended quarry.

2. (of hunting hounds) move towards a particular objective

> By which they will draw towards him, trying for the
> scent as they go. [266b]

3. pull, usually with the aid of a TERRIER, quarry from its place of refuge.

4 (of a GUNDOG) find birds by their body scent.

> Dogs which can draw in a superior manner, will
> scent birds at astonishingly long distances under
> favourable conditions of wind and temperature.
> [378]
> Drawing is the act of approaching the birds by the
> body scent. This manner of determining the location
> of the birds is commonly performed with much
> greater quickness and precision than by roading.
> [378]

5. select by chance the dogs to meet each other in matches.

draw the slot (obs.) of HOUNDS on the scent of a stag.

> When hounds pursue upon the scent, until they have
> unharboured the stag, they are said to draw on the
> slot. [151c]

drawer (obs.) HOUND used exclusively for DRAWING.

drawing *see* DRAW.

drawing up (of GUNDOG) coming close to a wounded bird.

> It is a fascinating sight to watch the dogs, especially
> if two are working together, ranging and quartering,
> or drawing up to a running grouse. [77]

drawn-up flank concave LOIN.

Drentse Partridge Dog DRENTSE PARTRIJSHOND.

Drentse Partrijshond [FCI] Dutch Setter.

The skull is broad, with imperceptible STOP, the MUZZLE a blunt wedge; deep-set amber eyes are set wide, the pendulous ears are high set. The neck is short and powerful, the chest deep, with the BRISKET in line with the elbow. Ribs are WELL SPRUNG with back ribs well developed. The back is rather longer than it is high. The tail is high set, carried low or SABRE fashion. The coat, brown or orange on a white ground, is dense, wavy and of medium length, forming moderate FEATHERING.

dress (of a FOXHOUND) groom for appearance at a show.

> A little dressing was badly needed. I mention no
> names or locality, but the pack I have in mind is now
> up to show form, thanks to a capable Master. [*297]

Drever [FCI] the most popular breed in Scandinavia, a HOUND used to hunt anything from hare to boar. Its excellent scenting powers and musical voice are much appreciated by Scandinavian hunters.

A compact dog, with a rectangular outline. The head is large and long, the dark brown eyes are clear and expressive, the ears of medium length, slightly rounded and pendulous. The neck is unusually long, with loose skin but no DEWLAP. The TOPLINE is level with a rounded CROUP, the chest falling to below the elbow level; the LOINS are strong and short. The tail is long and thick, carried below the level of the topline. The forelimbs are short but straight, with an elastic, slightly sloping PASTERN; the hindquarters are broad and well muscled, with low HOCKS. The coat is short, thick and close-fitting. All colours are acceptable with some white obligatory; white is also preferred on lower limbs and tail tip. Height about 35cm (13¾in).

drift tendency of a small or isolated population to become different from the main population.

drive 1. powerful thrust of the hind limbs; measure of forward propulsion achieved during movement.

> Hind legs showing drive. [203, BEAGLE]
> Sound, free and light movement essential with plenty
> of drive. [203, POODLE]

2. that quality in a HOUND which makes it determined to follow the scent at the maximum pace possible.

> The essential talents of a foxhound are to be found
> in his power of nose, drive and tongue. [221]

3. propensity of a hound or pack to make progress during the course of a hunt.

> Drive derives from sagacity combined with great
> scenting ability. [369]

4. keep a flock or herd of animals together and moving in the desired direction. [204]

droop (of the CROUP) steep slope.

> Hindquarters, strong, muscular and free from droop
> or crouch. [203, WIRE FOX TERRIER]

drooping hindquarters steeply sloping CROUP.

> Hindquarters drooping, broad and powerful. [203,
> DEERHOUND]

drop 1. lie flat; command, especially to a GUNDOG, to do so.

> That 'drop' or the left arm raised nearly perpen-
> dicular, or the report of a gun, means that he is to
> crouch down with his head close to the ground,
> between his feet, however far off he may be ranging.
> [184]

2. DROP EAR.

drop ear   ear carried pendulously.
> Ears Prick or drop. [203, SKYE TERRIER]

dropped   1. of ear carriage, pendulous.   2. *see* DROPPED HOCK.   3. lying flat, *see* DROP.

dropped hock   HOCK close to the ground, a result of weakness, injury or deformity, discernible in movement.

dropper   (obs.) CROSS-BRED GUNDOG.
> A cross between Setter and Pointer, I do not like. He is useless as a breeding dog, although certainly useful occasionally in the field; but his talents are uncertain and his temper is capricious. [186]
> The name given to the produce of the first cross between Pointer and Setter – are, in some few instances, fairly good. [123]
> We know now by experience that the first cross between the two (English Setter and Pointer); commonly called 'a dropper', is a very useful dog, possessing the properties of each, but it does not answer to go on breeding from it, either on the side of the sire or dam. [338]

dropsy   swelling caused by subcutaneous fluid.

Drótszörü Magyar Vizsla   HUNGARIAN WIRE-HAIRED VIZSLA.

drover   DROVER'S DOG.

Drover's Dog   extinct type of dog used, prior to the railways, to drive cattle over long distances.
> Bears considerable resemblance to the sheep-dog, and has usually the same prevailing black or brown colour. He possesses all the docility of the sheep-dog, with more courage, and sometimes a degree of ferocity. [406]
> This is a mixed breed, being a cross between the sheep-dog and the mastiff or hound, or sometimes the greyhound, pointer, or setter. [338]

Drury, W. D.   editor of *British Dogs: their points, selection and show preparation* (1903), and *Practical Kennel Management: a complete treatise on the proper management of dogs for the show bench, the field, or as companions, with chapters on diseases – their causes and treatment* (1901).

dry   free from surplus skin or flesh, esp. about the mouth, lips and neck; absence of DEWLAP.
> Head – Broad at the ears, wedge shaped, strong and dry (without loose skin). [6, NORWEGIAN ELKHOUND]
> A dry head and tight skin are faults [6, BASSET HOUND]

dry condition   lacking flesh and substance.

dry eye   KERATOCONJUNCTIVITIS SICCA.

dry scab   RINGWORM. [159]

dual champion   (esp. of gundogs) champion in both show and field.

dual dog   DUAL-PURPOSE DOG.
> The qualities that make a 'dual dog' are always to be appreciated, not deprecated. [6, VIZSLA]

dual-purpose dog   a dog capable of performing two functions, esp. a GUNDOG that will find and retrieve game.

duck feet   large and flat feet.

Ductus arteriosus   foetal blood vessel, connecting the aorta to the pulmonary artery, and which closes at birth.

Ductus diverticulum   inherited cardiac abnormality in which the arteriosus of the foetal heart remains partly open. (Mode of inheritance, ?)

Dudley   formerly used to describe a dog with a brown nose and light eyes.
> Dogs that have flesh-coloured noses, with which light-coloured eyes and generally yellowish-looking countenances are often associated, are called 'Dudley' because such animals originally came from that part of the Black Country known as Dudley. [221]

Dudley nose   light or flesh-coloured nose, when such is undesirable.
> Flesh-coloured (Dudley noses) or spotted (butterfly noses) are undesirable [6, ENGLISH SPRINGER SPANIEL]

Dufferin Harriers   NORTH DOWN.

duffleness   (of a coat) woolly quality.
> Coat . . . silky in texture, glossy and refined, with neither duffleness on the one hand, nor curl or wiriness on the other. [6, FIELD SPANIEL]

Duke of Beaufort's   hunted by the Dukes of Beaufort as a FOXHOUND pack since 1786, the extensive grassland and woodland COUNTRY lies in Gloucestershire, Somerset and Wiltshire. Former huntsmen include Philip Payne (1795–1817) and Will Long (1817–1858).

Duke of Buccleuch's   The hunt dates from 1827 when the 5th Duke of Buccleuch formed a pack in succession to that of George Baillie, which has hunted the country since 1787. The COUNTRY lies in and to the north of the Borders region.

Duke of Grafton's Hounds   GRAFTON.

Duke of Norfolk's Sussex Spaniel   NORFOLK SPANIEL [239]

Dulverton   hunt dating from 1875, the COUNTRY is largely grass and was split between the East and West Dulverton in 1940.

dumb rabies   form of RABIES in which the victim appears placid and quiescent.

Dumfriesshire   1. the COUNTRY has been hunted since 1816 for some years by a distinctive pack of black and tan HOUNDS.   2. former OTTERHOUND pack formed in 1889 to hunt all the Scottish rivers south of Ayrshire. HOUNDS were pure-bred Otterhounds. The pack was formed by David Bell Irving and hunted by members of the family until the 1980s.

Dummer   BEAGLE pack formed in 1939 to hunt a COUNTRY in Gloucestershire.

dummy   artificial RETRIEVE ARTICLE used in training dogs to retrieve.

Dungannon   private FOOT PACK of FOXHOUNDS since 1939.

Dungarvan   Irish HARRIER pack formed in 1941.

Dunhallow   FOXHOUND pack founded prior to 1745 to hunt a bank COUNTRY in County Cork.

Dunhound   running HOUND of a light beige-brown colour mentioned in *Sportsman's Dictionary*. (1735)

Dunker   [FCI] eponymous Norwegian SCENT-HOUND, which carries the name of Herr Wilhelm

Dunker who created the breed from local HOUNDS CROSSED with the RUSSIAN HARLEQUIN HOUND, from which the breed derives its unusual coloration. It is effectively indistinguishable, apart from in colour, from the HYGENHUND.

A powerful dog, with great stamina and a characteristic serious, almost surly, expression. The head is clean and fairly long, with pendulous ears of medium length. The neck is rather long, the chest capacious and the TOPLINE level. The limbs are well boned and strongly muscled. The coat is short, black and tan with a MARBLED SADDLE. Height 46–56cm (18–22in); weight 16–22kg (35–48½lb).

Dunkerstovare DUNKER.

Dunston HARRIER pack based on the Shotesham Harriers which had hunted the Norfolk COUNTRY since 1826.

Dupuy Pointer BRAQUE DUPUY.

Durham County Hunt hunt dating from the 17th century; former masters include Ralph Lambton, 1804–1838. The name was changed to South Durham in 1872.

Durham Light Infantry Beagles TEES VALLEY.

Dürrbächler BERNESE MOUNTAIN DOG. [312]

Dusicyon antarcticus Falklands Islands AGUARA. [380]

Dusicyon australis Falkland Island Fox (extinct).

Dusicyon canescens HOARY AGUARA. [380]

Dusicyon culpaeus Colpeo Fox, found in Ecuador and Tierra del Fuego.

Dusicyon griseus Argentine Grey Fox, Chiloe, found in Argentina and Chile.

Dusicyon fulvipes 'the dunfooted AGUARA, which is a short-legged foxy-looking animal.' [380]

Dusicyon gymnocerus South American Pampas Fox found in Argentina and Paraguay.

Dusicyon inca Peruvian Fox.

Dusicyon microtis Small-Eared Zorro, found in the forests of the Amazon and Orinoco basins.

Dusicyon sechurae Sechura Fox, also called Peruvian Fox, found in the deserts of north-west Peru and south-west Ecuador.

Dusicyon sylvestris type of AGUARA dog classified by Colonel Smith; 'the dog of the woods'. [380]

Dusicyon thous Common Zorro or Crab-Eating Fox, found in the open forests of Colombia and northern Argentina.

> This fox-like animal was first described by Prince Wied as a dog, but it is hardly likely that it was even a wild dog. . . . It was first of all found in the area between Brazil and Tierra del Fuego and also west of the Andes in Chile. [185]

Dusicyon vetulus Hoary Fox, found in central and southern Brazil.

dusting powder fine grooming powders for external use, which act as a cleaning agent.

Dutch Barge Dog SCHIPPERKE.

Dutch cap shortened hair on the skull of a POODLE trimmed in a ROYAL DUTCH CLIP.

Dutch clip ROYAL DUTCH CLIP.

Dutch Partridge Dog DRENTSE PARTRIJHOND.

Dutch Pug PUG.

Dutch Setter DRENTSE PARTIJOND.

Dutch Sheepdog SCHAPENDOES.

Dutch Shepherd Dutch herding breed similar in many respects to the BELGIAN SHEEP DOG, strongly built, deep chested and with well-muscled hindquarters. The three coat types are long, rough and short-haired in various shades of BRINDLE. Height 58–64cm (23–25in); weight 30kg (66lb).

Dutch Shepherd Dog HOLLANDSE HERDERSHOND.

Dutch Smoushond HOLLANDSE SMOUSHOND.

Dutch Spaniel WETTERHOUN.

Dutch Steenbrak descended from the old HOUND-like farm dogs CROSSED with German hounds (DEUTSCHE BRACKE), to which the breed is similar in appearance. [312]

Dutch Terrier HOLLANDSE SMOUSHOND. [225]

Dutch Water Spaniel WETTERHOND. [312]

duty DOG TAX.

> The five-shilling duty has not materially diminished the number of these vagrant curs, nor has it influenced the breeding of the dog in any way. [186]

dwarf anaemia inherited condition characterized by abnormally short limbs and large red blood cell (Mode of inheritance recessive.)

dwarf ocular inherited condition characterized by abnormally short limbs and eye lesions. (Mode of inheritance, recessive.)

Dwarf Beagle POCKET BEAGLE.

> 'the dwarf or rabbit beagle is a very small and delicate little hound, but with an excellent nose, and much faster than he looks. [338]

Dwarf Foxhounds FOXHOUNDS that are somewhat smaller than usual.

> These hounds were dwarf foxhounds, and only stood twenty or twenty-one inches, but they had been drawn from all the best kennels in England by Mr George Templar. [318]

dwarfism stunted growth with pituitary and primordial cause.

dwell linger on a scent; fail to make satisfactory progress.

Dyrehund NORWEGIAN ELKHOUND. [312]

Dyshormonogenetic goitre GOITRE.

dyskinesia condition in which voluntary movements are difficult or painful.

dysplasia abnormal growth of a particular part. *See also* HIP DYSPLASIA.

dystocia inherited tendency to difficulty in giving birth, often owed to the combined effect of several physical features – abnormally large heads, narrow or upright pelvic girdles, etc. – of certain breeds.

E

E gene symbol for extension series, no black MASK. [395]

e^m gene symbol for extension series, black MASK. [395]

e gene symbol for extension series, black coat fading to yellow. [395]

e^br gene symbol for extension series, BRINDLE. [395]

Eagle Farms (US) AMERICAN FOXHOUND pack, formed in 1915 to hunt a wooded and open COUNTRY in Pennsylvania.

ear hearing organ, usually in reference to external parts of.

ear canker CANKER.

ear carriage manner in which the ears are held, often indicative of the dog's mood.

ear cropping CROPPING.

ear cropping clamps CROPPING CLAMPS.

ear feather long hair on the ear flap, e.g. COCKER SPANIEL.

ear fringe long hair on the outer edge of the ear flap, e.g. BEDLINGTON TERRIER.

ear haematoma AURICULAR HAEMATOMA.

ear leather LEATHER.

ear mange PSOROPTIC, OTODECTIC, and RAILLIETA mange.

ear margin dermatosis seborrhoea forming encrustations along the edges of the ear flaps.

ear mark tattoo on the ear flap.

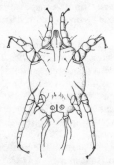

Ear mite.

ear mite parasitic mite which inhabits the ear canals: PSOROPTES CUNICULI. [*illus.*]

ear ossicles OSSICLES.

ear ring longer, unclipped hair on the ears, esp. on the KOOIKERHONDJE.

ears like a cobbler's apron (esp. of BORDER TERRIERS) heavy, rounded and immobile ears. (der. cobblers traditionally wore heavy leather aprons.)

ears like limp lettuce thin ears which should be erect but which wilt. (coined by Raymond Oppenheimer.)

ears sensitive in use ears which are alert and responsive to sounds.

ears set on high ears placed towards the top of the head.

ears set on low ears placed on the side of the head.

ears set on wide ears placed at the maximum distance apart.

ear, types of BAT, BEAR, BLUNT, BROKEN, BUTTON, CANDLE-FLAME, CROP, DEAD, DROP, FILBERT, FLARED, FLOP, FLYING, FOLDED, HOODED, HOUND, LOBULAR, PENDULOUS, PRICK, PROPELLER, ROSE, TROWEL-SHAPED, TULIP, VINE LEAF, V-SHAPED.

ear wax cerumen; yellowish substance forming naturally in the outer ear.

Earl of Berkeley's BERKELEY.

earth fox's underground refuge.

earth-dog dog used to work below ground, invariably a TERRIER.

earth-eating PICA.

earth-stopper hunt servant employed to close the entrances to EARTHs in which foxes might take refuge during the ensuing day's hunting.

earth-stopping *see* EARTH-STOPPER.
> A freshly drawn hole, perhaps an enlarged rabbit burrow, when noted should never be stopped or interfered with, as it is a certain sign a vixen has selected the spot for her future nursery. [235]

East African Dog strongly built, short-coated, pale fawn, strong-headed, PRICK-EARED primitive dog. [312]

east and west action EAST-WEST ACTION.

east and west mover (Am.) dog who has EAST-WEST ACTION.

East Antrim 1. Irish HARRIER pack formed in 1895 to hunt a COUNTRY in County Antrim. 2. former Irish STAGHOUND pack.

East Cornwall FOXHOUND pack founded in 1897 by the amalgamation of the East and North Cornwall.

East Devon pack founded in 1890 to hunt fox over a Devonshire wood and moorland COUNTRY.

East Down County Down hunt formed when the Lecale Harriers – themselves dating from 1768 – were given up in 1887.

East Dulverton DULVERTON.

East Essex dating from 1810 and hunting a plough and woodland COUNTRY in Essex.

East European Shepherd a Byelorussian herding breed very similar to a heavily built GERMAN SHEPHERD DOG, from which the breed is directly descended. Height 61–74cm (24–28in); weight 35–48kg (77–105½lb).

eastern expression oriental expression caused by obliquely placed and almond-shaped eyes. [*illus.* ALMOND EYES]
> Eastern or Oriental expression is typical of the breed. [203, AFGHAN HOUND]

Eastern Greyhound CHORTAJ.

East Java Dog   thick-coated PARIAH dog found in the Indonesian Islands.

> These dogs are nowadays to be found only in the mountains of Java. The hair is very thick, light brown, with a reddish tinge and black-brown stripes, of which one runs from the tip of the nose to the tip of the tail, and the others over the shoulder downwards. The limbs are light-brown, the under-part dirty-white with a brownish tinge. [185]

East Kent   dating from the 18th century, the hunt occupies a plough and woodland COUNTRY.

Easton   HARRIER pack formed in 1911 by the amalgamation of the Oakley Pack and the East Suffolk, both of which date from 1906 and which hunt a COUNTRY in Suffolk.

East Siberian Laika   LAIKA WASTATCHNO-SIBIRSKAIA.

East Surrey   former DRAGHOUND pack formed in 1916 to hunt LINES in Surrey.

East Sussex   Sir Augustus Webster formed the hunt in April 1853 to hunt a heavily wooded COUNTRY in East Sussex.

east-west action   toeing out: gait in which the forefeet are thrown out sideways. [*illus.* TOEING OUT]

east-west front   narrow shoulder placement or weak PASTERNS causing the forefeet to turn outwards.

easy keeper   GOOD DOER.

ecbolic   substance which causes uterine contractions.

Ecclesfield   former 15in BEAGLE pack formed in 1885 to hunt a COUNTRY in south Yorkshire.

echinococcus   infection caused by the larva of *ECHINOCOCCUS*.

Echinococcus tapeworm.

Echinococcus   genus of TAPE-WORMS. [*illus.*]

Echinococcus granulosus   species of tapeworm whose larva gives rise to hydatid cysts in the liver, kidneys and other organs of most mammals.

Echinococcus multilocularis species of tapeworm which gives rise to hydatid cysts principally in rodents and humans; the adult form is found in foxes and dogs.

Echinococcus vogeli   species of tapeworm which infects wild and domestic dogs with larval forms in rodents and humans.

Echinostoma iliocanum   intestinal FLUKE found in dogs, rodents and humans.

eclampsia   milk fever, a condition occurring esp. in nursing bitches and caused by inadequate intake or take-up of calcium.

E coli   intestinal bacterium.

ectoparasite   external parasite.

ectopic pregnancy   pregnancy which takes place outside the uterus.

ectromelia   inherited condition in which there is incomplete development of the long bones of the limbs. (Mode of inheritance, recessive.)

ectropic ureter   inherited tendency to incontinence. (Mode of inheritance, unclear.)

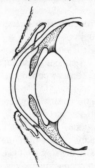

Ectropion.

ectropion   inherited eversion of the eyelids. (Mode of inheritance, familial.) [*illus.*]

eczema   nonspecific skin condition.

edema   (Am.) spelling of OEDEMA.

Edible Dog   (obs. colloq.) CHOW CHOW.

EEG   electroencephalogram.

eel stripe   line of darker hair along the spine.

> Dark eel stripe frequently occurs along back. [203, WEIMARANER]

effective population   that part of the population which will be bred from.

egg   fertilized ovum.

egg-shaped chest   ribs forming an oval shape.

egg-shaped head   smooth and rounded, as in BULL TERRIERS.

Eggesford   the hilly Devonshire COUNTRY was first hunted by Newton Fellowes in 1798. The hunt was known as Lord Poltimore's until 1875, when the COUNTRY was split to provide for the Dulverton and the present name was assumed.

Eglinton   1. dating from 1861, the pack hunts a moorland COUNTRY in Ayrshire. 2. (Can.) FOX-HOUND pack formed in 1929 to hunt a rolling grassland COUNTRY in Toronto. The hunt is an offshoot of the Toronto Hunt formed in 1843.

Egyptian Hairless Dog   probably extinct hairless breed from northern Africa.

> Normal in every way except for its teeth. It had no canine teeth nor any incisors in either jaw. [185]

Egyptian Sheepdog   ARMANT.

Ehlers-Danlos syndrome   inherited condition characterized by fragile bones and skin. (Mode of inheritance, dominant and recessive.)

Ehrlichia canis   species of tick which gives rise to tropical pancytopenia, hemorrhagic fever, tracker-dog disease, canine ehrlichiosis and tick fever.

ehrlichiosis   CANINE EHRLICHIOSIS.

Eimeria canis   protozoan parasite of dogs and cats.

ejaculate seminal fluid; the act of EJACULATION.

ejaculation expulsion of semen.

Ekia Wild African Dog. [338]

ekzema (obs. spelling) ECZEMA. [320a]

El Hor SALUKI.

elbow joint between forearm and upper arm.

elbow dysplasia inherited developmental defects of the elbow joint, especially in growing puppies, leading to forelimb lameness and arthritis. (Mode of inheritance, recessive.)

elbow subluxation inherited tendency to dislocation of the elbow joint leading to forelimb lameness. (Mode of inheritance, recessive.)

electro (pref.) pertaining to electricity.

electrocardiogram equipment used to measure the performance of the heart.

electroencephalogram equipment used to measure brain function.

electrolytes substances which split into ions when dissolved in water; electrolyte solutions are used to combat dehydration.

electrophoresis method of using electrical field to trace the movement of proteins.

electroretinography method of using light stimulation to record electrical changes in the retina.

Elghund group of Scandinavian SPITZ-type HOUNDS used to hunt elk (moose).

Elizabethan collar large ruff-like collar that forms a hood over the face and is used to prevent a dog from licking or scratching at injuries.

Elkhound [KC] typically SPITZ breed used to locate elk in the forests of Scandinavia, but although the general type is an old one the Elkhound, in both grey and black forms, was itself only standardized at the beginning of the 20th century.

The breed is compact and powerful, with a square outline and proud attitude. The head is wedge-shaped, with slightly oval eyes, small, pricked ears and very mobile and strong jaws. The neck is of medium length with a thick RUFF. The shoulders are sloping and the forelimbs are straight; the back is short and strong, the LOIN wide and the chest deep and broad with well-curved ribs. The STIFLE and HOCK are only moderately angulated. The tail is thickly PLUMED and carried tightly over the back. The coat is close and weather-resistant, with a dense undercoat and coarse, shaded grey topcoat. Height 49–52cm (19–20½in); weight 20–23kg (44–50½lb).

Elkridge ELKRIDGE-HARFORD.

Elkridge-Harford (US) crossbred FOXHOUND pack formed in 1934 as a result of the merger between the Elkridge and Harford hunts, to hunt a COUNTRY in Maryland.

Elterwater Terrier formerly a localized strain of Lakeland working TERRIERS.

emaciated (of condition) thin and wasted.

embolism blockage, usually a clot of blood, in a blood vessel.

embossed 1. (esp. of HOUNDS) branded. [319q] 2. (of HOUND) marked by the froth produced by an exhausted hunted deer. [159]

embryo unborn young prior to the development of major organs.

emesis expulsion of stomach contents through the mouth.

emetic agent which causes EMESIS.

emphysema abnormal presence of air in some part of the body, usually causing respiratory difficulty.

encephalitis inflammation of the brain.

encephalization quotient a measure of the degree to which the physical capacity of the brain exceeds that which is necessary to control basic body functions.

enchondral associated with cartilage.

endemic ENZOOTIC.

endo (pref.) pertaining to the lining or inside of.

endocardiosis common cause of cardiac disease caused by chronic fibrosis and thickening of the ventrical valves.

endocrine glands glands that secrete hormones into the blood.

endochronal ENCHONDRAL.

endometritis inflammation of the womb lining.

endometrium womb lining.

endoparasites internal parasites: includes worms and flukes, etc.

endoscope implement for making internal examinations.

endotheliochorial placenta those maternal vessels which form the contact between dam and unborn offspring.

endothelium lining of the heart cavities.

enema insertion of liquid into the rectum to stimulate the passage of faeces or to introduce nutrient.

Enfield Chace woodland COUNTRY in Hertfordshire and Middlesex hunted since 1935.

English Beagle [AKC] BEAGLE.

English Bloodhound [AKC] BLOODHOUND.

English Bulldog (obs. Eng. & Am.) BULLDOG.
> Well, of all dogs it stands confess'd
> Your English bulldogs are the best!
> I say it, and will set my hand to 't;
> Camden records it, and I'll stand to 't. [325]

English Bullmastiff [AKC] BULLMASTIFF.

English Cocker Spaniel [AKC] COCKER SPANIEL.

English Coonhound red- or blue-TICKED version of the BLUETICK COONHOUND.

English Foxhound [AKC] FOXHOUND.

English Pointer [AKC] POINTER.

English saddle clip one of the traditional CLIPs used on POODLES, and a variation on the LION CLIP.
> In the 'English Saddle' clip, the face, throat, feet, forelegs, and base of the tail are shaved, leaving puffs on the forelegs and a pompom on the end of the tail. The hindquarters are covered with a short blanket of hair except for a curved shaved area on each flank and two shaved bands on each hind leg. The entire shaven foot and a portion of the shaven leg above the puff are visible. The rest of the body is left in full coat but may be shaped in order to ensure overall balance. [6, POODLE]

English Setter [AKC, FCI, KC] breed of old but uncertain origin. The form of the modern breed is often credited to Edward Laverack, whose closely inbred STRAIN certainly had a considerable influence on the breed during the mid-19th century.

An elegant, active and friendly dog with keen working instincts. The head, which is carried proudly, is long and lean, with well-defined OCCIPUT and STOP, a deep, square MUZZLE and bright oval eyes. The folded, pendulous ears are set low and are of moderate length covered with silky hair. The lean and muscular neck is long, the shoulders WELL-LAID BACK, the limbs well muscled over round bone. The chest is deep and the ribs WELL SPRUNG; the back is short and the LOINS wide and slightly arched. STIFLES are well bent, thighs are long and well muscled. Movement is free, graceful and redolent of speed and stamina. The tail extends the line of the back. The silky coat – blue, orange, lemon or liver BELTON is preferred, without heavy patches of colour – forms FEATHERING under the BRISKET, behind the legs and under the tail. Height 61–68cm (24–26¾in).

> The English Setter . . . is a hardy, active, handsome Dog. Its scent is exquisite; and it ranges with great speed and wonderful perseverance. Its sagacity in discovering the various kinds of game, and its caution in approaching them, are truly astonishing. [51]

English Shepherd unrecognized breed developed in America from CROSSES between various British, usually Scottish, herding breeds and employed as a multi-purpose stock-herder.

The breed has a broad skull with high-set ears and a short MUZZLE. The body is fairly long and strongly made, the limbs are well boned and muscular. The coat is thick with abundant FEATHERING. The colour may be black and tan, TRICOLOUR, SABLE and white, or PIED. Height 46–58.5cm (18–23in); weight 18–27kg (39½–59½lb).

English Springer Spaniel [AKC, FCI, KC] along with the COCKER, this breed was first recognized by the KENNEL CLUB as a separate breed in 1892, but it has a much longer history than its relatively recent nomenclature might suggest. It has been used since the 17th century and before for springing game for hawks or to nets, or, later, for the gun.

Although racier in outline than other British land SPANIELs the Springer remains a COMPACT and strong breed. It is friendly and biddable. The fairly broad skull is of medium length, with a distinctive FLUTING between the eyes. The dark, ALMOND EYES are of medium size, the ears lobular and of good length. The neck is strong and muscular and the forelimbs straight and well boned. The chest is deep with WELL SPRUNG ribs, the LOIN muscular and slightly arched. The muscular hindquarters are WELL LET DOWN. The tail is low set, traditionally DOCKED. The close, straight, weather-resistant coat may be liver or black with white or tan. Height 51cm (20in).

English style clip CONTINENTAL CLIP with a rosette of longer hair left on the loins and, optionally, round the base of the tail.

English Toy Spaniel (Am.) KING CHARLES SPANIEL.

English Toy Terrier [Black and Tan] [KC] TOY version of the MANCHESTER TERRIER. Weight 3.5–5.5kg (7–12lb).

English Water Spaniel curly-coated SPANIEL briefly extant during the 19th century.

> It will not be denied that the English Water Spaniel is at least historically older than the Irish. [123]
>
> The name given at the end of the eighteenth century to a Collie-like dog which had possibly been bred from a Spaniel or Setter crossed with a Poodle. [184]
>
> The old-fashioned water dog our great grand-fathers used was the English water spaniel. Mostly liver and white in colour, with a curly coat, it was just such an animal as would be produced through a cross between the modern brown curly-coated retriever and an ordinary liver and white spaniel. [221]

English White Terrier extinct breed of TERRIER, basically a pure white version of the MANCHESTER TERRIER.

enostosis bony growth within the cavity or internal surfaces of long bones and bone cortex. (Mode of inheritance, familial.)

Entamoeba hartmanni harmless amoebic parasite found in the colons of dogs and the large intestine of humans.

Entamoeba histolytica amoebic parasite which causes amoebic dysentery and liver abscesses in dogs, humans, cats, rats, pigs and monkeys.

enter 1. introduce a HOUND or TERRIER to work.
> Dogs to be employed for particular purposes, are said to be 'entered' for them; the entering being, in fact, their earliest training; thus one is 'entered' for deer, another for foxes, and another for pheasants and partridges. [393]

2. put forward for competition. *See also* ENTRY.

enteritis inflammation of the mucous lining of the intestines producing abdominal pain, diarrhoea, dehydration and, in acute cases, dysentery.

enteropathic acrodermatitis inherited tendency to inflammation of the skin produced by defective zinc uptake. (Mode of inheritance, recessive.)

enterotomy surgery requiring an incision into the intestines.

entire of dog with two testicles fully descended into the scrotum.

Entlebucher dim. ENTLEBUCHER SENNENHUND.

Entlebucher Mountain Dog ENTLEBUCHER SENNENHUND.

Entlebucher Sennenhund [FCI] MOLOSSAN used as a PASTORAL GUARD, HERDER and DROVER.

A square, sturdy dog with a strong broad head and smooth, TRICOLOUR coat. Height 51cm (20in); weight 25–30kg (55–66lb).

entre chien et loup literally, between dog and wolf: dusk, the period of half-light between day and night.
> The best time to talk of difficult things is entre chien et loup, as the Guernsey folk say. [126]

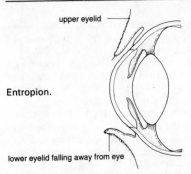

upper eyelid

Entropion.

lower eyelid falling away from eye

entropion inherited inversion of the eyelids resulting in extreme irritation and abrasion of the eyeball. (Mode of inheritance, uncertain.) [*illus.*]

entry 1. details submitted to enable a dog to compete. 2. new introduction esp. to a pack of HOUNDS or TERRIERS. 3. marks in a thicket left by a passing deer. [151c]

enzootic (of disease in animals) constantly present in an area or district, or during a particular season; equivalent of endemic in humans.

eosinophilic cyositis (Am.) EOSINOPHILIC GRANULOMA.

eosinophilic granuloma growth of non-pruritic nodules on the skin and mucous membranes of the mouth, causing difficulty in eating and, in extreme cases, in closing the mouth.

Épagneul ÉPAGNEUL FRANÇAIS.

Épagneul Bleu de Picardie [FCI] a blue, or black, version of the ÉPAGNEUL DE PICARDIE.

Épagneul Breton [FCI] BRITTANY.

Épagneul de Picardie French water SPANIEL built for speed and stamina.

The skull is large and rounded with a prominent OCCIPUT, the ears low set and luxuriously FURNISHED, the deep amber eyes have a frank expression. Forequarters are long and straight, hindquarters are muscular. The body is deep and fairly broad, the tail forms a TEAPOT curve and is profusely FEATHERED. The MOTTLED grey and tan coat is heavy and tends towards silkiness. Height 56–64cm (22–25in).

Épagneul de Pont-Audemer [FCI] compact and vigorous French water SPANIEL which combines the talents of POINTER and RETRIEVER. The breed's ancestry probably includes both the old FRENCH SPANIEL and the IRISH WATER SPANIEL.

The skull is rounded with a prominent OCCIPUT; the deep-set, amber eyes are rather small, the ears are flat, long and of medium thickness and covered in very curly hair which joins the characteristic curly TOPKNOT. The neck is muscular and lean, the forequarters long and sloping; the chest is broad and deep, the BRISKET is WELL LET DOWN and the LOINS short and muscular. The tail is traditionally DOCKED. The curly or waved coat is brown or grey with brown FLECKING. Height 52–58cm (20½–23in).

Épagneul Ecossais extinct French small SETTER

[150]; may be the same breed as the ÉPAGNEUL FRANÇAIS to which it is identical. [225]

Épagneul Français [FCI] SPANIEL bred of disputed origins but with obvious similarities with the SMALL MÜNSTERLÄNDER and the DRENTSE PARTRIJSHOND.

A quiet dog with a broad, slightly DOMED skull, short, strong neck, deep, broad chest and strong limbs. The low-set tail is long and well FEATHERED, the coat long, slightly waved and invariably brown over a white GROUND. Height 53–61cm (20¾–24in).

Épagneul Nain PAPILLON.

Épagneul Picard liver and white or tan and white or TRICOLOUR French GUNDOG. Height 56–61cm (22–24in); weight 20kg (44lb).

Actually a Setter in all essential respects. [225]

Épagneul Pont-Audemer [FCI] liver or liver and white, wavy-coated French GUNDOG. Height 51–58cm (20–23in); weight 18–24kg (39½–53lb).

epidemiology study of the incidence and cause of disease.

epidermis outermost layer of the skin.

epidermolysis bullosa inherited tendency to blistered skin, especially at points of pressure or trauma. (Mode of inheritance, familial.)

epididymis duct within the testes in which the sperm is stored.

epiglottis cartilaginous membrane at the entrance to the larynx.

epilepsy inherited disease in which there are spasmodic fits. (Mode of inheritance, complex.)

epiphora constant tear secretion which typically stains the coat under the inner corner of each eye.

epiphyseal aseptic necrosis LEGG-CALVÉ-PERTHES DISEASE.

epiphyseal dysplasia inherited condition in which there are abnormally shortened limbs and early generalized arthropathy. (Mode of inheritance, unclear.)

epiphysis widened end of a long bone.

Epirus Mastiff Grecian Mastiff, which, according to Drury, was heavier than the Assyrian version, but not as big or ferocious as the British breed.

episiotomy incision of the vulva to ease parturition.

epistasis propensity of an allele to mask the effects of others on different loci.

epistropheus AXIS.

epulis irregular-shaped growth on the gum, esp. in older dogs.

EQ ENCEPHALIZATION QUOTIENT.

equipage (Fr.) the entire hunt, including all its accessories.

Erdélyi Kopó [FCI] breed divided into short- and long-legged varieties used for hunting a variety of game in Hungary.

The head is reminiscent of that of a BEAGLE: the eyes oval and obliquely set, the pendulous ears oval in shape and falling without wrinkle. The neck is muscular and of medium length, with a slight DEWLAP. The chest is BARRELLED and long, the WITHERS well developed, and the TOPLINE straight to a moderately slanting CROUP; TUCK-UP is slight. The thick tapering STERN is set and carried low. The skin and coat are dark. In the long-legged variety, the coat is thick, dense and rough, invariably black but often with white spots on the forehead, chest, paws and tail. In the short-legged variety the coat is shaded brownish-red, again with white spots and with a smoky MASK. Height (long-legged) 55–66cm (21¼–26in); (short-legged) 45–50cm (17¾–19½in).

erect ear entire ear flap held vertically.

erect pastern vertical from ground to HOCK-joint.

Eridge prior to 1870 the vale and woodland COUNTRY was hunted by the West Kent Woodland; the present name was assumed in 1879.

Ermenti ARMANT.

erythema redness of the skin, usually following abrasion or injury.

erythrocyte antigens antigens used in the identification and matching of blood samples.

erythrocyte sedimentation rate measure of the extent to which red blood cells settle in a column of fresh citrated blood.

Erz Mountain Dachsbracke ALPENLANDISCHE DACHSBRACKE.

Eskdale former Scottish 16in BEAGLE pack formed in 1902 to hunt a COUNTRY in Cumbria.

Eskdale and Ennerdale Cumbrian and Lancashire hunt with a largely fell COUNTRY, dating in its present form from 1857.

Eskimo Dog [KC] originally a generic name applied to most or all types of SLED-DOG; the specific breed is now recognized by the KENNEL CLUB.

The breed is typically SPITZ in appearance, with a broad, wedge-shaped head, pricked ears and ALMOND EYES. The forequarters are strongly boned and muscled, the chest deep and the body COMPACT and powerful. The outer coat is long and coarse, the undercoat thick and weather-resistant. The coat may be of any colour. Height 51–69cm (20–27in); weight 27–48kg (59½–105½lb).

esophageal achalasia MEGAOESOPHAGUS.

Esquimaux Dog (obs.) ESKIMO DOG; formerly any dog with SPITZ characteristics and found in Arctic regions.

> Found over a wide geographical range, but although specimens from different parts differ from one another, they all present certain general and prominent features. [123]
> At home one would fear to encounter such hoop-spined, spitting, snarling beasts as the Esquimeaux dogs of Peabody Bay. But wolves as they are, they are far from dangerous: the slightest appearance of a missile or cudgel subdues them at once. [202]

Essex 1. pack dating from 1785; the arable COUNTRY lies entirely in Essex. 2. (US) AMERICAN FOXHOUND pack formed in 1912 to hunt a varied COUNTRY in New Jersey.

Essex and Suffolk hunting a plough and woodland COUNTRY, the pack dates from 1803 when it was known as Mr Newman's, the pack's founder.

Essex Farmers founded in 1913 to hunt an Essex COUNTRY which lies between the Crouch and the Blackwater.

Essex Union bank and ditch COUNTRY hunted by a pack which dates from 1822 when it was founded by Lord Petre.

Estonian Hound GONTCHAJA ESTONSKAJA.

Estrela Mountain Dog [KC] a PASTORAL GUARD developed in the Estrela Mountains of Portugal and Spain. A sturdy MASTIFF-type dog, affectionate with its owners, indifferent to others, and with a pronounced stubborn streak.

The head is long and powerful with a slightly rounded, broad skull, moderate STOP and tapering MUZZLE. The roof of the mouth is heavily pigmented with black. The oval eyes are of medium size with prominent brows. The ears are small, thin and triangular, and carried backwards against the skull. The neck is short with a characteristic protective tuft of hair under the throat. The forelimbs are straight, strongly boned and muscled. The TOPLINE slopes from WITHERS to CROUP; the chest is deep and WELL SPRUNG; the strong LOINS are short. Moderately ANGULATED hindquarters are well muscled. The FEATHERED tail reaches the HOCK where it rises to form a hook. Coat may be either long or short, thick, moderately harsh with a dense undercoat; colours may be fawn, BRINDLE or WOLF-grey. Height 62–72cm (24½–28½in).

estrum (Am.) OESTRUS.

etiology AETIOLOGY.

Eton College former 15–15½in BEAGLE pack formed in 1864 by the College to hunt a COUNTRY in Berkshire.

ETT ENGLISH TOY TERRIER.

Ettrick Forest private BEAGLE pack formed in 1955 to hunt a COUNTRY in Selkirkshire and Roxburghshire.

Eurasian EURASIER.

Eurasier [FCI] result of efforts made by Julius Wipfel to recreate the old type of GERMAN WOLFSPITZ using CROSSES between modern WOLFSPITZ, CHOW CHOWS and various spitz SLED-DOGS.

A powerful watchdog, friendly with its owners but distrustful of strangers. Typically SPITZ in appearance, with a distinctly lupine head, muscular neck, short chest, strong LOIN, level TOPLINE and muscular limbs, the hindlimbs being only slightly ANGULATED. The thick, STAND-OFF coat may be red, fawn, mahogany, WOLF grey, black or white. Height 48–61cm (18¾–24in); weight 19–32kg (42–70½lb).

European brown tick RHIPICEPHALUS SANGUINEAS.

European dog tick RHIPICEPHALUS SANGUINEAS. Also IXODES HEXAGONUS.

European-Russian Laika one of the larger LAIKAS, used principally for ground game. Typical SPITZ appearance; coat black with red, grey or fawn shading. Height 56cm (22in); weight 20kg (44lb).

euthanasia humane killing.

even bite teeth meeting without overlap. [*illus.* LEVEL MOUTH.]

even mouth teeth set regularly and in line.

everted membrane nictinans inherited curled THIRD EYELID causing runny and watering eyes. (Mode of inheritance, probably recessive.)

ewe neck long, thin, weak, concave neck, similar to that of a sheep. The curve of the neck is a mirror image of the normal, hence the synonymous expression 'Neck on upside down'. [*illus.*]

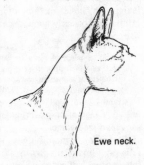

Ewe neck.

> To be penalised . . . concave neck, sometimes called a ewe neck or upside-down neck (the opposite of arched). [6, ENGLISH SPRINGER SPANIEL]

ex out of: having as DAM.

exchanging when GREYHOUNDS each move the hare from its course.

Exemption Show small show exempted from KENNEL CLUB(2) rules, usually but not invariably run in order to raise money for some worthwhile cause.

exercise area defined area or enclosure, set aside at shows within which dogs may excrete.

exertional rhabdomyolysis muscular collapse resulting from strenuous exercise, most often encountered in working SIGHTHOUNDS.

Exeter College former BEAGLE pack formed in 1903.

exhibitor one who enters and exhibits dogs at shows.

Exmoor founded in 1869 by Nicholas Snow, whose Mastership earned the pack the title of the Stars of the West, the COUNTRY is mostly moorland with a few big woods.

exocytosis benign new bone growth.

exotic dogs formerly a show classification which included principally foreign breeds.

> Sixth Division Class XXXII.
> Dogs Useful to Man in Various Foreign Countries: Esquimaux, Siberian, Tartar, Kamschatcan, Greenland, Canadina, Kangaroo Dogs, Kabyle Dogs, Dogs of the Bazaars of the East.
> Dogs Used for Human Food: Chinese (*Canis edibilis*), the Poul of New Irland, the edible dog of North America, the edible dog of the Polynesia.
> Dogs Untamed by Man: The East Indian Dhole, the Australian Dingo, the Himalayan Wahh, and the Indian Quao.
> Dogs Which Become Wild: The American Chestnut coloured dog, the dog of New Caledonia, of Sumatra, of the Cape of Good Hope, and of St. Domingo. [37]

expeditation surgical removal of the toes formerly performed as a means to prevent dogs from harassing game.

exposure keratitis drying and inflammation of the cornea owing to incomplete closure of the eyelids, and resulting from abnormality or injury. May also be caused by exposure to high winds.

expression 1. arrangement of the facial features contributing to characteristic appearance. 2. degree to which the phenotype of a gene varies.

extended trot trotting gait in which the limbs reach unusually far forward.

> Ideal fore-movement akin to the 'extended trot'; hackney action not desirable. [259, ENGLISH TOY TERRIER (BLACK AND TAN)]

extension allele individual gene which forms part of an extension series.

extension series a series of genes from different loci which have combined effect.

extensor brows long, bushy growths of hair above the eyes.

extensor dominance of the response of a four- to five-day-old puppy when subjected to stimulation, in which there is stretching and hollowing of the back and straightening of the limbs and tail. (This in contrast to the response of the newborn puppy which will curl up when stimulated – FLEXOR DOMINANCE).

extensor lid one of three, in the case of dogs, movable flaps of skin (eyelids) which protect the eye.

extensor rim edge of the eyelids surrounding the oral orifice.

extensors muscles which straighten the limbs.

extensor shape aperture formed by the eyelids.

extensor teeth upper canines.

extinction used in relation to LEARNING THEORY, to refer to a learned response that in the absence of REINFORCEMENT no longer performed.

eye 1. organ of sight. 2. intense gaze of a herding dog on the animals under its charge; concentration of a herding dog.

> Is the power of a dog to control sheep with its eyes? Dogs in which the power has not been sufficiently developed are spoken of as being 'loose eyed', which is another way of saying that they lack the power of concentration for efficient work. [252]

3. precautionary look from a dog that might be contemplating violence.

eye dog (esp. BORDER COLLIE) herding dog that appears to control stock by fixing it with its gaze.

eye rim that part of the eyelid which lies closest to the eye itself.

> Eye rims preferably completely black in black-spotted, and liver brown in liver-spotted. [203, DALMATIAN]

eye, types of ALMOND, BEADY, BOLTING, BULGING, CIRCULAR, DEEP SET, FISH, FULL, GLASS, GLOBULAR, GOOSEBERRY, HAW, JEWELLED, LIGHT, MARBLED, OBLIQUE, OVAL, PIG, RINGED, ROUND, TRIANGULAR, WALL.

eyeing *see* EYE(2) and (3).

eyelid EXTENSOR LID.

eyelid eversion ECTROPION.

eyelid inversion ENTROPION.

F

F1 F1 HYBRID.

F1 hybrid first generation of a CROSS between two breeds, LINES or STRAINS.

F2 F2 HYBRID.

F2 hybrid second generation of a CROSS between two breeds, LINES or STRAINS.

face forepart of the head.

face judging making decisions in the ring that are based not on the quality of exhibits but on the reputation of the exhibitors.

faced down of a dog that has been subdued in the face of an aggressive display.

factor (obs.) gene.

Factor VII one of thirteen elements associated with blood-clotting, the absence of which produces a relatively mild form of haemophilia.

Factor VII deficiency inherited anaemia. (Mode of inheritance, recessive.)

Factor VIII one of thirteen elements associated with blood-clotting, the absence of which produces Haemophilia A and Von Willebrand's disease.

Factor IX one of thirteen elements associated with blood-clotting, the absence of which produces Haemophilia B or Christmas Disease.

Factor X one of thirteen elements associated with blood-clotting, the absence of which produces Stuart-Prower Syndrome.

fading puppy syndrome often inexplicable death of very young puppies; a variety of agents are thought to be responsible.

faecal of, or pertaining to, faeces.

   faecal egg count method of determining the presence of intestinal parasite infection, by the presence or absence of the parasite's eggs in the faeces.

   faecal impaction accumulation of faeces in the rectum.

   faecal incontinence involuntary expulsion of faeces.

   faecalith impacted faecal mass requiring surgical removal.

   faecal marking dominance, or territorial behaviour, characterized by deliberate distribution of faeces.

faeces eating COPROPHAGY.

Fairfax (US) AMERICAN FOXHOUND pack formed in 1927 to hunt a rolling COUNTRY in Virginia.

Fairfax, Thomas author of *The Complete Sportsman* (1758).

Fairfield County (US) AMERICAN FOXHOUND pack formed in 1924 to hunt a hilly COUNTRY in Connecticut.

Fairforth Basset former rough and smooth BASSET pack formed in 1909 to hunt a COUNTRY in Kent.

fairy saddle growth of longer hair on the withers and part of the back.

faking any illicit method of preparing a dog for exhibition, formerly including excessive trimming of hair.

> This expression is one that is generally adopted by exhibitors when alluding to certain dishonourable practices which unprincipled persons resort to with the object of improving the appearance of their dogs or of concealing blemishes. [320]

Falkland Island Wolf *DUSICYON AUSTRALIS.*

fall 1. fringe of hair overhanging the face; veil. 2. shot feathered game.

   fall of hair 1. moulting. 2. FALL.

fallaway line of the CROUP.

falling apart of a dog which looks good when held in position but whose faults become apparent when it stands naturally or is moved.

Fallopian tube tube which runs from the ovary to the oviduct.

fallow 1. pale yellow or red.

2. species of deer.

false untrue, artificial.

   false dog mammal which looks like a dog but is of another species.

   false heat external signs of OESTRUS without ovulation.

   false point GUNDOG wrongly indicating the presence of a bird.

   false pregnancy symptoms of pregnancy in the absence of conception; pseudopregnancy.

   false rib ribs not connected to the sternum.

familial of, or relating to, the family; prevalent within a family.

   familial anaemia inherited nonspherocytic haemolytic anaemia. (Mode of inheritance, recessive.)

   familial necropathy inherited degeneration of the kidneys. (Mode of inheritance, recessive.)

   familial polyneuropathy PROGRESSIVE AXONOPATHY.

   familial selection selection based on the quality of a group of siblings rather than on the quality of an individual.

fancier one who belongs to the FANCY(2).

> He soon became the property of honest Tom Pritchard – as worthy a fancier as ever spunged a dog's mouth out, or fought one under the candles and a tin of lighted oil. [32]

fancy 1. take a particular interest in; collective noun for those who exhibit dogs at show.

> 'Orses and dorgs is some men's fancy. They're wittles and drink to me. [120]

2. those with a particular, usually illegitimate, interest in dogs.

> Dog stealing in London has now become the regular trade of men calling themselves 'the Fancy'. [166a]

fang CANINE TOOTH.

fanning redirect and so alter the course of a SHEEP DOG that is running out to gather sheep. [204]

Fan-tailed Greyhound BORZOI.

> They seldom hunt with anything but greyhounds, of which they possess a most beautiful species called the fan-tailed greyhound, which differs from the Italian in this respect, that it is covered with a long silken hair, instead of the short smooth coat which characterises the former, and is considerably larger. [39]

Farley Hill Beagles former 14in BEAGLE pack formed in 1919 to hunt a COUNTRY in Hampshire.

Farmington (US) AMERICAN FOXHOUND and DRAGHOUND pack formed in 1929 to hunt a pasture and woodland COUNTRY in Virginia.

Farndale dating from 1835, the COUNTRY in north Yorkshire is mostly moorland.

Farou BERGER DU LANGUEDOC.

Fartlek training training system used for SIGHTHOUNDS, and involving long distances covered at different speeds.

fatigue gait of very tired dogs, especially SLED-DOGS and those that have spent an exhausting day in the field: pace or amble in an effort to rest weary muscles.

fault 1. departure from that which the BREED STANDARD requires. 2. *at fault*: of HOUNDS that have lost the scent.

> When hounds are at fault, and cannot make it out of themselves, let the first cast be quick. [47]

favus type of RINGWORM.

fawn 1. pale tan. 2. deer in its first year. [151c]

Fawn Irish Setter Syndrome BLUE DOG SYNDROME.

FCI FEDERATION CYNOLOGIQUE INTERNATIONALE.

F coefficient measure of the degree of INBREEDING in an individual's PEDIGREE.

Feather.

feather 1. profuse growth of hair, especially on the rear of the legs and the underside of the tail but also on ears. [*illus.*]

> A good coat, the feather straight, and not too long, is indispensable to him as a protection from briars and brambles, and his legs should also be well-feathered. [186]

2. manipulate the vagina in order to stimulate uterine contractions.

feathered of limbs or tail that carries a profuse growth of hairs.

feathering 1. excited, rapid movement of a HOUND's or GUNDOG's STERN, esp. when on an uncertain scent.

> And as hounds know where the fox lies nearly as well as their master, Pillager and Pilgrim were quickly feathering on the line, but not yet venturing to speak. [344c]

2. FEATHERS.

> Abundant feathering on chest, under body and behind legs, but clean from hock to ground. [203, FIELD SPANIEL]

Featherstone Setter former variety of English Setter: ANGLESEY SETTER.

feathery of a coat that has FEATHERS.

fecund very fertile.

fecundity measure of fertility.

Federation Cynologique Internationale (FCI) organization, founded in 1911, which governs canine affairs in a number of countries throughout the world (notably excepting Britain and the USA).

feeder one whose duty it is to feed HOUNDS. [319]

Feist RAT TERRIER.

feisty (Am. colloq.) quarrelsome or spirited dog.

Fell Foxhound FELL HOUND.

> They arrived during the afternoon and were a mixed pack. Some were pure bred otter-hounds; some were fox-hounds crossed with otter-hounds. There were some ordinary fox-hounds and some Fell fox-hounds. I had never before seen a specimen of these last, and I certainly liked their appearance very much. [401]

Fell Hound type of FOXHOUND used to hunt the northern fell counties.

Fell Terrier working TERRIER developed among the hunts of the English Lake District. Strongly made, with a powerful head, dark, keen eyes, a strong MUZZLE and exceptionally large strong teeth. The neck is well muscled, the chest deep and narrow, the forelimbs straight and well muscled. The LOIN is fairly long and strong, the hindquarters powerful and moderately ANGULATED. The coat is hard, tight and close, and may be black, blue, or shades of liver. Height 28–38cm (11–15in); weight 5–8kg (11–17½lb).

felted coat coat matted into pads or strands.

femoral head necrosis LEGG CALVÉ PERTHES DISEASE.

femur thigh bone which joins STIFLE to hip. [*illus.* SKELETON]

fence instruction to a GUNDOG not to leave the enclosure occupied by it and its handler.

> That 'Fence' means that he is not to leave the place where you are. After being so checked a few times when he is endeavouring to quit the field, he will understand the word to be an order not to 'break fence'. [184]

Fennec Fox *VULPES ZERDA.*

feral of dog with domestic ancestry which lives in a semi-wild state.

Fermac private Irish pack of HARRIERS originally called the Mid Down Foot Harriers; the name was changed in 1959 and the pack reformed with 15in BEAGLES.

Fermanagh Irish HARRIER pack formed during the 18th century by the Enniskillen Fusiliers and Dragoons. The COUNTRY extends over the whole of Fermanagh and parts of Donegal, Tyrone and Monaghan.

ferrety (of feet) long, thin.

fertilization bring about development of the female ovum by the introduction of semen.

fetch 1. retrieve an object. 2. a command to retrieve. 3. drive sheep towards the shepherd.

fetlock (obs.) PASTERN.

> Faults . . . overbent fetlocks. [203, former IRISH WOLFHOUND]

fetomomy dissection of a dead foetus in utero.

fettle 1. restore to full working order.

> Cap: But fettle your fine joints 'gainst Thursday next,
> To go with Paris to Saint Peter's Church. [319p]

2. condition.

feuterer (18th cent. Fr.) KENNEL MAN or dog keeper. (der. *VAUTRIER*.)

fewterer (obs.) huntsman.

> And if the hare happe to come out to the greihoundes aforn the racches, and be bede, the fewterer that lette renne shuld blowe the dethe and kepe hur as hoole as he may to the hunters be come, and than shuld their rewarde the houndes. [125]

fianis excrement of boar, wolf, fox, marten or badger. [159]

fibrinoid leukodystrophy INHERITED CONGENITAL ICHTHYOSIS.

fibroblast immature cell with the capability of becoming a differentiated bone cell.

fibula smaller of the two bones which join the STIFLE and HOCK joints. [*illus.* SKELETON]

fibula tarsal bone CALCANEUS.

Field Ch. abbr. FIELD CHAMPION.

fiddle 1. pinched in the middle. 2. (of an exhibitor) adopt a dishonest ruse in order to confuse the judge. 3. (of a judge's behaviour) seem to be unable or unwilling to make a decision.

fiddle face elongated, concave foreface.

fiddle front out at elbow; pasterns turned in; feet turned out;

> Steepness in shoulder, fiddle fronts, and elbows that are out are serious faults [6, BASSET HOUND]

fiddle-headed untypically elongated head.

> Long, gaunt head in a breed which ought to be shorter in the head. [46]

field 1. HUNT FOLLOWERS.

> At a fixture at Stock House in 1828 there were 'two hundred and eighty-five horsemen' present, a very large field for that period. [318]

2. area in which a hunt takes place. 3. spectators at TRIALS. 4. environment.

Field Ch. abbr. pref. FIELD CHAMPION.

Field Champion [AKC] title awarded on achieving certain levels of success in AKC licensed FIELD TRIALS.

field immunity immunity to disease acquired as a consequence of the production of antibodies following a threat from infection encountered during normal life.

field money product of a collection formerly taken at the death of a hunted quarry. [47] Now replaced by CAPPING.

field sports pastimes which involve the pursuit of wild animals: hunting, shooting and fishing.

field trial test of canine skill and training for work.

Field Trial Champion (F.T.Ch.) [KC] title awarded on achieving success in FIELD TRIALS.

Field Spaniel [AKC, KC] breed created from existing GUNDOG breeds during the mid-19th century to form the ideal companion for the rough shooter. The breed is docile, active and independent.

The head is well chiselled with a pronounced OCCIPUT, raised brows, moderate STOP and with a long, lean MUZZLE. The hazel eyes are almond-shaped with tight lids; the pendulous ears are moderately long and wide. The neck is long and muscular, the shoulders sloping and WELL LAID BACK; forelimbs are straight with flat bone. The chest is deep, the ribs fairly WELL SPRUNG and the LOIN strong; the STIFLES are moderately bent with HOCKS WELL LET DOWN. The tail is traditionally DOCKED. The coat is long, flat and glossy with abundant FEATHERING to chest, underside and BREECHES, and may be black, liver or ROAN, with or without tan markings. Height 45.7cm (18in); weight 18–25kg (39½–55lb).

Fife the original pack was brought together in 1789 by Alexander Scrymgeour.

fighting pit enclosed area in which dogs fight.

> Made square at about 14 x 14ft., boarded all round at about 3ft in height [296]

Fila Brasiliero [AKC, FCI] breed created in Spain's South American colonies from MASTIFFS imported from Europe during the late 16th and early 17th centuries; used as a DROVER and TRACKER as well as a very effective GUARD.

The breed is typically MOLOSSAN, with a massive, powerful, rectangular head, deep MUZZLE and thick FLEWS. The neck is of exceptional strength and heavily muscled, with pronounced DEWLAP. The body is broad and deep, and slightly OVERBUILT. The coat is short and close over a thick and loose skin and may of any colour other than white or grey. Height 61–76cm (24–30in); weight 43kg (94½lb).

Fila da Terceiro comparatively short-legged, long-bodied, heavily built South American domestic guard dog with smooth, fawn or yellow coat, strong, blunt head and small, DROP EARS. Height 61cm (24in); weight 46kg (101lb). [312]

Fila de San Miguel CÃO DE FILA DE SAN MIGUEL.

Filaroides hirthi species of canine lung parasite.

Filaroides milksi species of canine lung parasite.

filbert ear triangular ear with rounded lower angle, similar to the shape of a filbert nut.

> Ears. Moderately sized, filbert shaped, set on low,

and hanging flat to cheek. [203, BEDLINGTON TERRIER]

filled   head that has no hollows or indentations. Viewed from front, eggshaped and completely filled, its surface free from hollows or indentations. [203, BULL TERRIER]

filled right up   (of MUZZLE) lacking STOP.

filled-up face   smoothly rounded head, without STOP or indentations.

fill-in   strongly developed bony structure below the eyes.

fill the eye   (of appearance) to please.

fimashings   quarry excrement. [159]

find   1. search, esp. for game.
Fully the half fell to the old dog's point, and I never saw him hunt or find better in my life. It was his twelfth 12th. [94]

2. instruction to a dog to search.
That 'Find' or 'Seek' means that he is to search for something which he will have great gratification in discovering. [184]

finder   1. DOG FINDER. [250]   2. slow HOUND able to follow a cold trail formerly used to find game.
And his hounds that be that day finders shall come to the lair or to the views and shall there be uncoupled, and they shall run, and enchase. Then hath the hunter great joy and liking. [125]

Finder   WATER SPANIEL devoted to particular tasks.
With these dogs also we fetch out of the water such fowl as be stung to death by any venomous worm, we use them also to bring us our bolts and arrows out of the water . . . for which circumstances they are called Inquisitores, searchers, and finders. [139]

fine   (usually of bone) slender, lightly constructed.

Fingal   Irish HARRIER pack formed in 1949 to hunt a COUNTRY in Counties Dublin and Meath.

finish   1. (Am.) gain the points necessary in America to be awarded the title of CHAMPION; MAKE UP. 2. (in OBEDIENCE training) to return to the starting position: sitting AT HEEL on the handler's left side.

Finkie   dim. FINNISH SPITZ.

Finland Dog   (obs.) FINNISH SPITZ.
In Finland there appears to be a breed resembling the Australian Dingo, but much more domesticated. [123]

Finnish Cock-eared Dog   FINNISH SPITZ.

Finnish Hound   FINSK STÖVARE.

Finnish Lapland Dog   LAPINKOIRA.

Finnish Lapphund   LAPINKOIRA.

Finnish Spitz   [AKC, KC] typically SPITZ breed, used as a hunting dog principally to locate Ptarmigan and Capercaillie, gamebirds that are also native to Scotland, which they oblige to perch in trees where the sportsman can then shoot them, indicating the place by means of a bark which the breed's supporters regard as melodious.
The head is rather long, with a slightly arched forehead, narrow MUZZLE and clean lips. The obliquely placed eyes are almond-shaped, the small ears sharply PRICKED. The neck is muscular with a dense RUFF, the square body deep chested with a pronounced TUCK-UP. Forelimbs are straight, hind-

quarters are strong and moderately ANGULATED. The tail is curved and PLUMED. The stiffish coat is semierect, with a short soft UNDERCOAT; always a rich red-gold or reddish-brown. Height 39–50cm (15¼–19½in); weight 14–16kg (31–35lb).

fins   profuse growth of hair on the feet, esp. in the LONG-HAIRED DACHSHUND.

Finno Laika   one of six European Russian LAIKA breeds identified in 1896 by Prince Andrew Shirinsky Shihmatoff. [380]

Finsk Spets   FINNISH SPITZ.

Finsk Stövare   lightly built and rather leggy SCENT-HOUND developed from other Scandinavian hounds during the 19th century. Of typical scenthound appearance, with a short, close, TRICOLOUR coat. Height 56–64cm (22–25in); weight 25kg (55lb).

Firehouse Dog   (obs.) DALMATIAN.

first cross   product of a mating between two dogs of different, pure breeds; the F1 generation.

first whipper-in   senior WHIPPER-IN.
Your first whipper-in being able to hunt the hounds occasionally, will answer another good purpose; it will keep your huntsman in order. [47]

Fisher   *Canis piscator*: type of dog reputedly used to locate fish.
The dog called the fisher, whereof Hector Boethus writes, which seeks for fish by smelling among rocks and stones, assuredly I know none of that kind in England, neither have I received by report that there is any such . . . except you hold opinion the beaver or Otter is a fish. [139]

fish eye   round, light-coloured eye.

fish-scale disease   INHERITED CONGENITAL ICHTHYOSIS.

fisting-hound   type of SPANIEL. [159]

fistula   abnormal aperture.

fit   convulsions, involuntary and unco-ordinated motor activity.

Fitzwilliam (Milton)   the hound PEDIGREE book goes back to 1760, at which time the pack was already well established under the mastership of Lord Fitzwilliam. The COUNTRY is largely plough, woodland and pasture.

fix   1. dishonest judging.   2. perform cosmetic surgery.   3. grip tenaciously with the teeth.
My people usually, I think, follow the hole, except when the earth is large, and the terriers have fixed the fox in an angle of it. [47]

fixation   point at which alleles become homozygous owing to drifts, selection or INBREEDING.

fixing   1. BREEDING(3) pattern aimed at producing fixation.   2. (of judging) creating a situation in which dishonesty can be practised.

flag   1. tail, esp. one that is long, FEATHERED and carried proudly.
The hounds must all work gaily and cheerfully, with flags up. [6, BEAGLE]

2. (esp. in GUNDOGS) to move excitedly a proudly carried tail.
The tail flags constantly while the dog is in motion. [6, GORDON SETTER]

3. article representing a human arm, used for the purpose of training guard dogs.

flagging 1. movement of the tail in a dog at POINT. 2. *See* FLAG(2).

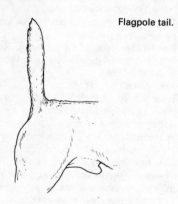

Flagpole tail.

flagpole tail long, vertically carried tail. [*illus.*]

flags flagstones or other hard surface upon which working HOUNDS were usually stood while being judged, hence 'on the flags'.

> On the flags they are light of bone, weak at the ankles often, and hare footed, but all acknowledge that they show wonderful sport in their beautiful native country. [316]

flanks vertical surfaces of the LOIN.

flapper racing FLAPPING.

flapper shooting shooting immature birds.

> Few dogs could equal him for flapper shooting, that vilest of sports, if followed before the unfortunate birds get strong on the wing – as unprofitable, too, for the table, as unsatisfactory to the real sportsman. [184]

flapping racing GREYHOUNDS on unlicensed tracks.

flapping track unlicensed GREYHOUND racing track.

flare BLAZE that is wider at the top than at the bottom.

Flared ears.

flared (of ears) proportionately large and carried at 90-degree angle to the head. [*illus.*]

flash over run the drag or an occupied holt.

flashings (esp. of CARDIGAN WELSH CORGIS) white markings.

> Usually with white flashings on chest, neck, feet, face and tip of tail. [6, WELSH CORGI, CARDIGAN]

flashy superficially attractive, eye-catching.

flat back level TOPLINE.

flat bone leg bone elliptical in section, rather than round.

flat catcher dog that achieves success more by flashiness than by real quality.

Flat-Coated Retriever [AKC, FCI, KC] popular 19th-century GUNDOG which has enjoyed a recent return to widespread popularity. An active dog of medium size and with a confident and kindly temperament. The head is long and moulded, the skull flat and fairly broad with slight STOP. The ears are small and lie close to the head, the eyes are dark brown or hazel. The neck is quite long, free from THROATINESS, and runs into a deep chest with well-defined BRISKET and fairly flat foreribs. The LOIN is short and square and the hindquarters muscular, with moderate bend of STIFLE. The tail is short, GAILY carried and well set on. The black or liver coat is fine and dense with good FEATHERING. Height 56–61cm (22–24in); weight 25–35kg (55–77lb).

flat croup horizontal CROUP, showing little or no slope.

flat feet absence of arch in the toes.

Flat Puppy Syndrome condition from which SWIMMERS suffer.

flat-ribbed of ribs lacking SPRING.

> With flat ribs and strong loins. [203, former BEARDED COLLIE]

flat-sided of ribs lacking roundness and with little spring.

> Flatsidedness and flanged ribs are faults. [6, GREYHOUND]

flea small, wingless, blood-sucking insect. *CTENOCEPHALIDES CANIS* is the species most commonly affecting dogs.

> The guerrilla fights the war of the flea, and his military enemy suffers the dog's disadvantages; too much to defend; too small, ubiquitous, and agile an enemy to come to grips with. [347]
> I do honour the very flea of his dog. [199a]

flea-bitten coat marked with small red marks or TICKS(2).

flea collar collar impregnated with insecticide.

flea comb fine-toothed comb used to remove fleas, their eggs and other fine debris.

fleck 1. (of a GREYHOUND) make a missed snatch at a hare. 2. small unevenly shaped spot of colour on a coat.

flecked (of coat) TICKED or speckled with secondary colour.

Fleethound (obs.) SCOTTISH DEERHOUND.

> For the Northern, or Fleet-hound, his head and nose ought to be slenderer and longer, his back broad, his belly gaunt, his joynts long, and his ears thicker and shorter – in a word, he is in all parts slighter made, and formed after the mould of a Greyhound. [53]

Fleming, Abraham translator of *Caius de Canibus Britannicis* (1756).

Flemish Draught Dog CHIEN DE TRAIT BELGE.

Flemish Hounds The HOUNDS of St Hubert, famous since the 8th century, under the name of Flemish

Hounds, were divided into two varieties – the black and the white. [81]

flesh 1. raw meat, especially when fed to HOUNDS. 2. (obs.) BODY, esp. when referring to condition.

> It requires a nice eye and great attention to keep them all in equal flesh. It is what distinguishes a good kennel huntsman. [47]

flesh-coloured nose unpigmented, pink nose.

flesh mark unpigmented patch on a nose.

fleshy cheek having well-developed masseter muscles.

fleshy ear having unusually thick LEATHERS, which in a GUNDOG or working TERRIER take a long time to heal after injury.

flewed having FLEWS. [159]

> So flew'd, so sanded; and their heads are hung
> With ears that sweep away the morning dew. [319k]
> The deep-flew'd hound
> Breed up with care, strong, heavy, slow, but sure. [328]

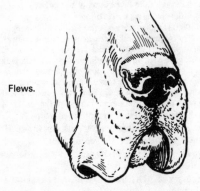

Flews.

flews pendulous, fleshy parts of the upper lips. [*illus.*]

> Heavy, square muzzle with well developed flews. [203, CLUMBER SPANIEL]
> Flews moderately deep, enclosing powerful jaw. [203, WEIMARANER]
> Flews straight with no sloppy droop. [6, ENGLISH SHEPHERD]

Flexi-lead spring-loaded, retractable lead.

flexion the closing of a joint.

flexor muscle which facilitates the bending of limbs.

flexor dominance of the tendency of newborn puppies to curl up when subjected to stimulation.

Flint and Denbigh bank and ditch COUNTRY in Clwyd dating from 1830 and founded by Sir Thomas Mostyn.

floating rib thirteenth rib, each of the rear pair, which are shorter than the rest and not attached to them. [*illus.* SKELETON]

flocked (of coat) soft and fine.

> Coat, long, flocked without curl covering entire head and body. [203, BOLOGNESE, Interim BREED STANDARD]

flooding discouraged methods of treating phobias by means of prolonged or intense exposure to the source of the phobia.

flop ear pendulous ear, as in a SPANIEL.

Florentine Spitz VOLPINO ITALIANO.

flower 1. (of SHAR PEI) BICOLOURed. 2. bicoloured tongue.

flowered Chinese description of a dog of two or more colours.

flown AWAY(1).

fluffy 1. (of coat) soft and woolly. 2. dog with abnormally soft coat.

> Very serious faults: Fluffies: A coat of extreme length with exaggerated feathering on ears, chest, legs and feet. [6, PEMBROKE WELSH CORGI]

Fluffy Poodle (obs.) name used formerly to distinguish groomed POODLES from those presented in corded coat.

> Shown with the hair combed and teased out till little of the curl is apparent, but the parts unshorn are a mass of soft fluffy hair on head, ears, shoulders, etc. [123]

fluke parasitic nematode which infects the blood, intestines, liver and lungs.

flush to put feathered game to flight.

> Now used to find, flush and retrieve game for gun. [203, ENGLISH SPRINGER SPANIEL]

fluting MEDIAN FURROW.

> Skull of medium length, fairly broad, slightly rounded, rising from foreface, making a brow or stop, divided by fluting between eyes. [203, ENGLISH SPRINGER SPANIEL]

fluttering lip thin FLEWS.

> Faults: . . . Loose lips hanging over the lower jaw (fluttering lips) which create an illusion of a deep muzzle. [6, GREAT DANE]

fly-away coat coat that does not lie flat to the body.

fly-away ear DROP EARS or semi-PRICK EARS which are held horizontally, pointing away from the head, when such carriage is normal for the breed, e.g. WHIPPET. *See also* FLYING EAR.

fly catcher dog that wins more than its actual quality suggests would be likely.

fly catching act of trying to catch imaginary flying objects. Possibly the product of a hallucinogenic minor seizure.

flyer exceptionally successful dog, esp. of a show dog or racing hound.

Flying ears.

flying ear ear which, by reason of injury, infection or habit, is carried horizontally when such carriage is abnormal for the breed. [*illus.*] *See also* FLY-AWAY EAR.

flying lips FLEWS.

flying trot   fast gait in which all four feet are simultaneously off the ground.

Fo Dog   Buddhist ivory, jade or porcelain symbol, usually presented in pair of dam and puppy, and intended to protect the well-being of the household.

foetal   of, or pertaining to, FOETUS.

foetal atrophy   atrophy and partial resorption of a dead feotus.

foetal rickets   ACHONDROPLASIA.

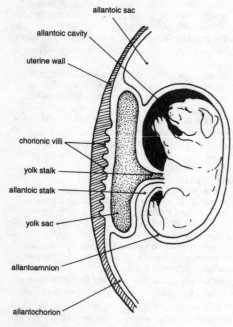

allantoic sac
allantoic cavity
uterine wall
chorionic villi
yolk stalk
allantoic stalk
yolk sac
allantoamnion
allantochorion

Foetus in utero, showing structure of the foetal unit.

foetus   unborn young, esp. after the stage at which it attaches itself to the uterine wall. [*illus.*]

foil   1. to obliterate or foul the scent of the quarry.
Yon crowding flocks, that at a distance gaze,
Have haply foil'd the turf. [328]
2. (occasionally) the scent of the quarry itself.
When a fox runs his foil in cover, if you suffer all your hounds to hunt on the line of him, they will foil the ground. [47]

foisting-hound   type of LAP-DOG. [159]

folic acid   one of the vitamins in the B complex.

folded ear   pendulous ears which have a vertical fold in the leather. [*illus.*]
Ears . . . set on low and falling in graceful folds. [203, BLOODHOUND]

follicle   pouch-like sac.

follicular mange   DEMODECTIC MANGE.

follower   one who follows HOUNDS but has no official capacity with the hunt. [387]

fontanelle   area on the skull of the foetus and neonate not covered by bone; the bones usually join soon after birth but remain open in HYDROCEPHALIC

Folded ear.

individuals and in some TOY breeds, esp. CHIHUAHUAS.

foot   terminal point of the limb.

foot harriers   HARRIERS whose FOLLOWERS are not mounted.

foot-hound   any HOUND followed on foot.
The Beagle is the foot hound of our country. [123]

foot-follower   one who follows HOUNDS on foot.
Notwithstanding the prejudice against 'foot-people' voiced by generations of fox-hunters, whose point of view was that of the 'thruster' quoted by Nimrod, who gave vent to the sentiment – when galloping past a prostrate and possibly injured fellow-sportsman – 'the pace was too good to enquire,' the genuine 'pedestrian sportsman' has a defined and indeed valuable place in the pursuit of the fox. [235]

foot-licking   common symptom of atopy.

foot pack   hunt that pursues its quarry on foot. HOUND pack that is hunted on foot.

footpad   one of five fleshy parts of the underside of the foot. [*illus. DIGITAL PAD*]

foot, types of   CAT, HARE, OVAL, PAPER, SLEW, SLIPPER, SPLAY.

footing   of a GUNDOG puzzling out a scent.
Show your pupil a few times out of doors how to work out a scent, by dragging a piece of bread unperceived by him down wind through grass, and then letting him 'foot' it out. [184]

foramen magnum   inherited large fissure in the OCCIPUTAL bone between the cranial cavity and spinal canal. (Mode of inheritance, uncertain.)

Forbe's disease   GLYCOGENOSIS TYPE III.

fore   at, or of, the front.

fore arm   that part of the foreleg between the elbow and carpus.

fore chest   STERNUM.

foreface   MUZZLE.
Skull and foreface of equal length. [203, SCOTTISH TERRIER]

foreface depth   depth from the upper surface of the MUZZLE to the lower surface of the underjaw.

forehand   front limbs and shoulders.

foreleg   either of the front limbs.

forelock   that part of the head hair which falls forward over the forehead; FRINGE.

fore pastern   METACARPAL BONES; part of the foreleg above the foot. [*illus. SKELETON*]

fore paw   foot of the foreleg.

forequarters forelimbs and shoulders.
Is composed of the shoulder, the upper arm [between it and the elbow], the fore-arm [below the elbow], the knee, the leg, and the foot. [338]

forequarter's angulation angles formed between the upper arm and humerus, and the humerus and scapula. [*illus.* ANGULATION, UPRIGHT SHOULDER, TERRIER FRONT]

foreign expression expression that is not typical of the breed.

Forest and District former 15½in BEAGLE pack formed in 1905 in succession to the Lyme Harriers to hunt a COUNTRY in Cheshire.

Forest Fox *CEREDOCYON THOUS.*

Forest Laws laws, originally devised by King Canute, which proscribed entry to the Royal Forests and imposed controls, often consisting of physical mutilation, on certain breeds of dog.

form 1. resting place of a hare.
2. (esp. of racing dogs) likelihood of success assessed on the basis of recent achievements.

forme fruste abnormal manifestation of a normal condition.

foster to nurse puppies born to another bitch.

foster-mother bitch that nurses puppies on the behalf of another.

Fotor SPANIEL GENTLE. [139]

Fouilloux, Jacques du *see* DE FOUILLOUX, JACQUES.

foul (of scent) spoil; overlay and obscure with another.

foul colour untypical and undesirable colouring.

foundation stock initial breeding stock, from which a breeding kennel will be established.

founder (obs.) nonspecific complaint causing lameness.
No dog of mine ever suffered from founder, or kennel lameness, which is, I believe, more commonly found amongst Hounds than any other dogs. [186]

founder effect propensity of foundation stock to transmit unusual or even unique features to closely inbred descendants.

founder principle FOUNDER EFFECT.

Four Burrow Cornish hunt with a pasture, moorland and plough COUNTRY dating from 1780, when both fox and hare were hunted under the mastership of Mr Turner MP.

four-eyed said of dogs that have a spot of colour above each eye. [159]

four-footed friend (lit.) dog.

Fousek Czechoslovakian POINTER. [312]

Fowey former HARRIER pack founded during the first half of the 19th century to hunt a COUNTRY in Cornwall.

fox *CANIS VULPES*, the foremost hunting quarry in Britain.
The fox and stoat are curious Little Chaps. One eats a lot he Don't kill, the other kills a Lot he Don't eat. [165]

fox box container for a bagman.

fox dog 1. any dog used to hunt foxes. 2. (obs.)

specific type of dog formerly used to hunt foxes.
The 'Fox-dog', in all probability, was the Southern Hound, a heavy, crook-kneed kind of baying Hound, which dwelt on the scent, and was incapable of killing a fox unless he hunted him to death. [186]
3. formerly thought to be the product of a biologically impossible CROSS between fox and dog.
So called ... because they spring from a union of a dog and a fox. [404]

fox encephalitis infectious canine HEPATITIS.

fox hunting pursuit of foxes with HOUNDS, which are followed by huntsmen, either mounted or on foot.
I have often observed in women of her type a tendency to regard all athletics as inferior forms of foxhunting. [382]
'Fox-'unting is indeed the prince of sports. The image of war without its guilt, and only half its danger. I confess that I'm a martyr to it – a perfect wictim – no one knows wot I suffer from my ardour. [344b]

fox trot economical and ground-consuming pace, between a walk and a trot. [50]

Fox-beagle small type of FOXHOUND.
I must mention an instance of extra-ordinary sagacity of a fox-beagle that once belonged to the Duke of Cumberland. [47]

Foxcatcher (US) AMERICAN FOXHOUND pack formed in 1912 to hunt a largely open COUNTRY in Delaware.

Fox Collie extinct Scottish SHEEP DOG. [150]

Foxhound [FCI, KC] HOUND used and developed by English foxhound packs, essentially a packhound and, except at the breed's own shows, seldom seen away from HUNT KENNELS.

A good Foxhound must have stamina, speed, drive and intelligence. The head should be broad with a well-defined STOP, the eyes deep and dark, the MUZZLE of fair length and strong. The silken, pendulous ears lie close to the head and taper towards the lower extremity; the neck is reasonably long and well muscled. The importance of good shoulders cannot be too strongly stressed; forelegs are straight and well boned, with elbows neither out nor TIED IN. The chest is deep but not overSPRUNG in the modern Foxhound; the TOPLINE may arch slightly over the powerful LOINS. Hindquarters are well muscled with moderate ANGULATION. Good feet, which should be compact, well padded and WELL KNUCKLED UP are of the utmost importance. The STERN should be carried proudly but never over the back, a GAY stern is an abomination. Nose – the ability to find and follow a scent – is vital while a good melodious voice adds to both aesthetic appeal and utility. Size varies according to the demands of the COUNTRY, the prevailing fashion and the master's preference.
The most perfect of his race is the foxhound – perfect in shape, in pace, in nose, in courage. Not one of his canine companions is his equal, for in addition to his merits as a mere quadruped, as a hound he is the reason for the maintenance of expensive establishments, for the breeding of high class horses,

and generally for giving an impetus to trade and causing a 'turnover' without which the agriculturalist might starve and the greatness of our country be placed in peril. [221]

Fox Paulistinha   TERRIER BRASILIERO.

Fox River Valley   (US) American and English FOX-HOUND pack formed in 1940 to hunt a grass, plough and woodland COUNTRY in Illinois.

Fox Terrier   terrier bred to go after foxes that have gone to EARTH. There are two varieties: SMOOTH FOX TERRIER and WIRE FOX TERRIER.

> The Fox Terrier was originally kept as an addition to every pack of foxhounds, being always so handy as to be up within a very few minutes of running to ground. [338]
> A terrier was a thoroughbred animal per se, but it could only be called a fox terrier when fit for the bolting of a fox. [338]
> He was small and fat and white, with a brown-and-black head; a fox terrier. My father said he had a lemon head – some such mysterious technical phraseology. [219]

foxy   of, or resembling, a fox.

> General foxy appearance is the chief characteristic of this working terrier. [203, former CAIRN TERRIER]

foxy head   head resembling that of a fox.

fragmented coronoid process   ELBOW DYSPLASIA.

Français Blanc et Noir   [FCI] black and white French pack HOUND, black and white being not only the most common colour among French pack hounds but considered to be the oldest.

A solidly built, well-balanced hound with a DOMED skull and prominent SUPRAORBITAL RIDGE; the STOP is not pronounced and the MUZZLE is slightly arched; ears are set at eye level and slightly VOLUTED; eyes are dark. The slightly DEWLAPped neck is rather long but strong. The shoulders are long and lean, the elbows carried close to the body and the limbs well boned. The BRISKET is WELL LET DOWN and the belly slightly drawn up. Hindquarters are long and well muscled with rather long feet. The long, elegant tail is thick at the root. The coat is short, dense and always black and white, with black, or occasionally tan, spots on the legs. Height 61–74cm (24–29in).

Français Blanc et Orange   [FCI] probably a descendant of the POITEVIN and the BILLY, it is now considerably reduced in number and distinguished from the FRANÇAIS TRICOLORE only by its orange and white coat.

Français Tricolore   [FCI] an elegant, well-built and muscular French HOUND with an elongated, slightly DOMED head, pronounced OCCIPUT, and a square MUZZLE. The eyes are large and brown, the pendulous ears broad and VOLUTED. The neck is long and muscular with a slight DEWLAP, the chest deep and long to a slight TUCK-UP. The shoulders are long and the elbows set under the body, the hindquarters are long and muscular with broad, WELL LET DOWN HOCKS. The coat, over a fine skin, is short and fine and always TRICOLOUR. Height 61–74cm (24–29in).

free action   FREE GAIT.

free from change   of a hound, esp. a BLOODHOUND, which can be relied upon not to change from a hunted to a fresh scent. [236]

free gait   natural, efficient and unexaggerated movement.

free return   concession allowing a bitch that has failed to conceive to return to the STUD-DOG for another mating at a subsequent season, without the need to pay another stud fee.

freighting capacity   measure of the ability to draw a loaded sledge.

> A working sledge dog, primarily assessed for 'freighting capacity' in arctic conditions. [203, ESKIMO DOG, Interim BREED STANDARD.]

French Black and White Hound   FRANÇAIS BLANC ET NOIR.

French Bulldog   [AKC, KC] claimed by some authorities to have its origins in Spain as a dog used to bait donkeys.

A sturdy and compact breed, with a broad, square, flat-skulled, deep MUZZLEd head, surmounted by characteristic BAT EARS. The body is short, COBBY, rounded and muscular, with wide shoulders and narrower LOINS. The short and muscular forelegs are set wide apart; the hindquarters are longer than the forelegs but equally muscular and create an overbuilt TOPLINE. The tail is naturally short. The short, close coat may be BRINDLE, PIED, or fawn. Weight 10.9–12.7kg (24–28lb).

French dog   type of dog described by FLEMING.

> There is also at this day among us a new kind of dog brought out of France. . . . And they be speckled all over with white and black, which mingled colours incline to a marble blue, which beautifies their skins and offers a seemly show of comeliness. These are called French dogs as is above declared already. [139]

french front   Very narrow front with PASTERNS turned outwards. [*illus.*]

Frenchie   dim. FRENCH BULLDOG.

French illness   (obs.) probably DISTEMPER.

French Mastiff   DOGUE DE BORDEAUX.

French front.

French Orange and White Hound   FRANÇAIS BLANC ET ORANGE.

French Pointer   BRAQUE FRANÇAIS.

> Is distinguished by a furrow between his nostrils, which materially interferes with the acuteness of smell. He is better formed and more active than either the Spanish or Portuguese dog, and capable of longer continued exertion; but he is apt to be quarrelsome, and is too fond of chasing the hare. [406]
> This is rather a nondescript animal, as he varies greatly throughout France, being in some districts very similar to the Spanish dog, while in others he

has evidently been crossed with the poodle, and resembles that dog very closely. [338]

French Poodle   common misnomer for the POODLE (which is of German origin).
> Next day she had him as handy as a French poodle, and looking about as sensible as one. [344c]

French Sheep Dog   BERGER.

French Short-haired Shepherd   BEAUCERON.

French Spaniel   ÉPAGNEUL FRANÇAIS.

French Tricolour Hound   FRANÇAIS TRICOLORE.

French White and Black Hound   FRANÇAIS BLANC ET NOIR.

French White and Orange Hound   FRANÇAIS BLANC ET ORANGE.

fresh find   previously hunted quarry found again after a long CHECK or after hunting another.

fresh fox   fox that HOUNDS have begun to hunt in the course of hunting another.
> A fresh fox broke away here, but hounds were stopped and put in again. After about five minutes they pushed their hunted fox out and he went over the wall, on through Standean Farm, and put in some work in the long ash plantation. [401]

Friesian Water Dog   WETTERHOUN.

frill   long hair on the chest.
> Abundant coat, mane and frill. [203, SHETLAND SHEEPDOG]

fringes   long hair on the rear of the legs, edges of the ears and underside of the tail. *See also* FALL.
> Ears . . . covered with short fine hair with fringe of whiteish silky hair at tip. [203, BEDLINGTON TERRIER]

frog-a-log   (Brit. rhyming slang) dog.

frog-faced   having a wide, short nose and receding jaw.
> It is evident that did the mouth not project beyond the nose, and had both jaws and nose been level, the nostrils would be flat against the part to which the dog was fixed, and the breathing would be stopped. When modern Bulldogs, as is sometime the case, have this defective formation, they are 'frog-faced' as it is termed. [133]

froggy   (esp. in the BULLDOG) of top lips that overhang a level or OVERSHOT jaw.

front   forelegs, chest, BRISKET and shoulders.

front, types of   BOWED, CABRIOLE, CHIPPENDALE, CROOKED, EAST-WEST, FIDDLE, FRENCH, GUN BARREL, HORSESHOE, NARROW, PIGEON, PINCHED, STEEP, STRAIGHT, TERRIER, TRUE, WIDE.

frontal bones   those bones of the skull which shape the forehead.

frontal plane   any vertical plane at right angles to the MEDIAN PLANE.

frosting   slight greying of the facial hair owed either to age or to a breed propensity.
> Frosting [white or grey] on the muzzle. [203, BELGIAN SHEPHERD DOG, MALINOIS, Interim]

froufrou   tuft of longer or more profuse hair on the tip of a tail.

frown   facial expression produced by breeds with wrinkling to the head, such as exhibited by the BASENJI.

F.T.Ch.   abbr. pref. FIELD TRIAL CHAMPION.

fucosidosis   inherited enzyme deficiency resulting in an excess of tissue fucose producing cerebral and neural degeneration. (Mode of inheritance, recessive.)

fugation   hunting COUNTRY. [159]

full blood   (Aust.) of a SHEEP DOG in whose pedigree CROSSES with another breed are so remote as to be negligible. [204]

Full Ch.   abbr. pref. FULL CHAMPION.

Full Champion   GUNDOG that has won its titles both in the ring and in the field.

full cry   hounds speaking in unison.

full drop ear   pendulous.

full eye   rounded and slightly protruding.

fullmart   polecat. [159]

full mouth   a complete set of teeth.
> A puppy is said to have its full mouth when its second teeth have been cut. [320]

full of running   reference to a strong, hunted fox.
> The fox was strong, he was full of running,
> He could run for an hour and then be cunning [249]

Fulton's Harriers   BISLEY.

fundus   that part of any curved organ, which is furthest from the opening.

fungal kerion   pustular eruption possibly caused by hypersensitivity to fungal growths.

fungus eczema   FUNGAL KERION.

furious rabies   rabies in which the symptoms take the form of extreme excitability, irritability and indiscriminate aggression.
> He shammed furious rabies, and bit all the babies,
> And followed the cats up the trees, and then ate 'em! [64]

Furness and District   former 15½in BEAGLE pack formed in 1886 to hunt a COUNTRY in Cumbria.

furnished   having well-developed body and FURNISHINGS.

furnishings   profuse growth of hair, longer than the main body hair, which contributes to an appearance characteristic of the breed.
> Dogs with semi-long hair are generally not as heavily furnished in the rear as the long-haired dogs. [6, PYRENEAN SHEPHERD]

furrow   depression down the skull from OCCIPUT to STOP.

furunculosis   bacterial infection of the skin producing suppurating perforations.

fused incisors   incisors that have grown together: inherited abnormality. (Mode of inheritance, familial.)

futurity stake   competition for dogs in which competitors are nominated at or prior to their birth.

fysteing hound   SPANIEL GENTLE.
> This puppitly and peasantly cur (which some frumpingly term fysteing hounds) serve in a manner to no good use except . . . to succour and strengthen quailing and quamming stomachs, to betray bawdery, and filthy abominable lewdness (which a little dog of this kind did in Sicilia). [139]

G

G gene symbol for progressive silvering/greying: black turns to blue in adults. [395]

Gabriel's Hounds distant sounds of a skein of wild geese are said to resemble the cry of HOUNDS. They are also said to resemble the cries of damned souls being whipped on by the Archangel Gabriel.

GAG GLYCOSAMINOGLYCOGEN.

Gaigeria HOOKWORMS.

gaily (of tail carriage) *see* GAY.

gait 1. movement.

> at the trot the gait is big, very lively, graceful and efficient. [6, IRISH SETTER]

2. demonstrate a dog's movement in the ring.

galacturia treatment of unweaned puppies by means of medicants given to the dam.

Galco Espagñol former var. spelling of GALGO ESPAGÑOL. [312]

Galecynus fossil canine ancestor.

Galgo Espagñol [FCI] SIGHTHOUND with origins in Andalusia and north into Castile. It seems likely that Moorish invaders were responsible for the prevalence throughout the Mediterranean region of a number of similar breeds.

The head is long and lean, the small ROSE EARS carried back; the BRISKET is deep and the ribs carried well back to a pronounced but not exaggerated TUCK-UP. The TOPLINE is straight and slightly higher than the withers. The overall conformation is typical of sighthounds. The long tail is carried low in a SABRE curve. The coat is short, shiny and black or tawny, sometimes streaked with black, on a white GROUND. Height 63–70cm (24¾–27½in); weight 30kg (66lb).

gallop 1. the fastest pace: a four-beat pace in which all four feet are off the ground at the same time and regain contact with the ground near hind first, then off hind, then fore and off fore. 2. (of heartbeat) rapid and irregular.

Galton's law statistical genetic proposition formulated by Francis Galton which is intended to define the range within which various characteristics will occur.

game 1. having the necessary courage to undertake its task, usually of a TERRIER, also of a fighting dog. Hence, gameness.

> The Hon. Gerald Lascelles, . . . told me that the Parson used to try a dog to the limit, kill him, and if he was really game, breed from his brother. [238a]

2. quarry which is so defined in law.

game laws law, originally promulgated by Canute, which define game and regulate when it may be taken.

game sense innate ability to find game.

> Very active with a keen game sense. [203, ENGLISH SETTER]

game test when two dogs have fought themselves to a standstill, one may be replaced by a fresh dog in order to test the gameness of its exhausted opponent.

Gamekeeper's Night Dog former name for the BULLMASTIFF.

gamete cells involved in sexual reproduction, spermatozoan (male) and ovum (female).

gametocyte cell which produces GAMETES.

gametogenesis the production of GAMETES.

Gammel Dansk Hønsehund [FCI] POINTER developed in Denmark during the early years of the 18th century, now used both as a pointer and as a TRACKER of wounded quarry. The skull is broad, the MUZZLE deep and the neck fairly short and strong, with pronounced DEWLAP. The body is greater in length with a deep, broad chest, level TOPLINE, WELL-LAID shoulders, muscular quarters and well-boned limbs. The white coat is short and dense with liver patches. Height 56cm (22in); weight 18–24kg (39½–53lb).

gang hitch large team of SLED-DOGS hooked in pairs to a central towline.

gangline TOWLINE.

gangliosidosis deficiency of the lipid storage system resulting in stunted growth and muscular dysfunction.

gangliosidosis GM1 inherited deficiency of the lipid storage system resulting in stunted growth and muscular dysfunction. (Mode of inheritance, recessive.)

gangliosidosis GM2 inherited condition causing muscular dysfunction, fits, poor sight and death. (Mode of inheritance, recessive.)

gangrene putrefaction of tissue.

ganning barking of foxes. [159]

Garrowby former HARRIER pack formed in 1906 to hunt a COUNTRY in Yorkshire.

Garswood ASPULL AND PENDLE FOREST.

Garth and South Berks lying mainly in Berkshire the bank and ditch COUNTRY was formed in 1962 by the amalgamation of the Garth, which dates from 1790, and South Berks, dating from 1843.

Gascon Saintongeois [FCI] created in the 1840s by Baron de Virelade, who used CROSSES between the GRAND GASCONY and the SAINTONGEOIS, both hounds formerly principally used for hunting wolves. The larger variety of the breed is used principally for deer and other large game, and the smaller variety for hare.

The head is lean with pronounced OCCIPUT, deep-set eyes, pendulous ears and a deep, FLEWED MUZZLE. The neck is inclined to throatiness, the chest is deep and capacious, and the LOINS strong. The tail is long and thin. The smooth coat is short, dense and TRICOLOUR on a solid white or TICKED GROUND.

Grand: height 63.5–71cm (24–28in); weight 30–32kg (66–70½lb); Petit: height 57–63.5cm (22½–25in).

Gascony Hound an American COONHOUND with – largely because of its blue TICKING and a relationship with imported French HOUNDS – a strong resemblance to the hounds of Gascony. The distinctive coloration gives rise to the breed's alternative name of Bluetick Coonhound. Rather more RACY and lightly boned than other Coonhounds, the speckled, glossy blue coat and the bugle voice are distinctive features. Height 51–69cm (20–27in); weight 20–36kg (44–79lb).

Gascony-type French Pointer BRAQUE FRANÇAIS DE PETITE TAILLE.

Gasehound (var. spelling) GAZEHOUND.

gaskins usually, the second thigh, but may also be applied to the thigh as a whole ÿ.
> The lower end of the second thigh [46]
> The thighs and second thighs (gaskins) are very muscular. [6, BLOODHOUND]

gastric of, or relating to, the stomach.

gastric dilation abdominal distension caused by fluid or gas.

gastric dilation-volvulus inherited tendency to gastric dilation leading to haemorrhage, ulceration and death.

gastric foreign body indigestible object within the intestinal tract, most commonly an unsuitable toy or inappropriate food.

gastric torsion bloat, the disposition to which is probably inherited.

gastritis inflammation of the stomach lining.

gastroenteritis inflammation of the lining of the lower digestive tract causing vomiting and diarrhoea.

Gaucher's disease GLUCOCEREBROSIDOSIS.

Gaussian curve graphic or mathematical representation of NORMAL DISTRIBUTION.

gaunt head long, angular and bony head.

gawcie tail (Scot.) of a well-FEATHERED tail carried curled over the back.
> Large, well furnished with hair, and carried pretty high, and with a good swirl – in fact, the term 'gawcie', which Burns uses to describe the Scotch Collie's tail, pretty accurately applies. [123]

gay (of tail carriage): see GAY TAIL; GAY STERN.

gay stern HOUND's tail carried over the back, an objectionable characteristic.

gay tail tail carried over the back.
> Tail customarily docked, carried erect; not over-gay. [203, AUSTRALIAN SILKY TERRIER, Interim]

gay-tike boy DOG-FANCIER. [280]

gaze 1. of a hunted deer that turns to face HOUNDS.
> . . . the poor frighted deer, that stands at gaze,
> Wildly determining which way to fly. [319vv]

2. to view a hunted otter.

Gazehound SIGHTHOUND.
> This breed is now lost, and it is very difficult to ascertain in what respects it differed from the greyhound. [338]
> This kind of dog, which pursues by the eye, prevails little, or never a whit, by any benefit of the nose that

is by smelling, but excels in perspicacity and sharpness of sight altogether, by the virtue whereof, being singular and notable, it hunts the Fox and the Hare. [139]

Gazelle Hound SALUKI.

gee order for a SLED-DOG team to turn right.

geea (regional Eng.) go; encouragement to HOUNDS.

geld (more usually of horses) castrate.

Gelert legendary dog, who killed the wolf that had slain his master's child, but was then killed by his master who assumed Gelert to be responsible for the child's death.
> 'Hell-hound! my child's by thee devoured,
> The frantic father cried;
> And to the hilt his vengeful sword
> He plunged in Gelert's side. [332]

gene constituent information-carrying parts of the chromosomes, upon which inherited characteristics are based.

gene composition the make-up of genes, which are formed from deoxyribonucleic acid (DNA), the basis for all life.

gene frequency measure of the prevalence of a particular gene, most frequently a mutant allele, within a defined population.

gene pair disparate pair of genes, often consisting of one normal gene and one mutant allele, on a particular locus.

gene pool sum of all the genes available in a breeding population.

gene segregation subject of Mendel's Second Law which states that when two genes with alternative alleles occur, each will independently segregate into its various effects.

gene symbols genes are labelled by standard letters, upper case denoting dominant genes, lower case recessive ones.

genealogy study of PEDIGREES.

generalized progressive retinal atrophy PROGRESSIVE RETINAL ATROPHY.

generalized tremor syndrome muscular tremors especially evident when excited, cause unknown.

Genesee Valley (US) English and crossbred FOXHOUND pack formed in 1876 to hunt pasture and woodland COUNTRY in New York State.

genetic concerned with inherited characteristics.

genetic assimilation BALDWIN/WADDINGTON EFFECT.

genetic bottleneck period during which the breeding population falls below that which is necessary to sustain a healthy population.

genetic constitution GENOTYPE.

genetic defects inherited undesirable characteristics.

genetic drift way in which the frequency with which genes occur tends to change over time to produce more or less examples of one or other characteristic.

genetic expressivity EXPRESSIVITY.

genetic fingerprinting an analysis of nucleic acids which identifies the offspring or parents of the tested animals.

genetic interval average time between birth and sexual maturity.

genetic linkage failure of genes to separate at meiosis.

genetic penetrance PENETRANCE.

genetic ratio measure of the frequency with which various phenotypes occur in a given population.

genetics that branch of science which deals with the way in which characteristics are inherited.

genic appertaining to the GENES.

genital appertaining to the external sexual organs.

genitals external reproductive organs.

genocopy phenotype which is a replica of a known genetic type to which it is either unrelated or distantly related.

genome entire collection of genes carried by an individual.

genotype sum of inherited characteristics, expressed in gene symbol.

genotype selection use of known inherited characteristics as a basis for the selection of breeding stock.

genuiscissio operation required by C11 Forest Laws which involved severing tendons behind a dog's knee in order to make it unable to run and so to harass forest game.

geophagia habit of eating soil, clay or earth.

German Boarhound GREAT DANE.

German Broken-coated Pointer STICHELHAAR.

German Bulldog BOXER.

German Hound DEUTSCHER BRACKE.

German Hunting Terrier DEUTSCHER JAGTERRIER.

German Long-haired Pointer DEUTSCHER LANG-HAARIGER VORSTEHHUND.

German Mastiff (obs.) GREAT DANE.

German Pinscher smooth-coated black-and-tan German GUARD. Height 40–48cm (15¾–18¾in); weight 11.5–16kg (24–35lb).

German Sausage Dog (colloq. disparaging) DACHSHUND.

> I knew a couple of elderly spinsters once who had a sort of German sausage on legs which they called a dog. [194]

German Sheep Dog small German herding dog.

> A small-sized breed, with bushy tail carried over the back, small muzzle, and shaggy coat, which is generally black or light fawn. [338]

German Shepherd Dog [AKC] GERMAN SHEPHERD DOG (ALSATIAN).

German Shepherd Dog (Alsatian) [KC] originally a PASTORAL GUARD and HERDER, the breed's ability to respond to training for a number of tasks has made it the breed of choice for most police and guard work as well as the most popular breed of dog worldwide. The breed is descended from the light-coloured German shepherd dogs to be found during the 17th century but only towards the end of the 19th century were efforts made, particularly in Würtenburg,

Hesse, Thuringia and Bavaria, to fuse various regional types into a homogenous breed. The breed's distinctly lupine appearance has earned it the name of 'Wolf Dog', its security work 'Police Dog' and its place of origin 'Alsatian'.

The breed is highly intelligent, strong, agile and has great stamina. The head is fairly broad and wedge-shaped with a strong MUZZLE. The high-set ears are carried erect; the neck is fairly long, the forequarters long and obliquely set. The body is long, the chest deep and the back straight, the CROUP curving downwards to the long tail. The hindquarters must not be OVER-ANGULATED. The coat is straight and hard, black, black and tan or SABLE; white is highly undesirable. Height 57.5–62.5cm (22½–24½in).

German Short-haired Pointer [AKC, KC] GUNDOG originally produced from CROSSES between several European HOUND and gundog breeds. The result was a slow, ponderous dog which was then refined by means of crosses with imported ENGLISH SETTERS to produce an exceptional and very biddable all-purpose gundog with a superlative nose.

The head is CLEAN CUT, with a broad, slightly rounded skull, imperceptible STOP and a powerful MUZZLE. The pendulous ears are broad, neither fleshy nor thin, and high set. The neck is muscular and slightly arched, the forequarters sloping, the limbs straight and well boned with slightly sloping PASTERNS. The chest is deep, the ribs WELL SPRUNG and the TUCK-UP pronounced with a wide, slightly arched LOIN. The hips are broad, the thighs strongly muscled and the STIFLES well bent. The tail is traditionally DOCKED and is carried at or below the horizontal. The coat is short, flat and COARSE, and may be black or liver, with or without white TICKS(2) or patches. TRICOLOURS are not acceptable. Height 53–64cm (20¾–25in).

German Spaniel DEUTSCHER WACHTELHUND.

German Spitz one of several closely related European SPITZ breeds which differ only in size and acceptable colour range. The KEESHOND is the largest of these, the Mittel of medium size, the Klein slightly smaller and the POMERANIAN the smallest of the four. Only the Klein and Mittel, however, are officially classified as varieties of the same breed.

Heads are typically spitz, broad in skull, narrowing through the MUZZLE, with OVAL EYES and small triangular high-set pricked ears. The neck is moderately short, the forelimbs straight, the chest deep and the body compact with a level TOPLINE and moderate TUCK-UP. The hindquarters are moderately ANGULATED. The tail is curled over the back and, like the legs, is well FEATHERED. The DOUBLE COAT consists of a soft and woolly undercoat with a fairly long, harsh topcoat, which forms an abundant FRILL round the neck and chest. Height: Klein 23–28cm (9–11in), Mittel 29–35.5cm (11½–13¾in).

German Spitz (Klein) [KC] GERMAN SPITZ.

German Spitz (Mittel) [KC] GERMAN SPITZ.

German Wire-haired Pointer [AKC, KC] wire-haired version of the GERMAN SHORT-HAIRED POINTER, from which it principally differs in that the outer coat is harsh and dense with a soft undercoat. Preferred colours are liver, with or without white, or black and white; solid black and TRICOLOURS are firmly discouraged. Height 56–67cm (22–26½in); weight 20.5–34kg (45–75lb).

German Wolfspitz large, extinct SPITZ originally used for hunting wolves.

germ cell GENE.

germ cell lineage the propensity of certain characteristics to persist from generation to generation.

germ line individuals which carry the same genes and thus maintain the existence of those genes.

germinal cells gonad cells which produce the gametes.

germinal mutation process giving rise to the production of mutant alleles.

gestation that period between conception and birth, which in the dog is usually 63 days, within a normal range from 58 to 68 days.

get 1. offspring of a male parent. [159]
> The beautiful foxhound type he put into all his get was remarkable, and it would be hard to find a kennel in which a trace of his blood could not be found. [316]

2. to sire. 3. make pregnant.

giant axonal neuropathy inherited disease characterized by ataxia, hypotonia, loss of feeling, and hind-limb reflexes. (Mode of inheritance, recessive.)

giant breed no official definition exists and there is considerable variation among unofficial ones, but generally includes those breeds whose body weight exceeds 50kg (110lb).

Giant German Spitz DEUTSCHER GROSSPITZ.

Giant Schnauzer [AKC, KC] developed originally as a DROVER and PASTORAL GUARD, this impressive breed has since developed as a very effective all-purpose guard. The breed is powerful, robust and squarely built, with speed and endurance.

The rather long head is strong with medium STOP punctuated by bushy eyebrows, the dark eyes are oval; the ears are V-shaped and high set, and traditionally CROPPED in countries which allow the operation. The neck is rather long, slightly arched and strong, the shoulders flat with strong, straight forelegs. The chest is rather broad and deep, the back straight but dropping slightly from WITHERS to hips, the hindquarters are strongly muscled. The tail is traditionally DOCKED, set high and carried at an angle to the TOPLINE. The coat is short and harsh with a good undercoat, and may be black, PEPPER AND SALT or shades of grey with an obligatory dark MASK. Height 60–70cm (23½–27½in).

Giardia canis intestinal protozoan parasite which causes GIARDIASIS.

giardiasis condition caused by *GIARDIA CANIS* and resulting in dysentery and diarrhoea.

giddiness TURNSIDE. [406]

Gierke's disease GLYCOGENOSIS TYPE I.

gig training cart for SLED-DOGS.

gigantism ACROMEGALY.

gingiva relating to the gums.

gingival hyperplasia inherited abnormal growth of gingiva resulting, in extreme cases, in an inability to close the mouth. (Mode of inheritance, familial.)

gingival hypertrophy GINGIVAL HYPERPLASIA.

gingival recession tendency of the gums to recede with age.

gingivitis inflammation of the gums.

girth circumference of the chest, in working TERRIERS customarily measured by spanning with the hands.

gista canis HOUND bread; a type of coarse bread formerly fed to dogs.

git 1. (regional Eng.) offspring. 2. produce (der. beget.).

give tongue *see* GIVING TONGUE.

giving tongue sound made by HOUNDS or TERRIERS, esp. when working.

Glaisdale north Yorkshire hunt with a moorland, pasture and plough COUNTRY, founded in 1877.

Glamorgan hunt dating from 1873 when the COUNTRY was hunted by Mr T.M. Talbot.

Glanmire former Irish HARRIER PACK formed in 1901 to hunt a COUNTRY in County Cork.

Glanzmann's disease THROMBASTHENIA.

Glanzmann-Naegli disease THROMBASTHENIA.

Glasgow Fancy Skye Terrier CLYDESDALE TERRIER. [123]

Glasgow Hounds LANARKSHIRE AND RENFREW-SHIRE.

Glasgow Smuts extinct Glaswegian fighting breed, a version of the BLUE PAUL.

Glasgow Terrier PAISLEY TERRIER.
> They [Paisley terriers] had silky coats, and were only pretty 'mongrels' bred from Skye terrier 'rejections,' and ought to be known as Glasgow or Paisley Skyes. [221]

glass eye pale blue eye.
> Glass eyes are preferred although the eyes may be of any color or combination of colors. [6, CATAHOULA LEOPARD DOG]

glatting (regional Eng.) hunting eels with dogs.

glaucoma disease of the optic disc, resulting in reduced vision or blindness.

Glaucoma I inherited eye disease resulting from increased pressure on the optic disc and causing blindness. (Mode of inheritance, recessive.)

Glaucoma II as GLAUCOMA I but mode of inheritance, dominant.

glaucous light blue coloration.
> In the glaucous or blue dogs a pearl, walleye or china eye is considered typical. [6, OLD ENGLISH SHEEPDOG]

gleet chronic nasal discharge.

Glen dim. IRISH GLEN OF IMAAL TERRIER.

Glendale NORTH NORTHUMBERLAND.

Glengarry Collie blue and white, sometimes with

tan, rough-coated, semi-PRICK EARED, wall-eyed SHEEPDOG from County Antrim.

Glenmore (US) AMERICAN FOXHOUND pack formed in 1930 to hunt a mountain and open rolling COUNTRY in Virginia.

Glen of Imaal Terrier IRISH GLEN OF IMAAL TERRIER.

Glenwerry Collie herding breed formerly to be found in County Antrim.

> A distinct, much valued species still existing in the glens of Antrim in the district around Conor. The breed originated from Scotland. . . . Their colour is blue and white, sometimes mixed with tan. The rough, profuse coat is weather resisting, the ears are mostly semi-erect, and the foremost characteristic is the inevitable wall-eye, which Nature has bestowed on every Glenwerry Collie. [295]

globoid cell leukodystrophy inherited lysomal storage disease resulting in neurological dysfunction. (Mode of inheritance, recessive.)

globular eye round and prominent eye.

glomerular lipidosis enlarged glomus cells which appear to have no clinical importance.

glomerulonephritis inherited kidney malfunction leading to excessive thirst, vomiting and urination. (Mode of inheritance, familial.)

glomerulonephropathy auto-recessive kidney disease characterized by weight loss, apathy, vomiting, polydipsia and polyuria in adult dogs of some breeds.

glomerus that part of the kidney in which the blood is filtered and cleansed.

glossopharyngeal defect BIRD TONGUE.

Glove Beagles (obs.) Elizabethan miniature BEAGLES.

> The favourite hound of the great Queen Elizabeth, and not the Beagle only, but also the Pocket variety of the breed, then called 'Glove', or 'Singing', Beagle. [123]

glucocerbrosidisosis inherited condition producing tremors and unco-ordinated, stumbling movement. (Mode of inheritance, familial.)

glucosuria RENAL TUBULAR DYSFUNCTION.

glycogenosis type I inherited glucose storage deficiency, producing hypoglycaemia.

glycogenosis type II inherited metabolic disorder, in which abnormal levels of glucose are stored in the body tissue.

glycogenosis type III neurological deterioration resulting from a starch and glucose deficiency.

glycogen storage disease any one of a group of metabolic disorders.

glycogen storage disease I GLYCOGENOSIS TYPE I.

glycogen storage disease II GLYCOGENOSIS TYPE II.

glycogen storage disease III GLYCOGENOSIS TYPE III.

glycoproteinosis neurological disease characterized by proliferation of Lafora bodies.

glycosaminoglycogen complex sugar associated with certain hereditary diseases.

Glyn Celyn BEAGLE pack formed in 1928 to hunt a COUNTRY in Powys.

GM1 abbr. GANGLIOSIDOSIS GM1.

GM2 abbr. GANGLIOSIDOSIS GM2.

gnar snarl. [159]

gnarl (obs.) snarl.

> Glo: Thus is the shepherd beaten from thy side,
> And wolves are gnarling who shall gnaw thee first
> [319d]

gnarler small HOUSE- or WATCH-DOG. [280]

go (as pref.):

go-by when a coursing GREYHOUND passes its opponent on a straight run and obtains a clear length's lead from a similar disadvantage.

go normal dog which early in life has been confirmed as suffering from CEA but in which symptoms have disappeared, making the animal appear and test as normal.

go sail (of a hunted stag) take to the water. [151c]

go to cry (of HOUNDS) respond to a summons from a FOLLOWER, or to the cry of other hounds.

go to ground 1. (of quarry) take refuge below ground.
2. (of a terrier) enter an underground refuge in order to eject the occupant.

go to the cherries go to the dog race-track.

go to the dogs 1. degenerate, spoil. 2. attend GREYHOUND races.

Goathland dating from 1650 the hunt lies in north Yorkshire and has a principally moorland COUNTRY with some woodland and pasture.

Gogerddan founded by Sir Richard Pryse, Bt. in 1600 the hunt lies in a Dyfed bank COUNTRY.

goggle eye GLOBULAR EYE.

going over (esp. of coat) losing peak condition.

Goitre inherited condition resulting in enlarged thyroid gland, sparse coat, nervousness and excitability; causes neonatal mortality. (Mode of inheritance, familial.)

Goldburn Irish BEAGLE pack formed in 1952 to hunt a COUNTRY in Counties Dublin, Meath and Wicklow.

Golden Jackal CANIS AUREUS.

Golden Retriever [AKC, FCI, KC] one of several explanations of the breed's origins involves a troup of Russian circus dogs bought by Lord Tweedmouth in about 1850. A more likely explanation is that Lord Tweedmouth acquired a yellow puppy from a litter of traditionally black FLAT-COATED RETRIEVERS and by mating this and its offspring with his strain of Tweedwater Spaniels and, possibly, other breeds, he produced a distinctive and reliable GUNDOG whose qualities made it very desirable to sportsmen.

The breed is intelligent, biddable and a willing worker. The broad skull and powerful MUZZLE are equally divided by a well-defined STOP. The dark brown eyes are set well apart, the ears set level with the eyes. The muscular neck is of good length, the shoulders WELL LAID, with a long scapula, and straight limbs. The chest is deep and WELL SPRUNG, the TOPLINE level and the body SHORT-COUPLED. The LOIN is strong, the rear limbs muscular with strong second thighs and well-bent STIFLES. Feet are cat-like.

The tail is carried level with the back. The gold or cream coat may be flat or wavy, forming good FEATHERING in the chest, BRISKET and the rear of the limbs. Height 51–61cm (20–24in).

Golden Retriever myopathy inherited muscle disease producing progressive stiff and awkward movement in young male GOLDEN RETRIEVERS. (Mode of inheritance, recessive.)

Golden's Bridge (US) AMERICAN FOXHOUND pack formed in 1924 to hunt a hill and dale COUNTRY in Connecticut.

Golden Valley pack founded in 1945 to replace Captain Nugent Hope's Hounds, the grass and moorland COUNTRY lies in Powys.

Goldie dim. (colloq.) GOLDEN RETRIEVER; gold COCKER SPANIEL.

gollies dim. GOLLIWOGS.

golliwogs (Brit. rhyming slang) the dogs; GREYHOUND racing. [142]

gonads sexual organs which produce the gametes, testes in the male, ovaries in the female.

gone AWAY (1).

gone away 1. of the pack when it has struck the scent and moved off at a fast pace. 2. hunting signal, issued by a cry or a call on a horn, that a fox has GONE AWAY(3). 3. of hunted quarry that has quit its place of refuge and is attempting to make its getaway.

gone to ground *see* GO TO GROUND.

Gontchaja Estonskaja Estonian hound: variety of the GONTCHAJA RUSSKAJA.

Gontchaja Russkaja Estonian Hound: developed principally as a HARRIER, the breed is typical of others used for that purpose. Slightly LONG CAST and solidly built, the short, dense coat carries a black SADDLE, white on chest, MASK and lower limbs, over drab yellow or dull tan GROUND.

Gontchaja Russkaja Pegaja Russian HOUND rather smaller than the FOXHOUND and with a close relationship to the eastern Scandinavian hound breeds. The breed is squarely built and CLEAN-HEADED with rounded, pendulous ears. The coat is short, usually TRICOLOUR with a MERLE SADDLE from which the breed derives its name. Height 56–66cm (22–26in).

good doer dog which thrives without special attention.

Goodpasture's syndrome auto-immune disease resulting in pulmonary bleeding; its existence in dogs is suspected.

Goodwood Hounds COWDRAY.

goori GOORIE.

goorie (NZ) a MONGREL; also a term of abuse.

goory GOORIE.

gooseberry eye light yellow or amber eye.

goose neck long, thin, arched neck. [*illus.*]

goose rump steeply sloping CROUP.

Faults – Roach back, swayback, goose rump. [6, AFGHAN HOUND]

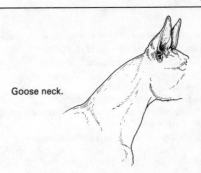

Goose neck.

goose-step gait characterized by exaggerated elevation of stiffly held forelegs.

Gordon Setter [AKC, FCI, KC] breed developed from the 17th century by successive Dukes of Gordon. A stylish, intelligent and bold dog built like a weight-carrying hunter, for speed as well as stamina.

The head is deep with a slightly rounded skull, well-defined STOP and long MUZZLE. The dark-brown eyes show a keen expression, the ears are thin and of medium size, low set and lying close to the head. The neck is long and arched, the forequarters well ANGULATED, with elbows close to the body and FLAT-BONED straight forelimbs. The body is of moderate length, the BRISKET deep with WELL-SPRUNG ribs; LOINS are slightly arched and the hindquarters broad and muscular with well-bent STIFLES. The well-FEATHERED tail is carried SCIMITAR fashion and tapers from a thick root. The black-and-tan coat is fine and flat forming feathering on ears, chest, brisket, tail and legs. Height 62–66cm (24½–26in); weight 25.5–29.5kg (56–65lb).

This variety of the modern setter had its name originally from the fact of being first introduced to the public from Gordon Castle, Fochabers, Banffshire, the Highland seat of the Dukes of Richmond and Gordon. For what length of time the family possessed the strain no one appears to know, but that it was not there in 1803, when Colonel Thornton visited the place, may be taken for granted, as that gallant sportsman, in his 'Northern Tour', makes no allusion whatever to any such dogs. [221]

Gorey and District Irish BEAGLE pack formed in 1957 to hunt a COUNTRY in counties Wexford, Wicklow and Carlow.

Gos d'Atura [FCI] a pastoral breed with origins in north-eastern Spain.

The head is comparatively large with a broad skull, deep STOP, and strong, bearded MUZZLE. The ears are high set, usually DROP but occasionally PRICKED. The body is long and muscular. The black, black-and-tan, tan, GRIZZLE, or black-POINTED tan coat may be long and wavy or short (Cerda). Height 46–51cm (18–20in); weight 18kg (39½lb).

Gos d'Atura Catala GOS D' ATURA.

Gos d'Atura Cerda GOS D' ATURA. [312]

Goshen (US) AMERICAN FOXHOUND pack formed in 1957 to hunt a wooded COUNTRY in Maryland.

Gosport and Fareham former 15in BEAGLE pack formed to hunt a COUNTRY in Hampshire.

gowler 1. (19th cent. obs. Brit. rhyming slang) a howler; a dog which howls.[142] 2. dog. [280]

Graa Dyrehund ELKHOUND.

Graafian follicle periodically produced sac attached to the lining of the ovary which ruptures during OESTRUS to release an ovum.

gracing contrac. (obs.) GREYHOUND racing.

grading system of assessment intended to quantify the value of animals intended for breeding. 2. FCI method by which judges indicate the quality of exhibits: 1st grade – typical and correct in conformation, a very good specimen; 2nd grade – a good dog without outstanding faults; 3rd grade – a dog with obvious faults, but still acceptable type and conformation; 0 grade – an untypical, bad-tempered or nervous dog, or one that has a disqualifying fault; KEP – cannot be judged, a dog shown in such poor condition, fat, thin, lame, untrimmed, etc., that its quality cannot be assessed by the judge.

grading up 1. (Aust.) process of breeding working SHEEP DOGS back to type after an OUTCROSS to another breed has been made. [204] 2. method of improving an inferior population by means of matings to superior stock.

gradualism theory that evolutionary processes do not take large or rapid steps resulting in rapid change, although it should not be concluded from this that evolutionary change is constant in either speed or direction.

Graduate KENNEL CLUB show class for dogs that have not won a CC but have achieved some level of success at previous shows.

Grafton hunted as the Duke of Grafton's Hounds from 1842 to 1861 when, until 1882, they were known as Lord Southampton's Hounds. The COUNTRY lies in Northamptonshire and Buckinghamshire.

Grahund 1. (obs. spelling) GREYHOUND. 2. medium-sized, powerfully built SPITZ, with long, straight, harsh, grey TOPCOAT over a soft grey UNDERCOAT; the powerful head is MASKED. Used for hunting and as a DOMESTIC GUARD. Height 51cm (20in). [312]

grain mite HARVEST MITE.

Grand Anglo-Français [FCI] group of three varieties of French Hound differentiated by coat colour: black and white, orange and white and TRICOLOUR. All three breeds are typically FOXHOUND in appearance, with short, smooth coats and elegant outlines. The tricolour is slightly smaller than the others but the average weight is about 30kg (66lb).

Grand Anglo-French Blanc et Noir [FCI] black-and-white variety of the GRAND ANGLO-FRANÇAIS.

Grand Anglo-French Blanc et Orange [FCI] orange-and-white variety of the GRAND ANGLO-FRANÇAIS.

Grand Anglo-French Tricolore [FCI] TRICOLOUR variety of the GRAND ANGLO-FRANÇAIS.

Grand Basset Griffon Vendéen [KC] short-legged version of the GRIFFON VENDEEN, which it resembles in every respect except that the height is 30–36cm (12–14in).

Grand Bleu de Gascogne [FCI, KC] one of the largest of the French PACKHOUNDS, principally used on deer and wild boar. The deep voice is a much prized characteristic of the breed.

A very strongly made, rather long-bodied dog with a large head, pronounced OCCIPUT, deep FLEWS and low-set, long, curled pendulous ears. The weather-resistant coat is smooth but not short and invariably black MOTTLED and patched over a white GROUND; POINTS (3) are tan. Height 60–70cm (23½–27½in).

Grand Gascon Saintongeois larger variety of the GASCON SAINTONGEOIS.

Grand Gascony GRAND BLEU DE GASCOGNE.

Grand Griffon Vendéen [FCI] one of the four varieties of GRIFFON VENDÉEN.

Grand Nite Champion title earned at American COONHOUND trials.

Grange Con and West Wicklow Irish BEAGLE pack formed in 1960 to hunt a COUNTRY in County Wicklow.

Granewilliam NORTH KILDARE.

granulocyte cell containing granules.

granulocytopathy inherited defective neutrophils resulting in recurrent infections. (Mode of inheritance, recessive.)

granuloma nodule of granulation tissue.

Grau BERGER DE LANGUEDOC.

graves residue from the manufacture of tallow candles, formerly made into cakes and fed to dogs. [159]

gravid pregnant; in whelp.

gray (obs.) BADGER.

Grayhound GREYHOUND, esp. from Scotland.

Great Anglo-French Tricolour GRIFFON VENDÉEN.

Great Anglo-French White and Black GRIFFON VENDÉEN.

Great Anglo-French White and Orange GRIFFON VENDÉEN.

Great Dane [AKC, KC] in spite of its name the breed's origins were in Germany where it was formerly used as a HOUND to hunt wild boar, an activity which required speed, stamina, strength and great courage.

The breed's sheer size is its most obvious characteristic. The long, proud head has a proportionately narrow skull and broad MUZZLE; the eyes are deep set and dark, except in HARLEQUINs in which WALL or odd eyes are permitted. The triangular, FOLDED and high-set, pendulous ears are CROPPED where the operation is permitted. The neck is long and arched, the shoulders well ANGULATED, and the FLAT-BONED forelegs straight. The BRISKET is very deep, with WELL-SPRUNG RIBS, arched TOPLINE and strong LOINS. The hindquarters are very muscular, with long SECOND THIGHS and well-turned STIFLES. The tail tapers from a thick root and is carried level with the back.

Movement is lithe and easy. The short, dense coat may be BRINDLE, fawn, blue-black or HARLEQUIN. Minimum height, bitches 71cm (28in), dogs 76cm (30in); minimum weight, bitches 46kg (101lb), dogs 54kg (119lb).

Great Danish Dog DALMATIAN. [406]

great dorsal muscle large, triangular muscle between the last dorsal vertebrae, the ribs and the head of the humerus.

Greater St John's Dog ancestor of the NEWFOUNDLAND, used by fishermen to retrieve objects from the sea.

Greater Swedish Elkhound JÄMTHUND. [312]

Greater Swiss Mountain Dog [AKC] short, black-and-tan Swiss draught dog. Height 58–71cm (23–28in); weight 60kg (132lb).

greater tubercle rounded, projecting tip of the humerus. [*illus.* SKELETON]

Great Gascony Blue GRAND BLEU DE GASCOGNE.

Great German Spitz DEUTSCHER SPITZ.

Great Pyrenees [AKC] PYRENEAN MOUNTAIN DOG.

Great Spitz DEUTSCHER SPITZ.

great trochanter upper part of femur, forming the hip-joint. [*illus.* SKELETON]

Great Vendéen Griffon GRIFFON VENDÉEN.

Great Water-Dog CANIS AQUATICUS MAJOR.

Grecian Greyhound type of GREYHOUND formerly to be found in Greece.
> Somewhat smaller than the English dog, and the hair is longer and slightly wavy, the tail also being clothed with a thin brush of hair. [338]

Grecian Mastiff EPIRUS MASTIFF.

Gredin former type of SPANIEL.
> In England this was a variety of Cocker. As represented by Buffon, it was probably a degenerate descendant of an English exportation. [239]

Greek Harehound HELLENIKOS ICHNILATIS.

Greek Herder SPARTIATE.

Greek Hound HELLENIKOS ICHNILATIS.

Greek Sheep Dog a determined and fearless, white-coated, Greek PASTORAL GUIDE, very similar to other white-coated pastoral breeds developed around the Mediterranean. Traditionally, the right ear is CROPPED allegedly to improve hearing. Height 63–71cm (24¾–28in); weight 34–45kg (75–99lb).

Greenland Dog GRØNLANDSHUND.
> Most of the Greenland Dogs are white; but some are spotted, and some black. They may rather be said to howl than bark. The Greenlanders sometimes eat their flesh. [51]

Green Spring Valley (US) American and English FOXHOUND pack formed in 1892 to hunt a rolling pasture and woodland COUNTRY in Maryland.

green yard ROUT.

Gre-hound (obs. spelling) GREYHOUND.

grew (obs.) GREYHOUND.

 grew-bitch (obs.) GREYHOUND bitch. [159]

 grew hound (obs.) GREYHOUND. [56]

grewnd (obs.) GREYHOUND. [*276]

grey BADGER.

Grey Collie syndrome CYCLIC HAEMATOPOIESIS.

Greydog 1. WEIMARANER. 2. mythical Kentucky dog said to appear in troubled times.

Grey Elk Dog ELKHOUND.

Grey Elkhound ELKHOUND.

Grey fox UROCYON CINEREOARGENTEUS.

Greyfriar's Bobby 'a little terrier dog' from Edinburgh, who, according to a story first published in the *Inverness Advertiser* in 1864, spent a lonely fourteen-year vigil at the graveside of his dead master, Auld Jock. Baroness Burdett-Couts later erected a statue to the dog's memory, which remains one of Edinburgh's attractions.

Legend claims that Greyfriar's Bobby was a SKYE TERRIER, and that his master, Auld Jock, was in the habit of taking his midday meal at John Trail's restaurant in Greyfriar's Place. One cold November day Bobby arrived at the restaurant alone and in a forlorn state; he returned in an even worse state the following day. Alarmed by the dog's obvious distress, Trail followed him when he left the restaurant and was led to Auld Jock's lifeless body. Auld Jock was buried in the Greyfriars Burial Ground, and the story has it that for the next fourteen years Bobby watched over the grave, taking leave only once a day, at the sound of Edinburgh's One O'Clock Gun, to eat at John Trail's restaurant.

In 1989, Forbes MacGregor, a Scottish journalist, discovered that no such person as Auld Jock had ever existed and that Bobby had belonged instead to a local policeman, John Gray. After John Gray's death on 8 February 1858, Bobby, who was by then about two years old, showed reluctance to leave his master's grave, and on several occasions thereafter he returned to the graveyard. However, he went to live in the home of a Mr Ritchie at 38 Candlemaker Row, although he also enoyed the hospitality of James Anderson, at 28 Candlemaker Row, and frequently visited John Trail to beg for scraps. He is said to have survived until his sixteenth year.

Greyhound [AKC, FCI, KC] archetypal British SIGHTHOUND used both for COURSING and as a racing dog. Muscular, powerful and symmetrical, it is a strongly built, but graceful, dog, renowned for its exceptional speed.

The head is long and lean with a flat skull, small ROSE EARS, strong jaws, and a long, arched and muscular neck. The forequarters are oblique and muscular, the forelegs long and straight with slightly sprung PASTERNS. The chest is deep, the flanks WELL TUCKED UP, and the LOIN powerful. The hindquarters are wide and muscular with WELL-LET-DOWN HOCKS; the long tail is set low. The fine, short coat may be black, white, red, blue, fawn, FALLOW or BRINDLE, with or without white markings. Height 68–76cm (26¾–30in).
> Various explanations have been offered of the etymology of the prefix 'grey', some contending that the colour is implied, others that it means Greek

(*Graius*), while a third party understand it to mean 'great'. . . . The greyhound . . . has the pure blue or iron grey colour very commonly; and although this shade is not admired by any lovers of the animal for its beauty, it will make its appearance occasionally. Hence it may fairly be considered a peculiarity of the breed, and this grey colour may, therefore, with a fair show of probability, have given the name to the greyhound. [338]

Greyhound Fox large and leggy type of fox with, especially during the winter months, a greyish coat. It is probably the old type of native fox, the smaller rufus form having been imported from France to satisfy the needs of southern hunting countries.

> Is the largest, and is chiefly found in the mountainous parts of England and Scotland. . . . His ears are long and erect, and his aspect wild. [51]

Grey Norwegian Elkhound ELKHOUND.

Greyhound polyarthritis inflammation of the joints found in young Greyhounds and some related breeds.

Greyhound racing sport in which Greyhounds pursue an artificial hare around a track.

greying series those genes which cause coat coloration to become progressively lighter with age.

Grey St. Luis Dog (obs. Ang.) GRIFFON NIVERNAIS.

griffon coarse-coated French breeds.

Griffon à Poil Dur Rough GRIFFON. [312]

Griffon à Poil Laineux Long-coated GRIFFON. [312]

Griffon Basset GRIFFON VENDEEN.

Griffon Belge [FCI] a larger version of the GRIFFON BRUXELLOIS.

Griffon Brabancon smooth-coated variety of the GRIFFON BRUXELLOIS.

Griffon Bruxellois [KC] a breed containing three varieties and which was originally developed as a vermin killer. Probably bred from the SMOUSHOND and other local TERRIER-like breeds and has since been somewhat miniaturized in two of its varieties.

A well-balanced, lively little dog with a square outline. The head is relatively large, with a wide, rounded skull, deep STOP, short MUZZLE and prominent chin. The large, round eyes are very dark, the small ears semi-erect and traditionally CROPPED. The mouth is slightly UNDERSHOT. The neck is of medium length and the shoulders WELL LAID. The chest is wide and deep, the forelimbs straight; the short body has WELL SPRUNG RIBS, a short LOIN and level TOPLINE. The hindquarters are well muscled with low HOCKS. The tail is customarily DOCKED. The coat is rough in the Bruxellois and Belge, smooth in the Brabancon, and may be MASKED red, black or black and tan. Weight 2.7–4.5kg (6–10lb).

Griffon Bleu de Gascogne [FCI] superlative and aristocratic French pack HOUND used extensively for hunting rabbit but originally for wolves.

The ARISTOCRATIC head is long and strong with wrinkled cheeks and a MUZZLE with curved BRIDGE. The deep chestnut eyes have thick lashes and exposed HAW. The ears are very low set, long, thin and curled. The CRESTED and DEWLAPped neck runs to massive forequarters with well-muscled forelimbs. The chest

is long, wide and deep, the LOIN flat and the back rather long. Hindquarters should be muscular with low HOCKS and moderate ANGULATION. The SICKLE TAIL is thick and long. The black-and-white FLECKED coat is profuse, thick and of medium length; the skin is black on lips and scrotum and black and white over the body. Height 58–70cm (23–27½in).

Griffon d'Arrêt à Poil Dur [FCI] a tough, multipurpose French GUNDOG. Originally known as the Korthals Griffon, the breed was developed from about 1874 by Eduard K. Korthals in Holland, and later in Germany, from breeds imported from France. The breed made its debut in the British show ring at a KC show in 1888, and was recognized by the AKC in 1887. The breed's ability to point and retrieve, its adaptability to any game, and especially its ability to work in water, are qualities of which its supporters are proud.

The breed has a large, strong head, long MUZZLE, low-set, pendulous ears, long neck and deep body with strong CRUPPER, long forequarters, and WELL-ANGULATED hindquarters. The tail is traditionally DOCKED. The coarse coat, which may be orange or chestnut, with white or steel-grey markings, is hard and coarse. Height 51–61cm (20–24in).

Griffon d'Arrêt à Poil Laineux [FCI] a woolly-coated, slightly smaller version of the GRIFFON D'ARRÊT À POIL DUR, developed by Emmanual Boulet during the 1870s.

The head and MUZZLE are broad and well FURNISHED, the ears pendulous, the neck rather long, and the chest broad and deep; the slightly arched LOINS are powerful; the tail is long and straight. The dull, straight coat is brown, with or without white markings, and may be slightly silky. Height 50–60cm (19½–23½in).

Griffon de Bresses said to be an ancestor of the Otterhound.

> the oldest hound in Europe, for it can be traced back to the ninth century . . . a rough-coated hound. [368]

Griffon d'Ecurie Stable Griffon.

Griffon Fauve de Bretagne [FCI] a robust French pack HOUND originally used on wolf but now re-employed on smaller game.

The breed has a comparatively small head with FOLDED pendulous ears, a strong neck, well-boned forelimbs, and a capacious chest with barrelled ribs carried well back to a strong LOIN. The hindquarters are muscular and the long tail high set. The rough coat is always WHEATEN or shades of red. Height 50–55cm (19½–21¼in); weight 27kg (39½lb).

Griffon Korthals GRIFFON D'ARRÊT À POIL DUR.

Griffon Nivernais [FCI] a rough-coated, long-legged HOUND which has been known in France since at least the 13th century, when the breed was known as Chien Gris de St Louis in recognition of Louis IX's interest in the breed.

The breed is rugged, almost to the point of being unrefined, a characteristic which is accentuated by the breed's rough coat and bearded head. The head is lean and rather long, the eyes dark and the FOLDED, pendulous ears rather short. The neck is light and lean, the shoulders close to the body and the forelimbs strong and straight with short PASTERNS. The body is deep in BRISKET, with a long back, and slightly arched over the LOIN. The SICKLE TAIL is WELL SET ON and well FURNISHED. The coat is long, harsh and shaggy and for preference WOLF-grey or blue-grey with tan PATTERN markings. Height 53–59cm (20¾–23¼in).

Griffon Vendéen   French SCENTHOUND breed which is divided into four varieties: the Grand, the Grand Basset, the Briquet and the Petit Basset. During the last 500 years the four varieties have arisen in response to the demands made by the game in which each was regarded as a specialist: wolf and boar for the Grand, and smaller game (especially hare) for the Basset, Briquet and Petit varieties.

All four varieties are strong and active working hounds with good voices; they are extrovert, independent yet eager to please. The skull is oval, the STOP well defined and the MUZZLE fairly short. The eyes are large and dark, the FOLDED, pendulous ears narrow and fine. The neck is long and supple, the shoulders clean and well laid, the back strong and level and the chest deep with well rounded ribs. The STERN is carried SABRE fashion. The untrimmed coat is rough, with a thick undercoat, and white with lemon, orange, TRICOLOUR or GRIZZLE patches. Height: Grand, 69cm (27in); Briquet, 56cm (22in); Grand Basset, 38–43cm (15–17in); Petit Basset, 34–38cm (13½–15in).

Grifhoundes   GREYHOUND. [159]

grin   a wrinkling of the lips in an expression that resembles the human grin.

grindle-tail   a TRUNDLE-TAIL dog. [159]

grizzle   coat colour produced by a mixture of hairs, each of which is BANDED with a light root, dark midsection and darker tip; agouti.

Groenendael   black variety of the BELGIAN SHEEP DOG.

Grønlandshund   [FCI] a typical northern SPITZ-type draught dog, used also for hunting. Height 64cm (24in); weight 40kg (88lb).

groomer   one who trims dogs.

Grosser Münsterländer   [FCI] LARGE MÜNSTERLÄNDER.

Grosser Münsterländer Vorstehhund   LARGE MÜNSTERLÄNDER.

Grosser Schweizer Sennenhund   Greater Swiss Mountain Dog. [312]

ground   predominant coat colour.

ground covering   of movement which carries the dog over the ground in an economical and efficient manner; covering ground.

ground game   non-flying game.

ground itch   prurient skin disorder associated with HOOKWORM infection.

group   bureaucratic subdivision of the domestic dog, each group containing recognized breeds that are considered to have something in common. Groups vary from kennel club to kennel club.

group system   judging at shows based on GROUPS.

Grove, The   TIPPERARY.

Grove and Rufford   formed in 1952 by the amalgamation of the Grove, which dates from 1948, and the Rufford, dating from 1949, the COUNTRY lies in Nottinghamshire, Derbyshire and Yorkshire.

growth hormone   secretion of the pituitary gland which stimulates growth.

growth hormone responsive dermatosis   alopecia and increased skin pigmentation.

growth rate   measure of the speed at which a foetus or a puppy increases in size.

gruntle   MUZZLE. [159]

GSD   abbr. GERMAN SHEPHERD DOG (ALSATIAN).

G series   abbr. GREYING SERIES.

GSP   abbr. GERMAN SHORT-HAIRED POINTER.

guard   1. GUARD DOG.   2. protect; command to do so.

guard dog   dog used to protect people, property or livestock.

guard hair   outer layer of coarse hairs.

> The undercoat with a longer guard hair growing through it. [6, AMERICAN ESKIMO DOG]

guide dog   dog trained to guide blind people.

Guildford and Shere   former BEAGLE pack formed to hunt a COUNTRY in Surrey.

Guillain-Barre syndrome   auto-immune-related disease of the peripheral nervous system rare in dogs.

gun   one of a shooting party who carries a gun.

gun-barrel front   having straight, vertical and parallel forelimbs.

gundog   1. specimen of a breed developed to work with shooters.   2. [KC] one of the GROUPS comparable to AKC Sporting.

gundog trial   organized competitive test of GUNDOG abilities.

gun shy   of a GUNDOG that will not work for fear of the noise made by guns.

> Gun-shyness is often supposed to be hereditary; but it is not so. [225]
> And a gun-shy dog being useless in the field is best destroyed, or if good-looking, kept for show purposes. [320]

Gutschen Hundle   BOTTOLO. [359]

gutter hunter   homeless dog which lives principally by scavenging.

> There is a class of dogs, not inaptly termed 'gutter hunters', that are constantly prowling and poking their noses into all sorts of unsavoury and insanitary places. These are poor wretches that are not properly fed, and are practically ownerless animals; they belong to people who ought not to have a dog. [106]

gynander   GYNANDROMORPH.

gynandromorph   individual with rudimentary male and female sex organs.

H

H standard gene symbol for hairlessness.

habituation learning 1. progressive adaptation to a stimulus. This may form part of a planned programme or it may happen spontaneously, as when a dog investigates the bush under which it found a rabbit yesterday. 2. Erasure of a CONDITIONED REFLEX by means of exposure to a CONDITIONED STIMULUS; the modification of unacceptable behaviour patterns by means of reward or praise.

hackles muscles over the WITHERS which enable an angry or fearful dog to increase its apparent size and look more formidable by erecting hair in that area.

hackney action exaggerated trot in which both front and rear limbs are lifted unusually high, sometimes adopted to prevent over-reaching. (der. the characteristic movement of hackney carriage horses.)

> Any tendency to throw feet sideways, or high stepping 'hackney' action highly undesirable. [203; PHARAOH HOUND]
> A high stepping 'hackney' action is a definite fault. [6; PHARAOH HOUND]

hackneyed illiterate reference to hackney action.

> Co-ordinated to permit a true hackneyed action. [203; MINIATURE PINSCHER]
> Lifting feet high when in motion, with no hint of hackneyed action or plaiting. [203; AFFENPINSCHER, interim BREED STANDARD]

hackney gait HACKNEY ACTION.

haemangiosarcoma malignant tumour which occurs in the spleen, liver, skin, heart and muscle, and causes severe bleeding.

Haemaphysalis leachii leachi yellow dog tick (East Africa). Small African species of tick, also found in Australia and Western Asia, which transmits canine babesiosis.

Haemaphysalis punctata tick common to Europe and North America, attacking all domestic animals.

haemarthrosis accumulation of blood within a joint cavity.

haematology study of blood diseases.

haematoma subcutaneous clotted blood.

haematopoiesis CYCLIC HAEMATOPOIESIS.

Haemobartonella canis nonpathogenic parasitic micro-organisms.

haemobartonellosis infection with HAEMOBARTONELLA CANIS.

haemolytic anaemia inherited dysfunction of the immune system leading to death. (Mode of inheritance, recessive.)

haemolytic PK anaemia inherited anaemia caused by immune response disorder, often associated with jaundice and frequently fatal. (Mode of inheritance, recessive.)

haemophilia condition in which the blood fails to congeal.

haemophilia A inherited disease caused by clotting factor VIII-C deficiency. (Mode of inheritance, sex-linked, recessive.)

haemophilia B inherited disease caused by clotting factor IX deficiency. (Mode of inheritance, sex-linked, recessive.)

haemophilia C inherited disease caused by clotting factor XI deficiency. (Mode of inheritance, autosomal, dominant.)

Haemophilus haemoglobinophilus bacteria found in infantile genitalia; effect uncertain.

haemorrhagic pancreatitis progressive abdominal pain caused by internal bleeding. *See also* ACUTE HAEMORRHAGIC PANCREATITIS.

haemostasis cessation of bleeding.

hairless dogs *See under* HAIRLESSNESS.

hairlessness inherited total absence of hair other than on legs and feet. Hairlessness may arise as a mutation in any breed and at any time. In a few breeds – in Africa, China, Turkey, Peru, Mexico and the United States – hairless specimens have been retained as the basis for breeds: PERUVIAN INCA ORCHID, INCA HAIRLESS DOG, CHINESE CRESTED DOG, XOLOITZCUINTLI, and XOLOITZCUINTLI TOY. The condition H appears to be invariably dominant with HH being a lethal condition resulting in embryonic death. There is also evidence that hairlessness is associated with dental irregularities. (Mode of inheritance, recessive.)

> Hairless dogs have imperfect teeth. [111]

Halden Hound HALDENSTÖVARE.

Haldenstövare [FCI] Norwegian SCENTHOUND developed from several imported HOUND breeds, and named after the town in which it originated. It was recognized by the FCI in the mid-1950s. Like other Scandinavian hounds, which must work in weather not conducive to good scent, the breed has an exceptional nose.

The overall appearance is that of a lightly built FOXHOUND. The skull is slightly DOMED and shows some OCCIPUT; the STOP is moderate, the MUZZLE straight and not heavily FLEWED. The pendulous ears reach the mid-point of the muzzle when extended; the eyes are dark, the neck CLEAN, long and well arched. Forequarters are long and sloping, with straight, strongly boned forelegs. The chest is deep, with WELL-SPRUNG ribs, a straight TOPLINE and a rounded CROUP. Hindquarters are muscular with well-bent HOCKS. The TRICOLOUR coat is smooth, short and very dense. Height 51–64cm (20–25in); weight 20–27kg (44–59½lb).

Haldon DART VALE AND HALDON.

Half-and-half formerly a CROSS between a TERRIER and a BULLDOG, used for dog-fighting.

Halifax Blue and Tan Terrier (obs.) YORKSHIRE TERRIER.

hallmark   those characteristics which are specific to particular breeds.

halloo   verbal signal, generally used to attract attention during a hunt. Becomes specific in meaning only when used in conjunction with another word, e.g. Halloo away! meaning that the quarry is departing.
> Never halloo unless you have a good reason for doing so. [266b]

Hall's Heelers   former breed of Australian HERDER. Hall crossed them (blue merle, smooth-haired Collies) with the Dingo . . . and these dogs became famous as 'Hall's Heelers'. [160]

halo   area of dark pigmentation around the eyes.
> Dark, round with black eye rims, surrounded by dark haloes, consisting of well pigmented skin. [203; BICHON FRISE]

Halti   proprietary head-collar, similar in design to a horse's head-collar, to which a lead can be attached. Originally developed to discourage dogs from pulling.

ham   well-developed muscles above the STIFLE-joint.
> Hocks well let down and the hams densely coated with a thick, long jacket. [203, former OLD ENGLISH SHEEPDOG]

Hambledon   pack dating from the 18th century. The COUNTRY lies principally in Hampshire.

hambling   surgical removal of the toes to prevent dogs from harassing game.

Hamilton   (Can.) ENGLISH FOXHOUND pack formed in 1958 to hunt an arable COUNTRY in Ontario.

Hamilton Hound   HAMILTONSTÖVARE.

Hamiltonstövare   [FCI, KC] created at the end of the 19th century by Count A.P. Hamilton (founder of the Swedish KENNEL CLUB). Imported FOXHOUNDS were crossed with German SCENTHOUNDS to produce a dog able to trail wounded quarry even in the worst scenting conditions.

An upstanding, well-proportioned and even-tempered hound with a rather long rectangular head, broad skull, well-defined STOP and fairly long MUZZLE. The eyes are dark brown, the pendulous ears high set. The neck is long and powerful, the forequarters muscular and WELL LAID with straight forelimbs. The chest is deep with moderately sprung ribs; the TUCK-UP is slight and the TOPLINE straight. Hindquarters are broad, powerful and WELL-ANGULATED. The tail is high set and may be held horizontally or with a slight upward SABRE curve. The close, weather-resistant DOUBLE COAT is tan, PATTERNed black and brown, with white on the chest. Height 46–60cm (18–23½in).

hamling   HAMBLING. [159]

Hampshire 'H.H.'   pack dating from 1745 when Mr Evelyn hunted the Hampshire COUNTRY which is now heavily wooded.

hanch   (regional Eng.) a sudden bite, a snap.

Hand Dog   dog trained to respond to hand signals.

handler   one who is in charge of a dog, and to whom the dog looks for instruction, esp. during competition.

hand-strip   remove dead coat, either with finger and thumb or with a stripping knife. Commonly used as a syn. for PLUCK.

handy   suitable for its purpose.
> You wish me to explain what I mean by hounds being handy. It respects their readiness to do whatever is required of them. [47]

Hanger, Colonel George   author of *Colonel George Hanger to All Sportsmen, and particularly to Farmers and Gamekeepers* (1814).

hanging ear   pendulous ear.

Hanover Hound   HANNOVERSCHER SCHWEISSHUND.

Hanoverian Hound   HANNOVERSCHER SCHWEISSHUND.

Hannoverscher Schweisshund   [FCI] HOUND used for following the blood trail left by wounded game and developed for this purpose during the 19th century.

The head is large, the capacious chest rounded, and the heavy body LOW ON THE LEG. The coat is red, streaked with black. Height 51–61cm (20–24in); weight 38–45kg (83½–99lb).

Hapa Dog   former smooth-coated variety of PEKINGESE.
> . . . is a variety of the Pekinese Spaniel, to which it is similar in general shape, the great difference being that the Hapa is a smooth-coated dog. [225]

haploid   number of paired cells in a chromosome: 38 in dogs.

Harada's disease   inherited inflammation of the eyes and skin. (Mode of inheritance, uncertain.)

harbour   1. the place in which a deer habitually rests. [151c]

hard   hard-bitten; strong.
> She's the hardest from Bedale to Bicester,
> In holt or in earth or in drain. [85b]

hard-bitten   impervious to pain; of a dog, usually a TERRIER or fighting dog, which accepts punishment without flinching and without being deterred from its purpose.
> Describing a plucky dog who will accept punishment without flinching. [320]
> A fine wiry-haired, 'hard-bitten' lot they are, with a good deal of eyebrow, and a grizzled moustache, and a wear-and-tear look about them. [186]

hard driving   generating strong propulsion from the hindquarters.

hard-driving action   movement which is exaggeratedly powerful and uneconomical.

hard-eyed   strong-eyed.

hard mouth   (in a GUNDOG) unwelcome propensity to damage retrieved game, or even dummy retrieve article.
> He is inclined to be hard-mouthed, i.e. he may bite and injure the game he ought to retrieve tenderly and without ruffling a feather. [221]

harde   (obs.) cord, rope or leather strap used to join two, three or four COUPLES(2) of HOUNDS.

Harderian gland   gland which lies between the THIRD EYELID and the cornea.

hardled   of COUPLED HOUNDs, joined with a HARDE.

hardpad   former name for distemper. (der. one of the symptoms of distemper: hardening of the foot pads.)

hard palate   roof of the mouth.

Hardy-Weinberg Law   law propounded by G. H. Hardy and W. Weinberg which states that in a large and stable population the frequency with which genes occur will not change from generation to generation.

hare   1. customary quarry of BEAGLES, HARRIERS and GREYHOUNDS; formerly the principal quarry for HOUNDS.

> I speak how the hare shall be hunted; it is to with that the hare is king of all venery; for all blowing, and the fair terms of hunting, come of the seeking and the finding of her, for certain it is a marvellous beast. [125]

2. coat coloration consisting of a mixture of lighter and darker hairs.

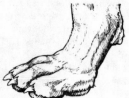

Hare foot.

hare feet   long, narrow feet, especially with elongated middle toes. [*illus.*]

> American hounds have a tall, light elegance, with rather light bone and 'hares feet' that again bring the Kerry Beagles to mind. [329]
> Hare feet are a fault. [6, LEONBERGER]

hare-finder   dog employed to find quarry taking refuge above ground.

hare hound   HOUND used to hunt hares.

harelike   HARE FEET.

> Feet – Thin and elongated (harelike). [6, PAPILLON]

harelip   CLEFT LIP.

hare-pie   of coat with patches of hare coloration on a white GROUND; dog with such coloration.

> Hare-pies and badger pies or blue pies are unfashionable, although frequently of surpassing beauty and excellence. [186]

Hare Stakes   show class confined to HOUNDS used to hunt hare.

Hare Indian Dog   SPITZ-like breed from the area around the Mackenzie River and Great Bear Lake in America, and used to hunt moose and reindeer.

> The dogs of the Hare Indians differ but very slightly from the Prairie Wolf, or Coyote. [123]
> This variety of dog is cultivated at present, so far as I know, only by the Hare Indians, and other tribes that frequent the borders of the Great Bear Lake and the banks of the Mackenzie. It is used by them solely in the chase, being too small to be useful as a beast of burthen or draught. The Hare Indian dog has a mild countenance, with, at times, an expression of demureness. It has a small head, slender muzzle; erect, thickish ears; somewhat oblique eyes; rather slender legs, and a broad hairy foot with a bushy tail, which it usually carries curled over its right hip. [298]

Hare Indians' Dog   HARE INDIAN DOG.

Harford   ELKRIDGE-HARFORD.

Hark   command to HOUNDS to pay attention to a speaking hound.

Hark forrard   huntsman's command to HOUNDS to direct them forward.

Hark in   encouragement to HOUNDS to join another which has found the scent.

harle   LEASH of GREYHOUNDS. [159]

Harlekinspinscher   variation of the PINSCHER with coat colour similar to that of a HARLEQUIN GREAT DANE.

harlequin   coat coloration usually consisting of small, unevenly shaped patches of black or blue on a lighter, usually white, GROUND.

> Harlequin; pure white underground with preferably all black patches or all blue patches, having appearance of being torn. [203, GREAT DANE]

harlequin Collie   COLLIE with harlequin colouring.

> a very well-marked variety of Collie is the Marled, or Marbled, sometimes incorrectly called the Tortoiseshell, and from the bizarre combination of colours it also gets the name of Harlequin. [123]

harlequin Great Dane   not a separate variety of the GREAT DANE but an attractive and very distinctive colour variation of the breed, characterized by splashes of black or blue against a white GROUND.

> I certainly think that no equipage can have arrived at its acme of grandeur until a couple of Harlequin Danes precede the pomp. [127]

harlequin merle   HARLEQUIN.

Harlequin Pinscher   HARLEKINPINSCHER.

harlou   (Fr.) hunting cry, associated with hunting wolves.

harness   1. arrangement of straps round a dog's chest and back, used as an alternative to a collar.   2. arrangement of straps used to attach a SLED-DOG to the tugline and then the gangline to enable it to pull.

harr   snarl angrily. [159]

Harrier   British packhound resembling a small FOX-HOUND, principally used by mounted followers for hunting hare, but occasionally used also for fox. Height 48–56cm (18¾–22in); weight 22–27kg (48½-59½lb).

> The true harrier is a dwarf southern hound, with a very slight infusion of the greyhound in him. [338]
> Occupies an intermediate station between the beagle and the fox-hound. [406]
> The harrier chases a hare in small circles, so that members can pull one rein and still maintain the usual grip on the saddle. [379]

Harrier of Bengal   DALMATIAN. [51]

hart   male deer, esp. red, aged five years or more.

hart of grease   an eight-year-old stag. [37a]

Harts Run   (US) AMERICAN FOXHOUND pack formed in 1940 to hunt a rolling woodland and open pasture COUNTRY in Pennsylvania.

harvest mites   parasitic larvae of THROMBICULIDAE, which normally infect rodents but can irritate other species and cause small lesions, especially on exposed skin.

Hatzrüde   archetypal form of German MASTIFF.

> Germany has several varieties of big dogs, such as the Hatzrüde, Saufanger, Ulmer Dogge and Rottweiler Metzgerhund. [225]

haulding of a dog driving sheep away from the handler. [103a]

haunch muscular development associated with the hips; buttocks.

haunch bones hip bones, especially the two ILIAC CRESTS. The haunch bones are especially prominent in some SIGHTHOUND breeds.

Haut-Poitou POITEVIN.

Havana Silk Dog BICHON HAVANAIS.

Havana Spaniel BICHON HAVANAIS.
> Has a softer coat [than the Manilla Spaniel] and in colour it may as often be brown as white. [225]

Havanese BICHON HAVANAIS.

Haw.

haw 1. properly used to refer only to the THIRD EYE-LID but more commonly to the pink inside surface of the lower eyelid. [*illus.*]
> Soft expression and not showing much haw. [203, SUSSEX SPANIEL]
> Eyes . . . showing a prominent haw. [6, BASSET HOUND]

2. order for a SLED-DOG team to turn left.

haw's syndrome protrusion of the NICTITATING MEMBRANE.

Hawaiian Poi Dog Ilio: *CANIS PACIFICUS.*

Hawker, Lt.-Col. Peter author of *Instructions to Young Sportsmen* (1816).

Hawkestone former OTTERHOUND pack founded by Sir Rowland Hill in 1870 to hunt the rivers Penk, Teme, Clun, Oni, Corve, Ledwyche, Rea, Monnow, Dore, Wye, Irfon, Ithon, Usk, Dee, Honddu, Towy, Cothi, Bran, Tivy, Cych, Clwyd, Elway, Tern, Roden, Lug and Ellesmere.

hawk eye yellow or amber eye.

hay shade of tan, especially in CHESAPEAKE BAY RETRIEVERS.

Haydon pack dating from prior to 1845. The Northumberland moorland COUNTRY is heavily wooded in some parts. During the late 1800s the hunt was known as the Roman Wall Hounds, then the Hexhamshire and Haydon, becoming the Haydon in 1899.

hazel (esp. of eyes) yellowish brown.

HC Highly Commended: sixth phase.

HDA HYPERTROPHIC OSTEOPATHY.

head 1. a deer's antlers. [151c]

2. the speed at which HOUNDs hunt.
> A great excellence in a pack of hounds, is the head they carry; and that pack may be said to go the fastest that can run ten miles the soonest. [47]

3. the front runners in a pack. [344c]

head, types of BOXY, CLEAN, COFFIN, CONICAL, EGG-SHAPED, OTTER, PIP, TRIANGULAR, TWO-ANGLED, VULPINE, WEDGE-SHAPED.

head up descriptive of HOUNDs lifting their heads from the scent.

headed of a hunted quarry which is turned from its intended path by interference from other than HOUNDS.
> Here, in heavy fog and rain, the fox was apparently lost, having been headed by the furze-cutters on the moor. [318]

heading and tailing process of drafting the fastest and slowest HOUNDs in a pack in order to achieve uniformity of pace among the remaining hounds.
> The object of the members of the hunt has been to keep down the pace of the pack, rather than increase it, and they oftener draft at the head than the tail. [344a]

Heading Hound MOLOSSUS. [186]

Headley Hunt ROCKY FORK–HEADLEY.

heam (obs.) membrane surrounding a newly born puppy. [159]

Hearing Dog dog trained to assist deaf people.

heartbeat rhythmic movement of the heart muscles, which varies from breed to breed but normally within the range of 70 to 100 per minute.

heart room deep and capacious chest.
> Chest deep and well developed with plenty of heart and lung room. [203, former ENGLISH SPRINGER SPANIEL]

heartworm *DIROFILARIA IMMITIS.*

heat OESTRUS.

heavy dogs of Sussex extinct progenitors of the SUS-SEX SPANIEL.

Heavy Finder SOUTHERN HOUND.
> Those who first designed the cross evidently intended and desired to combine the power of the two differ-ent races employed for destroying the fox – the Greyhound and the Heavy Finder, or Southern Hound. [186]

he-dog male dog.
> He fought with the he-dogs, and winked at the she-dogs,
> A thing that had never been 'heard' of before. [64]

hee (regional Eng.) call to summon a dog.

heel 1. 'hunt heel': hunt against the direction in which the quarry has travelled. 2. walk closely on the left side of the handler; command to a dog to do so.
> The spaniel, which so far has been kept rigidly to heel, seizes the opportunity to break away. [140]

3. (rarely) HOCK or TARSUS joint.

heel free walk at heel without being on a lead.

heel work (esp. of Obedience dogs) exercise involv-ing practice at walking to heel.

Heeler dog used for driving cattle which it per-suades to move by nipping at their heels. *See* LAN-CASHIRE HEELER, ORMSKIRK HEELER, AUSTRALIAN HEELER and WELSH CORGI.

heeling [AKC] walking at the heel of the handler.

height the distance between the highest point of the withers and ground level, when the dog is standing.

Heirer (obs.) HARRIER.
> The name 'Heirers' or Harriers is known to have
> been given to Hounds used for hare-hunting in the
> time of Henry V, but they were also used for hunt-
> ing deer. [186]

Hellenic Harehound HELLENIKOS ICHNILATIS.

Hellenic Hound HELLENIKOS ICHNILATIS.

Hellenikos Ichnilatis [FCI] SCENTHOUND indigenous
to Greece, principally used to hunt hare; originally
used as a packhound but now principally hunted as
part of a BRACE or team.
> The head is long, the skull rather narrow with a
slight OCCIPUT; eyes are deep set and of medium size;
the high-set ears are of medium length, flat, and
rounded at the tips. The neck is powerful, muscular
and without DEWLAP. The outline is rectangular, the
WITHERS are prominent, the LOINS slightly arched,
short and muscular. The high-set tail reaches the
HOCK. The black-and-tan coat is dense. Height
46–55cm (18–21¼in); weight 17–20kg (37½–44lb).

Hell Hound HOUNDS OF HELL.

helminth any parasitic worm.

helminthagogue vermifuge, something which expels
parasitic worms.

hemeralopia inherited inability to see in bright light.
(Mode of inheritance, recessive.)

hemivertebrae inherited asymmetrical vertebrae
development, not uncommon in some BRACHY-
CEPHALIC breeds. (Mode of inheritance, complex and
unclear.)

Henham former HARRIER pack formed in 1881 to
hunt a COUNTRY in Suffolk.

hepatatic encephalopathy inherited degenerative
brain disease resulting in excitability, tremor, com-
pulsive movement, blindness and death. (Mode of
inheritance, uncertain.)

hepatitis inflammation of the liver caused by infection or toxin. In some forms, it may be inherited.
(Mode of inheritance, sex-linked.)

hepatomegaly enlargement of the liver.

Hepatozoon canis protozoan parasite of the leucocyte and bone marrow causing debility, fever, weight
loss and hind limb paralysis.

herder dog used to control and direct the movement
of farm animals.

herding dog HERDER.

hereditary of that which is genetically transmitted
from one generation to the next.

hereditary collagen dysplasia EHLERS-DANLOS
SYNDROME.

hereditary defect defect transmitted from parent to
offspring.

hereditary myelopathy inherited muscular weakness, incontinence. (Mode of inheritance, recessive.)

hereditary sensory neuropathy inherited condition
in which there is reduced sensitivity to pain of the
feet and lower limbs leading to self-mutilation.

hereditary thrombasthenia blood abnormality arising from a platelet defect which produces anaemia.
(Mode of inheritance, dominant.)

hereditability measure of the extent to which a characteristic is genetically inherited.

heredity the transmission of characteristics from
one generation to another.

hermaphrodite animal who has the reproductive
organs of both sexes.

hermit (regional Eng.) an unruly creature, esp. an
unruly dog. [140]

hernia projection of an organ through the protective muscular encasement.

herring gut narrow, slab-sided chest.

Hertfordshire pack established in 1775 by the
Marchioness of Salisbury as the Hatfield
Hunt,;hounds were passed to the Herts. Hunt Club
in 1819 and for some time thereafter carried the name
of successive masters: Sir Thomas Sebright
(1828–1835); Mr Delme Radcliffe (1835–1839); Lord
Dacre 1839–1866); and Mr Gerard Leigh
(1866–1875). The varied COUNTRY has large areas of
woodland and plough.

Hertha Pointer short, yellow-coated Danish GUN-
DOG. Height 58–65cm (23–25½in); weight 22–27kg
(48½–59½lb).

Heterochromia iridis WALL EYE.

heterogametic sex that sex which produces both X
and Y chromosomes (the male in dogs).

heterophyte intestinal fluke of little pathogenic significance.

heterosis HYBRID VIGOUR.

heterotic expression exceptional vigour of the heterozygote compared with the homozygote.

heterozygosity measure of the proportion of heterozygous alleles carried by a group of animals.

heterozygote zygote in which the two alleles are dissimilar.

heterozygous of HETEROZYGOTE.

heterozygous advantage superiority of the heterozygote to homozygote.

heu gaze cry given when a hunted otter is sighted.

Hexhamshire and Haydon HAYDON.

Heythrop hunt dating from 1835 and occupying a
COUNTRY in Oxfordshire and Gloucestershire.
Former huntsmen include Stephen Goodall (1869–
1875).

hie on instruction to a GUNDOG to advance in the
direction indicated by a wave of the hand.
> That 'On' (the short word for 'hie-on'), or the fore-
> ward under-hand swing of the right hand, signifies
> that he is to advance in a forward direction (the
> direction in which you are waving). [184]

high in hock of dog with a long HOCK, which tends
to produce an exaggerated degree of hind-limb
ANGULATION.

high in station of dog with forelegs which are appreciably greater in length than the distance from elbow
to WITHERS.

high in wither of dog with a TOPLINE which falls
appreciably from the WITHERS.

Highland Collie (obs.) BEARDED COLLIE.
> In Scotland there is an old-fashioned sheep dog of

the same sort called the 'Highland or Bearded Collie'. [221]

An attempt made by writers to circumscribe the national character of this dog [the Scotch Collie] by calling him the Highland Collie, as though he were peculiar to the North of Scotland. [123]

Then there is the Scottish bearded, or Highland Collie, less popular still with the flock-master, a hardy looking dog in outward style, but soft in temperament, and many of them make better cattle than sheep dogs. [225]

Highland Greyhound   a former localized type of GREYHOUND.

Is a larger, stronger, and fiercer dog [than the Scotch Greyhound], and may be readily distinguished from the Lowland Scotch greyhound by its pendulous, and, generally, darker ears, and by the length of hair which almost covers the face. [406]

Highland Heeler   former type of smooth-coated Scottish COLLIE.

There is one strain of smooth Collie which calls for particular attention, and that is the variety called sometimes the Welsh Collie, and at others the Highland heeler. In colour this dog is a peculiar sort of greyish hue, to which the terms 'harlequin', 'plum-pudding', 'tortoiseshell', are all applied. He is usually found with one eye [sometimes both] 'wall-eyed', or 'China-eyed'. [320a]

Highland Terrier   former generic name applied to TERRIERS of Scottish origin.

After being called a Skye terrier, he became known as the Scotch terrier, the Scots terrier, and the Highland terrier; then others dubbed him the Cairn terrier and the Die Hard, whilst another move was made to give him the distinguishing appellation of the Aberdeen terrier. [221]

high mettled   eager; spirited; in prime condition.

Highly mettled fox-hounds are seldom inclined to stop while horses are close at their heels. [47]

high on the leg   of dog with long legs in relation to body length.

High Peak   HARRIER pack which has hunted a rugged moorland COUNTRY in Derbyshire since 1848.

high scent   BREAST-HIGH SCENT.

The high scent which a fox leaves, the straightness of his running, the eagerness of the pursuit, and the noise that generally accompanies it, all contribute to spoil harriers. [47]

high set ear   ear which is placed towards the TOPLINE of the skull.

Hillsboro   (US) American, English and crossbred FOXHOUND pack formed in 1932 to hunt a largely grassland COUNTRY in Tennessee.

Hilltown Harriers   (US) HARRIER, English and crossbred FOXHOUND pack formed in 1962 to hunt a hilly COUNTRY in Pennsylvania.

hill-worn   (esp. of a herding dog) debilitated by excessive work.

'Hi loost'   assurance to a GUNDOG that he is searching in the correct place; encouragement to continue doing so.

hind   female deer.

hindhand   that part of the body which lies behind the hips, CROUP, tail and hindquarters.

hindquarters   that part which lies behind the LOIN.

  hindquarters angulation   relative geometry of the bones of the hips and rear legs.

hip dysplasia   inherited condition in which there is abnormally shallow acetabulum and small or mis-shapen femoral head. (Mode of inheritance, polygenic.) [illus.]

hip joint   joint between femur and pelvis.

hips   PELVIS.

hip socket   cavity in the pelvis into which the femoral head fits.

histamine   the substance produced by body tissues during allergic reaction.

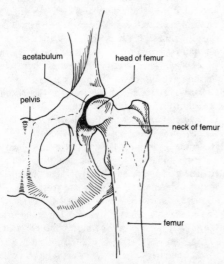

Normal hip joint.

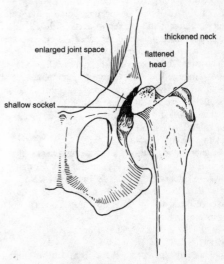

Severe hip dysplasia.

histiocytosis inherited skin, scrotal and nasal cancers. (Mode of inheritance, uncertain.)

histology microscopic examination and study of tissue samples.

hit off recover the scent after a CHECK.
> When his hounds came to a check, his cast was a bold one, quick and decisive, and by this means he either hit the scent again immediately, or lost his fox. [358]

hoareosporidium pellerdyi coccidia which causes mild inflammation of the tissues.

Hoary Aguara AGUARA dog. [123]

Hoary Fox *DUSICYON VETULUS.*

hock HOCK JOINT.

hock-joint tarsus: joint on the hind limb between lower thigh and PASTERN. Since the hock is a joint it cannot itself be long or short; terms such as long or short in hock refer to the distance between the hock joint and the ground. [*illus.* POINTS and SKELETON]

hock ring bracelet of trimmed hair around the HOCK of a POODLE.

hocks, types of BOW, COW, SICKLE, WELL-LET-DOWN.

hocks well let down short PASTERNS.

hocking out moving with the HOCKs turned outwards.

Hockley-in-the-Hole public gardens in Clerkenwell, London which, from Elizabeth's reign, provided a venue for bull- and BEAR-BAITING.
> Both 'Hockley-hole' and 'Mary-bone',
> The combats of my dogs have known,
> He'd Ne're like bullies coward-hearted,
> Attacks in publick, to be parted; [145f]

hocky of a dog with faulty HOCKs.

Hodgkin's Disease neoplastic disease of the lymph nodes.

hogback sharply ROACHED topline.

Hokkaido [FCI] native dog of the island of Hokkaido. Aboriginal people of Japan are the Ainu, their language is still spoken in parts of the island of Hokkaido; their native dogs, used as hunters and DOMESTIC GUARDS, carry both names.

The breed is, in every respect, typically SPITZ in appearance with a characteristic blue tongue. The DOUBLE COAT is short and erect. Height 46–53cm (18–20¾in); weight 20–30kg (44–66lb).

Hokkaido Ainou HOKKAIDO.

Hokkaido Dog HOKKAIDO.

Hokkaido-Ken HOKKAIDO.

Holcombe one of the oldest HARRIER packs in the UK. In 1617 the pack was present at Houghton Tower to celebrate the visit of King James I. HOUNDS are said to have been based on imported CHIEN DE GASCOGNE but the strain is now lost. The COUNTRY lies in Lancashire.

hold 1. (of a hunted stag) enter cover. [159] 2. restrict.

hold at bay prevent quarry from further flight, whilst awaiting the arrival of the hunt.

hold back warning to HOUNDS to remain within the space defined by WHIPs and huntsman.

hold hard 1. instruction to the HUNT-FOLLOWERS not to press too closely on HOUNDS. 2. order given to the forward WHIPPER to reduce his speed.

hold over command to HOUNDS: remain still.

hold up 1. restrict HOUNDS to a particular area or direction of travel. 2. stop HOUNDS while they are hunting. 3. prevent sheep from moving away from a particular place. [204]

Holderness the Yorkshire COUNTRY has been hunted since 1726 and in its present form since 1765 when William Bethell took over the mastership from Squire William Draper; father of Diana, the redoubtable lady to hounds.

holders canine teeth. [159]
> Jaws level and strong, with well-developed teeth, especially the canines or holders. [203, former RHODESIAN RIDGEBACK]

Holdfast proverbial name for a staunch dog.
> Brag is a good dog, but Holdfast is a better.
> [Proverb]

holding 1. the ability of a given area to attract and retain quarry. 2. of a scent which is barely good enough to enable hunting to proceed. [95]

Holinshed, Raphael author of *The Chronicles of England, Scotland and Ireland* (1577).

Hollandse Herdershond [FCI] group of three varieties – short-, long- and rough-coated – of PASTORAL GUARDS and HERDERS, similar in type to the closely related BELGIAN SHEEP DOG and GERMAN SHEPHERD DOG, to which the breed is undoubtedly related. The breed, though not enjoying great popularity outside Holland, is obedient, hardy and strong.

The rather lean head is of moderate length and fairly narrow with an intelligent expression. Dark, almond-shaped eyes are obliquely set, ears are rather small, high set and held stiffly erect. The chest is deep, slightly SPRUNG, the back short, the TUCK-UP slight. The tail is carried SABRE FASHION. The coat colour varies slightly between the varieties, but yellow, chestnut and brown are the basic colours.

Hollandse Herdershond Korthaarige short-coated variety of the HOLLANDSE HERDERSHOND.

Hollandse Herdershond Langhaarige long-haired variety of the HOLLANDSE HERDERSHOND.

Hollandse Herdershond Ruwhaarige rough-coated variety of the HOLLANDSE HERDERSHOND.

Hollandse Smoushond [FCI] Dutch wire-haired TERRIER, developed during the late years of the 19th century from reject WHEATEN GERMAN PINSCHERS. The breed came close to extinction during the Second World War but was revived during the 1970s.

The head is broad with a flat skull, short, strong MUZZLE and dark eyes. The ears are set level with the skull and fall forward close to the cheek. The chest is fairly deep, without excessive SPRING; the back is fairly long with a light arch over the strong LOIN. Forelimbs are straight and well boned, shoulders WELL LAID. Hindquarters long in thigh and with low-set HOCKS. The tail is thick and carried proudly. The dark straw-coloured, harsh coat is weather-resistant. Height 35.5–43cm (14–17in); weight 9–10kg (20–22lb).

> Differs little from the old fashioned British rough-coated terrier type. It is also a stable-yard dog; a man's rather than a lady's pet. [225]

holloa call made by hunters to encourage HOUNDS or attract attention.

hollow (of back) SWAY-BACKED.

Holme Valley BEAGLE pack formed in 1928 in succession to the HARRIER pack of the same name.

Holmfirth, Honley and Meltham former HARRIER pack formed in 1880 to hunt a moorland COUNTRY in west Yorkshire.

holt 1. otter's customary underground refuge. 2. (obs.) the home of a fox. [25]

Holy Cross Irish BEAGLE pack formed in 1926 to hunt a COUNTRY in County Tipperary.

homoeopathy treatment of disease by the use of minute quantities of natural drugs that produce symptoms similar to those of the disease.

homogametic sex sex which produces only one sort of gamete, in dogs the female.

homologous of similar type, nature or relative position.

homologous chromosome one of a pair of similarly shaped chromosomes.

homologous genes gene which occurs in different species and has the same effect.

homozygote a HOMOZYGOUS individual.

homozygous of individual carrying a particular gene in duplicate.

honde HOUND or dog. [159]

honourable scar evidence of injuries earned during legitimate work.

> Honourable scars from fair wear and tear not to be unduly penalised. [203, NORWICH TERRIER]

Hooded ears.

hooded ear pricked ear in which the PINNA curves forward at the tip and on the sides, thus forming a hood. [*illus.*]

hook and snivey a swindle in which a landlord is cheated into providing food for a dog. [280]

hook-up area enclosure close to the starting line of SLED-DOG race in which teams are harnessed.

Hookworm.

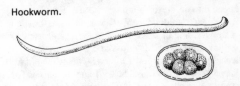

hookworm nematode of several species including *Ancylostoma, Necator* and *Uncinaria*. [*illus.*]

hookworm dermatitis inflammation caused by increased sensitivity of HOOKWORM-infested animals.

hoose disease caused by LUNGWORM infestation.

hormone glandular secretion which controls growth, sexual activity, and metabolism.

horn 1. instrument carried by a huntsman as an aid to controlling HOUNDS and maintaining contact with HUNT FOLLOWERS. 2. material of which the nails are composed.

> Feet . . . with well-developed knuckles and strong horn, which last is of the greatest importance. [6, ENGLISH FOXHOUND]

Hornchurch Beagles MID-ESSEX.

Horsell former 15in BEAGLE pack originally formed prior to 1875 as the Chertsey Beagles and became a private pack from 1875 to 1897 under the name of their owner Mr Bailey before assuming their present name. The COUNTRY lies in Surrey.

horseshoe front front in which the forelegs are, though straight, further apart at the elbows than at the feet. Normal in some breeds, eg. BEDLINGTON TERRIER.

Horsnell Beagles WEST SURREY AND HORSNELL.

Hospice Dog SAINT BERNARD.

Hottentot Dog (obs.) BASENJI.

Hottentot Hunting Dog (obs.) BASENJI.

hough disable by means of cutting or amputating the pads. [159]

hound sporting dog intended for the pursuit of quarry, whether by sight or scent.

> A hound is of great understanding and great knowledge, a hound has great goodness and hath great memory and great smelling. [215]
> In thee alone, fair land of liberty!
> Is bred the perfect hound, in scent and speed
> As yet unrival'd. [328]

hound colours range of colours found on PACK-HOUNDS: the most common include TRICOLOUR, tan and white, lemon and white, lemon PIED, HARE(2)-pied, blue MOTTLED; some packs also keep black-and-tan hounds. Working hounds, however, may be of any colour.

hound dog (Am.) HOUND.

> You ain't nothin' but a hound dog
> Cryin' all the time. [223]

hound ears pendulous, rounded ears.

hound glove HOUND PAD.

hound jog   economical trot.

hound-marked   colouring similar to that of FOX-HOUNDS or BEAGLES.

hound music   cry of hunting HOUNDS. [309]

hound pad   studded rubber pad or short-bristled material made in the form of a glove and used to groom short-coated HOUNDS and other breeds.

hound parlance   jargon adopted by those who hunt.

hound trail   artificial scent trail laid as a basis for competitive racing, esp. in northern England.

hound van   vehicles in which the pack is transported to and from the MEET.

hound work   skills exhibited by hunting HOUNDS.

Hounds of Hell   fabled HOUNDS which hunted lost souls.

> Lead on the unmuzzled hounds of hell,
> Till all the frighted echoes tell
> The blood-notes of the chase. [73]

house-dog   any type of dog which lives in the house.

> The shrewmouse eyes me shudderingly, then flees;
> and, worse than that,
> The housedog he flees after me – why was I born a
> cat? [80a]

Household Brigade   former DRAGHOUND pack formed in 1863 to hunt LINES(2) in Berkshire.

house-train   educate a puppy not to defecate in the house.

Hovawart   [FCI] German DOMESTIC GUARD. The name is derived from *hofewart*, an estate guard, also used to guard and herd farm stock. The breed dates from the 13th century and was rescued from oblivion in the early years of the 20th century and resuscitated by means of judicious CROSSES(2) with other breeds.

The head is strong and broad with a convex forehead; the ears are high set, V-shaped and fall close to the head. The neck is strong and moderately long, the forequarters straight and strong with WELL-LAID shoulders; the chest is broad and deep, the TOPLINE straight with a gently sloping CROUP. Hindquarters are WELL ANGULATED and strongly muscled. The tail reaches to below the HOCKs. The coat is black, black and tan, or FLAXEN, long, slightly wavy and dense. Height 53–68cm (20¾–26¾in); weight 25–40kg (55–88lb).

hover   holt, or more usually, a temporary place of refuge; hide. [186]

Howard County   (US) crossbred FOXHOUND pack formed in 1930 to hunt a rolling woodland COUNTRY in Maryland.

howl   mournful cry, associated with strong emotions whether of distress, pleasure or bewilderment.

> Every wolf's and lion's howl
> Raises from Hell a human soul. [52]

hoxing   GENUISCISSIO, excision of the sinews of the knee, a former method of exerting control over dogs.

Hrvatski Ovcar   [FCI] ancient cousin to the more popular PULI with origins in Croatian Yugoslavia. A reliable HERDER, self-reliant, fast and with abundant stamina.

The conical head has an oval skull with pronounced OCCIPUT. The eyes are almond-shaped and dark with a lively expression, the ears triangular and pricked. The neck is rather upright, moderately long and well muscled. The forequarters very oblique with a short upper arm; forelegs are straight to a sloping PASTERN and tightly padded, small feet. The ribs are WELL SPRUNG, the back short, with short, strong LOINS. The muscular hindquarters are moderately ANGULATED with a low HOCK. The tail is high set and well FEATHERED; some puppies are born without tails, others are traditionally DOCKED quite short. The black coat is fairly long, except on the face, and dense. Height 40–50cm (15¾–19½in).

Hrvatski Ovcarsk Pes   CROATIAN SHEEP DOG. [312]

Huby Beagles   DERWENT VALLEY.

huckle bones   protruding hip-bones, especially the ILIAC CRESTS.

huick holloa   cry which draws attention to a VIEW.

huick to . . .   instruction to HOUNDS to pay attention to a particular named hound, eg. 'Huick to Melody'.

human diploid cell vaccine   rabies vaccine based on inactivated virus grown on human lung tissue.

humeral   effect caused by body fluids.

humerus   long bone of the upper forelimb extending from elbow to the lower point of the scapula. [*illus.* SKELETON]

Hundred of Hoo Foxhounds   ROYAL ENGINEERS.

Hungarian Greyhound   MAGYAR AGAR.

Hungarian Hound   ERDÉLYI KOPÓ.

Hungarian Puli   [KC] PULI.

Hungarian Sheep Dog   MUDI. [312]

Hungarian Vizsla   [KC] one of the multi-purpose European GUNDOGs which has become a firm favourite among both exhibitors and sportsmen. Illustrations from 1,000 years ago depict Magyar sportsmen using very similar dogs to FLUSH winged game for falcons. The breed is lively, intelligent, robust and amenable to training whether for fur or feather, POINTING, or retrieving on land or in water.

The noble head is lean, the skull moderately wide with a distinct MEDIAN LINE and moderate STOP. The jaws are powerful and the nose brown. The eyes are oval and slightly darker than the coat, the ears are quite low set, a rounded V-shape, and drop forward close to the cheeks. The long neck is strong and moderately arched without DEWLAP. The forequarters are WELL LAID, the legs straight and well boned, and the PASTERN upright. The short back is level, the chest fairly broad and deep with a prominent sternum. TUCK-UP is slight and the CROUP is well muscled. Hindquarters have moderate ANGULATION. The tail is traditionally DOCKED to one third its length and is carried horizontally. The russet gold coat is short, straight, smooth and shiny. Height 53–64cm (20¾–25in); weight 20–30kg (44–66lb).

Hungarian Wire-haired Vizsla   wire-haired variety of the HUNGARIAN VIZSLA.

Hunsley Beacon   BEAGLE pack formed in 1960 in

succession to the Burton Constable Beagles to hunt a COUNTRY in Humberside.

hunt 1. pursue wild animals with hounds.
> A parcel of men, with vacant minds, meet at covert-side, the dogs smell a stink, they run, and the men gallop after them, that's hunting. [277]

2. establishment employed in hunting; (the) hunting party. 3. area in which hunting takes place. 4. (Am.) pursue or shoot wild animals.

hunt at force run quarry down with HOUNDS. [159]

hunt change CHANGE. [159]

hunt counter follow a scent contrary to the direction in which it was laid. [159]

hunt-follower one who follows HOUNDS but who has no official capacity with the hunt.

hunt heel HUNT COUNTER.
> The low-scenting hound is, moreover, brilliant in his work: he neither ties on the line nor hunts heel and can follow with his nose high. [369]

hunt kennels kennels and breeding establishment belonging to a hunt.

Huntaway New Zealand HERDER closely resembling a low-set BORDER COLLIE and differentiated from it principally by its black and rich tan coloration.

hunting 1. (Brit.) field sport involving pursuit of quarry with HOUNDS.
> We are more inclined and delighted with the noble game of hunting, for we Englishmen are addicted and given to that exercise and painful pastime of pleasure, as well for the plenty of flesh which our Parks and Forests do foster, as also for the opportunities and convenient leisure which we obtain, both which, the Scots want. [139]
> It is very strange, and very melancholy, that the paucity of human pleasures should persuade us ever to call hunting one of them. [196]
> [Of the English country gentleman galloping after a fox:] The unspeakable in full pursuit of the uneatable. [390]

2. (Am.) field sports generally, including shooting.

Hunting Dog *LYCAON PICTUS*.

hunting the clean boot following a natural trail laid by a human runner.

Huntingdon Valley (US) AMERICAN FOXHOUND pack formed in 1914 to hunt a hilly pasture COUNTRY in Pennsylvania.

huntsman person who is in charge of a pack of HOUNDS.

hup command to sit, almost exclusively used with working SPANIELS.

Hursley this woodland and plough Hampshire and Wiltshire COUNTRY has been hunted since 1836; for some years after 1839 the pack was known as the Hursley Subscription Hounds.

Hursley Subscription Hounds HURSLEY.

Hurworth pack founded in 1799 by the brothers Wilkinson; the COUNTRY lies in Durham and north Yorkshire.

hush puppy (Am.) deep-fried cornmeal cake, usually fed to dogs but, in times of hardship, also eaten by people.

Husky SIBERIAN HUSKY.

Hütespitz unrecognized medium-sized GERMAN SHEEP DOG.

Hyaena Dog *LYCAON PICTUS*.

H-Y antigen substance found on the Y chromosome, and which plays a part in testicular development and male sexual differentiation.

hybrid individual resulting from union between parents of two different species, usually infertile.

hybrid vigour elevated vigour of animals resulting from a first CROSS(2) between two PEDIGREE animals of different breeds.

hydatid HYDATID CYST.

hydatid cyst watery cyst formed by the larva of the tapeworm *Echinococcus*.

hydrocephalus abnormal enlargement of the cranium owing to accumulation of fluids, which is not uncommon in some small breeds with DOMED skulls.

hydrophobia (obs.) RABIES (der. fear of water from the inability to drink which is one of the early symptoms of rabies.)
> Hydrophobia is a kind of madness well known in every village, which comes from the biting of a mad dog. [75]

hydrophoby lay trick whereby a parent claims compensation for wounds alleged to have been inflicted on his or her child by a dog. [280]

Hygenhund [FCI] one of the relatively few eponymous breeds which carry the name of their originator, in this case F. Hygen, a Norwegian hunter and breeder, who crossed Dutch HOUNDS with a number of native hound breeds to produce this distinctive breed.

The head is rather broad, and slightly DOMED, the MUZZLE broad and deep, with CLEAN LIPS; the eyes are dark and the ears thin, soft and pendulous. The chest is long, deep and capacious, the TUCK-UP moderate and the back short, straight and powerful. The CROUP is long and slightly rounded. The forelegs are straight, solid and well muscled with sloping PASTERNS; the shoulders are WELL ANGULATED. The hindquarters are broad, muscular and well angulated. The coat is straight, slightly rough, dense and glossy; colours include chestnut, yellow-red (with or without black shading) and black and tan. Height 46–58cm (18–23in).

hyoid horseshoe-shaped bone under the tongue.

hyper (pref.) excessive; greater than normal.

hyperactive abnormally or frantically active.

hyperexcitability inclined to become abnormally excited.

hyperglycaemia condition in which there is an abnormally large amount of sugar in the blood.

hyperipoproteinaenia inherited metabolic disorder leading to fits. (Mode of inheritance, familial.)

hyperkalaemia inherited abnormally high concentration of blood potassium owing to renal abnormality. (Mode of inheritance, uncertain.)

hyperkeratosis thickening of the skin's horny layer.

hyperkinesis abnormally increased energy and restless movement; hyperactivity.

hyperplasia abnormal increase in the size of an organ or area of tissue owing to an increase in normal cell growth.

hypertension persistent high blood pressure, although normal blood pressure varies from breed to breed.

hyperthermia inherited abnormally high body temperature, nervousness and excitability. (Mode of inheritance, familial.)

hypertonic abnormally elevated tension of the muscles.

hypertrophic neuropathy inherited myelin production defect leading to early weakness, loss of reflexes and paralysis. (Mode of inheritance, recessive.)

hypertrophic osteodystrophy disease, principally found in the young of the large breeds, in which abnormal bone growth causes pain, swelling, fever, lethargy and anorexia.

hypertrophic osteopathy symmetrical abnormal growth of new bone on the extremities of the limbs and long bones.

hypertrophic pulmonary osteopathy HYPERTROPHIC OSTEOPATHY

hypertrophy abnormal enlargement of an organ.

hypo (pref.) deficient; defective.

hypofibrinogenaemia inherited blood fibrogen deficiency leading to mild or severe bleeding. (Mode of inheritance, dominant.)

hypomyelinogenesis inadequate synthesis of myelin, causing nerve development defect. It can be inherited, or caused by a virus or nutrient deficiency. Affected dogs are called tremblers. (Mode of inheritance, recessive.)

hypo-oestrinism reduced oestrogen levels, as with spayed females, sometimes associated with urinary incontinence.

hypopituitarism reduced pituitary gland activity resulting in dwarfism.

hypoplasia underdevelopment of an organ.

hypoproconvertinaemia inherited condition resulting in reduced levels of clotting Factor VII producing mild bleeding. (Mode of inheritance, recessive.)

hyposomatotropism growth-hormone responsive dermatosis.

hypostasis ability of alleles on one locus to mask the effect of alleles on a different locus.

hypothermia dangerously depressed temperature.

hypothyroidism inherited thyroid gland inactivity. (Mode of inheritance, uncertain.)

hypotrichosis reduced or absence of coat.

Hyrcanian Dog former type of MASTIFF.
  Said, on account of their extreme ferocity, to have been crossed with the tiger. [406]

hysterectomy surgical removal of the uterus.

hysteria mental disorder characterized by irrational behaviour and ataxia.

I

iatrogenic of illness caused by the action of a physician.

Ibizan Hound One of several SIGHTHOUNDS with origins around the Mediterranean and with a striking resemblance to representations of the Egyptian Anubis, of which the breed's supporters make much play. The breed's method of hunting utilizes eyesight, good scenting ability and alertness to sound made by quarry.

A superb hunter with abundant stamina and agility. The head is long and fine with a flat skull and prominent OCCIPUT; the MUZZLE is slightly convex, the almond-shaped, amber eyes clear and expressive, the mobile ears are large and carried upright. The neck is lean, long and muscular; the forequarters are steep with a short scapula, long legs and erect pasterns. The TOPLINE is level, falling away slightly along the CROUP. The chest is long and flat, the TUCK-UP pronounced. Hindquarters are long, straight and muscular with a long SECOND THIGH. The low-set tail is long and thin. The smooth or rough coat is red or tawny and white. Height 56–74cm (22–29in).

Ibizan Podenco IBIZAN HOUND.

Iceland Dog 1. LANSDK FAREHUND.
> Somewhat smaller than the Esquimaux . . . in other respects they resemble the other dogs of the Northern parts. [123]

2. *CANIS ISLANDICUS.*

Icelandic Sheep Dog ISLANDSK FAREHUND.

Iceland Spitz ISLANDSK FAREHUND.

ichthuosis inherited keratin deficiency leading to dry, rough and scaly skin. (Mode of inheritance, familial.)

ichthyosis nonspecific skin disease characterized by dryness, cracking, toughness and the development of a scaly or horny layer.

Icticyon [Speothos] venaticus short-legged wild dog found along the rivers of tropical Panama and Brazil. Height about 30cm (12in); length, including tail, about 75cm (29½in).

Ictidocyon fossil canine ancestor.

idiogram diagrammatic method of representing a KAROTYPE.

idiopathic condition which occurs without apparent cause.

idiopathic hyperaesthesia syndrome increased sensitivity resulting in self-trauma and reluctance to have the part touched, often resulting in ACRAL LICK DERMATITIS.

idiopathic epilepsy epilepsy which, whilst it does occur in dogs, is less common in them than in some other species.

Idstone, Rev. Thomas Pearce sometime editor of *The Field*, and author of *The Dog, with Simple Directions for his Treatment, and Notices of the Best Dogs of the Day and their Breeders and Exhibitors* (1872), and of *The Idstone Papers* (1872).

iliac crest the prominent, rounded tip of the ilium. [*illus*. SKELETON]

Ilio Hawaiian Poi Dog: *CANIS PACIFICUS.*

Ilirski Ovcar SARPLANINAC.

ilium one of the three components of the hipbone: the ilium forms the hip socket. [*illus*. SKELETON]

Illyrian Hound KELTSKI GONIC.

Illyrian Sheep Dog SARPLANINAC.

immotile cilia syndrome inherited lack of movement of ciliary structures of the eye. (Mode of inheritance, probably recessive.)

immune of, or relating to, IMMUNITY.

immune mediated polyneuropathy disease affecting several nerves.

immune system system of the body by which infections are combated naturally.

immunity ability to resist infection.

immunization promotion of immunity; process of promoting immunity, usually by VACCINATION.

impenetrance failure of a gene to express itself.

implantation attachment of a fertilized egg to the wall of the uterus.

impotence infertility.

in and in INBREEDING.
> Great mistakes have been made by masters of foxhounds in breeding too much in-and-in from near affinities, instead of having recourse to an alien cross. [266b]
> Breeding in and in, to a certainty, would enfeeble their intellects as surely as their constitutions. In this way has many a kennel been deprived of the energy and endurance so essential in a sportsman's dog. [184]

in-and-in breeding INBREEDING.
> Sir J. Sebright declares that by breeding in-and-in, by which he means matching brothers and sisters, he has actually seen the offspring of strong spaniels degenerate into weak and diminutive lapdogs. [111b]

inanition prolonged starvation.

inappetance loss of appetite.

in blood (of HOUNDS or TERRIERS) still excited by a recent kill.

inbred strain group of closely related animals.

inbreed select closely related animals for the purpose of mating. *See* INBREEDING.

inbreeding matings between closely related individuals intended to reproduce some desired characteristic.
> The whole system becomes enfeebled; the constitution is more liable to disease, and soon succumbs; the brain is weak; the circulation slow. Palsy, fits, dropsy, tumours, rickets, malformation of the limbs, cancer, every variety of disease attacks these highbred favourites, from which the tinker's mongrel escapes. [186]

With this particular pair, inbred to the uttermost, he had successfully surmounted a great risk. It was now touch and go whether he dared venture on one more cross to the original strain, in the hope of eliminating the last clinging of liver colour. [143b]

inbreeding depression loss of vigour as a result of excessive or unwise INBREEDING.

In-breeding or Sibbing is a fruitful source of constitutional weakness and loss of size amongst dogs, and if carried on too far is therefore a practice to be deprecated. [320]

Inca Dog INCA HAIRLESS DOG.

Inca Hairless Dog PERRO SIN PELO DEL PERU.

Inca Moonflower Dog PERRO SIN PELO DEL PERU.

incisive bone the skull bone that supports the INCISOR. [*illus.* SKELETON]

incisor each of the six front teeth which lie between the canine teeth, and which are adapted for cutting.

incomplete dominance when the heterozygote produces a phenotype intermediate between that which would have been produced by the two homozygotes.

incomplete penetrance of a gene which does not always totally express itself.

incontinence involuntary urination or defecation.

incus anvil bone of the ear.

independent culling involuntary CULLING; culling undertaken because of old age, sickness or injury.

Index SETTER. [139]

When he approaches near to the place where the bird is, he lays him down, and with a mark of his paws, betrays the place of the bird's last abode, whereby it is supposed that this kind of dog is called Index. [139]

Indian Dog HARE INDIAN DOG.

Against fawns and stags one ought to make use of Indian dogs; for they are strong, large, swift of foot, and spirited; and having these qualities they are able to endure hard tasks. [404]

Indian Haredog HARE INDIAN DOG. [123]

Indian Jackal *CANIS AUREUS.*

Indian Tail-less Dog type of dog mentioned by Ash. [37b]

Have little to recommend them. In appearance they resemble the Pomeranian, except that they have no tail, and are of a foxy colour; in fact, they are not unlike the latter animal, but they are heavier in bone, more stoutly built, and shorter in the body. [320a]

Indian Wild Dog *CANIS AUREUS.*

individual merit selection selection for BREEDING(3) based on the positive qualities of individuals.

infantile scurvy HYPERTROPHIC OSTEODYSTROPHY.

infection invasion of the body by organisms which cause disease.

infectious (esp. of disease) of that which can be transmitted to another via the air or via physical contact.

infectious canine hepatitis (CAV-1) HEPATITIS.

infectious canine tracheobronchitis KENNEL COUGH.

infertile unable to produce offspring; sterile.

infield land enclosed by a race-track.

inguinal hernia inherited groin hernia. (Mode of inheritance, threshold.)

inheritance transmission of characteristics from generation to generation.

inherited of that which is possessed by transmission from ancestors.

inherited achondroplastic dwarfism ACHONDROPLASTIC DWARFISM.

inherited congenital cerebellar hypoplasia CEREBELLAR ATROPHY.

inherited congenital hypotrichosis partial or complete absence of hair, sometimes associated with thyroid abnormality. Occurs sporadically in some breeds. (Mode of inheritance, uncertain.)

inherited congenital ichthyosis fish-scale disease: alopecia associated with areas of thickened and scaly skin. (Mode of inheritance, uncertain.)

in pup PREGNANT.

Inquisitors FINDERS. [139]

in season undergoing OESTRUS.

inseminate to introduce semen into.

insemination the process – artificial or natural – by which semen is introduced into a receptive female.

instinct innate ability to respond appropriately without prior experience.

A dog by instinct turns aside,
Who sees the ditch too deep and wide. [346]

inside hare artificial lure which, unusually, travels on the inside edge of a race-track.

instrumental learning process of learning in which a voluntary act is elicited by means of a reward or reinforcement.

INT gene symbol for lightest tan intensity. [395]

int gene symbol for darkest tan intensity. [395]

int^m gene symbol for intermediate tan intensity. [395]

Int. Ch. abbr. INTERNATIONAL CHAMPION.

integument (of tissue, ovule) outer protective covering.

intensity series those genes which control the intensity of coat colour.

inteotropic hormone PROLACTIN.

interbreed 1. CROSS(2). 2. INBREED.

interbreeding 1. breeding between two different breeds. 2. INBREEDING.

With Greyhounds also there has been much close interbreeding, but the best breeders agree that it may be carried too far. [111b]

interdigital between the toes.

interdigital cyst cyst which appears between the toes.

interdigital dermatitis inflamed, prurient skin condition between the toes, often resulting from licking, contact allergy or HOOKWORM penetration.

interdigital pyoderma infection between the toes, often caused by foreign objects or parasites.

interim applied to BREED STANDARDs that have not yet been finally approved.

intermediate inheritance inheritance of characteristics which are intermediate between those carried by the parents.

International Champion (Int. Ch.) title awarded to a dog that has achieved Championship status in one FCI country and won CACIBs in two or more countries under different judges.

International Sheep Dog Society (ISDS) governing body, with which WORKING SHEEP DOGS are registered. *See also* STUD BOOK NUMBER.

International Show show organized under FCI rules in which winners that are already National Champions may become entitled to the title INTERNATIONAL CHAMPION.

intersex animal that has an abnormal mixture of XX and XY cells, or is XXY, and thus exhibits some of the physical characteristics of each sex.

intersexuality inherited tendency to produce partial hermaphrodites. (Mode of inheritance, chromosomal, anamoly.)

intervertebral disc protrusion inherited painful and neurological problems sometimes leading to paralysis and caused by displacement of an intervertebral disc (slipped disc). (Mode of inheritance, polygenic.)

intestinal malabsorption inherited condition producing persistent diarrhoea, debility, weight loss and death. (Mode of inheritance, recessive.)

in the money (in competition) placed in the first three.

intrauterine within the uterus.

intrauterine contraceptive device device inserted in the uterine cavity in order to prevent pregnancy. The use is not widespread in dogs.

intravertebral between the bones of the spine.

intravertebral disc disease painful nerve defects of the invertebrae resulting in paralysis.

introvert human personality term also applicable to dogs and used to describe a cautious and self-contained attitude.

Inu (Jap.) DOG.

in use (obs. of bitches) IN SEASON.
Some dogs will not copulate with bitches until the last day or two they are in use. [218]

in utero within the uterus.

in vitro outside the body, usually of fertilization.

involuntary culling INDEPENDENT CULLING.

in whelp PREGNANT.

Inwood Buckhounds former private pack formed in 1913 to hunt wild roe deer in a COUNTRY in Somerset.

Ioujnorousskaia Ovtcharka [FCI] a PASTORAL GUARD native to the Ukraine. Very typical of the basically white long-coated herding breeds developed in the Mediterranean basin.

The head is strong, with pendulous ears and a characteristic FRINGE; the body is long with a deep capacious chest; the PUMP-HANDLE TAIL is thick coated. The coat is white, long and dense. Height 63–66cm (24¾–26in); weight 55–74kg (121–162lb).

Irfon and Towy FOXHOUND pack dating from 1909 when the pack was TRENCHER-FED and consisted of

rough-coated Welsh hounds; the varied COUNTRY is in Powys.

iris the coloured part of the eye which surrounds the pupil.

Irish Blue Terrier KERRY BLUE TERRIER.

Irish Brace novelty class at some informal shows for two dogs as dissimilar as possible.

Irish Glen of Imaal Terrier [AKC, FCI, KC] distinctive TERRIER breed with origins in the Wicklow Mountains of Ireland. Formerly used for BADGER-BAITING, DIGGING, and DRAWING and occasionally for dog fighting. Unusually among working terriers, it is mute when employed.

An unusual terrier of medium size but with heavy bone and substance. The skull is fairly wide, the STOP well defined and the MUZZLE tapering with strong jaws enclosing a perfect SCISSOR BITE. Eyes are brown, round and wide set; ears are small and may be ROSE or SEMI-PRICK. The body is of medium length, deep, with WELL-SPRUNG ribs forming a wide chest. The shoulders are broad and muscular, the bowed forelegs short and well boned. The TOPLINE rises to a strong LOIN. The hindquarters are muscular with well-bent STIFLES. The coat is of medium length and of harsh texture with a soft undercoat; it may be blue, BRINDLE or shades of WHEAT. Height 35–36cm (13¾–14in).

Irish Greyhound former name for the IRISH WOLFHOUND.

> I want you to procure a pair of Irish Greyhounds, a dog and a bitch of the same breed, but not castrated as I intend to breed from them. You know how devoted I am to the chase, and these dogs will provide an agreeable pastime, besides enabling me to hunt the wild boar with them. [167]

Irish pattern white (of coat colour) white confined to neck, chest and BRISKET.

Irish Red and White Setter [KC] old Irish GUNDOG breed which fell into obscurity following the popular success of the IRISH SETTER with which it is identical, except in colour. It was protected from total extinction by the recessive characteristic of its coat colour, and the enthusiasm of a few faithful supporters.

A more workaday dog than the Irish Setter, with a strong, athletic build. The head is broad, the skull DOMED below a distinct OCCIPUT; a good STOP leads to a square MUZZLE. The clean, brown eyes are round and slightly prominent, the ears fall close to the head; the very muscular neck is rather long and slightly arched, the shoulders WELL LAID, the forelegs well boned and the PASTERNS sloping. The strong, muscular body has a deep, WELL SPRUNG chest; the hindquarters are wide and powerful with well-bent STIFLE. The tail is carried level with the TOPLINE. The fine coat is pearly white with patches of solid red; some ROANing is permitted on the face and limbs. Height 58–69cm (23–27in).

Irish Red Setter IRISH SETTER.

Irish Red Terrier   IRISH TERRIER.

Irish Setter   [AKC, FCI, KC] old Irish GUNDOG
bred of uncertain origin whose elegance and demon-
stratively affectionate temperament have made it into
a popular companion.

The long, lean head has an oval skull with pronounced OCCIPUT; the deep MUZZLE is square ended;
the dark hazel eyes are almond shaped; the fine-tex-
tured ears are of moderate length, low set and hanging in a fold close to the head. The very muscular
neck is fairly long and slightly arched, the forequarters deep and WELL LAID, the forelegs straight and
well boned. The body is narrow in front with a deep
chest, WELL SPRUNG ribs and a TOPLINE which falls
gently from the WITHERS. The powerful, wide
hindquarters contribute to typically free-flowing
movement. The coat, which forms FEATHERING on
chest, under belly, the rear of the limbs and under
the tail, is a rich chestnut. Height 63–69cm
(24¾–27in).

Irish spotting   IRISH PATTERN WHITE.

Irish Terrier   [AKC, FCI, KC] the breed emerged
from among the variety of Irish TERRIER breeds as a
consequence of the growing interest in dog shows and
moves towards standard classification and nomenclature. Formerly widely known as 'Dare Devil'
because of its fearless attitude and enjoyment of a
fight. As its former involvement in BADGER-DIGGING
and dog fighting have become things of the past the
breed has become more amenable to discipline,
though the BREED STANDARD readily – even proudly
– admits that the breed is 'a little too ready to resent
interference on the part of other dogs'.

The head is long with a flat, clean skull and strong,
clean jaws. The eyes are small and dark, the ears
small and V-shaped. The neck is of fair length, the
shoulders long and WELL LAID, the moderately long
limbs straight and well boned. The chest is deep and
the body moderately long with a slightly arched,
muscular LOIN. Hindquarters are strong and muscular with moderately bent STIFLES. The tail is traditionally DOCKED and is carried GAILY. The coat is
harsh and wiry, red, red-WHEATEN or yellow-red,
with a small amount of white permitted on the chest.
Height 46–48cm (18–18¾in).

Irish Water Spaniel   [AKC, FCI, KC] although it
has been claimed that dogs proficient in water have
existed in Ireland for 6,000 years, the modern breed
dates from the mid-19th century. The breed may lay
justified claim to being the first of the multi-purpose
GUNDOGS and, though initially reserved with
strangers, it is a reliable and loyal sporting companion.

The DOMED skull is large, the strong MUZZLE long,
square and with gradual STOP. The small eyes are
almond-shaped; the ears, which hang close to the
cheeks, are long and oval in shape. The neck is
strong, arched and carries the head well over the line

of the back. The forequarters are sloping and powerful, the limbs straight and well boned. The chest is
deep, and barrel-shaped, the back short, broad and
strongly coupled with deep, wide LOINS.
Hindquarters are well ANGULATED and powerful. The
feet are round and spreading. The tail is naturally
short, low set and carried in line with the back. The
rich dark liver coat (called puce-liver by aficionados)
forms dense, tight, oily ringlets on the body, TOP-
KNOT, ears and limbs. The coat on the face and chest
is short and smooth. Height 51–58cm (20–23in).

Irish Wheaten Terrier   SOFT-COATED WHEATEN TER-
RIER.

Irish Wolfdog   IRISH WOLFHOUND.

> The last variety, and the most wonderful of all that
> I shall mention, is the great Irish wolfdog, that may
> be considered as the first of the canine species. This
> animal, which is very rare even in the only country
> in the world where it is to be found, is rather kept
> for show than use, there being neither wolves nor
> any other formidable beasts of prey in Ireland that
> seem to require so powerful an antagonist. [155a]

Irish Wolfhound   [AKC, FCI, KC] the extinction of
the wolf in Ireland rendered the purpose for which
this breed was originated obsolete. Thus, having been
in existence since prior to Roman times, it came close
to extinction itself, from which plight it was rescued
during the 19th century.

The most obvious characteristics of the breed are
its great size, power and gentle nature. The head is
long and carried proudly, the elliptical eyes dark, the
ROSE EARS small and standing away from the face.
The neck is rather long and muscular, the forequarters sloping, the limbs straight and strong. The chest
is deep and wide with a short back, arched LOINS and
pronounced TOUCH-UP. The tail is long and slightly
curved. The coat, which may be grey, BRINDLE, red,
black, white, fawn, WHEATEN or steel grey is rough
and harsh. Height greater than 71cm (28in), ideally
81–86cm (32–34in); weight over 41kg (90lb).

Iroquois   (US) American and crossbred FOXHOUND
pack formed in 1880 to hunt a meadow and woodland COUNTRY in Kentucky.

irregular bite   teeth unevenly spaced or out of alignment.

isabella   yellow-dun colour.

ischium   part of the pelvic girdle. [*illus.* SKELETON]

ISDS   abbr. INTERNATIONAL SHEEP DOG SOCIETY.

Iseland   Iceland dog; SHOCK-DOG. [159]

Island   pack formed in 1853 to hunt a COUNTRY in
Wexford.

Island Grey Fox   *UROCYON LITTORALIS.*

Islandsk Farehund   [FCI] breed developed in Iceland
as a HERDER, DOMESTIC GUARD and destroyer of vermin and which has much in common with other SPITZ
breeds with origins in northern Scandinavia,
Greenland and western Russia.

A compact, typically spitz breed, of medium size,
with vulpine head, strong, deep-chested body, curled
PLUME TAIL and thick coat of either long or medium

length, shaded WOLF SABLE, WHEATEN, off-white or black. Height 31–41cm (12¼–16in); weight 9–14kg (20–31lb).

Isle of Wight   1. BEAGLE pack formed in 1906 and re-formed in 1959.   2. FOXHOUND pack founded in 1845 to hunt imported foxes; the original hounds were supplied by the Crockford Harriers.

isoallele   allelic gene which differs from the normal when combined with a dominant mutant allele.

isolation syndrome   fear of human contact as a result of being reared in isolation or without pleasant human contact. Puppies so reared will, by the age of twelve weeks, develop a largely irreversible fear of human contact.

Istarski Gonič   hound with origins in Yugoslavia where it was principally used for hunting boar and admired as much for its voice as for its superb nose.

Built on typical SCENTHOUND lines the overall impression is of a lightly boned HARRIER. There are two varieties, the Istarski Kratkodlaki Gonič and the Istarski Ostrodlaki Gonič, which are separated by coat alone, whether smooth or coarse. White predominates with a small amount of lemon on the head. Height 46–53cm (18–20¾in).

Istarski Kratkodlaki Gonič   [FCI] short-haired variety of the ISTARSKI GONIČ.

Istarski Ostrodlaki Gonič   [FCI] coarse-haired variety of the ISTARSKI GONIČ.

Istrian Pointer   rough- or smooth-haired multi-purpose GUNDOG, predominantly white with light tan, red or black markings, long-headed and with DROP EARS. Height 48cm (18¾in); weight 20kg (44lb).

Istrian Sheep Dog   KRASKY OVCAR.

Istrian Short-haired Hound   ISTARKSI KRATKODLAKI GONIČ.

Istrian Wire-haired Hound   ISTARSKI OSTRODLAKI GONIČ.

Italian Greyhound   [AKC, KC] delicately constructed miniature SIGHTHOUND of great antiquity.

The narrow skull is long and flat, the STOP slight and the MUZZLE fine and long. The eyes are large and lustrous, the delicate ROSE EARS well set back. The long neck arches gracefully into long, sloping shoulders. The limbs are straight with fine but strong bone. The chest is deep and narrow, the TOPLINE arched over the loin. Hindquarters are muscular and long, with well-bent STIFLES, and HOCKS well let down. The tail is long and low set. The coat is short and glossy over a supple and fine skin. Colour may be black, blue, cream, fawn, red, with or without white. Weight 2.7–4.5kg (6–10lb).

> A gentleman, who is less often out in his opinions on such matters than in the elbows of his coat – (that is at the intervals of his inhabiting one), – assures us that, idle and heavy as he looks now, he is light as an Italian greyhound in the pit. [32]

Italian Hound   SEGUGIO ITALIANO.

Italian Mastiff   NEAPOLITAN MASTIFF. [312]

Italian Pointer   BRACCO ITALIANO.

Italian Short-haired Segugio   smooth-coated variety of the SEGUGIO ITALIANO.

Italian Spinone   [KC] SPINONE ITALIANO.

Italian Spitz   VOLPINO ITALIANO.

itton   CURRE.

Iveagh   Irish HARRIER pack formed in 1825 which hunted its County Down and Armagh COUNTRY until 1880. The pack was reformed in 1902.

Ivicene   IBIZAN HOUND.

Ixodes angustus   hard-bodied dog tick.

Ixodes canisuga   the tick most commonly found on the dog in Britain, but also occurs in North America and western Europe.

Ixodes cornuatus   dog tick which can cause paralysis.

Ixodes dammini   tick associated with the transmission of LYME DISEASE.

Ixodes hexagonus   dog tick, also found on sheep, occurring in Europe, America and North Africa. Transmits canine babesiosis. Sometimes known as the European dog tick.

Ixodes kingi   large, round-bodied dog tick.

Ixodes holocyclus   Tick found on ruminants, dogs and pigs, and the cause of Australian tick paralysis. Occurs in Australia and India.

Ixodes muris   small mouse tick, also found on dogs.

Ixodes ricinus   European sheep tick, also found on dogs, which can transmit canine babesiosis. Occurs in most parts of the world.

Ixodes rugosa   red-bodied tick found on dogs.

Ixodes texanus   localized American dog tick.

J

jabot frill of hair on the throat, esp. on SCHIP-PERKES.

Jack dim. JACK RUSSELL TERRIER.

jack 1. male of an animal [159], esp. a male hare.

> Or just a great jack, this gay morning
> Sense scorning. [85f]

> If a stout runner can keep within fairly easy distance of a pack of well-bred Beagles on the line of a lively Jack hare, he is in the sort of condition to be generally envied. [225]

> Old Tiney, surliest of his kind,
> Who, nursed with tender care,
> And to domestic bounds confined,
> Was still a wild Jack-hare. [102c]

2. implement used formerly to create an artificially short foreface on BULLDOGS.

> Formerly this shortness of face [in the Bulldog] was artificially obtained by the use of the 'jack', an atrocious form of torture, by which an iron instrument was used to force back the face by means of thumbscrews. [225]

> The instrument – a sort of vice – which was used in days gone by to hold in position the noses of bulldogs which had been forced back after the lip-string had been severed. The object of all this was to develop an artificial shortness of face, and it need scarcely be added that it was illegal as it was cruel. [320]

Jackal CANIS AUREUS; CANIS MESOMELUS.

jacke JAQUE.

jacket coat.

Jack Russell JACK RUSSELL TERRIER; PARSON JACK RUSSELL TERRIER.

Jack Russell Terrier popular TERRIER which formerly embraced a variety of types, the short, crook-limbed or heavy-bodied specimens of which would undoubtedly have been anathema to the reverend gentleman whose name they carry. In Britain breeders have steadfastly refused to become involved in any process which might lead to official recognition although the best Jack Russell Terriers are indistinguishable from the KC officially recognized PARSON JACK RUSSELL TERRIER.

Jämthund [FCI] one of the ELKHOUND breeds with origins in northern Sweden.

Basically a bigger and heavier version of the more widely popular Elkhound: a powerfully built SPITZ, with long, straight, harsh, grey topcoat over a soft grey undercoat; the powerful head is MASKED. Used for hunting elk and as a DOMESTIC GUARD. Height 59–64cm (23¼–25in).

Japanese dim. JAPANESE CHIN.

Japanese Akita [KC] one of the largest of the native Japanese breeds, originally used as a hunter for larger game and, probably only incidentally, for fighting.

The breed is physically impressive and typically SPITZ in appearance, with a broad, flat, bear-like skull, strong MUZZLE, and slightly rounded, triangu-lar, pricked ears. The powerful neck is thick and fairly short, the body fairly long with a deep wide chest. The tail is long and thick, and usually carried curled over the back. The short, stiff coat may be of any colour or combination of colours. Height 61–71cm (24–28in); weight 34–50kg (75–110lb).

Japanese Chin [AKC, KC] oriental TOY breed of considerable antiquity, which has its origins in both royal and religious symbolism, the lion-like appearance being created in tribute both to Buddha and to royalty. The breed is undoubtedly closely related, in appearance and purpose, to the PEKINGESE but whether its origins are in China or Japan remains a matter for inconclusive debate.

A lively, intelligent and good-natured little dog. The head is relatively large, the broad skull rounded between the eyes; the MUZZLE is very short. The eyes, which have an expression of permanent astonishment, are large, dark and wide set. The V-shaped ears are small, high and wide set. The neck is proudly carried and the forelimbs finely boned and straight; the body is compact and square in outline. The hindquarters show a good TURN OF STIFLE. The tail curls over the back. The profuse, long, silky coat forms plumes on ears, chest, behind the legs, tail and belly, and may be black or shades of red and pearly white; never TRICOLOUR. Weight 1.8–3.2kg (4–7lb).

Japanese Fighting Dog JAPANESE AKITA and TOSA.

Japanese Pug JAPANESE CHIN.

> Not unlike our modern Toy Spaniels in general outline, for in his skull and retrousse nose he bears a great resemblance to these breeds. [320a]

Japanese river fever SCRUB TYPHUS.

Japanese Shiba Inu [KC] SHIBA INU.

Japanese Spaniel JAPANESE CHIN.

> Through the introduction of the black-and-tan Japanese Spaniel – of which I know at present a very fine specimen, brought over by Sir John Hay – black-and-tan King Charles were produced. [320a]

Japanese Spitz [KC] small SPITZ breed created during the late years of the 19th century to satisfy a demand for small HOUSE-DOGS.

The breed is typically spitz in every characteristic with black-rimmed, dark, almond eyes and black lips and nose, contrasting sharply with a profuse, STAND-OFF white coat. Height 28–36cm (11–14in).

Japanese Terrier NIPPON TERRIER.

Japanese Tosa TOSA.

Japanese Wolf CANIS LUPUS HODOPHYLAX.

jaque canine armour.

> Jaque, also a jacke or coat of maile; and thence a jacke for the bodie of an Irish Greyhound, etc., made commonly of a wild boares tanned skinne and put on him when he is to coape with that violent beast. [98]

jaundice yellow-tinged skin caused by liver malfunction.

Javanese Dog SIGHTHOUND native to Java.
> Every Javanese of rank has large packs of dogs with which he hunts the muntjak, the deer of that country. The dogs are led in strings by the attendants until they scent the prey: they are then unloosed, while the sportsmen follow, but not at the speed which would distinguish the British sportsman. [406]

jaw panosteitis inherited inflammation of the jaw bones. (Mode of inheritance, familial.)

Jed Forest FOXHOUND pack dating from 1884; the COUNTRY includes moorland, pasture and plough.

jejunum part of the intestines, so called because it is generally empty. [406] (der. L. *jejunus*, fasting.)

Jelly Dog (colloq.) BEAGLE. (der. the breed's association with the hare, which is eaten with redcurrant jelly.)

Jelly Hound type of HOUND formerly to be found chiefly in Wales.
> What was known as the Jelly hound descended from the original Margram pack. They were mostly black-and-tans, with a heavy, bloodhoundy look about them, not much more than 21 inches in height, somewhat finer in the throat than the average Welsh hound, and possessing the most wonderful voices. [383]

jerky pulse WATER HAMMER PULSE.

Jersey former DRAGHOUND pack.

Jesse, George R. author of *Researches into the History of the British Dog* (1866).

jewelled of eye in which the iris has a ruddy tinge; sometimes also applied to a WALL EYE.

jingler bells and other trinkets threaded on a wire ring and used to create noise to encourage SLED-DOGS.

jinked of an animal injured in the LOINS or back. [159]

John Peel Foxhounds BLENCATHRA.

jolly (obs.) said of a skittish in-season bitch. [159]

Jones Terrier archetypal NORWICH TERRIER popularized during the 1920s by Frank Jones (also known as 'Roughrider Jones'), who made a living out of selling horses and dogs to students at Cambridge.

jowl 1. FLEWS.
> But if the guy is strange-looking the dogs are even stranger-looking, because they have big heads, and jowls that hang down like an old-time faro bank dealer's, and long ears the size of bed sheets. [306]

2. (regional Eng.) howl.

judge 1. person appointed to assess the merits of dogs in competition.
> The judge should be a man of order, possessed of a natural ability for clear and accurate comparison and rapid analysis; he must be able almost at a glance to take in the whole animal and to roughly estimate its approach to his ideal standard of excellence for the breed; to mentally dissect the several properties of each one, and to place them in the order in which they approach nearest to his idea of perfection. [106a]
> I have known a man act as a judge of fox terriers

> who had never bred one in his life, had never seen a fox in front of hounds, had never seen a terrier go to ground, had never seen either otter, weasel, or foumart outside the glass case in which they rested on the wall in the bar parlour. [221]

2. carry out the duties of a judge.
> I show
> Thou judgest.
> He gets first prize
> She protests
> We make a row
> Ye get into hot water
> They complain to the Secretary
> It [the dog] has a fit. [239]

judge the wrong end of the lead base assessment on the reputation of the handler rather than on the quality of the dog.

jugal ZYGOMATIC.

jugelow dog. [280]

Jugoslovenski Drobojni Gonič JUGOSLOVENSKI TROBOJNI GONIČ.

Jugoslovenski Ovcarski Pas-Sarplaninac [FCI] Yugoslavian Sheep Dog, a PASTORAL HERDER and GUARD, closely related to the ANATOLIAN SHEPHERD DOG, but with origins in the part of former Yugoslavia now called Illyria.
The head is broad in skull and strong in MUZZLE, with short V-shaped, pendulous ears; the neck is strongly muscled and the chest deep and capacious. The back is fairly short and broad, and the limbs well boned and muscular. The long tail is carried SCIMITAR fashion. The dense coat may be either rough or smooth, with a good undercoat, and may be any colour from black to white, whether solid or shaded. Height 56–61cm (22–24in); weight 25–37kg (58–81½lb).

Jugoslovenski Planinksi Gonič [FCI] Yugoslavian Mountain Hound, originating in the south west of former Yugoslavia, where it is principally used to hunt smaller, occasionally larger, game, including wild boar.
A long-headed dog, with MEDIAN FURROW, moderate STOP, and a long MUZZLE; the rounded, pendulous ears are high set and fairly short, hanging close to the head. The body is long with a deep, broad chest, WELL-SPRUNG RIBS, and a deep, short LOIN. Legs are of medium length, well-boned and strongly muscled. The short coat has a black SADDLE over red or tan, and a white BLAZE on the chest is permitted. Height 45-55cm (17¾–21¼in).

Jugoslovenski Posavski Gonič [FCI] typical of other HOUNDs with origins in Yugoslavia, but with a thick, wiry coat, which is red or WHEATEN, with or without white markings. Height 46–58cm (18–23in); weight 18kg (39½lb).

Jugoslovenski Trobojni Gonič [FCI] Yugoslavian Tricolour Hound. An ancient and rare SCENTHOUND used to hunt small game.
The head is of medium length, with well-defined OCCIPUT, strong MUZZLE and CLEAN LIPS; the eyes are

brown and the rounded, pendulous ears are high set and carried flat against the cheeks. The forequarters are WELL ANGULATED, and the legs straight with PASTERNS of moderate length; the feet are rounded with well arched toes and springy pads. The body is broad and deep, the ribs slightly rounded, with broad, short LOINS and a broad, sloping CROUP. The hindquarters are muscular and well angulated; the SABRE TAIL is fairly long. The TRICOLOUR coat is short, dense and glossy. Height 46–56cm (18–22in).

junior any dog between the age of six and eighteen months.

junior class 1. [KC] show class designated for JUNIORS. 2. FCI show class for dogs between nine and fifteen months old on the day of the show.

junior handling [KC] competition in which the ability of young people to handle dogs in the ring is assessed; the handling skill and not the quality of the dogs is the deciding factor.

junior showmanship (Am.) JUNIOR HANDLING.

Junior Warrant [KC] award made by the KC to dogs that have won a certain number of points at shows before they cease to be JUNIORS.

Jura Hound JURA-LAUFHUND.

Jura-laufhund [FCI] a black-and-tan, thick-coated SCENTHOUND of Swiss origin. The Jura-LAUFHUND is very reminiscent of a lightly built BLOODHOUND.

Jura-laufhund, type Saint-Hubert black version of the JURA-LAUFHUND.

Jura Neiderlaufhund smaller version of the JURA-LAUFHUND. Height 33–42cm (13–16½in); weight 15–18kg (33–39½lb).

juvenile cellulitis inherited condition causing inflamed facial tissue. (Mode of inheritance, familial.)

juvenile osteodystrophy CANINE JUVENILE OSTEODYSTROPHY.

juvenile pyoderma skin disease of the head, stomach and anal area, associated with swelling of the jaw lymph glands, which causes fever and weight loss; frequently fatal. Cause unknown.

K

K standard gene symbol for kinky coat.

Kabuli Hound (obs.) AFGHAN HOUND.

Kabyle Dog AIDI.

Kaffir Dog Hottentot Dog: BASENJI.

Kai Dog BRINDLE, short, coarse-coated, SPITZ-type SIGHTHOUND of Japanese origin. The breed's alternative name of Tora Dog refers to the breed's striped brindle coat, *tora* being Japanese for tiger. Height 46–58cm (18–23in); weight 16–21kg (35–46lb).

Kaikadi TERRIER-like breed from the Indian Deccan plateau where it is used to kill vermin and hunt small game.

The breed has a long, lean head with prominent eyes and PRICK EARS, its legs, too, are unusually long and thin. The coat is smooth, a mixture of white, tan and black.

Kalagh type of AFGHAN HOUND that has long hair on the head and ears, but short hair on the body.

Kamschatka Dog type of GREENLAND DOG.
> Commonly black or white. They are strong, nimble, and active, and are very useful in drawing sledges. [51]

Kangal ANATOLIAN SHEPHERD DOG.

Kangal Dog ANATOLIAN SHEPHERD DOG.

Kangaroo Dog AUSTRALIAN GREYHOUND.
> Now a decided and distinct breed, with certain famous strains that are sought after and that win distinction in their classes at the Colonial shows. In general appearance the dog resembles a heavy Greyhound. [225]

Kaninchen Dachshund KANINCHTECKEL.

Kaninchteckel DACHSHUND developed principally for hunting rabbit.

Kansas Jack Rabbit American hare closely resembling the European variety.

Karabash ANATOLIAN SHEPHERD DOG.

Karabash Dog ANATOLIAN SHEPHERD DOG.

Karelian Bear Dog KARJALANKARHUKOIRA.

Karelian Bear Laïka RUSSO-EUROPEAN LAÏKA.

Karelian Laïka RUSSO-EUROPEAN LAÏKA.

Karelischer Barenhund KARJALANKARHUKOIRA.

Karelo-Finnish Laïka typically SPITZ breed developed on the Russian/Finnish borders to hunt small game.

The breed has round eyes, a thick neck exaggerated by a thick RUFF, and a rather long back; its light build and bushy, curled tail contribute to a distinctive appearance. The dense, stand-off coat may be red, fawn or black with a white BLAZE, chest, legs and tail tip. Weight 11.5–14kg (25–31lb).

Karelsk Björnhund KARJALANKARHUKOIRA.

Karelskaja KARELO-FINNISH LAÏKA.

Karjalankarhukoira [FCI] large and powerful SPITZ breed with origins in western Russia. Used for hunting bear but also used on elk, wolves and smaller game, the breed's courage and stamina are remarkable.

The strong head is broad, with a powerful MUZZLE; the body is well muscled. The dull, black coat is straight and stiff with white markings to chest, BLAZE, legs and tail tip. Height 48–59cm (18¾–23¼in); weight 20–23kg (44–50½lb).

Karjalankarhukoira **Karelsk** **Björnhund** KARJALANKARHUKOIRA.

Karjalan Karkuloirat former name of the Karelian Bear Dog: KARJALANKARHUKOIRA.

karotype the way in which chromosomes are arranged within the cell nucleus.

Karski Ovčar [FCI] PASTORAL GUARD with origins in Yugoslavia.

The breed has a powerful head and MUZZLE, a rather long, deep back, and sturdy limbs. The tail is bushy. The exceptionally dense, weather-resistant SABLE coat provides protection in the harsh conditions in which the dog works. Black muzzle and SPECTACLES contribute to a characteristic expression.

Karst Sheep Dog KARSKI OVČAR.

Karst Shepherd KARSKI OVČAR.

karyogram IDIOGRAM.

karyology study of the chromosome nucleus.

Kaukasische Schäferhund KAVKASKAIA OVTCHARKA.

Kavkaskaia Ovtcharka [FCI] herding breed to be found in varied forms throughout the former Soviet Union.

It is usually a large dog with a broad skull, strong MUZZLE, and lupine appearance. The body is deep and long, the PLUMED TAIL curled over the back. Height 63.5–71cm (25–28in); weight 46–65.5kg (101–144lb).

KC abbr. KENNEL CLUB(2).

keel underside of the BRISKET, esp. in DACHSHUNDS.

keeper 1. a canine DOMESTIC GUARD.
> Borrowing his name of his service, for he does not only keep farmers' houses, but also merchants' maisons, wherein great wealth, riches, substance and costly stuff is reposed. [139]

2. dim. gamekeeper.
> I strolled on a little, and soon heard the beat of rapid footsteps behind me, as a hard-featured old keeper ran up. [170]

Keeper's Dog dim. Gamekeeper's Dog; a MASTIFF.

Kees dim. KEESHOND.

Keeshond [AKC, KC] DOMESTIC GUARD said to have been popular among Dutch bargees, hence its alternative name of Dutch Barge Dog. A typically SPITZ breed with a wedge-shaped vulpine head, pricked ears and almond-shaped eyes framed by characteristic SPECTACLES. The long, arched neck is furnished with a profuse RUFF. The body is short and COMPACT, presenting an overall square outline. The limbs are well boned and strongly muscled, the hindquarters carrying profuse light-coloured TROUSERS. The PLUMED, black-tipped tail is carried over the back at all times. The black, shaded grey, coat is harsh and erect. Height 43.2–45.7cm (17–18in).

The name may be derived from Cornelis, or Kees, de Gyzelaar, a late 18th-century Dutch patriot, or possibly from the breed's association with the patriots – the Dutch word for rabble.

Kelb-tal Fenek PHARAOH HOUND.

Kelef K'naani CANAAN DOG.

Kelpie dim. AUSTRALIAN KELPIE.
> King trained his Kelpie and ran her in the first Sheepdog Trials in Australia, held at Forbes, New South Wales, in 1872, . . . her many pups born over the succeeding years were sold as Kelpie's pups, and this probably led to the naming of the breed. [160]

Keltski Gonič powerful, harsh-coated Bosnian HOUND used for a variety of both large and small game. Height 55cm (21¼in).

ken (Jap.) dog (as in Tosa Ken, Ainu Ken, etc.).

Kendal and District former pure-bred OTTERHOUND pack formed in 1903 to hunt the Wharfe, Nidd, Derwent, Esk and their tributaries.

kenede (obs.) KENNELled. [159]

kenet (obs.) small variety of running HOUND.

Kenette KENET.

Kenettys KENET.

kenled having given birth. [159]

kennel 1. place in which dogs are housed.
2. holt or EARTH.
> Before the dawn he had loved and fed
> And found a kennel, and gone to bed. [249]

3. to harbour quarry. [159] 4. breeder's establishment. 5. place of temporary boarding for dogs.

kennel blind able to see merit only in one's own dogs, a debilitating malady among some breeders.

kennel boy man who takes care of the KENNEL and its inhabitants.

kennel club organization set up to govern canine affairs. 2. KENNEL CLUB (KC).

kennel cough acute, sometimes highly infectious respiratory condition characterized by coughing spasms, fever, nasal discharge and swollen lymph glands. Infective agents vary from viruses, bacteria, mycoplasmas and allergic conditions.

kennel hare captive hare alleged to have been formerly kept to train FOXHOUNDS and STAGHOUNDS. (Unlikely to be true.)
> Stories are told of the kennel-hare – a hare kept on purpose, and which is sometimes shown to the fox or stag hounds. The moment that any of them open, they are tied up to the whipping post, and flogged, while the keepers at every stroke call out 'Ware hare!' [406]

kennel huntsman person responsible for the care of HOUNDS.

kennel lameness lameness of uncertain cause affecting several inhabitants of a kennel.
> This is a kind of lameness connected with, or attributable to, the kennel. [406]

kennel maid woman who takes care of the kennel and its inmates.

kennel man person who takes care of the kennel and its inmates.
> A good kennel man is a most valuable person, a bad one is a constant source of embarrassment to his master and a danger to his charges. [320]

kennel sickness former name applied to an outbreak of contagious diarrhoea among kennel inmates.

kennel terriers TERRIERS, sometimes of well-defined STRAINS, kept in HUNT KENNELS. [123]

kennel tick *RHIPICEPHALUS SANGUINEUS.*

kennel type breeder's STRAIN; of a type within a breed that can be discerned as hailing from a particular KENNEL(4).

Kennel Club (KC) UK KENNEL CLUB.

kennelitis unreasonable suspicion and fear of humans resulting from lack of early socialization of dogs reared in kennels.

kennels KENNEL(4); HUNT KENNELS.

Kentucky Shell Heap Dog fossil dog found in southern states of America.

keout mongrel CUR. [159]

keratitis inherited inflammation of the cornea. (Mode of inheritance, recessive.)

Kergie CORGI.
> The Kergie is a small, smooth-haired dog, low-to-ground, red in colour, with a little white, and very like a fox minus the brush. He is used as a cattle-dog, like a Lancashire Heeler. He will kill rats, but will not go to ground, although there may be exceptions, of course. Kergies often have wall-eyes, and Sealyhams show this trait occasionally. [238a]

Kerry Beagle one of several Irish breeds which experienced a period of decline that brought them close to the point of extinction. The breed's demise has been prematurely announced by some canine authorities. The Scarteen Foxhounds, based in County Limerick have, since 1781, hunted a pack composed entirely of Kerry Beagles. The pack is popularly known as the Black and Tans.

The breed is basically an IRISH FOXHOUND, very similar to an old-fashioned BLOODHOUND, comparatively lightly built and lacking that breed's exaggerations. Similar in appearance to the Bloodhound, the short coat is usually black and tan but other colours are not unknown. Height 58cm (23in).
> In reality not a Beagle at all, usually a black-and-tan hound the size of a Foxhound, and with much of the appearance and many of the characteristics of the old Southern Hound. [123]
> Seems now to be practically extinct, although so recently as 1870 the Scarteen pack in Tipperary was composed entirely of this breed. [225]
> Richardson, in 1851, writes of a Kerry beagle, which, he says, is 'a fine, tall, dashing hound, averaging twenty-six inches in height, and occasionally, individual dogs attain to twenty-eight inches. He has deep chops, broad, pendulous ears, and when highly bred is hardly to be distinguished from an indifferent bloodhound.' [221]

Kerry Blue Terrier [AKC, FCI, KC] large and characteristically Irish TERRIER breed developed for a catholic range of sports about whose precise nature it is perhaps best not to enquire too deeply.

A COMPACT and powerful terrier, with a long, lean head, dark eyes with keen expression, and small V-shaped DROP EARS. The REACHY NECK runs into flat shoulders, and a SHORT-COUPLED deep-chested body. The forelimbs are straight and well boned, the hindquarters large and well-developed, with short HOCKS. The profuse, wavy, trimmed coat is soft and silky and in adults always blue with or without black POINTS(3). Juveniles are often black. Height 46–48cm (18–18¾in); weight 15–16.8kg (33–37lb).

Keswick (US) AMERICAN FOXHOUND pack formed in 1896 to hunt a rolling woodland and pasture COUNTRY in Virginia.

Kibble Hound short-legged version of the old SOUTHERN HOUND.

> Besides these [Old English Hounds] there is a variety called the 'Kibble-Hound', produced by a mixture of the Beagle and the Old English Hound. [51] Applied to such as were short and crooked in the leg, as if broken, and, in that sense, the Dachshund, the Basset, and some of our Dandie Dinmont Terriers, may be called Kibble-hounds. [123]
> So long ago as 1590 the Southern, or Talbot, was rendered shorter on the leg, and faster, by crossing, and then he was called a 'Kibble Hound', and in the time of James I they ran 'together in a lumpe . . . both at sente and view'. [186]

kicked-up toe KNOCKED-UP TOE.

kid-fox fox cub. [159]

Kildare hunt dating from 1766 after which amalgamation with the Bishopscourt Hunt in 1793 formed the present establishment which hunts fox over a COUNTRY in County Kildare and Wicklow.

Kilfeacle Irish BEAGLE pack formed in 1955 to hunt a COUNTRY in County Tipperary.

Kilkenny hunt dating from 1797; former masters include Isaac Bell (1908–1921).

kill dead quarry.

Killeagh Irish HARRIER pack formed in 1949 to hunt a COUNTRY in County Cork.

Killenaule Irish TRENCHER-FED BEAGLE pack formed in 1960 to hunt a COUNTRY in County Tipperary.

Killinick Irish HARRIER pack formed in 1921 to hunt a COUNTRY in County Wexford.

Killultagh, Old Rock and Chichester Irish HARRIER pack formed in 1876 on the amalgamation of the Killultagh and Old Rock and Chichester, which date from 1832. The COUNTRY lies in County Antrim.

Kilmoganny Irish HARRIER pack formed in 1918 as the Carrick Harriers; the name was changed in 1922. The COUNTRY lies in southern Kilkenny.

Kilrush Irish BEAGLE pack formed in 1958 to hunt a COUNTRY in County Limerick.

kinesiology science of animal locomotion.

kinetic balance balance while in motion.

King Charles Spaniel [AKC, FCI, KC] TOY SPANIEL breed associated with King Charles I.

The breed is gentle, affectionate and reserved. Its DOMED skull is comparatively large, with a well-defined STOP and square MUZZLE. The eyes are large and expressive. The ears are pendulous, very long and well FEATHERED. The body is deep, and short. The gait is free and active. The long, silky coat may be black and tan, TRICOLOUR, BLENHEIM or RUBY. Weight 3.6–6.3kg (7½–13½lb).

King of Terriers usually refers to the AIREDALE TERRIER, the largest of the TERRIER breeds.

Kingmik name by which the ESKIMO DOG is known to the natives of northern Canada.

King's Shropshire Light Infantry BEAGLE pack formed in 1964 to hunt a COUNTRY in Devon.

King, William author of 'Reasons and proposals for laying a tax upon dogs, humbly addressed to the House of Commons', by Lover of His Country (1740).

Kingwood (US) American, English, and crossbred FOXHOUND pack formed in 1962 to hunt a wooded and open COUNTRY in New Jersey.

kink 1. sharp bend, esp. in a tail; a deformity.
> Tail set low, without kink or twist. [203, BEARDED COLLIE]

2. a dog which behaves in an unpredictable manner.

kink tail tail that has an abnormally sharp, angled bend along its length.

kinky (of coat) wavy.

kin selection tendency among wild animals to favour mates with which they have genes in common, thus increasing the chance that those genes will survive.

Kirghiz Borzoi TAIGAN.

Kirghiz Greyhound Southern Siberian COURSING HOUND, with silky FEATHERING on ears, legs and RINGED TAIL; the larger dogs tend to have a coarser coat. Weight 28–41kg (61½–90lb). [150]
> kept by the Kirghiz, on the steppes of Central and Southern Siberia and Turkestan. [225]

Kirkham former HARRIER pack formed in 1814 to hunt a COUNTRY in the Lancashire Fylde.

Kishu [AKC] one of several SPITZ HOUND breeds developed in the various regions of Japan; a close relative of the KAI and SHIKOKU.

The coarse coat is short, and straight. Height 43–46cm (17–18in).

Kishu Inu KISHU.

kissing spots KISS MARK.
> tan spots on the side of the cheeks. [46]

kiss mark tan mark on the cheek or forehead of some breeds.

Kit Fox *VULPES MACROTIS*.

Kleiner Münsterländer [FCI] SMALL MÜNSTERLÄNDER.

Klinefelter's syndrome condition resulting in abnormally small fibrous testes, occasionally seen in dogs.

knee STIFLE-joint.

kneecap PATELLA.

knee cutting GENUISCISSIO.

knep (regional Eng.) a playful bite.

knitting WEAVING.

knobber second-year hart. [159], possibly a misspelling of KNOBBLER.

knobbler two-year-old hart. [151c]

knocked-down hip fracture of the ilium, seen most often in working or racing SIGHTHOUNDS.

knocked-up toe injury to the digital flexor tendon common in coursing and racing dogs and working SIGHTHOUNDS.

knocking cry of HARE HOUNDS. [159]

knuckle PASTERN-joint.

knucklebone TALUS.

knuckle over (of the carpal joint) to protrude forward beyond the vertical line of the forelimbs. [*illus.*]
Forearm . . . must not bend forward or knuckle over. [203, DACHSHUND]

knuckled up (of toes) strongly arched.
The feet strong and well knuckled up. [6, BLOODHOUND]

Knuckling over.

knuckling over *see* KNUCKLE OVER.
Knuckling over highly undesirable. [203, PETIT BASSET GRIFFON VENDEEN]

Koban Copegi ANATOLIAN SHEPHERD DOG.

Kombia former native of southern India used principally as a hunting dog, now thought to be extinct in its pure form.

Komondor [AKC, FCI, KC] largest of the herding breeds developed in Hungary. Used principally as a PASTORAL GUARD the breed is strong, wary of strangers and must be treated with respect.

The head is short, the skull arched, the STOP moderate and the MUZZLE broad. The medium-sized, pendulous ears are U-shaped. The body is broad and deep, and the overall outline rather longer than high. The white coat falls in long, thick cords to provide protection against both weather and combatants. Height 60–80cm (23½–31½in); weight 36–51kg (79–112lb).

Kooichi Dog (var. spelling) KUCHI.

Kooiker Dog KOOIKERHONDJE.

Kooikerhondje wavy-coated, red and white Dutch GUNDOG. Height 35–41cm (13¾–16in); weight 9–11kg (20–24lb).

Korel Laika one of six RUSSIAN-EUROPEAN LAIKA

breeds identified in 1896 by Prince Andrew Shirinsky Shihmatoff. [380]

Korthals GRIFFON D'ARRÊT À POIL DUR.

Korthals Griffon GRIFFON D'ARRÊT À POIL DUR.

Kostroma Hound GONTAJA RUSSKAJA.

Krabbe's disease GLOBOID CELL LEUKODYSTROPHY.

Krasky Ovčar dense-coated, iron-grey Yugoslavian PASTORAL GUARD. Height 54–61cm (21–24in); weight 24–40kg (55–88lb).

Kromfohrländer [FCI] TERRIER-like companion breed of recent origin, produced by Frau Ilse Schleifenbaum in what is now North Rhine-Westphalia.

The breed has a broad skull, rather heavy V-shaped ears which fold on a line with the skull, a noticeable STOP and a broad MUZZLE. The body is rather long, the chest deep, the long tail is carried below the level of the back. The medium-length coat is rough and with shades of tan on a predominantly white GROUND. Height 38–43cm (15–17in); weight 12kg (26½lb).

k-selection process of selection for those qualities which, in the wild, lead to success in the face of competition. Desirable qualities include: long life, large size and power, and small numbers of well-cared-for offspring. The effect of a similar form of selection may be observed among kennels – and their owners.

Kuchi Tanjore vermin killer, with long, thin legs and a heavily FEATHERED tail. Height about 25cm (10in); weight about 7kg (15½lb).

Kurran Valley Hound one of several former names for the AFGHAN HOUND.

Kurzhaar GERMAN SHORT-HAIRED POINTER.

Kurzhaariger GERMAN SHORT-HAIRED POINTER.

Kurzhaariger Kaninchenteckel short-haired rabbiting DACHSHUND.

Kuvasz [FCI] Hungarian PASTORAL HERDER and GUARD, very typical of other white, heavily coated herding breeds which have their origins in Europe's mountain ranges. The name is derived from the Turkish word for guard and is said to suggest that the breed's origins may lay further east than Hungary.

The head is noble and powerful, with well-developed MEDIAN FURROW, long, pointed MUZZLE and oblique, dark eyes. The ears are high set and fall to the side of the skull. The neck is rather upright, the ribs deep and only moderately rounded; there is a rise over the CROUP to a long tail; hindquarters are muscular but not over ANGULATED. The DOUBLE, weather-resistant coat is rough and wavy and invariably white or ivory. Height 66cm (26in); weight 40–60kg (88-132lb).

Kyi Leo breed developed since 1972 in America from CROSSES(2) between the LHASA APSO and the MALTESE. Smaller than but very similar to the Lhasa Apso.

kyphosis abnormal curvature of the spine.

Kyushu KISHU.

L

Lab dim. LABRADOR RETRIEVER.

Labrador dim. LABRADOR RETRIEVER.

Labrador Retriever [AKC, FCI, KC] probably developed from imports of small NEWFOUNDLAND dogs, known as the St John's breed, CROSSED(2) with British native GUNDOGS during the early years of the 19th century. The breed is strongly built, active and good-tempered, with an excellent nose and soft mouth; it is generally an eager and biddable worker.

The broad skull and powerful MUZZLE are separated by a well-defined STOP, the medium-sized eyes may be brown or hazel, the ears hang close to the head and are set well back. The neck is clean and powerful, the forequarters long and sloping with straight, well-boned limbs. The chest is wide, deep and WELL SPRUNG, the LOINS strong and short. Hindquarters are strong with WELL-LET-DOWN HOCK and a good TURN OF STIFLE. The distinctive tail is very thick at the base, tapers gradually and must not curl over the back (the BREED STANDARD uses the phrase 'otter tail'. The coat is short, dense, flat and hard with a weather-resistant undercoat, and may be black, yellow or liver, always self-coloured, though a small white spot on the chest is permitted. Height 54–57cm (21–22½in).

Labrit unrecognized southern French SHEEP DOG.

lachrymal of or relating to tears, especially of the glands or ducts that secrete tears.

  lachrymal gland glands or ducts, situated in the inner corners of the eyes, which produce tears.

lacing moving with the rear legs unusually close together.

Lacoena impossible CROSS between a dog and a fox.
  Dog bred of a bitch and a fox. [139]

lactation the process of a bitch's producing milk.

lactogenic hormone PROLACTIN.

lady pack (of HOUNDS) pack consisting entirely of bitches.

Laekenois [FCI] BELGIAN SHEEP DOG.

Lafora bodies large bodies which normally surround the neurons and which may proliferate in cases of neurological disease, especially glycoproteinosis, a disease of the central nervous system which gives rise to seizures. Similar symptoms also recur in Lafora's disease.

Lafora's disease a familial form of epilepsy. *See* LAFORA BODIES.

Lagotto TRUFFLE DOG.

laid-back (of the angle formed by the scapula and the humerus) ANGULATED.
  Shoulder-blades well laid back. [203, BASSET HOUND]

Laïka group of Russian hunting SPITZ breeds. (der. from *Iajatj*, to bark, a reference to the way in which these breeds mark their quarry. [312]) The first dog to be sent into space was a Laïka.

Laïka Roussko-Evropeiskaia [FCI] large, strong and impressive SPITZ breed built on the same lines as the AKITA and the KARELIAN BEAR DOG; used to hunt bear, wolf, boar and elk. Height 53–61cm (20¾–24in); weight 20–23kg (44–50½lb).

Laïka Wastatchno-Sibirskaia [FCI] a distinctly lupine breed, originally used as a DRAUGHT and hunting dog and developed in Eastern Siberia. The lupine appearance is accentuated by a thick, rather stand-off coat which is often black, grey or white but may also be red, tan or PIED. Height 56–64cm (22–25in); weight 18–23kg (39½–50½lb).

Lajka Ruissisch Europaisch RUSSIAN-EUROPEAN LAIKA.

Lake Dog *CANIS FAMILIARIS PALUSTRIS.* [312]

Lakeland Terrier [AKC, FCI, KC] small TERRIER with origins in the English lake district, and which now exists in two distinct and quite separate forms, one of which is officially recognized, the other used principally for sporting purposes and appearing publicly at hunt and working terrier shows.

Although the KC BREED STANDARD emphasizes the breed's workmanlike appearance and fearless demeanour the officially recognized breed is no longer involved with its original purpose in life. The flat skull is refined, the MUZZLE powerful and not over long; the eyes are dark, and the V-shaped ears are alertly carried and set neither high nor low. The REACHY NECK is slightly arched, the shoulders WELL LAID and the limbs straight and well boned. The chest is narrow, the back moderately short; the strong, muscular hindquarters have long thighs and WELL-TURNED STIFLES. The tail is traditionally DOCKED and carried GAILY. The dense, harsh coat may be black or blue and tan, WHEATEN-red GRIZZLE, liver, blue or black; deep tans are not encouraged. Height not more than 37cm (14½in); weight 6.8–7.7kg (15–17lb).

The working Lakeland differs from the recognized variety in that the head is broader, shorter and altogether more powerful; the back is slightly longer to enable the terrier to gallop across country and to manoeuvre underground. The coat, exceptionally hard and dense, is weather-resistant and does not produce the copious FURNISHINGS which are such a feature of the recognized breed. Weight up to about 9kg (20lb).

Lake of Two Mountains (Can.) ENGLISH FOXHOUND pack formed in 1946 to hunt a wooded COUNTRY in Quebec.

Lalanders' Dog BAT-EARED FOX.

Lamarck, Jean Baptiste Pierre Antoine de Monet (1744–1829) French naturalist who propounded a theory, LAMARCKISM, which suggests that acquired characteristics may be inherited. It has since been discredited.

Lamarckism discredited theory which suggested that acquired characteristics can be inherited.

lamb clip coat CLIP used for companion POODLES in which the coat on MUZZLE, neck, feet and base of tail is clipped very short, while the coat over the rest of the body is reduced to about 1cm (½in) long. A popular variation of this clip leaves longer hair on the legs from elbow to PASTERN. A POMPOM is usual.

lame (of movement) unsound.

La Medera PERRA DE AGUA ESPAÑOL.

Lamerton Harriers SPERLING.

La Mesta PERRA DE AGUA ESPAÑOL.

lamina cribrosa perforated roof of the nasal cavity.

lamping using long dogs to hunt at night with the aid of spotlights, carried by hand or, less sportingly, affixed to a vehicle.

Lanarkshire and Renfrewshire FOXHOUND pack originally hunted by the Glasgow Hounds and the Robertson Hunt in 1771; the existing pack was formed in 1820 but the COUNTRY has since been restricted by industrial development.

Lancashire Heeler [KC] recently recognized DROVER developed in the Fylde area of Lancashire and with links with Viking invaders, though whether the cattle dogs of Lancashire, Wales and Scandinavia have origins in Sweden or Britain remains a matter for debate.

The breed is low set, active and strong and combines herding qualities with the instincts of a vermin-killer. The flat skull is wide and tapers towards the eyes, the almond eyes are dark, the ears either pricked or DROP, though the latter should be mobile. The moderately long neck joins WELL LAID shoulders and amply boned forelimbs with PASTERNS that turn slightly outwards. The chest is WELL-SPRUNG with ribs carried well back to a CLOSE COUPLING. Hindquarters are muscular with WELL-LET-DOWN HOCKS. The tail is set high and forms a partial curl. The coat is short and black and tan. Height 25–30cm (10–12in).

land spaniel (obs.) generic term used to differentiate between dogs used principally for wild fowling and those used for land-based quarry.

> You shall observe, that although any dogge which is of perfit and good sent, and naturally addicted to the hunting of feathers, as whether it be a land-spaniell, water-spaniell, or else the Mungrell between either or both those kindes, or the Mungrels of either of these kindes, either with the shallow flewed hounds, the tumbler, lurcher, or indeede, the small bastard Mastiffe, may be brought to this perfection of Setting. [245a]

Landilo Farmers' FOXHOUND pack founded during the Second World War to succeed the Penlan; the Dyfed COUNTRY is well wooded.

Landseer [FCI] black-and-white variety of the NEW-FOUNDLAND. (der. Sir Edwin Landseer.)

Landseer Newfoundland BICOLOURED variety of the LANDSEER.

Lane Basset type of BASSET bred by Charles Lane of Franqueville, Baos, Seine-Inférieur.

> Decidedly of a plainer type, weak in colour, lighter in bone, and noticeably longer in the leg, the head broader and somewhat flat, with shorter ears. [225]

Lane Hound smooth-coated type of BASSET HOUND bred by Charles Lane. [123]

Langehren breed that was noted in the Forest Laws of Canute as being 'too small to do harm to the King's deer'. [123]

The derivation of the name suggests that the breed had long ears. DRURY suggests that they were the ancestors of the Talbot and, eventually, the FOXHOUND.

Langhaar GERMAN SHORT-HAIRED POINTER.

Langhaar Hollandse Herdershond long-coated variety of the HOLLANDSE HERDERSHOND.

Langhaariger Kaninchenteckel long-haired variety of the KANINCHTECKEL.

Langhaariger Teckel long-haired variety of the DACHSHUND.

lank (of the body) long, lean.

> Long, low and lank – he is twice as long as he is high. [6, former SKYE TERRIER]

lap-dog small or TOY companion dog.

> No louder shrieks to pitying heav'n are cast,
> When husbands, or when lap-dogs breathe their last. [288a]
> The pampered lap-dog in the midst of his comforts has one great thorn in his side, one perpetual misery to endure, in the perfumes which please his mistress. [182b]

Lap-dog Beagle POCKET BEAGLE.

> According to Blaine, the earlier varieties [of Beagles] varied from the deep-flewed diminutive type of the old Southern hound to the fleet and elegant Foxhound Beagles; to which we may as the pigmy breed called 'Lapdog Beagles'. [320a]

Lapinkoira [FCI] Finnish Lapphund, a herder and DRAUGHT dog used by northern nomadic herdsmen.

Typically SPITZ in appearance with a short dense coat which may be of virtually any colour. Height 46–53cm (18–20¾in).

Lapinporokoira [FCI] Lapland Herder used by northern nomadic herdsmen to control and guard herds of reindeer.

A medium-sized, rather short-haired SPITZ breed with deep, broad chest, strong LOINS and well-boned muscular limbs. The red-tinged black and tan coat is dense, stiff and rough. Height 43–56cm (17–22in).

Lapland Dog (obs.) SAMOYED. [123]

> In all respects similar to a wolf, excepting the tail, which is bushy and curled like those of the Pomeranian race. [406]

Lapland Herder LAPINPOROKOIRA.

Lapland Laika one of six EUROPEAN-RUSSIAN LAÏKA breeds identified in 1896 by Prince Andrew Shirinsky Shihmatoff. [380]

Lapland Reindeer Dog LAPINPOROKOIRA.

Lapphund [FCI] Swedish version of the LAPINKOIRA and physically very similar. The preference is for a solid coloured dark brown or black coat but some white is allowed on collar, chest and feet. Height 40–46cm (15¾–18in).

Lapplandsk Spets [FCI] LAPPHUND.

Lapponian Herder LAPINPOROKOIRA.

Lapponian Shepherd LAPINPOROKOIRA.

Lapponian Vallhund LAPINPOROKOIRA.

Large Blue Gascony Hound BASSET BLEU DE GASCOGNE.

Large-eared Cape Dog *OCTOCYON MEGALOTIS*.

Large English-French Hound GRAND ANGLO-FRANÇAIS.

Large French-English Pointer ANGLO-FRANÇAIS GRAND.

Large French Pointer BRAQUE FRANÇAIS DE GRANDE TAILLE.

Large Münsterländer [KC] one of a group of German GUNDOGS, principally used on winged game. The Large Münsterländer became differentiated from the rest during the early years of this century and has developed into a valued multi-purpose gundog.

The head is long, with a slightly rounded skull, strong jaw, clean, dark brown eyes, broad, high-set, pendulous ears, and a strong, slightly arched neck. The chest is wide and deep, the shoulders WELL LAID, forelegs straight. The back is firm, the COUPLINGS short, with a slightly rounded CROUP. Hindquarters are WELL ANGULATED and muscular; the feet are round and WELL KNUCKLED UP; the tail is thick at the base and carried in line with the back. The straight coat is long and dense, always black and white with patches or FLECKS. Height 59–61cm (23¼–24in); weight 25–29kg (55–64lb).

Large Portuguese Hound PODENGO PORTUGUÊS.

Large Portuguese Rabbit Dog PODENGO PORTUGUÊS.

Large Rough Water-dog described by BEWICK [51] as 'web-footed, swims with great ease, and is used in hunting ducks and other aquatic birds', and probably the CURLY-COATED RETRIEVER's ancestor.

Large Spanish Hound SABUESO ESPAÑOLE DE MONTE.

Large Swiss Mountain Dog GREATER SWISS MOUNTAIN DOG.

Large Vendéen Basset GRAND BASSET GRIFFON VENDÉEN.

Large Vendéen Griffon Grand GRIFFON VENDÉEN.

Large Water-dog former unidentified breed which DRURY said 'was one of the ancestors of the large-sized Poodle'.

Larrye extinct French SCENTHOUND; one of the ancestors of the BILLY, and formerly used for hunting wolf.

Lartington HARRIER pack formed in 1919 in succession to the Stockton Foot Harriers.

larva juvenile which assumes adult form following metamorphosis.

larva migrans larva which is capable of moving about the body tissues.

laryngeal of, or relating to, the LARYNX.

laryngeal paralysis acquired or congenital defect of the nerves of the larynx, resulting in noisy respiration. (Mode of inheritance, dominant.)

laryngostenosis inherited restriction of the larynx causing laboured breathing. (Mode of inheritance, familial.)

larynx cavity of the throat in which vocal cords are contained.

Larzac BERGER DE LANGUEDOC.

latch-key dogs dogs which have owners but are obliged to roam the streets throughout the day.

lateral at the side of.

lateral epicondyle lower tip of the humerus. [*illus.* SKELETON]

Latissimus dorsi broad back muscle which retracts the forelimbs.

Latvian Hound short dense black and tan Russian SCENTHOUND. Height 40–48cm (15¾–18¾in).

Lauderdale FOXHOUND pack which hunts a largely pasture COUNTRY that lies in the Scottish Borders region. The hunt itself dates from 1889 though the country had, since 1826, been previously hunted by the Lothian Hounds. In 1910 Mrs Scott Plummer's private pack was amalgamated with the Lauderdale to form the present establishment.

Laufhund (Swiss) a HOUND that is followed on foot.

Lauray (US) AMERICAN FOXHOUND pack formed in 1953 with DRAGLINES over a COUNTRY in Ohio.

lave-eared long-eared. [159]

Laverack setter eponymous STRAIN of ENGLISH SETTER.

> Without doubt, to the late Mr Edward Laverack, who died in April, 1877, the present generation is indebted for the excellence of the setter, both in form and work, as he is found to-day, and, with few exceptions, the very best dogs are actual descendants of the Laverack strain. That there is, however, such a thing as a 'pure Laverack' to be found now in 1892 I very much dispute. [221]

law 1. (sporting) start given to hunted quarry.
> When the devoted deer was separated from his companions, they gave him, by their watches, law, as they called it, for twenty minutes; [386]

2. period of time allowed to elapse after the advertised time of a MEET in order to accommodate latecomers.
> And now, time being up, and a quarter of an hour's law being given to boot – for Hazey was always in a greater hurry to leave off than he was to begin – all parties having at length got together, the cavalcade moved off in a cluster, hounds first, Hazey next, supported on either side by Lucy and Facey. [344c]

3. (obs.) carry out surgical operation, which was required by law, to restrict a dog's ability to hunt. 4. distance a coursed hare is allowed to run before GREYHOUNDS are SLIPped(3).

Layard, Daniel Peter author of 'An essay on the bite of a mad dog' (1762).

Layback.

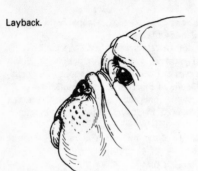

layback 1. the receding profile of BRACHYCEPHALIC breeds. [*illus.*]
> Term applied to the skull of the Bulldog to indicate the receding line of profile in the head. [46]

2. angle which the scapula makes with the upper arm.

lay on start HOUNDS on the scent.

lead strap or cord restraint attached to a dog's collar and held by the dog's HANDLER.

lead dog foremost dog in a team of SLED-DOGS.

leader dominant dog in a pack.

leading leg forelimb which strikes the ground first and in front of the other when a dog is cantering.

leaky-roof track (Am.) FLAPPING TRACK.

leam collar or leash for HOUNDS. [159]

leam hound HOUND led on a leash. [159]

lean cheek having tightly fitting cheek muscles; no FLEWS or wrinkling.

lean head CLEAN HEAD.

learning theory models based on experiments which demonstrate how animals acquire new patterns of behaviour.

leash 1. LEAD.

2. three HOUNDS, usually restrained together.

3. COURSING.
> But it was not until eleven years after this period that the Waterloo Cup was instituted [in 1836], to win which is the highest ambition of followers of the leash. [225]

leash laws legislation which governs circumstances when it is necessary to keep a dog on a leash.

leashed hounds LEASH(2).

Leash Hound LIMIER.
> The Leash Hound or Limier, was the 'Rachel', or guiding one of the pack, used for harbouring the deer. He was led for this purpose, and trained for this one thing. [186]

leather pendulous ear flap.
> Leathers, thin, small to medium in size, covered with coat and fringe. [203, SOFT-COATED WHEATEN TERRIER]
> leather hard from base to tip. [203, SWEDISH VALLHUND]
> Leather thick in texture and inside ear well furnished with hair. [203, AUSTRALIAN CATTLE DOG]
> Leathers never long enough to come below the muzzle. [6, PEKINGESE]

leather ends of ears that are short-coated or hairless at the tips, but otherwise well-furnished.

Lebanon Valley OLD CHATHAM.

Lebrel IRISH GREYHOUND.

Lecale Harriers EAST DOWN.

Ledbury pack whose COUNTRY lies in Herefordshire, Worcestershire and Gloucestershire. It has been hunted since 1810, the pack then being known as the Mathon and Colwall.

Lee, Rawdon author of *A History and Description of the Modern Dogs of Great Britain and Ireland:* 1st vol. *Non-sporting* (1894); 2nd vol. *including Toy, Pet, fancy and Ladies' Dogs* (1899); and 3rd vol. *Sporting* (1893).

lees (obs.) LEASH for dogs. [159]

leg any one of the four limbs.

leg-cocking display posture, involving the raising of one hind leg, adopted during urination by males, and some females.

leg, types of BANDY, CHAIR, LEGS WELL UNDER BODY. *See also* FRONT, HOCKS.

legs well under body legs set well underneath the body, resulting from correct ANGULATION.

Legg-Calvé Perthes disease inherited femoral head necrosis leading to lameness.

leggy long in the leg.

Leighton, Robert prolific author whose works include *The Complete Book of the Dog* (1925), *Dogs and All About Them* (1910), *The New Book of the Dog* (1907), and *Your Dog* (1924).

Leishmania peruviana protozoan parasite which infects humans and may infect dogs.

Leix (Queen's County) FOXHOUND pack re-established in 1899 as the Queen's County Hunt; the name was changed to the Queen's County in 1904, and in 1908 to the Queen's County and Castlecomer; the present name was adopted in 1918.

Lelaps former type of SIGHTHOUND.
> We slipped our dogs, and last my Lelaps too,
> When none of all the mortal race would do. [411]

Leman probably a variation of LEMOR.
> God send every Gentleman,
>   Down a down!
> Such hawks, such hounds, and such a Leman!
>   With a down! [28]

lemon belton predominantly yellow BELTON.

Lemor SCENTHOUND mentioned by Juliana BERNERS. [123]
> Dame Juliana Berners, writing in her '*Book of St Albans*' published in 1486, does not appear to mention the bloodhound, or sleuth hound, but the Lemor or Lymer is no doubt the same dog, and so called because it ran the line of scent, and not, as it has been asserted, because it was the custom to run it in a leash. [221]

length distance from the top point of the WITHERS to the back of the hips.

lens luxation inherited displacement of the eye lens. (Mode of inheritance, recessive.)

Lentiginosis profusa inherited dark pigmented skin. (Mode of inheritance, familial.)

Leonberg Newfoundland (obs.) LEONBERGER. [123]

Leonberger [AKC, KC] dog which was created by Heinrich Essig, with the deliberate intention of reproducing the appearance of the heraldic lions which support Leonberg's coat of arms.

A MOLOSSAN breed with a broad DOMED skull, deep MUZZLE, brown eyes, high-set, rounded ears, a moderately long, clean neck, deep chest, good TUCK-UP and strong LOINS. The limbs are WELL ANGULATED and strongly boned and muscled. The tail is bushy and carried at half-mast. The coat is of medium softness, smooth, thick and dense, usually shades of yellow, fawn or red, with a dark MASK. Height 70–76cm (27½–30in).

leonine of, or bearing resemblance to, a lion.
Leonine in appearance. [203, CHOW CHOW]

Leon Mastiff MASTIN DE LOS PIRINEOS.

Leopard Cur native American breed used by settlers in the southern States as a DOMESTIC and PASTORAL GUARD, HERDER, hunter and fighting dog.

The overall outline is similar to the heavier COON-HOUNDs, the head is strong, the body is powerfully muscled. The coat is smooth and PATTERNED in the characteristic leopard-spotting, though black and tan, blue, BRINDLE and yellow are also allowed. Weight 20–35kg (44–77lb).

leopard-spotting blue or yellow MERLE coat PATTERN characteristic of the LEOPARD CUR.

Leopard Tree Dog LEOPARD CUR.

Leporarius name by which FLEMING referred to the GREYHOUND. [139]

Lepte autumnale *TROMBICULA AUTUMNALE.*

Leptospira genus of bacteria of the group leptospirosa.

Leptospira interrogans serovar canicola leptospirosa principally associated with dogs but also found in pigs, cattle, humans and a number of wild species.

Leptospira interrogans serovar icterohaemorragiae leptospirosa found in dogs as well as rats, pigs, cattle and humans.

leptospirosa group of bacteria which attack the liver.

leptospirosis highly infectious and fatal disease caused by leptospirosa; symptoms include jaundice and nephritis. Vaccines provide effective protection.

Lesser St John's Dog ST JOHN'S DOG.

Lesser Water-Dog *CANIS AQUATICUS MINOR.*

let down 1. take a sporting dog out of training. Some schools of thought holding that, in summer the pack should be let down for some months and only walked out or turned into a grass yard. [257]
2. of HOCKS that are close to the ground.
Hindquarters . . . with well let down hocks. [203, SAMOYED]

let-go match system of BULL-BAITing in which dogs were loosed in relays.

lethal fatal.

lethal chamber container in which dogs are killed by gassing or electrocution.

lethal gene gene which carries a characteristic that results in the death of the offspring.

lethal oedema inherited condition leading to the birth of grossly bloated, non-viable puppies. (Mode of inheritance, recessive.)

let-loose match BULL-BAITING in which the bull is not tied to a ring. [157]

leucocyte white blood cell.

leucocyte antigen complex the principal canine histiocompatibility complex.

leucocytosis temporary increase in the number of white cells in the blood.

leucodystrophy rare inherited condition resulting in motor dysfunction. (Mode of inheritance, recessive.)

leucorrhoea chronic vaginal discharge, usually whitish or greyish, a symptom of METRITIS or VAGINITIS.

leu in verbal encouragement to HOUNDS to enter cover or to TERRIERS to venture underground.
The whips crept to the sides to view,
The Master gave the nod, and 'Leu,
Leu in. Ed-hoick, ed-hoick. Leu in!' [249]

leukaemia LYMPHOSARCOMA.

leuth place from which GREYHOUNDS are SLIPped(3) for COURSING.
As I stood in the leuth with the sun pouring on my back the sweat dropped off me on to the dogs' backs. I slipped about twenty couples, and by the time I had finished had a real hearty thirst. [401]

Levararios HARRIER. [139]

level even; straight.

level back TOPLINE in which WITHERS and HAUNCH are the same height.
Back level, medium length. [203, CAIRN TERRIER]

level bite pincer bite; LEVEL MOUTH.

level gait movement with little rise and fall.

level jaw pincer bite; LEVEL MOUTH.

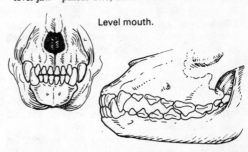
Level mouth.

level mouth teeth meeting without overlap, though some BREED STANDARDS use the phrase to describe a mouth in which the upper teeth overlap the lower, which is usually referred to as a SCISSOR BITE. [*illus.*]
Mouth – Level and strong. [203, FIELD SPANIEL]

leveret young hare.

Levesque one of the eponymous breeds, named after its originator Rogatien Levesque who in the later years of the 19th century CROSSED(2) several French and English HOUND breeds to produce a worthy addition to the French BATARDs.

A long-headed, heavy-eared, slenderly built typical SCENTHOUND, with TRICOLOUR coat. Height 66–71cm (26–28in).

Levinarius LYEMMER. [139]

And it is called in latin Levinarius, a Levitate, of lightness, and therefore may well be called a light hound. [139]

Leviner LYEMMER. [139]

Lhasa Apso [AKC, FCI, KC] breed said to have been bred in the form and colour of a small lion as a compliment to Buddha. Originally used as a sentinel in the temples, the breed reached the west in 1921 and has since become rightfully popular. The name is variously said to derive from *Abso* (to bark) or as a corruption of *Rapso* (a goat).

A gay and confident breed, sturdy and heavily coated. The head is fairly narrow with medium STOP and a straight MUZZLE. The oval eyes are dark, the ears pendant, the mouth a REVERSE SCISSOR BITE. The strong neck is well arched, the shoulders WELL LAID, and the body rather longer than the height at the WITHERS; the chest is well ribbed, the TOPLINE level and the LOIN strong. Forelegs are straight, hindquarters muscular and WELL ANGULATED. The tail is high set and carried well over the back; the tail is often KINKED. The coat is heavy, straight and profuse on all parts of the body and may be golden, sandy, honey, dark GRIZZLE, SLATE, SMOKE, PARTICOLOUR, black, white or brown. Height 25.4cm (10in).

Lhassa Terrier (obs.) LHASA APSO.

An interesting little breed formerly found under the inappropriate name of Bhuteer Terrier. [123]

liam 1. LEAD or LEASH.

You must be provided with a Bloodhound, Draughthound, or Sluithound, which must be led in a Liam. [53]

2. HOUND normally kept on a LEASH.

lib castrate. [159]

Liberian Dog two main sources provide conflicting descriptions of this breed: 1. small, broad-headed, PRICK-EARed reddish-brown short-coated primitive dog. [312] 2. unrecognized West African TERRIER. [150]

libido sexual urge.

lice 1. (Fr.) bitch HOUND. 2. (Fr.) BROOD-BITCH. 3. external slow-moving white or pale-red parasites of the order PHTHIRAPTERA.

licence official permit to own a dog, available on payment of a fee.

lick dermatitis ACRAL LICK DERMATITIS.

lick granuloma ACRAL LICK DERMATITIS.

Liddesdale hunting a moorland COUNTRY which bestrides the border between England and Scotland, the hunt dates from 1808 and includes among its former masters John Dodd (1900–1943).

lift 1. take HOUNDs off the scent in order to overcome some difficulty, not an action appreciated by those who enjoy seeing hounds work.

He is half inclined to lift them again. If it weren't that they were hunting so well, he would do it. [344c]

2. take HOUNDS that have lost the scent to a place where it is known to exist.

3. (joc.) a supposed disease which causes dogs to lift a hind leg in order to urinate.

4. (of a SHEEP DOG) persuade sheep to begin to move in the desired direction. [204]

ligament tendon which connects two moving parts.

light eye of eye less dark than is desirable.

light in hindquarter lacking muscular development.

light sedge dark WHEATEN coat colour.

Shades ranging from light sedge to chocolate. [6, LABRADOR RETRIEVER]

lightening polygene series of genes which have the effect of lightening the colour of the coat.

Ligonier Valley (US) BEAGLE pack formed to hunt cottontail rabbit over a pasture COUNTRY in Pennsylvania.

like produces like unreliable belief that dogs will reproduce their own characteristics.

like to like mating between dogs of similar appearance; ASSORTIVE MATING.

But, as it is found by experience that in this particular 'like produces like', it is only necessary to be assured that the parents possessed this internal formation, whatever it may be, in order to be satisfied that their descendants will inherit it. [338]

lime LEASH or thong. [159]

Limer LIMIER.

Limerick 1. FOXHOUND pack whose present establishment replaced a scratch pack in 1828. 2. Irish HARRIER pack formed in 1917.

Limestone Creek (US) AMERICAN FOXHOUND and DRAGHOUND pack formed in 1939 to hunt a COUNTRY in New York State.

Limier (Fr.) old type of silent hunting SCENTHOUND used to locate quarry; LEASH HOUND.

You can readily understand that this Limier, though a 'Slugghounde', was a favourite of kings and princes. [186]

Limit class (KC) show class for dogs that have not won three CHALLENGE CERTIFICATES under three different judges or seven or more first prizes in all at Championship shows in Limit and Open classes, confined to the breed, where Challenge Certificates were offered for the breed.

limit dextrinis GLYCOGENOSIS TYPE III.

Limnatis africana leech found in the vagina, urethra and nasal cavity of dogs and other species.

line 1. dogs closely related for several generations and bred by one KENNEL(4); a family. 2. track or trail followed by HOUNDs.

With nose to the ground he holds his line
Be it over the plough or grass. [272j]
Then babel broke forth, as the hounds, converging from every quarter, flung themselves on the line. [329b]

3. mate. The reference may be to *line*, as in cover the inner surface.

I have met with several dogs, like Ponto, who refused to line a bitch till the last day or two of heat. [218]

line-breeding breeding between fairly distantly related animals in order to concentrate the genes of a particular individual.

line hunter HOUND which does not deviate from the scent.

> Besides, this same trend thus defines the line-hunter: 'A hound which will not go a yard beyond the scent, and keeps the pack tight. [266b]

lineage PEDIGREE.

> For every longing dame select
> Some happy paramour; to him alone
> In leagues connubial join. Consider well
> His lineage; what his fathers did of old. [328]

line ferret LINER. [238a]

liner line ferret; ferret, usually a large and strong one, which is worked attached to a thin cord which can be traced to discover the ferret's whereabouts underground.

> Shortly two terriers were missing, and we found them marking a hole. So, in with the 'liner', and a twenty minutes' dig produced seven rabbits. [401]

line-up (of showing) short-list of dogs lined up before a judge and from which he or she selects the winners.

lining act of mating; an act which produces a line.

linkage propensity of two or more genes located on the same chromosome to act together.

linkage disequilibrium measure of the tendency of linked genes, alleles, to occur together with certain alleles on another locus, so that characteristics carried by different genes may tend to go together, WALL EYES and MERLE coat may be an example of linkage disequilibrium.

linkage map representation of the arrangement of genes on a chromosome.

Linlithgow and Stirlingshire hunt dating from 1775 when it was founded by Sir William Augustus Cunynghame; the COUNTRY consists of pasture, plough and moorland.

Linnaeus, Carolus Latinized name of Carl von Linne (1707–1778), a Swedish naturalist who devised a classification system for the natural world.

Linognathus piliferus louse specific to dogs.

Linognathus setosus louse found on dogs and foxes.

Linton former BEAGLE and Beagle/HARRIER CROSS pack formed in 1886 to hunt a COUNTRY in Kent.

linty (of coat) soft and dense.

> Double coat with a soft linty undercoat and a harder topcoat. [203, DANDIE DINMONT TERRIER]

lion (of coat colour) light yellowish tan.

> Color – White or red (from light, yellowish-red called 'lion' to deep red). [6, IBIZAN HOUND]

lion clip basic coat CLIP for adult show POODLES in which the MUZZLE, throat, feet and LOINS are clipped short, while the topknot and coat on the chest, neck and shoulders is left long. The tail is finished with a POMPOM, and the forelegs are ornamented with BRACELETS, the hind legs with STIFLE and HOCK RINGS. Variations on this clip include the ENGLISH SADDLE CLIP, and those used commonly on the LÖW-CHEN and PORTUGUESE WATER DOG.

As soon as the coat grows long, the middle part and hindquarters of these dogs, as well as the muzzle, are clipped. At the end of the tail the hair is left at full length. [6, PORTUGUESE WATER DOG]

Lion Dog LÖWCHEN.

> Appears to be crossed between the poodle and the Maltese dog, being curly like the former, but without his long ears and square visage. He is now very seldom seen in this country. [338]
> Is a diminutive likeness of the noble animal whose name it bears. [406]
> Canis leoninus, is exceedingly small, with long hair, like the foregoing [Shock dog] on the fore part of the body; that on the hind parts being shorter and smooth. [72b]

lion jaw CRANIOMANDIBULAR OSTEOPATHY.

lip-fold dermatitis skin disease found in breeds with heavily wrinkled facial skin or heavy, folded FLEWS.

lipid storage disease inherited cellular metabolic disorder resulting in excessive tissue lipids. (Mode of inheritance, recessive.)

lipoma benign tumour associated with obesity.

lippy of heavy or full lips.

Liptok SLOVAC CUVAC.

Liseter (US) private BEAGLE pack formed in 1928 to hunt cottontail rabbit.

listed dog [AKC] dog entered at shows run under AKC rules prior to registration with that body; equivalent of the British 'Registration applied for'.

Lithuanian Hound black-and-tan HOUND of recent origin developed from imported European SCENT-HOUNDs in order to develop a versatile breed suitable for hunting hare, fox and boar. Height 53–61cm (20¾–24in).

litter 1. young born to one conception; siblings.

> And somehow I knew that a litter of four
> Lay curled in a box at the vestry door. [272a]

2. the act of giving birth.

> The hare had littered in running; the same happened to my bitch in coursing. By instinct the former ran, the latter coursed: and thus I found myself in possession at once of six hares and as many dogs, at the end of a course which had only begun with one. [291]
> It was a litter, a litter of five,
> Four are drowned and one left alive,
> He was thought worthy alone to survive: [43]

Little Danish Dog *CANIS VARIEGATUS.*

little dog (colloq.) BEAGLE.

Littlegrange Irish HARRIER pack formed in 1942 to hunt a COUNTRY in East Meath and South Louth.

Little Lion Dog LÖWCHEN.

Little Prospect Foot (US) private BEAGLE pack formed in 1952 to hunt hare, cottontail rabbit and fox.

liver shade of brown.

liver belton BELTON.

Llanidloes Setter extinct variety of the ENGLISH SETTER.

> It seems to me that this Welsh setter is no more than an ordinary English setter, with little distinguishing type, excepting a coarse, hard, curly coat, and a thick, though long, head, may be deemed to constitute type. [221]

This is a very ancient and well-known breed, but I am sorry to say that it is dying out. They are particularly stout and hardy dogs, never tire, and unflinching in their endeavours to find game. A close, compact animal, and very handsome. The old pure breed was milk-white, or, as it is called there, a 'chalk-white'. [218]

Llangeinor FOXHOUND pack founded in 1885 to hunt a hilly COUNTRY in Glamorgan; the original hounds came from the Llanharan Pack. The pack did not function from 1925–1941, during which time the country was hunted by the Bwllfa Hounds.

Llangibby FOXHOUND pack which tradition holds was founded by Sir Trevor Williams in 1641; the varied Gwent COUNTRY includes some area of reen.

Llanharan Pack LLANGEINOR.

Llewellin Setter type of ENGLISH SETTER developed during the mid-years of the 19th century by Purcell Llewellin and now absorbed into the wider breed.

loaded of superfluous muscular development of the scapula in relation to the humerus.

> Shoulders well laid back, muscular, not loaded. [203, BASENJI]

lobe-shaped ear LOBULAR.

lobster stoat. [159]

lobular (of ears) pendulous and rounded. [*illus.*]

> Ears Thick, fairly large and lobular. [203, SUSSEX SPANIEL]
> Ears – lobular, long, of fine leather, well feathered [6, COCKER SPANIEL]

lock TIE.

> Another idea some have is that a dog cannot get a bitch in whelp unless he is locked. This is not the case. [218]

Lobular ear.

lock jaw TETANUS.

locus position occupied by a gene on the chromosome.

lodge holt.

loin vertical surfaces between the ribs and hips. [*illus.* POINTS]

London (Can.) ENGLISH FOXHOUND pack formed in 1885 to hunt fox and DRAG(2) over a rolling pasture COUNTRY in Ontario.

London fog (20th cent. Brit. rhyming slang) dog. [280]

long cast long-bodied.

Longcoat Chihuahua [KC] CHIHUAHUA.

long-coupled measure of the distance between back ribs and pelvis. [*illus.*]

long day the provision of artificial light to extend the apparent daylight hours and thus to stimulate breeding.

long dog 1. SIGHTHOUND, esp. a LURCHER.

> A longdog is a dog that is long everywhere; long

head, long neck, long legs and a long tail, be it pure-bred or cross-bred. [375]

2. GREYHOUND. [159]

Long-eared Fox BAT-EARED FOX.

Longendale former 14in to 15in BEAGLE pack formed in 1902 as the Carlecotes to hunt a COUNTRY in south Yorkshire. The present name was assumed in 1909.

Long-Haired Dachshund [KC] DACHSHUND.

Long-haired Dutch Shepherd LANGHAAR HOLLANDSE HERDERSHOND.

Long-haired Hollandse Herdeshond HOLLANDSE HERDESHOND.

Long-haired Rabbit Dachshund LANGHAARIGER KANINCHENTECKEL.

Long-haired Whippet unrecognized long-haired variety of the WHIPPET.

long hound SIGHTHOUND.

> In an instant the long hounds leap up, half a dozen at a time. [193]

Long Lake (US) AMERICAN FOXHOUND pack formed in 1959 to hunt a pasture and woodland COUNTRY in Minnesota.

long net net placed across a field to entrap running quarry.

> Not so the long net. Nothing escapes from it. I have caught Deer, Fox, Badger, Cat, Hare, Rabetts, Hedgehogs and I once caught a Policeman. [165]
> I refer to long nets, which are used for running round or across a piece of covert to catch the rabbits as they are bustled about by the dogs. [45]

Longreen (US) AMERICAN FOXHOUND pack formed in 1957 to hunt a rolling pasture and woodland COUNTRY in Tennessee; a DRAG(2) is hunted on Thanksgiving Day.

longtail (colloq.) GREYHOUND or LURCHER. [91]

look out below hunt-official stationed downstream of where OTTERHOUNDS are hunting.

loose (esp. of HOUNDS) unleash.

loose-coupled having a weak, and usually long, LOIN.

loose-eyed of a SHEEP DOG which lacks the power and concentration to control sheep by means of intense expression.

loose in elbow having an unusual degree of flexibility at the elbow joint, usually used to refer to elbows which turn outwards.

loosely strung (of body) BODY LOOSELY STRUNG.

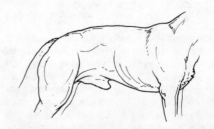

Long-coupled.

lope easy, economical canter.
> He slipped between the rails with hope new-born
> And loped across the stubble to the sound. [272e]

lop-eared having pendulous ears. [159]

Lorarius LYEMMER [139]

Lord Coventry's Hunt CROOME.

Lord Dacre's HERTFORDSHIRE.

Lord Leconfield's FOXHOUND pack founded in 1773 by Lord Egremont and amalgamated with the Chiddingfold in 1942.

Lord North's Basset former 13in BASSET pack formed in 1908 to hunt a COUNTRY in Oxfordshire.

lordosis COITAL CROUCH.

Lord Poltimore's EGGESFORD.

Lord Southampton's Hounds GRAFTON.

Lord Waterford's WATERFORD.

Los Altos (US) American, English and crossbred FOXHOUND pack formed in 1952 to hunt a DRAG(2) over a wooden hilly COUNTRY in California.

lost back (esp. in a SLED-DOG) torn lumbar muscles.

Lothian Hounds LAUDERDALE.

Loudon (US) AMERICAN FOXHOUND pack formed in 1894 to hunt an open rolling COUNTRY in Virginia.

Louisiana Catahoula CATAHOULA LEOPARD DOG.

Loulou Finnois FINNISH SPITZ.

louse parasitic insect of the order PHTHIRAPTERA. Infestation causes irritation; severe infestation may result in anaemia.

loused off (N. Eng.) loosed-off, syn. with THROW OFF.
> The writer always says where he 'threw off'. This is comparable with the custom of the fell packs of the Lake District where they still refer to where they 'loused off' rather than where they met. [101]

Louth formed in 1817 to hunt a bank and ditch COUNTRY in County Louth.

Löwchen [AKC, KC] BICHON-type breed probably more associated with middle Europe than with the Mediterranean region. A dog CLIPped in the manner of the Löwchen is to be seen on 16th-century illustrations and may well be regarded as an early specimen of the breed. On the edge of extinction after the Second World War, it has since made a spectacular return to popularity.
The breed's appearance owes much to the traditional LION CLIP in which the coat is styled. The breed is alert, active, sturdy and gay. The head is short, the skull wide, the large, round eyes dark, the ears pendulous. The neck is slightly arched and carried proudly. The short, strong body has a level TOPLINE and moderate TUCK-UP. Forelegs are straight, hindquarters well turned and muscular. The tail is carried gaily. The coat which may be of any colour or combination of colours is long, wavy and silky. Height 25–33cm (10–13in).

Löwchen [Little Lion Dog] LÖWCHEN.

lower stickle bottom STICKLE.

Lowlands Herder POLISH LOWLAND SHEEP DOG.

low on the leg of a dog whose body is low-slung; proportionally short-legged.

low set (esp. of ears, tail) placed below the level which might be regarded as normal.

low-set hocks HOCKS that are close to the ground; short from hock to PASTERN.

Lowther EAMONT.

lozenge (esp. in CAVALIER KING CHARLES SPANIELS) small patch of white on the forehead.
> Markings evenly divided on head, leaving room between ears for the valued lozenge mark or spot [a unique characteristic of the breed]. [203, CAVALIER KING CHARLES SPANIEL]
> The lozenge is unique and highly desirable, though not essential. [6, CAVALIER KING CHARLES SPANIEL]

LTH PROLACTIN.

Lucas Terrier CROSSBRED type of TERRIER produced by Sir Jocelyn Lucas, which narrowly failed to achieve official recognition during Sir Jocelyn's lifetime and afterwards lost support.

Lucernese Hound LUZERNER LAUFHUND.

Lucern Hound LUZERNER LAUFHUND.

Luchak a short-haired variant of the AFGHAN HOUND.

Ludlow originally founded sometime prior to 1780, the hilly Worcestershire, Herefordshire and Shropshire COUNTRY has been hunted regularly since 1854.

lugs (colloq.) ears. [73f]

lumbar appertaining to the LOINS.

lumbar vertebrae vertebrae of the loin region, between the thoracic vertebrae and the sacrum. [*illus.* SKELETON]

lumber 1. useless size or bone; an encumbrance.
> Judges are apt to select the very largest specimens as prize dogs, which is mistaking lumber for quality. [186]
> Strong and powerful, without lumber – athletic rather than racy. [203, IRISH RED AND WHITE SETTER]
2. to move in a heavy, ungainly way.

lumbosacral luxation injury to the bones, blood vessels or nerves of the lumbar vertebrae.

lumbosacral stenosis weakness caused by a reduction, usually congenital, in the diameter of the spinal canal, often characterized by self-mutilation of the lumbar region and tail.

lumen cavity within soft tissue, esp. in blood vessels and the intestines.

Lundehund NORWEGIAN LUNDEHUND.

Lunesdale FOXHOUND pack which has hunted a north Lancashire and Cumbrian COUNTRY, with occasional breaks, since 1932.

Lunesdale and Oxenholme former STAGHOUND pack formed in 1866 to hunt a COUNTRY in Lancashire and Cumbria.

lungworm group of parasitic worms which inhabit the respiratory tracts or pulmonary arteries, including *Filaroides hirthi, Filaroides milksi, Oslerus osleri* and *Angiostrongylus*. Symptoms of infestation include chronic cough and respiratory distress.

lupoid of dog which has the characteristics of a wolf.

lurche LURCHER. [246]

Lurcher ubiquitous CROSSBRED SIGHTHOUND of varied size and appearance depending on its parentage and the type of game for which it is intended. A dog with considerable intelligence, stamina and speed. CROSSES(2) between a sighthound, GREYHOUND, WHIPPET, DEERHOUND or SALUKI, and a TERRIER (usually BEDLINGTON or BORDER), or a BORDER COLLIE, or occasionally STAFFORDSHIRE BULL TERRIER, various GUNDOGS and HOUNDS or guarding breeds, are skilfully used to produce the desired article.

> Although this dog is not used by the fair sportsmen in this country, yet he must be recognised as a distinct and well-known cross. . . . He is par excellence the poacher's dog. [338]
> Less and shorter than the Greyhound, and its limbs stronger: its body is covered with a rough coat of hair, most commonly of a pale yellow colour; its aspect is sullen, and its habits, whence it derives its name, are dark and cunning. [51]
> Originally a cross between the greyhound and the shepherd's dog, retaining all the speed and fondness for the chace belonging to the one, and the superior intelligence and readiness for any kind of work which the latter possessed. [406]
> A poacher to his eyelids, as all the lurcher clan,
> Follows silent as a shadow, and clever as a man. [85e]

lure artificial quarry used to train SIGHTHOUNDS or GUNDOGS.

lure coursing artificial COURSING using an inanimate object as the quarry.

luteinizing hormone hormone secreted by the pituitary gland which causes ovulation in the female and secretion of testosterone in the male.

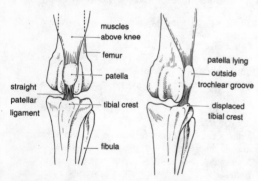

muscles above knee
femur
patella
straight patellar ligament
tibial crest
fibula

patella lying outside trochlear groove
displaced tibial crest

Normal stifle joint.   Luxated patella.

luxating patella inherited condition in which the patella slips to either side of the trochlean groove. Caused by a deformity of the STIFLE joint. (Mode of inheritance, uncertain, probably polygenic.) [*illus.*]

luxation dislocation.

Luzerner Laufhund [FCI] Swiss SCENTHOUND used on deer and boar and differentiated from other European hounds principally by its heavily TICKED, TRICOLOUR, smooth coat. Height 46–59cm (18–23¼in).

Luzerner Niederlaufhund [FCI] short-legged variety of the LUZERNER LAUFHUND. Height 33–41cm (13–16in).

lyam thong or LEASH used to lead HOUNDs [159]

lycanthropi madmen whose condition was formerly blamed on the influence of wolves. [159]

Lycaon pictus hunting dog, found in the savannah of the Ivory Coast, Somalia and South Africa.

Lyciscus CROSS between a dog and a wolf. [139]

Lyemmer formerly a lightly built HOUND.

> So called from its being led in a thong, and slipped at game. . . . It is now unknown to us. [51]

lying hound dog or HOUND that gives false evidence of being on the trail.

Lyme disease painful inflammation of the joints caused by *Borrelia burgdorferi* which is transmitted by *Ixodes dammini*; endemic in the United States.

Lyme Harriers FOREST AND DISTRICT.

Lyme Mastiff former STRAIN of MASTIFF kept at Lyme Hall in Cheshire.

> The Lyme Hall breed [of Mastiff] is considered the purest and most valuable strain of blood in the kingdom, but owing to the jealousy with which it has always been guarded by the Legh family, to which it belongs, the general public have been unable to judge its merits by either personal observation or experience. [320a]

Lymer HOUND which is lead on a LIAM.

lymph yellow opalescent liquid collected from various bodily tissues and returned to the blood via the lymphatic system.

lymphatic of, or secreting, LYMPH.

lymphatic system those parts of the body which are involved in the collection of lymph.

lymphatic thyroiditis inherited auto-immune disease in which thyroid follicles are progressively destroyed. (Mode of inheritance, familial.)

lymphocyte leucocyte associated with cellular immunity.

lymphocytic of, or relating to, LYMPHOCYTE.

lymphocytic leukaemia CANINE MALIGNANT LYMPHOMA.

lymphocytic thyroiditis auto-immune disease responsible for most hypothyroidism in dogs; characterized by thyroid dysfunction.

lymphoedema inherited localized chronic swelling. (Mode of inheritance, dominant.)

lymphoid LYMPH-like; of the nature of lymph.

lymphoma CANINE MALIGNANT LYMPHOMA.

lymphomatomatoid granulomatosis pulmonary tumour, rare in dogs.

lymphosarcoma inherited malignant tumour of the lymph gland. (Mode of inheritance, complex.)

lysis destruction of a cell.

lysosome that part of a cell which contains the enzymes which assist normal destruction processes.

lyssa 1. RABIES. 2. cartilage under a dog's tongue which was formerly thought to be a worm responsible for rabies.

M

M   gene symbol for MERLE.

Macellaio Herder   SICILIAN BRANCHIERO

Macellaio Herding Dog   SICILIAN BRANCHIERO.

Ma-chu-goua   heavily built SIGHTHOUND, short-coated and with a characteristic ridge. It is probably extinct in its pure form.

Mackenzie River Dog   primitive PARIAH dog used as a hunter and draught dog by the Indians of the Canadian North West Territories. According to LEIGHTON it is the same as the HARE INDIAN DOG but other authorities suggest that this is a regional variant.

Macroom   pack re-established in 1949 to hunt a COUNTRY in County Cork.

macrothrombocytosis   the presence, in the blood of some breeds, of relatively small numbers of abnormally large platelets with no clinical evidence of platelet dysfunction.

mad dog   dog suffering from rabies.

> At a general meeting of the parishioners of Eccles, near Manchester, it was unanimously agreed to strike off from the poor's-rate all paupers who shall after the 20th instant keep dogs. They also agreed to pay five shillings for every mad dog killed in their parish. [29]

made up   1. having attained the title of Champion.   2. having attained all the attributes of maturity.

> A dog is said to be 'made up' when he is fully developed. [320a]

Magellanic Dog   CANIS MAGELLANICUS.

magpie   (of coat colour) black and white.

> The old black-and-white hounds of the Oakley country, which were known as the Oakley magpies in the early days of the Peterborough Hound Show, were changed both in colour and character under Mr Arkwright's reign, until year after year they beat all competitors at the show. [318]

Magyar Agar   Hungarian SIGHTHOUND very similar to a lightly built GREYHOUND. Height 63–70cm (24¾–27½in); weight 22–31kg (48½–68lb).

Magyar Vizsla   [FCI] HUNGARIAN VIZSLA.

Mahratta Dog   YOUATT suggested that this West-Indian SIGHTHOUND was the same as the DHOLE; he was mistaken. It is a typical, smooth-coated small GREYHOUND, with both speed and endurance. The most common colours are slate blue and tan on a white GROUND. Height about 56cm (22in).

Mahratta Greyhound   Indian SIGHTHOUND, smooth-coated, deep-chested and compact.

maiden   1. unmated dog or bitch.   2. a dog of either sex which has yet to win in adult competition.

Maiden class   (KC) show class for dogs that have not previously won an adult class at a show.

main-earth   principal EARTH in a hunting COUNTRY; the largest and most frequently used earth.

Majestic Tree Hound   COLD-NOSEd SCENTHOUND developed for tracking big cats. A large, powerful and ponderous breed with exceptionally long, FOLDED ears and with well-developed FLEWS and DEWLAP. The coat is short and of any colour or combination of colours. Height 79cm (31in); weight 45kg (99lb).

Major Birkbeck's   former 14½in BEAGLE pack formed in 1909 to hunt a COUNTRY in Norfolk.

Majorca Sheep Dog   Ca De Bestiar: PERRO DE PASTOR MALLORQUIN.

Major David Davies'   former private 12–14in BEAGLE pack formed in 1909 to hunt a COUNTRY in Powys.

major gene   gene which has considerable effect on the phenotype.

Major Sir Robert Walker's   former private HARRIER pack formed in 1910 to hunt a COUNTRY in east Yorkshire.

making cut   remaining in the competition when all but a previously determined number have been eliminated.

making game   tail action which indicates that a GUNDOG is aware of the presence of game but has yet to locate it.

making the wheel   of a tail that curls over the back to form a complete circle. [*illus.*]

> Tail . . . curled high over the back 'making the wheel' when alert. [203, PYRENEAN MOUNTAIN DOG]

Makhmal   (var. spelling) BAKMULL.

malabsorption   impaired ability to utilize food, either inherited or developed. (Mode of inheritance, uncertain.)

Malamute   dim. ALASKAN MALAMUTE.

Making the wheel.

malar bone   ZYGOMA.

Malinois   [FCI] one of the four varieties of BELGIAN SHEEP DOG.

Mallassezia pachydermatis   a yeast found on the skin of atopic dogs.

mallophaga   sub-order of PHTHIRAPTERA.

Mallorquin Bulldog   PERRO DE PRESA MALLORQUIN.

Maltese   [AKC, FCI, KC] the Maltese was the TOY dog against which CAIUS and FLEMING directed such stern criticism. The breed is undoubtedly an old one and of Mediterranean origin.

The proudly carried head has a well-defined STOP and relatively broad MUZZLE; the dark eyes are oval with dark HALOes, the pendulous ears long and well FEATHERED. The body is short and COBBY and the limbs short but well formed. The coat is silky and always white. Height 25.5cm (10¼in).

Maltese Dog MALTESE.

Maltese Little Lion-dog light-tan MALTESE, purposely bred so but unrecognized and not popular. [123]

Maltese Spaniel MALTESE.

mammary gland teat; gland that secretes milk. There are usually two rows of four situated along the stomach.

  mammary gland tumour cancer with an inherited predisposition. (Mode of inheritance, complex.)

mammotropin PROLACTIN.

Manawatu Hunt (NZ) pack formed in 1909 to hunt hare over a COUNTRY in Manaku.

Manchester Terrier [AKC, FCI, KC] smooth-coated descendant of the old English BLACK AND TAN TERRIER with origins in the rat pit. An elegant, COMPACT and sporting dog with a long, lean head, small dark eyes and small V-shaped ears. The neck is fairly long and muscular, the shoulders CLEAN, narrow and WELL LAID BACK. The body is short with WELL-SPRUNG RIBS, slight arch and pronounced CUT-UP. The hindquarters are strong and muscular. The tail is short, thick at the base and tapering. The short, smooth and glossy coat is always jet black with closely defined tan POINTS(3). Height 38–41cm (15–16in).

Mandarin Pug former name for the PEKINGESE.
  In 1870 a black and white Japanese spaniel, such as we have now, was entered at a Crystal Palace dog show by Mr P. Gordon. It was called a Mandarin pug, and said to be one of the four taken at the sacking of the Summer Palace in Pekin. [221]

mandible major bones forming the lower jaw. [*illus.* SKELETON]

mandibular prognathism inherited abnormal forward protrusion of the lower jaw. (Mode of inheritance, unclear.) [*illus.* UNDERSHOT]

mandrake plant whose roots were said to be shaped like a human body and have the power to cure ills. It was, however, necessary to avoid touching the roots when uprooting the plant and it was customary to tie a dog to it to provide the necessary final pull.

mane ruff; profuse growth of hair on and under the neck.
  Not overcoated; bitches tend to carry less coat and mane than dogs. [203, TIBETAN SPANIEL]

maned wolf *CHRYSOCYON BRACHYURUS.*

mange skin disease caused by any one of several genera of mites, each of which causes a particular type of mange: demodectic, sarcoptic, otodectic, psoroptic. Each type of mite attacks a particular part of the body and produces specific symptoms, although each will cause localized hair loss.

mangey of dog suffering from MANGE.
  A regular course of whey and vegetables, during the hot months, must certainly be wholesome, and is, without doubt, the cause that a mangey hound is an unusual sight in my kennel. [47]

mangie (obs. var. spelling) MANGY. [363]

mangy of dog suffering from MANGE.
  He was a miserable-looking object, a sort of Lurcher, of a dirty red colour, with ribs showing like the bars of a gridiron through his mangy side. [182c]

manifestation degree to which the effect of genes is apparent.

Manila Spaniel BICHON formerly to be found in the Philippines; LEIGHTON suggests that it is the same breed as the HAVANESE.

mannosidosis accumulation of cellular sugars.

manteau (specifically of the SLOUGHI) SADDLE.

mantle dark-shaded coat on the shoulders, back and flanks; also referred to as a SADDLE.

manufacturing defect defect which is present at birth but which has arisen during pregnancy.

manyhew (obs.) MANGE. [159]

marbled 1. coat patched with a darker shade of the GROUND colour. 2. TICKED.
  Possessing a similar meaning to that we attach to 'mottle', 'ticked', or 'flecked'. [221]

  marbled eye eye with a mixture of two or more colours.

Marbled Collie HARLEQUIN COLLIE. [123]

marbles (colloq.) testicles.

Maremma Sheep Dog [KC] Italian PASTORAL GUARD and HERDER characterized like other European herders, by its lush, white coat, abundant substance and apparent strength.

  The large head is conical, the eyes dark and bold, the ears rather small and pendulous. The jaws are powerful with CLEAN LIPS. The forequarters are long and sloping, with well-boned limbs. The TOPLINE is slightly OVERBUILT, the hindquarters wide and powerful. The well-FURNISHED tail is low set and hangs to between the HOCKS. Height 60–73cm (23½–28¾in); weight 30–45kg (66–99lb).

Marie-Bamberger's disease HYPERTROPHIC OSTEOPATHY.

Marie's disease HYPERTROPHIC OSTEOPATHY.

mark 1. indicate the position of quarry or the object of a search; (of HOUNDS, TERRIERS) BAY at, or cluster round, the mouth of an underground retreat in which quarry has taken refuge, hence 'mark to ground'.
  And on the shore he'll mark without a frown
  A flap-eared doggie, bandy-legged and brown. [222a]
  Only one or two rats had bolted when the ferrets came out so badly bitten that they could not be put in again. I knew there were a lot more because the dogs kept marking the holes. [401]
  Hounds ran nicely from Longmuir by North Nains ... to Bellencrief, where, in darkness rendered more intense by thick mist, they marked their fox to ground. [*306]
2. (of a GUNDOG) watch the fall of shot gamebird in order to judge its landing place and then retrieve it; command to a gundog so to do. 3. otter footprint; spur; seal. 4. (of territory) *see* URINATION MARKING.

  mark to ground MARK.

Markham, Gervase author of *Country Contentments* (1615).

Markiesje recently created variety of the DRENTSE PATRIJSHOND.

marking hound HOUND which can be relied upon to MARK at an occupied place of refuge.

markings arrangement of coat colour, especially of darker colour on a lighter GROUND.

> All colours and markings, including white, allowed. [203, SIBERIAN HUSKY.]

Marland former HARRIER pack established in 1910 as a BEAGLE pack but converted to harriers in 1912. The COUNTRY was in north Devon.

Marlborough (US) AMERICAN FOXHOUND pack formed in 1936 to hunt a rolling pasture and woodland COUNTRY in Maryland.

Marlborough College BEAGLE pack formed in 1952 to hunt a COUNTRY in Wiltshire around the school.

Marlborough Spaniel formerly a larger version of what is now the KING CHARLES SPANIEL.

> Is higher on the legs [than the Blenheim], which need not be so fully feathered. He has much longer muzzle and a flatter skull. The Marlborough possesses many of the attributes of a sporting Spaniel. [225]

marled of MERLE coat coloration.

Marled Collie HARLEQUIN COLLIE. [123]

marshall official at a race or COURSING meeting.

Maryboro' Irish BEAGLE pack formed in 1957 to hunt a COUNTRY in County Cork.

mask 1. dark upper skull. 2. dark MUZZLE.
> Dark mask confined to muzzle, distinctly contrasting with colour of head. [203, BOXER]

3. short coat on the head in dogs who have long or rough body coats. 4. the head of a HOUND's quarry; a trophy.

> We shall learn before it's over
>   Just how far a fox can roam,
> And the pace of a night rover
>   When his mask is set for home [272g]

mask, types of BALD, CLOVERLEAF.

masseter cheek muscles.

massiveness having impressive size relative to the breed.

Masson Hound one of three types of BASSET HOUND which, according to DRURY, existed in England.

mast cell tumour inherited skin tumour. (Mode of inheritance, complex.)

Master 1. of HOUNDS or of FOXHOUNDS: *see* MASTER OF FOXHOUNDS, MASTER OF HOUNDS.

> A Master must therefore be a millionaire, an Adonis, a loss to the diplomatic service, and possessed of all the virtues and aspirations of the early Christian martyrs with none of their ultimate recompense. [379]

2. male person to whom a dog shows a particular allegiance.

Master Agility dog (MAD) (Am.) the highest title awarded in AGILITY competition.

master hair GUARD HAIR.

Master of Foxhounds (MFH) person responsible for a pack of FOXHOUNDs and its affairs.

Master of Game (1410–1413) the oldest book on field sports in the English language, written by Edward, Duke of York, the grandson of King Henry III and Master of Game to King Henry IV.

Master of Hounds (MH) person responsible for a BEAGLE, HARRIER or OTTERHOUND pack and its affairs.

Mastie (16th cent. Brit.) MASTIFF. [139]

mastiff generic term for breeds characterized by large powerful heads, massive size and great strength.

Mastiff [AKC, FCI, KC] the ancestors of the Mastiff were taken from Britain by the Romans for use in the gladiatorial arena and as dogs of war. Solid and heavily built, it is one of the most physically impressive of all the breeds.

The head is square, flat and broad, the MUZZLE short, the small eyes wide set; the small ears are thin and lie close to the skull. The neck is arched and very muscular, the forequarters sloping and heavily muscled. The chest is wide and deep, the ribs well rounded and the LOINS wide and muscular. The tail is high set, long, and thick at the root. The coat is short and close, apricot fawn, silver fawn or dark BRINDLE fawn; a black MASK is obligatory. Height 70–76cm (27½–30in); weight 80–86kg (176–189lb).

> Probably the breed was imported from Middle Asia, until it became distributed throughout Europe, and in unsettled times it was used in these islands as a terror to the thief, whence its name 'Masa thefe', or, according to William Harrison (1586), 'Master theefe'. [186]
> Those who in quarrels interpose
> Must often wipe a bloody nose.
> A Mastiff old true English blood
> Lov'd fighting better than his food. [145f]

Mastiff Fox large subspecies of fox formerly found in northern England.

> Is rather less [than the Greyhound Fox]; but his limbs are more strongly formed. [51]

Mastin (Sp.) MASTIFF.

Mastin d'Aragon MASTIN DE LOS PIRINEOS.

Mastin de Español MASTIN ESPAÑOL.

Mastin de Extremadura MASTIN ESPAÑOL.

Mastin de la Mancha MASTIN ESPAÑOL.

Mastin de Leon MASTIN ESPAÑOL.

Mastin de los Pirineos [FCI] MOLOSSAN with origins in the mountains between France and Spain.

A strong and elegant breed with a large, broad head with slightly rounded skull and pronounced OCCIPUT. The eyes are small and dark with prominent HAW; the pendulous ears are small and pointed. The neck is slender but well muscled, the forequarters well boned and muscular, with straight limbs and close-arched toes. The body is long and rises slightly from WITHERS to an upright CROUP; the chest is broad and deep and the LOIN strong and supple. The tail is long, SCIMITAR curved and well FEATHERED. The skin is white or pink, except the lips which are black, with a thick, rough white coat with golden or grey patches on the head and sometimes on the body and root of the tail. Height 70–80cm (27½–31½in); weight 55–70kg (121–154lb).

Mastin Español [FCI] a powerful, commanding PASTORAL GUARD which can also double up as a hunter of boar and other large game.

The head is broad and slightly rounded, with a powerful, black-FLEWED MUZZLE, small eyes with prominent HAW, and small, pendulous pointed ears. The neck is strong and muscular with symmetrical DEWLAP. The forequarters are long, the forelegs straight and well boned, and the feet WELL KNUCKLED. The chest is broad and deep, the LOINS strong. The TOPLINE slopes slightly from WITHERS to CROUP and the strong tail is carried in a slight curve. The coat is fine and thick and varies in colour from grey to fawn and red, with golden and grey-patched white also acceptable. The skin is rosy white. Height 60–70cm (23½–27½in); weight 50–60kg (110–132lb).

Mastino Napoletano [FCI] Italian MOLOSSAN GUARD and former gladiatorial breed of impressive size and demeanour. The breed is of ancient origin though rescued from the point of extinction only after the Second World War. The breed's majestic bearing coupled with its great size and apparent strength is impressive, its loose fitting skin an important breed characteristic.

The head is large, broad and short, with rather rounded eyes, small ears and pronounced STOP. The skin forms heavy wrinkles over the brows and MUZZLE; the FLEWS are heavy. The short, strong neck surmounts sloping shoulders, and heavily boned, strongly muscled forelegs with sloping PASTERNS. The body is broad, rather long with a broad and muscular CROUP and powerful hindquarters. The tail is thick and traditionally DOCKED. Movement is slow, deliberate and bear-like. The short, dense coat is hard in texture and usually black, but blue, grey and brown (from fawn to red) are permitted. Height 50–75cm (19½–29½in).

match 1. any contest – including show, fighting - or series of contests, decided on a knock-out basis, between pairs of dogs.

> At the Boarded-house, in Marybone fields, on Monday, the 24th of this instant July, will be a match fought between the wild and savage panther and twelve English dogs, for 300£. [23]

2. (esp. of fighting dogs) bring two dogs together.

match meeting meeting at which a series of MATCHes between SHOW-DOGS takes place. The KC limits the number of dogs taking place to 64.

mate copulate. (Am.=breed.)

maternal antibody temporary and limited protection from disease derived from maternal milk.

maternal impression discredited belief that a pregnant female's experiences can have an effect on the appearance or temperament of her offspring.

Mathon and Colwall LEDBURY.

Mâtin French breed corresponding to a LURCHER or COLLIE.

> The French mâtin is not a very distinct dog, comprehending an immense variety of animals, which in

England would be called lurchers, or sheep dogs, according to the uses to which they are put. [338]

Mâtin Belge BELGIAN MASTIFF.

matrilineal of the female line; in line of female descent.

matron bitch that has had a number of litters.

maungy (var. spelling) MANGY.

Maupin Dog type of FOXHOUND developed by General Maupin in America during the 1850s and used as a component in the creation of the WALKER and AMERICAN FOXHOUNDS.

Mauthe Dog ghostly black SPANIEL said to haunt Peel Castle, in the Isle of Man.

maxilla either of the two symmetrical bones which form the upper jaw. [*illus.* SKELETON]

McCarthy Water Spaniel (obs.) one of three 19th-century varieties of IRISH WATER SPANIEL, also called the Southern Water Spaniel, formerly found in southern Ireland. [295]

MCV abbr. MINUTE CANINE VIRUS.

Meadow Brook (US) American, English and CROSSBRED FOXHOUND pack formed in 1877 as the Queen's County Hounds to hunt DRAG(2) over an arable and woodland COUNTRY in New York State. The pack was converted to hunting fox in 1890 when Thomas Hitchcock imported Mr Salkeld's pack from Cumberland.

mealy (of coat colour) dull tan.

measurable breeds (Am.) any of those breeds which, at American shows, are subject to a height disqualification.

Meath FOXHOUND pack dating at least from 1723. In 1813 the private packs of Messrs Pollock and Gerrard joined forces to form the Clongill Hunt, the name of which changed to the Meath Hunt in 1932.

meatus nasal cavity. [406]

Mecklenburg (US) American, English and CROSSBRED FOXHOUND pack founded in 1956 to hunt fox and DRAG(2) over a woodland, creek and swamp COUNTRY in North Carolina.

meconium chrome-yellow fluid found in the intestines of newborn puppies; the first faeces.

Medelan Russian MOLOSSAN breed formerly used for hunting bear, now thought to be extinct.

> I suppose the last possible descendants of the original dogs of war were the great Medelans owned by the late Tsar of Russia, and kept by him at the summer palace of Gatchina. These dogs were the size of a calf, and quite capable of killing a man single-handed. They were used for rousing bears out of the thickets in summer and from their hibernating quarters in winter. [383]

median furrow MEDIAN LINE.

median line shallow furrow running, in some breeds, from OCCIPUT to STOP; scissura.

> There is a slight furrow or median line extending from the stop to halfway up to skull. [6, TIBETAN MASTIFF]

median plane imaginary plane from nose to tip of tail about which dogs are symmetrical.

mediastinum cavity between the lungs in which the heart is situated.

Medium Griffon Vendeen BRIQUET GRIFFON VENDÉEN.

Medium Pinscher PINSCHER.

Medium Portuguese Hound PODENGO PORTUGUÊSA MEDIO.

Medium-sized Portuguese Podengo PODENGO POR-TUGUÊSA MEDIO.

medulla central part of an organ.

meestle dog. [280]

meet rendezvous for HOUNDS and FOLLOWERS before commencing hunting.

> During the latter period of his life the word 'meet' came into use, as designating the appointment or place of meeting of hounds, to which he had an equal dislike. I remember a juvenile sportsman saying to him one day, when out hunting, 'Where is the meet tomorrow?' Upon which he replied, 'There will be a leg of mutton on my table tomorrow at six o'clock, if that is what you mean, and I shall be happy if you will come and partake of it. [358]

megakaryoblastic leukaemia rare canine disease characterized by internal bleeding, anaemia and early death.

megaoesophagus dilation of the oesophagus, a condition which may be congenital or inherited as a secondary symptom of myaesthenia gravis. (Mode of inheritance, unclear.)

meiosis process of cell division which results in halving the diploid number of chromosomes prior to formation of gametes with the full haploid number.

meiotic of, or relating to, MEIOSIS.

meiotic drive propensity of alleles to exert a major chance of finding a successful gamete.

melanism propensity to be black or very dark.

Melbourne Hunt (Aust.) FOXHOUND pack formed in 1854 to hunt fox over an undulating COUNTRY in Victoria.

Meleager participant in the Calydonian wild-boar hunt.

Melita Dog MALTESE.

> Here the stone says it holds the white dog from Melita, the most faithful guardian of Eumelus. [Inscription on a Greek tomb]

Melitaeus SPANIEL GENTLE. [139]

Melitoeos SPANIEL GENTLE. [139]

Melton Mowbray town in Leicestershire formerly regarded as the centre of fox-hunting in the shires but perhaps now best known as the place in which the major British pet-food company is situated.

melon pips tan spots on the brows.

> Coat . . . black tan and white with tan melon pips and mask. [203, BASENJI]

membrane nicotans THIRD EYELID.

membranoproliferative glomerulonephritis progressive enlargement of the kidney glomeruli, resulting in blood-infused urine, protein deficiency and reduced resistance to disease.

meme hypothetical unit which enables a gene to survive in spite of its effect on the phenotype.

Mendel, Gregor Johann Austrian monk from the Augustinian monastery at Brünn who, in 1860, discovered the basic laws of inheritance from his experiments with peas, and thus founded the science of genetics.

Mendelian of, or relating to, the theory of genetics as expounded by MENDEL.

Mendelian character product of a major gene which is simply inherited.

Mendelian factor (obs.) GENE.

Mendelian inheritance theory that the means of inheritance, the genes, do not blend: although genes may create an effect intermediate between the information that each may carry, the genes themselves do not blend and are therefore available to pass on their intact information to future generations.

Mendelian trait characteristic which is governed by the basic laws of inheritance.

Mendelism (obs.) elementary genetic principles.

Mendip Farmers hunted as the Mendip Hunt since 1760, the COUNTRY lies in the county of Avon.

Mendip Hunt MENDIP FARMERS.

mengrell (obs. spelling) MONGREL.

meningitis inherited inflammation of the brain. (Mode of inheritance, uncertain.)

mephitic trail (lit.) scent trail.

> With a pack of hounds the Terrier is used to go to earth after the fox . . . so that his more powerful enemies may pursue him – guided by the mephitic trail. [106]

merle (of coat coloration) blue-grey FLECKED with black. The colour is associated with inherited deafness and ocular defects. (Mode of inheritance, dominant.)

merle eye blue-grey eye.

merle series various genes which give rise to MERLE coat coloration or in certain combinations to white and sometimes deaf dogs.

merled incorrect version of MARLED. [123]

Merry (US) private BEAGLE pack formed in 1958 to hunt cottontail rabbit.

merry of tail, esp. in the COCKER SPANIEL, which is in ceaseless motion.

mesanigiocapillary glomerulonephritis MEMBRANO-PROLIFERATIVE GLOMERULONEPHRITIS.

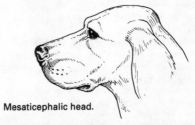

Mesaticephalic head.

mesaticephalic skull form intermediate between DOLICHOCEPHALIC and BRACHYCEPHALIC; skull that gives a CEPHALIC INDEX of about 70–75. [illus.]

messan (esp. Scot. and N. Eng.) small useless MONGREL dog.

> But wad hae spent an hour caressan,
> Ev'n wi' a Tinkler-gipsey's messan. [73e]

messenger CARRIER. [139]

messet (regional Eng.) MESSAN.

Messrs Lett's former Irish HARRIER pack formed in 1888 to hunt a COUNTRY in County Wexford.

metabolic toxic retinopathy SUDDEN ACQUIRED RETINAL DEGENERATION.

metabolism physical and chemical processes by which the body is maintained.

metacarpal of the METACARPUS.

metacarpal bones METACARPUS.

metacarpal pad each of the five thick spongy growths on the underside of the forefeet which form the protective surface on which dogs walk. [*illus.* DIGITAL PAD]

metacarpus part of the forelimb joining the carpus to the foot; the bones of this part. [*illus.* SKELETON]

metachromatic leucodystrophy inherited progressive degeneration of the nerves. (Mode of inheritance, recessive.)

Metamora (US) AMERICAN FOXHOUND pack formed in 1928 to hunt over a hilly grass and woodland COUNTRY in Michigan.

metaphyseal osteopathy HYPERTROPHIC OSTEODYSTROPHY.

metastasis transfer of disease from one organ to another.

metatarsal of the METATARSUS.

metatarsal bones *see* METATARSUS.

metatarsal pad large, roughly triangular spongy growth at the rear of the foot; communal pad. [*illus.* DIGITAL PAD]

metatarsus part of the hind limb joining hock to foot; the bones of this part. [*illus.* SKELETON]

metoestrus that part of the female reproductive cycle which follows OESTRUS and ends with DIOESTRUS, and characterized by early development of the corpus luteum. [*illus.* OESTRUS]

Metorchis albidus liver fluke found in dogs, foxes, and also in birds and humans.

Metorchis conjunctus liver fluke found in dogs, foxes and other carnivorous species.

metritis inflammation of the uterus.

meute (Fr.) the pack.

meute de chien (Fr.) PACKHOUND.

Mexican Hairless Dog XOLOIZCUINTLE.

Meynell founded in 1816 by Hugo Charles Meynell, the COUNTRY lies in Derbyshire and Staffordshire. Former huntsmen include Fred Gosden (1901–1906).

MFH abbr. MASTER OF FOXHOUNDS.

> Vot's an MP compared to an MFH? Your MP lives in a tainted hatmosphere among other MPs, and losses his consequence by the commonness of his office, and the scoldings he gets from his constituents; but an MFH holds his levee in the stable, his levee in the kennel, his levee in the 'unting field – is great and important everywhere – has no one to compete with him, no one to find fault, but all join in doing honour to him to whom honour is so greatly due. [344]

MH abbr. MASTER OF HOUNDS.

Mha Kon Klab extinct African primitive dog with characteristic ridge. [222]

MHE abbr. HAEMANGIOSARCOMA.

Miacis primitive canine ancestor.

Miami Valley (US) ENGLISH FOXHOUND pack formed in 1960 to hunt fox and DRAG(2) over a steep, wooded COUNTRY in Ohio.

Michuacaneus ALCO. [380]

Mick (colloq.) IRISH TERRIER.

microphthalmia inherited abnormally small eyes. The condition may be inherited, and related to MERLE coloration, but may also be the product of nutritional deficiency during pregnancy. (Mode of inheritance, recessive.)

Microsporidia genus of fungus species responsible for RINGWORM.

Microsporidia canis commonest of the species of fungus which cause RINGWORM.

Microsporidia distortum one of the species of fungus which cause RINGWORM, occasionally seen in dogs.

Microsporidia gypseum one of the species of fungus which cause RINGWORM, found in infected soil.

Microsporum fungi associated with skin disease and hair loss.

Mid-Antrim Irish HARRIER pack formed in 1875 to hunt a COUNTRY in County Antrim.

Mid-Asian Shepherd Dog SREDNEASIATSKAIA OVTCHARKA.

Mid-Asiatic Borzoi TASY.

Middle Asian Ovtcharka SREDNEASIATSKAIA OVTCHARKA.

Middleburg (US) AMERICAN FOXHOUND pack formed in 1906 to hunt over a grass and arable COUNTRY in Virginia.

Middlebury (US) AMERICAN FOXHOUND pack formed in 1945 to hunt a rolling COUNTRY in Connecticut.

middle ear that part of the ear which contains the three ossicles.

Middle-sized Anglo-French Hound ANGLO FRANÇAIS DE MOYENNE VENERIE.

Middleton and Middleton East FOXHOUND pack formed in 1953 by the amalgamation of the Middleton, which dates from 1764, and the Middleton East, which was founded in 1921; the COUNTRY lies in the Yorkshire wold.

Middleton Orange County MOC.

Mid-Down Foot Harriers FERMAC.

Mid-Essex BEAGLE pack formed in 1947 as the Hornchurch Beagles; the name was changed in 1952. The COUNTRY is in Essex.

Mid-Kent former STAGHOUND pack formed in 1868 to hunt a COUNTRY in Kent.

Midland (US) American, English and CROSSBRED

FOXHOUND pack formed in 1950 to hunt over a pasture and woodland COUNTRY in Georgia.

Midland Hunt Club (Aust.) FOXHOUND pack originally formed in 1848 with HOUNDS imported from the DUKE OF BEAUFORT'S pack; the present name was adopted in 1917. Kangaroo, wallaby, deer and hare are hunted over a heath, pasture and woodland COUNTRY in Tasmania.

Midleton Irish BEAGLE pack formerly known as Mr Byrne's Beagles, formed to hunt a COUNTRY in County Cork.

Mid-limit class [KC] show class for dogs that have not won three CHALLENGE CERTIFICATES or five or more first prizes in all at Championship shows in Mid-limit, Limit and Open classes, confined to the breed, where Challenge Certificates were offered for the breed.

Mid-Surrey Farmers' Drag Hounds former DRAGHOUND pack formed in 1926 in succession to the Banstead Drag.

migration introduction of new bloodlines into a breed, part of a breed or a KENNEL(4).

Mikado Terrier NIPPON TERRIER.

Mikawa Inu recent product of CROSSES(2) between the smooth CHOW CHOW and the NIPPON INU.

milk fever ECLAMPSIA.

milk rash skin rash caused by allergic reaction to one or other of the constituents of milk.

milk tooth first tooth; first deciduous tooth; puppy tooth.

Millbrook (US) AMERICAN FOXHOUND pack formed in 1907 to hunt over a woodland and plough COUNTRY in New York State.

Mill Creek (US) American, English and CROSSBRED FOXHOUND pack formed in 1920 to hunt fox and DRAG(2) over a wooded COUNTRY in Illinois.

Millwood (US) English and CROSSBRED FOXHOUND pack formed in 1927 to hunt fox and coyote over a rolling wooded COUNTRY in Kansas.

Milvain (Percy) FOXHOUND pack founded in 1921 to hunt a Northumberland COUNTRY.

mimic gene gene which produces a similar phenotype to another.

mincing (of action, gait) prancing movement, deficient in forward impetus.

> Action very distinctive, rather mincing, light and springy in slower paces and slight roll when in full stride. [203, BEDLINGTON TERRIER]

Minehead HARRIER pack formed in 1891 to hunt fox over a Somerset COUNTRY.

mineralocorticoid any of that group of hormones originating in the adrenal cortex and exercising effect on the mineral content of extracellular fluids.

Miniature Black-and-Tan Terrier ENGLISH TOY TERRIER.

Miniature Bulldog formerly a small variety of the BULLDOG.

Miniature Bull Terrier [AKC, KC] small version of the BULL TERRIER. Height not more than 35.5cm (14in).

Miniature Dachshund any one of three miniature varieties of DACHSHUND: wire-haired, short-haired or long-haired.

Miniature Long-haired Dachshund [KC] small version of the Long-haired DACHSHUND. Weight not more than 5 kg (11lb).

Miniature Pekingese SLEEVE PEKINGESE.

Miniature Pinscher [KC] a small version of the PINSCHER characterized by its HACKNEY GAIT. Height 25.5–30cm (10–12in).

Miniature Poodle one of the three main varieties of the POODLE. Height 28–38cm (11–15in).

Miniature Schnauzer [KC] smaller version of the SCHNAUZER. Height not to exceed 33–35.6cm (13–14in).

Miniature Smooth-haired Dachshund [KC] small version of the Smooth-haired DACHSHUND. Weight not more than 5kg (11lb).

Miniature Wire-haired Dachshund [KC] small version of the Wire-haired DACHSHUND. Weight not more than 5kg (11lb).

Mini Dachsi dim. (colloq.) MINIATURE DACHSHUND.

minor gene gene which has little effect on the phenotype.

Minor Limit class [KC] show class for dogs that have not won two CHALLENGE CERTIFICATES or three or more first prizes in all at Championship shows in Minor Limit, Mid-limit, Limit and Open classes, confined to the breed, at shows where Challenge Certificates were offered for the breed.

minor puppy 1. puppy between six and nine months old. 2. [KC] show class for such puppies.

Min Pin dim. (colloq.) MINIATURE PINSCHER.

Minute Canine Virus (MCV) CANINE PARVOVIRUS TYPE 1.

mirled (incorrect spelling) MARLED. [123]

misalliance unplanned and unwanted mating.

miscellaneous breed [AKC] any breed that is not sufficiently numerous to warrant its own register; equivalent to the UK's RARE BREED.

Miscellaneous class [AKC] show class for breeds awaiting entry to the AKC STUD BOOK, and equivalent to the UK's ANY VARIETY for rare breeds.

mismarked of dog that has coat coloration or markings not conforming to that which is acceptable for the breed.

mismating MISALLIANCE.

Mistabella SPITZ-like, European farm dog found during the Middle Ages but no longer extant; a probable ancestor of the European spitz breeds.

mistress female person to whom a dog shows a particular allegiance.

Mitchelstown Irish BEAGLE pack formerly known as the Mitchelstown Harriers and reformed in 1960 to hunt a COUNTRY in County Cork.

Mitchelstown Harriers MITCHELSTOWN.

mite any one of several species of arthropods

associated with mange, usually characterized by their small size.

mitosis process by which the division of cells leads to the production of tissue and organs.

mitral insufficiency inherited heart dysfunction. (Mode of inheritance, complex.)

mob kill a quarry without having given due LAW (1) and (4).

MOC (US) BEAGLE pack formed in 1961 to hunt, on foot and mounted, cottontail rabbit over a COUNTRY in Virginia.

Modbury HARRIER pack which hunts fox over a Devon COUNTRY and was founded in the mid-19th century.

Moddr Rhu the red dog; (Gaelic) IRISH SETTER.

modelled CHISELLED.

modifier gene gene which exerts influence over the effect of another gene, it is now generally accepted that most genes may modify the effects of most other genes.

molar of each large tooth at the rear of the jaw, which is adapted for grinding.

mole 1. raised spot on the face, from which there usually grows hair. 2. (of coat) short and soft.
> Mole type coats undesirable. [203, GERMAN SHEP-HERD DOG (ALSATIAN)]

molero persistent soft spot in the skull produced by failure of bones to unify, esp. in CHIHUAHUAS and some other TOY breeds.

Moller-Barlow's disease HYPERTROPHIC OSTEODYS-TROPHY.

Molosscicus MOLOSSUS. [139]

Molossan MOLOSSUS; MOLOSSOID.

Molossi inhabitants of Eastern Epirus where the huge Roman war and guard dogs are said to have originated.

Molossian Hound large ancient breed, ancestor of the MASTIFF breeds. [370]

molossoid of animal with the characteristics of a MOLOSSUS; of, or relating to, Molossus.

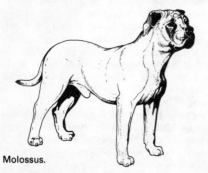

Molossus.

Molossus large and sturdy dog whose origins are in Molossia. [139] [*illus.*]
> After the name of a country in Epirus called Molossia, which harbours many stout, strong, and sturdy Dogs of this sort. [139]

Monday morning disease CANINE HYPOXIS RHAB-DOMYOLYSIS.

Mongolian Dog extinct French breed, similar in appearance to the POODLE.
> It resembles the Poodle in general shape, but itsre-markable for its very thick and closely packed coat of white hair, . . . the head is long, with drop ears, and a square muzzle. It is somewhat high on the leg, and round bodied. [225]

mongrel dog whose parents are not purebred; dog of unknown ancestry.
> The first cross between two separate breeds is an undoubted 'mongrel', a shapeless nondescript, blending generally the malformations and the faults of both types. [186]
> He was a ghastly mongrel – I tremble to think of the many different breeds of dogs that have gone to his making – but he had Character, he had Heart, he had an unconquerable zest for life. [374]
> He wa'n't no common dog, he wa'n't no mongrel; he was a composite. A composite dog is a dog that's made up of all the valuable qualities that's in the dog breed – kind of a syndicate; and a mongrel is made up of the riffraff that's left over. [365]

mongrelize breed indiscriminately.
> With the exception of a few kennels of choice blood, and which have been most carefully guarded, I fear, nay I am sure, the setter has greatly degenerated and mongrelised. [218]

monkey rack (colloq.) privileged ringside seats for dignitaries at dog shows.

Monkey Dog (colloq.) AFFENPINSCHER.

Monkey Terrier (colloq.) AFFENPINSCHER.

Monkstown Irish HARRIER pack formed in 1915 to hunt a COUNTRY in County Cork.

Monmouth County (US) HARRIER pack formed in 1885 to hunt fox and hare over a hill and lowland COUNTRY in New Jersey.

Monmouthshire established as the Monmouthshire Hunt Club in 1835 in succession to Squire Lewis's private pack, the Gwent COUNTRY is largely grass with some big woodlands.

Monmouthshire Hunt Club MONMOUTHSHIRE.

monogenic of character influenced by a single gene.

mono-nephrosis inherited condition resulting in the absence of one kidney. (Mode of inheritance, familial.)

monophyletic of individuals descended from a com-mon ancestor, correctly used to refer to species of wild dogs (all of which descend from a single ances-tor species) but usefully used to describe breeds that descend from a single ancestor.

monorchid strictly any male with only one testis, but often applied to individuals with one testicle descended into the scrotum.

monorchidism inherited condition in which the male dog has only one testicle. (Mode of inheritance, unknown.)

Montainboeuf extinct French SIGHTHOUND, one of the ancestors of the BILLY.

Montgomery HARRIER pack founded prior to 1939 by C.N. de Courcy Parry to hunt a hilly COUNTRY.

Montpelier (US) AMERICAN FOXHOUND pack formed in 1924 to hunt over a hilly, heavily wooded COUNTRY in Virginia.

Montreal (Can.) ENGLISH FOXHOUND pack formed in 1826 to hunt over an arable and pasture COUNTRY in Montreal.

Mooner night GUARD. [139], a type of dog mentioned by TOPSELL. [359]
> Because he does nothing else but watch and ward at an lynch, wasting the wearisome night season without slumbering or sleeping, baying and wailing at the Moon. [139]

Moonflower Dog PERRO SIN PELO DEL PERU.

Moore County (US) American and CROSSBRED FOXHOUND pack formed in 1914 to hunt fox and DRAG(2) over a rolling woodland COUNTRY in North Carolina.

Mooreland (US) American, English and CROSSBRED FOXHOUND pack formed in 1961 to hunt over an arable and woodland COUNTRY in Alabama.

Mops popular European name for PUG (der. *mopsen,* to grumble), possibly a reference to the breed's tendency to snore or, perhaps, its rather disgrunted expression.

Mopshund (Ger.) PUG. [225]

Morden Harriers WORCESTER PARK AND BUCKLAND.

Morocco Deerhound (obs.) PHARAOH HOUND.

Morpeth Northumbrian hunt founded in 1818 to hunt a largely grassland COUNTRY.

morph variant within a polymorphic population.

morphogenesis process by which structures become differentiated during early growth.

mort horn call sounded at the death of quarry during a hunt.

morula early stage in the development of an egg before cells have begun to change into more complex matter.

mosaic individual resulting from somatic mutation.

Moscow Long-haired Toy Terrier Soviet TOY breed of recent origin, with long coat of various colours. Height 20–28cm (8–11in); weight 2–3kg (4½–6½lb).

Moscow Watchdog MOSCOVSKAYA STOROJEVAYA.

Moskovskaya Storojevaya a recently created DOMESTIC GUARD with MOLOSSAN characteristics.

The head is large, the chest wide and deep, the body powerful; the limbs are heavily boned and muscular, and the tail is long and heavily feathered. The coat, invariably red and white, is long and dense. Height 64–69cm (25–27in); weight 45–68kg (99–149½lb).

Moskovskaya Storodzevay Sobaka MOSCOVSKAYA STOROJEEVAYA.

Moth (colloq.) PHALENE.

motion sickness TRAVEL SICKNESS.

motor skills ability to exert precise control over movement.

mottled (of skin or coat markings) randomly distributed small patches of dark colour on a lighter GROUND.

moucher 1. person or dog searching for game, usually without permission; a poacher or his dog. 2. a stray dog searching for food.

mougrell one who hunts on foot. [280]

moult (of coat) to shed, whether cyclically – as in all but a few breeds – or as a result of stress. Moulting tends to take place in spring when winter coat is shed, but may also take place in autumn in order to facilitate the growth of winter coat.

Mountain Cur SCENTHOUND produced in the Ohio River Valley from CROSSES(2) between imported and native HOUNDS. Of varied size and appearance but usually stocky with a BRINDLE, black-and-tan, blue, WHEATEN or tan coat of medium length. The tail is traditionally DOCKED or may be naturally short. Weight 16–29kg (35–64lb).

Mount St Bernard Dog SAINT BERNARD. [338]

mouse-hound weasel. [159]

mousell MUZZLE. [159]

mousey 1. of an insipid coat colour. 2. lacking personality, esp. of an under-sized racing dog.

moustache growth of hair on the upper jaw, either side of the nose.

mouth 1. (of HOUNDS) GIVE TONGUE on the scent.
> Between two dogs, which hath the deeper mouth. [319f]

2. (of GUNDOG) damage a retrieved bird; *see also* HARD MOUTH.

mouth, types of CROOKED; LEVEL; PARROT; SCRAMBLED; SHARK; SOFT; WRY. See also BITE, TYPES OF.

move gait; assume motion. In dogs, usually trot.

move close (of gait) move with hind limbs unusually and undesirably close together. [*illus.*]

move off (of HOUNDS) leave the MEET to go to the first DRAW(2).

moves like a train (cliché) of dog whose movement is powerful, true and rhythmic.

move straight move with all four limbs retaining a vertical line when in action.

Moving close behind.

Mr Baily's WEST SURREY AND HORSNELL.

Mr Butcher's Beagles former 15in BEAGLE pack formed to hunt a COUNTRY in Yorkshire.

Mr Byrne's Beagles MIDLETON.

Mr Connock Marshall's former name of the EAST CORNWALL.

Mr Delme Radcliffe's HERTFORDSHIRE.

Mr Gerard Leigh's HERTFORDSHIRE.

Mr Haight Jr's Litchfield County (US) American, English and CROSSBRED FOXHOUND pack formed in 1929 to hunt a rolling pasture COUNTRY in Connecticut.

Mr Hubbard's Kent County (US) AMERICAN FOX-HOUND pack formed in 1931 to hunt a pasture COUNTRY in Maryland.

Mr Harry Geach's BEAGLE pack formed in 1944 to hunt a COUNTRY in Lincolnshire.

Mr Holt Needham's SPARKFORD VALE.

Mr Humble's BRAES OF DERWENT.

Mr Jefford's (US) AMERICAN FOXHOUND pack formed in 1917 to hunt a rolling COUNTRY in Pennsylvania.

Mr J. Hutchinson Driver's former HARRIER pack which succeeded the Ripley and Knaphill Harriers; formed in 1738 to hunt a COUNTRY in Surrey.

Mr Newman's ESSEX AND SUFFOLK.

Mr Nigel Wheatcroft's private BEAGLE pack formed in 1953.

Mr O'Hara's former Irish HARRIER pack formed in 1909 to hunt a COUNTRY in County Sligo.

Mr Scott Plummer's LAUDERDALE.

Mr Seymour Allen's SOUTH PEMBROKESHIRE.

Mr Shirley's former private Irish HARRIER pack formed in 1912 to hunt a COUNTRY which was principally in County Monaghan.

Mrs Pryse-Rice's former privately owned HARRIER pack formed in 1894 on the basis of Mr Pryse-Rice's pack of FOXHOUNDS. The COUNTRY was in Dyfed.

Mr Stewart's Cheshire (US) ENGLISH FOXHOUND pack formed in 1914 to hunt an open COUNTRY in Pennsylvania.

Mr T.P. Lewes' former private OTTERHOUND pack formed to hunt the Ayrton, Ystwyth, Rheidol and their tributaries.

Mr W. Thompson's former OTTERHOUND pack formed in 1903 to hunt the Wharfe and its tributaries.

mucoarteritis degeneration of the heart and arterial system owing to abnormally high fat intake.

mucoplysacharidosis inherited metabolic disorder producing mental retardation, stunted growth and ocular defects. (Mode of inheritance, familial.)

Mudhol Hound small, finely built Indian SIGHT-HOUND with a long head and smooth black-and-tan coat. Weight 9–14kg (20–31lb).

Mudi [FCI] Hungarian HERDER and general-purpose farm dog. Height 35.5–51cm (14–20in); weight 8–13kg (17½–28½lb).

mullerian system embryonic female genitalia.

Mullion and District BEAGLE pack formed in 1953 to hunt a COUNTRY in Cornwall.

Multiceps multiceps TAENIA MULTICEPS.

multifactorial POLYGENIC.

multifocal retina dysplasia inherited ocular defect characterized by the existence of several small defective areas in the retina and tapetum; vision appears not to be disturbed. (Mode of inheritance, recessive.)

multilobular chondroma and osteoma disfigurement and brain disturbance caused by the growth of nodule masses on and in the head.

multiparous producing multiple offspring after each pregnancy.

multiple alleles mutant allele series produced by a normal gene.

multiple epiphyseal dysplasia inherited condition producing displacement of the cartilage between long bones.

multiple factor POLYGENES.

multum in parvo (L.) much in little. Used to describe the PUG's COMPACTness and strength surprising for its size.

Multyfarnham WESTMEATH.

mumbling (of GUNDOG) playing with game while retrieving it; mouthing.

> Whose buzz the witty and the fair annoys,
> Yet with ne'er tastes, and beauty ne'er enjoys,
> So well-bred spaniels civilly delight
> In mumbling of the game they dare not bite. [288]

Münchener (obs.) [AKC] GIANT SCHNAUZER.

Müncher Dog (obs.) GIANT SCHNAUZER.

muschel BURR.

> Ears . . . with very strongly developed burr (muschel) at the base. [6, ST BERNARD]

muscle contractile tissue of the body, which makes movement possible.

muscle bound excessive development of MUSCLE.

muscle fibre deficiency inherited tendency to weakness; uncertain movement. (Mode of inheritance, recessive.)

muscle tone quality of muscular development.

muscular of, or relating to, MUSCLE.

muscular dystrophy inherited degenerative disease of the muscles. (Mode of inheritance, sex-linked.)

musculation arrangement and disposition of MUSCLES.

mush encouragement to a SLED-DOG team. The term has been popularized by authors, and is seldom used by real sled-dog drivers.

mush dog SLED-DOG.

musher driver of a SLED-DOG team.

music sound made by HOUNDS in pursuit of their quarry.

> I have known many good hounds of the Devonshire pied sort, and they have always been keen workers, with beautiful music. [316]
> What music doth a pack of dogs make to any man, whose heart and ears are so happy as to be set to the tune of such instruments! [377]
> My love shall hear the music of my hounds, Uncouple in the western valley: let them go; [319k]
> The 'Musical din' of the Hounds still continued to have its charms & I still continued to follow them. [51a]

musick (obs.) MUSIC.

> When the wild Musick charms my ravish'd Ear, How dull, how tasteless Handel's Notes appear! [360]

Muskberry the County Cork hunt has existed since 1742.

Mustard and Pepper Terrier DANDIE DINMONT TERRIER.

mutagenic   of influences capable of causing mutation.

mutant   product of mutation.

  mutant gene   allele which has been spontaneously changed by external forces so that its expression will differ from that of the normal gene.

mutation   spontaneous phenotype change resulting from changed DNA structure.

mute   of a HOUND or TERRIER that works silently.

  The mute hound on the scent who hides it or keeps
  it secret not only does not try to help but makes
  every effort to outdistance all assistance and all company. [369]

  The white hound runs at the head of the pack,
    And mute as a mouse is he,
  And never a note he flings us back
    While the others voice their glee. [272j]

  As we have seen, the first essential, next to size and
  pluck, is we must have a dog that will 'speak' and
  not be mute. [283a]

mutilation   unnecessary surgery carried out to alter appearance or facilitate control.

muton   smallest measure of mutation.

mutt   dog. [280]

mutted up   guarded by a dog. [280]

mutuel   American equivalent of the Tote in which odds are derived from the amount of money wagered on the dog in question.

muzzle   1. nose and jaws; foremost part of the head. [*illus*. POINTS]

  Their muzzles were fast bound;
  Their collars were of gold with rings set round. [86]
  There was once a god in Egypt, when the gods they
  first began,
  Brave Lufra saw, and darted forth,
  She left the royal hounds mid-way,
  And dashing on the antlered prey,
  Sunk her sharp muzzle in his flank
  And deep the flowing life-blood drank. [314c]

2. device worn on the head to prevent dogs from biting. In Britain the design and standard of such is controlled by British Standard 7659: Specification for Dog Muzzles.

  There was no muzzling order then, in the seventies,
  and quite a common sight was the independent dog,
  usually a cur, roaming the streets in search of stray
  scraps of food. [182c]

  It is ordered that any person who shall suffer his or
  her mastiff dog to go about unmuzzled in the day
  time shall forfeit 6d. and that any person who shall
  suffer his or her mastiff dog to go about at night
  shall forfeit 12d. if it be unmuzzled, and 6d. if it be
  muzzled. [9]

muzzle band   (of BOSTON TERRIER) white marking on the MUZZLE.

muzzle, types of   BLUNT, PINCHED, POINTED, SHORT, SQUARE, SNIPY, TAPERING, TRUNCATED, WEDGE-SHAPED.

Muzzling Orders   (UK) The Metropolitan Police Act, 1867: British legislation intended to control the spread of rabies.

my word   (early 20th-cent. Brit. rhyming slang) dog turd. [142]

myasthenia   weakness caused by nerve abnormalities.

  myasthenia gravis   inherited episodic muscular weakness. (Mode of inheritance, recessive.)

Mycobacterium marianum   MYCOBACTERIUM SCROFULACEUM.

Mycobacterium scrofulaceum   bacteria which causes a tuberculosis-like disease in dogs.

Mycobacterium tuberculosis   tuberculosis bacterium, rarely found in dogs.

Mycoplasma cynos   bacteria associated with pneumonia.

mycosis   fungal disease.

  mycosis fungoides   malignant disease of the skin and lymph glands.

Mydding Dogge   (obs. OE) dog that scavenges among refuse.

mydriasis   dilation of the pupil.

myelin   sheath that surrounds nerve fibres.

myelitis   inflammation of the spinal cord.

myelopathic paralysis   progressive ataxia and paralysis of the hind limbs.

myelopathy   disease of the spinal cord.

myometrium   smooth muscular covering of the uterus which during the birth process rhythmically contracts to aid expulsion of the foetus.

myopathy   inherited muscular disease or weakness; unco-ordination. (Mode of inheritance, recessive.)

Myopia   (US) American, English and CROSSBRED FOXHOUND pack formed in 1882 to hunt DRAG(2) over a pasture and woodland COUNTRY in Massachusetts.

myotitis   inflammation of the muscles causing painful swelling and lameness.

  myotitis ossifans   inherited generalized inflammation of the muscles and abnormal bone growth, rarely seen in dogs. (Mode of inheritance, probably familial.)

myotonia   any disease producing involuntary muscle spasms.

  myotonia congenita   inherited muscular weakness; unco-ordination; stiffness of the muscles and inability to move, worsening with age and excitement. (Mode of inheritance, probably recessive.)

myotonic myopathy   MYOTONIA CONGENITA.

N

Naas Irish HARRIER pack formed in 1920 to hunt a COUNTRY in County Wicklow.

NAF abbr. NAME APPLIED FOR.

nail 1. (of a dog with its quarry) to take violent hold of.

> In vain the last double, for Jezebel's nailed him! Whoohoop! in the open the veteran dies. [61]

2. claw of the feet.

nailer reliable HOUND or TERRIER eminently suitable for its purpose.

naked dog any one of several hairless breeds.

Name Applied For suffixed to a dog's name for the purposes of entering competition before official Kennel Club registration has been confirmed.

name disc engraved disc attached to a dog's collar providing information about its ownership.

Nantucket (US) BEAGLE pack formed in 1926 to hunt jack rabbits on Nantucket Island.

nape the top of the neck adjacent to the base of the skull and below the OCCIPUT.

narcolepsy inherited tendency to fits precipitated by excitement or exercise. (Mode of inheritance, uncertain.)

narcolepsy cataplexy syndrome NARCOLEPSY.

nares nostrils.

narrow front forequarters in which the forelegs are close together and parallel.

nasal appertaining to the nose.

nasal bone the small bone of the nasal cavity, above the incisive bone. [*illus.* SKELETON]

nasal gleet (obs.) nasal discharge.

> Or ozoena, is usually the result of cold, or the sequel to a common catarrh. There is a discharge of mucous or muco-purulent matter from the nostrils, sometimes tinged with blood, and generally of a foetid odour. [320a]

nasal pyoderma skin disease affecting upper surface of the MUZZLE. Cause unknown.

nasal septum cartilaginous membrane which separates the nasal cavities.

naso-labial line groove between the two halves of the nose.

> The nostrils should be broad with a naso-labial line between them. [203]

natural dock born without a tail or with an unusually short tail.

> Occasionally a puppy is born with a natural dock. [6, WELSH CORGI (PEMBROKE)]

natural selection process of breeding which results in the survival of individuals able to withstand conditions pertaining in the wild, and in which process there is no external interference.

Navarro Mastiff MASTIN DE LOS PIRINEOS.

Navarro Pointer PERDIGUEIRO NAVARRO.

Neapolitan Mastiff [AKC, KC] MASTINO NAPOLETANO.

neck junction between head and WITHERS; (skeleton) cervical vertebrae.

neckline light strap, running from a SLED-DOG's collar to the towline.

neck on upside down EWE NECK.

neck, types of ARCHED, CRESTED, EWE, GOOSE, SWAN.

necropsy autopsy; study of the dead body, usually to ascertain cause of death.

necrosis death of part of the whole.

necrotizing myelopathy inherited spinal cord degeneration. (Mode of inheritance, dominant.)

Nederlandsche Herdershonden DUTCH SHEPHERD.

negative adaptation HABITUATION LEARNING.

negri bodies round or oval masses found in the nerves of animals infected with rabies.

neider (Swiss) short-legged HOUND; BASSET.

Nejdi smooth-coated SALUKI.

nematode type or group of parasitic worm which includes ROUNDWORMS as distinct from flatworms.

Nenets Herding Laïka Russian pastoral breed developed by the Nentsy nomads principally for herding reindeer.

Typically SPITZ in appearance with a powerful head, sharply pricked ears and a deep-chested body of considerable substance. The coat is exceptionally profuse, with thick RUFF and BREECHES; colour may be black, grey, white, whether solid or PIED. Height 41–46cm (16–18in); weight 19–23kg (42–50½lb).

neonatal appertaining to the time soon after birth.

neonatal maladjustment syndrome condition in which a puppy wanders aimlessly, feeds infrequently and is at risk of becoming chilled. Seems most often to follow a difficult birth; prognosis is poor.

neonate newborn offspring.

neoplasm abnormal new growth of tissue.

neoteny strictly an evolutionary tendency of juvenile forms to reproduce, and for their offspring to retain juvenile characteristics. Used more loosely to refer to the persistence of juvenile physical and behavioural characteristics into adulthood. The attraction of some TOY breeds is partially based on this quality.

Nepalese Hound large MASTIFF breed from Tibet whose existence was doubted by IDSTONE.

> Supposing we yield to such a theory as that the Nepalese Hound is the original of all breeds, a doctrine some naturalists have endeavoured to establish? [186]

Nepalese Mastiff NEPALESE HOUND.

nephropathy (FN) inherited kidney degeneration.

nessletripe runt of a litter. [159]

neuroaxonal dystrophy inherited progressive loss of muscular co-ordination, causing tremors. (Mode of inheritance, recessive.)

neurogenic muscular atrophy inherited progressive weakness of the neck and limb muscles. (Mode of inheritance, familial.)

neuronal abiotrophy inherited early onset of progressive neural tetraplegia and muscle atrophy. (Mode of inheritance, recessive.)

neuronal ceroid lipofuscinosis CEROID LIPOFUSCI-NOSIS.

neuropathy any tendency to reduced ability to feel pain as a result of nerve abnormality or degeneration.

neuroticism human behavioural characteristic also applicable to dogs and used to describe excessive responses to anxiety or excitement.

neuter castrate or spay; a dog having been so treated.

neutral mutation (of genes) mutation which confers neither advantage or disadvantage on the individual.

neutropenia condition in which there is a decrease in the number of white blood cells present in the blood.

neutrophilia condition in which there is an increase in the number of white blood cells present in the blood.

Newbridge former Irish 13½in BEAGLE pack formed in 1907 to hunt a COUNTRY in County Kildare.

Newcastle and District former 15½in BEAGLE pack formed in 1908 to hunt a COUNTRY in Northumberland and north Yorkshire.

Newcastle Setter former variety of ENGLISH SETTER.
> But local strains of the general variety (of English Setters) as it is diffused throughout the country. [221]

New College, Magdalen and Trinity former 15½in BEAGLE pack formed in 1896 by New College, Oxford, and in 1902 becoming the joint property of New College and Magdalen, to hunt a COUNTRY in Oxfordshire.

Newfie dim. NEWFOUNDLAND.

New Forest 1. former 12½–13in BEAGLE pack formed in 1901 to hunt a COUNTRY in Devon. 2. hunt dating from 1780 and whose COUNTRY lies in Hampshire and Wiltshire and consists largely of wood and moorland. Former masters include John Warde, 1808–1814.

New Forest Buckhounds BUCKHOUND pack formed in 1854 to hunt a COUNTRY in the Hampshire New Forest.

Newfoundland [AKC, FCI, KC] a breed with characteristics very similar to the modern Newfoundland was described by Captain Richard Banks in 1620. The breed was used by local fishermen to retrieve objects from the sea and as a draught dog. A massively boned dog with great strength and extremely active.

The head is broad and massive with pronounced OCCIPUT; the MUZZLE is short and clean. The forelegs are straight, the body well ribbed with a broad back and muscular loins. The hindquarters are strong, the feet large and webbed. The black or brown, DOUBLE COAT is dense, oily and water-resistant. White dogs

with black markings are referred to as Landseers. Height 66–71cm (26–28in); weight 50–69kg (110–152lb).
> The only object within doors upon which she bestows any marks of affection, in the usual style, is her dog Chowder; a filthy beast from Newfoundland, which she had in a present from the wife of a skipper in Swansey. [327]

New Guinea Singing Dog CANIS HALLSTROMI.

New Holland Dog DINGO. [406]

New Ireland Dog white or cream, PIED variant of the NEW ZEALAND NATIVE DOG, regarded as both a companion and a culinary delicacy by its aboriginal owners.

Newmarket and Thurlow FOXHOUND pack whose plough COUNTRY lies in Suffolk and Cambridgeshire and has been hunted since 1793. Former masters include Squire Osbaldeston, 1827.

Newry Irish HARRIER pack formed in 1820 to hunt a COUNTRY in Counties Down and Armagh.

New South Wales Wolf DINGO.
> Has been called a Dog; but its wild and savage nature seems strongly to point out its affinity to the Wolf; to which, in other respects, it bears a great resemblance. [51]

New Zealand Huntaway HUNTAWAY.

New Zealand Native Dog short-coated PARIAH, used as a DOMESTIC GUARD, a dietary supplement and a source of fine skins by its Maori owners.

The wedge-shaped head, PRICK EARS, curled tail and variable colours are typical of the type.

New Zealand Sheep Dog type of shepherd dog developed from imported herding breeds to satisfy the needs of New Zealand sheep farmers; the breed is noted for its HUNTAWAY abilities.

NFC NOT FOR COMPETITION.

Niam Niam edible dog from the upper reaches of the Nile. [181a]

nick 1. propensity of a mating to produce top quality offspring. [204]
> Should the cross nick, however, spare no pains to continue it, if circumstances will enable you to do it. [266b]

2. (cosmetic surgery) cut the tendons in order to alter tail carriage or correct a deformed tail.

nick leg one leg striking another during movement.

nictitating membrane rudimentary THIRD EYELID.

nidicolous of puppy born blind and helpless.

night blindness PROGRESSIVE RETINAL ATROPHY.

night cur thievish dog.
> The farmers of the country and upland dwellers, call this kind of Dog a night cur, because he hunts in the dark. [139]

Nihon Terrier JAPANESE TERRIER.

Nippon Inu smaller version of the JAPANESE AKITA.

Nippon Terrier created during the 19th century from imported TERRIERS to satisfy the Japanese desire for small, domestic breeds. The breed is unrecognized outside Japan.

The head is fine, small and elegant, the body is muscular and fine skinned, with a smooth, predominantly white, black-or-tan FLECKED coat. Tail traditionally DOCKED. Height 30–38cm (12–15in); weight 4.5–6kg (10–13lb).

Nite Champion title awarded to HOUNDS which receive more than 100 points in American Coonhound trials.

Nivernais de Petite Taille former small variety of the GRIFFON NIVERNAIS.

Nivernais Griffon GRIFFON NIVERNAIS.

nobble 1. cheat. [280]. 2. use dishonest means to prevent a dog from winning.

nociceptor pain receptor, stimulated by injury.

no course a course which is declared void for whatever reason.

no go of a course that has been declared void as a consequence of both dogs having become UNSIGHTED.

non-additive traits dominant and epistatic effect of certain polygenes.

non-slip retriever dog that does not hunt for fresh game but retrieves shot game.

nonspecific of ailment or condition which may arise as a result of any one of several causes.

non-sporting of breeds not used for sporting purposes: not a HOUND, GUNDOG or TERRIER.

Non-sporting Group 1. [AKC] a number of breeds, grouped together for the purposes of classification, which includes those breeds – other than WORKING or TOY – which the AKC do not consider to have been developed for sporting purposes. 2. [KC] of the three groups – UTILITY, working and toy – which include all breeds that the KC currently regard as not having been developed for sporting purposes.

The AKC and KC do not entirely agree about which breeds should be included, and both differ from the FCI.

non-uniting anconeal process UN-UNITED ANCONEAL PROCESS.

Nootka Sound Dog name under which an unidentified dog formerly exhibited by the London Zoological Society was known.

Nordic Spitz NORRBOTTENSPETS.

Nordiske Sitz-hunde NORWEGIAN BUHUND.

Norfolk and Suffolk FOXHOUND pack which derives from the Norwich Staghounds which began hunting CARTED stag in 1610. The hunt was converted to foxhounds in 1964.

Norfolk Lurcher traditionally a CROSS between a COLLIE and a GREYHOUND.

Norfolk Retriever former localized type of English RETRIEVER of doubtful provenance.

> Our convictions are most decidedly against believing the Norfolk Retriever to be anything but a mongrel, related in some degree to the modern Retriever proper. [320a]
> A coarse, liver-coloured dog, sometimes to be seen in the marshy districts of East Anglia, which some people claim as a distinct breed. [225]

There is supposed to be a Norfolk retriever, but this is no special strain, being black, brown, black and tan, or any other colour; an undoubted cross between an ordinary field spaniel and some other retriever. Such cross-bred dogs are useful on the 'Broads' when the shooting season is on, and, being hardy, are, when trained, perhaps better adapted to wildfowl shooting than the more attractive and better cared for varieties. [221]

Norfolk Spaniel liver-and-white SPANIEL breed formerly to be found in eastern England.

> As almost any liver-coloured and white moderately large dog is called by this name, more Norfolk Spaniels are used than any other. [186]
> The epithet of Norfolk was derived from a Duke of that cognomen, who established an improved breed of sporting Spaniel, and has nothing to do with the county – in fact, it was probably at first interchangeable with Sussex, the native home of the Duke in question. [123]
> Resembles a thick-made English setter in shape and general proportions, but is of a smaller size, seldom exceeding 17 or 18 inches in height. The colour is black and white, or liver and white. [338]
> From a cross with the terrier a black and tan variety was procured, which was cultivated by the late Duke of Norfolk, and thence called the Norfolk Spaniel. [406]
> I am somewhat at a loss to know why the ordinary liver and white spaniel came to be distinguished by the Spaniel Club as the Norfolk spaniel. [221]

Norfolk Terrier [AKC, FCI, KC] short-legged, short-coated, short-backed, stocky TERRIER with a wide, slightly rounded skull surmounted by PRICK EARS. The coat may be red, WHEATEN, tan, GRIZZLE, or black and tan. Height 25–26cm (10–10¼in).

normal curves graphic or mathematical representation of NORMAL DISTRIBUTION.

normal distribution measure of the frequency with which any trait occurs within a given population.

normal gene gene which produces a normal phenotype.

Normalgrosse Teckel Smooth-haired DACHSHUND.

normal phenotype typical appearance for the breed.

Norman Artesian Basset BASSET ARTESIAN NORMAND.

Normandy Basset BASSET ARTESIAN NORMAND.

Norman Hound French HOUND.

> Adapted for the pursuit of all kinds of the larger game in the French forests. He is a heavy, strong dog, somewhat coarse in bone, in shape approaching the Bloodhound rather than our Foxhound. [225]

Norrbottenspets [FCI] small SPITZ breed originally used for hunting. Differs from other spitz in that the white coat, spotted with black, brown or tan, is unusually short and the tail not tightly curled. Height 41–43cm (16–17in); weight 12–15kg (26½–33lb).

Norris's Drops formerly a supposed remedy for distemper. [47]

Norsk Buhund NORWEGIAN BUHUND.

Norsk Elghund [FCI] NORWEGIAN ELKHOUND.

Norsk Elghund [Gra] NORWEGIAN ELKHOUND.

Norsk Elghund [Sort] Black Norwegian Elkhound: SVART NORSK ALGHUND.

Norsk Lundehund NORWEGIAN LUNDEHUND.

North African Jackal *CANIS ANTHUS.*

North American Wild Dog COYOTE.

North Buckinghamshire BEAGLE pack formed in 1939.

North Cornwall founded in 1824 to hunt fox in a bank and wall COUNTRY.

North Cotswold dating from 1868 when the Earl of Coventry gave up part of his Berkeley COUNTRY.

North Dartmoor BEAGLE pack formed in 1960.

North Down Irish HARRIER pack formed in 1881 to succeed the Dufferin Harriers; the COUNTRY lies in County Down.

North-East Cheshire DRAGHOUND pack formed in 1962 to hunt a COUNTRY in Cheshire.

Northeasterly Hauling Laïka NORTH-EASTERN SLEIGH-DOG.

North-Eastern Sleigh Dog large and powerfully built Manchurian SLED-DOG, white, black or, less commonly, red, black and tan, or PIED. It has a thick, DOUBLE-COAT, with a strong head, short, stiffly pricked ears, short neck and a characteristic MANE. Height 58cm (23in).

Northern Counties former OTTERHOUND pack formed in 1903 on the basis of local packs which had been in existence since prior to 1873. The COUNTRY consisted of the rivers Tweed, Till, Glen, Whitadder, Blackadder, Aln, Coquet, Wansbeck, Font, Pont, Blyth, Tyne, Derwent, Wear, Tees, Leven, Swale, Codbeck, Ure and their tributaries as well as the Northumbrian lakes.

Northern Counties Fox Terrier (obs.) BEDLINGTON TERRIER.

Northern Dhole fierce, wild dog, a subspecies of *CUON ALPINUS* (formerly *Cyon albinus*).

Northern Hound 1. type of FOXHOUND formerly to be found in north-eastern England. 2. name used by DRURY to refer to the SCOTTISH DEERHOUND.

Northern Water Spaniel (obs.) one of three 19th-century varieties of IRISH WATER SPANIEL. [295]

North Herefordshire established in 1826 the COUNTRY is largely pasture with some woodland.

North Kildare former Irish HARRIER pack formed in 1906 as the Grangewilliam. The present name was taken in 1909.

North Kilkenny founded in 1934 to hunt part of the Kilkenny COUNTRY.

Northland (Aust.) BEAGLE cross FOXHOUND pack formed in 1953 to hunt DRAG(2) over a lowland pasture COUNTRY in Tasmania.

North Ledbury founded in 1905 the hilly woodland COUNTRY lies in Worcestershire and Herefordshire.

North Lonsdale founded in 1947 to hunt a COUNTRY in southern Cumbria.

North Mayo Irish HARRIER pack formed in 1840 to hunt hare, fox and deer.

North Norfolk HARRIER pack formed by the amalgamation of local packs in 1871.

North Northumberland hunt founded in 1882 as the Glendale to hunt a COUNTRY in the Cheviots.

North Pembrokeshire hunt founded in 1866 and united with the South Pembrokeshire in 1885.

North Shropshire hunt founded in 1823.

North Staffordshire hunt whose COUNTRY has been hunted since 1825 when Charles Wicksted hunted his own HOUNDS.

Northumberland Terrier possibly the BORDER TERRIER; DRURY cites the breed as one of the BEDLINGTON's ancestors.
> No doubt some famous dogs of the breed of old Northumberland Terriers were long ago located about Thropton, Rothbury, Felton, and Alnwick. [123]

North Warwickshire hunt founded in 1832 to hunt a COUNTRY vacated by the Warwickshire.

North-west Indian Greyhound RAMPUR DOG.

North Wexford Irish BEAGLE pack formed in 1955 to hunt a COUNTRY in County Wexford.

Norwegian Black Elkhound SVART NORSK ALGHUND.

Norwegian Buhund [KC] typical SPITZ breed used for a variety of rural tasks. The body is lightly built and COMPACT, the head broad but lean with a tapering MUZZLE. The ears are sharply pricked and the eyes dark and expressive. The body is strong and short, with a deep chest and short COUPLINGS. The DOUBLE COAT is harsh to the touch and may be WHEATEN, black, red or WOLF-SABLE. Height 45cm (17¾in).

Norwegian Elkhound [AKC] ELKHOUND.

Norwegian Hound DUNKER.

Norwegian Lundehund [KC] developed on the Norwegian island of Vaerog to locate Puffins' nests and retrieve eggs from them. The breed's six-toed feet, closable ear orifices and unusually flexible neck are unique characteristics.

The wedge-shaped head with pronounced STOP and strong MUZZLE, sharply pricked triangular ears and slanted eyes are typically SPITZ. The body is rectangular with a sloping CROUP and high-set densely coated tail which does not curl. The coat is rough and DOUBLE, reddish-brown or FALLOW, with black POINTS(4). Height 32–38cm (12½–15in); weight 6–7kg (13–15½lb).

Norwegian Puffin Dog NORWEGIAN LUNDEHUND.

Norwegian Sheep Dog NORWEGIAN BUHUND.

Norwich former STAGHOUND pack formed in 1809 to hunt a COUNTRY in Norfolk.

Norwich Staghounds NORFOLK AND SUFFOLK.

Norwich Terrier [AKC, FCI, KC] DROP-EARed counterpart of the NORFOLK TERRIER, to which it is identical in every respect except ear carriage.

nose 1. generally used to refer to the MUZZLE, specifically to the scenting organ at the tip of the MUZZLE. 2. scenting ability.

They say the old boy's got a better nose than any of his hounds. [309]

Excellent nose, persevering hunter and tracker. [203, DACHSHUND]

nose out discover by means of scent.

nose, types of BROWN, BUTTERFLY, DUDLEY, RAM'S, ROMAN, SELF-COLOURED, SMUDGE.

nose work tracking; follow a scent trail.

nostril aperture in the nose.

Not for Competition suffixed to the name of dog who will attend a show but will not compete. Such a dog will attend usually for the purpose of providing companionship to a younger inexperienced dog that will be shown.

Nova Scotia Duck Tolling Retriever [AKC, FCI, KC] breed developed in Yarmouth County, Nova Scotia, to serve the dual purpose of attracting water fowl to within the range of guns and then retrieving the shot birds.

A COMPACT, well-boned and strongly muscled dog with a wedge-shaped head, wide-set eyes, triangular ears set well back, and a deep-chested body. The slightly wavy, DOUBLE, weather-resistant coat may be red or orange with lighter shading. Height 45–51cm (17¾–20in); weight 17–23kg (37½–50½lb).

November 1st traditionally the date on which the formal fox-hunting season starts in Britain.

Novice class (KC) show class for dogs that have not won a CHALLENGE CERTIFICATE or three or more first prizes at a Championship show (some classes excepted).

nursing bitch bitch with unweaned puppies.

nyctalopia inability to see in reduced light levels; night blindness.

Nyctereutes procyonoides Racoon-dog. Species found in the forests of Indochina, south-eastern Siberia, Japan, a small wild canid formerly valued for its pelt and as a consequence hunted to extinction in eastern Asia where it was formerly to be found.

nymphomania neurotic compulsion to have sexual intercourse, esp. in females.

nystagmus regular involuntary eye movement.

O

Oak Brook (US) AMERICAN FOXHOUND pack formed in 1944 to hunt over a wooded COUNTRY in Illinois.

Oakenclough Beagles BLEASDALE.

Oak Grove (US) AMERICAN FOXHOUND pack formed in 1945 to hunt fox and occasional DRAGS(2) over a swampy lowland and pasture COUNTRY in Tennessee.

Oakley dating from 1800, the hunt operates in a heavily ploughed COUNTRY which lies in Bedfordshire, Buckinghamshire and Northamptonshire.

Oakley Foot BEAGLE pack formed in 1958 to hunt a COUNTRY in Leicestershire.

Obedience the sport at which a dog is tested on the accuracy with which it carries out set commands.

  Obedience Dog dog trained for the purpose of competing at OBEDIENCE.

  Obedience test one of a number of competition exercises that make up an OBEDIENCE TRIAL.

  Obedience trial organized competition of OBEDIENCE comprising a number of standard tests, each to suit a specific level of training.

obesity the condition of being abnormally and unhealthily fat.

Oblique eye.

oblique eye eye in which the outer corners are higher than the inner corners. [*illus.*]

oblique shoulder WELL-LAID shoulder.

occiput high part at the back of the skull; peak or apex. [*illus.* POINTS]

occipital of, or relating to, the OCCIPUT.

  occipital crest OCCIPITAL PEAK.

  occipital peak OCCIPUT.
    The skull is long and narrow, with the occipital peak very pronounced. [6, BLOODHOUND]

  occipital tuberosity protrusion of bone at the back of the skull, forming the OCCIPUT. [*illus.* SKELETON]

occlusion manner in which teeth in the upper and lower jaws meet when the mouth is closed.

OCD abbr. OSTEOCHONDRITIS DISSECANS.

ocular of, or relating to, the eye.

  ocular dermoids inherited corneal cysts. (Mode of inheritance, probably recessive.)

  ocular larva migrans eye defects caused by migration of larval *Toxocara canis*.

oedema swollen tissue. *See also* LETHAL OEDEMA.

OES abbr. OLD ENGLISH SHEEPDOG.

oesophageal of, or relating to, the OESOPHAGUS.

  oesophageal achalasia MEGAOESOPHAGUS.

  oesophageal dysfunction inherited condition resulting in difficulty in swallowing. (Mode of inheritance, probably autosomal dominant.)

  oesophageal dysphagoia inherited difficulty in swallowing owing to malfunction of the oesophagus. (Mode of inheritance, dominant.)

  oesophageal osteosarcoma disorder of the oesophagus associated with *Spirocerca lupi* infestation.

oesophagus that part of the alimentary canal between the pharynx and stomach; the gullet.

oestrogen female hormone which induces OESTRUS.

oestrous of, or relating to, OESTRUS.

  oestrous cycle regular recurrence of OESTRUS. Domestic dogs come into oestrus on average about once every seven months, while wild canids and primitive breeds have an annual oestrus, usually in autumn.

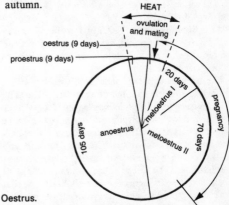

Oestrus.

oestrus that part of the sexual cycle during which ovulation occurs. [*illus.*]

Ogar Polski [FCI] one of several HOUND breeds which have a similar appearance to the BLOODHOUND and probably derive from a common root. A ponderously massive and imposing breed with a short, black and tan coat. Height 56–66cm (22–26in); weight 25–32kg (55–70½lb).

Old Berkeley FOXHOUND pack dating from the 18th century and hunted by successive Earls of Berkeley until 1801 when it became a subscription pack. The COUNTRY lies principally in Buckinghamshire and Hertfordshire.

Old Berkshire hunt that in its present form dates from 1830, but it has been in existence since 1760; hunts fox in a COUNTRY lying in Berkshire and Oxfordshire.

Old Charlton Hunt COWDRAY.

Old Chatham   (US) American and CROSSBRED FOX-HOUND pack formed as the Lebanon Valley in 1926 to hunt over a meadow and plough COUNTRY in New York State.

Old Chatham Foot   (US) BEAGLE pack formed in 1952 to hunt cottontail rabbit over a COUNTRY in New York State.

Old Country Bulldog   AMERICAN BULLDOG.

Old Danish Bird-dog   GAMMEL DANSK HØNSEHUND.

Old Danish Honsehund   GAMMEL DANSK HØNSE-HUND.

Old Danish Pointer   GAMMEL DANSK HØNSEHUND.

old dog encephalitis   progressive mental and motor dysfunction, blindness, circling in old dogs, and associated with distemper virus.

Old Dominion   (US) American and CROSSBRED FOX-HOUND pack formed in 1924 to hunt a grass, plough and woodland COUNTRY in Virginia.

Old English Bob-tailed Sheepdog   OLD ENGLISH SHEEPDOG.

Old English Bulldog   BULLDOG. [123]

Old English Hound   SOUTHERN HOUND.
> Distinguished by its great size and strength . . . it is endued with the most exquisite sense of smelling . . . The breed . . . is now almost extinct. [51]

Old English Mastiff   MASTIFF.

Old English Sheepdog   [AKC, FCI] formerly known as the Bobtail and principally used as a cattle drover, the breed's strength and soundness were essential to its purpose in life.

The breed is squarely built and muscular with a distinctive ambling gait and unusual bark. The skull is capacious with well-defined STOP, the MUZZLE strong, the eyes, which are set well apart, may be blue. The ears are small and carried close to the skull. The arched neck is strong. The body is short and COMPACT with WELL-SPRUNG RIBS, the hindquarters are muscular. The tail is either naturally absent or DOCKED very short, hence the name Bobtail. The coat is harsh and profuse, either grey or blue, with white. Height 56cm (22in); weight 30kg (66lb).

Old English Terrier   rough-coated BLACK AND TAN terrier, now subsumed into the WELSH TERRIER. Early authorities disagreed as to the identity of the breed. It is likely that as the old Black and Tan Terrier became differentiated into distinct localized breeds, the name was adopted by the briefly popular OLD ENGLISH WHITE TERRIER.

Old English Water Spaniel   extinct variety of SPANIEL.

Old English White   AMERICAN BULLDOG.

Old English White Terrier   extinct breed of English terrier which was in every respect except colour similar to the present MANCHESTER TERRIER.

old man   (of a BULLDOG) mature dog.
> A term applied principally by bulldog breeders, but by others also, to an animal that has matured. Thus a backward puppy is sometimes referred to as one that is likely to be all that is required when he has a little more of the old man about him. [320]

Old Shock   goblin, said to appear in the form of a calf or large dog. [159]

Old Spanish Pointer   PERDIGUEIRO NAVARRO.

Old Surrey and Burstow   FOXHOUND pack dating from the 17th century, prior to 1866 the pack consisted of HARRIERS. The COUNTRY lies in Sussex and Surrey.

Old Welsh Grey Sheep Dog   WELSH GREY.

Old Yaller   (Am. colloq.) CAROLINA DOG.

olecranon   upper part of the ulna. [*illus.* SKELETON]
   olecranon process   point of the elbow.

olfactory   pertaining to smell.
   olfactory nerve   group of nerves situated at the forefront of the skull which are associated with the ability to discern scent.

oligodendroglia cells   cells associated with the nervous system.

ololygmancy   art of foretelling the future by the howling of dogs.

Olpe Hound   DEUTSCHE BRACKE.

on   1. of HOUND following a scent.   2. of TERRIER that has reached his quarry underground.   3. dim. HIE ON.

on   (as prep.):
   on his/her toes   lively.
   on the flags   (esp. of PACKHOUND) competing in a show.
   on the leg   of dog with long legs in proportion to the size of the dog.
> The Irish setter is rather more 'on the leg' than the English dog. [37]

Oncicola canis   intestinal parasite infestation which causes cysts on the walls of the intestine.

on heat   (of bitch) in season; undergoing OESTRUS.

onion head   smooth head, lacking in desirable wrinkle.

oocyte   immature cell which develops into an ovum.

oogenesis   production of oocytes.

oogonia   cells which produce oocytes.

open   (of HOUNDS) begin to GIVE TONGUE.

open-angle glaucoma   primary glaucoma in which the anterior chamber remains open, forming an open angle which impairs the passage of light and thus reduces vision.

Open class   1. (KC) show class for all dogs of the breeds for which the class is provided and which are eligible for entry at the show.   2. (FCI) show class for dogs more than twenty-four months old on the day of the show.

open coat   of a coat which should be tight but which is loose and parted.

open couplings   long and loose COUPLINGS.
> Open couplings highly undesirable. [203, FLAT-COATED RETRIEVER]

open foot   foot in which the toes are widely spread, usually a fault.
> I would not reject a well-shapen puppy in all other respects, for merely somewhat of an open foot, provided his ankles or fetlocks were good. [266b]

opening meet the first formal MEET of the season proper, in the UK traditionally 1 November for fox-hunting.

open marked of coat that has spotted markings on a white GROUND, esp. on a HOUND.

open pyometra *see* PYOMETRA.

open show (KC) show open to all comers but which does not have CHALLENGE CERTIFICATES on offer.

Opisthorchis tenuicolis parasitic fluke which invades the bile duct causing abdominal pain, diarrhoea and jaundice.

Opisthorchis viverrini parasitic liver fluke, causing abdominal pain, diarrhoea and jaundice.

Opotiki Hunt (N.Z.) pack formed in 1932 to hunt hare over a pasture COUNTRY in Opotiki.

oral appertaining to the mouth.

oral metering signals, whether relating to taste or texture, which originate in the mouth and inhibit further feeding.

orange belton (of coat colour) orange and white TICKING, esp. in an ENGLISH SETTER.

Orange County (US) AMERICAN FOXHOUND pack formed in 1903 to hunt over a rolling COUNTRY in Virginia.

orb eyeball.

orbit cavity within the skull which contains the eye. [*illus.* SKELETON]

orbital muscles ridge of muscles above the eyes which contribute to the development of the brows.

organelle structure within a cell.

oriental expression expression created by obliquely placed, almond-shaped eyes.
> Eastern or Oriental expression is typical of the breed. [203, AFGHAN HOUND]

Ormond hunt dating from 1778 when it was founded in County Offaly by Lord Lismore.

Ormskirk Heeler (obs. var.) LANCASHIRE HEELER.

Ormskirk Medicine formerly a supposed remedy for rabies.
> I have heard that the Ormskirk Medicine is also very good. I have given it to several people in my neigh-bourhood, and, I believe, with success. [47]

orthopaedics branch of medicine appertaining to the bones.

orthoselection selection exercised over related individuals over time in order that change proceeds in a certain direction.

Osbaldiston, William Augustus author of *The British Sportsman* (1792).

os calcis CALCANEUS.

Oslerus osleri parasitic filarid found in the bronchial passages.

ossicles small bones of the middle ear.

osteoarthritis degenerate disease of the joints.

osteochondritis dissecans inherited malformation of the cartilage especially between the femur and humerus. (Mode of inheritance, polygenic.)

osteodystrophia fibrosa condition in which there is gradual replacement of bone with fibrous tissue.

osteodystrophy bone disease resulting from abnormal development during growth, or distortion caused by abnormal metabolism in adults.

osteodystrophy I OSTEODYSTROPHY.

osteodystrophy II HYPERTROPHIC OSTEODYSTROPHY.

osteogenesis imperfecta inherited condition in which the bones are abnormally brittle. (Mode of inheritance, familial.)

osteopathy 1. any bone disease. 2. a system of therapy based on mechanicals and the manipulation of body structures.

osteophyte bony growth.

osteoporosis condition in which the bones become light and porous.

osteosarcoma malignant tumour of the leg bones, common in dogs. (Mode of inheritance, familial.)

Österreichischer Bracke-Brandlbracke OSTERREICH-ISCHER GLATTHAARIGE BRACKE.

Österreichischer Glatthaarige Bracke racily built smooth-coated, black-and-tan HOUND principally used for tracking larger game. The ears are broad and pendulous, the skull broad and the body deep-chested and athletic in appearance. Height 46–59cm (18–23¼in); weight 23kg (50½lb).

Österreichischer Kurzhaariger Pinscher [FCI] DOMESTIC GUARD which has become uncommon.
> The body is rather long and broad, the head strong with a powerful MUZZLE and curved STOP; the short ears are dropped. The coat is short and smooth and may be black, brown, fawn or BRINDLE, with or without white on chest, muzzle and lower legs; black and tan is also acceptable. Height 51cm (20in).

Ostiah Laïka one of five Siberian LAÏKA breeds identified in 1896 by Prince Andrew Shirinsky Shihmatoff. [380]

Oswestry Corporation Hounds TANATSIDE.

Otago Hunt (NZ) pack formed in 1896 to hunt DRAG(2) and hare over farmland in Dunedin.

other end of the lead HANDLER of a SHOW-DOG. Usually used in reference to judging, when it is occasionally alleged that some judges habitually judge 'the other end of the lead'.

otitis inflammation of the ear.

otitis externa inflammation of the external ear, producing discharge and pain resulting in head shaking and scratching.

otitis media inflammation of the middle ear, causing symptoms similar to those of otitis externa.

otoascariasis mite infestation of the ear.

otocephalic syndrome inherited hydrocephalus, cranial abnormalities, agnathia and neurological abnormalities. (Mode of inheritance, familial.)

Otocyon megalotis Bat-eared Fox, also known as the Large-eared Cape Dog, found in the grasslands of southern Africa, southern Zambia, Ethiopia and Tanzania.

Otodectes cynotis parasitic ear mite which causes OTODECTIC MANGE.

otodectic mange inflammation of the external and

middle ear, associated with thick brown crusts and dermatitis, and caused by the mite *Otodectes cynotis*.

otorrhoea discharge from the ear.

Ottawa Valley (Can.) ENGLISH FOXHOUND pack formed in 1873 to hunt fox, but since 1930 it has hunted DRAG(2) over a COUNTRY in Ontario.

otter *Lutra vulgaris*, fish-eating member of the weasel family, formerly hunted in Britain, for which purpose the OTTERHOUND was bred.

otter head (esp. in BORDER TERRIER) head resembling that of an otter.

otter hunting the pursuit of otters with hounds, which are followed by huntsmen on foot.

otter pole bamboo or ash, metal-shod staff used by otter-hunters to assist them when moving through water.

otter tail (esp. in LABRADOR RETRIEVER) thick and flat tail resembling that of an otter.

> Tail . . . should be clothed thickly all round with the Labrador's short, thick, dense coat, thus giving that peculiar 'rounded' appearance which has been described as the 'otter' tail. [6, LABRADOR RETRIEVER]

Otter Dog OTTERHOUND.

> Otter-hunting was practised in the time of King John, with what were known as 'Otter-dogs' and the huntsman was supplied with two horses. [186]
> Of these otter-dogs – a cross between the old southern hound, the Scotch terrier, and water-spaniel – there were specimens in the Islington Agricultural Hall, looking, however, naturally enough, 'like fish out of water' [383]

Otter Terrier any leggy CROSSBRED terrier suitable for work to OTTER.

> Any cross-bred creature was called a Scotch terrier, especially if he appeared to stand rather higher on the legs than the ordinary terrier; if he were on short legs he was an 'otter' terrier. [221]

Otterhoun WETTERHOUN.

Otterhound [AKC, FCI, KC] old HOUND breed developed solely to satisfy the peculiar demands made of hounds used to hunt otter.

A rough-coated, squarely built hound, with a long, fairly narrow head, long, peculiarly FOLDED ears and a powerful MUZZLE. The chest is deep and the TOPLINE level. The hindquarters are strong and well muscled with moderate ANGULATION. The feet are large, thickly padded and webbed. The STERN is set high. Movement is a loose shambling walk, with an efficient long-striding action at faster paces. The coat, of any recognized HOUND COLOURS, is dense, rough and weatherproof. Height 60–67cm (23½–26½in).

out and outer hunter who runs unreasonable risks in order to stay with HOUNDS.

> And the fishmonger, previous possessor of the grey, loudly affirmed, with many oaths which it is unnecessary to repeat, that 'Muster Sawyer always was a hout-and-houter, and has gone audacious!' [338b]

out at elbow of dog whose elbows protrude.

> Such hounds as are out at the elbows, and such as are weak from the knee to the foot, should never be taken into the pack. [47]

out at shoulder of dog whose scapula is not closely set against the ribs.

out at walk (of puppies, especially HOUNDS) boarded with a keeper to be educated. *See* PUPPY WALK.

outbred of dog produced without line- or inbreeding.

outbreed avoidance of line- or inbreeding; OUT-CROSS.

outcross 1. dog that is mated for the purpose of introducing unrelated animals to a PEDIGREE.

> An outcross is introduced when the breed operated upon is declining in stamina or is in danger of extinction. [225b]

2. mate closely bred animal with one to which it is not related.

out of born of: having as DAM.

out of coat of dog that is sparsely coated.

outlaw gene gene whose deleterious effect persists because of the gene's favoured place on its own locus.

out of mark of an otter which is lying up in a holt whose entrance is below water level and thus cannot readily be MARKed by HOUNDS.

outside rabbit artificial lure which runs on the outside edge of an American GREYHOUND race-track.

ova pl. OVUM.

oval chest chest in which the depth is greater than the width.

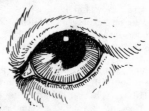

Oval eye.

oval eyes normally elongated eyes with rounded inner and outer corners. [*illus.*]

oval foot slightly longer version of what is generally referred to as a CAT FOOT.

> Feet oval, toes strong, well arched, and tight, two centre toes slightly advance of two outer. [203, WELSH CORGI (PEMBROKE)]

ovariohysterectomy SPAYING.

ovary each of the two female reproductive organs which produce ova and oestrogen.

over (of OTTERHOUNDS) *see* PASS OVER.

over-angulated (usu. of shoulder or hindlimb) that has a greater degree of ANGULATION than is desirable for the breed.

overbirdiness (Am.) of GUNDOG that repeatedly searches the same piece of ground for game.

overbuilt of TOPLINE that, while straight, is higher at the CROUP than at the WITHERS. [*illus.*]

over-dominance when the Aa heterozygote dominates both the AA homozygotes.

Overbuilt back.

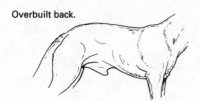

overfill excessive bone or muscle on the head and MUZZLE.

Overhang.

overhang pronounced BROW. [*illus.*]
overhung 1. (of mouth) former term for OVERSHOT. [320] (Usually used to refer to breeds in which the condition was desirable.) 2. (of eyes) having pronounced brows.
overlaps of a mutant gene producing an apparently normal condition.
overlay different, usually darker, coat colour that lies over the main coat.
overreach (esp. at trot) extend the feet, when moving, further than is necessary or desirable. At trot, this will cause the hind feet to overtake the forefeet.
over-run pass that which is being followed. HOUNDS may over-run their quarry, hunt-FOLLOWERS may over-run hounds.

> When hounds come to a check, a huntsman should observe the tail hounds: they are least likely to over-run the scent. [47]

Overshot bite.

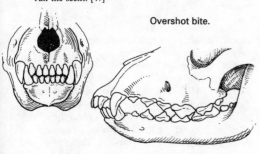

overshot bite bite in which the teeth of the upper jaw overhang those of the lower jaw to the extent that there is a gap between the teeth when the mouth is closed. [*illus.*]
overshot jaw OVERSHOT BITE.
overtipped of semi-PRICK EARS that break too near the skull in breeds in which this is undesirable.
over-tread excessive development of KNUCKLEs.

> Their forelegs drumsticked without crooks,
> Straight, without over-tread or bend,
> Muscled to gallop to the end [249a]

oviduct that part of the reproductive tract in which the ova are fertilized.
Ovtcharka group of Russian guard dogs.
Ovtcharka de Russie Meridionale SOUTH RUSSIAN OWTCHARKA.
ovulation process of producing ova. [*illus*. OESTRUS]
ovum unfertilized gamete produced by the female.
Owczarek Nizinny POLISH LOWLAND SHEEP DOG.
Owczarek Podhalanski [FCI] PASTORAL GUARD with origins in Hungary and Czechoslovakia.

> The breed is strongly made and muscular, with a lupine head and strong, MANEd neck. The thick coat may be straight or wavy and is either pure white or cream in colour. Height 61–86.5cm (24–34¼in); weight 45–69kg (99–152lb).

Owczarek Polski Nizinny POLISH LOWLAND SHEEP DOG.
Owczarek Tatrzanski OWCZAREK PODHALANSKI.
own (esp. of HOUNDs) indicate that scent has been found.
  own the scent HOUNDs being able to recognize and follow the DRAG.

> It is obvious that the reasons why hounds are brought to a check is that they no longer own the scent. [235]

Owtchah SOUTH RUSSIAN OWTCHARKA.

> The huge rough sheep-dog of Russia, known as the Owtchah, which is found in great numbers all along the valley of the Dnieper. [221]

Owtcharka Russian sheep-herding breeds.
Oxford University DRAGHOUND pack formed some years prior to 1862 to hunt LINEs(2) in Oxfordshire.
Oyuki Terrier NIPPON TERRIER.
ozoena (obs.) nasal discharge.

> The discharge from the nostril is abundant and constant, sometimes fetid. The Schneiderian membrane, of more than usual sensibility in this animal, is exposed to man cases of irritation, and debilitated and worn out before its time. [406]

P

P standard gene symbol for pink-eyed dilution. [395]

p 1. abbr. puppy. 2. abbr. parents.

PA abbr. PROGRESSIVE AXONOPATHY.

pace (of gait) move the legs on each side slowly and in unison to produce a two-beat tempo and a decided roll of the body.

> The American Eskimo should trot not pace. [367]

Pachon de Vitoria PERDIGUEIRO NAVARRO: unrecognized Spanish GUNDOG. [150]

pack 1. group of dogs, usually HOUNDS, TERRIERS or wild canids, acting in unison for the purpose of hunting.

> Everyone has observed how much more dogs are animated when they hunt in a pack, than when they pursue their game apart. We might, perhaps, be at a loss to explain this phenomenon, if we had not experience of a similar in ourselves. [183]

2. of the feel of a closely clipped coat, esp. in the POODLE. 3. that part of a LION-CLIPped POODLE's coat which is left over the LOIN and rump.

packhound HOUND which customarily hunts with a pack, esp. FOXHOUNDS, BEAGLES, HARRIERS.

pack sense of the way in which HOUNDS support one another's efforts.

Pack Stake trial class for more than two HOUNDS working together.

pad 1. each of the five defined fleshy parts of a dog's foot. 2. foot of a badger, fox or otter taken as a trophy. 3. walk in a quiet and deliberate manner.

padding 1. obs. SEAL. 2. movement in which the front feet are lifted higher than necessary, to avoid heavy contact with the ground, produced by a combination of strong rear action and upright shoulder construction. 3. thickening of the lips.

> The upper lip is thick and padded, filling out the frontal space created by the projection of the lower jaw. [6a]

paddle move the feet in an arc to the side instead of in a straight line. [*illus.*]

> Should not move close behind nor paddle nor plait in front. [203, BEAGLE],

paddock fenced area used for exercise.

paddock judge person in charge of arrangements immediately prior to a GREYHOUND race.

Paddling.

Pai small type of short-legged house-dog, used to scavenge for table scraps in 1st century AD china.

Paisley Terrier CLYDESDALE TERRIER. [123]

Pakuranga Hunt (N.Z.) pack formed in 1874 to hunt over farmland in Papakura.

palate roof of the mouth, partly hard and partly soft, which separates the mouth cavity from the respiratory passages.

Pale Fox VULPES PALLIDA.

palpation manual external exploration in order to discover the whereabouts of internal foreign objects or to diagnose pregnancy by feeling for tell-tale signs.

palpebral fissure opening between the eyelids, the shape of which is described in BREED STANDARDS when referring to the eye.

Pampas Fox DUSICYON GYMNOCERUS.

pancreas glandular organ situated high in the stomach which secretes insulin.

pancreatic of, or relating to, the PANCREAS.

pancreatic acinar atrophy inherited condition caused by insufficient secretion of digestive enzymes. (Mode of inheritance, recessive.)

pancreatic atrophy inherited condition in which degeneration of the pancreas leads to increased appetite, undigested stools and loss of condition. (Mode of inheritance, recessive.)

pancreatic gastrinoma tumour of the pancreas, rarely seen in dogs.

Pandy BEAGLE pack formed in 1961 to hunt a COUNTRY in Gwent.

panis caninus DOG BREAD. [141]

panmixis random mating.

Pannonian Dog former dog of war.

> used in war as well as in the chace, and by whom the first charge on the enemy was always made. [406]

pannus DEGENERATIVE PANNUS.

panosteitis inherited condition in which there is inflammation of parts of bones. (Mode of inheritance, uncertain.)

pants BREECHES.

paper foot thin and flat foot or pad.

> Flat feet, splayed feet, paper feet etc, are to be heavily penalized. [6a]

papers (colloq.) registration documents issued by the appropriate KENNEL CLUB.

papilla small protuberance on or in the body.

papillomatosis warts.

Papillon [AKC, FCI, KC] a delicately constructed though surprisingly robust TOY SPANIEL breed with origins in France. The name derives from the French word for butterfly, a reference to the appearance of the large, obliquely erect, wing-like ears; DROP-EARed specimens are, in reference to their closed 'wings', referred to as Phalene (moth).

The rounded skull is flanked by very large, obliquely set, slightly rounded, heavily FRINGED ears; the STOP is well defined and the muzzle finely pointed. The medium-sized, dark-rimmed eyes are rounded. The sloping shoulders are well developed, the forelegs straight and finely boned with long, HARE FEET. The body is fairly long, with WELL-SPRUNG RIBS and strong LOINS. Hindquarters are WELL TURNED. The tail is long, arched over the back, and well fringed. The abundant coat is long and silky, white with patches of any colour other than liver. Height 20–28cm (8–11in).

Papuan Dog small, short-coated, PRICK EARed primitive dog. [222]; unrecognized NEW GUINEA NATIVE DOG. [150] (Definitions taken from sources that disagree.)

Paragonimus kellicotti parasitic fluke found in the lungs and causing bronchitis. Occurs in America and Asia.

parahormone natural substance which exerts hormone-like influence over the function of an organ or organs.

parainfluenza condition caused by CANINE PARAIN-FLUENZA VIRUS.

parakeratosis condition causing thickening of the horny layer of the skin.

parallel tracking of movement in which the forefoot and hind foot on each side of the body travel down separate but parallel lines.

paralysis inability to move.

paraphymosis inability to retract the penis.
> a condition in which the penis, having protruded, the glans refuses to retract again. It thus becomes strangulated, and much swelling and great pain is the result. [320a]

paraplegia paralysis of the hind limb or limbs.

parasite creature which lives in or on another from which it derives its nourishment.

parasitic otitis OTOASCARIASIS.

parathyroid gland endocrine gland situated near the thyroid gland.

paresis mild form of paralysis.

par force medieval form of hunting in which the quarry was allowed to run at will.

pariah FERAL dog.
> This is the general name in India for the half-reclaimed dogs which swarm in every village, owned by no one in particular, but ready to accompany any individual on a hunting excursion. [338]
> Even a dog that gets fierce with hunger and loneliness 'll throw you a tender look if you're kind to him. Pariahs have their private feelings. [178]
> Many of these London pariahs were wretched-looking objects, full of sores and old scars, some like skeletons and others with half their hair off from mange and other skin diseases. [182b]

Park BEAGLE pack formed in 1962 to hunt a COUNTRY principally in Dorset.

Parkfield former 14½in BEAGLE pack formed in 1906 to hunt a COUNTRY in Cheshire.

paronychia inflammation of the nails and surrounding tissue.

parrot mouth OVERSHOT BITE.

Parson dim. PARSON JACK RUSSELL TERRIER.

Parson Jack Russell Terrier [KC] the first officially recognized TERRIER of the type bred by the eponymous parson. The aim of breeders is to preserve the old-fashioned type of FOX TERRIER which was brought to perfection by the Parson and which is very different from the squat, barrel-ribbed, short-backed, shrill-voiced terriers which also carry the Parson's name.

The breed conforms with the classic working terrier prescription of 14 inches (36cm) high and 14 pounds (6½kg) in weight as is necessary for any terrier intended to run with hounds and GO TO GROUND(2) to fox. The head is moderately broad and flat, with a shallow STOP and strong MUZZLE. The dark almond eyes are fairly deeply set, the small V-shaped ears drop forward close to the head, the fold following the line of the skull. The neck is muscular and of good length, forequarters are long and sloping, legs straight and strong. The chest is moderately deep, the back strong and the LOIN slightly arched. Hindquarters are muscular with good ANGULATION and short HOCKS. The tail is high set and strong, traditionally DOCKED. The coat may be rough or smooth, always harsh, close and dense over a thick skin and is entirely white or white with tan, lemon or black patches preferably confined to head and the root of the tail. Height 35–36cm (13¾–14in).

partial dominance INCOMPLETE DOMINANCE.

particoloured (of coat) two-coloured, neither colour dominant; pinto.
> Parti-colored dogs shall be disqualified. [6, POODLE]

parturition the process of giving birth.

parvovirus group of viruses which, during the 1970s, extended their range to include the canine species. Two forms occur in dogs: CANINE PARVOVIRUS TYPE 1 (CPV-1) (also called Minute Canine Virus (MCV)) and CANINE PARVOVIRUS TYPE 2 (CPV-2). The development of effective vaccines and of field immunity has reduced what was initially a high mortality rate.

Severe cases of both types of parvovirus are characterized by blood-infused, foul-smelling diarrhoea, enteritis, rapid dehydration and probable death within 24 hours. Puppies which survive may develop PARVOVIRUS MYOCARDITIS.

parvovirus myocarditis residual heart damage sometimes caused by severe attacks of parvovirus and resulting in the early death of affected puppies.

pass (of HOUNDS) over-run the DRAG.

pass over (of HOUNDS) fail to MARK.

pastern metacarpus, that part of the leg between the carpus, wrist, and the foot. [*illus.* POINTS]

pastern, types of BARE, BROKEN, SLOPING, SUNKEN, UPRIGHT.

pastoral guard dog used to protect farm stock from predators.

pastoral herder dog used to control livestock under the direction of its handler.

Pastore Abbruzzese MAREMMA SHEEP DOG.

Pastore Maremmano-Abbruzzese MAREMMA SHEEP DOG.

patch solid colour marking on coat that is predominantly of another colour, usually white.

patchy tongue incompletely pigmented tongue.

pate 1. head of an otter taken as a trophy. 2. badger. [159]

patella kneecap; STIFLE-joint. [*illus.* SKELETON]

patellar of, or relating to, the PATELLA.

patellar dislocation condition in which the patella is displaced from its normal position.

patellar luxation inherited dislocation of the patella resulting in characteristic hind-limb hopping movement. (Mode of inheritance, polygenic.)

patellar subluxation partial or temporary dislocation of the patella.

patent ductus arteriosus inherited abnormal persistence of foetal open lumen. (Mode of inheritance, threshold.)

paternity testing any one of several methods of ascertaining the true sire of a puppy or puppies.

pathogenesis development of a disease.

pathogenic causing disease.

Patterdale Terrier (popular misnomer) FELL TERRIER.

Patti Indian PASTORAL GUARD, black-and-tan coated and wolf-like in appearance, formerly owned by Tamil nomads but now uncommon in its pure form.

patrilineal of descent via a male line.

paunchy (of abdomen) loose and flabby, lacking muscular development.

Pavlovian conditioning development of links between stimuli and responses.

paw foot.

PDA abbr. PATENT DUCTUS ARTERIOSUS.

peach fawn (of coat colour) warm pale tan.
Colour in the Whippet is absolutely of no importance to a good judge, though possibly what is known as the peach fawn is the favourite among amateur fanciers. [225]

peak 1. OCCIPUT.
Head and skull, long and fine with slight peak. [203, POODLE]
2. syn. widow's peak, as in the IRISH WATER SPANIEL.

Pearce, Thomas (pseudonym Idstone), author of *The Dog: with Simple Directions for his Treatment, and Notices of the Best Dogs of the Day and their Breeders or Exhibitors* (1872).

pearl eye silvery coloured eye.
Eyes . . . If blue, a pearl, China or walleye is considered typical. [6, OLD ENGLISH SHEEPDOG]

pear-shaped (of body) broad, rounded chest and narrow loins, as in the BULLDOG.

Peat Dog CANIS FAMILIARIS PALUSTRIS. [312]

pectineus muscle muscle on the inner thigh.

pectoral muscle muscle which runs along the sternum.

pedalling 1. (of movement) hind limbs moving in an exaggerated and circular manner without imparting drive. 2. of a sled driver resting one foot on the runner and helping to propel the sled with his other foot.

pedes truncatus amputation of the feet formerly carried out to prevent dogs from harassing game. [141]

pediculosis louse infestation.

pedigree 1. genealogical history.
2. form on which genealogical information – pedigree – is recorded. 3. dog whose parents are of the same breed.

pedigreed (Am.) of dog having a PEDIGREE.

peg metal spike or screw which is driven into the ground and to which a dog may be tied.
The peg is one of the most useful of the keeper's breaking instruments. It should be made with a joint and metal ferrule, like the old-fashioned parasol, as one of considerable length, suited for sandy or loose soil, can thus be carried easily in the pocket. The line can be whipped round this in an instant, and the dog secured to learn the mystery of the 'down charge', or 'waiting' and guarding gun or game. [186]

peg-dog GUNDOG trained to sit beside the shooter as he awaits the arrival of game put up by BEATERS. (der. the position occupied by each shooter is marked by a numbered peg.)
You may be lucky enough to be able to purchase a dog who was intended for trials and did not quite make the grade, but is of a higher standard than the usual peg-dog or rough-shoot dog. [*114]

Peintinger STEIRISCHE RAUHAARIGE HOCHGESBIRGSBRACKE.

Peintinger Bracke STEIRISCHE RAUHAARIGE HOCHGESBIRGSBRACKE.

Peke dim. PEKINGESE.

Pekinese (obs. spelling) PEKINGESE.
But the country has now been flooded with the Pekinese, and one is made to loathe it from the constant sight of it in every drawing-room and railway carriage and motor-car and omnibus, clasped in a woman's arms. [182b]

Pekinese Spaniel (obs.) PEKINGESE.
He [the Chow Chow] yields to the Pekinese Spaniel the claim to be the Royal dog of China. [225]

Pekingese [AKC, FCI, KC] a popular TOY breed of ancient Chinese origin. The breed is one of several oriental breeds whose lion-like appearance is said to have been created as a compliment to Buddha. The breed itself was long confined to aristocratic ownership and appreciated for its appearance, for the comfort and companionship it provided, as a sentinel and as a food taster.

The breed is small, though thick set and unusually heavy for its size. Bitches tend to be larger than dogs. The head is large, broad and flat, the MUZZLE short and broad, the lustrous eyes large, round and dark. The thick neck is very short, the forequarters short, thick and heavily boned, the forelegs slightly bowed. The body is short and broad with a narrow waist. Hindquarters are lighter than the forequarters, the feet are large and flat, the high set, thickly PLUMED tail carried over the back. The long, profuse coat is coarse, with a thick undercoat, and forms a dense MANE on the neck and abundant FEATHERING on chest, ears, limbs and feet. All colours and combinations of colour other than albino and liver are acceptable. Weight not over 5kg (11lb) for dogs and 5.5kg (12lb) for bitches.

> When the Mings were eventually ousted by the Manchurian Ch'ing dynasty in the seventeenth century, the Pekingese dog was firmly reinstated in the Forbidden City and, for the next 200 years, enjoyed a privileged status unrivaled by any other variety of pet before or since. [317]

Peking Palace Dog (obs.) PEKINGESE.

Peking Palasthund (obs.) PEKINGESE.

Pelger-heut anomaly inherited heart murmurs of no clinical significance. (Mode of inheritance, dominant.)

Pelon (obs.) MEXICAN HAIRLESS DOG.

> A most outlandish and repulsive looking little brute, with not a vestige of down or hair on its blue-grey (or sometimes purplish) skin, excepting a few stiff bristles standing up over the eyebrows and the ears, which only serve to accentuate the perfect bareness of the skin, which in the true breed shows a strange finely wrinkled appearance. [221]

pelt skin with attached hair, esp. of an otter but also commonly of the BORDER TERRIER.

pelvic of, or relating to, the PELVIS.

pelvic limb the hind limb.

pelvis rigid group of bones which form the hips. [*illus.* SKELETON]

Pembrokeshire hunt created by an amalgamation of the North and South Pembrokeshire in 1894. The banked COUNTRY is largely pasture and woodland.

Pembroke Welsh Corgi WELSH CORGI (PEMBROKE).

pemphigus vulgaris one of a group of related skin disorders in which the skin develops shallow ulcers especially involving the mucoid membranes.

pen drive sheep into a small fenced paddock. Penning is one of the exercises in a SHEEP DOG TRIAL. [204]

pencilled (obs., of a coat) PILY.

> A pily or pencilled coat is the typical one, according to the club's standard. [46a]

pencilling 1. black lines running along the top surface of the toes.

> Black pencilling on toes and black streak under jaw permissible. [203, GORDON SETTER]

2. black lines running from the outer corner of the eyes.

Pendle Forest and Craven HARRIER pack hunting a pasture and moorland COUNTRY on the borders of Lancashire and Yorkshire and formed in 1945 by the amalgamation of the Pendle Forest (formed in 1930) and the Craven Harriers (which dated from the 18th century).

pendulous of ear which hangs down the side of the head and is incapable of being erected.

penetrance degree to which a gene masks the effects of another.

Penhow BEAGLE pack formed in 1959 as the Penhow Mousehounds but recognized in 1962 under the title of Penhow Beagles; the COUNTRY is in Gwent.

Penhow Mousehounds PENHOW.

Penistone former 22–24in HARRIERS or old SOUTH-

ERN HOUND pack formed in 1260 under the mastership of Sir Elias de Midhope to hunt a COUNTRY in Yorkshire.

Pentyrch dating from 1946 the hunt occupies a COUNTRY around the river Taff.

pepita parti-colour, esp. in the MUDI.

Pepper and Mustard Terrier breed kept by DANDIE DINMONT.

> The Deuke himself has sent as far as Charlieshope to get ane o' Dandie Dinmont's Pepper and Mustard terriers. [314]

pepper and salt (of coat colour) mixture of black and grey hairs.

> The typical pepper-and-salt color of the topcoat results from the combination of black and white hairs, and white hairs banded with black. [6, STANDARD SCHNAUZER]

peppering of a coat which is interspersed with darker hairs.

> An intensely pigmented medium gray shade with 'peppering' evenly distributed throughout the coat. [6, GIANT SCHNAUZER]

peptic oesophagitis inflammation of the oesophagus sometimes occuring as a consequence of anaesthesia.

Per Ardua (RAF) BEAGLE pack formed by the RAF Beagling Association in 1951 to hunt a COUNTRY in Lincolnshire.

Percy FOXHOUND pack formed in 1850 to hunt a Northumbrian largely grassland COUNTRY.

Perdigueiro (Portuguese) POINTER.

Perdigueiro Burgales PERDIGUEIRO DE BURGOS.

Perdigueiro de Burgos [FCI] the Spanish POINTER, a breed brought close to its present form during the 18th century but having existed as a heavier, less active breed for many years prior to that date.

The breed is unusually large and heavy for a Pointer. The head and MUZZLE are strong, the body well muscled; the coat is short and smooth, with liver TICKS(2) and patches on a white GROUND. Height 55–66kg (121–145lb).

Perdigueiro Navarro an old, Spanish, unrefined POINTER breed which was revived in its old form during the early years of the 20th century, but remains unrecognized.

The skull is strong, the MUZZLE square with a characteristic DOUBLE NOSE and heavy FLEWS; the muscular neck carries a heavy DEWLAP; the body is strong and well muscled. The coat is smooth or long-haired, with orange or liver markings on a white GROUND. Height 51–61cm (20–24in).

Perdigueiro Português [FCI] the breed's ancestors were used in the 14th century to PUT UP feathered game for falcons and were probably closely related to Spanish dogs which performed similar tasks.

The head is broad with distinct MEDIAN LINE and STOP, the ears rather heavy and pendulous. The chest is deep, and the forequarters well muscled. The coat is usually short and smooth, predominantly white with chestnut or yellow patches. Height 51–56cm (20–22in).

performance testing method by which the inheritable traits carried by a particular dog are assessed.

perianal fistula inherited tendency to inflammation and ulceration of the anal sinuses. (Mode of inheritance, familial.)

perianal pyoderma PERIANAL FISTULA.

pericardium tough tissue surrounding the heart.

perinatal occurring immediately prior to or just after birth.

perineal hernia pelvic diaphragm defect found in elderly male dogs, with protrusion of the contents of the abdomen and bladder through the pelvis.

perineum area between the anus and the genital organs.

period of gestation period from conception to birth: 63 days.

peripheral vestibular disease inherited head tilt; lack of balance. (Mode of inheritance, recessive.)

peritoneopericardial communication PERITONEO-PERICARDIAL HERNIA.

peritoneopericardial hernia hernia of the peritoneum, which may cause diarrhoea, vomiting and heart failure.

peritonitis inflammation of the peritoneum.

peritoneum membrane which lines the abdomen and encloses the viscera.

Perkiomen Valley Hunt WHITELANDS–PERKIOMEN VALLEY.

perro (Sp.) dog.

Perro de Agua Español [FCI] Spanish GUNDOG breed suitably adapted for work in water and sharing a number of characteristics with other gundog breeds adapted for the same specialized purpose and which probably all share a common ancestry.

The head is powerful and the ears are carried close to the cheeks. A strongly made, square-bodied dog with a deep, well-ribbed chest and WELL-ANGULATED, muscular limbs. The coat is thick and curly, black, brown or fawn. Weight 9kg (20lb).

Perro de Pastor Catalan CATALAN SHEEP DOG.

Perro de Pastor Catalan de Pelo Largo GOS D'ATURA.

Perro de Pastor Catalan de Pelo Corto GOS D'ATURA CERDA.

Perro de Pastor Mallorquin short, dark BRINDLE or black-coated Spanish PASTORAL GUARD. Height 48–56cm (18¾–22in); weight 21–27kg (46–59½lb).

Perro de Presa Canario short, BRINDLE or fawn-coated Spanish MOLOSSAN DOMESTIC and PASTORAL GUARD. Height 52–65cm (20½–25½in); weight 38–50kg (83½–110lb).

Perro de Presa Mallorquin [FCI] impressive MOLOSSAN breed originally developed on the island of Mallorca for dog-fighting and bull-baiting.

A powerful breed much reminiscent of old-fashioned BULLDOGS. The head is large, powerful, and black MASKED; the MUZZLE is strong, with small, thin ROSE EARS; the neck is muscular and the body fairly long and distinctly OVERBUILT. The tail is long

and strong. The short, hard coat may be BRINDLE, fawn or shades of red. Height 48–56cm (18¾–22in); weight 38–48kg (83½–105½lb).

Perro Flora PERRO SIN PELO DEL PERU.

Perro Mastin del Pireneo Pyrenean Mastiff: MASTIN DE LOS PIRINEOS.

Perro sin Pelo del Peru [FCI] Peruvian companion breed nicknamed Moonflower because the Incas sought to protect these hairless dogs from strong sunlight by exercising them only at night.

The breed is in many ways indistinguishable from other hairless breeds. The head is of medium width with unusually small eyes, the neck is fairly long and gracefully arched. The fine-boned, slender body stands on delicate but WELL-ANGULATED limbs. The soft, pliable skin is smooth and MOTTLED. Height 39.5–51cm (15½–20in); weight 9–13kg (20–28½lb).

Persian Greyhound SALUKI.

> an elegant animal, beautifully formed in all points, and resembling the Italian in delicacy of proportions. . . . About 24 inches high. The ears are pendulous like those of the Grecian dog, and hairy like those of the English setter, but in other respects he resembles the English smooth greyhound. [338]
> More delicately framed than the English breed; the ears are also more pendulous, and feathered almost as much as those of a King Charles' spaniel. Notwithstanding, however, his apparent slenderness and delicacy, he yields not in courage, and scarcely in strength, to the British dog. [406]

persistent hyperplastic primary vitreous inherited persistence of embryonic eye tissue producing a white or opaque pupil, sometimes associated with micropthalmia. (Mode of inheritance, familial.)

persistent pupillary membrane inherited remnants of non-vascular tissue across the iris and cornea producing opacity. (Mode of inheritance, familial.)

persistent right aortic arch inherited heart murmur. (Mode of inheritance, threshold.)

perspiration sweat. The sweat glands of dogs are largely confined to the tongue.

Perthe's Disease LEGG CALVÉ PERTHES DISEASE.

Peruvian Fox DUSICYON SECHURAE.

Peruvian Hairless Dog PERRO SIN PELO DEL PERU.

Peruvian Inca Orchid PERRO SIN PELO DEL PERU.

pet dog canine companion.

Peterborough Hound Show premier show for working PACKHOUNDS in Britain. Stems from a show first run in 1859 which moved to various venues before finding a permanent home at the East of England Agricultural Society showground.

Petit Basset Griffon Vendéen [FCI, KC] one of the four varieties of GRIFFON VENDÉEN.

Petit Berger BERGER DES PYRENEES.

Petit Bleu de Gascogne [FCI] a smaller variety of the GRAND BLEU DE GASCOGNE, which it resembles in every respect but size. Height 49.5–60cm (19¼–23½in).

Petit Brabançon [FCI] the smooth-coated version of the GRIFFON BRUXELLOIS which the FCI classifies as a separate breed.

Petit Braque Français [FCI] the small variety of the Braque Français: BRAQUE FRANÇAIS DE PETIT TAILLE.
Petit Chien Lion LÖWCHEN.
Petit Gascon-Saintongeois [FCI] smaller version of the GASCON SAINTONGEOIS.
Petit Griffon Bleu de Gascogne [FCI] a rough-coated version of the GRAND BLEU DE GASCOGNE which it resembles in all respects other than that the coat is wiry and the height 49.5–60cm (19½–23½in).
pet quality no ability to work and insufficient merit to achieve success in the show ring.
pettigrew (obs.) PEDIGREE. [159]
Pevensey Marsh BEAGLE pack formed in 1947 to hunt a COUNTRY in Kent.
phagocytes cells which combat disease.
phalanges bones of the toes and feet. [*illus.* SKELE-TON]
Phalene [FCI] DROP-EARed PAPILLON.
  Ears of the drop type, known as Phalene, are similar to the erect type, but are carried drooping and must be completely down. [6, PAPILLON]
phantom pregnancy condition in which some or many of the symptoms of pregnancy are apparently manifested in an unmated bitch.
Pharaoh Hound [AKC, FCI, KC] a breed developed in Malta from HOUNDS bred by Phoenician traders and claimed to be one of the oldest breeds in the world: it is said that the breed has a 5,000-year history behind it. It hunts its traditional quarry – hare and rabbit – both by scent and sight. Breed enthusiasts claim that the Pharaoh Hound has the ability to blush.
  The head is triangular, with a wedge-shaped, powerful MUZZLE. The large ears are broad, high set and erect, the eyes small and deep set; the neck is long and slender, but very muscular. The body is narrow, the chest only moderately let down, the LOIN well muscled. Forelimbs are straight and flat boned with short, straight PASTERNS; hindquarters are long with a slightly bent STIFLE. The short glossy coat is chestnut or rich tan, with or without white markings. Height 53–56cm (20¾–22in).
pharynx that part of the alimentary canal between the mouth and the oesophagus.
phenocopy having a similar external appearance to another. (Not inherited.)
phenotype physical appearance; visible characteristics influenced by environment and inheritance.
pheromone secreted chemical substance which acts as a sexual attractant.
Philipino Edible Dog PHILIPPINE ISLANDS DOG.
Philippine Islands Dog herding dog native to the Philippine Islands, which is also used as a culinary delicacy.
Philippine Native Dog PHILIPPINE ISLANDS DOG.
philtrum junction between the right and left sides of the lips, a continuation of the NASO-LABIAL LINE.
phobia excessive or persistent unreasonable fear. Dogs are especially susceptible to the development of phobias during the early socialization and fear-imprinting periods of puppyhood, when experiences – positive or adverse – make a lasting impression.
photophobia aversion to light; abnormal sensitivity to light.
Phthiraptera order of parasitic insects commonly referred to as lice. Two suborders exist: Mallohaga, biting lice; and Siphunculata, sucking lice. [*illus.*]

Phthiraptera.

Phu Quoc Dog a medium-sized DOMESTIC GUARD dog from Thailand, which is now the object of interest outside its native land. Perhaps because of the characteristic ridge of hair along its spine, is sometimes thought to be one of the ancestors of the RHODESIAN RIDGEBACK. The extinct Mha Kon Klab also had a ridged back.
  A dark brown, powerful spitz-type breed with a characteristic curious growth of coat along the back, near the shoulders, that hair pointing forward towards the head. [225]
phylogeny study of a species' evolution.
physaloptera canis spirurid parasite infesting the stomach, and which causes inflammation and excessive production of mucous, vomiting, anorexia and debility.
physaloptera rara spirurid parasite infesting the stomach and duodenum producing symptoms similar to those of *p. canis*.
pica depraved appetite; a tendency to eat unsuitable objects.
Picardy Shepherd BERGER DE PICARD; CHIEN DE BERGER DE PICARDIE.
Picardy Spaniel ÉPAGNEUL BLEU DE PICARDIE.
Piccoli Brabantino PETIT BRABAÇON.
Piccolo Levriero Italiano [FCI] ITALIAN GREY-HOUND.
pick PICK-UP(2).
Pickering (US) AMERICAN FOXHOUND pack formed in 1911 to hunt over a wooded COUNTRY in Pennsylvania.
pickers-up people employed to recapture GREY-HOUNDS after their course is over. 2. people employed to collect shot game especially in the absence of GUNDOGS.
picket line STAKE OUT.
pick of litter best puppy in the litter.
  The bitch from the Belvoir, the dog from the Quorn –
  The pick of their litter our puppy was born. [388a]
pick up 1. end an organized dog fight: if an owner decides that his dog has been beaten he may pick it up and remove it from the ring, thus conceding the match. 2. retrieve shot game, either during or after a shoot.

pi-dog PARIAH dog.

Piedmont (US) AMERICAN FOXHOUND pack formed in 1840 to hunt an arable and pasture COUNTRY in Virginia. Former Masters include Mr Paul Mellon. Legend has it that a fox with two brushes runs at full moon but has yet to be killed.

pie dog PARIAH dog. [129]

piebald (of coat colour) black and white, neither dominant.

 piebald spotting (of coat colour) having white areas on a predominantly darker GROUND.

pied (dim.) PIEBALD.

pies 1. those colours that have two components.
 Colors . . . The various 'pies' compounded of white and the colour of the hare and badger, or yellow, or tan. [6, ENGLISH FOXHOUND]
 2. dogs that are PIED.

pigeon breast prominent sternum.

pigeon dizzying (Am.) callous method of training a GUNDOG to be steady to live game, it involves swinging a live pigeon round until its dizziness temporarily prevents flight so that it can be used as a training aid.

pigeon-toed of dog whose feet turn inwards.

pig eye small, sunken eye.

pig jaw (obs.) MANDIBULAR PROGNATHISM.
 This formation, called overshot, or pig-jawed, is met with in various breeds of dogs, but if at all excessive is most objectionable. [123]
 If the upper jaw protrudes, the Setter is said to be 'pig-jawed'; many well-bred Setters have this formation, which I much dislike, although I prefer it to the under jaw protruding, which makes a Setter hideous. [186]

pigmentation colouring.

pile dense, soft undercoat.

pily coat close coat consisting of two layers: a soft undercoat and a coarser topcoat.

Pimpernel (Royal Signals) BEAGLE pack formed in 1952 to hunt a COUNTRY in Dorset. In 1956 the name was changed from RASC Pimpernel Beagles to Pimpernel; 'Royal Signals' was added in 1962.

pincer bite level mouth: incisor teeth of upper and lower jaw meeting tip to tip without overlap. [*illus.* LEVEL MOUTH]

pinched front undesirably narrow front.

pincher jaw OVERSHOT BITE.

pineal of the PINNA.

 pineal alopecia inherited hair loss on the ear flap. (Mode of inheritance, uncertain.)

pink hunting pink: hunt uniform, the attire worn by the members of a hunt, and which consists of a scarlet coat.

pinna ear flap; LEATHER.

pinscher (Ger.) TERRIER-like dog: AFFENPINSCHER; DOBERMANN PINSCHER; HARLEKIN PINSCHER; MINIATURE PINSCHER; PINSCHER; STANDARD PINSCHER.

Pinscher [FCI, KC] originally developed to control rural vermin, and to serve as a DOMESTIC GUARD, it is an extremely active and tractable dog.

The head is long and narrow, with a short, pointed MUZZLE; the ears are upright and sharply pointed when traditionally CROPPED, but fall neatly to the side of the cheeks in their natural state. The neck is long, lean and arched, the shoulders well sloped, and the forelimbs straight with small round feet. The body is square in outline, with a deep chest, moderate TUCK-UP, and strong quarters; the high-set tail is traditionally DOCKED short. The short, hard, glossy coat may be black and tan, or solid black, blue or silver-grey. Height 40–48cm (15¾–18¾in).

pinto (of coat colour) evenly distributed patches of black and white.
 Pinto has white background with large evenly placed patches covering head and more than one-third of body. [6a, AKITA]

Pin-toed front.

pin toes toes which point inwards. [illus.]

 pin toeing moving with the toes pointing inwards.

pin wire (of coat) exceptionally hard and short.

pipe huntsman's call.
 The pipe of the huntsman is an unerring guide to all. [266b]

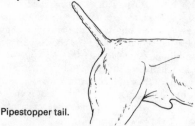

Pipestopper tail.

pipestopper tail long, thin tail. [*illus.*]
 A 'pipe stopper tail' is as inelegant as it must be to the majority obscure. [123]
 Anything approaching a 'Pipestopper' tail being especially objectionable. [6, SMOOTH FOX TERRIER]

Pipewell BEAGLE pack formed in 1927 as the Pipewell Foot Beagles to hunt a COUNTRY in Northamptonshire.

Pipewell Foot Beagles PIPEWELL.

pip head (derog.) any dog with a rounded skull, round eyes and weak MUZZLE.

pips tan spots on the brows of black and tan breeds; MELON PIPS.

pisiform any rounded pea-sized structure, but especially the carpal accessory.

pit enclosure in which organized dog fighting, or the baiting of another animal by dogs, takes place.

From the centre of the unceiled, hugely-rafted roof of a spacious building, hung an iron hoop, stuck round with various lengths of tallow candles, lighting an ovalpit in which two savage bull-dogs were rolling and tearing each other about, under the auspices of their coatless masters, who stood at either end applauding their exertions. A vast concourse of ruffianly spectators occupied the benches rising gradually from the pit towards the rafters. [344]

pit dog   dog used to fight in bear- or dog-fighting pit.

pit weight   weight of a dog after training for an organized fight.

Pit Bull   dim. AMERICAN PIT BULL TERRIER.
At his voice the pit bull eschewed the manners of the bull pit,
And assumed those of the pulpit. [262]

Pit Bull Terrier   dim. AMERICAN PIT BULL TERRIER.

pitch   CROSS(2).

pitted   (of teeth) disfigured by infection.
Pitted teeth from distemper or allied infections should not be penalized. [6, GORDON SETTER]

Pittenween Terrier   a variety of Scottish working TERRIER, now extinct.

pituitary alopecia   growth-hormone responsive dermatosis.

pituitary dwarfism   inherited juvenile panhypopituitarism resulting in slow and abnormal growth, retention of puppy hair and teeth, immaturity and shortened life-span. (Mode of inheritance, recessive.)

pituitary gland   endocrine gland at the base of the brain concerned with skeletal and sexual development.

pituitary hypoplasia   inherited absence or incomplete development of the pituitary gland.

pituitrin   hormone produced by the PITUITARY GLAND.

placed   of dog who has been awarded a position in the PLACINGS.

placenta   vascular organ developed during pregnancy which supplies oxygen and nutriments to the foetus.

placings   order in which winners in a competition are arranged by the judge: [KC] First; Second; Third; Reserve; Very Highly Commended; Highly Commended; and Commended.

plaiting   of movement in which the forefeet move towards and across each other.
Plaiting, crossing or rolling are highly undesirable. [203, SMOOTH COLLIE]

planes   the surfaces of the head.

Plas Machynlleth   HARRIER pack formed in 1894 to hunt a COUNTRY in Powys.

plasma thromoplasin antecedent   inherited blood-clotting factor XI deficiency producing mild bleeding. (Mode of inheritance, recessive.)

plasmid   small piece of self-replicating genetic material which exists outside the chromosome.

platelet   blood cell involved in clotting.

plates   flat growths of neglected, matted hair, esp. on KOMONDORS.

Cords of an adult strong and heavy, and felt-like to touch. If neglected, forms into large, matted plates. [203, KOMONDOR]

platter hound   (obs.) TRENCHER-FED HOUND. [186]

pleasant-faced   (obs.) of a long-nosed specimen of a short-nosed breed.
An old-fashioned expression used to describe a dog belonging to a short-muzzled breed which possesses a long muzzle or face. [320]

pleitropy   tendency of a gene to exert influence over more than one characteristic.

Plizeilich Soldatenhund   DOBERMANN.

plodding   of movement in which the feet hit the ground heavily.
No hackney action or plodding. [203, SALUKI]

Plott Hound   BRINDLE, short-coated American SCENTHOUND. Height 56cm (22in); weight 23kg (50½lb).

pluck   remove dead hair with finger and thumb. STRIP.

Plume.

plume   GAILY carried, FEATHERED tail. [*illus.*]
Light plume on top (of tail) where curled. [203, KEESHOND]

plumed   of a well-feathered tail that is carried over the back.
Tail . . . proudly curved or plumed over the back. [6, JAPANESE CHIN]

Plum Pudding Dog   DALMATIAN, first recorded use 1897.

pluralism   modern interpretation of Darwinism which argues that evolution is driven by other factors in addition to natural selection. The concept is, in modified form, applicable to domestic dogs in that breeders' preference, competitive success, general popularity, veterinary skill and other factors may exert influence over breed phenotype.

PNA   (abbr.) ABIOTROPHY.

pneumonia   inflammation of the lungs.

poacher   one who takes game illegally.
If I Had been Born an idiot and unfit to carry a gun – though with Plenty of Cash – they would have called me a Grand Sportsman. Being Born Poor, I am called a Poacher. [165]

Poacher's Dog   LURCHER.

Pocadan   KERRY BEAGLE.

Pocket Beagle   diminutive BEAGLE, as owned by Queen Elizabeth I. Efforts to reproduce the breed have been made in America.

Podenco   [FCI] a small COURSING dog native to

Spain and developed principally for coursing small game, such as rabbits.

Podenco Andaluz SIGHTHOUND little known outside Andalusia, and very similar in appearance to other Mediterrnean sighthounds. The breed has three coat types – harsh, long and short – and three sizes. Height 43–48cm (17–18¾in).

Podenco Canario [FCI] SIGHTHOUND which originates in the Canary Isles and with strong similarities with the Mediterranean sighthounds. Height 53–64cm (20¾–25in).

Podenco Ibicenco [FCI] IBIZAN HOUND.

Podengo Português [FCI] a group of SIGHTHOUNDS principally used for hunting rabbit and other small game. In appearance they are typical of other sighthounds of Mediterranean origin, and may have either smooth or rough coats, which are usually yellow or fawn, but may occasionally be black with white markings. The group has three main varieties distinguished by size: the PODENGO PORTUGUÉSA GRANDE; the PODENGO PORTUGUÉSA MEDIO; and the PODENGO PORTUGUÉSA PEQUEÑO.

Podengo Portuguésa Grande yellow, tan, or grey-and-white, smooth- or rough-coated Portuguese SIGHTHOUND. Weight 30kg (66lb).

Podengo Portuguésa Medio tan or grey-and-white, smooth- or rough-coated Portuguese SIGHTHOUND. Height 39–56cm (15¼–22in); weight 16–20kg (35–44lb).

Podengo Portuguésa Pequeño small, fawn and white, smooth- or rough-coated Portuguese SIGHTHOUND. Height 20–30cm (8–12in); weight 4–6kg (9–13lb).

Pohjanpystykorva NORRBOTTENSPETS.

Poi Dog HAWAIIAN POI DOG.

poikilocytosis presence of mis-shapen red cells in the blood.

point 1. (of a GUNDOG having found a bird) stop, stiffen and look in the direction of the bird; the way in which POINTERS indicate the presence and position of game.

> When we came out of the wood, we saw him pointing with a foot up. [92]
> Both dogs came to a dead point near the stream, and then drew for at least a quarter of a mile. [337]
> So firm does the habit of pointing become, that it is said that Mr Gilpin, the artist, painted a brace of pointers, Pluto and Juno, the property of Colonel Thornton, while in the act, and that they stood an hour and a quarter without moving. [393]

2. (of anatomy) junction. 3. *see* POINTS(2).

point of elbow that part of the forelimb at which the humerus and the radius and ulna meet, the point itself is usually taken as the upper surface of the olecranon.

point of hock junction between the femur and the tibia and fibula.

point of shoulder joint formed by the scapula and humerus.

point scaling method of assessment involving the allocation of POINTS(2) to various conformational attributes.

pointed of coat colour in which the muzzle and ears – and often also the feet and tip of tail – are of a darker colour than the base colour.

Pointer [AKC, FCI, KC] like several of the GUNDOG breeds, the Pointer pre-dates the use of guns for sporting purposes, being originally used to indicate, by pointing, the position of game which would then be taken by hawks or GREYHOUNDS.

A quintessentially English breed, graceful, ARISTOCRATIC but with outstanding functional qualities which combine a kind and biddable nature with strength, endurance and speed. The skull is of medium breadth with a pronounced OCCIPUT and STOP. The MUZZLE is slightly concave, the LEATHERS thin, pointed at the tips and pendulous. The arched, muscular neck is long, the shoulders WELL LAID and long, the legs straight and firm, the BRISKET WELL LET DOWN, the ribs carried well back and the COUPLINGS short with prominent haunch bones. The tail tapers from a thick root and is carried level with the back. The hindquarters are very muscular with WELL-TURNED STIFLES and WELL-LET-DOWN HOCKS. The fine, smooth coat is hard, white, with TICKS(2) or patches of lemon, orange, liver or black, SELF-COLOURS and TRICOLOURS are also acceptable. Height 61–69cm (24–27in).

> Again, dogs of all kinds when intently watching and slowly approaching their prey, frequently keep one of their fore-legs doubled up for a long time, ready for the next cautious step; and this is eminently characteristic of the pointer. [111a]
> 'Shooting flying' came into vogue about the year 1730; and this may be taken to be about the date of the introduction of the pointer to England. [221]
> See how the well-taught pointer leads the way:
> The scent grows warm; he stops; he springs the prey. [145d]
> The name Pointer, derived from the Spanish 'punta', implies that the first ancestors of the breed must have come from Spain. [123]
> The general introduction, therefore, of firearms into the field sports may, we think, be correctly taken as the final cause of the Pointer. [320a]

Pointing Wire-haired Griffon GRIFFON D'ARRÊT À POIL DUR.

points 1. (of anatomy) the main bones or parts of the body; qualities. [*illus.*]

> Natália: I know that Leap is still young, he's not a full-grown hound yet. But for points and action, not even Volchanietsky has a better dog. [87]

2. it was formerly the practice to ascribe a value, measured in points, to each attribute mentioned by the BREED STANDARD. The practice, which led to the parts rather than the quality of the whole being assessed, has been discontinued. 3. any or all of the extremities, esp. MUZZLE and ears, sometimes also feet and tail. 4. (of coat) dark spots or markings on a paler GROUND. 5. [AKC] awards which count towards the title of champion.

Poitevin [FCI] a French PACKHOUND developed

Points of the dog.

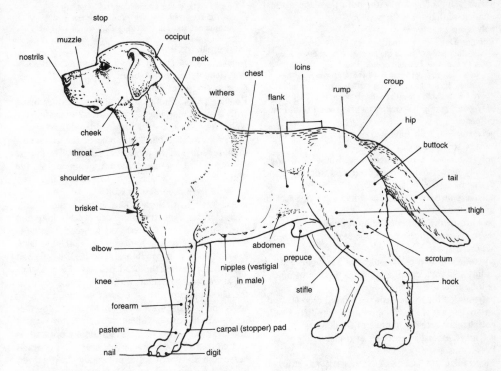

during the 18th century by the Marquis Francois de Larrye.

Typically HOUND-like in appearance, rather RACY for his size and with a narrow head with pronounced OCCIPUT. The short, smooth coat is usually TRI-COLOUR or orange and white. Height 61–71cm (24–28in).

Poitevin-Normand robust CROSS between the Poitevin and the heavier Normandy hounds.

Police Dog dog used by police forces to search, track or apprehend criminals. The herding breeds are the most often used, the GERMAN SHEPHERD DOG being the most common in Britain, USA and Australia.

Poligar Hound unrecognized Indian SIGHTHOUND. The Greyhound of Southern India. [225]

Polish Greyhound CHART POLSKI.

Polish Hound OGAR POLSKI.

Polish Lowland Sheep Dog [KC] Polish breed which represents an intermediate stage between the CORDED HERDERS of eastern Europe and the coarser-coated HERDERS of western Europe.

A medium-sized, COBBY dog with a lively but biddable disposition. The slightly DOMED skull is fairly broad, with a MEDIAN FURROW, the STOP is well defined and the MUZZLE fairly short. The oval eyes are hazel to brown; the heart-shaped, fairly high-set ears fall forward close to the cheeks. The neck is strong, quite long and clean. The shoulders are WELL LAID BACK and the forelimbs straight with some spring of PASTERN. The body is slightly longer than high, with a deep BRISKET, pronounced WITHERS, level back, slight TUCK-UP and a short, sloping CROUP. Hindquarters are broad, muscular and WELL ANGULATED. Some puppies are born without tails; those which are not are traditionally DOCKED. The coat is long, harsh, dense and shaggy, and of any colour. Height 40–52cm (15¾–20½in).

Polish Mountain Dog OWCZAREK PODHALANSKI.

Polish Mountain Herder OWCZAREK PODHALANSKI. [222]

Polish Sheep Dog POLISH LOWLAND SHEEP DOG.

Polish Water Dog extinct medium-sized Polish GUNDOG.

poll (of HOUND) top of the head.

Polski Owczarek POLISH LOWLAND SHEEP DOG.

Polski Owczarek Nizinny [FCI] POLISH LOWLAND SHEEP DOG.

Polski Oyan Polish Hound: OGAR POLSKI.

Poltalloch Terrier (obs.) WEST HIGHLAND WHITE TERRIER. [225]

Polugar dog very short-haired version of the WILD DOG OF DAKHUN. [406]

polyarthropathy disease in more than one joint.

polycystic having several cysts.

polydactylism the condition of having more than the normal number of digits on the foot, accepted as normal in some breeds.

polydactyly of a dog with more than the normal number of digits.

polydipsia excessive thirst.

Polygar Dog (var. spelling) POLUGAR DOG.
> In other parts of India the natives chase the wild hog with a coarse Polygar breed. The dog is taught to seize the hog between the hind legs when he has turned his head to meet some other assailant, and to retain the hold until the hunters come up. [184]

polygene group of genes which exert combined influence.

polygenic of trait inherited as a result of the influence of several genes.

polyglandular auto-immune syndrome in dogs, usually associated with thyroid and adrenal gland dysfunction.

polymorphic characteristic which is present in several forms.

polyneuropathy inherited disease involving nerves in several parts of the body. (Mode of inheritance, probably recessive.)

polyostotic fibrous cysts inherited cysts between the radius and ulna, causing lameness. (Mode of inheritance, familial.)

polyostotic fibrous dysplasia inherited blood coagulation defect. (Mode of inheritance, familial)

polyphagia excessive intake of food.

polyuria excessive secretion of urine.

Pom dim. POMERANIAN.

Pomeranian [AKC, KC] TOY SPITZ miniaturized from larger German pastoral spitz breeds, and popularized in Britain by Queen Victoria.

A COMPACT, SHORT-COUPLED vivacious little dog with a typically vulpine head, oval eyes, small, erect ears and a rather short neck set into WELL-LAID shoulders. Forelegs are straight and fine boned, the back is short and the chest well ribbed and fairly deep. The tail is high set and carried over the back. The undercoat is thick and soft, the topcoat long, straight and harsh, and of any colour. Weight 1.8–2.5kg (4–5½lb), with dogs tending to be smaller than bitches.

Pomeranian Sheep Dog uncommon, white, SPITZ-type German herding breed. Height about 56cm (22in).

Pomeranian Wolf-dog PASTORAL GUARD used to protect sheep from wolves. [338]

Pommerscher Hütehund POMERANIAN SHEEP DOG. [222]

Pompe's disease GLYCOGEN STORAGE DISEASE II.

pompom hair trimmed to form a ball on the tail, legs or hips, esp. in POODLES.

pompon (Am.) POMPOM.

Pomyoleanian Dog corruption of POMERANIAN introduced by R.D. Blackmore. [221]

Pont-Audemer Spaniel ÉPAGNEUL DE PONT-AUDEMER.
> Épagneul Pont-Audemer, properly speaking, a Setter, is a most original-looking animal, . . . The head in particular is quite distinct. It is extremely

long and tapers to a pointed muzzle. The hair is short to the forehead, but the skull is surmounted by a prominent top-knot of long hair which falls in a point towards the eyes, and almost overlaps the pendant ears. [225]

pooch 1. (Am.) a small and useless but attractive dog, usually of mixed breed; a pet dog. [280] 2. (Eng. colloq.) any dog.

Poodle [AKC, FCI, KC] formerly a GUNDOG breed with a particular talent for working in water, for which its natural coat is ideally adapted and which has produced the basis for some of the CLIPS now often regarded as the product of fashion. The largest of the three, sometimes four, varieties is the Standard, from which the Miniature and Toy varieties have been developed.

An intelligent, elegant and active breed with a characteristic light, free gait. The head is long and fine, with a slight OCCIPUT on a broad skull; the almond eyes are dark and expressive, the LEATHER low set, long and pendulous. The neck is of good length, and carries the head proudly. Forequarters are strong and muscular, with WELL-LAID shoulders; the chest is deep with WELL-SPRUNG ribs, the back short and the TOPLINE level to broad LOINS. Muscular hindquarters have well-bent STIFLES; feet are small and oval; the tail, which is traditionally DOCKED, is carried GAILY. The characteristic coat is profuse and harsh and always of solid, preferably clear, colour; all solid colours are acceptable. Height: Standard over 38cm (15in); Miniature 28–38cm (11–15in); Toy under 28cm (11in).
> The poodle was probably originally a water spaniel, but he is now used solely as a house dog, in this country at all events. [338]

poodle clip any one of the styles into which the coats of POODLES are traditionally trimmed: PUPPY CLIP, ENGLISH SADDLE CLIP, ENGLISH STYLE CLIP, CONTINENTAL CLIP, LAMB CLIP, LION CLIP, ROYAL DUTCH CLIP, SADDLE CLIP, SPORTING CLIP, and WORKING CLIP.

Poodle-Pointer PUDELPOINTER. [225]

Poodle Sheep Dog SCHAFPUDEL.

poop 1. puppy. [159] 2. excrement. 3. excrete.

pooper-scooper implement designed for the removal of canine excrement, an idea born out of the rising public awareness of the health risks associated with dogs' fouling in public places.

pop-hole small door, usually with a shading flap, providing access from a kennel to an outdoor run.

population number of individuals within a defined group.

population genetics study of inheritance patterns within a population.

Porcelaine [FCI] French SCENTHOUND of ancient origin used principally on deer and hare. The name is a reference to the breed's unusually short, smooth and shiny white coat.

The DOMED skull, finely CHISELLED head, FOLDED

pendulous ears and finely boned body are characteristics of the breed. Height 56–59cm (22in–23¼in).

Portman FOXHOUND pack which has hunted a Dorset, Wiltshire and Hampshire COUNTRY since prior to 1857 when Mr Farquarson gave up his pack and the second Lord Portman formed the present pack. The country has large tracts of downland and woodland.

Portuguese Cattle Dog CÃO DE CASTRO LABOREIRO.

Portuguese Fishing Dog CÃO DE AGUA PORTUGUÊS.

Portuguese Hound PODENGO PORTUGUÊS.

Portuguese Podengo PODENGO PORTUGUÊS.

Portuguese Pointer type of GUNDOG formerly to be found in Portugal.

> Resembles the Spanish in form, but is furnished with a bushy stern, and looks like a cross with the oldfashioned spaniel. [338]
> With a slighter form than the Spanish one, is defective in the feet, often crooked in the legs, and of a quarrelsome disposition. He soon tires, and is much inclined to chase the hare. The tail is larger than that of the spaniel, and fully fringed. [406]

Portuguese Rabbit Dog PODENGO PORTUGUÊS.

Portuguese Sheep Dog CÃO DA SERRA DE AIRES; ESTRELA MOUNTAIN DOG.

Portuguese Warren Hound PODENGO PORTUGUÊS.

Portuguese Watch Dog RAFEIRO DO ALENTEJO.

Portuguese Water Dog The appearance of the Portuguese Water Dog has much in common with other GUNDOG breeds that are principally intended for work in water; doubtless several share a common ancestry.

The head is strong, with STOP exaggerated by a profuse TOPKNOT; ears have thin, heart-shaped LEATHERS set fairly high. The neck is relatively short, the WELLSPRUNG ribs carried well back, and the BRISKET deep. The back is short with pronounced TUCK-UP. The tail is carried curled over the back. The coat may be long or curled, brown or black, with or without white markings, or entirely white. Height 40–56cm (15¾–22in); weight 16–25kg (35–55lb).

Posavac Hound JUGOSLOVENSKI POSAVSKI GONIČ.

Posavski Gonic JUGOSLOVENSKI POSAVSKI GONIČ.

post-distemper convulsions fits resulting from residual brain damage following distemper.

post-distemper encephalitis mental and motor dysfunction associated with distemper virus.

posterior caudal drawer sign instability of the STIFLE-joint caused by cruciate ligament rupture.

posterior chamber luxation LENS LUXATION.

Post-graduate class (KC) show class for dogs that have not won a CHALLENGE CERTIFICATE or five or more first prizes at Championship shows in Post-graduate, Minor Limit, Mid-limit, Limit and Open classes.

postnatal after birth.

postpartum postnatal; after birth.

postpartum endometritis inflammation of the uterine cavity following birth.

potage mixture of bread, meat and blood formerly fed to HOUNDS.

pot-casse the supposed bell-like tone of the bark of certain breeds.

> His bark is loud with a distinct 'pot-casse' ring in it. [6, OLD ENGLISH SHEEPDOG]

pot gut distended abdomen.

pot-hook tail tail carried in a high curve over the back.

> Tail high set, carried well over the back but not like a pot-hook [203, LHASA APSO]

pot hunt (of competitor) deliberately seek out weak competition in order to increase the chances of winning trophies.

pot hunter (disparaging) one who POT HUNTS.

potlicker inferior GREYHOUND.

Potomac (US) AMERICAN FOXHOUND pack formed in 1910 to hunt a rolling wooded COUNTRY in Maryland.

Potsdam Greyhound slightly larger version of the ITALIAN GREYHOUND.

> Breed of Italian origin, much favoured by Frederick the Great, who kept many of them as companions. [225b]

potter dwell on the scent; make no progress.

pouch loose fold of skin on the HOCK-joint.

> Wrinkles of skin may appear between hock and foot, and at rear of joint a slight pouch resulting from looseness of skin. [203, BASSET HOUND]

pounding of faulty movement in which the front stride is shorter than the rear stride, causing the forefeet to strike the ground heavily and deliberately. It often leads to dog being DOWN IN PASTERN.

poverty of blood (obs.) debility previously thought to have been 'a result of constitutional weakness or bad feeding'. [320a]

Powder Puff 1. coated specimen of the CHINESE CRESTED. 2. tail of a hare. [91]

powder-puff dilution genetic factor which gives rise to coated specimens of CHINESE CRESTED dogs.

Powinder Dog Kooichi Dog: KUCHI.

PP standard gene symbol for POWDER-PUFF DILUTION.

PRA abbr. PROGRESSIVE RETINAL ATROPHY.

Prairie Wolf CANIS LATRANS.

prancing exaggerated bouncy movement lacking forward propulsion.

prefix KENNEL(4) name used before the dog's individual name.

pregnancy period between mating and birth during which the foetus is carried in the womb.

pregnant of bitch in pregnancy: in whelp.

premium list (Am.) SCHEDULE.

premolar each of the 16 teeth situated at the side of the jaws immediately behind the canines and in front of the molars. Normally there are four on either side of each jaw.

prenatal before birth.

prenatal lethal genes that kill puppies prior to their birth.

prepatent period time that elapses between infection and when effective treatment can commence.

prepotent of dog who has a powerful ability to transmit his characteristics to his offspring; of dog in whose offspring there is visible evidence of that dog's parentage.

prepuce the skin protecting the penis.

presbycusis loss of hearing owing to advancing age.

presence demeanour that attracts favourable attention, especially in the show ring.

presphenoid anterior part of the sphenoid bone at the base of the skull.

press encourage HOUNDs to hunt more quickly than the scent or their ability will allow. [47]

prick ear erect and, usually, pointed ear.

pricker 1. hunt servant employed to drive deer out of dense cover or to isolate a particular deer. [386] 2. member of the FIELD formerly used to rouse a hunted hare. [344]

pricking putting HOUNDs onto the scent by taking them to the visible tracks left by the hunted animal, formerly regarded as unsporting, nowadays as legitimate.

prick-lugged (obs.) PRICK EARed. [159]

primary ciliary dyskinesia IMMOTILE CILIA SYNDROME.

primary glaucoma disease of the eye involving increased pressure within the eye and consequent distortion of the optic disc, leading to visual defects and blindness unless treated.

primary hairs GUARD HAIRS.

primary sex ratio percentage of male sperms present at fertilization.

primary teeth milk teeth; deciduous teeth.

primiparous producing offspring for the first time.

primordial dwarfism inherited generalized disproportionate growth. (Mode of inheritance, uncertain.)

Prince Charles Spaniel TRICOLOURed CAVALIER KING CHARLES SPANIEL.

This is a black-white and tan Spaniel, identical in every respect with the King Charles, though it is not nearly so old a variety. [123]

private marks various means by which individual HOUNDs were formerly identified.

These 'private marks', as they are called in the kennel, are generally made on the lips, the deaf ears, or by cutting off the ear buttons; another way of marking them is, by dipping a thread into wet gunpowder, or Indian ink, and drawing it with a needle under the inside skin of the ear, in the shape of a T, a V, an X, or any other device which may take the marker's fancy – it is a neat way of doing the business and attended with less pain than clipping the lips or ears. [371]

prize card printed card presented as a symbol of an award.

professional handler person who, for a fee, prepares a dog for and takes charge of it during competition.

progeny offspring.

progeny test method of assessing the value of a sire by testing his offspring.

progesterone steroid hormone concerned with fertility and the control of oestrus.

progesterone assay method of determining pregnancy by measuring hormone levels.

prognathism MANDIBULAR PROGNATHISM.

prognosis likely outcome, esp. of disease or injury.

progressive axonopathy inherited disease of the peripheral and central nervous system. (Mode of inheritance, recessive.)

progressive central retinal atrophy inherited progressive degeneration of the retina resulting in blindness. (Mode of inheritance, familial.)

progressive lens luxation inherited condition in which the lens of the eye is displaced, producing irritation and leading to blindness. (Mode of inheritance, recessive.)

progressive muscular dystrophy inherited progressive weakness of the muscles; awkward movement. (Mode of inheritance, sex-linked.)

progressive peripheral retinal atrophy inherited progressive degeneration of the retina resulting in blindness. (Mode of inheritance, recessive.)

progressive retinal atrophy group of inherited degenerative eye diseases which vary in age of onset. Initially producing impairment of vision in bright light and progressing to impairment – though not always total blindness, in all conditions. (Mode of inheritance, unclear.)

progressive silvering genetic effect caused by the incompletely dominant gene G producing coats with an intermixture of white hairs in a darker coat, the number of white hairs increasing as the dog ages.

projectile vomiting vomiting often without prior retching in which the contents of the stomach are ejected forcefully. It may be a symptom of pyloric obstruction.

prolactin pituitary hormone which leads to the development of mammary tissue and milk secretion.

prolapse displacement of an organ.

prominent (of eye) rounded and bulging; (of hip bones) protuberant.

pro-oestrus period of heightened follicular activity during OESTRUS.

propeller ear ear held horizontally and at right angles to the head.

properties (obs.) desirable markings. [250]

prophylaxis prevention or control of disease.

propped stance stance in which the feet are firmly planted unusually far in front of and behind the dog, often indicative of a stubborn reluctance to move.

proppy of dog that has upright shoulder and STIFLE, lacking ANGULATION.

proscolex early stage in the development of a TAPEWORM.

prostate gland gland which surrounds the neck of the bladder whose secretion is a constituent of semen.

prostatic of, or relating to, the PROSTATE GLAND.

prostatic calculi stones originating in the urinary tract which lodge in the prostate.

prostatic fluid constituent of semen secreted by the prostate gland.

prostatitis inflammation of the prostate causing pain, abnormal movement, bloody urine, and constipation.

prosternum protrusive brisket.

prosthesis artificial replacement for part of the body.

prostoglandin fatty substance which exerts a hormone-like influence.

proteinuria presence of proteins in the urine.

protoplasm contents of a cell.

protozoa free-living parasitic or commensal unicellar structures.

proud on heat; a proud bitch is a bitch in season.
> Give particular orders to your feeder to watch over the bitches with a cautious eye, and separate such as are going to be proud, before it is too late. [47]

proud tail gay tail.

Prudhoe and Derwent BRAES OF DERWENT.

prurigo (obs.) incessant itching. [320a]

pruritus itching.

pseudo-achondroplastic dysplasia EPIPHYSEAL DYSPLASIA.

pseudo-achondroplastic dystacia EPIPHYSEAL DYSPLASIA.

pseudo-Cushing's syndrome growth-hormone responsive dermatosis.

pseudocoprostasis constipation caused by matted hair around the anus, confined to badly kept long-haired dogs.

pseudocyesis PSEUDOPREGNANCY.

pseudohaemophilia Von-Willebrand's disease: ANGIOHAEMOPHILIA.

pseudohermaphroditism condition of having sexual organs of one sex but the characteristics of both.

pseudopregnancy phantom pregnancy; exhibition of some or all the signs of being pregnant without being so.

Psoroptes cuniculi ear mite causing psoroptic mange.

psoroptic mange mange caused by PSOROPTES CUNICULI.

Psowaya Barsaya BORZOI.

psychogenic megacolon enlargement of the colon caused by a reluctance to defecate.

pteryplegia art of shooting birds in flight.

ptyalism 'excessive secretion of the salivary glands.' [320a]

puberty period of development when the sexual organs become active.

pubis bone forming the front of each side of the pelvis. [*illus.* SKELETON]

puce dark liver with a blue or purple tinge.
> Dark liver or puce denoting unmistakably a recent cross with the black or other variety of Field Spaniel .[6, SUSSEX SPANIEL]

puce-liver purplish-tinged liver peculiar to the IRISH WATER SPANIEL.
> Rich dark liver with purplish tint or bloom peculiar to the breed and sometimes referred to as puce-liver. [203, IRISH WATER SPANIEL]

Puckeridge hunt that was once part of the Puckeridge and Hertfordshire, which existed as one pack from 1725 and divided in 1782.

Pudelpointer [FCI] breed developed during the late years of the 19th century by Baron von Zedlitz. What emerged was a breed with all the dash and nose of the POINTER and the retrieving instinct and amenable temperament of the POODLE.

The breed resembles a heavily built, rough-coated Pointer. The head is broad, the STOP sharp, the MUZZLE long and slightly upturned. The BIRD-OF-PREY EYES are large and round and the pendulous ears are of medium size and set close to the skull. The neck is lean and muscular and the shoulders broad, long and well muscled; the forelimbs are straight with the elbow set far back. The body is short, the chest very deep and moderately broad; the belly is WELL-TUCKED UP, the CROUP long and sloping. The hindquarters are WELL ANGULATED and muscular; the feet are round and tight with thick pads. The coat is exceptionally hard, rough and thick, light brown or brown. Height 60–65cm (23½–25½in).

puerperal occurring immediately after birth.

puerperal metritis infection of a pregnant uterus.

puerperal tetany ECLAMPSIA.

puff decorative sphere of hair left on the end of a POODLE's tail.

Pug [AKC, KC] the origins of the Pug are sufficiently obscure to have produced a variety of stories, probable and improbable, well researched and imaginative. BUFFON suggested that the breed was a miniature MASTIFF.

The breed is square and COBBY, COMPACT and WELL KNIT, with an air of self-importance combined with a happy disposition. The head is large and BRACHYCEPHALIC, but not APPLE-HEADED or UPFACED. The eyes are very large, round and expressive, the small and thin ears were formerly CROPPED close to accentuate the roundness of the head. The mouth may be slightly UNDERSHOT but never WRY. The thick neck is slightly CRESTED, the forelimbs are very strong, the shoulders well sloped and the chest wide and well ribbed. The body is short and cobby and the TOPLINE level; the hindquarters are very strong. The tail, known as the twist, is desirably DOUBLE CURLED. The coat is fine and smooth and may be silver, apricot, fawn or black, always with a black MASK and TRACE. Weight 6.3–8.1kg (13½–17½lb).
> The drawing-room pug, ugliest of man's [the breeder's] many inventions [182b]

pug (rare, Eng.) fox. [40]

pug-jawed OVERSHOT, possibly a misunderstanding and corruption of pig-jawed. [87]

pug-nosed of a flattened nose like a pugilist or, possibly, the dog of the same name.
> a squint, a pug-nose, mats of hair . . . betray character. [132]

Puli [AKC, FCI] the breed's name derives from the Hungarian word for leader, a reference to the fact

that this ancient PASTORAL HERDER and GUARD is followed by his charges.

The breed's most apparent characteristic is its luxuriant, CORDED coat, which provides protection from
weather and adversaries. The head is rather small,
and fine with a DOMED skull, well-defined STOP and
blunt, rounded MUZZLE. The eyes are dark brown,
the ears rather low set and V-shaped. The mouth is
pigmented with black FLEWS and red tongue. The
neck is muscular, the forequarters WELL LAID and the
forelimbs straight and muscular. The WITHERS are
high, the chest deep, the LOIN short and strong and
the rump short with a tightly curled tail.
Hindquarters are muscular and WELL ANGULATED
with LOW-SET HOCK; TOPLINE slopes slightly from
WITHERS; feet are round and tightly padded. The gait
is quick-stepping and short. The corded coat may be
black, rusty black, white, or one of various shades of
grey or apricot. Height 37–44cm (14½–17½in);
weight 10–15kg (22–33lb).

pull out (of judge) select for inclusion in the final
LINE-UP.

pulmonary oedema condition characterized by
watery fluid within the heart leading to laboured
breathing and, immediately prior to death, blood-
tinged nasal discharge.

pulmonic valve stenosis inherited heart murmur and
fibrillation. (Mode of inheritance, threshold.)

pulse rate the speed at which the heart beats,
counted at any one of several pulse points. In a dog,
the normal pulse rate varies between 70–100 beats
per minute, larger breeds generally having a slower
rate than smaller ones.

Pumi [FCI] Hungarian hunter and GUARD developed during the 17th and 18th centuries by
CROSSING(2)native breeds, especially the PULI, with
shepherd dogs imported from France and Germany.

The slightly rounded skull, the long MUZZLE,
oblique eyes and high-set, erect, mobile, heavily
FRINGED ears impart a distinctive appearance. The
neck is rather upright and slightly curved, the forelimbs straight with sloping PASTERNS; the chest is
deep with rather flat ribs, the TOPLINE falls to the
rump, the back is short. The high-set tail is carried
horizontally and is traditionally DOCKED. The DOU-
BLE COAT is rough and tangled, but not matted as in
the Puli, and is usually grey over a heavily pigmented
skin. Height 33–45cm (13–17¾in); weight 8–13kg
(17½–28½lb).

pump-handle tail tail that falls steeply from the rump
before curving into a horizontal position. [*illus.*]

pumping PEDALLING.

punch through (of a SLED-DOG's feet) break through
a thin crust over softer snow.

punchy of snow which has a light, hard crust of
insufficient thickness to support a sled and dog team.

punishing jaw strong, well-muscled jaw with correct
dentition.

Pump-handle tail.

pup 1. dim. PUPPY.
> Buy a pup and your money will buy
> Love unflinching that cannot lie. [209c]

2. give birth. [320a]

pupil dark circular aperture at the centre of the eye.

puppy 1. dog under twelve months of age.

Puppy class 1. (KC) show class for dogs of six and
not more than twelve months of age on the first day
of the show. 2. (FCI) show class for dogs of
between six and nine months of age on the day of
the show.

puppy clip clip traditionally used on the coat of
immature POODLES. Also called the working clip.
> A Poodle under a year old may be shown in the
> 'Puppy' clip with the coat long. The face, throat,
> feet, and base of the tail are shaved. The entire
> shaven foot is visible. There is a pompom on the end
> of the tail. In order to give a neat appearance and a
> smooth unbroken line shaping of the coat is per-
> missible. [6, POODLE]

puppy farm place in which puppies are bred, often
in unsuitable and sometimes inhumane conditions,
for sale to dealers.

puppy head gland syndrome JUVENILE PYODERMA.

puppy mill (Am.) PUPPY FARM.

puppy pyoderma IMPETIGO.

puppy show show confined to puppies.

puppy strangles JUVENILE PYODERMA.

puppy walk 1. place where puppies are reared and
educated on behalf of their owner. 2. rear puppies
in this manner.
> The Puppy Show is held in order that the simpletons
> who have walked a puppy, or even a couple, may
> put on their Sunday clothes and realise how much
> better their puppy looks than the other people's.
> [379]

puppy-walker one who rears and educates puppies,
usually for a hunt, before returning them to the
pack.

pure blood having well-bred parents of the same
breed.
> Thus we arrive at the necessity for 'good breed', or
> 'pure blood', as the same thing is called in a dif-
> ferent language, both merely meaning that the ances-
> tors, for some generations, have been remarkable for
> the possession of the qualities most desired. [338]

pure-bred of dog who has parents of the same
breed.
> 'What's that you say?' exclaimed Bawcombe. 'Be
> you saying that Tory's old Tom's son? I'd never
> have taken him if I'd known that. Tom's not pure-

bred – he's got retriever's blood.' [182]

pure-finder (obs.) one who collects dog dung from the streets. [280]

purling WEAVING.

Purple Ribbon awarded by the American United Kennel Club to a dog which is known to have been pure-bred for at least six generations, the three most recent being UKC registered.

puss hare.

pussing hunting hare.

put by (obs.) keep a bitch in secure confinement while she is IN SEASON.

> When bitches are not intended to breed, they are carefully 'put by', that is to say, they are secluded from the dog, and during that time they are in great measure deprived of their usual exercise. [338]

put away (obs.) PUT DOWN.

> If I can, I drop on a likely-looking one about a year old who was going to be 'put away' on account of the tax. [45]

put down 1. humanely put to death. 2. prepared for show so that an exhibit looks at its best in the ring. 3. unplaced by the judge. 4. eject an otter from its refuge. 5. lay an artificial trail for HOUNDS. 6. release a BAGMAN.

put down the line of dog that is not placed among the show winners.

putty nose DUDLEY NOSE.

> Putty or 'Dudley' noses and white patches on the nose are serious faults. [6, CAVALIER KING CHARLES SPANIEL]

put up 1. to give a dog a prize at a show. 2. put birds to flight.

> My faithful Punch ranges about and puts up a quail. [38]

puzzle 1. PUZZLE PEG. [166a]
2. (of a sporting dog) seek for the scent.

puzzle peg metal bar suspended vertically from a GUNDOG's collar in order to assist in its training. Not now in common use.

> You have to be careful, probably to select the puppy from parents who hunt with their heads up instead of carrying them an inch or so from the ground, so you may have fair expectations that your puppy will follow suit. Should he not do so, the only thing to do will be to hunt him for a time with a 'puzzle peg'. This can be purchased at most gunmakers' or saddlers'; it acts as a kind of bowsprit, projecting some 8in. from the dog's under jaw, and, by the point of the peg sticking in the ground as soon as he stoops, prevents him from lowering his head to snuffle about. [106]

puzzling see PUZZLE(2).

pyloric sphincter muscular valve between the stomach and the intestine.

pyloric stenosis congenital condition usually associated with BRACHYCEPHALIC breeds and the cause of frequent vomiting and poor growth.

pyoderma skin disease characterized by the production of pus. Some forms may be inherited. (Mode of inheritance, uncertain.)

pyometra infection of the uterus, occurring in two forms: closed pyometra in which the cervix is closed and the pus retained in the uterus (hence the absence of discharge); and open pyometra, in which the cervix remains open, facilitating the discharge of pus. The first form is the most serious, and can be fatal; the latter is easier to treat and is often referred to as purulent metritis.

pyometritis PYOMETRA.

pyorrhoea copious discharge of pus.

Pyrame *CANIS BREVIPILIS*.

Pyrenean Mastiff MASTIN DE LOS PIRINEOS.

Pyrenean Mountain Dog [KC] a superlative PASTORAL HERDER and GUARD developed in the Pyrenees but with a strong family likeness to several other European mountain pastoral breeds.

The breed's great size and power are enhanced by an elegant head and glamorous coat. The head is strong, with a level skull and imperceptible STOP; the almond-shaped eyes are dark brown, the ears small and triangular. The neck is fairly short and muscular, with some DEWLAP. The shoulders are powerful and the forelegs straight and well boned. The chest is broad, the TOPLINE level and the LOINS strong; hindquarters are powerful with prominent haunches and a sloping CROUP. The tail is thick at the root and carried low except when the dog is excited when it curls over the back. The gait is slow and powerful with a tendency to PACE at slow speeds. The coat, which is mainly white with patches of BADGER(2), WOLF-grey or yellow, is a profuse mixture of fine and coarser straight hair which form an abundant MANE and FEATHERING to the rear of the limbs, underside of the body and tail. Height 65–70cm (25½–27½in); weight 40–50kg (88–110lb).

Pyrenean Sheep Dog CHIEN DE BERGER DES PYRENEES.

Pyrenean Shepherd Dog CHIEN DE BERGER DES PYRENEES.

Pyrenean Wolfhound MASTIN DE LOS PIRINEOS.

> look well fitted to tend mountain sheep, and to defend them from the attacks of such predatory animals as wolves and foxes. Their coats are thick and shaggy, especially in the vicinity of the neck, and very wiry, frequently of a rufous colour, slightly tawny, and of a lighter shade on throat, chest and lower legs. The height appears to range from about 28in to 30in. The tail is rather long and tufted. [123]

Pyrenees-type French Pointer BRAQUE FRANÇAIS DE GRANDE TAILLE.

pyrexia FEVER.

pyriform veterinary term meaning pear-shaped.

Pytchley FOXHOUND pack famous for its large, undulating grassland enclosures. The COUNTRY lies in Northamptonshire and Leicestershire. It was founded in 1750 by the Earl Spencer and has included John Warde (1797–1808) and 'Squire' Osbaldeston (1827–1834) among its masters. Former huntsmen include Charles Payne (1848–1865), Will Goodall (1874–1895) and Frank Freeman (1906–1931).

Q

q   1. long arm of a chromosome.   2. symbol used to represent the frequency with which the rarer of a pair of alleles occurs.

QRS complex   QRS WAVE.

QRS wave   pattern produced on an electrocardiogram.

quack   unqualified veterinary practitioner.

quadriplegia   1. inherited inability of young puppies to stand and walk; head tremors; defective vision. (Mode of inheritance, recessive.)   2. TICK PARALYSIS.

quadriplegic   puppy suffering from QUADRIPLEGIA; swimmer.

qualitative variation   tendency for change due to the effect of major genes.

quality   having desirable attributes.

quantitative variation   absence of uniformity.

Quantock   STAGHOUND pack formed in 1902 to hunt a COUNTRY in the Quantock Hills.

quarantine   period of isolation either to allow disease to develop for the purpose of treatment, or to prevent its transmission.

  quarantine kennel   place in which dogs undergo a period of quarantine.

Quarme   former HARRIER pack established in 1860 to hunt a large COUNTRY in Devon and Somerset.

quarry   1. object of the chase. (der. L. *corium*, entrails of a hunted animal, with which HOUNDS were rewarded.)

  Fort. This quarry cries on havoc. O proud death. [319c]

2. (obs.) the entrails of hunted animals formerly fed to HOUNDS as a reward.

  Ross. Were, on the quarry of these murder'd deer,
  To add the death of you. [319i]

quarter   (esp. of GUNDOG) systematically search ground for the presence of quarry or scent.

  To complete his education he must be made staunch to 'bird, dog and gun' – to back his partner – to quarter his ground thoroughly and honestly – to know his place. [4]

quarters   hindquarters.

Queen Anne front.

Queen Anne front   forequarters in which the legs are bowed and the elbows protruding. [*illus.*]

Queen's County   LEIX (QUEEN'S COUNTY).

Queen's County and Castlecomer   LEIX (QUEEN'S COUNTY).

Queen's County Hounds   MEADOW BROOK.

Queensland Heeler   (obs.) AUSTRALIAN CATTLE DOG.

quest   1. search for, especially of quarry but sometimes also of objects.   2. (regional Eng.) DRAW(4).

quien   dog. [280]

quiz   (19th-cent. colloq.) an odd-looking dog or person.

Quorn   celebrated FOXHOUND pack hunting a COUNTRY which lies principally in Leicestershire. The hunt dates from 1698 when Thomas Boothby formed what is regarded to have been the first pack to concentrate its attention on foxes. He hunted the pack for fifty-five seasons until 1753 when Hugo Meynell took over the mastership until 1800, forty-seven seasons later. Other masters include Asheton Smith (1806–1817), and 'Squire' Osbaldeston (1817–1821 and 1823–1827). Former huntsmen include Jack Treadwell (1857–1863) and Frank Gillard (1808–1870).

  When Meynell took over the Quorn he found the pace too slow for his liking. The only way to kill a good fox was to run him hard so that he never got too far ahead, and gradually a type of hound was evolved which was fast, compact, well-nosed, full of stamina and capable of sticking to a line. [175]

R

Rabbit Beagle POCKET BEAGLE.
> On the hunting bill of fare were Mr Jolliffe's foxhounds, Mr Meager's harriers, the Derby staghounds, the Sanderstead harriers, the Union fox-hounds, the Surrey fox-hounds, rabbit beagles on Epsom Downs, and dwarf fox-hounds on Woolwich Common. What a list to bewilder a stranger! [344b]

Rabbit Dachshund KANINCHTECKEL.

rabbit dog 1. dog used for hunting rabbits, usually a small type of LURCHER. 2. any TERRIER.
> My belief is that the pure-bred sheep-dog is indeed the last dog to revert to a state of nature; and that when sheep-killing by night is traced to a sheep-dog, the animal has a bad strain in him, of retriever, or cur, or 'rabbit-dog', as the shepherds call all terriers. [182]

rabies incurable viral disease found in all warm-blooded animals, and in most parts of the world. Symptoms progress from restlessness, to apparent fear of any disturbance, manic aggression, paralysis, and – once symptoms have appeared – inevitable death.
> The dog to-day that guards your babies
> To-morrow turns and gives them rabies. [262]
> The victory over rabies, that most dreaded of diseases, lifted Pasteur into indisputable fame. [117]

Raby Hunt founded in 1816 as the private FOXHOUND pack of the Earl of Cleveland to hunt fox in a COUNTRY in north Yorkshire.

race marshall person in charge of arrangements immediately prior to and during a race.

race out (of a racing GREYHOUND) give maximum effort right up to the finishing line.

rache 1. (obs. Scot.) female of a type of BLOODHOUND. [139]
> There are among the Scotch, besides the common domestic dogs, three kinds of dogs, which you will not [I think] find anywhere else in the world: . . . the second [ane rache] is used for discovering by scent horses, wild beasts, birds, nay, even fishes lurking among stones. [56]

2. scenting hound. [159]
> Raches run on every side,
> In furrows they hope me to find. [30]

racing Greyhound GREYHOUND bred to run on the track.

racing sled lightweight sled used exclusively in speed competitions.

Racoon-dog NYCTEREUTES PROCYONOIDES.

Racoon-like dog NYCTEREUTES PROCYONOIDES.

racy of dog with long body and legs; slender.

racy hindquarters long thighs, without exaggerated bend, and low HOCKS.
> Hindquarters Racy [203, BORDER TERRIER]

radius the shorter, thinner of the two long bones of the forearm which run from elbow to wrist. [illus. SKELETON]

Radley College BEAGLE pack formed by the college Bursar in 1940 to hunt a COUNTRY in Oxfordshire.

Radnor (US) AMERICAN FOXHOUND pack formed in 1883 to hunt a rolling COUNTRY in Pennsylvania.

Radnorshire and West Herefordshire hunt formed in 1868 to hunt a hill and grass COUNTRY.

Rafeiro do Alentejo [KC] Portuguese PASTORAL GUARD. The breed is strongly made, with a broad skull, short pendulous ears, powerful, short neck and deep, broad body. The limbs are well boned and muscular. Height 76cm (30in); weight 43–50kg (94½–110lb).

RAF abbr. REGISTRATION APPLIED FOR.

rage syndrome inherited condition characterized by intermittent, unprovoked and hysterical aggression, most commonly associated with gold COCKER SPANIELS. (Mode of inheritance, probably familial.)

ragged long and loose.
> The couples must be wide, even to raggedness, and the topline of the back should be absolutely level. [6]

railbird (Am.) RAILER.

railer GREYHOUND which runs close to the inside rail, thus taking the shortest course from start to finish.

raillieta mange mange caused by one of the *Raillietia* parasites, and characterized by intense itching and moist, reddened skin.

Raillietia auris parasitic ear mite causing RAILLIETA MANGE.

Raillietia caprae parasitic ear mite causing RAILLIETA MANGE.

Rajapalayam tall and impressive Indian guarding breed similar in general appearance to the GREAT DANE. Weight 54kg (119lb).

rake grooming tool used to remove dead hair from long-haired breeds.

Rampur Dog Indian SIGHTHOUND very similar to, but slightly larger than, the SLOUGHI. The pronounced STOP is an unusual feature to find on a sighthound as are the light eyes which contrast with and accentuate the colour of the smooth grey coat. Height 65–71cm (25½–28in); weight 22.5–30kg (49½–66lb).
> Somewhat resembles a small Deerhound, but his chief characteristic is the absence of hair, which leaves his body smooth. [320]
> Also called the North-west Indian Greyhound – is a stoutly built dog of typical greyhound conformation.

Rampur Greyhound RAMPUR DOG.

Rampur Hound 1. RAMPUR DOG.
> Also called the North-West Indian greyhound – is a stoutly built dog of typical greyhound conformation . . .
> Unlike the Afghan hound there is no feather on the ears, tail etc. [46]

2. (obs.) AFGHAN HOUND.
> This is an Eastern breed which in shape and make

resembles the greyhound, but he is built on more
substantial lines. He is, moreover, a hairless dog by
nature, but specimens kept in this country usually
develop a soft fluffy coat, owing doubtless to the
coldness of our climate. Some excellent specimens of
this breed were brought home by his majesty King
Edward on his return from his tour of India in 1876.
[320]

Rat tail.

Ram's nose.

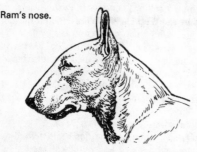

ram's nose MUZZLE that has a convex upper line,
as is typical of the BULL TERRIER. [*illus.*]

random mating mating carried out without prior
consideration.

range (of GUNDOG) search for game.
> Ranging is the act of beating out the ground in a
> more or less irregular and informal manner, the dog
> in a great measure exercising his own judgement in
> conducting it. [378]

rangy tall and long but strongly built.

ranula cyst under the tongue.

Rapidan (US) AMERICAN FOXHOUND pack
formed in 1959 to hunt a woodland and pasture
COUNTRY in Virginia.

Rappahannock (US) AMERICAN FOXHOUND pack
formed in 1926 to hunt a hilly COUNTRY in Virginia.

rare breed [KC] any breed that has not been
allocated CHALLENGE CERTIFICATES. *See also*
MISCELLANEOUS BREED.

rascal (obs.) animal that is so thin it is fit neither
to hunt nor to be hunted. [159]

rasper formidable fence.

Rastreador Brasiliero one of several breeds that owe
their existence to one individual breeder, in this case
Oswalde Aranha Filho, whose efforts to produce a
dog capable of hunting jaguar created an unusually
impressive breed.
> The skull is broad and flat, the STOP shallow, the
> ears long and pendulous, and the eyes pale yellow.
> The neck is strong and the body deep and muscular.
> The SABRE TAIL is carried proudly. The white coat,
> with blue, tan or black markings, is short and harsh.
> Height 63–69cm (24¾–27in); weight 22–27kg
> (48½–59½lb).

ratches (var. spelling) RACHES. [50]

rate admonish verbally; scold harshly; esp. to
HOUNDS (der. berate.) [388a]

rat pit enclosure in which rat-killing competitions
formerly took place. Now an illegal 'sport'.

rat tail long, thin tail covered with smooth hair.
[*illus.*]
> A rat-like Tail is insisted upon, not as of absolute
> use in any way, but as a sign of high breeding, with-
> out which it is well known the greyhound is
> comparatively valueless. [338]
> Defects . . . teapot curve or inclined forwards from
> the root. Rat tail with absence of brush. [6, BEAGLE]

Rat Terrier unrecognized American breed of mixed
type which is said to have been named by President
Theodore Roosevelt. The head is unusually small, the
MUZZLE inclined to SNIPYness, the ears may be
pricked or DROP; colour varies. Three sizes are recognized: standard – height 35.5–58.5cm (14–23¼in),
weight 16kg (35lb); mid-sized – height 20–35.5cm
(8–14in), weight 3–4kg (6½–9lb); and toy – height
20cm (8in), weight 2–3kg (4½–9lb).

rattle note sounded on a hunting horn to mark a
kill; MORT.

rattle-headed of a dog that lacks intelligence.
> The rattle headed dog, particularly if he has a hobby,
> is a real trouble to his handler. Devoid of intelli-
> gence, he performs his work as it may happen, and
> never comprehends the meaning or application of his
> education except the simplest parts which are related
> to the simplest work. [378]

ratty tail RAT TAIL.
> Disqualifications . . . ratty tail. [6, BEAUCERON]

Rauhaariger Kaninchteckel rough-coated KAN-
INCHTECKEL.

Raza Fina (obs.) CHIHUAHUA.
> The true Chihuahua, which is very small, has smooth
> hair, different colours except black (which is off
> colour), fine nose, large prominent eyes, slender feet
> with long thin claws, and a curious small round
> depression in the skull, between the ears, which is
> the distinguishing characteristic of the breed. [221]

RBIS abbr. RESERVE Best in Show.

reach measure of the forward movement achieved
at each step.

reaching of movement in which the forelegs are
carried well forward at each stride.
> Straight, free and balanced (movement) with good
> reaching forequarters. [203, MANCHESTER TERRIER]

reachy action long-striding, economical movement.

reachy neck long and slender neck.

ream scent left on the water surface by a hunted
otter.

recessive gene gene whose effect can be obscured by
that of another.

recessive traits those characteristics inherited via a
recessive gene, whose presence may be obscured by
a dominant gene or genes.

recheat (obs.) notes sounded by a huntsman when
hounds are at FAULT. [319l]

recklin (regional Eng.) the smallest in a litter; runt.

recombinant individual with newly introduced alleles not present in the population as a whole.

recover 1. rediscover the scent after a check. 2. start a hare from its FORM. [159]

rectal appertaining to the RECTUM.

    rectal paralysis inability to pass faeces owing to failure of rectal muscles.

    rectal prolapse protrusion of the wall of the rectum through the anus.

    rectal stricture constriction of the rectum resulting in difficulty in passing faeces, small faeces, abdominal distension and constipation.

rectum that part of the large intestine which runs from the pelvis to the anus.

red colour ranging from rich fawn to chestnut.

Red-and-White Setter IRISH RED AND WHITE SETTER.

> There is also another Irish Setter, red and white, of which now there are but few kennels left, . . . These dogs are highly spoken of by their breeders, who state that they have all the characteristics of the red dog, with the additional advantage of being more readily distinguished on the moor. [123]

Red-and-White Spaniel WELSH SPRINGER SPANIEL.

Redbone Coonhound legend has it that the Redbone, one of the most popular of the COON-HOUND breeds, derives from dogs imported by Scottish immigrants during the 18th century; legend does not suggest what these dogs might have been.

    The breed is a handsome, strong SCENTHOUND with a deep voice and excellent NOSE(2). The coat, which is always red, is short, dense and hard. Height 66cm (26in); weight 22–31.5kg (48½–69½lb).

Red Chester (obs.) CHESAPEAKE BAY RETRIEVER.
> At one time the variety was known to the wildfowlers and others in the area as the 'red Chester', or 'brown Winchester'. [37]

Red-coon Dog REDBONE COONHOUND.

Red Dog *CUON ALPINUS.*

Red Fox *CANIS VULPES.*

Redland (US) AMERICAN FOXHOUND pack formed in 1930 to hunt a rolling, heavily wooded COUNTRY in Maryland.

red mange DEMODECTIC MANGE.
> Of the two terms, blotch or surfeit, and red mange, we feel naturally inclined to give the former to the more simple kind of type of eczema, retaining the latter name of red mange for the more virulent. [320a]

red sesame coat colour synonymous with red SABLE; red with a light overlay of black hair.
> Red sesame (red sable). This color is red with a sparse black overlay. 'Red sesame' that does not show the proper red color or has too heavy an overlay of black hair is a fault. [6, SHIBA KEN]

Red Setter IRISH SETTER.
> The blood-red, or rich chestnut or mahogany colour, the deep rich red, not golden, nor fallow, nor fawn, but deep, pure, blood-red is the colour of an Irish Setter of high mark. [37]

red speckle (of coat colour) coarse ROAN; small red ticks on a white ground.
> The color should be a good even red speckle all over including the undercoat (not white or cream) with or without darker red markings on the head. [6, AUSTRALIAN CATTLE DOG]

Redtick Coonhound ENGLISH COONHOUND.

reduction division that part of the process of meiosis when the number of chromosomes is halved.

redwater fever BABESIOSIS.

Red Wolf *CANIS RUFUS (NIGER).*

Reedwater Foxhounds BORDER.

Reedwater Terrier (obs.) BORDER TERRIER, so called because of the breed's use by the REEDWATER FOX-HOUNDS.

referee adjudicator between the conflicting opinions of judges.

register record details of a dog's breeding with the appropriate KENNEL CLUB.

Regular Class class whose definition is set out by the regulating KENNEL CLUB, as distinct from a Special Class.

Rehpinscher MINIATURE PINSCHER.

Reindeer Herding Laïka NENETS HERDING LAÏKA.

reinforcement reward or praise following the desired response during training in order that the dog associates the response with a pleasurable experience and so is more likely to repeat the response.

Reisenschnauzer GIANT SCHNAUZER.

relaie (obs.) pack of fresh HOUNDS used to replaced tired ones. [159]

renal appertaining to the kidneys.

    renal carcinoma cancer of the kidney, with a tendency to grow quickly to a large size.

    renal cortical hypoplasia inherited kidney insufficiency leading to poor growth and weakness. (Mode of inheritance, familial.)

    renal cystadenon carcinoma cancers that originate in the kidneys, grow very large and spread to other organs.

    renal cystic adenocarcinoma inherited kidney and skin tumours. (Mode of inheritance, familial.)

    renal dysplasia inherited small and misshapen kidneys, causing loss of appetite and weight; and leading to death. (Mode of inheritance, familial.)

    renal osteitis fibrosa RENAL SECONDARY OSTEODYSTROPHIA FIBROSA.

    renal rickets RENAL SECONDARY OSTEODYSTROPHIA FIBROSA.

    renal secondary osteodystrophia fibrosa renal failure associated with jaw deformation, tooth loss and facial swelling, caused by retention of phosphates.

    renal tubular dysfunction inherited kidney malfunction leading to thirst and excessive urination, loss of weight and poor coat condition. (Mode of inheritance, familial.)

Renart original French name for a fox, taken from the German *Reginhart*, a personal name. Caxton mistranslated the word as *Reynard*.

repeat mating mating between the parents of an earlier litter.

reproductive cell gamete.

reproductive cycle OESTROUS CYCLE.

reproductive tract that part of the female anatomy from ovaries to vulva; that part of the male anatomy from accessory glands to external genitalia.

reproductive trait anomaly uncommon, probably inherited, conditions which affect reproduction or the reproductive organs.

reproductive value assessment of the probable number of an individual's future female offspring.

Resasti Itrski Gonic WIRE-HAIRED ISTRIAN HOUND.

research dog dog used to facilitate research esp. used as the subject of laboratory experiments.

Reserve award which acts as an insurance against any higher placings being disqualified. Thus a Reserve Best in Show or Reserve CC are placed immediately behind the Best in Show or CC winner. In show classes, however, Reserve is the placing behind the third-placed dog but in front of those that are commended in some way.

restorer (obs.) one who profits by returning stolen dogs to their owners.
> One of the most successful restorers was a shoe-maker, and mixed little with the actual stealers; the dog-dealers, however, acted as restorers frequently enough. If the person robbed paid a good round sum for the restoration of a dog, and paid it speedily, the animal was almost certain to be stolen a second time, and a higher sum was then demanded. [250]

retained placenta placental material remaining in the uterus; failure to expel placental material during parturition, a potential cause of metritis.

retained testicle CRYPTORCHIDISM.

retina part of the eyeball that is sensitive to light.

retinal dysplasia inherited blindness caused by retinal detachment. (Mode of inheritance, recessive.)

retrieve fetch game or article.

retriever those breeds of GUNDOG which are intended for finding and recovering shot game.

reverse scissor bite slightly UNDERSHOT BITE; exact opposite of the SCISSOR BITE.
> Scissor or reverse scissor bite. [203, TIBETAN TERRIER]

reversion reappearance of a wild ancestral phenotype.

Reynard popular name for a fox, originally coined by Caxton in his *Reynard the Fox*.
> In the earliest days in which there are any records of foxhunting, Reynard was pursued by a mixed pack of 'Fox-dogs', Terriers, Greyhounds, and nets. [186]

rhinosinusitis inflammatory condition of the nasal passages.

Rhipcephalus sanguineus tick that occurs in most mammals and birds, including dogs. Known as the European dog tick or European brown tick, sometimes known as the kennel tick, it is nonetheless found in all parts of the world. Transmits *Anaplasma, Babesia, Borrelia, Coxiella, Pasteurella, Rickettsia*.

Rhodesian Lion Dog RHODESIAN RIDGEBACK.

Rhodesian Ridgeback [AKC, FCI, KC] an impressive breed developed to hunt lion. Imported breeds contributed size and strength; native breeds the ability to work in Africa's hostile climate and the ridge from which the name is derived, and which very few breeds, anywhere in the world, carry.

A handsome, strong and active dog with a broad, flat skull, reasonably well-defined STOP, long, deep and powerful MUZZLE, round, bright eyes, and high-set rounded ears carried close to the head. The neck is fairly long and strong, the forequarters muscular; the chest is very deep and the back and LOINS strong. Hindquarters are muscular with a good TURN OF STIFLE. The tail is long and carried in an arc. The coat is short and dense and always light WHEATEN to red, the characteristic dagger-shaped ridge extending from the WITHERS to the haunch. Height 61–67cm (24–26½in).

rib each of the long bones that are attached to the thoracic vertebrae and enclose the lungs, and of which there are two types: the sternal (or true) rib; and the floating (or false) rib. [*illus.* SKELETON]

  ribcage the structure enclosing the lungs and consisting of the ribs and sternum.

ribbed up having ribs which contribute to a COMPACT appearance.
> A dog is said to be well ribbed up when his back ribs are long and his loins powerful and deep. [320]

Ribblesdale Buckhounds former pack formed in 1906 to hunt wild deer in a COUNTRY in Lancashire.

ribbon award of excellence at American dog shows.
> No dog to receive a ribbon if he behaves in vicious manner towards handler or judge. [6, ENGLISH SPRINGER SPANIEL]

rickets disease of the bones resulting in deformity in which the shafts of the limb bones are bent. The condition is caused by a deficiency of either vitamin D or phosphorous, or both.

Rickettsia conorii bacteria which causes boutonneuse fever in humans and dogs.

Rickettsia rickettsii bacteria which causes spotted fever.

Rickettsia tsutsugamushi bacteria which causes scrub typhus.

ridge distinctive coat pattern along the spine of some breeds.
> Ridge clearly defined, tapering and symmetrical, starting immediately behind shoulders and continuing to haunch. [203, RHODESIAN RIDGEBACK]

ridgil unilateral CRYPTORCHID. [159]

Riesenschnauzer [FCI] GIANT SCHNAUZER.

rig (regional Eng.) MONORCHID.

riggot unilateral CRYPTORCHID or an incompletely castrated animal. [159]

ring 1. defined area in which judging takes place at a show. 2. group of RESTORERS. 3. circular.

  ring craft the art of handling a dog in the show ring in order to present it to its best advantage.

  ring stern RING TAIL.

Ring tail.

ring tail   tail carried in a circle below the level of the TOPLINE. [*illus.*]

ring walk   track of a stag. [159]

ringworm   fungal infection resulting in hair loss. In dogs, the fungi species are *Microsporum canis, Microsporum gypseum* and *Trichophyton mentagrophytes*.

ringed eyes   eyes encircled with, usually, darker markings; SPECTACLES.

ringer   illegal substitute, esp. in GREYHOUND racing.

ringing work   (of HOUNDS) hunting within a small area and giving voice with enthusiasm.

> They quickly found a fox and after some ringing work went away, the line for two or three miles being parallel with a branch of the Shropshire Union Canal. [*297]

riot   HOUNDS hunting something other than their legitimate quarry.

> And though they trotted up so quiet
> Their noses brought them news of riot. [249]
> Young ones properly awed from riot, and that will stop at a rate, may be put into the pack, a few at a time. [47]

Ripley and Knapp Hill Harriers   BISLEY.

ripple coat   wavy coat.

Riverdale Beagles   former 14in old-fashioned blue-MOTTLED BEAGLE pack formed in 1911 to hunt a COUNTRY in Essex.

Riverstown   Irish BEAGLE pack formed in 1896 to hunt a COUNTRY in County Cork.

roach back   *see* ROACHED.

Roach back.

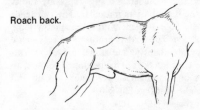

roached   arched TOPLINE. (der. the shape of a fish's back.) [*illus.*]

> Topline not roached but rather approaching hollowness. [203, CHESAPEAKE BAY RETRIEVER Interim Breed Standard]
> A topline showing a roach or dip is a serious fault. [6, SILKY TERRIER]

roading   (of a GUNDOG) finding birds by the scent they have left on the ground.

> Roading is the act of following the trail of the birds with more or less quickness by the foot scent. [378]

roadwork   exercise of a dog on roads as part of a programme to induce fitness.

roan   of a basically white coat in which individual or small flecks of coloured hairs are intermixed.

> White speckled with brown [brown roan], with or without large brown patches. [293, ITALIAN SPINONE]

Robenhaus Dog   *CANIS FAMILIARIS PALUSTRIS.* [222]

Robert   (obs.) fox.

> There had been no time for reflection, and in a moment Reynard, or Robert as we sometimes call him, was on the ground bleeding his life out. [182b]

Rochdale   former HARRIER pack which existed at least since the late 17th century when Alexander Butterworth was Master. The COUNTRY was in east Lancashire.

Rockbridge   (US) AMERICAN FOXHOUND pack formed in 1947 to hunt a rolling COUNTRY in Virginia.

rocking horse   dog with excessive rise and fall, esp. of the WITHERS, when moving.

Rockwood   HARRIER pack established about 1868 to hunt a COUNTRY in west Yorkshire.

Rocky Fork   1. (US) BEAGLE pack formed in 1954 to hunt cottontail rabbit over a COUNTRY in Ohio.   2. ROCKY FORK-HEADLEY.

Rocky Fork-Headley   (US) American and English FOXHOUND pack formed in 1940, by merging the Rocky Fork hunt, formed in 1925, with the Headley hunt, formed in 1935, to hunt fox and DRAG(2) over a hilly, wooded COUNTRY in Ohio.

rocky mountain spotted fever   SPOTTED FEVER.

Rodbery Terrier   BEDLINGTON TERRIER. Incorrect version of Rothbury. [46a]

rod-cone dysplasia   inherited impairment of night vision leading to blindness. (Mode of inheritance, recessive.)

Rodersham and Isle of Sheppey   former BEAGLE pack formed in 1893 to hunt a COUNTRY in Kent.

roebuck   male roe deer.

roebuck mark   dark mark on the back of the thigh above the HOCK, a characteristic of the GRAND GASCON SAINTONGEOIS but also sometimes seen on other breeds.

roll   1. the equivalent of sparring for dogs intended for use in organized dog fights. The roll is usually against an inferior opponent unlikely to harm the fighting dog.

> Then in his first training roll against an experienced but toothless dog, he had killed his opponent before Dexter could stop him. [131]

2. WRINKLE.

rolling action   movement in which the body sways about its long axis.

rolling gait   ROLLING ACTION.

> Rolling gait attributable to long body and short legs. [203, CLUMBER SPANIEL]
> Free, slight rolling gait. [203, NEWFOUNDLAND]

rolling motion   ROLLING ACTION.

> Characteristic rolling motion accentuated by barrel-shaped rib cage. [203, IRISH WATER SPANIEL]

Rolling Rock (US) American and CROSSBRED FOX-HOUND pack formed in 1921 to hunt over a rolling COUNTRY in Pennsylvania.

roman nose MUZZLE with convex topline.

Roman Wall Hounds HAYDON.

Rombout (US) AMERICAN FOXHOUND pack formed in 1929 to hunt a wooded, rolling COUNTRY in New York State.

rome growl or roar.

Romney Marsh 1. hunt whose COUNTRY lies principally in Kent and has been hunted since 1858. 2. former HARRIER pack formed in 1858 to hunt a COUNTRY in Kent.

ronyon MANGY animal.

root of muzzle (esp. in BOXER) junction between STOP and foreface.

root of tail junction between tail and body.

rope walking moving with all four feet hitting the ground on a single line; SINGLE TRACKING.

ropey of dubious quality.

roquet DOGUIN.
> With a round head, short muzzle, large eyes, small pendulous ears, slender limbs, turned tail upwards and forwards. Colour often slaty or blackish, with white about the limbs. [37]

Rose ear.

rose ear small ear normally folded back to reveal the BURR. [*illus.*]
> 'Rose ear' correct, i.e. folding inwards at back, upper or front inner edge curving outwards and backwards, showing part of inside of burr. [203, BULLDOG]
> Ears – Rose or half-pricked and not large. [6 STAFFORDSHIRE BULL TERRIER]

Roseneath Terrier localized Scottish type of working TERRIER.
> Local examples of the working terrier, as, for example, the Roseneath, which is often confused with the Poltalloch. [225]

Rose Tree (US) AMERICAN FOXHOUND pack formed in 1859 to hunt a COUNTRY in Pennsylvania.

rosette tan patch on the chest of characteristically patterned black-and-tan dogs.

Ross HARRIER pack formed prior to 1820 to hunt a COUNTRY in Herefordshire.

rotary motion continuous forward movement in which the feet, viewed from the side, follow an uninterrupted circular motion.
> When trotting, should have strong rear drive, with apparent rotary motion of hindquarters. [203, DOBERMANN]

Rothbury Terrier (obs.) BEDLINGTON TERRIER.

Rott dim. ROTTWEILER.

Rottie dim. ROTTWEILER.

Rottweil Dog (obs.) ROTTWEILER.
> Metzgerhund, or butcher's dog of the town of Rottweil in South Germany, in which district it is, or was, largely used by the knights of the cleaver for driving cattle. [225]

Rottweiler [AKC, FCI, KC] an archetypal MOLOSSAN breed which carries the characteristic black-and-tan coloration common to a number of breeds with origins in central Europe. Originally developed as a cattle drover and guard in the district surrounding Rottweil in southern Germany.

A stalwart, COMPACT and powerful dog with a broad skull, well-developed ZYGOMATIC ARCH, deep MUZZLE, almond-shaped eyes and small, pendant ears. The neck is of fair length and very strong, the forequarters long and sloping, the body broad and deep. The hindquarters are strongly muscled with WELL-ANGULATED HOCKS. The tail is customarily DOCKED very short. The gait is purposeful and conveys an impression of great strength. The coat, which is always black and tan, is of medium length with a good undercoat. Height 58–69cm (23–27in).

rough (of coat) shaggy.

Rough Beagle CROSS between a medium-sized BEAGLE and a rough TERRIER.
> Another variety is the Rough, or Wire-haired, Beagle. The absolute purity of his descent is doubtful, a cross more or less remote of the Terrier or the Otterhound being generally alleged, He is, however, a quaint, hard little hound found useful in a very rough country, and should in all respects be a copy of the ordinary Beagle, excepting for a stiff, dense, wiry coat. [338]

Rough-coated Bohemian Pointer ČESKY FOUSEK.

Rough Collie [KC] a Scottish herding breed characterized by its profuse, rough coat.

The wedge-shaped head tapers from skull to MUZZLE without STOP or break; the ears are small and semi-erect, the eyes almond shaped. The neck is of fair length, the shoulders sloping, the body rather long and the hindquarters muscular. The gait tends to be CLOSE(2) but straight with a reasonably long, effortless stride. The coat is profuse and very dense with a very abundant FRILL; SABLE and white, TRI-COLOUR or BLUE MERLE are the permitted colours, all with white on the collar, lower limbs, tail tip and BLAZE. Height 51–61cm (20–24in).

Rough Greyhound LURCHER.
> Is identical in shape and make with the pure greyhound, and the two can only be distinguished by their style of running when at work or play; the deerhound, though depending on his nose, keeping his head much higher than the greyhound. [338]

Rough-haired Bohemian Pointer ČESKY FOUSEK.

Rough-haired Dutch Shepherd RUWHAAR HOLLANDSE HERDERSHOND.

Rough-haired Italian Hound SEGUGIO ITALIANO A PELO FORTE.

Rough Scotch Deerhound rough-coated SCOTCH

GREYHOUND. STONEHENGE differentiates between the Scotch Greyhound and the DEERHOUND: the two, he says, were identical in shape and make and could be distinguished only by their style of running, the Deerhound keeping his head much higher than the Greyhound.

round 1. circular. 2. *see* ROUNDING.

  round bone femur.

Round eye.

round eye eye with circular aperture. [*illus.*]
> Eyes . . . Moderate size, round, neither sunken nor prominent. [203, FRENCH BULLDOG]

round foot CAT FOOT.

round head skull that appears circular when viewed from any angle.

Roundworm.

roundworm nematode; a group of parasitic worms, circular in section, affecting various animals including dogs. *Toxocara canis* and *Toxascaris leonina* are the roundworms most commonly found in dogs. [*illus.*]

rounding former practice of trimming the leather of FOXHOUNDS' ears in order to improve their appearance and allegedly reduce the chance of damage.
> The operation of rounding the ears is not now practised in some kennels, but if skilfully done it does not cause much pain, and saves them being torn in thick coverts. [47]
> The small rounded ear of the foxhound is due to the rounding irons of the huntsman, who removes a large portion of the pup's ears in order to save them from the tears and scratches which they would inevitably encounter in 'drawing'. [338]
> The frequent deafness of the pug is solely attributable to the outrageous as well as absurd rounding of his ears. The almost invariable deafness of the white wire-haired terrier is to be traced to this cause. [406]
> The ear matters little, as masters of Hounds persist in 'rounding' them, although in drawing a covert or thorny break I believe that the ear is a natural protection to the eye, and that it is given for that purpose. [186]

Roundway former HARRIER pack formed about 1865 to hunt a COUNTRY in Wiltshire.

rout (obs.) place to which impounded strays were taken after the customary three days in the pound. [159]

Route Irish HARRIER pack formed in 1930 to hunt a COUNTRY in north Derry and Antrim.

routed of a stray which, having been kept for the requisite three days, is taken from the pound to the ROUT, or green yard, where it was formerly kept until claimed. [159]

Roxby and Cleveland Hunt former name of the CLEVELAND.

Royal Agricultural College former BEAGLE pack formed in 1893 to hunt a COUNTRY in Gloucestershire.

Royal Air Force Beagles former BEAGLE pack formed by the RAF to hunt a COUNTRY in Buckinghamshire and Middlesex.

royal antlers topmost branches on a stag's head. [151a]

Royal Artillery 1. former DRAGHOUND pack formed in 1866 to hunt LINES(2) in Kent. 2. formed in 1908 as a HARRIER pack but recognized as a FOXHOUND pack in 1946.

Royal Buckhounds pack of STAGHOUNDs formed by King Henry VI some time prior to 1499 and maintained until 1901 when it became the Berkshire and Buckinghamshire Farmers'.

royal collar 1. ELIZABETHAN COLLAR. 2. RUFF, usually white.

Royal Dutch clip style of coat clip used on companion POODLES, in which the feet, MUZZLE and neck are clipped very close, leaving a moustache. The topknot, ears, WITHERS, fore- and hindquarters are clipped fairly short, while the body and crest of the neck are clipped very short. A POMPOM is optional.

Royal Engineers former 14½in BEAGLE pack formed in 1907 in succession to the Hundred of Hoo Foxhounds to hunt a COUNTRY in Kent.

Royal Rock BEAGLE pack formed in 1845 to hunt a COUNTRY in Cheshire.

rp gene symbol for rippled coat.

Rubarth's disease infectious canine HEPATITIS.

rubber jaw RENAL SECONDARY OSTEODYSTROPHIA FIBROSA.

rubbing rag poor quality show dog.

ruby (of coat colour) rich, dark red.

  ruby eye eye tinged with red.

Ruby Spaniel solid red CAVALIER KING CHARLES SPANIEL.
> Twenty years ago this variety was almost unknown, except as a freak of nature, when one would occasionally appear in a litter of pure-bred black-and-tans. [123]

rudder 1. tail of an otter. 2. any tail which resembles that of an otter, most often applied to GUNDOGS, esp. LABRADORS.

ruff thick growth of long hair round the neck; MANE.

> The male carries more of a 'ruff' than the female. [6, SAMOYED]
>
> The neck itself should be long, convex in its upper outline, without any tendency to a dewlap or to a 'ruff' as the loose skin covered with long hair round the neck is called. [338]
>
> In males [neck] may appear shorter due to dense ruff. [203, FINNISH SPITZ]

rufus coloration (of coat) red.

rufus polygenes genes which act together to create RUFUS COLORATION.

Rumanian Sheep Dog medium-coated Rumanian PASTORAL GUARD, white with tan spotted head. Height 61–66cm (24–26in); weight 32–42kg (70½–92½lb).

rum bugher (19th-cent colloq.) a valuable dog; a likely target for a dog thief.

rump upper part of the hindquarters. [*illus.* POINTS]

run avidly pursue quarry.

> Just as we fancy that the hounds never run nowadays as they used, when we had lungs to holloa and nerves to ride. [388b]

run heel BACKTRACK.

run on keep a puppy beyond the time when it would usually go to a new home, usually done in order to ascertain its qualities.

run over (Am. of a HOUND) overrun the scent.

> One bad run-over, or loss, almost always gives the fox enough time to get far enough away to bring the pack to the trail. [378]

runner 1. dog taking part in a competition in which running is involved. 2. wounded bird incapable of flight. 3. quarry hunted at BLOODHOUND trials.

> The quarry at bloodhound working trials is, of course, a human runner. Some people, who know nothing about trials, shudder at the idea of being asked to be a quarry for bloodhounds, picturing themselves running, exhausted, over the fields with a baying hound at their heels. [236]

running fits CANINE HYSTERIA.

Running Treeing Walker smaller and faster version of the TREEING WALKER COONHOUND.

runt small weak puppy; the smallest in a litter.

Ruppel's Fennec *CANIS FAMELICUS*.

rupture (of muscle) tear.

Russell 1. fox, contraction of Dan Russell. (der. *Rossel* or, possibly, of *russet*, a reference to the colour of a fox.)

> Daun Russel, the fox, stert up at oones,
> And by the garget hente Chaunteclere
> And on his bak toward the wood him bere. [86]
> Sir Russel Fox then leapt to the attack,
> Grabbing his gorge he flung him o'er his back
> And off he bore him to the woods, [86]

2. dim. JACK RUSSELL TERRIER.

russet gold (of coat colour in the HUNGARIAN VIZSLA) reddish brown.

Russian Black Terrier TCHIORNY TERRIER.

Russian Drab Yellow Hound GONTCHAJA RUSSKAJA.

Russian-European Laïka impressive, large and strong SPITZ breed developed to hunt large game in inhospitable country. The coat is fairly short and usually black and white. Height 53–61cm (20¾–24in); weight 20–23kg (44–50½lb).

Russian Greyhound BORZOI.

> About 26 or 27 inches high, with short pricked ears, turned over at the tip; he is rather thin and weak in the back and loins, and long on the leg. The coat is thick, but not long, excepting the hair of the tail, which is fanlike, with a spiral twist of a peculiar form. [338]
>
> Principally distinguished by its dark-brown or iron-grey colour – its short semi-erect ears – its thin lanky body – long but muscular legs – soft thick hair, and the hair of its tail forming a spiral twist, or fan [thence called the fan-tailed dog,] [406]

Russian Harlequin Hound GONTCHAJA RUSSKAJA PEGAJA.

Russian Hound GONTCHAJA RUSSKAJA.

Russian Piebald Hound GONTCHAJA RUSSKAJA PEGAJA.

Russian Pointer former type of GUNDOG supposed to hav originated in Russia.

> Is a rough, ill-tempered animal, with too much tendency to stupidity, and often annoyed by vermin. He runs awkwardly, with his nose near the ground, and frequently springs game. He also has the cloven or divided nose. [406]

Russian Retriever RUSSIAN SETTER.

Russian Samoyed Laïka NENETS HERDING LAÏKA.

Russian Setter probably the type of GUNDOG (probably a yellow FLATCOATED RETRIEVER) from which the GOLDEN RETRIEVER was bred, and which was called the Russian Setter in an effort to avoid the stigma which might otherwise have been attached to attempts to breed from rejects of an established breed.

> I contend that, for all kinds of shooting, there is nothing equal to the Russian or half-bred Russian setter, in nose, sagacity, and every other necessary qualification that a dog ought to possess. . . . The actual form of the Russian setter is almost entirely concealed by a long woolly coat, which is matted together in the most extraordinary manner. [338]
>
> I have heard of Russian Setters, but I have never seen one worthy of the name, nor do I think that such an animal is bred or cultivated by the Muscovites. [186]

Russian Shepherd Dog OVTCHARKA.

Russian Spaniel a typical, strongly made, working SPANIEL with a silky white coat with black, brown or liver markings. Height 38–43cm (15–17in).

Russian Terrier TCHIORNY TERRIER.

Russian Wolfhound BORZOI.

Russo-European Laïka RUSSIAN EUROPEAN LAÏKA.

Russo-Finnish Laïka closely related and very similar to the FINNISH SPITZ, but with a fawn rather than a red coat.

Ruwhaar Hollandse Herdershond rough-coated, BRINDLE, grey, red, gold or blue Dutch HERDER and PASTORAL GUARD. Height 58–63cm (23–24¾in); weight 30kg (66lb).

Ryburn Foot Harriers former HARRIER pack formed to hunt a COUNTRY in west Yorkshire.

S

s abbr. sire.

S gene symbol for spotting, solid colour. [395]

S^g gene symbol for slate-grey. [395]

S^i gene symbol for spotting, Irish spotting. [395]

S^p gene symbol for spotting, piebald. [395]

S^w gene symbol for spotting, extreme white piebald. [395]

Saarloos Wolfdog SAARLOOS WOLFHOND.

Saarloos Wolfhond [FCI] AGOUTI, WOLF-grey or brown, dense short-coated, Dutch lupoid herder. Height 70–75cm (27½–29½in); weight 36–41kg (79–90lb.)

sable (of coat colour) red, brown or tan, overlaid and intermixed with black.
> All black, all grey, or grey with lighter or brown markings referred to as Sables. [203, GERMAN SHEPHERD DOG (ALSATIAN)]

sabre (of tail) *see* SABRE TAIL.

sabre tail tail carried in a gentle and uniform curve.
> Stern carried well up and curving gently, sabre-fashion. [203, BASSET HOUND]
> Tail . . . has but a slight curve and is carried like the blade of a saber. [6, PETIT BASSET GRIFFON VENDEÉN]

Sabueso Español [FCI] Spanish PACKHOUND with, colour and size apart, many of the characteristics of ST HUBERT or BLOODHOUNDS. The breed offers two varieties, the Sabueso Españole de Monte being by far the most common. The head is strongly peaked, the FLEWS well developed and the pendulous ears are heavily folded. The limbs are well boned, straight and short, the neck carries a well-developed DEWLAP. The chest is deep and WELL SPRUNG, the TOPLINE level. The STERN is carried SABRE fashion. The coat is short and smooth and may be red or black and white. Height 56cm (22in).

Sabueso Españole de Monte variety of the SABUESCO ESPAÑOL.

Sabueso Españole Lebrero The less common variety of the SABUESO ESPAÑOL. It has a red with IRISH PATTERN WHITE short coat. Height 51cm (20in).

sacral of, or relating to, the SACRUM.

sacral vertebrae vertebrae associated with the hips.

sacram CROUP.

sacrum the three fused bones that lie between the pelvis and form the link between the lumbar and coccygeal vertebrae. [*illus.* SKELETON]

saddle 1. that part of the back occupied by the saddle on a horse. 2. patch of colour or growth of hair over the back in the place, shape and relative size of the saddle on a horse.

saddle back 1. long back, especially one that dips behind the withers. 2. a back with SADDLE(2).

saddle clip ENGLISH SADDLE CLIP.

sagace (obs.) HOUND that hunts by scent.

Sagax scenting HOUND.
> We may know these kind of Dogs by their long, large

and bagging lips, by their hanging ears, reaching down both sides of their chaps, and by the indifferent and measurable proportion of their making. [139]

sagittal crest hind part of the OCCIPUT.

sagittal suture junction of the frontal bones of the skull which over the brows forms the MEDIAN LINE or furrow.
> Arch across skull of a rounded, flattened curve, with depression up centre of forehead from median line, between eyes, to halfway up sagittal suture. [203, MASTIFF]

St Bernard [AKC, KC] breed developed in Alpine hospices with the specific purpose of searching for and helping to rescue lost travellers. Although undoubtedly of ancient origin the breed's fortunes have fluctuated over the years, partly because of the restricted breeding base and partly because religious dogma banned female dogs from the hospices. With the advent of dog shows, however, the breed quickly established a far wider popularity and is now an international, easily recognized favourite.

The breed's principal characteristic is its great size. The head is massive, the STOP steep and the MUZZLE rather short. The medium-sized ears fall close to the cheeks; eyes are dark and clean. The slightly arched neck is long, thick and muscular, the forequarters broad and sloping, the legs straight and well boned. The body is broad, with well-rounded ribs, broad strong LOIN and heavily boned, muscular hind limbs. The feet are large with strongly arched toes. The tail is long, high set and normally carried low. The coat may be rough or, less commonly, smooth and is white with large patches of orange, mahogany or red BRINDLE. Height, the greater the better.

St Bernardshund [FCI] ST BERNARD.

St Columcill said to have been able to cure rabies.

St Germain Pointer BRAQUE ST GERMAIN.

St Eustace patron saint of dogs in southern Europe. [225]

St Hubert patron saint of hunting.

St Hubert Bloodhound CHIEN DE ST HUBERT.

St Hubert Hound extinct form now subsumed into the CHIEN DE ST HUBERT.
> Black hounds, called St Huberts, are described as mighty of body, with legs low and short, not swift in work, but of good scent. [123]
> The hounds which we call Saint Hubert's hounds, are commonly all blacke, yet never-the-less, the race is so mingled at these days, that we find them of all colours. These are the houndes which the Abbotts of St Hubert have always kept some of their race or kynde, in honour or remembrance of the Saint, which was a hunter with St. Eustace. . . . This kind of Dogges hath bene dispersed through the Countries of Hennault, Lorayne, Flanders and Bourgoyne, they are mighty of body, never the less their legges are low and short, likewise they are not swift, although they be very good of scent, hunting

chaces which are farre straggled, fearing neither water nor cold, and doe more covet the chaces that smell, as foxes, bore, and such like, than other, because they find themselves neither of swiftness nor courage to hunt and kill the chaces that are lighter and swifter. [363]

Two dogs of black Saint Hubert's breed,
Unmatched for courage, breath, and speed. [314c]

St Hubert's Day 3 November, formerly the opening day of the British hunting season.

On fam'd St Hubert's feast, his winding horn
Shall cheer the joyful hound and wake the morn.
[145d]

St Hubert-type Jura Hound type of BLOODHOUND developed in the Jura Mountains between Switzerland and France. Essentially a lighter-bodied, more agile version of the bloodhound. Height 46–59cm (18–23¼in).

St John's Dog ST JOHN'S RETRIEVER.

St John's Retriever extinct smaller type of NEWFOUNDLAND, an ancestor of the LABRADOR RETRIEVER.

The other the best for every kind of shooting, he is oftener black than of any other colour and scarcely bigger than a Pointer. He is made rather long in the head and nose; pretty deep in the chest; very fine in the legs; has short or smooth hair; does not carry his tail so much curled as the other; and is extremely quick and active in running, swimming, or fighting. [166a]

The St John's breed of these dogs [Newfoundlands] is chiefly used on their native coast by fishermen. Their sense of smelling is scarcely to be credited; and their discrimination of scent in following a wounded pheasant through a whole covert full of game, or a pinioned wildfowl through a furze brake or a warren of rabbits, appears almost impossible. [221]

St Partridge's Day formerly a humorous reference to 1 September, the traditional day on which the British partridge shooting season opens.

St Roch St Roch and his dog were inseparable companions, and legend claims that St Roch refused to enter Heaven unless his dog was also admitted. It is not recorded how this information became available.

Saintongeois GASCON SAINTONGEOIS.

saliva enzyme-rich secretion of the salivary glands which promotes the first stages of digestion.

salivary gland each of the glands in the mouth which secret saliva.

salt (obs.) IN SEASON. [159]

Then they grow salt and begin to be proud; yet in ancient time, for the more enobling of their race of dogges, they did not suffer them to engender till the male were foure yeare olde, and the female three: for then would the whelpes proove more stronge and lively. [419]

Saltersgate Farmers' pack whose forest and moorland COUNTRY lies in Yorkshire and has been hunted since 1939.

Saluki [AKC, FCI, KC] archetypal Arab SIGHTHOUND, from which most other Mediterranean sighthounds are derived and which many resemble.

The pride which Bedouin nomads took in their dogs led them to designate Salukis as El Hor, the hound, which then avoided the effect of religious rules about contact with dogs.

A graceful, dignified, aristocratic and independent breed imbued with great speed and stamina. The head is long and narrow, the eyes large and oval, the ears long and mobile. The supple neck is long and well muscled, the shoulders WELL LAID and muscular, the forelegs straight with strong, sloping PASTERNS. The chest is deep and long, the TOPLINE slightly arched over the LOIN. Hindquarters are wide and muscular. The feet are of moderate length, slightly webbed with the inner toes noticeably longer than the outer ones. The tail is low set, long and curved. The coat is always smooth and silky and may be long (*Shamir*), or short (*Nejdi*); white, cream, fawn, golden red, GRIZZLE, silver and deer-grizzle, TRICOLOUR, black and tan, or variants of these are all acceptable colours. Height 58.4–71.1cm (23–28in).

In the poems of Abu Newas, a court poet of AD 800, he writes, 'Oh, my Huntsman, bring me my dogs brought by the kings of Saluk,' and this may be an explanation of the name, for Saluk is a long since vanished town of Arabia, and Saluk in Arabic means hound. [37b]

The word slughi is colloquial Arabic, in classical Arabic saluki; to the Arab it means a 'hound' or 'greyhound', and not a 'kelb', the despised dog of Islam. [37]

Samojed [FCI] SAMOYED.

Samoyed [AKC, KC] breed developed by nomadic Samoyede people as a HERDER and PASTORAL GUARD along the shoreline eastwards from the Kara Sea and into Siberia.

A dog of typically SPITZ appearance and with a characteristic smiling expression which reflects the breed's affectionate nature. The wedge-shaped head is flat, broad and powerful, the foreface gently tapered. The lips are black as are the rims round the slanted, almond eyes. Ears are erect, slightly rounded and thick, the neck strong and arched. Forequarters are WELL LAID, with straight, well-boned limbs. The chest is deep with WELL SPRUNG ribs, the LOIN exceptionally strong, and the back broad and very muscular. The muscular hindquarters are WELL ANGULATED. The tail is long, thickly coated and, when not at rest, carried over the back. Feet are long and rather flat. The double coat has a close, soft undercoat and a harsh, straight, stand-away topcoat of silver tipped white, white and biscuit, or cream. Height 46–56cm (18–22in).

The Samoyed dog takes its name from a Nomadic tribe who live in that vast tract of Tundra country which extends from the Eastern shores of the White Sea in Northern Russia to the River Khatanga in Western Siberia. [207]

Samoyed glomerulopathy inherited progressive renal failure, lethargy and weight loss, associated with the SAMOYED. (Mode of inheritance, dominant.)

Samoyed Laïka one of five Siberian LAÏKA breeds

identified in 1896 by Prince Andrew Shirinsky Shihmatoff. [380]

Samoyed smile characteristic expression of the SAMOYED.

> Lips – Should be black for preference and slightly curved up at the corners of the mouth, giving the 'Samoyed smile'. [6, SAMOYED]

Sanction show KC-licensed event in which entry is limited to members of the promoting society.

sand (obs.) courage, esp. in a fighting dog.

> Some time back, when she belonged to a bulldog fancier who liked to try what 'sand' his pets had, she fought for two hours and a quarter. [31]

Sandanona (US) BEAGLE pack formed in 1948 to hunt brown hare and cottontail rabbit over a COUNTRY in New York State.

Sand Fox *VULPES RUEPPELLII.*

Sandhurst BEAGLE pack formed in 1935 to hunt a COUNTRY in Surrey.

sand toe lameness in racing GREYHOUND caused by impact against hard ground.

Sanguinarius BLOODHOUND. [139]

Sanshu Dog SPITZ-type medium-sized guard dog developed in Japan during the early years of the 20th century from native Japanese and imported spitz breeds. The coat is shades of tan and red, black and white, or black and tan. Height 41–46cm (16–18in).

Sanshu Inu SANSHU DOG.

Sao Paulo typhus ROCKY MOUNTAIN SPOTTED FEVER.

SAP abbr. SERUM ALKALINE PHOSPHATE.

sapling immature GREYHOUND.

> The term sapling is applied to a Greyhound whelped on or after January 1st of the same year in which the season of running commenced. [123]

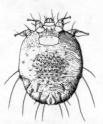

Sarcoptes: sarcoptic mange mite.

Sarcoptes genus of mites. [illus.]

sarcoptic mange intensely pruritic, often generalized skin condition, caused by mites of the genus *Sarcoptes*.

sarcoptic mite mite of the *Sarcoptes* genus, causing SARCOPTIC MANGE.

Sarcocystis bertrami parasitic protozoa which causes cysts in the horse and dog.

Sarcocystis cruzi parasitic protozoa of dogs and cattle, the cause of weight loss, fever and anaemia.

Sarcocystis equicania SARCOCYSTIS BERTRAMI.

Sarcocystis miescheriana parasitic protozoa of dogs and pigs.

SARD abbr. SUDDEN ACQUIRED RETINAL DEGENERATION.

Sar Planina SARPLANINAC.

Sarplaninac Yugoslavian HERDER and PASTORAL GUARD.

The head is broad, the V-shaped ears drop close to the cheek, and the expression is one of determination. The body is deep and strong with well-boned, WELL-ANGULATED quarters. The tail is long and carried low. The medium-length coat is grey, tan, white or black. Height 56–61cm (22–24in).

Sar Tip larger and more powerful version of the SARPLANINAC. [312]

saturation supposed effect described in a discredited theory propounded by Bruce Lowe which claimed that repeat matings resulted in the dam's blood becoming saturated with the blood of the sire so that successive litters of puppies became progressively more like their sire. [320]

Sauerland Basset Hound WESTPHALIAN DACHSBRACKE.

Sauerland Dachsbracke WESTPHALIAN DACHSBRACKE.

saved his brush of a fox that has evaded hounds.

Savernake Forest Buckhounds BUCKHOUND pack reformed in 1956.

Save Valley Hound JUGOSLOVENSKI POSAVSKI GONIČ.

Savoy Sheep Dog BERGER DE SAVOY.

saw-horse stance standing stubbornly on splayed legs and feet.

scabies SARCOPTIC MANGE.

scaling method of assessing performance or quality by allocating points to various aspects.

scalp 1. skin covering the upper part of the skull.

> Scalp should be free from wrinkles. [6, AIREDALE TERRIER]

2. disparaging reference to the attitude taken by some ambitious judges towards the collection of official approval to judge more breeds.

scapula shoulder blade. [*illus.* SKELETON]

Scarteen (The 'Black and Tans') Irish FOXHOUND pack founded some time prior to 1781 and hunted for about 200 years by members of the Ryan family; the name derives from the colour of the pack's distinctive KERRY BEAGLES.

scent odour left by quarry.

> The most favourable condition for scent is when the earth is warmer than the air. [71]

scent marking tendency of dogs to mark territory or companions with spots of urine.

scenthound HOUND which hunts by following a scent.

scenting hound SCENTHOUND.

Schafpudel rare and possibly extinct German HERDER and PASTORAL GUARD with a distinctive PIED or shaded-white, corded coat. Height 61cm (24in).

Schapendoes [FCI] Dutch HERDER with a strong physical resemblance to the BEARDED COLLIE.

A strong-headed dog: the skull is broad and flat with a well-defined MEDIAN FURROW. The back is long, broad and strong, the chest deep and WELL SPRUNG. The thick and shaggy coat is most commonly blue-grey or black but all other colours are acceptable. Height 43–51cm (17–20in).

schedule advance notice of classes, judges, time and place for a show.

Schiller Hound SCHILLERSTÖVARE.

Schillerstövare [FCI] Swedish HOUND which carries the name of its founder Per Schiller.

The breed is lightly and elegantly built, short-coated, and always tan with a black SADDLE. Height 48–61cm (18¾–24in).

Schipperke [AKC, FCI, KC] breed which evolved as a DOMESTIC GUARD on Flemish barges but which was brought to popularity in Britain about the turn of the century.

A distinctly SPITZ-type breed with a foxy head; the oval eyes are dark, the ears sharply erect, the shortness of the neck is accentuated by an abundant RUFF. The chest is deep, the back short and strong, and the quarters WELL ANGULATED. Many puppies are born tailless; those that are not are traditionally DOCKED. The coat is dense and harsh, with MANE and FRILL and well-developed CULOTTES on the thighs. Weight 5.4–7.3kg (12–16½lb).

> Schipperkes have always been kept as watch-dogs on the Flemish canal barges, and that, no doubt, is the origin of the name, which is the Flemish for 'Little Skipper', the syllable 'ke' forming the diminutive of 'Schipper'. [225]

Schistosoma mekongi parasitic worm found in the blood vessels, bladder and uterus.

Schistosoma rodhaini parasitic worm found in dogs and rodents.

Schistosoma spindale parasitic worm found in the blood vessels.

Schmitt's syndrome POLYGLANDULAR AUTO-IMMUNE SYNDROME.

Schnauzer [FCI, KC] a group of three breeds which differ only in size, the largest being the GIANT SCHNAUZER, the middle-sized variety the Schnauzer and the smallest the MINIATURE SCHNAUZER. All three sizes have strong TERRIER temperamental and physical characteristics, the miniature version being classified as a terrier in some countries. The three varieties are all of German origin.

The head is long and strong with a moderately broad skull, prominent brows, medium STOP and a strong bearded and moustached MUZZLE with tight lips. The eyes are oval and sheltered by bushy brows. Ears are V-shaped, set high and drop forward, or they are traditionally CROPPED; the moderately long, strong neck is slightly arched and clean. Shoulders are flat and WELL LAID, the forelegs straight. The deep, moderately broad chest has a strong breast-bone, the back is straight and strong and falls slightly to the hindquarters. The LOIN is short, the WELL

ANGULATED hindquarters muscular. Feet are cat-like. The traditionally DOCKED tail is set and carried high. The coat is harsh and wiry and may be black, pepper and salt, or shades of grey. Height 45.7–48.3cm (18–18¾in).

Schutzhund the training and testing to assess the aptitude and training of guard breeds, esp. GERMAN SHEPHERD DOGS.

Schweisshund BLOODHOUND.

> Has many of the characteristics of the Bloodhound. In the neighbourhood of Hanover he is popular as a limier, and is used for the purpose of tracking wounded deer. [225]

Schweizerischer Laufhund [FCI] the name Laufhund points to a HOUND used by hunters on foot. The breed is probably the product of CROSSES between native Swiss hounds and some of the more lightly built French hound breeds.

The breed is lightly built, lightly boned and leanly muscled. The head is long with a pronounced OCCIPUT and wide, folded pendulous ears. Colour ranges from yellow to red on a white GROUND. The coat is always dense but may be smooth or rough. Height 46–61cm (18–24in).

Schweizerischer Niederlaufhund [FCI] short-legged version of the SCHWEIZERISCHER LAUFHUND.

Schoshundle BOTTOLO. [359]

scimitar (of tail carriage) SCIMITAR TAIL.

scimitar tail similar to a SABRE TAIL but with a more exaggerated curve.

> Tail . . . with a curve like a scimitar. [203, DANDIE DINMONT TERRIER]
> Tail – Set low, scimitar shaped. [6, BEDLINGTON TERRIER]

 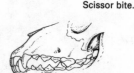

Scissor bite.

scissor bite most common canine dental formation in which the teeth of the upper jaw are very slightly forward of but touching those of the lower jaw in a slight overlap, in precisely the same manner as the blades of scissors meet. Sometimes wrongly used to refer to teeth which meet edge to edge (*see* PINCER BITE). [*illus.*]

> Jaws strong with a perfect, regular and complete scissor bite, i.e. upper teeth closely overlapping the lower teeth and set square to the jaws. [203, DANDIE DINMONT TERRIER]

scissura median line between the eyes at forehead.

> Scissura not too deep. [6, GERMAN SHORT-HAIRED POINTER]

sclera outer, usually white, membrane of the eyeball.

S colour series those genes which control the distribution of colours on an otherwise white coat.

scoot drag the anus along the ground to relieve irritation commonly thought to be indicative of worm infestation, but is more frequently a symptom of anal gland impaction.

score allocate points according to the degree of excellence, a method of assessing the quality of measurable characteristics.

Scotch Colley (obs.) generic name for Scottish shepherd dogs. [126]

Scotch Collie usually refers to the ROUGH COLLIE, although other collie breeds have their origins in Scotland.

Scotch Deerhound DEERHOUND.
> He is also named the Rough Greyhound, and the Northern, or Fleethound. [123]

Scotch Greyhound formerly a stronger version of the GREYHOUND.
> Has the same sharpness of muzzle, length of head, lightness of ear, and depth of chest, as the English dog; but the general frame is stronger and more muscular, the hindquarters more prominent, there is evident increase of size and roughness of coat, and there is also some diminution of speed. [406]
> In shape the Scotch Greyhound resembles the ordinary smooth variety, but he is rather more lathy, and has not quite the same muscular development of loin and thigh, though, the bony frame being more fully developed, this is perhaps more apparent than real. [338]

Scotch Terrier formerly applied to any Scottish TERRIER but now principally used to refer to the SCOTTISH TERRIER.
> The Scotch Terrier is generally low in stature, seldom more than 12 or 14 inches in height, with a strong muscular body and short stout legs; his ears are small and half-pricked; his head is rather large in proportion to the size of his body, and the muzzle considerably pointed; his scent is extremely acute, so that he can trace the footsteps of all other animals with certainty; he is generally of a sand-colour or black. [151a]

Scottie (var. spelling) SCOTTY.

Scottish Deerhound [AKC, FCI] DEERHOUND.

Scottish Highland Greyhound probably the DEERHOUND.
> Formerly used by the chieftains of that country in their grand hunting parties. [51]

Scottish Terrier [AKC, FCI, KC] breed refined to a standard type during the later years of the 19th century by Captain Gordon Murray and Sewellis Shirley, the founder of the Kennel Club. In the process the old varied working TERRIER types were discarded and a breed evolved which, whilst it retained terrier characteristics, was not built for the life of a working terrier but rather to attract attention in the show ring and as a domestic companion.

The head is long with a flat skull, distinct STOP, strong foreface, wide-set, dark-brown, almond-shaped eyes and pointed erect ears. The neck is muscular, the shoulders long and sloping with the well-boned forelegs set behind the BRISKET. The rounded chest is fairly broad and is hung between

the PASTERNS. The back is short and muscular with a level TOPLINE. The hindquarters are powerful, the tapered tail is carried upright. The double coat is wiry and dense and may be black, BRINDLE or WHEATEN. Height 25.4–28cm (10–11in).

Scotty dim. (colloq.) SCOTTISH TERRIER.

Scotty cramp inherited muscular stiffness and hypertension caused by serotin deficiency, and associated with the SCOTTISH TERRIER. (Mode of inheritance, recessive.)

Scotty jaw CRANIOMANDIBULAR OSTEOPATHY.

scrambled mouth misplaced incisors.

scratch 1. line across a dog-pit which fighting dogs must cross in order to continue hostilities.
> If a dog won't go to the scratch out of his corner, he loses the fight. [250]
> I saw a dead dog win a fight. I set him up – and he crawled up to the white line, snarled, and died. The other had two hind-legs broke, and would not come to scratch. [383]

2. starting position which is furthest from the finish in a handicap race.

Scratch Beagle Club CHESHIRE.

scratch pack pack composed of HOUNDS collected from different sources.
> They were sitting there with their hounds and their terriers, and whilst the scratch pack rolled and dried themselves amongst the earlier summer flowers, we were gazing in astonishment at an otter weighing 25½lb – one that we had killed ourselves with the aid of our two hounds and terriers. [221]

Screen former Irish HARRIER pack formed in 1855 to hunt a COUNTRY in County Wexford.

screw dermatitis inflammation of the fold of skin which occurs in breeds with SCREW TAILS.

screw tail short tail tightly spirally curled.
> Tail, set-on low; short, fine, tapering, straight or screw. [203, BOSTON TERRIER]

scrotum pendulous envelope of skin containing the testicles. [*illus.* POINTS]

scrub typhus disease of man, dogs and rodents, transmitted by *Thrombicula akamushi*.

scummer (obs.) dog that spreads or smears its faeces. [159]

sealing wax HAW. [103]

Sealydale Terrier unrecognized breed produced in Southern Africa from CROSSES between SEALYHAM TERRIERS and AIREDALE TERRIERS. [312]

Sealyham Terrier [AKC, FCI, KC] breed carrying the name of its place of origin, Sealyham in Haverfordwest, Wales, the home of Captain Owen Tucker Edwardes who, during the 1800s, set about the task of producing a TERRIER ideally suited to hunting and badger-digging. Using a number of native terrier breeds he achieved remarkable success, both in achieving his original aim, and in producing a breed that was quickly taken up by the show ring fraternity. Thus it was quickly converted into a larger, heavier and more glamorous dog than Captain Edwardes had envisaged or that would have suited his purpose.

The wide, DOMED skull carries dropped, rounded ears, and a square jaw; the eyes are round and dark; the neck is fairly long and thick, the shoulders WELL LAID, and the broad, deep, WELL-SPRUNG chest well let down. Forelegs are short and straight. The hindquarters are unusually powerful with well-bent STIFLES. The traditionally DOCKED tail is carried erect. The coat is long, hard and wiry and may be all white or carry patches of lemon, brown, blue or BADGER-PIE on head and ears. Height up to 31cm (12¼in); weight 8.2–9kg (17½–20lb).

> It was a rather stocky little beast with shaggy white hair and occasional rakishly placed patches of black. There was a suggestion of Sealyham terrier about it, but that was almost blotted out by hosts of reminiscences of other breeds. [278]

searcher finder. [139]

searing iron tool formerly used in the application of a cautery.

season 1. OESTRUS. 2. prescribed time within which game may legitimately be hunted. [50]

seat hare's resting place; form. [328]

Seavington pack whose COUNTRY lies in Dorset and Somerset; the hunt was established as a HARRIER pack in 1863 by Tom Naish.

sebaceous appertaining to SEBUM.

 sebaceous cyst benign cyst formed by an accumulation of sebum.

 sebaceous gland gland that secretes sebum, usually through the follicles.

sebum fatty secretion which lubricates the hair and skin.

Sechura Fox DUSICYON SECHURAE.

secondary glaucoma GLAUCOMA produced as a consequence of some other condition.

secondary sex ratio percentage of males born.

second cross offspring of a first CROSS mated to a dog of either of the breeds of its purebred parents.

second mouth mouth in which the permanent teeth have replaced the milk teeth.

second thigh that part of the rear leg between STIFLE and HOCK.

> Thighs long and powerful with muscular second thigh. [203, AIREDALE TERRIER.]

Seçoviano Spanish GREYHOUND. [222]

sectorial teeth CARNASSIAL TEETH.

sedge colour resembling dead grass: a dull tan.

Sedgefield (US) AMERICAN FOXHOUND pack formed in 1927 to hunt a rolling COUNTRY in North Carolina.

seeing-eye dog (Am.) GUIDE DOG for the blind.

> First and foremost, every blind man using a Seeing Eye dog gets his primary points of orientation at street corners. When it comes to the end of a block the dog guides his master straight to the kerb ahead and stops. [164]

seek 1. FIND. 2. (to a GUNDOG) command to find.
 seek back BACKTRACK.

seen retrieve retrieve of game or article that was visible to the GUNDOG at the time of its being shot or dropped, thus enabling the dog to mark its fall and then retrieve it, without scenting or searching.

segregation process during meiosis when homologous chromosomes migrate to opposite ends of the cell to enable each to unite with separate gametes.

Segugio Italiano [FCI, KC] Italian DOLICHOCEPHALIC HOUND breed, lightly built on lines that suggest speed, but a dog that will hunt all day. The coat whether rough (Segugio Italiano a Pelo Forte), or smooth (Segugio Italiano a Pelo Raso) is hard and invariably black and tan or shades of red. Height 51–56cm (20–22in).

Segugio Italiano a Pelo Forte rough-coated version of the SEGUGIO ITALIANO.

Segugio Italiano a Pelo Raso smooth-coated version of the SEGUGIO ITALIANO.

Segusian CELTIC BEAGLE. [295]

> These dogs are called Segusians, deriving their name from a Celtic people, amongst whom, I suppose, they were first bred and held in repute. . . . For they manifest nothing different from others in their mode of finding or hunting their game, having no peculiarity, unless one were to speak of their shape, which I scarce think worth while, except merely to say that they are shaggy and ugly, and such as are most high-bred are most unsightly. . . . For their voice is dolorous and pitiful, and they do not bark on scent of their game, as if eager and savage, but as if plaintively whining after it. [138]

Seidenspitz extinct German TOY DOG. [150]

> A not very common German toy breed, in general appearance something between a Maltese and a Pomeranian. [225]

selection process, either natural or artificial, by which a breeding population is produced.

 selection index an individual's total score on the SELECTION SCALES divided by the maximum total score expressed as a percentage.

 selection intensity measure of the number of puppies which pass the process of selection compared with the number actually produced.

 selection scales means by which grading, from poor to excellent in a number of steps and for several characteristics, is carried out.

selective breeding SELECTION.

self-coloured of one solid colour.

 self-coloured nose nose of identical colour to the coat.

self-hunter dog that seizes any opportunity to go off alone on illicit sporting expeditions.

> He is not a self-hunter – that is, he does not skulk off poaching. [186]

self-marked self-colour interrupted by paler, usually white, markings on chest, feet and tail tip.

self-tailed dog dog born without a tail or with an exceptionally short tail.

> Many of them (Cur Dogs) are whelped with short tails, which seem as if they had been cut: these are called Self-tailed Dogs. [51]

self-whelper bitch that does not require surgical assistance to give birth.

semen fluid containing sperm.

 semen defects inherited defective sperm: missing and deformed tails, deformed heads, feeble movement. (Mode of inheritance, complex and influenced by nutrition.)

semi-dominance INCOMPLETE DOMINANCE.

semi-drop ear erect ear that falls over at the tip.

Semi-prick ears.

semi-erect ear PRICK EAR in which the apex drops slightly forward. [*illus.*]

semi-hare foot foot intermediate in shape between the oval and HARE FOOT.

semi-lethal of gene that causes the death of some individuals that inherit it.

seminal pertaining to SEMEN.

seminal fluid fluid in which the semen is transported; the main component of the ejaculate.

seminal vesicle gland in which seminal fluid is produced.

seminoma inherited tumour of the testes. (Mode of inheritance, uncertain.)

semi-prick ear SEMI-ERECT EAR.

send out (esp. of POINTERS) CAST(2).

Sennowe Park HARRIER pack formed to hunt a COUNTRY in Norfolk.

Sennybridge and District Farmers' pack formed in 1950 to hunt a Powys COUNTRY.

sensory neuropathy inherited loss of digital and lower limb sensitivity; self-mutilation. (Mode of inheritance, recessive.)

sentine (obs.) kennel. [159]

sepsis presence of toxins in the blood or tissues.

septicaemia condition arising as a result of sepsis.

septum strip of cartilage between the nostrils.

sequence order in which the feet and legs move during a single stride.

serology way in which an antigen-antibody reacts.

serotonin hormone found in the blood, intestinal mucous, pineal body, and central nervous system, which is essential to gastric and muscular activity.

Serra da Estrela Dog (obs.) ESTRELA MOUNTAIN DOG.

serratus-ventralis trunk muscle.

serum that part of a fluid which remains liquid after solid matter has been extracted, i.e. blood serum.

serum alkaline phosphate enzyme associated with liver function.

service (of stud-dog) mate.

service pup term used among shepherds to refer to a puppy given to the owner of its sire in lieu of a stud fee.

sesamoid small bone embedded in a joint or tendon.

set 1. point: indicate the presence of game.
A keeper nearly always breaks in his young dogs to point (or 'set' as some term it), if their ages permit it, on favourable days in Spring, when the partridges have paired. [184]
2. stand in an aggressive or threatening posture.
3. position; put.

set-on 1. relationship between tail and back. 2. point at which the tail meets the back. 3. (of ears) relationship with the skull.

set-to originally organized dog fight; now commonly any spontaneous fight between dogs.
A volley of yells and plaudits rent the building as the white dog pinned the brindled one for the fourteenth time, and the lacerated animal refused to come to the scratch, and as the pit was cleared for a fresh 'set-to', Slender Billy, with a mildness of manner contrasting with the rudeness of the scene, passed our party on, and turned out two coal-heavers and a ticket-porter, to place them advantageously near the centre. [344]

set up (of a SHOW-DOG handler) stand the dog in a position that will enhance its appearance and thus attract the judge's attention.

seton thin strip of fabric drawn under the skin by means of a needle, formerly used as a primitive method of vaccination, the seton being impregnated with vaccine; nowadays principally used to keep a wound open allowing infection to drain away.

sett underground home of a badger.

setter type of GUNDOG used to find feathered game.
Serviceable for fowling, making no noise either with foot or with tongue, while they follow the game. These attend diligently upon their Master and frame their conditions to such beckoning, motions, and gestures, as it shall please him to exhibit and make, either going forward, drawing backward, inclining to the right hand, or yielding toward the left. [139]

setting dog any breed of SETTER or any dog used for SETting.
Before I wade further into this discourse I show you what a setting dogge is. You shall understand that a Setting Dogge is a certaine lusty land spanell, taught by nature to hunt partridges, before and more than any other chase whatsoever, and that with all eagernesse and fiercenesse, running the fields over so lustily and busily as if there were no limit in his desire and furie; yet so qualified and tempered with art and obedience, that when he is in the greatest and eagerest pursute, and seems to be most wilde and frantik, that even thus one hem or sound of his master's voyce makes him presently stand, gaze about him, and looke in his master's face, taking all directions from it whether to procede, stand still, or retire. [245]

settled of a pack that has gathered and is confidently hunting a LINE(2).

severe pathesis inherited muscle wasting; intolerance of exercise. (Mode of inheritance, recessive.)

Sewero-Wostotschnaja Jesowaja Sobaka NORTH-EASTERN SLEIGH DOG.

Sewickley (US) AMERICAN FOXHOUND pack formed in 1922 to hunt DRAG(2) over a hilly COUNTRY in Pennsylvania.

sex gender.

sex chromosome either of the X or Y chromosomes which determine the sex of the individual.

sex determination prenatal process by which the gender of puppies is controlled, whether by natural or artificial means.

sex-limited gene gene which is expressed in only one sex, but is not associated with the X/Y chromosome.

sex-limited inheritance inheritance of characteristic normally carried by one or the other sex, for example mammary or testicle development.

sex-limited trait characteristic expressed in one sex only.

sex-linked gene gene which is present only on the X or, less probably, the Y chromosome.

sex-linked trait characteristic produced by a SEX-LINKED GENE.

sex mosaic chromosomal anomaly in which cells appropriate to both sexes are present.

sex ratio the number of males compared with females expressed as a percentage.

sex reversal inherited female sex reversal: the presence of rudimentary male genitalia in females. (Mode of inheritance, recessive.)

shackatory (obs.) a HOUND. [159]

shacked (obs.) rough-haired. [159]

shackle-hammed (obs.) bow-legged. [159]

shag-haired (obs.) rough-coated. [152]

shaghayred (obs.) rough-coated.
> His countenance like a lion, his brest great and shaghayred. [152]

Shakerag (US) American and crossbred FOX-HOUND pack formed in 1943 to hunt over a wooded, arable and swampland COUNTRY in Georgia.

shaker dogs GENERALIZED TREMOR SYNDROME.

shallow brisket rib cage in which there is undesirable absence of depth.

shallow chest SHALLOW BRISKET.

shambling action (of movement) lazy; not smart or well co-ordinated.
> Very loose and shambling at walk. [203, OTTER-HOUND]

Shamir long coated SALUKI.

shank thigh.
> Hind legs: . . . with well-muscled thighs or upper shanks. [6, MINIATURE PINSCHER]

Shannon Spaniel (obs.) IRISH WATER SPANIEL. [295]

Shantung Terrier (obs.) LHASA APSO.

Shar Pei [AKC, FCI, KC] American recreation of a type of Chinese fighting dog now close to extinction in its pure form in China. The breed's extraordinary appearance, with its bristled coat and deeply wrinkled skin, quickly brought it to a dangerous level of popularity and consequent commercialization that amounted to a callous exploitation of the breed, the effects of which subsequent breeders are trying hard to eliminate.

A powerful and aloof breed with a large head, broad, flat skull, wrinkled forehead, moderate STOP and well-padded MUZZLE. The tongue is blue-black or pink-spotted. The CLEAN, dark, almond-shaped eyes are of medium size; the thick, triangular ears are very small, wide set, and drop forwards close to the top of the skull. The neck is short and powerful, the chest broad and deep with a short, powerful LOIN. Forequarters are muscular and WELL LAID; the well-boned forelegs are straight with sloping PASTERNS; hindquarters are strong and moderately angulated. The tapering tail is set very high and carried in a tight curl over the back. The skin is exceptionally loose, creating folds and the coat is short, hard and bristle-like; black, red and shades of fawn or cream are permitted. Height 46–51cm (18–20in).

shape (in training) use repeated reinforcement in order to inculcate the desired response.

shark mouth markedly OVERSHOT BITE.

sharp of dog that is inclined to bite without provocation.

sharp-tipped (of ears) pointed and erect.

Shaw, Vero author of *The Encyclopaedia of the Kennel* (1913).

shawl (Am.) MANE.
> Neck . . . covered with a mane or 'shawl' of longer hair that is more pronounced in dogs than bitches. [6, TIBETAN SPANIEL]

sheath PREPUCE.

shed 1. discard coat periodically, usually seasonally, or as a result of trauma.
> The Akbash dog sheds seasonally. [6, AKBASH DOG]
2. separate one or more sheep from a flock. Shedding is one of the exercises in SHEEP DOG trials. [204]

she-dog female dog; BITCH.
> He fought with the he-dogs, and winked at the she-dogs,
> A thing that had never been heard of before. [64]

sheep dog dog bred for the purpose of working with sheep; shepherd's dog. *See also* STOCK DOG.

sheep dog trial competition to test the herding skills of SHEEP DOGS.

sheep setter (obs.) dog used to find lost sheep, especially those buried in snow.
> The great matter, in either case, is their extrication: for which dogs are often employed, bearing the name of 'sheep setters', and some of them acquiring renown for such services throughout a wide range of country. [393]

shelly insubstantial, lacking substance.

Sheltie dim. SHETLAND SHEEP DOG.

Shenkottah large and powerful hunting dog from northern India, said to have had great courage and strength. Probably now extinct in its pure form.

Shepherd's Dog *Canis Domesticus*; PASTORAL HERDER. [139]
> Our shepherd's dog is not huge, vast, and big, but of an indifferent stature and growth. . . . This dog either at the hearing of his master's voice, or at the wagging and whistling in his fist, or the shrill and hoarse hissing brings the wandering wethers and straying sheep, into the self same place where his master's will and wish, is to have them. [139]

This useful animal, ever faithful to his charge, reigns at the head of the flock; where he is better heard, and more attended to, than even the voice of the shepherd. . . . They have one, sometimes two extra toes on the hind feet, though they seem not to be of much use. [51]

Shepherd's Hound (obs.) SHEPHERD'S DOG. [139]
The shepherd's hound is very necessary and profitable for the avoiding of harm and inconvenience which may come to men by the means of beasts. [139]

Shepherd Spitz HÜTESPITZ. [312]

Shetland Collie (obs.) SHETLAND SHEEP DOG.

Shetland Sheep Dog [AKC, FCI, KC] diminutive herding breed from the Shetland Isles; in spite of its very similar appearance, it is not a miniature version of the ROUGH COLLIE.

The breed is affectionate towards its owner but reserved with strangers. The wedge-shaped, proudly carried head has a moderately wide, flat skull with prominent OCCIPUT; the slight STOP divides the head equally; the almond eyes are obliquely set; ears are small, high set and carried semi-erect with the tips falling forward. The arched neck is muscular, the shoulders well laid and the chest deep with WELL SPRUNG RIBS; the TOPLINE is level and the CROUP slopes gradually to a low-set tail; hindquarters are broad and powerful, the feet oval with well arched toes. The coat is long and harsh with a soft under-coat and a profuse MANE and FRILL with abundant feathering. Any colour from pale gold to deep mahogany is permitted, as are TRICOLOURS and MERLES (WALL EYES are permitted in the latter). Height 35.5–37cm (14–14½in).

Shiba [FCI] SHIBA INU.

Shiba Inu [AKC] a medium-sized, Japanese, strongly vulpine SPITZ breed used for hunting small game.

The wedge-shaped head, broad, flat skull, strong MUZZLE, sharply pricked ears and oblique eyes are typically spitz. The back is short and level with a strong LOIN. The tail is high set and carried over the back. The coat, in shades of tan or red or black and tan, is thick and upstanding. Height 34–42cm (13½–16½in).

Shih Tzu [AKC, FCI, KC] The breed's name translates from the Chinese for Lion Dog, and it is very much part of the family of small, short-faced, heavily coated dogs which have their origins in and around China.

This friendly yet independent breed is sturdy and heavily coated with a characteristic chrysanthemum-like face. The broad, round head carries a shock of hair which falls over the large, dark, round eyes, the short, square MUZZLE is bearded and whiskered; the ears are long and pendulous and again heavily coated; the mouth is slightly UNDERSHOT. The arched neck carries the head proudly; the shoulders are WELL LAID and the short forelegs well boned and as straight as possible; the chest is broad and the body slightly longer than high. The heavily PLUMED tail is carried

over the back. The long coat may be of any colour, preferably with a white BLAZE on the forehead and a white tail tip. Height not more than 26.7cm (10½in); weight 4.5–7.3kg (10–16lb).

Shika Inu larger version of the SHIBA INU.

Shika Kyushu Nippon Inu a compact, medium-sized Japanese SPITZ breed.

Shikoku Inu SHIKOKU.

Shikoku one of several SPITZ breeds from Japan, the Shikoku has origins in and around Osaka. Originally used to track and course deer, it is a typical spitz breed in every respect with a short, harsh, BRINDLE or red coat. Height 43–53cm (17–20¾in).

Shillelagh and District pack formed in 1958 to hunt the COUNTRY in County Wicklow vacated by the Coollattin Hunt.

Shiloh Shepherd lush-coated, unrecognized version of the GERMAN SHEPHERD DOG (ALSATIAN) originally developed in New York State from the early 1960s.

Shirley, Sewellis Evelyn founder of the UK's KENNEL CLUB.

Shock-dog *CANIS MELITACUS.*
This dog is now almost unknown. But formerly he was very generally kept as a toy dog. He is said to have been a cross between the poodle and small spaniel. [338]
is traced by Buffon, but somewhat erroneously, to a mixture of the small Danish dog and the pug. [406]

shock-headed of dog with a luxuriant and some-what unruly growth of hair on the head.
Shock-headed with hair falling well over the eyes. [203, former SHIH TZU]

shoot event organized for the purpose of shooting game; shooting party.

shooting brake *see* BRAKE.

Shorncliffe former DRAGHOUND pack formed some years prior to 1886 to hunt LINES(2) in Kent.

short (of body part; anatomy) slight in length; atrophied.

short backed of a dog with little distance between WITHERS and CROUP.

short bodied SHORT-COUPLED.

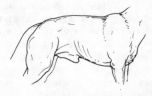

Short-coupled.

short-coupled of a dog in which there is little distance between back ribs and hips. [*illus.*]
In short-coupled and well ribbed-up dogs there is little space between ribs and hips. [203, AIREDALE TERRIER]
Body – Short coupled and sturdy with no waist or tuck-up [6, SHIH TZU]

short mandible inherited underdeveloped lower jaw. (Mode of inheritance, recessive.)

short spine inherited abnormally short, curved spine. (Mode of inheritance, recessive.)

Short-haired Catalan Herder GOS D'ATURA CERDA. [222]

Short-haired Dachshund variety of DACHSHUND.

Short-haired Dutch Shepherd KORTHAAR HOLLANDSE HERDERSHOND.

Short-haired Hungarian Vizsla variety of HUNGARIAN VIZSLA.

Short-haired Italian Hound SEGUGIO ITALIANO A PELO RASO.

Short-haired Skye Terrier (obs.) CAIRN TERRIER.
> If the pioneers of Cairn terriers had had their way, these dogs would now be known as Short-haired Skyes; but the Kennel Club, recognizing the confusion that would have arisen in connection with the older breed, wisely refused their sanction, so a less cumbersome but equally suitable name was chosen. [37]

Short Transylvanian Hound red and tan, short, coarse-coated Hungarian HOUND. Height 46–56cm (18–22in).

Shotesham Harriers DUNSTON.

shough rough-coated HOUND. [319i]

shoulder scapula and muscular attachments.

shoulder height the distance from ground to the WITHERS when the dog is standing upright.

show 1. competitive event at which the physical appearance and conformation of dogs are assessed. 2. exhibit. 3. the appearance of amniotic fluids during the process of birth.

show bred bred with the intention of producing a quality that enables it to be exhibited at SHOW.
> About this time I bought a little show-bred, wire-haired bitch which turned out a topper and which I named 'Squib'. [401]

show colour (in bitch during OESTRUS) secrete discharge suffused with blood.

show dog dog exhibited at show, especially one that has achieved some success.

show ring area – usually square – designated for the purpose of exhibiting dogs.

show slip slender lead with integral collar worn by dogs when being exhibited in the show ring.

Shower of Hail Setter type of SETTER formerly found along the north-west coast of Ireland, which was distinguished by its red coat sprinkled with small white spots. [332a]

showing haw of eyelids that expose some of their inner surface, an undesirable characteristic in most breeds and acceptable in very few.
> Eyelids should be reasonably tight, without any excessive haw. [203, ST BERNARD]

showing teeth of a mouth, characteristic of some BRACHYCEPHALIC breeds, in which the incisors are exposed even when the mouth is closed.

showmanship ability of dog or handler to attract the judge's attention and approval.

Shropshire BEAGLE pack formed in 1935 to hunt a COUNTRY in Shropshire.

Shropshire Fox-terrier extinct ancestral British working TERRIER.
> 'The Cheshire Terriers (or Shropshire, for the sorts are identical), were perhaps best known to the world through the kennel of Mr Stevenson of Chester, whose blood was mainly obtained from Mr (Domville) Poole.' [320a]

Shropshire Terrier SHROPSHIRE FOX-TERRIER.

shy 1. pull away from. 2. fearful. 3. artificial hide behind which the SLIPPER takes cover.

shy breeder dog or bitch of unreliable fertility or low libido.

shy feeder dog which habitually refuses to eat or requires encouragement to do so.

sib dim. SIBLING.

sib-mating mating between brother and sister.

sib-selection selection based on the quality of an entire litter.

sibbing (obs.) close INBREEDING, especially matings between siblings.
> In-breeding or sibbing is a fruitful source of constitutional weakness and loss of size amongst dogs, and if carried on too far is therefore a practice to be deprecated. [320]

Siberian Dog ESQUIMAUX DOG. [406]

Siberian Husky [AKC, FCI, KC] the breed whose strength and ruggedness has made enormous contributions to exploration, surveys and scientific work in the Arctic and Antarctic. Originally developed as a DRAUGHT DOG by the Siberian Chukchi nomads and originally known by that name. The breed was withdrawn from the Antarctic after decades of service out of fears, which many regarded as unfounded, that non-indigenous species might introduce disease to which native species lack immunity.

A demonstrative, friendly breed with no suspicion of strangers or aggression towards them. The head is strongly vulpine, with almond-shaped eyes and pricked triangular ears set closely together. The neck is arched and proudly carried, the forequarters WELL LAID, with straight forelimbs, sloping PASTERNs and flexible, strong wrists. The body has a level TOPLINE and is of medium length; the chest is broad and deep and the LOINS slightly arched and well muscled; the hindquarters are well muscled with well-defined, low HOCKS and oval, well-furred feet. The tail is similar to a fox's BRUSH – round and well furred. The DOUBLE COAT is thick and weather-resistant with a furry undercoat and a dense coat of GUARD HAIRS which are neither harsh nor silky. All colours and all markings are acceptable. Height 51–60cm (20–23½in); weight 35–47kg (77–103½lb).

Siberian Wolfhound (obs.) BORZOI.

sibling each of the offspring born to the same parents. In dogs the term is usually confined to littermates.

Sicilian Branchiero CANE CORSO.

Sicilian Dog breed mentioned by DRURY, quoting Strabo.
> There is a town in Sicily called Melita, whence are

exported many beautiful dogs, called *Canes Melitei*. They were peculiar favourites of the women; but now [AD 25] there is less account made of these animals, which are not bigger than common ferrets or weasels. [123]

Sicilian Hound   CIRNECO DELL' ETNA. [222]

sick   (Am.) encourage or order a dog to attack. Two-legged white dogs sicking four-legged dogs on your and my mother. [405]

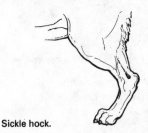

Sickle hock.

sickle hock   HOCK in which the metacarpal bones are not vertical and form a more than usually acute angle with the fibula and tibia. When standing or moving, the line from hock to foot slopes forward creating a sharp angle with the thigh producing stilted, uneconomical gait. [*illus.*]
Faults . . . over-angulated (sickle) hocks. [6, ALASKAN MALAMUTE]

sickle tail   sharply curved tail forming the outline of a sickle.
Sickle or uncurled tail highly undesirable. [203, JAPANESE AKITA Interim BREED STANDARD]
The tail is carried over the back, in a sickle position, full curl or double curl. [6, SHIBA KEN]

side-gaiting   CRAB.
Faults – Single tracking. Sidegaiting. Paddling in front or high hackney knee action. [6, MINIATURE SCHNAUZER]

side-lay   collective noun for fresh HOUNDS kept to replace others tired during the course of a hunt. [159]

Side-striped Jackal   CANIS ADUSTUS.

side-wheel   PACE.

side-wind   CRAB.

Sidney Silky   misspelling SYDNEY SILKY.

Sid Vale Harriers   AXE VALE.

Sieger   (Ger.) male CHAMPION.

Siegerin   (Ger.) female CHAMPION.

sighthound   HOUND that hunts by sight.

silent retinal syndrome   SUDDEN ACQUIRED RETINAL DEGENERATION.

silent whistle   high-pitched whistle which can be heard by dogs but not usually by humans.

Silky   1. former name for the now extinct PAISLEY TERRIER. [123]   2. dim. (colloq.) AUSTRALIAN SILKY TERRIER.

Silky Terrier   dim. AUSTRALIAN SILKY TERRIER.

Silky Toy Terrier   AUSTRALIAN SILKY TERRIER.

silver eye   WALL EYE.

silvering   progressive greying of the coat imparting a silver sheen; an inherited characteristic. (Mode of inheritance, incomplete dominance.)

Silverton   pack founded in 1863 to hunt a Devonshire banked COUNTRY.

Simian Fox   CANIS SIMENSIS.

Simian Jackal   CANIS SIMENSIS.

simple mongrel   (obs.) a first or F1 CROSS.
All these dogs are simple mongrels and are produced by a com-mixture of two pure races. [72]

sinew   tendon.

sinewy   (of limbs) long and muscular.

Singing Beagle   GLOVE BEAGLE. [123]

Singing Dog   BORNEO SINGING DOG.

single coat   coat that has no undercoat.

single-track   (of gait) to move with each of the four feet striking the ground along a single line, a gait typical of foxes.
Single tracking at trot is normal. [203, ALASKAN MALAMUTE]
Correct conformation will lend to single track movement. [203, CHESAPEAKE BAY RETRIEVER, Interim BREED STANDARD]
Moving at a slow walk or trot, they will not single-track. [6, SAMOYED]

Single-tracking action.

Sinnington   hunt dating from about 1680 when it was founded by the Duke of Buckingham and continued as a TRENCHER-FED pack until 1891.

siphunculata   sub-order of PHTHIRAPTERA, also called Anoplura.

Sir Sister   (US) BEAGLE pack formed in 1903 to hunt cottontail rabbit over a COUNTRY in Massachusetts.

Sir Thomas Sebright's   HERTFORDSHIRE.

Sir Watkin Williams-Wynn's   although the first Sir Watkin was killed in a hunting accident in 1749 no information exists about a pack at that time; during the next 100 years the family formed packs but none appears to have survived long. The present pack was formed in 1843 to hunt a COUNTRY in Cheshire, Shropshire, and Clwyd.

sire   male parent.

sit   position in which the hindquarters are rested on the ground while the forelegs remain upright; command to a dog to assume this position.

sit square   (esp. OBEDIENCE DOG) sit at right angles to the way in which the handler is facing.

sit to flush   (GUNDOG) remain in the sitting position after a FLUSH.

sit to shot   (GUNDOG) remain in the sitting position while the shot is taken and until the command to retrieve is given.

skeletal   of, or relating to, SKELETON.

skeletal lethal   inherited multiple skeletal defect. (Mode of inheritance, dominant.)

skeletal scurvy   CANINE HYPERTROPHIC OSTEODYSTROPHY.

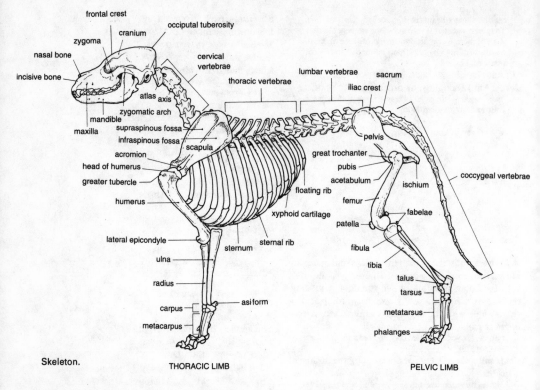

frontal crest
occiputal tuberosity
cranium
zygoma
nasal bone
incisive bone
cervical
vertebrae
lumbar vertebrae   sacrum
iliac crest
thoracic vertebrae
atlas axis
zygomatic arch
mandible
maxilla
supraspinous fossa
infraspinous fossa
scapula
acromion
head of humerus
greater tubercle
humerus
lateral epicondyle
ulna
radius
carpus
metacarpus
asiform
sternum
sternal rib
xyphoid cartilage
floating rib
acetabulum
pubis
great trochanter
pelvis
ischium
femur
patella
fibula
tibia
talus
tarsus
metatarsus
phalanges
fabelae
coccygeal vertebrae

Skeleton.   THORACIC LIMB   PELVIC LIMB

skeleton   the bones of the body, forming the frame. [illus.]

skewbald   (coat colour) brown patches on a white GROUND.
> Wolf grey, all black and all white, skewbald and piebald unacceptable. [203, ESTRELA MOUNTAIN DOG, Interim BREED STANDARD]

ski-jorring   short race in which the driver uses skis instead of a sled.

skin pH   measure of alkalinity or acidity of the skin. In dogs the normal range is from 5.5 to 7.2.

Skioku   BRINDLE or red, short, harsh-coated Japanese SPITZ. Height 44–56cm (17½–22in).

skirt   (of HOUNDS) to run wide of the pack, leaving others to do the work.
> Skirting – although a proof of intellect, or rather, cunning – is often the cause of much mischief, and always spoils the business-like appearance of things. [266b]

skirter   HOUND that runs on the flanks of the pack and so contributes little to the enterprise.
> He should be particularly attentive to the headmost hounds, and should be constantly on his guard against a skirter. [47]

skulk   collective noun for a group of foxes.

skull   the bones of the head.

skully   of head that has prominent or over developed skull.

Skycastle   (US) BASSET pack formed in 1960 to hunt cottontail rabbit over a COUNTRY in Pennsylvania.

Skye Terrier   [AKC, FCI, KC] although the TERRIERS of the Isle of Skye have been known for at least 400 years the present version of the breed has developed from the small utilitarian breed to become a glamorous show-dog, the transformation coinciding with the increased popularity of dog shows during the later years of Queen Victoria's reign, who was herself an ardent admirer of the breed.
  The breed is a one-man dog, suspicious of strangers, who would be wise to take a similar attitude. The outline is long and low. The powerful, long head has a strong MUZZLE, dark eyes, ears which may be either PRICK or DROP and a strong jaw. The slight CRESTED NECK is long, the shoulders broad and the oval chest deep. The body is long and low; the hindquarters are strong and muscular; forefeet are larger than those at the rear. The FEATHERED tail hangs down in repose but may also be carried level with the TOPLINE. The coat is soft and woolly underneath with an outercoat of long, straight, flat hair which may be black, grey, fawn, or cream with black POINTS(3). Height 25cm (10in); length 103cm (40½in).
> As far as I can discover, the first mention of a 'Skye terrier' as such is made in Colonel H. Smith's work of 1843, in which he gives a picture of the 'Isle of Skye terrier', a dog with large ears, a long shaggy coat, and, as far as can be judged from the illustration, short legs. [37]
> Most of the Skye Terriers about London are crossed with the spaniel, giving them that silky coat and jet

black colour which are admired by ladies, but mark impurity of blood. [338]

The Skye terrier originated, as a little severe concentration will suggest, in the islands of the Hebrides. They are short-legged and shaggy-coated, and were used to bolt otters and foxes before sophisticated London women degraded them to the level of tea-table sycophants. [383]

slab-sided of dog in which there is an absence of spring of rib, when some spring is desirable.

The ribs forming the thorax show a rib spring and are not flat or slab-sided. [6, GERMAN SHORT-HAIRED POINTER]

slack 1. (of a pack of HOUNDs) lack determination or purpose. [266b]
2. weak; poor.

slack back concave TOPLINE, especially when due to poor muscular condition.

slack loins having a long and poorly muscled COUPLING.

Slagterhunden (obs.) DANISH BROHOLMER.

Slaley Hounds BRAES OF DERWENT.

slanting pastern SLOPING PASTERN.

slats LOINS.

Great-chested, muscled in the slats. [249a]

sled wheelless vehicle pulled by dogs.

sled bag bag containing essential sled-race equipment.

sled-dog dog used to pull a sled.

Sleeve Dog SLEEVE PEKINGESE.

So small as to be carried in the sleeves of a Chinese coat. Hence they are called sleeve-dogs. Some resemble the old-fashioned short-bow-legged pugs, which may have been originally introduced into Europe from China. [221]

Sleeve Pekingese very small PEKINGESE: in China such dogs were carried in the capacious sleeves of their owner's gown, hence their name.

slench (obs.) sneak away to hunt alone. [159]

slete (obs.) encourage a dog to attack, especially livestock. [159]

Sleughhound SLEUTH-HOUND.

sleuth the track of an animal, hence SLEUTH-HOUND. [159]

Sleuth Dog SLEUTH-HOUND.

Sleuth-hound BLOODHOUND. (der. Old Norse *sleuth*.)

In Scotland it [the Bloodhound] was distinguished by the name of the Sleuth-Hound. [51]

slew feet (esp. of the forefeet) feet in which the toes point outwards.

Slinfold a former HARRIER pack formed in 1820 to hunt fox and hare in a Surrey and Sussex COUNTRY.

slip 1. lightweight lead with integral collar which does not disturb the outline of SHOW-DOGS. 2. double-collared leash by which COURSING HOUNDs can be simultaneously released.

I see you stand like Greyhounds in the slips,
Straining upon the start [319f]
Remembered thou my greyhounds true?
O'er holt or hill, there never flew

From slip or leash, there never sprang
More fleet of foot or sure of fang! [314a]

3. release HOUNDs from their slips in order to pursue their quarry.

The dogs were slipped; a general halloo burst from the whole party, and the stag wheeling round, set off at full speed. [315]

slipping patella LUXATING PATELLA.

slipping stifle LUXATING PATELLA.

slipper 1. one who releases HOUNDs from their SLIPS(2).

slipper foot long, oval foot.

Feet . . . may be neatened to avoid the appearance of 'boat' or 'slipper' feet. [6, HAVANESE]

sloping falling; inclining.

Sloping back.

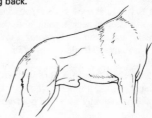

sloping back a TOPLINE which falls evenly from WITHERS to CROUP. [*illus.*]

sloping pastern PASTERN that is not vertical.

Forequarters . . . strongly boned with slightly sloping pasterns. [203, BASSET FAUVE DE BRETAGNE]

sloping shoulder scapula which is inclined towards 45 degrees.

slot a deer's footprint. [144]

slot in find the whereabouts of a harboured stag by tracing its SLOTS.

Slough-dog BLOODHOUND.

At one time he was kept for tracking moss-troopers, and guarding the various fords, he was called the Sloughdog, as he followed them over bogs and 'sloughs' to make them disgorge their booty. [186]

Slough-hound SLUGHOUND.

Sloughi [FCI, KC] The SIGHTHOUND of northern Africa and valued by the Arabs for its ability to COURSE both small and larger game.

The head is strong with a broad, flat skull and wedge-shaped MUZZLE. The eyes are large and dark, the ears rounded triangles carried close to the head; the neck is long and elegant with a finely pleated DEWLAP. The chest is not too broad and barely reaches the point of elbow; the TUCK-UP is pronounced and the TOPLINE fairly level to an oblique CROUP. Haunches are prominent; the hindquarters are muscular with good angulation; feet are long and thin. The coat is fine but tough and may be of any shade of SABLE or fawn with or without a black MASK. Height 65–70cm (25½–27½in).

Slouth-hound SLEUTH-HOUND.

For example, in the fourteenth century he (the

Bloodhound) was called the Sleuth or Slouth Hound, the word 'slouth', probably meaning scent. [186]

Slovac Čuvač SLOVENSKÝ ČUVAČ.

Slovakian Chuvach SLOVENSKÝ ČUVAČ.

Slovakian Čuvač SLOVENSKÝ ČUVAČ.

Slovakian Hound SLOVENSKÝ KOPOV.

Slovakian Kuvasz SLOVENSKÝ ČUVAČ.

Slovakian Pointing Griffon SLOVENSKÝ HRUBORSTY OHAR.

Slovakian Shepherd Dog SLOVENSKÝ CUVAC.

Slovakian Wire-haired Pointer CESKÝ FOUSEK.

Slovenský Čuvač [FCI] a Czechoslovakian PASTORAL GUARD and HERDER with strong similarities to other heavily coated, predominantly white breeds of Europe's mountain areas.

The head is wedge-shaped with a rounded skull, the ears V-shaped, the neck strong and the chest deep. The coat is thick and DOUBLE and is invariably a shaded warm white. Height 71cm (28in); weight 48kg (105½lb).

Slovenský Hruborsty Ohar [FCI] CESKÝ FOUSEK.

Slovenský Kopov [FCI] a superlative TRACKER from Czechoslovakia principally used for boar and large game.

A long-backed, strongly made dog, similar in type to the Polish Hound. The coarse black-and-tan coat is sleek and lies close to the body. Height 46–51cm (18–20in); weight 20–22kg (44–48½lb).

Slovenský Tchouvatch SLOVENSKÝ ČUVAČ.

Slow-hound probably an ancestor of the old SOUTHERN HOUND and remarkable for the patient manner in which it could follow a faint COLD SCENT.
> Now of these hounds there are divers kinds, as the Slow Hound, which is a large great dog, tall and heavy, and are bred for the most part in the best countries of this kingdome, as also in Cheshire and Lancashire and most woodland and mountainous countreys. [245a]

Slughi SLOUGH.
> The Arab speaks of the Slughi as el hor ('the noble one'). According to the Arab, the name is derived from Saluk, a long-since-vanished town in Southern Arabia, once famous for its armour and its hounds, or from 'Seleukia', of the Greek Empire in Syria. [37]

Slughound breed possessed by James I, probably a BLOODHOUND or Scotch wolfdog. [159]

Sluithound BLOODHOUND.
> To find out the hart or Stag, where his harbour or Lare is, you must be provided with a Bloodhound, Draughthound, or Sluithound, which must be led in a Liam; and for the quickening his scent, it is good to rub his nose with vinegar. [53]

slut (obs. Am.) BITCH. (der. Old Danish *slodde*, via Old English *slutte*, meaning untidy.)
> The dog was of a dingy red color and the slut, black. [324]

Sluth-hound BLOODHOUND.
> There are among the Scotch, besides the common domestic dogs, three kinds of dogs, which you will not (I think) find anywhere else in the world: . . . the

third kind (ane sluth hownd) is not larger than the scent-following dogs: but is usually reddish with black spots, or black with reddish spots. [56]

Smalandsstövare [FCI] a lightly made SCENTHOUND originating in mid-Sweden, and used for hunting small game.

COMPACT and light, with a square outline. The head is long and lean with dark eyes and high-set, rounded pendulous ears; the neck is moderately long, the chest well let down, with WELL-SPRUNG ribs. The back is short, and the CROUP long, broad and gently sloping. The tail is either long and carried SABRE fashion or naturally short. The forelimbs are straight, the hindquarters WELL-ANGULATED and strongly muscled. The coat is smooth, thick and glossy, invariably black and tan. Height about 48cm (18¾in).

Small Bernese Hound BERNER NEIDERLAUFHUND.

Small Bleu de Gascony PETIT BLEU DE GASCOGNE.

Small Blue Gascony Griffon PETIT GRIFFON BLEU DE GASCOGNE.

Small-eared Dog CANIS MICROTIS.

Small-eared Zorro DUSICYON MICROTIS.

Small English-French Hound ANGLO-FRANÇAIS DE PETITE VENERIE.

Small French Pointer PETIT BRAQUE FRANÇAIS.

Small Gascony Blue PETIT BLEU DE GASCOGNE.

Small German Spitz POMERANIAN.

Small Jura Hound JURA-NEIDERLAUFHUND.

Small Lucernese Hound LUZERNER NEIDERLAUFHUND.

Small Münsterländer [KC] a diminutive version of the LARGE MÜNSTERLÄNDER, from which it differs only in size. Height 43–56cm (17–22in).

Small Portuguese Hound PODENGO PORTUGUÊSA PEQUEÑO.

Small Swiss Hound SCHWEIZER NEIDERLAUFHUND.

Small-toothed Dog CANIS PARVIDENS.

Small Vendéen Basset PETIT BASSET GRIFFON VENDÉEN.

Smaller Bernese Hound BERNER NIEDERLAUFHUND.

Smaller French Pointer BRAQUE FRANÇAIS DE PETIT TAILLE. [222]

Smaller Jura Hound JURA NIEDERLAUFHUND.

Smaller Lucern Hound LUZERNER NIEDERLAUFHUND.

Smaller Swiss Hound SCHWEIZERISCHER NIEDERLAUFHUND.

smeller an article impregnated with the runner's scent in BLOODHOUND working trials.

smellers stiff, long hairs that grow on the MUZZLE.
> The removal of the long 'smellers' from the muzzle, however, is an easy matter if the dog is not inclined to bite. If he is, it is generally a good plan to get a friend to perform the operation, care being taken, however, only to remove the smellers and long eyebrows, nothing more. [37]

smeuse (obs.) a hare's tracks. [159]

Smithfield Collie extinct British DROVER.

Smithfield Drover extinct 19th cent. British droving breed.

Smithtown (US) American, English and CROSSBRED FOXHOUND pack formed in 1900 to hunt fox and drag over a rolling, wooded COUNTRY in New York State.

Smooth dim. SMOOTH FOX TERRIER.

smooth (of coat hair) short and straight and lying close to the skin.

Smooth-coat Chihuahua [AKC, FCI, KC] smooth-haired variety of the CHIHUAHUA.

Smooth-coated Fox Terrier SMOOTH FOX TERRIER.

Smooth Collie [AKC, FCI, KC] a smooth-coated variety of the more popular ROUGH COLLIE.

Smooth-faced Berger de Pyrenees medium-sized French HERDER with shaggy coat, which may be HARLEQUIN, BRINDLE, fawn, blue or grey with or without white. Height 41–56cm (16–22in).

Smooth-faced Pyrenean Shepherd Dog SMOOTH-FACED BERGER DE PYRENEES.

Smooth Fox Terrier smooth-coated variety of the FOX TERRIER, and recognized by the AKC, FCI and KC as Fox Terrier (Smooth). The smooth coat is the only feature distinguishing it from the WIRE FOX TERRIER. An alert, eager and fearless terrier developed in the English shires to work with FOXHOUNDS during the middle years of the 18th century, and attaining considerable popularity during the closing years of the 19th.

The skull is flat, with little STOP, and a chiselled foreface; the ears are small and V-shaped, and BREAK(5) above the line of the skull; the eyes are small, dark and deeply set. The neck is fairly long, CLEAN and muscular, the shoulders long and sloping, and the forelimbs straight and well boned; the chest is deep, the back short and the TOPLINE level; the LOINS are powerful and slightly arched. Hindquarters are strong and muscular with good TURN OF STIFLE; feet are small and cat-like; the high-set tail is customarily DOCKED and is carried GAILY. The smooth, hard, dense coat may be totally white, or may be marked with tan, black, or black and tan, although white must always predominate. Weight 6.8–8.2kg (15–18lb).

Smooth Griffon GRIFFON BRABANCON.

Smooth-haired Dachshund [AKC, FCI, KC] smooth-haired variety of the DACHSHUND.

Smooth-haired Istrian Hound ISTARSKI KRATKOD-LAKI GONIČ.

Smooth-haired Rabbit Dachshund KURZHAARIGER KANINCHENTECKEL.

Smousbart SMOUSHOND.

Smoushond shaggy, almost ragged-looking, small TERRIER-like dog, originally used as a STABLE DOG. It has a strong head, short MUZZLE and square body with a hard, rough, beige or grey coat. [222]

smudge small, dark, usually circular, mark on a dog's head.

smudge nose SNOW NOSE.

smut of a whole-coloured BULLDOG with black MASK or MUZZLE.

Whole or smut (i.e. whole colour with black mask or muzzle). [203, BULLDOG]

smutty of the tendency of tan markings to encroach into areas where they are not wanted, especially in classically marked black-and-tan dogs.

smutty nose brown or tan nose.
Some smutty-nosed, some tan, none bald. [249a]

snap bite suddenly and sharply.
Delighted in her pert Bow-wow:
But now she snaps if you don't mind:
'Twere lunacy to love her now. [80]

snap coursing former sport in which captive rabbits were COURSEd within an enclosure by SNAP-DOGS. The winner was the dog that snapped at the greatest number of rabbits.

snap-dog 1. former name for the WHIPPET [123]. One improbable explanation for the use of this name comes from Edward Ash:
At one time the breed was known as the 'snap-dog', because of the habit dogs had when running to snap each other.

Other explanations suggest that the name derives from the dog's tendency to snap at the rabbits which it was used to COURSE. There may also be a connection between 'snap' and the Northern English dialect term for food (rabbits being a welcome addition to the larder). [229] 2. (obs.) LURCHER. (possibly der. *snap*, the beneficiary of another's theft.) [253]

snap tail tail that lies closely along the TOPLINE.

snar (obs.) snarl. [159]

snarl threatening expression in which the lips are drawn back to reveal the teeth, accompanied by growling sound; threaten in this way.
My caress provoked a long, guttural snarl.
You'd better let the dog alone,' growled Mr. Heathcliff in unison, checking fiercer demonstrations with a punch of his foot. [63]

snatch (usually of a GREYHOUND) make an unsuccessful effort to bite running quarry.

snatch of hocks the degree of thrust from the HOCKS when a dog is moving.

sniffer dog dog used to discover contraband goods, usually drugs or explosives, by means of scent.

snip that part of a BLAZE which surrounds the nose.
Head solid black, white blaze, snip or star allowed. [203]

snipy of a muzzle that is long and pointed, similar to the beak of a snipe.
Muzzle broad, well filled under eye. Not snipy. [203, MALTESE]

snow hook anchor used to secure temporarily a team of SLED-DOGS.

snow nose nose that loses pigment during cold weather, producing pink markings; most often exhibited in dogs of arctic origin.
Pink streaked 'snow nose' acceptable. [203, ALASKAN MALAMUTE, Interim BREED STANDARD]
The pink-streaked 'snow nose' is acceptable. [6, SIBERIAN HUSKY]

snow-shoe feet large, flat feet, but not thin or open.

Their feet are of the 'snowshoe' type, tight and deep, with well-cushioned pads, giving a firm and compact appearance. [6, ALASKAN MALAMUTE]

snub-line cord used to attach a dog team and sled to a stationary object.

socks white markings to the feet, ankles or lower legs, not extending beyond the HOCK or knee.

socialization early learning process by which young puppies are accustomed to new sights, sounds and experiences.

soft back a TOPLINE which sags between WITHERS and CROUP.

Soft-coated Wheaten Terrier [AKC, FCI, KC] one of several TERRIER breeds with origins in the Irish counties of Kerry and Cork.

A hardy and strong dog with well-developed terrier instincts, spirited and game. The skull is flat and fairly long, the STOP well defined and the jaws strong. The dark hazel eyes are of medium size, the ears V-shaped and FOLDED close to the skull. The neck is of moderate length and slightly arched; the forequarters are WELL LAID and the limbs are straight. The chest is fairly wide, the body COMPACT with short, powerful LOINS and a strong, level back; hindquarters are muscular with WELL-LET-DOWN HOCKS and WELL-ANGULATED STIFLES. The tail is traditionally DOCKED and carried GAILY, but never over the back. The loosely waved coat is soft and silky and always the colour of ripe wheat. Height 46–49cm (18–19in); weight 16–21kg (35–46lb).

soft mouth (of a GUNDOG) mouth that is able to retrieve game without mouthing or damaging it.

soft palate that part of the palate which lies to the rear of the mouth.

so-ho hunting cry which indicates the presence of a sitting hare. [383]

solid colour (usu. of coat) one, uniform colour.

soma cells of the body tissue, as distinct from germ cells and the mind.

somatic of, or relating to, SOMA.

 somatic mutation mutation of the body cells giving rise to unusual features which are seldom inherited.

Somerset (US) private BASSET pack formed to hunt over a COUNTRY in Virginia.

Sonangi ALUNK.

sorty 1. typical of its breed. 2. collective noun for a group of dogs of identical appearance.

soss lap; drink like a dog. [159]

sound of animal in good order, physically and temperamentally.

sour mug dog fighting terminology for a BULLDOG.

South and West Wilts said to be probably the oldest pack of FOXHOUNDS in England: the hunt dates from the last decade of the 17th century. Former masters include Isaac Bell, 1925–1934.

South Canterbury (NZ) BEAGLE pack formed in 1881 on the basis of Beagles imported from Devonshire. Hare is hunted over a flat, well-drained sheep COUNTRY in South Canterbury.

South County Dublin Irish HARRIER pack formed in 1932.

South Dorset pack dating from 1806. The COUNTRY is largely grass.

Southdown pack formed in 1843 to hunt a Sussex downland COUNTRY.

South Durham DURHAM COUNTY HUNT.

South Herefordshire 1. hunt dating from 1869 when Harcourt Capper hunted the hilly country. 2. BEAGLE pack formed in 1938 to hunt a COUNTRY vacated by the BUSHEY HEATH.

South Notts pack whose COUNTRY was hunted from 1667 by the Earl of Lincoln; with few intermissions, it has been hunted by the South Notts since 1775.

South Oxfordshire pack founded by the Earl of Macclesfield in 1845; the COUNTRY is largely arable with some big woodlands.

South Pembrokeshire based on the Cresselly Hunt, which dates from before 1789. The present name dates from 1844, although from 1893 to 1923 the Cresselly was revived as a private pack under the name of Mr Seymour Allen's. The name reverted to the South Pembrokeshire in 1929. The COUNTRY is largely pasture with some woodland and little plough.

South Pool HARRIER pack formed in 1871 by the amalgamation of the Bowden Harriers and the Marlborough Harriers to hunt a COUNTRY in south Devon.

South Russian Ovtcharka IOUJNOROUSSKAIA OVTCHARKA.

South Russian Sheep Dog IOUJNOROUSSKAIA OVTCHARKA.

South Russian Shepherd Dog IOUJNOROUSSKAIA OVTCHARKA.

South Russian Steppe Hound STEPPE BORZOI.

South Staffordshire pack dating from 1775. The hunt's present form derives from arrangements made by Lord Anglesey in 1835.

South Tetcott pack formed in 1916 to hunt a wooded Devon and Cornwall COUNTRY.

South Union County Cork hunt established prior to 1830 from which time it was hunted by Thomas Walton Knolles until 1889.

South Wold pack which, from 1820 to 1822, was known as the Gillingham, the present name being adopted in 1822. The COUNTRY lies in Lincolnshire and contains a great deal of plough.

Southern Cur efficient and relentless TRACKER developed in the southern states of America for use on racoon and similar game.

A clean headed dog of unusually variable size, strongly made and muscular with a deep chest. The medium-sized ears are black as are the MUZZLE and areas surrounding the mouth, from which the breed derives its alternative name of Black Mouth Cur. The coat is short and shaded from yellow to fawn. Height 40–64cm (15¾–25in); weight 20–43kg (44–94½lb).

Southern Dhole formerly *CYON JAVANICUS*, southern subspecies of *CUON ALPINUS*.

Southern Hound old-fashioned, heavily built, slow-hunting type of FOXHOUND, formerly found in the south of England.

> A heavy, 'crook-kneed' kind of baying Hound, which dwelt on the scent, and was incapable of killing a fox unless he hunted him to death. [186]

Southern Illinois Open (US) CROSSBRED FOXHOUND pack formed in 1961 to hunt over a rolling COUNTRY in Illinois.

Southern Water Spaniel (obs.) one of three 19th-century varieties of IRISH WATER SPANIEL, also called the McCarthy Water Spaniel. [295]

spanell (obs.) spaniel.

> Howe necessary a thing a Spanell is to Falconrie, and for those that use that pastime, keeping hawkes for their pleasure and recreation. I deeme no man doubteth, as well to spring and retrieve a fowle, being flowen to the marke, as also divers other ways to assist and aydfe falcones and goshawkes. [363]

spangel (obs.) spaniel. [159]

spaniel a group of GUNDOGS used for finding game; *CANIS EXTRARIUS*.

> The common sort of people call them by one general word, namely Spaniel. As though these kind of Dogs came originally and first of all out of Spain. The most part of their skins are white, and if they be marked with any spots, they are generally red, and somewhat great withal, the hairs not growing in such thickness but that the mixture of them may easily be perceived. [139]
>
> Happiest of spaniel race,
> Painter, with thy colours grace:
> Draw his forehead large and high,
> Draw his blue and humid eye,
> Draw his neck so smooth and round,
> Little neck with ribbons bound! [346a]

Spaniel Gentle Toy SPANIEL, a chamber companion; a pleasant playfellow.

> These dogs are little, pretty, proper, and fine, and sought for to satisfy the delicateness of dainty dames, and wanton women's wills, instruments of folly for them to play with and dally withal, to trifle away the treasure of time, to withdraw their minds from commendable exercises, and to content their corrupted consciences with vain disport. [139]

Spanish Bulldog MASTIN ESPAÑOL. [222]

Spanish Greyhound GALGO ESPAÑOL.

Spanish Hound SABUESO ESPAÑOL.

Spanish Mastiff MASTIN ESPAÑOL.

Spanish Pointer PERDIGUERO DE BURGOS.

> Originally a native of Spain, was once considered to be a valuable dog. He stood higher on his legs, but was too large and heavy in his limbs and had widely spread, ugly feet, exposing him to frequent lameness. His muzzle and head were large, corresponding with the acuteness of his smell. [406]
>
> The Spanish Pointer was, I believe, a liver-and-white dog, with a great preponderance of liver-colour. He was very seldom ticked or flecked on his white, and bore a close resemblance to that well-known picture of the breed by Reinagle, in which he is represented with a very heavy head and jowl, deep flews, sunken, large eyes, and tremendous bone and muscle. [186]

Spanish Warren Hound PODENCO.

Spanish Water Dog PERRO DE AGUA ESPAÑOL.

Sparkford Vale a HARRIER pack formed in 1888 to hunt a COUNTRY in Somerset. From 1895 to 1905 the pack was known by the Master's name, Mr Holt Needham.

Spartan Dog (obs., lit.) BLOODHOUND.

> O Spartan dog
> More fell than anguish, hunger or the sea. [319m]

Spartiate a Greek PASTORAL HERDER, in many respects a smaller version of the GREEK SHEEP DOG.

spay surgically neuter a female.

Spaynel (obs. spelling) SPANIEL. [86]

speak 1. bark; customary command for a dog so to do. 2. (of HOUNDS) give voice when on the scent.

specialist judge who has a particular interest, whether as breeder or exhibitor, in the breed he happens to be judging.

speciality club (Am.) a club which confines its interests to a single breed (UK, a breed club).

Speciality Show (Am.) a show confined to a single breed.

speckled (of coat) flecked; TICKED.

spectacles lighter markings round the eyes of a dark-MASKed dog.

> Well defined 'spectacles' shown as a delicately pencilled black line slanting from outer corner of eye to lower corner of ear. [203, KEESHOND]

Speletti Dog short-legged version of *CANIS FAMILIARIS PALUSTRIS* constructed by Gandert. [312]

Speothos venaticus Bush Dog, found in the forests of Panama, south-eastern Brazil, east of the Andes.

Sperling a former HARRIER pack formed in 1880 when they were known as the Lamerton Harriers; the present name was adopted in 1887. The COUNTRY lies in Devon.

sperm germ cells or gametes produced by the male.

sperm agglutinins antibodies which occur in dogs infected with *Brucella canis*.

sperm count assessment of the quality and number of sperm in a sample of semen.

spermacytes early stage in the development of SPERM.

spermatid immature SPERM.

spermatogenesis cell divisions which produce SPERM.

spermatooza SPERMATOZOA.

spermatozoa pl. SPERMATOZOON.

spermatozoan mature male germ cell.

spermatozoon SPERM.

spey SPAY.

sphincter circular muscle surrounding an orifice.

sphingomyelitis inherited nervous disorder.

spina bifida developmental abnormality.

spinal of, or relating to, the SPINE.

spinal column SPINE.

spinal cord that part of the nervous system which is enclosed within the spine.

spinal dysraphism inherited condition in which

there is incomplete closure of the neural tube leading to characteristic 'bunny hopping' movement of
the rear limbs. (Mode of inheritance, familial.)

spinal muscular atrophy inherited wasting of the
spinal muscles. (Mode of inheritance, recessive.)

spine vertebral column, running from the back of
the head to the tip of the tail.

sphingomyelin lipidosis SPHINGOMYELINOSIS.

sphingomyelinosis inherited deficiency of nervous
tissue resulting in retarded growth and nervous
abnormalities. (Mode of inheritance, recessive.)

Spinone SPINONE ITALIANO.
> Somewhat allied to the Barbet in general appearance
> and the nature of his work is the important gun-dog
> known in Italy as the Spinone. [225]

Spinone Italiano [FCI] a multi-purpose GUNDOG
native to Italy.

The head is long, the skull flat with a prominent
OCCIPUT and a MEDIAN FURROW, the deep yellow or
ochre eyes are large and round, the ears triangular
and pendulous; the short neck is muscular and the
shoulders WELL LAID and strong with the points set
wide apart; the forelimbs are straight with strong oval
bone. The body is square in outline and solid, with
a broad, deep chest and a TOPLINE which falls slightly
from WITHERS to croup; the hindquarters are muscular with WELL-LET-DOWN HOCKS and vertical
METATARSALS; the forefeet are round, the hind feet
oval. The tail is traditionally DOCKED and carried in
line with the CROUP. The tough, thick coat may be
white, with or without orange, or brown with white
markings or speckles. Height 58–69cm (23–27in);
weight 29–39kg (64–86lb).

spinner a dog that habitually turns round and
round about its own axis. The behaviour is thought
to be either the product of neurological disturbance
or a ritualized effort to escape from a small enclosure in which the dog is confined for long periods.

Spirocera artica parasitic worm of dogs, foxes and
wolves.

Spirocerca lupi parasitic worm of the oesophagus,
major arteries and stomach, which produces nodules
that cause obstruction.

Spirometra erinacei small parasitic intestinal TAPE-
WORM.

Spirometra mansoni small parasitic intestinal TAPE-
WORM.

Spirometra mansonoides small parasitic intestinal
TAPEWORM.

Spirura rytipleurites parasitic worm of the alimentary tract.

spit-dog TURNSPIT.

spit-turner (obs.) TURNSPIT. [159]

spitz group of dogs which share similar physcial
characteristics consisting of pointed MUZZLES and
ears, vulpine heads and curled, usually bushy, tails.

splash (of coat) irregularly shaped, occasional
mark.
> Splash of white on chest, toes and tip of tail accept-

able. [203, NEWFOUNDLAND]

splayed 1. of foot: SPLAY FOOT. 2. (obs. of bitch)
neutered.

splay foot foot in which the toes are widely separated and not well knuckled.

spleen lymphoid organ situated in the abdominal
cavity.

splenomegaly abnormal enlargement of the spleen.

split heat SPLIT OESTRUS.

split oestrus OESTRUS in which early signs subside
and recur some weeks later, most likely to occur at
a bitch's first season but occurs sporadically at any
time. Ovulation may not occur.

spondylosis painful degeneration of the spine in
which movement is impaired.

  spondylosis deformans painful, inherited chronic
  lumbar vertebrae disease. (Mode of inheritance,
  familial.)

spontaneous ovulation naturally occurring ovulation
during the OESTROUS CYCLE.

spoon ear BAT EAR. [221]

spoon-shaped foot OVAL FOOT.

Spooner's and West Dartmoor pack formed in 1880
to hunt a Dartmoor COUNTRY.

sport 1. the use of dogs or hounds in pursuit of a
quarry. 2. an animal which unexpectedly differs
from the normal phenotype. 3. (obs.) of a puppy
which differed from others in the litter, as with a
yellow puppy in a litter of black LABRADORs, or
a liver-spotted puppy in a litter of black-spotted
DALMATIANS.

sporting breeds breeds originated for use in sport:
HOUNDS, TERRIERS, and GUNDOGS.

sporting clip one of the traditional CLIPs used on
POODLES.
> In the 'Sporting' clip, a Poodle shall be shown with
> face, feet, throat, and base of tail shaved, leaving a
> scissored cap on the top of the head and a pompom
> on the end of the tail. The rest of the body and legs
> are clipped or scissored to follow the outline of the
> dog, leaving a short blanket of coat no longer than
> one inch long. The hair on the legs may be slightly
> longer than that on the body. [6, POODLE]

Sporting Group 1. [AKC] a number of breeds,
grouped together for the purposes of classification,
which includes those breeds that the AKC consider
to have been developed for sporting purposes. 2.
[KC] of the three groups – GUNDOG, HOUND and
TERRIER – which include those breeds that the KC
currently consider to have been developed for sporting purposes.

The AKC and KC do not entirely agree about
which breeds should be included, and both differ
from the FCI.

spot chestnut mark in the centre of the Blenheim
KING CHARLES SPANIEL's skull.
> Wide, clear blaze with the 'spot' in centre of skull,
> should be a clear chestnut red mark about the size
> of a penny. [203, KING CHARLES SPANIEL]

Spotted Coach Dog DALMATIAN. [186]

spotted fever   fever caused by *Rickettsia rickettsii*, and characterized by skin eruptions. Spotted fever is a generic term which includes Rocky mountain spotted fever and BOUTONNEUSE FEVER.

spotting series   series of genes that gives rise to spotted coats ranging in colour from solid, through IRISH SPOTTING, and PIEBALD to extreme white piebald.

spread   1. the wide chest of a BULLDOG. [103]   2. spaced.

spread foot   foot in which the toes are widely separated and lacking arch.

spread hocks   BOWED HOCKS.

spreader   that part of a SLED-DOG harness which spreads the straps to prevent them from rubbing against a dog's legs.

spring   put birds to flight.
'Why, your dog'll spring all the birds out of shot,' observed Mr Sponge. [344d]

springer   any of those breeds originally intended to SPRING birds either for hawks or to be taken in nets; now used to perform the same function for shooters.

spring gag   instrument used to keep a dog's mouth open to facilitate dentistry.

Springer Spaniel   either one of two SPANIEL breeds used to SPRING game: ENGLISH SPRINGER SPANIEL and WELSH SPRINGER SPANIEL.

Springing Spaniel   (obs.) SPRINGER.
The true English-bred springing spaniel differs but little in figure from the setter, except in size, varying only in a smaller degree, if any, from a red, yellow or liver-coloured and white. They are nearly two-fifths less in height and strength than the setter, delicately formed, ears long, soft, and pliable, coat waving and silky, eyes and nose red or black, the tail somewhat bushy and pendulous, always in motion when actively employed. [348]

spring of rib   degree of arch in the ribcage.

Spring Valley   (US) AMERICAN FOXHOUND pack formed in 1961 to hunt fox and DRAG(2) over a pasture, plough and woodland COUNTRY in New Jersey.

springy action   movement with a pronounced bounce.
Smooth and springy (movement) with style of a high order. [203, AFGHAN HOUND]

springy gait   SPRINGY ACTION.
Free, long-striding, springy gait. [203, LARGE MÜNSTERLÄNDER]

Sproughton   former BEAGLE pack formed in 1909 to hunt a COUNTRY in Suffolk; during the 1916 season the pack was loaned to officers of the 4th Cyclist Brigade and was subsequently destroyed.

sprung   (usu. of rib, also of PASTERNS) *see* SPRING OF RIB.
Fore-ribs moderately sprung, back ribs deep. [203, Smooth Fox Terrier]

spur   1. DEW-CLAW.   2. an otter's footprint.

square head   head with strong, deep MUZZLE and broad skull.

squat   1. low to the ground, having abnormally short legs.   2. crouch, the position adopted by a urinating bitch.

squint   common misnomer for the characteristic expression of the JAPANESE CHIN.
Most desirable that white shows in the inner corners, giving characteristic look of astonishment (wrongly called squint), which should on no account be lost. [203, JAPANESE CHIN]

Squirrel Dog   (colloq.) PAPILLON. (der. translation of the Fr. colloq. term, *Le Chien Ecureuil*, a reference to the breed's PLUMED TAIL and mischievous attitude.)

squirrel tail   tail which is carried parallel with the TOPLINE.

Sredneasiatskaia   Ovtcharka   [FCI]   MID-ASIAN SHEPHERD DOG.

stable dog   a dog of any type, and usually of small or medium size, kept in stables as a GUARD, but more especially in order to control vermin.

Stabyhoun   a Dutch GUNDOG with a broad skull, well-defined STOP and high-set ears. The chest is deep and the back rather long. The coat, which forms FURNISHING on tail and hindquarters, is long, black, chocolate, or orange and white, TICKED or ROAN. Height 50–53cm (19½–20¾in); weight 15–20kg (33–44lb).

stae   1. (obs.) bait animals. [159]   2. (obs.) set dogs upon. [159]

Staff College and Royal Military Academy DRAGHOUND pack formed in 1869 by officers of the Staff College to hunt LINES(2) in Berkshire.

Staffordshire   BEAGLE pack formed in 1929 as the Staffordshire Otterhound Beagles; the name was changed in 1935.

Staffordshire Bull Terrier   [AKC, FCI, KC] a gladiatorial breed developed in the industrialized British Black Country and formerly used for baiting and fighting; nowadays it is an engaging and rightly popular companion and SHOW-DOG though the breed has lost none of its courage, strength or tenacity.

The head is short and deep with a broad skull, strong masseter muscles, pronounced STOP and short MUZZLE; the medium-sized eyes are round and dark, the ears ROSE or half-pricked, the lips CLEAN and tight and the mouth furnished with large, well-placed teeth. The short neck is muscular, the shoulders WELL-LAID and the straight forelegs well-boned; the feet turn slightly outwards. The CLOSE-COUPLED body has deep BRISKET, WELL-SPRUNG RIBS and strong LOINS; hindquarters are well bent and powerful; the PUMP HANDLE TAIL is set low. The short, smooth coat may be red, fawn, white, black or blue, with or without white. Weight 11–17kg (24–37½lb).

stag   1. male deer.   2. six-year-old male deer. [151c]

staggard   four-year-old male deer.
the stag is called . . . the fourth [year], a staggard. [151c]

Staghound   1. HOUND used to hunt deer, including those in surviving packs of stag- and BUCKHOUNDS, although these are often bred from large FOXHOUNDS.
I have no hesitation in asserting that the true Staghound is extinct. [186]

2. (obs.) SCOTCH DEERHOUND. [123].
> By his side jogged a large, iron-grey staghound of most grave demeanour, who took no part in the clamour of the canine rabble. [187]

stained of ground or water that has been disturbed by the passage of HOUNDS or hunt-FOLLOWERS.

Staintondale hunt that was formed, according to tradition, following the gift of a Charter by King John, but no reliable evidence records the event. The COUNTRY runs along the Yorkshire coast and contains both woodland and moorland.

stake competition in which the prize money is made up of a percentage of entry fees.

staked of show at which dogs are fastened to stakes, an alternative to benching: stakes are driven into the ground at convenient intervals.

stake out 1. length of chain along which resting SLED-DOGS are secured at intervals. 2. restrict a dog's freedom by fastening it to a stake.

stale line old and fading scent trail. [344c]

stallion male HOUND or any dog of pronounced masculine appearance.
> The massive quarters and deep ribs were a sign of the stoutness that is so necessary for a real stallion hound. [316]

stance posture, esp. that adopted in the SHOW RING to demonstrate a dog's physical appearance to best advantage.

stanch STAUNCH. [328]

stanchion vertical structural component of a sled.

stand 1. command to a dog to stop in a standing position. 2. (of a bitch) show willingness to be mated by adopting a stance in which the tail is lifted up and to the side and the hindquarters lifted. 3. appointed place in which GUNS stand during a formal shoot.

Standard dim. BREED STANDARD.

Standard German Spitz DEUTSCHER SPITZ.

Standard Mexican Hairless XOLOITZCUINTLE.

Standard Pinscher former KC name for the PINSCHER.

Standard Poodle largest of the three main varieties of POODLE. Height over 38cm (15in).

Standard Schnauzer medium-sized SCHNAUZER.

Standard Smooth-haired Dachshund largest smooth-haired Dachshund.

stand-off (of coat) erect.

stantype (colloq.) type described by the STANDARD.

stapes the ear stirrup.

staphylococci bacteria often implicated in suppurating infections.

star small white mark on the chest.
> White on chest (called 'The Star') [203, PHARAOH HOUND]

staring of a coat in poor condition with a tendency not to lie flat.
> High on their bent backs erect
> Their pointed bristles stare. [328]

Stars of the West EXMOOR.

starter 1. official who gives the signal to start a race. 2. (obs.) 'The Welsh "Spaniel", or "Springer", is also known and referred to in Wales as a "Starter".' [123, quoting Mr Williams of Ynisygerwn]

starting-box TRAP.

starting one off winning or giving the first CC with or to a particular dog.

static balance of weight evenly distributed on all four feet.

station (of SHOW-DOG) place in position, in a manner which will enhance the dog's appearance; set-up.

staunch (of HOUND) reliable; trustworthy; not inclined to riot.

stay command to remain in the same place.

stayer a racing dog capable of winning over long distances.

steady of sporting dogs that stick to the task in hand.

stealer 1. One of the types of dog which FLEMING listed under Venatici but about which he offered no further information. 2. DOG-STEALER. [250]

Steenbrak unrecognized Dutch farm dog. [150]

steep front forequarters in which the upper arm and scapula incline to the vertical.

Steinbracke medium-sized German HOUND with a light, lean head, dark, expressive eyes, broad pendulous ears and a long muscular neck. The chest is deep and the back short and straight, sloping from WITHERS to CROUP. The forelimbs are well boned with elbows turned slightly outwards; hindquarters are broad and muscular with long, moderately angulated legs. The feet are long and oval. The TRICOLOUR coat is dense and hard.

Steirische Rauhhaarige Hochgebirgsbracke [FCI] a rough-coated HOUND with origins in Austria, developed during the last quarter of the 19th century by Herr Peintinger.

The head is fairly long and narrow, with a well-defined STOP; the fairly small, pendulous ears fall close to the cheeks; the chest is not deep but the ribs are carried well back to a strong LOIN; the TOPLINE is level. Forelimbs are straight and the hind limbs muscular and WELL ANGULATED; the STERN is long. The red or WHEATEN coat is rough, hard and wiry. Height 43–53cm (17–20¾in); weight 15–15.5kg (33–38½lb).

Stenezkajapastuschja-Laïka North Russian SAMOYED LAÏKA. [222]

stenosis abnormal constriction of a hollow organ.

stenotic nares narrowing of the nostrils.

Stephen's Cur STEPHEN'S STOCK.

Stephen's Stock unrecognized American HOUND, developed by Hugh Stephens and regarded as a separate mountain cur breed of the early 1970s.

The hound is small and COMPACT but with abundant hound qualities. The sleek, smooth coat is always black, with or without white on the chest. Height 40–59cm (15¾–23¼in); weight 16–25kg (35–55lb).

Steppe Borzoi solid-coloured, short-coated Soviet SIGHTHOUND. Height 61–71cm (24–28in).

stern the tail, most usually of HOUNDs but occasionally of other breeds.
> Their sterns all spirit, cock and feather. [249a]

stern high of a TOPLINE which rises from WITHERS to STERN.
> Others rise in an almost straight line to the root of the tail, and are known as 'stern-high'. [225]

sternal of, or relating to, the STERNUM.

sternal rib true rib; each of the long curved bones that run between the thoracic vertebrae and the STERNUM. [*illus.* SKELETON]

sternum breast bone; BRISKET. [*illus.* SKELETON]

Stevenstone pack dating from prior to 1859 when the hunt was known as the North Devon Hunt; from 1859–1895 and from 1900–1907 it was known as the Hon. Mark Rolle Hunt. The COUNTRY lies in north Devon and is a mixture of pasture, plough and moorland.

steward official appointed to assist in organizing the exhibitors in the show-ring.

Stichelhaar German GUNDOG with a strong family likeness to the GERMAN WIRE-HAIRED POINTER, POINTING GRIFFON and PUDEL POINTER.

The distinctive head is broad, strong and well furnished with brows, moustache and beard; the chest is deep and the TOPLINE slopes from WITHERS to CROUP; the limbs are well boned and muscular. The rough brown and white, ROAN or TICKED coat is thick. Height 56–66cm (22–26in); weight 20kg (44lb).

stickle barrier formed by hunt-FOLLOWERS across a waterway to obstruct an otter's passage. [238a]

Sticker's sarcoma CANINE TRANSMITTABLE VENEREAL TUMOUR.

stifle the knee-joint, the junction between the lower end of the femur and the upper ends of the tibia and fibula. [*illus.* POINTS]

stifle band shaved band between the STIFLE RING and HOCK RING of a POODLE.

stifle ring BRACELET of trimmed hair round the STIFLE of a POODLE.

still-born (of puppy) dead at birth.

stilted (of gait/movement) restricted, straight-legged.

stilty (of conformation) high on the leg and with insufficient ANGULATION.

stimulus generalization the tendency of a response to a certain stimulus being repeated to other similar stimuli.

sting (usu. of a tail) tapering to a sharp point.
> The genuine sort has a tail thick at the root, and gradually tapering to an absolute point, or sting. [186]

stock 1. group of animals used for breeding purposes: breeding stock. 2. livestock.

stock dog 1. (Aust.) SHEEP DOG or cattle-HERDER. 2. (obs.) STUD-DOG.

> I had a little rat dog – a black tan terrier of the name of Billy – which was the greatest stock dog in London of that day. He is the father of the greatest portion of small black tan dogs in London now, which Mr Isaac, the bird-fancier in Princess street, purchased one of the strain for six or seven pounds. [250]

Stockard's paralysis progressive hind-limb weakness, inco-ordination and paralysis.

Stockford (US) private BASSET pack formed in 1913 to hunt hare and cottontail rabbit over a COUNTRY in Pennsylvania.

stockhaarig (esp. of the ST BERNARD) short-coated.
> Coat – Very dense, shorthaired (stockhaarig). [6, ST BERNARD]

stockings white markings which extend up the legs as far as the elbow or above the STIFLE.

Stockton Foot Harriers LARTINGTON.

Stoke Hill former 14½in BEAGLE pack formed in 1912 to hunt a COUNTRY in Somerset.

Stokesley Farmers' BEAGLE pack formed in 1937 to hunt a COUNTRY in north Yorkshire.

Stonehenge John Henry WALSH.

stones (colloq.) TESTICLES.

Stonewall Irish HARRIER pack formed in 1912 to hunt a COUNTRY in County Limerick.

stool faeces.

stoop (of HOUNDs) hunt with their MUZZLEs on the ground.

stop 1. depression at the bridge of the nose. [*illus.* POINTS]
> There must be no 'stop', the line from occiput to nose end straight and unbroken. [203, BEDLINGTON TERRIER]
> The amount of stop can best be described as moderate. [6, ENGLISH SPRINGER SPANIEL]

2. deliberately block an earth. 3. (usu. of GREYHOUNDs) prevent from running by illicit means, usually involving the administering of a drug.

stop-hound HOUND that hunts slowly. [70]

stopper pad CARPAL PAD.

Storrington BRIGHTON FOOT.

stout STAUNCH. [47]

stövare (Scandinavian) SCENTHOUND.

stove up of a SLED-DOG which is lamed during work.

Stowe a school BEAGLE pack formed in 1962 to hunt an extensive COUNTRY in Northamptonshire and Buckinghamshire.

Strabane 1. pack founded in 1948 to hunt a COUNTRY in Counties Donegal and Tyrone. 2. former Irish HARRIER pack formed in 1863 and amalgamated thirty years later with the Derry Harriers.

strabismus ocular defect; a squint.

straight back TOPLINE which neither dips nor rises along its length, though the straight line may not be parallel with the ground.

straightbred PEDIGREE(3) animal.

straight front forequarters in which the forelegs are vertical, parallel and straight.

straight hock a HOCK-joint that lacks ANGULATION.

straight-running WHIPPET and TERRIER racing on a short straight racetrack.
> Somehow, straight running, as the sport for which the Whippet is chiefly used is called, did not catch on in the South as it already had in the North. [123]

straight shoulder UPRIGHT SHOULDER.

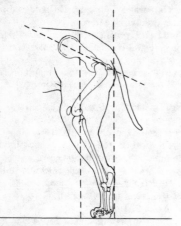

Straight stifle.

straight stifle STIFLE lacking ANGULATION. [*illus.*]

strain group of dogs in which there is a strong family resemblance resulting from interlinked relationships through several generations.

strangles JUVENILE PYODERMA.

stray dog of no fixed abode or, in legal terms, one that cannot be identified.

street (of racing dog) win by a considerable margin by means of sheer speed.
> The Irish dog had literally streeted his four opponents, and run in devastating style. [91]

street dog dog which habitually wanders the streets; 'latch-key dogs'.
> To which may be added the dogs called street dogs, which resemble no particular kind, because they proceed from races which have previously been several times mixed. [72]

Strellufstöver a short-legged Danish HOUND developed by Christian Frandsen during the early years of the 20th century.
> A short-legged, long-bodied hound with a deep chest, long tail and harsh coat of any HOUND COLOUR. Height 30–38cm (12–15in).

strene (obs.) canine copulation. [159]

Streptococci aerobic bacteria responsible for a wide range of sickness, including septicaemia, strangles, food poisoning and pneumonia.

stride distance covered by one foot in the process of a single step.

strip remove excessive hair, usually with a STRIPPING KNIFE. *See also* PLUCK.

Striped-tail Dog CANIS EUROSTICTIS.

stripping knife sharp-bladed and toothed instrument used to facilitate the removal of unwanted coat.

stroke (of hunting OTTERHOUNDS) full pace.

strong-eyed of a SHEEP DOG that causes sheep to move by staring at them in a threatening manner.
> My father taught me how to prevent the several faults that the strong-eyed young dog will assuredly make if not taken in time. [227]

strunt (obs.) tail.
> ''s a pretty little dog! 's a pretty little doggy! – ay! – yes! – he is, yes! – Wag thy strunt, then! Wag thy strunt, Rexie!' [219]

Stuart-Prower anaemia STUART-PROWER SYNDROME.

Stuart-Prower syndrome inherited clotting deficiency leading to serious bleeding in neonates. (Mode of inheritance, dominant.)

stub inherited spinal abnormalities, including an abnormally short tail and spina bifida. (Mode of inheritance, dominant.)

stub-bred of fox that is born and reared above ground. [235]
> And is it not proverbial that what are called stub-bred foxes are generally stoutest runners? [266b]

stubby of an unusually short tail, whether naturally so or DOCKED.

stud 1. breeding establishment. 2. male used for breeding.

stud-dog STUD(2).

stud fee payment made for the services of a STUD-DOG.

Stud Book 1. (of kennel clubs) publication, usually annual, which provides details of the breeding, date of birth and breeder of elite registered animals. 2. (of ISDS) publication listing all BORDER COLLIE/WORKING SHEEP DOGS registered.

Stud Book Number the unique number allocated to a dog listed in the STUD BOOK.

stump naturally short tail.
> Disqualifications. Tail cropped or stump. [6, BELGIAN TERVUEREN]

stumpointed (obs.) of a frightened rabbit that runs towards the dogs. [159]

Stumpytail Cattle Dog tailless variety of the AUSTRALIAN CATTLE DOG.

Stuttgart disease CANINE LEPTOSPIROSIS.

style PRESENCE.

Styrian Rough-haired Mountain Hound STEIRISCHE RAUHHAARIGE HOCHGEBIRGSBRACKE.

subacute of relatively short duration; intermediate between acute and chronic.

sub-aortic stenosis AORTIC SUBVALVULAR STENOSIS.

subclinical without obvious symptoms, often the early stages of a disease or a mild form of it.

subcutaneous under the skin.

subluxation partial dislocation.

subscription pack pack of HOUNDS maintained by the subscriptions of FOLLOWERS.
> After the death of Thomas Humble in 1841 the old trencher fed Prudhoe Hounds had a temporary rise in the world and, under the Mastership of Thomas Ramsay, became a subscription pack. [101]

substance good development in which the body is strongly built.

subvital gene gene that reduces the vigour of the individual without producing any other apparent effect.

sucking fits (obs.) ECLAMPSIA. [46]

Sudan Greyhound extinct Sudanese small coursing HOUND. [150]

sudden acquired retinal degeneration atrophy of the retina in mature dogs, resulting in blindness. Cause unknown.

suffix kennel name which appears after the dog's individual name, usually indicative that the owner is not the breeder.

Suffolk pack whose COUNTRY was hunted by the Duke of Grafton from about 1845.

Suliot Dog extinct type of BOARHOUND.
> The Suliot dog is one of the largest breeds known. In the war between the Austrians and the Turks, the Moslem soldiers employed many to guard the outposts . . . One of these was presented to the King of Naples, and was reputed to be the largest dog in the world, being little less than four feet high at the shoulder. [393]

Sumatra Battak BATTAK.

Sumatra Wild Dog BATTAK.
> . . . possessing the countenance of a fox, the eyes oblique, the ears rounded and hairy, the muzzle of a foxy-brown colour, the tail bushy and pendulous, very lively, running with the head lifted high, and the ears straight. [406]

summit the highest part of the skull.
> Ears . . . continuing the outline across the summit. [6, MASTIFF]

Sun Dog golden, red-coated version of the PEKINGESE.

sunken pastern DOWN IN PASTERN.

Sunnyland Irish 16in BEAGLE pack formed in 1915 to hunt a COUNTRY in County Down.

Sunnylands Beagles former Irish 14½in BEAGLE pack formed to hunt a COUNTRY in County Down.

Suomenajokoira [FCI] FINNISH HOUND.

Suomenpystykorva [FCI] FINNISH SPITZ.

superfeotation production of multiple offspring at one parturition which result from ova released and fertilized at different times.

superficial pigmentary keratitis abnormal pigmentation of the cornea owing to chronic keratitis. Seen mainly in BRACHYCEPHALIC breeds.

superovulation production, often artificially induced, of an unusually large number of ova.

suppuration the exuding of pus.

Supreme Champion Non-existent title much used by advertisers, usually to refer to the Best in Show winner at Crufts Dog Show.

Surrey Farmers' former DRAGHOUND pack.

Surrey Union pack dating from 1799; the bank and ditch COUNTRY contains extensive woodlands.

survival value the measure of a characteristic's influence over the survival of the individual and, therefore, of its offspring.

suspended trot fast trot with a long stride resulting in the hind feet striking the ground in front of the forefeet; because all four feet are momentarily off the ground together there appears to be a slight hesitation at each half stride.
> A suspended trot, which is a long far-reaching stride, with a slight hover before placing foot to ground. [203, IBIZAN HOUND]

suspension the instant when all feet are off the ground at trot.

Sussex Spaniel [AKC, FCI, KC] a determined and tireless worker of dense cover, this distinctive English SPANIEL is also a well-mannered companion who lacks the flightiness of some other more popular GUNDOG breeds.

The overall appearance is one of massive solidity combined with energy and activity. The skull is wide and slightly DOMED with MEDIAN FURROW and pronounced STOP; the large eyes are hazel in colour and show little HAW; the low-set ears are thick, lobular and lie close to the skull. The strong, slightly arched neck is long with slight throatiness, the forequarters sloping with strong, rather short forelimbs with large knees and short, sloping PASTERNS. The chest is deep, the back and LOIN strong. The hindquarters are muscular with large HOCKS, the round feet are well padded; the low-set tail is traditionally DOCKED. The flat, abundant coat is of a rich golden liver colour. Height 38–41cm (15–16in); weight 23kg (50½lb).

Svart Norsk Älghund black-coated variety of the ELKHOUND, seldom seen outside Scandinavia.

Swaledale former HARRIER pack formed about 1790 to hunt an extensive moorland COUNTRY in Yorkshire.

swamp back back with a decidedly concave TOPLINE.
> Some dogs dip very considerably some distance behind the shoulders before the upward curve of the spine begins, and these are known as 'swampbacked'. [225]

swan neck GOOSE NECK.

Sway back.

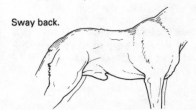

sway back concave TOPLINE. [*illus.*]
> Roach and sway backs highly undesirable. [203, BULLMASTIFF]
> Excessively long, roached or swayed back must be penalized. [6, GERMAN SHORT-HAIRED POINTER]

sweat gland gland which secretes perspiration. In the dog these are largely confined to the tongue and feet; sweating is not an important means of losing heat in dogs.

Swedish Beagle small HOUND used to drive hares to the GUNs. [320a]

Swedish Cattle Dog SWEDISH VALLHUND.

Swedish Dachsbracke DREVER.

Swedish Elkhound JÄMTHUND.

Swedish Grey Dog GRAHUND. [312]

Swedish Herder Spitz SWEDISH VALLHUND. [312]

Swedish Lapphund LAPPHUND.

Swedish Lapp Spitz LAPPHUND.

Swedish Vallhund [KC] a CORGI-like dog which also shares a common purpose and, in all probability, a common ancestry with those breeds.

A relatively short-legged and long-bodied dog, which displays vigilance, physical courage and great energy. The head is broad, lean and vulpine, with ricked, pointed ears, oval, dark brown, expressive eyes and a strong MUZZLE. The neck is long and proudly carried, the shoulders long and *well* ANGULATED, the forelegs straight; the chest is broad and deep, the ribs fairly WELL SPRUNG; the TOPLINE is level with a short, powerful CROUP. The tail is naturally short, never more than 10cm (4in) in length. The shaded grey coat is hard and dense with a good undercoat. Height 33–41cm (13–16in); weight 9–14kg (20–31lb).

Swift Fox *VULPES VELOX.*

swimmer FLAT PUPPY SYNDROME.

swine-chopped (obs. except among HOUND breeders) OVERSHOT.

> Never breed from a 'Swine chopped' hound – it is also very hereditary. [235]
> Ideally, should such a mouth be discovered among a litter of whelps they should all be put down and a note made of the line to be avoided. . . . It is extremely important for the future of Foxhound Breeding that swine chops should not be perpetuated, and no hound with this defect, however good in its work, should be bred from. [257]

swing dog each of the two dogs that run immediately behind the leader in a sled team.

swinging action movement in which the legs are brought forward without perceptible flexion.

> Legs carried straight forward with a swift long tireless swinging action. [203, BASENJI]

Swiss Hound SCHWEIZERISCHER LAUFHUND.

Swiss Laufhund SCHWEIZERISCHER LAUFHUND.

swivel part of the spring-clip to which the lead is attached, and which prevents twisting.

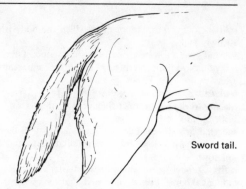

Sword tail.

sword tail long thick tail, tapering at the tip and carried straight, either up or down, as seen in the LABRADOR RETRIEVER. [*illus.*]

swore (obs.) snarl. [159]

Sydney Silky AUSTRALIAN SILKY TERRIER.

Sydney Silky Terrier AUSTRALIAN SILKY TERRIER.

sylvatic rabies that form of rabies which tends to occur among the inhabitants of woodland, including foxes and wolves.

symbiosis two or more species living together for mutual benefit. (Some authorities include parasitism in which benefit is not mutual.)

symmetrical of SYMMETRY.

> Hounds of three kinds are kept for the hunting of hares by scent – dwarf Foxhound bitches, rough Welsh Harriers (many of them of surpassing excellence), and the true Harrier, which is a dwarf Southern Hound, and in the present day quite as symmetrical, muscular, and perfect as the Foxhound. [186]

symmetry balance of all parts in which there is good proportion and no exaggeration.

> Taller the better, provided symmetry is maintained. [203, ST BERNARD]

syndrome combination of symptoms which tend to occur together or have a single cause.

synergist agent which acts in co-operation with, or enhances the effect of, another.

synovial fluid lubricant within a joint secreted by the synovial membrane.

systematic desensitization method of treating fear and anxiety by inducing an inappropriate response to the cause of the fear or anxiety.

T

T gene symbol for TICKING. [395]
tab ear flap; leather.
table-top back broad and level back.
tachycardia abnormally rapid heart beat.

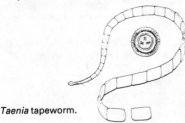

Taenia tapeworm.

Taenia genus of large TAPEWORMS, which includes the seven species commonly found in dogs. [*illus.*]
Taenia brauni probably a subspecies of *TAENIA SERIALIS* and with a similar lifecycle.
Taenia hydatigena species of tapeworm found in the small intestine of dogs, which excretes gravid segments that are picked up by sheep and goats in which the larva forms cysts in the brain, viscera and muscles. The cycle is completed when dogs eat uncooked meat. People eating or handling meat which has not been properly cooked may also ingest larvae which may then form potentially life-threatening cysts.
Taenia krabbei species of tapeworm which has a lifecycle in which the larval form is found in cysts in the muscles of wild ruminants. These are passed to dogs and other canids which have contact with infected animals; in the dog the worms mature and excrete gravid segments which are, in turn, picked up by wild ruminants.
Taenia lycaontis species of *Taenia* specific to wild dogs.
Taenia multiceps species of tapeworm which has a lifecycle in which the larval form is found in cysts in the brain and spinal cord of sheep and goats. These are passed to dogs and other canids which have contact with infected animals; in the dog the worms mature and excrete gravid segments which are, in turn, picked up by sheep and goats.
Taenia ovis species of tapeworm which has a lifecycle in which the larval form is found in cysts in the heart and skeleton of sheep and goats. These are passed to dogs and other canids which have contact with infected animals; in the dog the worms then mature and excrete gravid segments which are, in turn, picked up by sheep and goats.
Taenia pisiformis species of tapeworm which has a lifecycle in which the larval form is found in cysts in the liver and peritoneal cavity of hares and rabbits. These are passed to dogs and other canids which have contact with infected animals; in the dog the worms

mature and excrete gravid segments which are, in turn, picked up by hares and rabbits.
Taenia serialis species of tapeworm which has a lifecycle in which the larval form is found in cysts in the abdomen of hares and rabbits. These are passed to dogs and other canids which have contact with infected animals; in the dog the worms mature and excrete gravid segments which are, in turn, picked up by hares and rabbits.
taeniacide substance that kills tapeworms.
taeniafuge substance that produces the expulsion of tapeworms.
taeniasis tapeworm infestation.
TAF abbr. TRANSFER APPLIED FOR.
Taffy (colloq.) WELSH TERRIER.
taffy grooming compound illicitly used to enhance the colour of some show TERRIERS.
tag 1. the tip of the tail. 2. identity disc worn on the collar.
Tagan TAIGAN.
Tahl-Tan Bear Dog native North American Indian dog developed for hunting bear and other large game. Now possibly extinct as a pure breed but still among the breeds recognized by the Canadian Kennel Club. The breed had no firm type.

The head was usually a broad wedge, with either PRICK or DROP EARS. The body was sturdy and agile, the back rather long; the proudly carried, BRUSH-like tail was a distinctive feature of the breed. The coat was thick and weather-resistant, usually black patched on white or, less often, tan on white. Height 30.5–38cm (12¼–15in); weight up to 6.5–7kg (14½–15½lb).
Taigan SIGHTHOUND developed on the borders between Mongolia and China. The breed is remarkably similar to the SALUKI and is principally used for COURSING small game. Height 56–71cm (22–28in).
tail 1. that part of the spine consisting of the caudal vertebrae, which extends beyond the CROUP. 2. rear, esp. of HOUND pack; remove hounds to the rear of the pack. 3. catch and lift a quarry, esp. badger, by the tail. 4. DOCK. [406]
tail chasing neurotic or playful behaviour in which a dog chases its own tail.
tail gland hyperplasia alopecia and moist dermatitis of the root and anterior part of the tail, probably resulting from hormonal imbalances.
tail feather FEATHER.
tail set precise relationship between tail and body.
tail hounds HOUNDS that run at the rear of the pack.

> Halloos seldom do any hurt, when you are running up the wind; for then none but the tail hounds can hear you. [47]

tail short inherited abnormally short tail. (Mode of inheritance, probably dominant.)

tail, types of BEE-STING, BOBBED, CARROT, CHRYSANTHEMUM, COCK, COIN, CORKSCREW, CRANK, DOCKED, FLAG, FLAGPOLE, GAWCIE, GAY, KINK, OTTER, PIPESTOPPER, PLUME, POT-HOOK, SABRE, SCIMITAR, SCREW, SQUIRREL, STERN.

Talbot variously described as the extinct white version of what has now become the BLOODHOUND or as a peripatetic GUARD.

> Although many writers have endeavoured to find the origin of the bloodhound in the Talbot of ancient days, there is no reason to believe that the former had as great a connecting link with the latter as the foxhound with other hounds, of both this country and of the Continent. [221]
> The Normans brought to this country a big, upstanding hunting dog known as the Talbot hound, forerunner of those Talbot hounds which were used in medieval England as guards for the pack-trains of merchandise which crossed and re-crossed England. [383]

Talley House former HARRIER pack formed in 1906 to hunt a COUNTRY in Shropshire and Powys.

Tall Hungarian Hound TALL TRANSYLVANIAN HOUND.

Tallow Irish BEAGLE pack formed in 1957 to hunt a COUNTRY in Counties Waterford and Cork.

Tall Transylvanian Hound black-and-tan, short, coarse-coated Hungarian HOUND. Height 56–66cm (22–26in); weight 30–35kg (66–77lb).

talus proximal TARSUS BONE.

Talybont pack dating from 1929, whose COUNTRY lies in Powys.

Tamar Valley BEAGLE pack formed in 1960 to hunt a COUNTRY in Cornwall.

tan reddish brown.

tan brindle BRINDLE patterning in which the underlying colour is a shade of tan.

tan pattern usually associated with black but sometimes with a darker shade of tan, in which tan is confined to a spot on each cheek and above each eye, to the MUZZLE, under jaw and throat, chest, lower limbs, the vent and underside of the tail.

Tanheath (US) BEAGLE pack formed in 1958 to hunt cottontail rabbit over a COUNTRY in Massachusetts.

Tanatside the Powys COUNTRY has been hunted by a HARRIER pack, known as the Confederate Hunt, since about 1754; in 1795 the Rev. T. Lloyd and his son hunted a pack known as the Oswestry Corporation Hounds. From 1828 the pack became known as the Tanat Side Harriers, which hunted fox from 1926 when David Davies introduced a DRAFT of Welsh Foxhounds. Harriers were given up in 1928.

Tanat Side Harriers TANATSIDE.

tandem selection (of breeding) method of selection in which priority is given to different characteristics in turn.

taneous (of the head, esp. terriers') coffin-shaped.

Tank Corps Basset Hounds former BASSET pack formed in 1919 to hunt a COUNTRY in Dorset.

tapering head head that uniformly narrows from skull to MUZZLE.

tapering jaw jaw that narrows from STOP to nose.

tapetum covering of a group of cells.

tapetum lucidum reflective layer at the back of the eye.

tapeworm cestode; a group of parasitic worms, segmented, flattened, ribbon-like, affecting various animals including dogs. The genera most commonly affecting dogs are *DIPYLIDIUM, ECHINOCOCCUS, TAENIA*.

Tara Irish HARRIER pack formed at the beginning of the 19th century as the Bellinter Harriers.

tarier (obs.) TERRIER. [159]

tarre (obs.) urge dogs to fight.

> Arth: And like a dog that is compell'd to fight,
> Snatch at his master that doth tarre him on. [319n]

tartar of a dog, most often a TERRIER, which is indiscriminately aggressive.

Tasy SIGHTHOUND developed on the Kirhiz Steppe and principally used for hunting small game. Remarkably similar in every respect to the SALUKI. Height 56–71cm (22–28in).

Tatra Mountain Sheep Dog OWCZAREK PODALANSKI.

Tatra Sheep Dog OWCZAREK PODALANSKI.

Tatra Shepherd OWCZAREK PODALANSKI.

Taunton Vale the banked Somerset COUNTRY is largely grass but also contains large woodlands and has been hunted since 1876.

taut coat short, close coat over a tight-fitting skin.

tavele TICKED or ROANED. [*115]

tawny light tan.

> The beest hewe of rennyng houndes and moost common for to be good is iclepid broun tawne. [125]

Tawny Brittany Basset BASSET FAUVE DE BRETAGNE.

Taw Vale BEAGLE pack formed in 1962 to hunt a COUNTRY in Devon.

Tay-sach's disease GANGLIOSIDOSIS GM2.

Tazi AFGHAN HOUND.

TD abbr. pref. suffix. TRACKING DOG.

TDEx TRACKING DOG EXCELLENT.

team abbr. suffix. more than two dogs, esp. SLED-DOGS, usually of the same breed, working in unison.

team dog one of a team.

tarsal of, or relating to, the TARSUS.

tarsal bones *see* TARSUS.

tarsal pad CARPAL PAD.

tarsus the HOCK or ankle joint, which lies between the upper end of the cannon bone (metatarsus) and the lower end of the tibia; the seven bones from which this is composed. [*illus*. SKELETON]

TBC Hunt abbr. TINTAGEL, BOSCASTLE AND CAMELFORD HUNT.

Tchiorny Terrier [FCI] a russian DOMESTIC GUARD and vermin killer.

The strong head is heavily FURNISHED, the V-shaped ears are pricked, and the body strong and square. The PEPPER AND SALT coat is coarse and fairly long. Height 63.5–71cm (25–28in).

TCP CANINE EHRLICHIOSIS.

teapot tail   tail which is carried in an upward curve but which drops towards its end.

> Failing this, breeders find they have that greatest trouble to the Gordon breeder, the 'teapot' tail or a long stern with a curl at the end, badly carried in action. [37]

tear-staining syndrome   dark brown stains running from the inner corner of the eyes and caused by excessive production of fluid from the tear glands, most often seen in BRACHYCEPHALIC or breeds with profuse facial hair.

teaser   1. IN-SEASON female used to stimulate a dog to provide semen for use in artificial insemination.   2. (obs.) type of HOUND. [159]

teat   mammary gland.

teazer   TEASER.

Techichi   extinct Central American progenitor of the CHIHUAHUA, thought to have been heavy boned, long coated and mute.

> A much more likely story of the origin of the Chihuahua breed is that it was derived from a prior breed known as the Techichi, which the Toltecs of the seventh century took over from the yet earlier culture of the Mayans. [84]

Teckel   DACHSHUND. [123]

Teddy-bear Dog   (colloq.) CHOW CHOW.

Tedworth   hunt founded in 1826 by Assheton Smith; the Wiltshire and Hampshire COUNTRY contains a great deal of downland.

teehokois   dog or dogs. [280] (Partridge speculatively suggests a corruption of Iroquois, presumably a reference to dog soldiers.)

Tees Valley   BEAGLE pack founded on the basis of the former Durham Light Infantry Beagles, formed in 1850 to hunt a COUNTRY in Yorkshire.

teeth   DENTITION.

teething   the process during which the teeth erupt.

telangiectisasis   abnormal distension of blood cells within an organ.

telegony   discredited theory which suggests that the sire of a previous litter will exert influence over subsequent litters by different sires.

Telemonian   Malaysian aboriginal breed used as a DOMESTIC GUARD, a vermin-killer and as a dietary supplement. The breed is an accomplished climber and shares with the BASENJI, which the breed closely resembles, the inability to bark.

   The head is vulpine and wrinkled with slightly rounded PRICK EARS, the back is rather long and the tail long and straight. The coat is short and smooth, usually SABLE or tan and white. Height 38–48cm (15–18¾in); weight 8–13kg (17½–28½lb).

telophase   final stage in mitosis and meiosis.

Teme Valley   pack dating from 1892; the hunt occupies a pasture, woodland and downland COUNTRY in Shropshire, Herefordshire and Powys.

temperature   dog's normal body temperature is 38.3–38.7°C (100.9–101.7°F).

tender-mouthed   of a GUNDOG that retrieves without damaging the bird.

Tenerife Dog   BICHON FRISE.

tenesmus   ineffectual straining to pass excreta.

tenter   (regional Eng.) DOMESTIC GUARD dog; a dog which barks at intruders and thereby takes care of the home.

Tepeizeuintli   XOLOIZCUINTLE.

teratogenic agent   any influence which results in defective embryos.

term   duration of pregnancy, in dogs sixty-three days after conception.

terminal crossbreeding   production of an F1 generation without further CROSSBREEDING.

terminal ring   the curl at the end of the tail in some breeds.

Termino Hound   one of the three types of BASSET HOUND identified when the breed was first introduced to Britain. They were light TRICOLOURS, lemon-and-white, or blue-MOTTLED, with strongly ROMAN NOSES and slightly higher on the leg than the other types. [123]

teroures   Dame Juliana Berner's spelling of TERRIERS, suggestive of the possibility that the word may have the same root as terrify rather than *terra*.

terrarius   TERRIER. [139]

terrier   type of dog intended to harass or kill its quarry, sometimes used as an adjunct to HOUNDs, as a destroyer of vermin, or for gladiatorial purposes.

> Another sort there is which hunts the Fox and the Badger or Grey only, whom we call Terriers. [139]
> Not many years ago, any dog under 35 lbs. in weight, provided he had his ears cut short, was called a Terrier, unless his owner preferred describing him as a Bull Terrier, a Bulldog, or a Pug. [186]

terrier couplings   COUPLINGS(2).

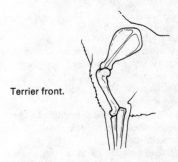

Terrier front.

terrier front   having short and almost vertical upper arms and a tendency to tied-in shoulders. Undesirable in some terriers. [*illus.*]

terrier man   person employed by a HUNT(2) to take charge of the TERRIERS and to supervise their work.

terrier pad   flat brush with short, stiff bristles, often of metal, used to groom hard-coated TERRIERS.

terrier trials   tests of the ability of TERRIERS to work below ground, sometimes conducted as competitions.

The 'earth' for terrier trials should be a wooden conduit (or shore as we say in Ireland) of square section, the inside measurement being 7½in wide. It is to be sunk in the earth so as to be entirely covered, no light being allowed to penetrate. In order that it may resemble the real thing as much as possible, the tunnel should follow a winding course with many angles. . . . The whole length of the earth should be not less than 50ft. [270]

Terrier Brasiliero typical, fairly long-bodied, finely boned TERRIER with a broad skull, DROP EARS, well-defined STOP and rather SNIPY MUZZLE. The smooth coat is always TRICOLOUR with white predominant. Weight about 6.5–9kg (14½–20lb).

Terrier Noir Russe CHORNYI.

territorial aggression behaviour instigated by a desire to defend what is regarded as home territory.

Terry former long-legged TERRIER of Scottish origin, now extinct.

The old hard and short-haired 'Terry' of the West of Scotland was much nearer in shape to a modern Fox-terrier, though with a shorter and rounder head, the colour of his hard, wiry coat mostly sandy, the face free from long hair, although some show a beard, and the small ears carried in most instances semi-erect, in some pricked. [128]

tertiary sex ratio number of males at puberty expressed as a percentage of the number of females.

Tervueren [FCI] one of four varieties of BELGIAN SHEPHERD DOG.

Tetcott founded in 1896 to hunt a grassland COUNTRY in Cornwall.

tesing (obs.) RINGWORM. [159]

test cross BACKCROSS mating carried out in order to gather information.

test mating mating carried out with the primary intention of gathering information by assessing the results.

testes pl. TESTIS.

testicle TESTIS.

testicular of, or relating to, TESTICLE.

  testicular feminization inherited tendency in males to have female sex organs. (Mode of inheritance, probably sex linked.)

testis male reproductive gland, which produces testosterone and spermatozoa.

testosterone sex hormone produced in the testes and responsible for the development of male physical and behavioural characteristics.

tetanus fatal disease caused by bacteria in which the facial muscles become paralysed. Also called lockjaw.

tetraplegia paralysis of all four limbs.

tetrology of Fallot inherited lethal multiple defect of the heart. (Mode of inheritance, threshold.)

Texan Wolf *CANIS NIGER SEU RUFUS.*

Texas Fever BABESIOSIS.

Thai Ridgeback Dog Thai DOMESTIC GUARD, probably now extinct in its homeland.

The breed has a broad, vulpine head with sharply pricked ears, and a long, deep-chested back; the tail

is SCIMITAR-shaped. The coat is short and smooth, fawn, black or blue, with black MASK and white on chest and lower legs. The distinguishing ridge of contra-growth hair begins between two rosettes of hair over the WITHERS and continues along the spine to end between the HUCKLE BONES. Height 56–66cm (22–26in); weight 23–34kg (50½–75lb).

Thambai Indian SIGHTHOUND principally used for COURSING hare.

Thanet and Herne 1. hunt whose Kent COUNTRY contains large woodlands, much pasture and some marshland; it has been hunted intermittently since 1873. 2. former HARRIER pack formed in 1762 as the Thanet Harriers; the Isle of Thanet pack was formed in 1813 and in 1895 amalgamation of the two packs brought the change to the present name.

Thelazia californiensis parasitic worm which invades the tear ducts and conjunctiva.

Thelazia callipaeda parasitic worm which invades the tear ducts and conjunctiva.

theobromine toxic substance found in chocolate and cocoa waste products, to which some dogs, as well as other animals, have a low level of tolerance.

thermoreceptor nerve ending stimulated by variations in temperature.

Thibet Dog TIBETAN MASTIFF. [338]

Thibet Mastiff TIBETAN MASTIFF.

In general contour they bear a resemblance to our English Mastiff, although the rough, dense coat and black colour form a strong contrast [with] our home breed. [338]

thick set (of body) squat, broad and solidly built.

Thievish Dog possibly LURCHER. [139]

the thievish Dog, which at the mandate and bidding of his master steers and leers abroad in the night, hunting Coneys by the air. [139]

thigh area between hip and STIFLE.

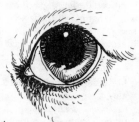

Third eyelid.

third eyelid rudimentary eyelid in the inner corner of each eye. [*illus.*]

thoracic of, or relating to, the THORAX.

  thoracic vertebrae those vertebrae that form that part of the spine between the cervical and lumbar vertebrae, and which provide attachment for the ribs. [*illus.* SKELETON]

  thoracic limb the forelimb.

  thoracic-lumbar disc disease inherited various vertebrae problems. (Mode of inheritance, complex.)

  thoracic hemivertebrae inherited anomaly in which

one side of the thoracic vertebrae are under developed. (Mode of inheritance, recessive.)

thorax   the part of the body – excluding limbs – between the neck and the abdomen.

Thornton Terrier   extinct, extremely RACY type of TERRIER created by Colonel Thomas Thornton.

thoroughbred   (of appearance) redolent of quality.

Thorpe Satchville   former BEAGLE pack formed to hunt a COUNTRY in Leicestershire.

threshold   character   polygenically   determined characteristic which appears abruptly.

throatiness   (of the throat) having loose flesh; DEWLAP.

> Neck long and strong, set into well laid shoulders, without throatiness. [203, PETIT BASSET GRIFFON VENDÉEN]
> Neck . . . free from throatiness. [6, IRISH SETTER]

throaty   of THROATINESS.

thrombastenia   inherited blood clotting deficiency. (Mode of inheritance, dominant.)

Thrombicula autumnale   harvest mite: one species of the family Thrombiculidae.

Thrombiculidae   family of acarine mites including *Thrombicula autumnale*, and which are one cause of digital dermatitis.

thrombocythaemia   inherited increase in the number of blood platelets. (Mode of inheritance, uncertain.)

thrombocytopenia   decrease   in   the   number   of platelets in the blood, a condition that may be drug-induced   or   resulting   from   an   auto-immune dysfunction.

thrombocytosis   THROMBOCYTHAEMIA.

thrombopathia   blood disorder characterized by poor blood coagulation, resulting from the failure of platelets to release the necessary agent.

thrombus   accumulation of blood within the vascular system.

throw   stamp; produce invariably. Of dog or bitch whose offspring invariably carry some particular quality.

throw back   young that bears strong resemblance to some ancestor. [123] Unexpected outcome of a mating, which is the product of some recessive characteristic carried by both parents.

throwing coat   shedding dead coat; moulting.

throwing tongue   (usu. of HOUNDS or TERRIERS) giving voice.

> He does his best to find a fox; throws his tongue when he is sure he has found him, and not before. [266b]

thrown out with the rubbish   (of a SHOW-DOG) rejected by the judge at a show as unworthy of any prize.

throw off   set HOUNDS to begin hunting.

> We found a hare in a few minutes after throwing off. [92]

throw up   lose the scent.

> They were running gaily, when suddenly they threw up. Backwards and forwards they cast, but they could make nothing of it. [318]

thrust of hock   DRIVE.

thumb mark   clearly defined black spot on the PASTERN, toes or chin.

> All above colours have black pencilling on toes without thumb marks. [203, MINIATURE PINSCHER]
> The Blenheim often carries a thumb mark or 'Blenheim spot' placed on the top and the centre of the skull. [6, ENGLISH TOY SPANIEL]

Thuringia Pinscher   former name for the DOBERMANN, changed on Louis Dobermann's death in 1984.

thyroid gland   largest of the endocrine glands situated in the neck which produces a hormone essential to normal growth and metabolism.

thyroiditis   inherited thyroid inflammation. (Mode of inheritance, familial.)

thyroxine   hormone produced by the thyroid gland.

Tibetan Apso   LHASA APSO.

Tibetan Dog   TIBETAN MASTIFF.

Tibetan Fox   *VULPES FERRILATA.*

Tibetan Mastiff   [KC] an ancient and impressive, heavily coated MOLOSSAN breed with origins in the Asian uplands. The breed comes to maturity very slowly and is an aloof but determined GUARD.

The head is broad and strong with a massive skull, well-defined OCCIPUT and STOP; the MUZZLE is fairly broad and strong with moderate FLEWS. The wide-set eyes are dark brown and expressive, the triangular ears pendulous and low set; the neck is muscular, arched and well MANEd, the forequarters WELL LAID and the limbs straight with sloping PASTERNS. The back is straight and muscular, the chest deep and the powerfully muscled hindquarters WELL ANGULATED. The CAT FEET are large and well FEATHERED. The tail is set high and carried over the back. The DOUBLE COAT is long and thick and may be black, black and tan, brown, or shades of gold and grey. Height, bitches more than 61cm (24in); dogs more than 66cm (26in).

Tibetan Sand Fox   *VULPES FERRILATA.*

Tibetan Spaniel   [AKC, FCI, KC] neither a true SPANIEL nor with any discernible connection to Spain, the Tibetan Spaniel is a snub-nosed TOY breed with characteristics to be found in several breeds of oriental origin. The breed is said to have originally been used as a religious counterpart of the British TURNSPIT, to turn prayer wheels rather than a roasting joint.

The breed is small, active and alert. The DOMED head with its slight STOP and medium-length MUZZLE is small but carried proudly; the eyes are dark and forward facing, the pendulous ears are of medium size. The short neck is strong and set in slightly bowed forequarters, the body is rather long, the PLUMED tail curls over the back. The coat is silky with MANE and FEATHERING being important features. All colours and combinations of colours are permitted. Height 25.4cm (10in); weight 4.1–6.8kg (9–14lb).

Tibetan Terrier   [AKC, FCI, KC] an Eastern

domestic and monastic companion, with little, if any, link with TERRIERS or their customary vocations.

The breed is sturdy, lively and good-natured with a skull of moderate width, marked STOP, large expressive, round eyes and V-shaped, heavily FEATHERED ears. The forequarters are heavily feathered, the shoulders flat and the legs straight; the body is muscular, COMPACT and square in outline; the HOCKS are low set and the STIFLES well bent. The fairly high set, well-feathered tail is of medium length and carried over the back. The DOUBLE COAT consists of a woolly undercoat and fine topcoat of white, golden, cream, grey, black, PARTI- or TRICOLOURed. Height 35.6–40.6cm (13¾–16in).

Tibetan Wolf   CANIS LUPUS CHANCO.

tibia   the thicker of the two long bones which run from the STIFLE to the HOCK, and located in front of the fibula. [illus. SKELETON]

tick   1. blood-sucking parasitic arachnid. There are many species that affect domesticated animals, most of which will also attack the dog. For those that are most commonly found on dogs, see DOG TICK. 2. Marking on coat, hence TICKED.

tick fever   BABESIOSIS.

tick paralysis   muscular dysfunction of the limbs caused by some species of tick: *Dermacentor venestus, Ixodes holocyclus*.

tick worry   general term for the debilitating effect of prolonged tick infestation.

ticked   (of coat) small, darker markings, irregularly and randomly distributed on a lighter GROUND.

Tickham   hunt founded in 1832 to hunt an arable and woodland COUNTRY in Kent.

ticking   see TICK(2).

ticking series   those genes which give rise to a TICKED coat.

tick-tack   (20th-cent. Am. rhyming slang) a race track, usually for horses, but occasionally for dogs. [142]

tie   characteristic position during canine copulation in which dog and bitch face in opposite directions, tied together by the bitch's sphincter muscles grasping the dog's penis, which must be enlarged in order for the tie to be fully effective. The belief that the achievement of the tie is entirely dependent on the bitch is erroneous.

tie-dog   dog that is usually tied up, a guard dog.
The names Tie-dog and Bandog intimate that the mastiff was commonly kept for guard. [225]

tied in   elbows set under the body which restrict movement.
The feet are turned out, and then there is a want of liberty in the play of the whole shoulder, because the elbow rubs against the ribs, and interferes with the action. [338]

T'ien Ken   Chinese canine deity.
The heavenly dog, or T'ien Ken, is a power of considerable antiquity, and in one of the main streets of Pekin a temple is dedicated to the god Erh Lang, the destroyer of dragons and protector of dogs. It is he that owns the dog which is heard howling in the sky and which occasionally commences to eat the sun. [37]

T'ien Kow   Chinese spectral dog, said to descend in the night to mutilate men.

Tiger Dog   KAI DOG.

Tiger Mastiff   (obs.) GREAT DANE.
Right at the head of the list of giants among Domestic dogs stands the Great Dane, Boarhound, Tiger Mastiff, or German Mastiff. [123]

tight-fitting jacket   short, close coat.

tight-lipped jaw   lips without FLEWS.

tike   (var. spelling) TYKE. [214]

tike-lurker   dog thief. [280]

tike-lurking   dog stealing. [280]

timber   quality of skeletal development; substance.

Timber Ridge   (US) private BASSET pack formed in 1946 to hunt cottontail rabbit, Kansas jack rabbit and fox over a COUNTRY in Maryland.

Timber Wolf   CANIS LUPUS.

Timmon's Biter   extinct 19th-century Australian HERDER developed from imported COLLIES crossed with native DINGOS.

tinea   RINGWORM.

tin hare   (Aust.) artificial hare used in GREYHOUND racing.

Tinker's Cur   large dog which carries a Tinker's equipment and also acts as a GUARD.
With marvellous patience they bear big budgettes fraught with Tinkers tools, and mettle to mend kettles, porridge pots, skillets, and chafers, and other such like trumpery . . . they love their masters liberally, and hate strangers spitefully, whereupon it follows that they are to their masters in travelling a singular safeguard, defending them forcibly, from the invasion of villains and thieves. [139]

Tintagel, Boscastle and Camelford Hunt   former name for the NORTH CORNWALL.

Tipperary   pack dating from before 1820 when William Barton hunted a private pack known as the Grove; the present name was assumed in 1826.

titlere   (obs.) HOUND. [159]

Tiverton   1. pack founded before 1841 to hunt a Devon banked COUNTRY with much pasture and plough; from 1873 to 1892 the hunt was known as William Rayner's Hunt. 2. former STAGHOUND pack formed in 1896 to hunt a COUNTRY in Devon and Somerset.

Tivyside   hunt that has existed intermittently since the early 1700s, and in its present form dates from 1937 when it was reformed as the Tivyside Farmers'.

Tivyside Farmers'   TIVYSIDE.

tod   fox, esp. in 19th-century Scotland but formerly also in England.
The thummart, willcat, brock, an' tod,
Weel kend his voice thro' a' the wood. [73e]

toeing-in   stance or gait in which the forefeet rotate towards each other, pointing inwards.

toeing-out   stance or gait in which the forefeet rotate away from each other, pointing outwards. [illus.]

Toeing-out.

toe pie kick a dog.

to-ho command, formerly used to cause GUNDOGS to stop.
> Some recommend that in addition to the long established 'to-ho' as a command to stop, that for going on should be 'go on'. [380]
> That to-ho, or the right arm raised nearly perpendicularly, means that he is to stand still. [184]

Toller NOVA SCOTIA DUCK TOLLING RETRIEVER.

tongue 1. cry of hunting HOUNDs, hence 'give tongue'.
2. chorus made by kennelled dogs.

tonsillitis inflammation and swelling of the tonsils.

toot (obs.) whine or cry. [159]

topcoat the outer layer of hair which provides protection against the elements. If the dog has an undercoat the topcoat is invariably the coarser of the two.

top dog 1. alpha dog. 2. (of fighting dogs) winner.
> I know that the world, that the great big world
>> Will never a moment stop
> To see which dog may be in the fault,
>> But will shout for the dog on top. [44]

topknot profuse growth of hair on the skull.
> Silver-blue or fawn top-knot. [203, AUSTRALIAN SILKY TERRIER, interim BREED STANDARD]
> Skull well balanced and mounted by a long 'top-knot', [203, AFGHAN HOUND]

Topline.

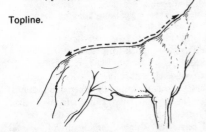

topline profile of the back from OCCIPUT to base of tail. [*illus.*]

top stickle STICKLE formed upstream from where OTTERHOUNDS are hunting.

Tora Dog KAI DOG.

Toronto and North York (Can) ENGLISH FOXHOUND pack formed in 1843 to hunt fox and DRAG(2) over a rolling arable and pasture COUNTRY in Toronto.

Torrington Farmers' hunt formed in 1939 to hunt a Devon COUNTRY.

torsion abnormal twist, esp. of an internal organ.

toruli digitales pads of the feet.

Tosa [FCI] Japanese fighting dog par excellence, which combines the aggression, unflinching disregard of pain and agility of other fighting breeds, with the size and strength of the MOLOSSAN breeds. A truly formidable animal.

The skull is broad, the MUZZLE powerful with PUNISHING JAWS. The neck is rather short and unusually thick and muscular; the body is broad, rather long and very muscular, the limbs being heavily boned and strong. The coat is short, hard and dense, usually a solid red with some white, but colour is not an important consideration in Japanese pits. Height 62–65cm (24½–25½in); weight 90kg (198lb).

Tosa Inu TOSA.

Tosa Ken TOSA.

Tosa Token TOSA.

total score sum produced by scoring. *See* SCORE.

tottering action movement which lacks forward impetus and appears unsteady.

tottering gait TOTTERING ACTION.

Tower Hill (US) private BEAGLE pack formed in 1956 to hunt cottontail rabbit over a COUNTRY in Massachusetts.

tourniquet tight bandage used to restrict the flow of blood.

towline line which runs from dog sled to leader, to which the rest of the team are fastened and through which they pull the sled.

Towy and Cothi hunt formed in 1914 as a TRENCHER-FED pack to hunt a COUNTRY in Dyfed.

towzy (Scot.) rough-coated.
> Come, my auld, towzy, trusty friend,
>> What gars ye look sae dung wi' wae? [174]

toxaemia poisoning resulting from bacterial infection.

toxascariasis symptoms arising as a consequence of *toxascaris* infestation.

Toxascaris leonina parasitic intestinal roundworm.

Toxocara canis parasitic nematode found in the small intestine, with larval infestation of muscular tissues, lungs and alimentary tract. Foetal infestation occurs via the placenta, hence the presence of the parasite in the majority of newborn puppies.

toxocariasis symptoms arising as a consequence of *Toxocara* infestation.

toy of small companion dog; a lap dog.

Toy Bulldog extinct small British companion dog. [150]

Toy Fox Terrier AMERTOY.

Toy German Spitz Deutscher Zwergspitz: POMERANIAN.

Toy Group a number of small breeds, grouped together for the purposes of classification, but which does not include all the diminutive breeds – the AKC, FCI and KC Toy Groups differing slightly from one another.

Toy Manchester Terrier ENGLISH TOY TERRIER (BLACK AND TAN).

Toy Poodle smallest of the three main varieties of POODLE. Height under 28cm (11in).

Toy Spaniel CAVALIER KING CHARLES SPANIEL and KING CHARLES SPANIEL.

Toy Xoloitzcuintle solid, patched or MOTTLED, hairless Mexican toy. Height 28–30cm (11–12in).

trace 1. dark stripe in the coat running along the spine.
> A black line or trace should run from the shoulders to the end of the tail. [186]

2. part of SLED-DOG harness.

trachea air passage within the neck.

trachelectomy cervical excision.

tracheobronchitis inflammation of the trachea and bronchia.

track scent trail; follow such a trail.

tracker TRACKING DOG.

tracker-dog disease CANINE EHRLICHIOSIS.

Tracking Dog [AKC] dog that has successfully completed the first AKC's Tracking Dog Test and achieved the required standard.

Tracking Dog Excellent [AKC] dog that has successfully completed the advanced Tracking Dog Test and achieved the required standard.

tracking harness harness used instead of a collar on a young or enthusiastic tracking dog.

tracking leash long leash, usually about 3m (10ft) in length, which allows a tracking dog freedom to work without risk of the handler foiling the line but which still enables the handler to retain control.

tracking line TRACKING LEASH.

trackless hare hare that leaves no scent.

Traders Point (US) CROSSBRED FOXHOUND pack formed in 1931 to hunt DRAG(2) and occasionally fox over a rolling COUNTRY in Indiana.

trail 1. line of scent left by the quarry; follow such a scent. 2. shouted request for a sled team to move over to allow another to overtake. 3. route over which a sled-team runs.

Trail Hound type of hound used to race over an artificial trail.

trail hunt (obs.) HOUND TRAIL, hence trail hunting.
> This 'trail hunting' is a favourite diversion in the north of England, and special strains of lightly-built foxhounds are used for the purpose. The line is generally run over an uneven country, and may extend for any distance between four and ten miles. Hounds are started at the same place, and the one coming in first, having completed the course, which was laid with fox's entrails, bedding, or some other strong scenting matter, wins the prize. [221]

trained off of dog that has lost racing form as a result of excessive training.

training mill (Am.) treadmill on which fighting dogs are brought to peak fitness.
> I was taken to a place last night where I saw seven or eight fighting dogs, some of them under training, and one actually being exercised on the training mill. [37]

Tranaki Hunt Club (NZ) pack formed in 1905 to hunt hare over open COUNTRY in New Plymouth.

transfer amend registration details following change of ownership.

Transfer Applied For (TAF) denotes that application has been made to the Kennel Club for transfer of ownership.

transhumance system of sheep husbandry in which both shepherds and PASTORAL GUARDS are used to protect sheep from predators. [204]

transplacental of transmission through the placenta, usually from DAM to foetus.

Transylvanian Hound HUNGARIAN HOUND.

trap 1. box, with spring-loaded door, from which a GREYHOUND is released at the start of a race. 2. mechanical device used to catch wild animals.

trap hare hare which has been taken unharmed in a trap for the purpose of being set down before HOUNDS.
> I had once some conversation with a gentleman about the running of my trap-hares, who said he had been told that catching a hare, and tying a piece of ribbon to her ear, was a sure way to make her run straight – I make no doubt of it; and so would a canister tied to her tail. [47]

trash (obs.) restrain on a leash.
> Iago: Which thing to do,
> If this poor trash of Venice, whom I trash
> For his quick hunting, [319m]
> Lord: Huntsman, I charge thee, tender well my hounds;
> Trash Merriman, the poor cur is embossed; [319q]

trash-cord thin cord, long or short, attached to a dog's collar and allowed to trail behind the dog as it runs.
> You must, however, make constant use of the trash-cord, that potent instrument by which, as Floyd discovered in the beginning of last century, all dogs may be broken. [123]

Trawler Spaniel extinct British TOY SPANIEL. [150]
> Sometimes confounded with the Cocker Spaniel, but this is a great mistake, as it is of entirely different type. It is supposed, without any certainty, to be descended from the original curly King Charles and the old-fashioned curly Sussex Spaniel. [225]

treadmill TRAINING MILL.

Tredegar Farmers' pack formed in 1947 to hunt a COUNTRY in Powys.

Treeing Coonhound either one of two COONHOUND breeds which, in common with other coonhounds, drive their quarry up trees and then mark their position by BAYing.

Treeing Tennessee Brindle amalgam of several COONHOUND varieties.

A broad-skulled dog with heavy pendulous ears, strong MUZZLE and characteristic broad nose. The body is solid, strong and square, the legs well boned and muscular. The short, smooth coat is always BRINDLE of various shades. Height 40–61cm (15¾–24in); weight 18–22.5kg (39½–49½lb).

Treeing Walker Coonhound of the various COONHOUND varieties, the Treeing Walker is, in appearance at least, closest to the breed's FOXHOUND ancestry.

A medium-sized hound with a refined head, strong neck and rather long back; the limbs are well boned and muscular. The coat is short and smooth, preferably TRICOLOUR but PARTICOLOURED dogs are acceptable. Height 51–69cm (20–27in); weight 22.5–34kg (49½–75lb).

trembler (colloq.) dog suffering from HYOMYELINO-GENESIS.

trencher-fed of PACK HOUNDS which, in ones and twos, are lodged in the homes of individual keepers.
> 'Trencher fed' packs of hounds are not so numerous as once was the case, though such are still to be found. They get their name from the fact that they are not kept in kennels, but individual hounds have separate homes with supporters of the hunt, and are regularly got together each morning a hunt is to take place. [221]

tret (obs.) leather strap for restraining HOUNDS. [159]

Treweryn (US) private BEAGLE pack formed in 1924 to hunt cottontail rabbit over a COUNTRY in Pennsylvania.

triangle (in showing) form of route taken by a handler and dog at the request of the judge, who, while standing at the apex of the triangle, is able to examine hind movement as the dog moves away, its lateral movement as the dog moves along the base of the triangle and its front movement as the dog returns to the apex of the triangle.

triangular like a triangle.

triangular ear V-SHAPED EAR.

Triangular eye.

triangular eye oval eye with sharply defined angles. [*illus.*]
> Eyes . . . Nearly triangular. [203, AFGHAN HOUND]

Trichomonas canistomae parasitic protozoan found in the mouth.

Trichophyton mentagrophytes fungal infection of the hair and skin, causing a type of RINGWORM in cattle, dogs, horses, pigs and sheep.

Trichuris vulpis parasitic WHIPWORM found in dogs and foxes.

trichurosis condition induced by *Trichuris* infestation, of which blood-infused diarrhoea is symptomatic.

tricolour (of coat) three-coloured, esp. white, black and tan.

Tri-country (US) American and CROSSBRED FOX-HOUND pack formed in 1962 to hunt a pasture, swamp and wooded hill COUNTRY in Georgia.

tricuspid valve one of the valves in the heart.

trim 1. barber the coat in order to create a desired appearance.
> Personally, when I am the adjudicator, I turn down without the slightest hesitation trimmed specimens. There is another fine argument in favour of non-trimming, for by the universal adoption of this rule no one is penalised, all exhibitors are on a dead level, and true sport is assured. [69]

2. secondary coat colouring.
> Leopards are to be preferred and may come in blue/grey/black/liver/red/white and patched. Trim may be black/white/tan/red/buff. [6, CATAHOULA LEOPARD DOG]

Tring and District Farmers former DRAGHOUND pack formed as a revival of the Hemel Hempstead Draghounds to hunt LINES(2) in Hertfordshire.

Trinity Foot former 14–15½in BEAGLE pack formed by Trinity College, Cambridge in 1962.

trip unsuccessful attempt by COURSING GREY-HOUND to kill the hare but which knocks it off its legs.
> Unsuccessful effort to kill, is where the hare is thrown off her legs, or where a greyhound flecks her, but cannot hold her. [*305]

tripe hound (Aust.) SHEEP DOG.

triple mongrel (obs.) the offspring of two MON-GRELS, a term coined in an attempt to define degrees of CROSSBREEDing(2).
> lastly there are dogs which may be called triple mongrels, because they are produced by two mixed races. Of this kind are the Artois and Islois dogs, which are produced by the pug dogs and the bastard pug dog. [72]

trisomy presence of a third chromosome.

trochanter *see* GREAT TROCHANTER.

Trombicula autumnale harvest mite: parasitic mite which causes intense irritation and dermatitis, especially of the feet, legs and belly.

trombiculidiasis dermatitis resulting from *Trombicula* infestation.

trophy 1. that part of a quarry which is retained for exhibition, a stag's head for example. 2. object won in competition.

tropical canine pancytopenia CANINE EHRLICHIOSIS.

trot fast two-beat gait in which diagonally opposite fore and hind feet move in unison resulting in two diagonally opposite feet being in contact with the ground at any one time.

trouserings BREECHES.
> The impression of a somewhat exaggerated bend in the stifle due to profuse trouserings. [6, AFGHAN HOUND]

Trowbridge former 14in BEAGLE pack formed in 1903 to hunt a COUNTRY in Wiltshire.

trowel-shaped ear ear that is wider in the middle than at the skull and then narrowing to a point.

trucking (Aust.) the process of loading or off-loading sheep from trucks to yards, work calling for specialized abilities in the dogs used.

true action movement in which the legs and feet move forwards without deviation to right or left.

Free [movement], covering adequate ground; straight and true in front and rear. [203, LABRADOR RETRIEVER]

True Blue Hunt   CATTISTOCK.

True Fennec   *VULPES ZERDA.*

true front   forequarters correct for the breed.

truffle dog   dog used to search for truffles, often a POODLE/TERRIER CROSS.

> a variety of the poodle, or at any rate a crossbred poodle. [221]
>
> Is nothing more or less than a bad, small-sized Poodle, and is never, or very rarely, met with under the designation Truffle-dog. Its cultivation is due to the existence of truffles, which it is employed to discover when they are lying in the ground by the help of its acute nose. [225a]

trumpet   temple.

Trumpington Terrier   archetypal NORWICH TERRIER.

> Upon graduation from Cambridge in 1899, E Jodrell Hopkins remained in the town to open a livery stable on Trumpington Street. . . . Hopkins also kept stable terriers, and eventually his particular strain was dubbed 'Trumpington'. [293]

trundle-tail   (obs.) curly-tailed dog. [159]

try back   return along the line of the scent.

tryndeltaylles   TRUNDLE-TAIL.

Trypanosoma ariarii   *TRYPANOSOMA RANGELI*

Trypanosoma brucei   protozoan blood parasite.

Trypanosoma cruzi   protozoan blood parasite; infestation is often fatal.

Trypanosoma escomeli   TRYPANOSOMA BRUCEI.

Trypanosoma evansi   protozoan blood parasite.

Trypanosoma gambiense   protozoan blood parasite; infestation gives rise to chronic disease.

Trypanosoma guatamalense   *TRYPANOSOMA RANGELI.*

Trypanosoma hominis   *TRYPANOSOMA GAMBIENSE.*

Trypanosoma nigeriense   *TRYPANOSOMA GAMBIENSE.*

Trypanosoma pecaudi   *TRYPANOSOMA BRUCEI.*

Trypanosoma rangeli   protozoan blood parasite.

Trypanosoma ugandense   *TRYPANOSOMA GAMBIENSE.*

Tschika   CHINESE GREYHOUND. [312]

Tsutsuga mushi disease   SCRUB TYPHUS.

Tuareg Sloughi   AZAWAKH.

tubercle   *See* GREATER TUBERCLE.

tuberculosis   disease caused by MYCOBACTERIUM infection.

tucked up   1. exhausted. [316]
2. looking miserable, especially with flanks drawn in.

   tucked-up abdomen   pronounced TUCK-UP.

   tucked-up flank   having narrow or drawn in LOINS.

tuck-up   profile of the underbelly.

> Back has natural arch over loin creating a definite tuck-up of underline. [203, BEDLINGTON TERRIER]

tufter   slow and reliable HOUND, with good nose used to discover the whereabouts of deer prior to the pack being put on.

tugline   line on a sledge which runs from the harness to the gangline and through which the dog exerts its force.

Tulip ears.

tulip ear   erect ear shaped like a tulip petal. [*illus.*]

Tullow Hunt   CARLOW.

tumbler   small type of dog principally used for hunting rabbits, possibly a WHIPPET.

> These Dogs are somewhat lesser than the hounds, and they be lanker and leaner, besides that they be somewhat pricke eared. A man that shall mark the form and fashion of their bodies, may well call them mongrel Greyhounds if they were somewhat bigger. [139]

tumoral calcinosis   CALCIUM GOUT.

tumour   abnormal growth resulting from cell multiplication within tissue.

Tunguse Laïka   one of five Siberian LAÏKA breeds identified in 1896 by Prince Andrew Shirinsky Shihmatoff. [380]

tubinate bones   the bones which give added support to the delicate scroll-like bones in the nasal cavity. [356]

Turbith's mineral   formerly a supposed remedy for rabies. [47]

Turkish Greyhound   former small eastern SIGHTHOUND.

> a small and almost hairless dog, of the greyhound kind. [338]

turn   1. (of a GREYHOUND) cause the hare to deviate from her chosen course.   2. of a fighting dog ceasing to face its opponent. [131]   3. process by which a STUD-DOG achieves the position indicative of being TIEd.

turn loose match   system of bull-baiting in which several dogs were simultaneously loosed to bait the tethered animal; the alternative system was the LET-GO MATCH.

turn of stifle   bend of STIFLE; angle of the stifle-joint.

turnside   (obs.) fits caused by worm infestation. [338]

turnspit   any dog with short, often crooked, legs, used to walk within a hollow wheel in order to turn a spit on which meat is roasting.

> Is generally long-bodied, has short crooked legs, its tail curled upon its back, and is frequently spotted with black upon a blue-grey ground. It is peculiar in the colour of its eyes; the same Dog often having the iris of one eye black, and the other white. [51]

turn up   1. the exaggerated upward curve of the underjaw in a BRACHYCEPHALIC head. [*illus.*]

> Chin prominent with good turn up [203, AFFENPINSCHER Interim BREED STANDARD]

Turn up.

2. impromptu but supervised fight between dogs, hence (fig.) an unexpected occurrence.
> By way of a finish, however, we had one turn-up between a Spanish bull-dog and an animal called Blood – a cross between a Spanish bull-dog and an English mastiff. [266a]

TVT CANINE TRANSMITTABLE VENEREAL TUMOUR.

twang sound made by a hunting horn.
> The horn was twanging a long way on
> For the only hound that was still astray. [272b]

Tweed-side Spaniel TWEED WATER SPANIEL.
> He had been for some years entirely sightless, and was led about by a large brown Tweed-side spaniel, of whose intelligence wonderful stories are told. [184]

Tweed Spaniel TWEED WATER SPANIEL.
> A Tweed Spaniel came nearest to him in docility. [94]

Tweed Water Spaniel (obs.) one of three 19th-century varieties of IRISH WATER SPANIEL. [295]

Twelfth 12 August, 'The Glorious Twelfth', the first day of the British grouse shooting season.

Twici, William huntsman to Edward II and author of *L'Art de Venerie* (c. 1328), the oldest known book devoted to hunting.

Twist.

twist (in a PUG) tightly curled tail. [*illus.*]
> Tail (twist) High set, curled as tightly as possible over hip. [203, PUG]

twisted jaw jaw that is out of alignment, in which the teeth do not meet evenly when the mouth is closed. [*illus.* WRY MOUTH]

twitch (obs.) DISTEMPER.

two-angled head profile in which the lines formed by the skull and MUZZLE are not parallel.
> Faults – Two-angled head. [6, SHETLAND SHEEPDOG]

two-ply coat DOUBLE COAT.

tying-up syndrome CANINE HYPOXIC RHABDO-MYOLYSIS.

tyke formerly any rough, shaggy MONGREL dog, now principally used to refer to working terriers.
> Toby was the most utterly shabby, vulgar, mean-looking cur I ever beheld: in one word, a tyke. He had not one good feature except his teeth and eyes, and his bark, if that can be called a feature. [65]
> For the love of a tyke for his master
> Can never be measured in gold. [357]

tympanista DANCER. [128]

Tynan and Armagh Irish HARRIER pack formed during the mid-19th century as the Tyn Harriers, a private pack, which in 1880 amalgamated with the Armagh Harriers.

Tynan Harriers TYNAN AND ARMAGH.

Tynedale the Northumbrian grass COUNTRY has been hunted by the present pack since 1854 when the Old Northumberland pack was dissolved.

type sum of qualities which distinguish one breed (breed type), or dogs from one kennel (kennel type), from others.
> It is extremely difficult to define in words the general outline and symmetry of a Collie, but it may be summed up in one word 'type'. [41]
> If one thinks of it the principle is wrong crossing what is practically two distinct breeds. You lose all type. [316]

Tyro class [KC] show class for dogs that have not won a CHALLENGE CERTIFICATE or five or more first prizes at Open or Championship shows (some classes excepted).

Tyroglyphus genus of acarine mites which infest grain and vegetable products, causing itching and mild dermatitis on contact with skin.

Tyrolean Hound OSTERREICHISCHER GLATTHAARIGE BRACKE.

Tyroler Bracke OSTERREICHISCHER GLATTHAARIGE BRACKE.

Tyrolese Hound OSTERREICHISCHER GLATTHAARIGE BRACKE.

U

UAP UN-UNITED ANCONAL PROCESS.

U-CD abbr. suffix UKC COMPANION DOG.

U-CDX abbr. suffix UKC COMPANION DOG EXCELLENT.

UD abbr. suffix AKC UTILITY DOG.

UDT abbr. suffix AKC UTILITY DOG TRACKER.

UDTX abbr. suffix AKC UTILITY DOG TRACKER EXCELLENT.

UKC UNITED KENNEL CLUB.

UKC Companion Dog dog that has successfully completed the UKC's Companion Dog obedience tests.

UKC Companion Dog Excellent dog that has successfully completed the UKC's more advanced Companion Dog obedience tests.

ulcer defect caused by the sloughing of dead tissue.

ulceromembraneous stomatitis viral infection of the mouth, particularly of the gums and mucous membranes, characterized by inflamed, ulcerated gums and slimy, discoloured saliva.

Ullswater pack formed in 1880 to hunt a mountainous Cumbrian COUNTRY.

Ulmer Dog (obs.) GREAT DANE.

ulna the longest bone of the foreleg, and located behind the radius. [*illus.* SKELETON]

ulnar of, or relating to, the ULNA.

   ulnar physis closure inherited deformed ulna. (Mode of inheritance, recessive.)

ulutation (obs.) howling. [159]

umbilical of the UMBILICUS.

   umbilical cord cord by which the developing foetus is attached to the placenta and through which it receives nourishment.

   umbilical hernia inherited tissue protrusion through the umbilical ring. (Mode of inheritance, probably recessive.)

umbilicus navel: scar at the site of the umbilical cord's attachment, barely discernible in dogs.

umbrella short VEIL.

   Long hair overshadows eyes like an umbrella. [203, HUNGARIAN PULI]

Umbrian Dog a cowardly SCENTHOUND.

   The Umbrian dog runs away even from the enemies whom he has himself discovered. Would that he had as much courage and pluck in fight as he has loyalty and sagacity of scent! [154]

unbroken (esp. of GUNDOG) untrained.

   Shot, who was, as a matter of fact, quite unbroken, tore off after them. [241]

Uncinaria genus of canine HOOKWORMS.

Uncinaria stenocephala common species of canine HOOKWORM, found also in the cat and fox.

uncinariasis HOOKWORM infestation, characterized by mild anaemia and enteritis.

uncoiling (Am) of SCENTHOUND's spiral CAST from a CHECK.

unconditioned response natural reflex response to a given stimulus.

unconditioned stimulus any natural stimulus which elicits a response.

uncouple separate HOUNDS that are COUPLED together.

undercoat soft coat which lies below the coarse TOPCOAT and provides insulation.

underdog (of fighting dogs) the dog underneath, and therefore the probable loser.

Undergraduate class [KC] show class for dogs that have not won a CHALLENGE CERTIFICATE or three or more first prizes in adult competitions at Championship shows.

undergrowth (obs.) UNDERCOAT.

   He was short and compact everywhere, with the very best coat that could be – short, hard and dense – with plenty of undergrowth, and a thick skin. [318, FIELD SPANIEL]

underground mutton (Aust.) rabbit.

underhung (of bite) UNDERSHOT.

Undershot bite.

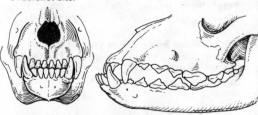

undershot of a bite in which the lower jaw protrudes beyond the upper jaw. [*illus.*]

underslung (of bite) UNDERSHOT.

undescended testes CRYPTORCHIDISM.

unearth eject a quarry, esp. a fox, from its EARTH.

   By birth and call of nature preordained
   To hunt the badger and unearth the fox
   Among the impervious crags. [402]

unentered (usu. of sporting dogs) not yet introduced to work.

   Shortly afterwards he had bought five-and-twenty couple of unentered bitches at Rugby Hound Sale. [309]

unharbour oblige a deer to leave its place of retreat.

   Unharbour'd now the royal stag forsakes
   His wonted lair; he shakes his dappled sides,
   And tosses high his beamy head. [328]

unilateral cryptorchid dog with only one testicle descended into the scrotum.

unit character characteristic determined by a single gene.

United continuation of a TRENCHER-FED pack formed in 1837 to hunt a COUNTRY which lies in Shropshire and Powys.

United Farmers former Irish HARRIER pack formed to hunt both hare and fox over a COUNTRY in County Cork.

United Hunt Club pack founded in 1871 to hunt a COUNTRY in County Cork.

United Kennel Club a privately owned US registry originally founded in 1898 to provide registration facilities for PIT BULL TERRIERS. It now registers a large number of breeds including several that are not recognized by other kennel clubs.

unkennel eject a quarry from its refuge.
> Ford: I'll warrant we'll unkennel the fox, let me stop this way first. So, now uncape. [319j]
> From a gentry steeped in pots,
> From unkennelers of plots,
> Libera nos, etc. [99]

unkindly (obs.) out of condition.
> When a dog looks unkindly in his coat, though he has been physicked, give him three doses of powdered glass, as much as will lie heaped up on a shilling to each dose. [161]

unlay (obs.) (of HOUNDS) uncouple.
> Than thei aught unlay for advauntage of the houndes, for so shal thei the sonner have hym at abay. [125]

unlike-to-unlike mating ASSORTIVE MATING.

unseen retrieve retrieve of shot game or article that was not visible to the GUNDOG at the time of its being shot or dropped, thus demanding the dog's use of scent in order to locate it.

unsighted of a COURSING dog that loses sight of its quarry.

unspoilt (usu. of GUNDOG) untrained.

unsteady (usu. of HOUNDS) inclined to riot.
> I am sorry to hear that your hounds are so unsteady. It is scarcely possible to have sport with unsteady hounds. [47]

untraining (Am.) process of retraining, especially to change behavioural trends.

Un-united anconal process inherited failure of the anconal process to unite with the ulna. (Mode of inheritance, polygenic.)

Un-united coronoid process ELBOW DYSPLASIA.

up order to a GUNDOG to seek above ground level.
> That 'Up' means that he is to sniff with his nose high in the air for that which he is in search. [184]

upfaced (of MUZZLE) short, turned up.
> Muzzle short, blunt, square, not upfaced. [203, PUG]

upper arm HUMERUS.

upright shoulder scapula closer to vertical than is desirable. [*illus.*]

upsweep TURN-UP.

up-water cry used to indicate that a hunted otter has swum upstream.

uraemia accumulation of protein waste in the blood.

Urcane type of dog alleged, by FLEMING, to be 'bred of a bear and a dog'. [139]

Urcanus type of dog alleged, by FLEMING, to be 'bred of a bear and a BANDOG'. [139]

Upright shoulder.

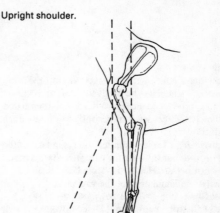

ureter tube which transports urine from the kidney to the bladder.

urethra duct within the penis which conveys semen and urine.

uric acid excretion inherited inability to convert uric acid to allantoin. (Mode of inheritance, recessive.)

urinary appertaining to urine.
  urinary calculi CYSTINE UROLITH.

urination marking method of reinforcing territorial possession by depositing drops of urine in strategic places, mainly associated with dogs but also used by dominant bitches.

Urocyon littoralis localized species of fox found in the Californian Santa Barbara Islands.

urogenital system male urinary and reproductive tract.

uterine of, or relating to, the UTERUS.
  uterine inertia absence of contractions during birth. There are two forms: primary uterine inertia characterized by the failure of the bitch to begin contractions that will produce puppies; and secondary uterine inertia, which occurs after contractions have begun but then cease, perhaps owing to exhaustion or to an obstruction.

uterus womb; bitch's internal organ in which the foetus develops.
  uterus horns twin branches of the upper part of the uterus.

Utility Dog [AKC] dog that has successfully completed the AKC's Utility Obedience tests.

Utility Dog Excellent [AKC] dog that has successfully completed the AKC's more advanced Utility Obedience tests.

Utility Dog Tracker [AKC] dog that has successfully completed the AKC's tracking test.

Utility Group [KC] a number of breeds, grouped together for the purposes of classification. Largely consisting of miscellaneous NON-SPORTING breeds.

uveodermatitis inherited dermatitis associated with multiple eye defects. (Mode of inheritance, familial.)

V

vaccina VACCINE.

vaccination introduction of VACCINE into the body in order to stimulate the production of antibodies.

vaccine product containing dead or attentuated viral bodies, dispensed intravenously to stimulate the production of antibodies.

Vaghari Dog Indian hunting dog similar to the GREYHOUND but showing the PARIAH's characteristic of a PROUD TAIL. Height 51–61cm (20–24in).

vaginitis inflammation of the vagina.

Valee Sheep Dog POLISH LOWLAND SHEEP DOG.

Vale of Clettwr pack whose Dyfed COUNTRY is well wooded and has extensive mountain land and has been hunted by the pack since 1923.

Vale of Clwyd BEAGLE pack formed in 1936 as the Arnold House Beagles; the name was changed in 1939 to Mr Eyton's Beagles and to the Vale of Clwyd Beagles in 1953. The COUNTRY is in Clwyd.

Vale of Lune HARRIER pack formed in 1866 to hunt a COUNTRY on the borders of Westmorland, Lancashire and Yorkshire.

Vale of the White Horse VWH.

Vallhund [FCI] SWEDISH VALLHUND.

valvular incompetence inherited failure of heart valves to close completely causing heart murmurs and inefficient operation of the heart. (Mode of inheritance, unclear.)

Vanjari BANJARA GREYHOUND.

variety dogs distinguished from others of the breed by their size, colour or coat quality; a sub-breed.

varmint (colloq.) quarry, especially fox.

varmint-looking (obs.) varminty. [250]

varminty (esp. nowadays, of a TERRIER) hard-bitten and workmanlike expression.
Possessed of no small amount of self-esteem with a varminty expression. [203, WEST HIGHLAND WHITE TERRIER]

vascular haemophilia ANGIOHAEMOPHILIA.

vas deferens excretory duct of the testes, which carries sperm to the duct from the seminal vesicle to produce a complete ejaculate.

vasectomy surgical removal of the vas deferens as a means of creating sterility.

Västgótaspets [FCI] SWEDISH VALLHUND.

vauntlay (obs.) the SLIPPING(3) of HOUNDS too soon when stag hunting, permissible only on the last drive or when the stag is nearly finished. [149]

Veadeiro Catarinense Brazilian HOUND which combines the qualities of both SCENT- and SIGHTHOUNDS.

veil layer of long, fine coat hairs.
In Powder Puffs coat consists of an undercoat with soft veil of long hair, veil coat a feature. [203, CHINESE CRESTED DOG]

veiled coat coat with an overlay of long, fine hairs.

Veloce GREYHOUND.

In the old days, judging from such models as the sculpture of the Hound on the Arch of Constantine, The veloces, or Greyhounds, were 30 inches high (using Trajan's slave with the spear as a scale). [186]

Venatici group of hunting dogs in which FLEMING included HARRIERS, TERRIERS, BLOODHOUNDS, GAZEHOUNDS, GREYHOUNDS, LEVINERS or LYEMMERS, TUMBLERS and STEALERS.

venatio (obs.) collective noun for sporting breeds. [139]

vénerie (Fr.) the art of hunting with HOUNDS.

vent 1. area surrounding the vulva and anus.
Under tail tanned, vent tanned by marking as narrow as possible so that it is covered by tail. [203, MANCHESTER TERRIER]
2. opening, especially one that discharges pus.

Ventreres extinct, strongly made HOUND, a type of ALAUNT, used also for bear-baiting. [215]

ventricular septal defect congenital defect of the heart producing murmur, palpable thrill and poor tolerance of exercise.

veuuersator TURNSPIT. [139]

vermifuge substance which kills parasitic worms.

vertagus TUMBLER. [139]

vertebra each of the bones of the spine, pl. vertebrae.

vertebrae osteochondrosis inherited lesions of the spinal column producing lameness. (Mode of inheritance, familial.)

Vertragus CELTIC GREYHOUND.

Vertraha CELTIC GREYHOUND. [295]
The Vertraha, coloured with yellow spots, swifter than thought or a winged bird it runs, pressing hard on the beasts it has found, though less likely to find them when they lie hidden. [295]

vertebral of, or relating to, VERTEBRAE.

vertebral column spine.

vertebral osteochondrosis SPONDYLOSIS DEFORMANS.

Vertregusi CELTIC GREYHOUND.

Very Highly Commended fifth place in a show class, sometimes derogatorily referred to as 'Very Highly Condemned'.

vet dim. VETERINARY SURGEON.

vet check veterinary inspection carried out prior to a competition or sale.

Veteran Class [KC] show class for dogs of an age specified in the schedule, but at least five years old on the first day of the show.

veterinarian (formerly Brit; now commonly Am.) VETERINARY SURGEON.

veterinary of the treatment of disease in animals.

veterinary nurse veterinary assistant who has successfully completed the appropriate course of training. Nurses are qualified only to assist a qualified vet.

veterinary practitioner 1. (US) a registered vet who practises on his own account or is employed by another. 2. (UK) a vet on the supplementary register of the Royal College of Veterinary Surgeons, a concession to vets whose veterinary education was interrupted by war service.

veterinary surgeon any qualified practitioner of veterinary medicine.

VHC VERY HIGHLY COMMENDED.

vice bite PINCER BITE.

Vicmead (US) CROSSBRED FOXHOUND pack formed in 1921 to hunt over a pasture and woodland COUNTRY in Delaware.

Victorian Pom (Ang.) the larger varieties of GERMAN SPITZ.

view (of HOUNDS or their FOLLOWERS) see the quarry, especially of fox-hunting. [401]

Vikhan large and strong Indian PASTORAL GUARD noted for its fierce, independent temperament.

Villaticus (obs.) MASTIFF. [139]

villus PROCESS which projects from a surface in order to increase surface area.

Vine pack whose country lies principally in Hampshire and has been hunted since 1770.

vine-leaf ear ear in which the LEATHER is divided into three, or more, distinct areas, giving some resemblance to the shape of a vine leaf.
> Ears: Large, vine leaf shaped, well covered with straight hair. [203, CLUMBER SPANIEL]

Virelade GASCON SAINTONGEOIS.

viral of, or relating to, VIRUS.

viral tracheitis KENNEL COUGH.

virus small infectious agent which replicates by using its host's biological processes in the course of which it gives rise to a variety of diseases.

visceral larva migrans condition caused by the migration of larval worms through the tissues, most commonly owed to *Toxocara canis* infestation.

visit (of sexually receptive females) attend in order to mate: females are said to 'visit' the male.

vitality degree to which the normal signs of health are present either in an individual or in a population.

vital sign any indication that life has not been terminated.

vixen female fox.

Vizsla dim. HUNGARIAN VIZSLA.

Vlaamsche Trekhond CHIEN DE TRAIT BELGE.

Vogool Laïka one of five European-Russian LAÏKA breeds identified in 1896 by Prince Andrew Shirinsky Shihmatoff. [380]

vohunazga dog type of hunting dog. [407]

voice (in HOUNDS) CRY.

Volpino Italiano white or, rarely, SABLE, Italian toy SPITZ with long, thick coat. Height 28 (11in); weight 4.5kg (10lb).

von Gierke's disease GLYCOGENOSIS I.

von Willebrand's disease ANGIOHAEMOPHILIA.

V-shaped ear ear which gradually and uniformly tapers to a point. [*illus.*]

V-shaped ears.

Vulpes fox genus of the family CANIDAE.

Vulpes bengalensis Bengal Fox, found in the open forest and steppes of northern India, Pakistan and Nepal.

Vulpes cana Blanford's Fox, found in the mountain steppes of Afghanistan. A fox with an exceptionally long tail and ears; the colour is grey to buff with a dark dorsal stripe, white underbelly and dark tail tip.

Vulpes chama Cape Fox, found in the South African grassland.

Vulpes corsac Corsac Fox, found in the south Russian and Manchurian steppes. A long-eared fox with a shaded red to yellow coat.

Vulpes ferrilata Tibetan Fox, found in Tibet. One of the largest foxes, it has a red coat, with white shading, a white-tipped BRUSH and white feet.

Vulpes macrotis Kit Fox, found in the dry grassland of south-west USA and northern Mexico. It has large ears, a short head and usually has a red coat flecked with grey. Weight about 2kg (4½lb).

Vulpes pallida Pale Fox, found in the deserts of Senegal. The ears are large and rounded, the head short and feline, the coat a sandy buff and the BRUSH black-tipped. Weight about 2kg (4½lb).

Vulpes rueppellii Sand Fox, found in the deserts of Morocco and Afghanistan. One of the larger foxes. The ears are exceptionally large, the coat a light buff with a light dorsal stripe and MASK.

Vulpes velox Red Fox, also called Swift Fox, found in the grasslands of northern America; a subspecies of VULPES MACROTIS and very rare.

Vulpes zerda Fennec Fox or True Fennec, characterized by its very large ears, largely vegetarian but also eats eggs and, possibly, small birds and mammals. The head is short, eyes large, the coat sandy-red to yellow or cream, the BRUSH black-tipped. A tiny Fennec no more than 20cm (8in) in height; weight about 1.5kg (3lb).

vulpicide one who shoots foxes and regarded by foxhunters as the lowest form of animal life.
> It is as bad as being a vulpicide in a fox-hunting country, which leaves nothing more to be said. [212]

vulpine of foxes; foxlike.

vulva external part of the female genitalia.

VWD VON WILLEBRAND'S DISEASE.

VWH Vale of the White Horse, a hunt invariably referred to by its initials, formed in 1824 to hunt a COUNTRY in Gloucestershire.

W

W abbr. WIDE RUNNER.

waddling action action with pronounced lateral movement, often associated with poor muscular development and obesity.

waddling gait WADDLING ACTION.
> There was an Old Man of Kamschatka,
> Who possessed a remarkably fat cur;
> His gait and his waddle
> Were held as a model
> To all the fat dogs in Kamschatka. [220]

wag waving motion of a dog's tail, said to be indicative of pleasure. Vertical wagging of the tail was formerly regarded as an early symptom of rabies.
> Does his tail wag horizontally or perpendicularly? That has decided the fate of many dogs in Enfield. [213]

Wah (obs.) DHOLE.
> A central and southern India dhole, with a large, flat head and black muzzle, a ferocious-looking, heavily built dog with a rather short tail, tan-coloured, with white underparts and a dark tip to tail. This dog hunted in packs and was said to have a deep, growling bay. [380]

waisted of a dog with narrow LOINS.

Walchia americana American harvest mite, the cause of TROMBICULIDIASIS.

Walhampton Basset former BASSET pack formed in 1889, and hunted by the Marquis of Conyngham as the Slane Bassets from 1903 to 1910. The COUNTRY lies in Leicestershire.

walk 1. take a dog out for exercise. 2. rear and socialize a HOUND puppy away from the pack with which it is intended to hunt. *See* AT WALK.
> To reach the required high standard some sixty to seventy couple of puppies would be sent to walk each year. [101]

3. slowest gait, in which three paws are in contact with the ground at any one time, feet being lifted in the sequence: right hind, right fore, left hind, left fore.

Walker Foxhound unrecognized, Virginian variety of SCENTHOUND derived from the ENGLISH FOX-HOUND and used as a component in the production of the TREEING WALKER COONHOUND.

Walker Hound WALKER FOXHOUND.

walking dandruff (colloq.) CHEYLETIELLOSIS.

Wallace County BIRCHWOOD.

wall eye an eye in which absence of pigment in the iris results in a very light, usually, blue eye. Less correctly used to describe an eye in which the cornea has become opaque.
> A Yorkshire Buckhound, having black spots upon his back, red ears, and a wall-eye, and PR. upon his near shoulder. [15]

Wallis Sheep Dog extinct European breed of SHEEP DOG, probably one of the progenitors of the Alpine PASTORAL GUARD breeds.

walrus puppy neonate suffering from ANASCARA.

Walsh, John Henry canine author and journalist who wrote under the pseudonym 'Stonehenge', and whose works include *The Dog in Health and Disease* (1872).

wanderer puppy suffering from NEONATAL MALADJUSTMENT SYNDROME.

wanlace (obs. Scot.) HOUNDS driving quarry towards nets or marksmen.

wappe formerly a HOUSE-DOG which FLEMING variously describes as one that warns of intruders by barking and as a TURNSPIT.
> Wappe comes from the natural sound Wau which the dog makes when barking to attract attention. Hence originally it was Wauppe. But for the sake of euphony, a vowel changing to a consonant, we say Wappe. [139]

wapper-jaw (obs.) wry mouth. [159]

wappet (obs.) yelping cur. [159]

wappynge 1. (obs.) yelping. [159] 2. (obs.) mongrel cur. [159]

warded (obs.) var. MATED.
> I should always advise that bitches be warded twice, the last three or four days of their being in season. [218]

war dog dog formerly used to harass the enemy or to carry messages or to search for the wounded on the battlefield in times of war.
> The war dogs, which were also big game dogs, were formidable in appearance and fierce as to temperament; added to which they were provided with spiked collars and not infrequently armour-clad, so that their capture or their despatch was not easy of accomplishment. [123]

Ward Union former Irish STAGHOUND pack formed in 1830 by the amalgamation of the Duber and Hollywood packs. The COUNTRY was in Counties Dublin and Meath.

'Ware (usually directed at a HOUND or hunt-FOLLOWER) take care. Contrac. *beware*.
> An acquaintance of mine, when he hears any of his servants say, "Ware horse!' halloos out, "Ware horse! 'ware dog! and be hanged to you!' [47]

warmint phonetic spelling of varmint, used by both Surtees and Dickens to imitate London pronunciation.
> At Bill Sike's feet, sat a white-coated, red-eyed dog; who occupied himself, alternately, in winking at his master with both eyes at the same time, and in licking a large, fresh cut at one side of his mouth, which appeared to be the result of some recent conflict. 'Keep quiet, you warmint! keep quiet!' said Mr Sikes, suddenly breaking silence. [120b]

warm tan rich, dark mahogany colour.

warner MONGREL HOUSE-DOG which barks to warn of the presence of intruders.
> They resemble no notable shape, nor exercise any worthy property of the true perfect and gentle kind, it is not necessary that I write any more of them, but to banish them as unprofitable implements . . .

unprofitable I say for any use that is commendable, except to entertain strangers with their barking in the day time, giving warning to them of the house, that such and such is newly come, whereupon we call them admonishing dogs. [128]

Warragal (Aust. Aboriginal) DINGO.
> The pure Dingo, or Warragal, as it is called by the natives, is only now met with in the far interior of Australia. [123]

warranty limited guarantee, of soundness or suitability for some particular purpose. More commonly used in respect of horses than of dogs.

Warrenton (US) CROSSBRED FOXHOUND pack formed in 1816 to hunt over a rolling grassland COUNTRY in Virginia.

Warrigal (var. spelling) WARRAGAL.

wart canine viral papillomatosis; small excrescence on the skin produced by abnormal growth of the papillae.

Warwickshire 1. FOXHOUND pack founded in about 1780 to hunt a COUNTRY in Warwickshire, Gloucestershire and Worcestershire. Former huntsmen include Lord Willoughby de Broke, 1881–1898, and Bob Champion, 1922–1927. 2. former 15in BEAGLE pack formed in 1903 to hunt a COUNTRY in Warwickshire.

watch-dog dog used to warn of the presence of intruders.
> Everybody praised him for his affectionate disposition and his value as a watch-dog, and I was told that his mother, now dead, had been greatly prized, and was the smallest red dog ever seen in that part of Hampshire. [182b]

Watch-dogge (obs. spelling) WATCH-DOG. [319r]

watch eye WALL EYE.

watchman KEEPER. [139]

water bag membrane which encloses the puppy and amniotic fluids in the womb, and which appears immediately prior to birth.

Water Dog 1. any dog developed or trained for the purpose of retrieving game from water. 2. Zoroastrian holy dog which afforded protection against drought. [407] 3. early type of SPANIEL described at length by Nicholas Cox. 4. early anglicized name for the POODLE or its ancestors. [123]

water drawer any large dog used for turning the pulley which lifted buckets from a well. [139]

Waterford pack founded in 1840, which – apart from a period from 1884–1859 when the COUNTRY was hunted by Lord Waterford's, and from 1859–1900 when it was hunted by The Curraghmore – has been hunting fox in County Wexford ever since.

water hammer pulse lateral, grossly exaggerated heart pulses, usually a prelude to collapse.

water-logged puppy bloated, non-viable puppy: LETHAL OEDEMA.

Waterloo (US) AMERICAN FOXHOUND pack formed in 1943 to hunt over a hilly grass and woodland COUNTRY with some swamps in Michigan.

Waterloo Cup premier British COURSING competition open only to nominees considered to be of appropriate quality. WATERLOO STAKES.

Waterloo Plate COURSING stake for GREYHOUNDS beaten in the second round of the WATERLOO CUP.

Waterloo Purse COURSING stake for GREYHOUNDS beaten in the first round of the WATERLOO CUP.

Waterloo Stakes comprising the Waterloo Cup, Plate and Purse, COURSING stakes run on Viscount Leverhulme's estate at Altcar.

Waterloo Trophy WATERLOO STAKES.

water-pie (fig., colloq.) drastic slimming diet for dogs.

water-rug rough-coated HOUND used to hunt aquatic quarry, probably a forerunner of the OTTERHOUND and the rough-coated WATER SPANIELS.

waters amniotic fluids.

water shy of a GUNDOG which, for whatever reason, refuses to retrieve from water.

Waterside Dog (obs.) AIREDALE TERRIER. [320a]

Waterside Terrier (obs.) AIREDALE TERRIER.

Water Spagnell (obs.) spelling of WATER SPANIEL.
> Unto all these smelling Dogs, I may also adde the water Spagnell, called in French barbati, and in Germany wasserhund; who is taught by his maister to seeke for things that are lost by words or tokens. These will take waterfoule, and hunt otters and beavers, and watch the stroke of the gun when the fouler shooteth. They use to sheare their hinder parts, that so they may be less annoyed in swimming. [359]

Water Spaniel extinct type of dog, probably an ancestor of the POODLE, used to PUT UP(2) water fowl and to retrieve from water.
> That kind of dog whose service is required in fowling upon the water, partly through a natural forwardness, and partly by diligent teaching, is imbued with that property. This sort is somewhat big, and of a measurable greatness, having long rough, and curled hair, not obtained by extraordinary trades, but given by natures appointment . . . cut and notted from the shoulders to the hind legs, and to the end of his tail . . . that being bare and naked, by shearing of such superfluity of hair, they might achieve the more lightness, and swiftness, and be less hindered in swimming. [128]

Waterville former Irish 20–23in black-and-tan KERRY BEAGLE pack formed in 1820 to hunt a COUNTRY in County Kerry.

waupe TURNSPIT; WAPPE.
> He is also called Waupe, of ther natural noise of his voice Wau, which he makes in barking. [128]

wavy coat characteristic, usually found in long or coarse-haired breeds, which causes the coat to appear rippled.

Wayne WAYNE–DUPAGE.

Wayne–DuPage (US) AMERICAN FOXHOUND pack formed in 1940 by the merger of the Dupage, formed in 1928, and the Wayne, to hunt fox and DRAG(2) over a plough and woodland COUNTRY in Illinois.

WCRA (UK) WHIPPET CLUB RACING ASSOCIATION.

weak dog SHEEP DOG which lacks the determination to control stubborn or recalcitrant sheep.

weaning process of education which results in puppies eating independently and not being reliant on their DAM's milk. Though some variation exists from breed to breed the process usually begins when puppies are about three weeks old and should be complete by the time they are about five weeks old.

wear 1. debility resulting from overwork, especially in SHEEP DOGS; hillworn. 2. HOLD UP(3).

Weardale BEAGLE pack formed in 1950 as a revival of the Wear Valley Beagles which had hunted the Durham COUNTRY from 1860 to 1939.

Wear Valley Beagles WEARDALE.

weasley of a dog with a long, low-slung body and a TOPLINE that falls from the WITHERS before rising over the LOINS.

> Low weasley body. [203, DANDIE DINMONT TERRIER]

Weaving.

weaving unsound gait in which the elbows are thrown outwards as the limb is brought forwards, causing corresponding movement in the PASTERNS, and the forefeet to be turned outwards; also occasionally referred to as knitting and purling. [*illus.*]

> A stiff, stilted, hopping or weaving gait highly undesirable. [203, DANDIE DINMONT TERRIER]
> But crossing or weaving of the legs, front or back, is objectionable. [6, IRISH SETTER]

wede (obs.) madness, especially. that characteristic of RABIES. [159]

Wedge-shaped head.

wedgy (esp. of the head) lacking modelling or chiselling. [*illus.*]

weedy (of body) poorly developed; stunted.

weepy of eye, from which there is continual discharge, usually the result of infection or irritation.

weighing sling support used in the process of assessing the weight of fighting dogs.

weighting method by which the importance given to different characteristics in a breeding programme is measured.

weight-pulling organized competition in which dogs are required to pull a loaded trolley or sled over a measured course against time, the body weight of the dog being taken into account when deciding the winner.

Weil's disease LEPTOSPIROSIS.

Weimaraner [AKC, FCI, KC] German GUNDOG breed characterized by its distinctive pale-grey coat and light-amber eyes. It was developed during the early years of the 19th century from various CROSSES, including SCHWEISSHUNDS, ST HUBERT HOUNDS and POINTERS. By 1810 Grand Duke Karl August of Weimar had produced a uniform type but it was not until 1897 that the breed received official recognition in Germany. The breed was recognized by the American Kennel Club in 1943 and by the Kennel Club in 1959.

A powerful, well-balanced dog with a strong hunting instinct and a friendly, fearless and protective temperament. The ARISTOCRATIC head is moderately long with moderate STOP and prominent OCCIPUT; the high-set ears are long and lobular, the neck CLEAN. Overall the dog presents a square outline, with strong, straight forelegs and moderately ANGULATED, well-muscled hindquarters; the tail is traditionally DOCKED. The uniform grey coat may be long or short. Height 58–71cm (23–28in); weight 32–39kg (70½–86lb).

Weimaraner Vorstehund (obs.) WEIMARANER.

Weimer Pointer (obs.) WEIMARANER, although LEIGHTON suggested that this was a smaller version of the breed:

> A smaller and less muscular dog than the more common national type of Germany, with a narrower head and a softer coat. . . . The average height is 23 inches. [225]

weir (obs.) SHED(2). [103a]

well angulated having the correct angulation for the breed in question.

well bred having an aristocratic pedigree.

> He is a little, very alert, well-bred, intelligent Skye, as black as a hat, with a wet bramble for a nose and two cairngorms for eyes. [336]

well cut up of dog with pronounced and desirable TUCK-UP.

Wellfort former Irish BEAGLE pack.

well-hung (colloq.) of animal with large and prominent testicles.

well-knit 1. (of body) powerful and strongly muscled. 2. of foot with toes close together. [*illus.*]

well knuckled up of foot with strongly arched toes.

> Feet well knuckled up and strongly padded. [203, BEAGLE]

well laid WELL LAID BACK.

Well-knit toes.

well laid back usually of a shoulder in which the scapula forms a right angle with the humerus.
>Shoulders well laid back, muscular, not loaded. [203, BASENJI]

well let-down (of brisket) having appreciable depth from BACKLINE through the chest to the brisket; (of hock) having appreciable distance between STIFLE and HOCK.

well let-down brisket *see* WELL LET-DOWN.

well let-down hock *see* WELL LET-DOWN.

well ribbed up (of ribcage) capacious, WELL-SPRUNG.
>Not slack, but deep in the back ribs – that is, well ribbed-up. [218]
>Good round widely-sprung ribs and deep in back ribs. [203, ENGLISH SETTER]

well sprung (of ribcage) correctly rounded for the particular breed.
>Deep brisket, well sprung ribs. [203, WELSH SPRINGER SPANIEL]

well-sprung rib *see* WELL SPRUNG.

well tucked up of dog with pronounced, highly arched TUCK-UP.

well turned (of shoulder or STIFLE joint) having the correct degree of ANGULATION for the particular breed.
>Well turned stifles. [203, POINTER]
>Powerful, well bent and well turned stifles. [203, AFGHAN HOUND]

Well Vale former BEAGLE pack formed to hunt a COUNTRY in Lincolnshire.

Welsh Beagle rough-coated BEAGLE, probably extinct as a pure breed.

Welsh Black and Tan extinct breed of WELSH SHEEP DOG.
>To-day the old Welsh Black-and-Tan, the Hillman, the Old Welsh Grey and the Red Heeler seem to have gone into oblivion, purely through neglect. [181a]

Welsh Cocker (obs.) WELSH SPRINGER SPANIEL.
>There is also in Wales the smaller-sized red-and-white Spaniel known as the Welsh Cocker. [123]

Welsh Collie grey, smooth-coated, WALL-EYED COLLIE, probably now extinct as a pure breed. [401]

Welsh Corgi Welsh herding breed, of which there are two varieties – WELSH CORGI (CARDIGAN) and WELSH CORGI (PEMBROKE) – that are distinguished principally by the former's having a long tail, and the latter's being either traditionally DOCKED or born

tailless, although other differences are also apparent to the discerning eye. Opinions vary as to whether the two breeds were brought to Britain by Viking raiders or whether similar breeds in Scandinavia have their origins along the west coast of Britain; another similar breed, the LANCASHIRE HEELER, is to be found in the Fylde. All three were, and are used for herding cattle.

Welsh Corgi (Cardigan) [AKC, FCI, KC] active, long-bodied Welsh herding dog, sturdy and LOW ON THE LEG. The head is strongly vulpine with a wide, flat skull, moderate STOP and tapered MUZZLE; the eyes are wide set and may be blue in MERLE dogs; the rather large ears are erect; the neck is muscular, the shoulders sloping and the forelimbs short, slightly bowed and strongly boned. The chest is deep and fairly broad with prominent sternum; hindquarters are strong and WELL ANGULATED; feet are round and well padded; the tail is similar to a fox's BRUSH. The coat is hard and short and may be of any colour with or without white. Height 30cm (12in).

Welsh Corgi (Pembroke) [AKC, FCI, KC] the STANDARD for this breed is in many respects similar to that of the WELSH CORGI (CARDIGAN), the principal differences being that the ears of the Pembroke are of medium size, the forelimbs should be as straight as possible, the feet oval and the tail short, preferably naturally so; the coat is of medium length and may be red, SABLE, fawn, or black and tan, with or without white. Height 25.4–30.5cm (10–12in).

Welsh Cur former type of SHEEP DOG native to Wales.
>The Welsh Cur, was, in the eye of the Welsh law, exalted to the name and dignity of Shepherd's Cur when it was proved he could perform the duties of the Sheepdog. [123]

Welsh Foxhound rough-coated FOXHOUND native to Wales.
>The Welsh hound looks like no other hound, nor like a hound at all. It prefers to wear its hair on end, is voracious, and usually lurks in a butcher's shop. But it can kill foxes. In fact, it can kill anything. [379]

Welsh Grey extinct breed of Welsh herding dog, formerly found in the Snowdonia region where it was principally used to herd goats.

Welsh Harrier rough-coated WELSH HOUND, now extinct as a pure breed.
>This is a rough or shag-haired hound, more resembling the Otterhound than our modern Harrier, in shape as well as coat. He is much smaller than the Otter-hound, but may be used for otter-hunting. [123]
>Many Hounds – Welsh Harriers, for instance – will hunt anything with a hairy skin, unless they are broken from it. [186]

Welsh Heeler extinct Welsh cattle-HERDER, probably an ancestor of the WELSH CORGI (CARDIGAN).
>This is no special variety of the sheep dog at all, but any ordinary animal such as is used by shepherds, and more especially by drovers, the latter training him to bark and bite at the heels of cattle – hence the misleading name which has been given to him. [221]

A very well-marked variety of Collie is the Marled, or Marbled, sometimes incorrectly called the Tortoiseshell, and from the bizarre combination of colours it also gets the name of Harlequin. The name of Welsh Heeler has also been given to this variety from the way the dogs have of heeling the driven cattle. [123]

Welsh Hillman WELSH COLLIE.

Welsh Hound WELSH FOXHOUND.

They were designated the Welsh hounds, and most truly did they preserve the ancient system in every respect. Many of them were the old-fashioned, rough coated hounds; a breed which I imagine now to be extinct, except for the purpose of otter-hunting. [358]

Welsh Setter curly-, hard-coated extinct GUNDOG breed.

The coat was white with lemon markings confined to the head and ears; the tail was short and flat, similar to that of an otter.

Welsh Sheep Dog WELSH COLLIE.

He was rather short-haired, like the old Welsh sheep-dog once common in Wiltshire, but entirely black instead of the usual colour – blue with a sprinkling of black spots. [182]

Welsh Shepherd's Cur WELSH CUR. [123]

Welsh Springer Spaniel [AKC, FCI, KC] a COMPACT, active and kindly dog built for physically demanding work in the field. A likely ancestor of the breed is mentioned by FLEMING.

The skull is slightly DOMED, the STOP well defined and the square MUZZLE of medium length; the eyes of medium size and CLEAN, the VINE-LEAF EARS are set moderately low and are, compared with other spaniels, small. The neck is long and muscular, the forelimbs straight and well boned; the chest is WELL SPRUNG with a deep BRISKET; the LOIN is slightly arched and muscular. Hindquarters are strong and muscular, the feet are round and cat-like; the tail, traditionally DOCKED, is carried low. The straight, silky coat is always rich red and white. Height 46–48cm (18–18¾in).

Welsh Terrier [AKC, FCI, KC] The breed made its British show ring debut at Carnarvon in 1884 and was recognized by the Kennel Club in 1902. Its appearance and ancestry show strong links with the extinct ENGLISH BLACK AND TAN TERRIER.

The BREED STANDARD requires that the breed be game and fearless but not aggressive. The flat skull is of moderate width, the STOP gentle and the jaws powerful; the dark eyes are small and well set in; the V-SHAPED EARS are set fairly high and fall forward close to the cheek. The neck is slightly arched and of moderate length, the shoulders long and sloping, and the forelimbs straight with ample bone. The back is short, the chest well ribbed and the LOIN strong; thighs are muscular and HOCKS are WELL LET DOWN; feet are small and cat-like. The traditionally DOCKED tail is not carried too GAILY. The wiry, hard, CLOSE coat may be black and tan or black-GRIZZLE and tan. Height 39cm (15¼in).

Welsh Wire-coated Hound WELSH FOXHOUND.

Sometimes termed the Welsh Foxhound. In truth, he is simply a Welsh breed of hound used sometimes for hunting fox, sometimes hare, and often the otter. [123]

West Cumberland former OTTERHOUND pack formed in 1830 to hunt the Duddon, Esk, Mite, Irt, Ehen, Calder, Derwent, Ellen and their tributaries.

West Cumberland Beagles BLACK COMBE AND DISTRICT.

West Down Irish BEAGLE pack formed in 1913 to hunt a COUNTRY in County Down.

West Dulverton DULVERTON.

Western hunted from about 1820, the Cornwall COUNTRY is largely pasture and woodland.

Western Siberian Dog SAMOYED. [123]

Westfälische Dachsbracke [FCI] short-legged German HOUND principally used to hunt hare and fox and to track wild boar.

The skull is broad and flat, the MUZZLE rather long and slightly arched, the eyes light brown, the rounded pendulous ears broad at the base. The strong neck is rather long; the TOPLINE is hollowed behind the WITHERS and arched over the broad LOINS, which fall to a sloping CROUP; the chest is long and the TUCK-UP moderate. Forelimbs are straight and strong, the quarters muscular and WELL TURNED; the long, high-set tail is carried as an extension of the spine. The short, dense coat may be of any colour, other than black and chocolate, with more or less white. Height 30–36cm (12–14in).

West Greenland Husky the largest of two Greenland breeds of DRAUGHT DOG.

West Highland dim. WEST HIGHLAND WHITE TERRIER.

West Highland White Terrier [AKC, FCI, KC] Colonel Malcolm of Poltalloch, Argyllshire, who was instrumental in developing the breed from earlier strains of white SCOTTISH TERRIERS, is credited with naming and introducing the breed to the show ring in about 1900. It was recognized by the Kennel Club in 1907 and has since become one of the most popular of the terrier breeds.

A gay and alert breed, active and game. The slightly DOMED skull tapers slightly to a distinct STOP accentuated by bony ridges over the eyes; the dark, wide-set eyes are slightly sunk, the ears small and carried firmly erect. The neck is muscular and the shoulders WELL LAID, the forelimbs short, muscular and straight; the back is level, the LOINS broad and the chest deep and well ribbed; hindquarters are strong and muscular, the forefeet larger than the hind feet and thickly padded; the jauntily carried tail is naturally short and trimmed in the shape of a carrot. The white DOUBLE COAT is harsh, long and straight. Height 28cm (11in).

West Hills (US) AMERICAN FOXHOUND pack formed in 1940 to hunt fox and coyote over a steeply wooded COUNTRY in California.

Westie dim. (colloq.) WEST HIGHLAND WHITE TERRIER.

West Kent pack whose woodland and pasture COUNTRY was hunted from about 1776 by John Warde and became known as the West Kent from about 1830.

West Kent Woodland ERIDGE.

Westmeath 1. FOXHOUND pack dating from 1854 and preceded by private packs which had hunted the COUNTRY since at least 1740. 2. former Irish HARRIER pack formed in 1906 as a private pack called the Multyfarnham.

Westminster Dog Pit notorious London venue for bear- and badger-baiting and for dog fighting, owned during the early years of the 19th century by Charlie Aistrop. [177]

Westmoreland (US) AMERICAN FOXHOUND pack formed in 1916 to hunt DRAG(2) over a pasture COUNTRY in Pennsylvania.

West Norfolk pack founded in 1534 by Sir Thomas le Strange. Part of the bank and ditch COUNTRY was hunted from 1896–1934 by the Downham Harriers, which later became the Downham Foxhounds.

West Percy offshoot of the Percy which assumed its present name in 1919; from 1893–1904 the moorland COUNTRY was hunted as the Callaly Hounds and from 1904–1917 as the Coquetdale Hunt.

Westphalian Basset DACHSBRACKE.

Westphalian Bracke DACHSBRACKE.

Westphalian Dachsbracke DACHSBRACKE.

Westphalische Dachsbracke DACHSBRACKE.

West Russian Coursing Hound smooth, thick-coated SIGHTHOUND, of various colours. Height 64–66cm (25–26in).

West Siberian Laïka Soviet SPITZ, variety of LAÏKA differentiated from the European-Russian form by its longer head and ears, and its short STAND-OFF coat, which may be white, grey, tan, red or black, solid or with white. Height 53–61cm (20¾–24in); weight 18–23kg (39½–50½lb).

West Somerset a vale COUNTRY with some large woodlands, which has been hunted since 1946.

West Street founded prior to 1843 as a HARRIER pack to hunt a COUNTRY in Kent.

West Suffolk former STAGHOUND pack formed in 1891.

West Surrey WEST SURREY AND HORSNELL.

West Surrey and Horsnell former 15½in BEAGLE pack formed in 1882 as the Epsom and Ewell Beagles which were amalgamated with the Surbiton Beagles in 1888; the present name was assumed in 1909. The name was changed in 1921 after amalgamation with the Horsnell Beagles, which had been formed in 1874 as Mr Bailey's, the name being changed in 1897.

wet eczema ACUTE MOIST DERMATITIS.

wet neck neck with superfluous skin on the throat, DEWLAP.

Wetterhoun [FCI] Dutch water GUNDOG which has been in existence at least since the early 17th century and was originally used for hunting otters, hence the alternative name of Otterhoun. A rather boisterous and strong breed but one which is an effective all-purpose gundog which excels in water.

The head is strong, the rather small ears pendulous. The body is broad and deep with the ribs carried well back to a strong LOIN with very slight TUCK-UP; limbs are strong and well boned. The coat is tightly curled and weatherproof and may be black or liver with or without white, and with or without TICKING. Height 53–59cm (20¾–23¼in).

Wexford founded as a private pack by Colonel Pigott in 1780.

Whaddon Chase the COUNTRY lies in Buckinghamshire and has been hunted by the pack since 1920; former huntsmen include Harry Goddard, 1906–1911, and Frank Woodward, 1938–1947.

whalpet (Scot.) WHELP. [73e]

whappet (obs.) prick-eared CUR. [159]

wheaten (of coat colour) pale gold, similar to ripe wheat.

Wheatland the Shropshire COUNTRY includes both grass and woodland and has been hunted since 1811 when the pack was TRENCHER-FED.

wheat-sensitive enteropathy inherited inability to digest wheat products. (Mode of inheritance, uncertain.)

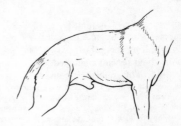

Wheel back.

wheel back arched TOPLINE; exaggerated ROACH BACK. [*illus.*]

wheel dogs pair of dogs which run directly in front of the sled.

whelp 1. give birth. 2. unweaned young, especially but not exclusively, of dogs.

whelpe (obs. spelling) WHELP. [163]

whelping process of giving birth.

whelping box specially designed container in which a bitch can give birth.

whicker (obs.) rapid movement of a hot or tired dog's tongue.

> The thump of a retriever's tail, the whicker of his dripping tongue. [279]

Widford former 14in BEAGLE pack formed to hunt a COUNTRY in Hertfordshire.

William Rayner's Hunt TIVERTON.

Wilton the Wiltshire, Dorsetshire and Hampshire

COUNTRY has been hunted since 1869. In 1884 the hunt became known as the Cranbourne; the present name was assumed in 1897.

Wimbush private BEAGLE pack formed in 1960 to hunt a COUNTRY in Essex.

whimper low sound made by excited or unhappy dogs.

whine low incessant noise made by an unhappy dog.

whip contrac. WHIPPER-IN. [249]

> Tom Dansey was a famous whip,
> Trained as a child in horsemanship
> Entered, as soon as he was able,
> As boy at Caunter's racing stable. [249]

Whip-dog Day generally 18 October, St Luke's Day; 10 October in Hull. The day was formerly appointed to round up and dispose of stray dogs.

> Whenever, after this, a dog showed his face while the annual preparation was going on, he was instantly beaten off. Eventually this was taken up by the boys, and until the introduction of the new police, was rigidly put in practice by them every 10th of October. [17]

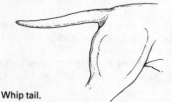

Whip tail.

whip tail long, thin tail. [*illus.*]

whip muscle sartorius muscle, especially of GREY-HOUNDS and, less often, of other SIGHTHOUNDS.

whipper-in hunt servant employed to help control a pack of HOUNDS at exercise or in the field.

> Now, huntsman, get on with the head hounds; the whipper-in will bring on the the others after you; [47]
> Most huntsmen, I believe, are jealous of the whip-per-in: they frequently look on him as a successor. [47]
> Holland, with Henry Petty at his back,
> The whipper-in and huntsman of the pack. [78]

whippers persons formerly employed to rid churches and churchyards of dogs and of tramps.

> It were verie good the dog whipper in Paules would have a care of this in his unsavourie visitation everie Saturday, for it is dangerous for such of the queenes liedge people as shall take a viewe of them fasting. [263]

Whippet [AKC, FCI, KC] a small SIGHTHOUND developed in northern England originally for rabbit-ing but now also used for racing over a short straight course.

A muscular, elegant and adaptable dog, built for speed. The head is long and lean, with a flat skull, slight STOP, bright, oval eyes, fine ROSE EARS and strong jaws. The arched neck is long and muscular, the shoulders oblique with clearly defined WITHERS; the forelegs are straight and the PASTERNS slightly sprung. The chest is very deep, the back broad and arched over the loin. Hindquarters are broad and muscular with well-bent STIFLES. Feet are well knuck-led and pads thick. The tail is long and tapering. The short, fine coat may be of any colour or mixture of colours. Height 44–51cm (17½–20in).

> In shapes and forms of dogges; of which there are but two sorts that are usefull for mans profit, which two are the mastiffe and the little whippet, or house dogge; the rest are for pleasure and recreation. [350]

Whippet Club Racing Association formed, by the Whippet Club, in 1968 to govern WHIPPET racing in a manner commensurate with Kennel Club objectives.

Whippet coursing former pursuit of captive rabbits within an enclosed area.

> Whippet coursing was a cruel sport. It was often run on any field or open space available. Rabbits were put down some yards away from the slipper who held the two dogs competing and the dog who picked up the rabbit first won the course. There seem to have been few if any rules. [297]

whippet racing short, handicapped sprint over a straight course usually 200yd long, but may vary from 150–250yd. At one end of the course there is either a SLIPPER or TRAP and, at the other, either people who attract the dogs' attention or an artificial lure. A good whippet covers the distance in some-thing under 12 seconds.

whippit (obs.) WHIPPET.

> Kind of dog between a greyhound and a spaniel. [159]

Whipworm.

whipworm parasitic worm of the genus *Trichuris*, which has a thick head end and thin whip-like rear end. [*illus.*]

whirl WHORL.

Whisht Hound mythological spectral HOUND of Dartmoor.

> The Dartmoor Whisht Hounds, heard baying on the moors and seen running round in a circle, are said to be the spirits of unbaptised children, doomed to hunt for ever. During the day they hide away in Hound's Tor and Hunt's Tor, and prefer when hunting to take the Abbot's Way on Dartmoor. [37]

whiskers correctly, the sensory hairs, but sometimes used to describe any coarse hair on the MUZZLE or chin.

white coat colour, signified by *w*, inherited as a recessive; white dogs have pigmented nose, eyes and exposed skin areas.

White Cavalier romantic term for the BULL TERRIER.

White Cuban (obs.) HAVANA BICHON.

White English Terrier ENGLISH WHITE TERRIER.

Whitelands Hunt WHITELANDS–PERKIOMEN VALLEY.

Whitelands–Perkiomen Valley (US) AMERICAN FOX-HOUND pack formed in 1959 by the merging of the Whitelands Hunt, formed in 1914, and the Perkiomen Valley Hunt, formed in 1924, to hunt over a hilly woodland and pasture COUNTRY in Pennsylvania.

white merle solid-white-coated dogs with whole or partially blue irises, small eye bulbus; they are usually partially or wholly deaf and are invariably sterile. The condition is produced by the homozygous MM gene.

White and Black French Hound CHIEN FRANÇAIS.

white spotting inherited characteristic in which white markings appear on a darker body colour.

White Terrier ENGLISH WHITE TERRIER.
Probably the first White Terrier which appears in an illustration occurs in the illuminated manuscript, showing the Ordinance of Charles the Bold in 1473. [37]

whitelie individual showing an untypical predominance of white coat colouring for its breed.
Whitelies: Body color white with red or dark markings. [6, PEMBROKE WELSH CORGI]

White Toy Terrier miniature version of the ENGLISH WHITE TERRIER.
Occasionally diminutive White Terriers of 3lb or 4lb weight turn up at a show, but do not seem as yet to be looked on as worthy of distinct classification. [37]

Whitney reflex reflex action, identified by Dr Leon Whitney, stimulated by pinching the base of the penis which causes a STUD-DOG to thrust vigorously towards the bitch.

Whitten effect tendency for synchronized seasons to occur among a group of females owing to the presence and interest of a male; the 'me too' syndrome.

whoa hopeful request for SLED-DOGS to stop.

whole-coloured self-coloured; of one colour.
'Whole-coloured', most preferable colours being red, red wheaten, or yellow red. [203, IRISH TERRIER]

whoopsie (euph.) excrement.

whorl spiral growth of hair, usually on either side of the anus and, sometimes, on the neck and shoulders.

who-whoop cheer which marks a kill by HOUNDS.

whripe (obs.) whimper. [159]

whule (obs.) whine or howl. [159]

whurr (obs.) growl. [159]

Wick and District BEAGLE pack formed in 1909, disbanded during the First World War and re-formed in 1924 as a BASSET pack. The Basset pack was disbanded in 1936 and the Beagle pack re-formed. The COUNTRY lies in Somerset.

wicket (Am.) device used at shows to measure the height of dogs.

Wicklow originally known as the Wicklow Harriers, the hunt dates from 1938 and assumed its present name in 1957.

Wicklow Harriers WICKLOW.

wide runner GREYHOUND that habitually chooses to run on the outside of the track. Such a dog is indicated in the racecard by 'W', and often seeded in an outside TRAP to avoid its interfering with other runners.

widow's peak triangular marking between the ears with the point reaching towards the eyes.

wild dog undomesticated dog.
When the Man waked up he said, 'What is Wild Dog doing here?' And the Woman said, 'His name is not Wild Dog any more, but the First Friend, because he will be our friend for always and always and always. [209a]

Wild Dog of Africa African PARIAH.
He is an outcast. He obtains a scanty living by the offal which he gathers in the towns, or he is become the perfect wild dog, and scours the country for his prey. His modern name is the deab. [406]

Wild Dog of Australia DINGO.
The newly discovered southern continent was, and some of it still continues to be, overrun by the native wild dogs. Dampier describes them, at the close of the last century, as 'beasts like the hungry wolves, lean like so many skeletons, and being nothing but skin and bone'. [406]

Wild Dog of Dakhun inhabitant of the mountains of Karnatak in south west India, mentioned as a true wild dog by old sources but probably a FERAL dog.

Wild Dog of Van Diemen Land DINGO.
When Van Diemen Land began to be colonized by Europeans, the losses sustained by the settlers by the ravages of the wild dogs were almost incredible. [406]

Wildehond LYCAON PICTUS.

Wild's Harriers late 18th-century, Manchester-based pack of HARRIERS.

wind catch (the scent).
Tit: But if you hunt these bear-whelps, then beware: The dam will wake, an if she wind you once [319t]

Windermere HARRIER pack formed in 1860 to hunt a moorland and fell COUNTRY in Westmorland.

Windhound (Am.) SIGHTHOUND.

Windmill Hill Dog Neolithic archaeological remains of a dog recovered from near Avebury by Alexander Keiller in 1928.

windspill (obs.) kind of GREYHOUND. [159]

winging gait in which there is dishing and horizontal rotation of the feet while the forelegs swing forward during movement.

winners (AKC) Best of Sex, i.e. Winners Dog and Winners Bitch are respectively the Best Dog and Best Bitch.

Winners Bitch (AKC) winner of the show class composed of first-prize winners from the five other bitch classes; equivalent to the Kennel Club's BEST BITCH.

Winners Class 1. (AKC) show class composed of winners from the five regular classes, equivalent to the Kennel Club's BEST OF SEX. 2. (FCI) show class for all dogs awarded a first grade in previous classes, plus the best Juniors and Young Adults.

Winners Dog (AKC) winner of the show class

composed of first-prize winners from the five other dog classes; equivalent to the Kennel Club's BEST DOG.

winter infertility   tendency for OESTRUS to be absent during periods of dark and cold weather.

Wire   dim. WIRE FOX TERRIER.

wire   (of coat) hard and coarse, usually also rippled.

Wire-coated Welsh Hound   WELSH TERRIER.

Wire Fox Terrier   although this variety of the FOX TERRIER is probably older than the SMOOTH variety it did not become popular until the early years of the 20th century.

The BREED STANDARD is exactly the same as that of the SMOOTH FOX TERRIER except that the coat is very wiry in texture and a maximum height of 39cm (15¼in).

Wire-haired Beagle   extinct version of the BEAGLE.
> Another variety is the Rough, or Wire-haired, Beagle. The absolute purity of his descent is doubtful, a cross more or less remote of the Terrier or the Otterhound being generally alleged. [123]

Wire-haired Continental Pointer   WIRE-HAIRED POINTING GRIFFON.

Wire-haired Dachshund   [KC] short, straight, harsh-coated version of the DACHSHUND. There should be a dense UNDERCOAT, bearded chin, bushy eyebrows and harsh coat on legs and feet. There are two sizes: miniature and standard.

Wire-haired Istrian Hound   orange or yellow-and-white, short, wire-haired Yugoslavian HOUND. Height 46–51cm (18–20in); weight 16–23kg (35–50½lb).

Wire-haired Pointing Griffon   GRIFFON D'ARRÊT À POIL DUR.

Wire-haired Rabbit Dachshund   RAUHAARIGER KANINCHTECKEL.

Wirral   former HARRIER pack formed in 1868 to hunt a COUNTRY in Cheshire.

Wissahickon   (US) American and CROSSBRED FOX-HOUND pack formed in 1955 to hunt a rolling COUNTRY in Pennsylvania.

witch   hare. (der. witches were formerly thought to be capable of assuming the form of a hare.)
> How high the pale he leapt, how wide the ditch,
> When the hound tore the haunches of the witch!
> [145d]

witch's milk   milk secreted by newborn puppies and other young mammals.

withers   highest part of the scapula, the point to which the height of a dog is traditionally measured.
[*illus.* POINTS]
> Approximate height: Dogs 48cm (19in) at withers; Bitches 46cm (18in) at withers. [203, WELSH SPRINGER SPANIEL]

wluine   (obs.) female wolf. [159]

wobbler   puppy suffering from WOBBLER SYNDROME.
  wobbler syndrome   CERVICAL SPONDYLOSIS.

Woburn pack   extinct strain of COLLIES used, during the late 18th century, by shepherds on the Duke of Bedford's estates.

Wold Greyhound   extinct, Yorkshire strain of long-haired, curly-tailed SIGHTHOUNDS.
> The Wolds greyhounds were long-haired, curly-tailed dogs, with straight, firm legs, round hard foxhound feet and incredibly swift powers of closing up on the prey. [83]

wolf   1. *CANIS LUPUS*.
> Rapacious animals we hate:
> Kites, hawks and wolves deserve their fate. [145g]
> He peeped through the chinks of his rude door, and there sat a great red wolf moaning melodiously with his nose high in the air. [294]

2. greyish coat colour.

wolf cub   juvenile wolf.

wolf dog   1. dog used to hunt wolves.   2. CHOW CHOW.
> Sometimes called the Wolf-dog, probably on account of its being used in packs for hunting purposes in the North of China. [123]

3. IRISH GREYHOUND. [338]   4. GERMAN SHEPHERD DOG (ALSATIAN).

wolf grey   (of coat colour) canine equivalent of AGOUTI coloration in rodents, a brownish-grey colour.

wolf sable   (of coat colour) even distribution of black, brown or grey hair throughout.

wolf's claw   (Am.) DEW-CLAW of the hind limb.
> Faults . . . the fifth toe on the hind legs appearing at a higher position and with wolf's claw or spur.
> [6, GREAT DANE]

Wolferton   one of Her Majesty the Queen's Kennel Club registered affixes, which derives from a village on the Sandringham estate.

Wolffian duct   rudimentary structure in which male sex organs develop.

Wolff–Parkinson–White syndrome   excitability associated with abnormally rapid heartbeat and fibrillation.

Wolfhound   dim. IRISH WOLFHOUND.
> With sternest Wolves he does engage
> And acts on them successful rage. [284]

Wolfspitz   1. larger and probably the original version of the POMERANIAN.
> Original type of Pomeranian, through which the derivation of the breed is traceable step by step through the dogs of Lapland, Siberia, Norway, and Sweden, to the wolf's first cousin, the Eskimo dog. [225]

2. (obs.) KEESHOND.

Wolver   (US) private BEAGLE pack formed in 1913 to hunt cottontail rabbit over a COUNTRY in Virginia.

Wolverston   former 13½in BEAGLE pack formed to hunt a COUNTRY in Essex.

Woodbrook   (US) American, English and CROSS-BRED FOXHOUND pack formed in 1925 to hunt DRAG(2) over a prairie COUNTRY in Washington.

Woode   (obs.) mad, rabid, thought to have been caused by a worm under the dog's tongue.
> And if that worme were taken from hem thei shuld never wax woode, but therof make I noon affirma-cioun. [125]

Woodfield   1. (US) private BEAGLE pack formed in

1950 to hunt cottontail rabbit over a COUNTRY in Ohio.

Woodland   former 17in BEAGLE pack formed to hunt a COUNTRY in Durham.

Woodland Pytchley   pack hunting a COUNTRY which lies entirely in Northamptonshire; the division from the Pytchley itself was made in 1874.

woodnesse   (obs.) RABIES.

Woodside   (US) AMERICAN FOXHOUND pack formed in 1961 to hunt over a hilly COUNTRY in South Carolina.

Wood Spaniel   SPRINGER SPANIEL.
> The ordinary Wood Spaniel, or Springer, by which name the larger breed is distinguished from the smaller one, or Cocker, is not only one of the most ancient of sporting dogs, but is certainly the most useful. [186]

woof   imitative of a dog's bark.

woopsie   WHOOPSIE.

Worcester Park and Buckland   former 15½in BEAGLE pack formed in 1886 by Charles Blake, in succession to the Morden Harriers, to hunt a COUNTRY in Surrey. In 1921 the pack amalgamated with the Buckland Beagles.

Worcestershire   FOXHOUND pack dating from prior to 1813 when the first master resigned.

work back   restore, in exchange for a fee, a stolen dog to its rightful owner. [280]

working certificate   document issued at Field trials for GUNDOGS and by Masters of Hounds for TERRIERS which affirms that a particular dog is capable of carrying out certain tasks.

working clip   PUPPY CLIP.

working dog   any dog which carries out the task for which its breed was intended.

Working Group   [AKC, KC] collection of pastoral and guard breeds grouped together for the purposes of show classification. The AKC and KC do not entirely agree about which breeds should be included in the group, and both differ from the FCI.

working retriever clip   style of coat CLIP peculiar to the PORTUGUESE WATER DOG.
> In order to give a natural appearance and a smooth, unbroken line, the entire coat is scissored or clipped to follow the outline of the dog, leaving a short blanket of coat no longer than one inch in length. At the end of the tail the hair is left at full length. [6, POR-TUGUESE WATER DOG]

Working Sheep Dog   The name under which the working BORDER COLLIE is registered by the International Sheep Dog Society (ISDS).

working terrier   any TERRIER which is used for the purpose for which the breed is intended.

working trial   competition in which the working qualities of dogs are assessed.

World Champion   title awarded to the dog that wins BEST OF BREED at the FCI WORLD SHOW.

World Show   annual peripatetic event organized by the FCI. The winners are awarded the title of World Champion.

worm   generic term for any endoparasitic helminth. Dogs are susceptible to a number of types of worm, including roundworm, tapeworm, heartworm, hookworm, and whipworm.

wormer   substance which kills parasitic worms.

wormian bones   sutural bones; bones joined by fibrous tissue which restricts or prevents movement, esp. the bones of the skull.

worming the tongue   operation formerly carried out to remove the tendon on the underside of the tongue, which was formerly thought to contain a worm which caused rabies: if the 'worm' was removed the dog would be protected against the disease.
> The violence used in stripping down the tendon is so great, and the lacerated fibrous substance is so much on the stress, and its natural elasticity is so considerable, that it recoils and assumes the appearance of a dying worm, and the dog is said to have been wormed. For the sake of humanity, as well as to avoid the charge of ignorance, it is to be hoped that this practice will speedily cease. [406]

wormy   of dog infested with internal parasites.

worry   1. (of HOUNDS) kill.
> Who-whoop! They have him! They're round him; how
> > They worry and tear when he's down!
> 'Twas a stout hill-fox when they found him: now
> > 'Tis a hundred tatters of brown! [388]

2. (of several dogs) attack an individual.
> Mr Heathcliff and his man climbed the cellar steps with vexatious phlegm: I don't think they moved one second faster than usual, though the hearth was an absolute tempest of worrying and yelping. [63]

3. (of any dog) attack farm stock or domestic animals.
> The bear and the badger are baited with the same barbarity; and if the rabble can get nothing else, they will divert themselves by worrying cats to death. [330]

4. hold in the teeth and shake.

wowl   (obs.) howl. [159]

wrench   turn of less than a right angle made by a coursed hare.

wrethchcock   smallest and weakest in a litter; a runt.

Wrinkle.

wrinkle   (usu. of ears) loose, folded skin.   2. (in PEKINGESE) roll of skin between eyes and nose. [*illus.*]

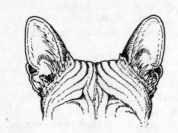

Wrinkling.

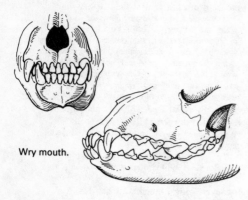

Wry mouth.

wrinkling (esp. of the head) having wrinkles. [*illus.*]
Faults . . . wrinkling too deep (wet) or lacking (dry).
[6, ALASKAN MALAMUTE]

wrist CARPAL JOINT.

wrist bones CARPAL BONES.

wry crooked.

wry face WRY MOUTH.
A 'wry-faced' dog is one having the lower jaw
twisted. [253]

wry mouth lower jaw laterally displaced so that the
teeth do not occlude correctly. [*illus.*]
A wry mouth is a serious fault. [6, BRUSSELS
GRIFFON]
Serious fault: Wry mouth. [6, BOSTON TERRIER]

wryneck SCREW TAIL.

Wurtemburg Pointer extinct large German
GUNDOG.
A heavy, thick-set dog which approaches the hound
in character. His ears are noticeably large. In colour
he is brown, brindle about the back and head, with
light tan-and-white markings, the white being plen-
tifully ticked with brown, which reminds one of a
speckled trout. The height at the shoulder may be
27 inches, the weight from 60 to 75 pounds. [225]

Wye Valley former OTTERHOUND pack formed in
1897 to hunt the Wye, Cowbridge, Ewenny, Ogmore,
Ely, Garron, Ledden, Olway, Monnow, Usk and
Troth.

Wylye Valley pack formed in 1919 to hunt a
COUNTRY that extends over the Wiltshire downs.

Wyre Forest BEAGLE pack formed in 1947 to hunt
a COUNTRY in Worcestershire and to the west.

XYZ

X chromosome pair of chromosomes found only in the female.

X-linked characteristics which are transmitted by genes present only on the X-chromosome.

xanthomatosis abnormal accumulation of lipid fats, often associated with diabetes mellitus.

Xarnelo (obs.) PODENCO IBICENCO.

xiphoid process pointed piece of cartilage supported by bone at the rear end of the sternum.

Xoloizcuintle [FCI] hairless breed with origins in Mexico, probably a mutant PARIAH which has been cultivated because of its unusual appearance.

The head is broad with imperceptible STOP, the ears large and mobile; the mouth lacks premolars. The body is long, the skin is smooth and warm to the touch and may be charcoal-grey or shades of chocolate or liver; unpigmented areas occur but are not encouraged. Height 33–37cm (13–14½in).

XX sex reversal of dogs which carry an XX karotype: if a Y-effect gene is also present such animals may be hermaphrodites.

XXX chromosome abnormality producing female sterility.

XX/XXY mosaic chromosomal anomaly in which a number of the body cells contain an extra Y chromosome.

XXY male hermaphrodite resulting from chromosome abnormality.

xysma small pieces of what appears to be body tissue, sometimes to be found in diarrhoea stools.

XY/XX mosaic chromosomal INTERSEX.

Yama Vedic god of death who was guarded by two dogs.

> Do thou hasten past the two four-eyed, brindled dogs, the offspring of Sarama. In trust him, O Yama, to they two watch-dogs, four-eyed, road-guarding, and man-observing. The two brown messengers of Yama, broad of nostril and insatiable. [300]

yamph (obs.) bark like a small dog.

Yankee Terrier (obs.) AMERICAN STAFFORDSHIRE TERRIER.

yap 1. shrill bark, usually of toy dogs. 2. (obs.) cur. [159]

> Some there are that make a sharp yapping noise from the track and try to deceive one, making out the false to be true. [404]

yappy of a dog with a tendency to yap incessantly.

yapster dog. [280]

yard-dog dog kept, usually chained, in a yard to act as a GUARD.

> A velvet mien; an eye of amber, full
> Of that which keeps the faith with us for life,
> Lover of meal-times; hater of yard-dog strife;
> Lordly, with silken ears most strokeable. [289]

yarding (Aust.) working sheep within an enclosed area or yard. [204]

yawing CRABBING.

Y chromosome chromosome which causes the formation of the testes and, therefore, maleness.

Yell Hound WHISHT HOUND.

yellow (of coat colour) rich-cream.

Yellow Black Mouth Cur SOUTHERN CUR.

yellow body CORPUS LUTEUM.

yellow dog tick HAEMAPHYSALIS LEACHII LEACHII.

yellow distemper HEPATITIS. [406]

yellows JAUNDICE.

> As to the yellows, in nine cases out of ten, that comes from chill and exposure to damp, when in a weakened or unhealthy state; the dog is not strong enough to cast it off in the usual robust way, so straight it goes to the liver. [158]

yelp high-pitched cry of an excited dog, usually in fear or pain.

> Then Malapert yelped at Myngs's whip. [249]
> She would utter an inward yelp and lift a cold nose to my cheek, whimpering sorely. [172]
> For recreation he killed cats and frightened small children by yelping round their legs. [194]

yelper (obs.) a WHELP(2). [159]

yeth-hounds headless spectral HOUNDS, supposed to be the animated spirits of unbaptized children; Gabriel's hounds.

yip small nervous dog. [280]

Ynysfor 1. private FOXHOUND pack which has existed since 1765 to hunt a COUNTRY in Gwynedd. 2. former private OTTERHOUND pack.

yoeman-fewterer (obs.) FEWTERER. [159]

yoghurt therapy treatment of digestive disorders by administering live yoghurt, a source of Lactobacillus.

York and Ainsty pack whose Yorkshire COUNTRY has been hunted since 1821, though at times it has been split into North and South countries, each with its own pack.

Yorkie dim. (colloq.) YORKSHIRE TERRIER.

Yorkshire dim. YORKSHIRE TERRIER.

Yorkshire Blue and Tan (obs.) YORKSHIRE TERRIER.

> A modern breed altogether, having been almost unknown beyond the neighbourhood of Halifax until within the last few years. [338]

Yorkshire Blue and Tan Terrier (obs.) YORKSHIRE TERRIER.

Yorkshire Buckhound extinct, localized type of STAGHOUND.

> Lost also about the same time near Camberwell, a Yorkshire Buckhound, having black spots upon his back, red ears, and a wall-eye, and PR upon his near shoulder. [15]

Yorkshire Terrier [AKC, FCI, KC] probably the world's most popular TOY dog, which arrived on the scene as a product of the late 19th-century desire to create 'fancy' breeds.

Under the long, straight coat is a COMPACT, short-backed, sturdy TERRIER in miniature. The skull is flat, the rich-tan ears pricked, and the eyes dark and sparkling with intelligence and liveliness. The body coat is never wavy and is of a dark steel blue, the hair on the head is tan. Weight up to 3.1kg (6½lb).

Yorkshire Waterside Terrier   AIREDALE. [320a]

Youatt, William   veterinary surgeon, and author of *On Canine Madness* (1828) and *The Dog* (1845).

Young Adults class   [FCI] show class for dogs between fifteen and twenty-four months old on the day of the show.

yowl   howl dismally.

> The forester luckily was no at hame, sir; but the dogs made an awful noise, yowling at the stag. [337]
> 'I believe I seen a two – three of the white dogs running east awhile ago,' said the elderly farmer, 'and they yowling!' [329a]

Ytzcuinte Porzotli   variety of ALCO. [380]

Yugoslavian Herder   SARPLANINAC.

Yugoslavian Hound of the Save Valley   JUGOSLOVEN-SKI POSAVKSI GONIČ.

Yugoslavian Mountain Hound   JUGOSLOVENSKI PLANINSKI GONIČ.

Yugoslavian Shepherd Dog   JUGOSLOVENSKI OVCARSKI PAS-SARPLANINAC.

Yugoslavian Tricolour Hound   JUGOSLOVENSKI TROBOJNI GONIČ.

Zanzibar Dog   medium-sized, short-coated, dun-coloured primitive African hunting dog with wedge-shaped head, horizontally held ears and slightly curled tail. It is probably extinct in its pure form.

Zetland   pack whose COUNTRY lies in Durham and north Yorkshire and has much plough with areas of moor and woodland; it has been hunted by the pack since 1866.

Zollinger-Ellison syndrome   gastric acidity, islet cell tumours and pancreatic disturbance resulting in vomiting, anaemia, diarrhoea, loss of weight and debility.

zoonosis   any disease which can be transmitted from animals to man.

Zorian Laïka   one of six European-Russian LAÏKA breeds identified in 1896 by Prince Andrew Shirinsky Shihmatoff. [380]

Zulu Dog   primitive, semi-wild GUARD and hunting dog. Small but powerful, it has a short, sandy-coloured coat, square MUZZLE, and is very similar to the BASENJI in all but colour.

Zulu Sand Dog   ZULU DOG.

Zwergpinscher   [FCI] MINIATURE PINSCHER.

Zwergschnauzer   [FCI] MINIATURE SCHNAUZER.

Zwergspitz   [FCI] POMERANIAN.

Zwergteckel   [FCI] MINIATURE DACHSHUND.

zygoma   bone of the cheek, below the eye. [*illus.* SKELETON]

zygomatic   of, or relating to, the ZYGOMA.

  zygomatic arch   part of the ZYGOMA which curves up behind the eye to the back of the skull. [*illus.* SKELETON]

zygote   cell produced as a consequence of union between male and female gametes.

Bibliography

1   Adams, E. et al, *Deer, Hare and Otter Hunting*, Seeley, Service & Co. (London, 1934).
2   Addison, Thomas, in *The Spectator* [1711], Everyman's Library (London, 1979).
3   Aldin, Cecil, *Dogs of Character*, Eyre & Spottiswoode (London, 1927).
4   Alken, Henry, *The National Sports of Great Britain*, Thomas McLean (London, 1821).
5   Allan, E. and Blogg, R., *Every Dog* [1983], Oxford University Press (Oxford, 1990).
6   American Kennel Club, The, *Breed Standards*, Dog World (Chicago, 1990).
6a American Kennel Club, The, *The Complete Dog Book* [1935], Garden City Books (New York, 1956).
6b American Kennel Club, The, *The Complete Dog Book* 2nd edn [1941], Howell Book House Inc. (New York, 1956).
7   Anon, *Kings 1*, 14:11, The Bible (King James version).
7a Anon, *Kings 2*, 8:13, The Bible (King James version).
8   Anon, *Boke of Curtasye* [15th cent.]: from Vesey-Fitzgerald, Brian *The Book of the Dog*, Nicholson & Watson (London, 1948).
9   Anon, *By-law of Kendal Corporation* [1584].
10 Anon, *Chester Plays*.
11 Anon, *Coventry Mysteries* [1591?], Shakespeare Society (London, 1841).
12 Anon, Dimetian Code [12th cent.]: from *Ancient Laws and Institutions of Wales*, English Record Commission (1841).
13 Anon, *Dog Whippers* [1576]: from Ash, Edward, *Dogs: Their History and Development*, Ernest Benn (London, 1927).
14 Anon, Inscription on a Greek tomb: from D'Oyley, Elizabeth (ed.), *An Anthology for Animal Lovers*, William Collins Sons (London, 1927).
15 Anon, in *London Gazette* [1667]: from Jackson, Frank and Jean (eds), *Dog Tales*, Richard Marples & Partners (Manchester, 1981).
16 Anon, *Mercurius Publicus* [1660]: from Parson, Daniel (ed.), *In Praise of Dogs*, Country Life Books (London, 1936).
17 Anon, *Notes and Queries* [1852]: from Ash, Edward, *Dogs: Their History and Development*, Ernest Benn (London, 1927).
18 Anon, 'Daddy wouldn't buy me a Bow-wow': from Opie, Iona and Peter (eds), *The Oxford Dictionary of Nursery Rhymes*, Clarendon Press (Oxford, 1952).
19 Anon, *Observations upon Prince Rupert's White Dog called Boye* [1642]: from D'Oyley, Elizabeth (ed.), *An Anthology for Animal Lovers*, William Collins Sons (London, 1927).
20 Anon, *Pamphlet Reporting a Dialogue between Prince Rupert's Dog and Another* [1643]: from D'Oyley, Elizabeth (ed.), *An Anthology for Animal Lovers*, William Collins Sons (London, 1927).
21 Anon, *Poor Beasts* [n.d.]: from Silcock, Arnold (ed.), *Verse and Worse*, Faber & Faber (London, 1977).
22 Anon, *Proverbs* 17:12, The Bible (King James version).
23 Anon, in *Read's Weekly Journal* [1721]: from Parson, Daniel (ed.), *In Praise of Dogs*, Country Life Books (London, 1936).
24 Anon, *Samuel* 24:14, The Bible (King James version).
26 Anon, Summary of the Proceedings of Parliament, 16 August 1784.
27 Anon, 'The Comic Adventures of Old Mother Hubbard and Her Dog' [1805]: from Opie, Iona and Peter (eds), *The Oxford Dictionary of Nursery Rhymes*, Clarendon Press (Oxford, 1952).
28 Anon, *The Fallow Doe* [1611]: from D'Oyley, Elizabeth (ed.), *An Anthology for Animal Lovers*, William Collins Sons (London, 1927).
29 Anon, in *The Gentleman's Magazine* [1774]: from Parson, Daniel (ed.), *In Praise of Dogs*, Country Life Books (London, 1936).
30 Anon, *The Hare Maketh Her Moan* [15th cent.]: from D'Oyley, Elizabeth (ed.), *An Anthology for Animal Lovers*, William Collins Sons (London, 1927).

31   Anon, in *The Licensed Victuallers' Gazette* (1899).
32   Anon, in *The London Magazine* [1820]: from Parson, Daniel (ed.), *In Praise of Dogs*, Country Life Books (London, 1936).
33   Anon, *The Names of the Hare*.
34   Anon, *The Twa Corbies*.
35   Anon, 'Wilhelm the Dachs' in *Punch*: from D'Oyley, Elizabeth (ed.), *An Anthology for Animal Lovers*, William Collins Sons (London, 1927).
36   Arnold, Matthew, *Geist's Grave* [1867]: from Parker, Eric and Croxton-Smith, A. (eds), *The Dog Lover's Weekend Book*, Seeley, Service & Co. (London, 1950).
37   Ash, Edward, *Dogs: Their History and Development*, Ernest Benn (London, 1927).
37a   Ash, Edward, *The New Book of the Dog*, Cassell (London, 1938).
37b   Ash, Edward, *Practical Dog Book*, Cassell (London, 1938).
37c   Ash, Edward, *This Doggie Business*, Hutchinson & Co (London, 1934).
38   Astley, Sir, *Fifty Years of My Life* [1894]: from Parker, Eric, (ed.), *Game Pie*, Country Life Books (London, 1977).
39   Atkinson, J.A. and Walker, J.A., *Picturesque Representation of the Manners, Customs and Amusements of the Russians* [1812].
40   Ayto, J. and Simpson, J. (eds), *The Oxford Dictionary of Modern Slang*, Oxford University Press (Oxford, 1992).
41   Baker, G., *To My Mother*.
*41   Baker, T., *The Collie* [1900].
42   Banks, Sir J., *Journal of a Voyage to Newfoundland* [1768].
43   Barham, Richard H., *The Bagman's Dog* [1840]: from *The Ingoldsby Legends*, Oxford University Press (Oxford, 1929).
44   Barker, D., *The Under-dog in the Fight* [19th cent.].
45   Barkley, H.C., *Rat-catching for the Use of Schools*, Methuen & Co. (London, 1960).
46   Barton, Frank T., *The Kennel Encyclopaedia* [1903], Virtue & Co. (London, 1946).
46a   Barton, Frank T., *Terriers: Their Points and Management*, John Lang (London, 1907).
47   Beckford, Peter, *Thoughts on Hunting* [1781], Methuen & Co. (London, 1951).
48   Belloc, Hilaire, *Epitaph on the Favourite Dog of a Politician* [1896]: from Grigson, Geoffrey (ed.), *The Oxford Book of Satirical Verse*, Oxford University Press (Oxford, 1980).
49   Bengtson, Bo, Wintzell, A. and Swedrup, I., *Dogs of the World* [1977], David & Charles (Newton Abbot, 1982).
50   Berners, Juliana, *Boke of St Albans* [1468]: from Hands, Rachel, *English Hawking and Hunting in the Boke of St Albans*, Oxford University Press (Oxford, 1975).
51   Bewick, Thomas, *A General History of Quadrupeds* [1790], Ward Lock (London, 1970).
51a   Bewick, Thomas, *A Memoir* [1862], Oxford University Press (Oxford, 1979).
52   Blake, William, *Auguries of Innocence* [1789]: from D'Oyley, Elizabeth (ed.), *An Anthology for Animal Lovers*, William Collins Sons (London, 1927).
53   Blome, Richard, *The Gentleman's Recreation* [1686]: from Parker, Eric (ed.), *Game Pie*, Country Life Books (London, 1977).
54   Blood, Douglas and Studdert, Virginia (eds), *Baillière's Comprehensive Veterinary Dictionary* [1988], Baillière Tindall (London, 1990).
55   Blunt, William S., *Poetical Works* [1898]: from Parker, Eric (ed.), *Game Pie*, Country Life Books (London, 1977).
56   Boethius, Hector, *Description of the Scottish Kingdom* [1574]: Gilbert, John M., *Hunting and Hunting Reserves in Medieval Scotland*, John MacDonald (Edinburgh, 1979).
57   Border Terrier Club, *Breed Standard*, Border Terrier Club (Carlisle, 1921).
58   Boswell, James, *Life of Samuel Johnson* [1791], Everyman's Library (London, 1906).
59   Brewster, Sir David, *Memoirs of the Life, Writings, and Discoveries of Sir Isaac Newton* [1850], Constable & Co. (London, 1850).
60   Bromiley, M.W., *Physiotherapy in Veterinary Medicine*, Blackwell Scientific Publications (Oxford, 1991).

61   Bromley-Davenport, William, *The Dream of an Old Meltonian* [1866]: from de Broke, Lord Willoughby, *The Sport of our Ancestors*, Constable and Co. (London, 1921).

61a   Bromley-Davenport, William, *Lowesby Hall* [1866?]: from de Broke, Lord Willoughby, *The Sport of our Ancestors*, Constable and Co. (London, 1921).

62   Bronte, Anne, *The Tenant of Wildfell Hall* [1848], Oxford University Press (London, 1906).

63   Bronte, Emily, *Wuthering Heights* [1847], Collins, London.

64   Brooke, Rupert, *The Little Dog's Day* [1911]: from Parson, Daniel (ed.), *In Praise of Dogs*, Country Life Books (London, 1936).

65   Brown, Dr John, *Rab and his Friends* [1858], Everyman's Library (London, 1970).

66   Browning, Elizabeth Barrett, *To Flush, My Dog* [1862]: from Parson, Daniel (ed.), *In Praise of Dogs*, Country Life Books (London, 1936).

67   Browning, Robert, *Tray* [1880?]: from Menzies, Lucy (ed.), *The First Friend*, George Allen & Unwin (London, 1922).

*67   Bryden, H.A., *Hare Hunting and Harriers*, Grant Richards (London, 1903).

68   Buck, Pearl, *The Child Who Never Grew Up*.

69   Buckley, Holland, *The West Highland White Terrier*, Illustrated Kennel News Co. (London, 1911).

70   Budgell, Eustace, in *The Spectator* [1711], Everyman's Library (London, 1979).

71   Budgett, H.M., *Hunting by Scent* [1933], Eyre & Spottiswoode (London, 1937).

72   Buffon, Comte de Georges Louis Leclere, *Histoire Naturelle*, 36 vols [1746–89], trans. W. Smellie, *Natural History*: from Parson, Daniel (ed.), *In Praise of Dogs*, Country Life Books (London, 1936).

72a   Buffon, Comte de Georges Louis Leclere, *Histoire Naturelle*, 36 vols [1746–89], trans. Gmelin, *Natural History*: from Ash, Edward, *Dogs: Their History and Development*, Ernest Benn (London, 1927).

73   Burns, Robert, *Birthday Ode for 31 December* [1787]: from MacKenna, J. (ed.), *Poetical Works of Robert Burns*, Collins (London, 1952).

73a   Burns, Robert, *Epitaph on John Rankine* [1785]: from MacKenna, J. (ed.), *Poetical Works of Robert Burns*, Collins (London, 1952).

73b   Burns, Robert, *On the Late Captain Grose's Peregrinations through Scotland* [1785]: from MacKenna, J. (ed.), *Poetical Works of Robert Burns*, Collins (London, 1952).

73c   Burns, Robert, *Second Epistle to Robert Graham Esq. of Fintry* [1791]: from MacKenna, J. (ed.), *Poetical Works of Robert Burns*, Collins (London, 1952).

73d   Burns, Robert, *The Jolly Beggars: A Cantata* [1786]: from MacKenna, J. (ed.), *Poetical Works of Robert Burns*, Collins (London, 1952).

73e   Burns, Roberts, *The Twa Herds, or The Holy Tylyie* [1786]: from MacKenna, J. (ed.), *Poetical Works of Robert Burns*, Collins (London, 1952).

73f   Burns, Robert, *Twa Dogs* [1786]: from MacKenna, J. (ed.), *Poetical Works of Robert Burns*, Collins (London, 1952).

73g   Burns, Robert, *My Lord a Hunting* [1786]: from Mackenna J. (ed.), *Poetical Works of Robert Burns*, Collins (London, 1952).

73h   Burns, Robert, *On Glenriddell's Fox Breaking his Chain* [1786]: from MacKenna, J. (ed.), *Poetical Works of Robert Burns*, Collins (London, 1952).

74   Burrows, George T. *Gentleman Charles*, Vinton & Co. (London, 1951).

75   Burton, Richard, *Anatomy of Melancholy* [1624].

76   Butler, Samuel, *Hudibras* [1663]: from Grigson, Geoffrey (ed.), *The Oxford Book of Satirical Verse* Oxford University Press (Oxford, 1980).

76a   Butler, Samuel, *The Tattling Gossip of the Newsheets* (1678).

77   Buxton, Lord, *Fishing and Shooting* [1902]: from Parker, Eric (ed.), *Game Pie*, Country Life Books (London, 1977).

78   Byron, Lord, *English Bards and Scotch Reviewers* [1809] *Best of Dogs*, Hutchinson & Co. (London, 1949).

79   Caius, Dr Johannes, *De Canibus Britannicis* [1570], trans. Abraham Fleming, *Of Englishe Dogges* [1576], Denlinger (Washington DC, 1947).

80   Calverley, Charles S. *Disaster* [1862]: from Silcock, Arnold (ed.), *Verse and Worse*, Faber and Faber (London, 1977).

80a   Calverley, Charles S., *Sad Memories* [1862]: from Silcock, Arnold (ed.), *Verse and Worse*, Faber and Faber (London, 1977).

81   Canteleu, Count le C. de, *Les Races de Chiens Courans Français*, Imprimerie Vanbuggenhoudt Frères (Brussels, 1897).

82   Carlyle, Thomas, [1850], quoted in Parkes, Eric and Croxton-Smith, A. (eds), *The Dog Lover's Weekend Book*, Seeley, Service & Co. (London, 1950).

83   Carson, Ritchie, *The British Dog*, Robert Hale (London, 1981).

84   Casselli, Rosina et al, *The Complete Chihuahua*, Howell (New York, 1963).

85   Chalmers, Patrick, *Dogs of Every Day* [1928], Eyre & Spottiswoode (London, 1933).

85a   Chalmers, Patrick, *Green Days and Blue Days* [1912], Maunsell (London, 1920?).

85b   Chalmers, Patrick, *Jane – A Terrier, Green Days and Blue Days* [1912], Maunsell (London, 1920).

85c   Chalmers, Patrick, *Pancakes, Green Days and Blue Days* [1912], Maunsell (London, 1920?).

85d   Chalmers, Patrick, *The Last Drive, Dogs of Every Day* [1928], Eyre and Spottiswoode (London, 1930).

85e   Chalmers, Patrick, *The New Anubis, Green Days and Blue Days* [1912], Maunsell (London, 1920?).

85f   Chalmers, Patrick, *To A March Hare, Dogs of Every Day* [1928], Eyre and Spottiswoode (London, 1930).

86   Chaucer, Geoffrey, *Canterbury Tales* [1387], Penguin Classics (London, 1954).

87   Chekhov, Anton, *The Proposal* [1889], Oxford University Press (London, 1959).

88   Chesterton, G.K., *The Song of Quoodle* [1933]: from *The Collected Poems of G.K. Chesterton*, Methuen (London, 1932).

89   Churchill, C., *The Duellist* [1763]: from Grigson, Geoffrey (ed.), *The Oxford Book of Satirical Verse*, Oxford University Press (Oxford, 1980).

89a   Churchill, C., *The Ghost* [1762]: from Grigson, Geoffrey (ed.), *The Oxford Book of Satirical Verse*, Oxford University Press (Oxford, 1980).

89b   Churchill, C. *The Prophecy of Famine* [1763]: from Grigson, Geoffrey (ed.), *The Oxford Book of Satirical Verse*, Oxford University Press (Oxford, 1980).

90   Clark, Kenneth, *Another Part of the Wood* [1974]: from Parker, Eric (ed.), *Game Pie*, Country Life Books (London, 1977).

91   Clarke, H. Edwardes, *The Waterloo Cup*, Spur Publications (1978).

92   Cobbett, William, *Rural Rides* [1830], Everyman's Library (London, 1953).

93   Cofield, Thomas R. *Training the Hunting Retriever* [1959], D. van Nostrand (London, 1959).

94   Colquoun, J., *The Moor and the Loch* [1840]: from Parker, Eric (ed.), *Game Pie*, Country Life Books (London, 1977).

95   Colville, Robert, *Beagling and Otter-hunting*, Adamand Charles Black (Newton Abbot, 1940).

96   Corbet, G.B. and Hill, J.E., *World List of Mammalian Species* (1991).

97   Corbett, Jim, *Man Eaters of Kumaon* [1944], Oxford University Press (London, 1946).

98   Cotgrave, Randle, *A French and English Dictionaire* [1611]: from Parson, Daniel (ed.), *In Praise of Dogs*, Country Life Books (London, 1936), and Jesse, George R., *History of the British Dog*, Robert Hardwicke (London, 1866).

99   Cotton, Charles, *The Litany* [1675].

100   Cowell, J., *Cowell's Interpreter* [1607]: from Parson, Daniel (ed.), *In Praise of Dogs*, Country Life Books (London, 1936).

101   Cowen, G.A., *The Braes of Derwent Hunt* [1955], Northumberland Press (Gateshead, 1955)

102   Cowper, William, *John Gilpin* [1782], Frederick Warne (London, 1880?).

102a   Cowper, William, *Letter to Lady Hesketh* [1782]: from Parson, Daniel (ed.), *In Praise of Dogs*, Country Life Books (London, 1936).

102b   Cowper, William, *The Dog and the Water Lily* [1782]: from Menzies, Lucy (ed.), *The First Friend*, George Allen & Unwin (London, 1922).

102c   Cowper, William, *Epitaph to a Hare* [1785?]: from Parson, Daniel (ed.), *In Praise of Dogs*, Country Life Books (London, 1936).

103   Croxton-Smith, A. *About Our Dogs*, Ward Lock & Co. (London, 1931).

103a   Croxton-Smith, A., *Improving Sheepdogs* [1950]: from Parker, Eric and Croxton-Smith, A. (eds), *The Dog Lover's Weekend Book*, Seeley, Service & Co. (London, 1950).

104   Cummins, John, *The Hound and the Hawk*, Weidenfeld and Nicolson (London, 1988).

105   *Daily Telegraph*: from D'Oyley, Elizabeth (ed.), *An Anthology for Animal Lovers*, William Collins Sons (London, 1927).

106   Dalziel, Hugh, and Dear, H.C., *Breaking and Training Dogs* [1875], Upcott Gill (London, 1909).

106a   Dalziel, Hugh, *British Dogs* [1879], Upcott Gill (London, 1888–97).

107   Dana, C.A., *New York Sun* [1882], New York Sun (New York, 1882).

108   Daniel, William B., *Rural Sports* [1801]: from Parker, Eric (ed.), *Game Pie*, Country Life Books (London, 1977).

109   Darbyshire Ahr Pincher.

110   Darke, P.G.G., *Notes on Canine Internal Medicine* [1983], Wright (Bristol, 1986).

111   Darwin, Charles, *The Origin of the Species* [1859], Everyman's Library (London, 1971).

111a   Darwin, Charles, *The Expression of the Emotions in Man and Animals* [1872], John Murray (London, 1872).

111b   Darwin, Charles, *The Variation of Animals and Plants under Domestication* [1867], John Murray (London, 1875).

112   Daubuz, W., *Rules of Advice* [1840–55]: from Looker, Samuel J. (ed.), *The Chase*, Daniel O'Connor (London, 1922).

113   Davies, E.W.L., *Memoir of the Rev. J. Russell* [1878], Chatto & Windus (London, 1902).

114   Dawkins, Richard, *The Extended Phenotype* [1983], Oxford University Press (Oxford, 1992).

*114   Deeley, Martin, *Advanced Gundog Training*, The Crowood Press (Marlborough, 1990).

115   Denlinger, Milo G. et al, *The Complete Boxer* [1948], Howell Book House Inc. (New York, 1972).

116   de Prisco, A. and Johnson, J.B., *Canine Lexicon*, TFH Publications Inc. (New Jersey, 1993).

117   Descour, Louis, *Pasteur and His Work*.

118   Desmond, A. and Moore, J. *Darwin* [1991], Penguin (London, 1992).

119   Dewar, G. *The Faery Year* [1906]: from Parker, Eric (ed.), *Game Pie*, Country Life Books (London, 1977).

120   Dickens, Charles, *David Copperfield*, Oxford University Press (Oxford, 1987).

120a   Dickens, Charles, *Dombey and Son* [1846], Oxford University Press (Oxford, 1987).

120b   Dickens, Charles, *Oliver Twist* [1837], Oxford University Press (Oxford, 1987).

120c   Dickens, Charles, *The Fine Old English Gentleman* [1850], Oxford University Press (Oxford, 1987).

120d   Dickens, Charles, *The Pickwick Papers* [1836], Oxford University Press (Oxford, 1987).

121   Doughty, C.M., *Travels in Arabia Deserta* [1888]: from Ash, Edward, *Dogs: Their History and Development*, Ernest Benn (London, 1927).

122   Drayton, M., Idea, *The Shepherd's Garland* [1593]: from D'Oyley, Elizabeth (ed.), *An Anthology for Animal Lovers*, William Collins Sons, (London, 1927).

123   Drury, W.D., *British Dogs* [1903], Upcott Gill (London, 1903).

124   Edney, A.T.B. (ed.) *Heredity and Disease in Dogs and Cats* [1988], BSAVA (1988).

125   Edward, Duke of York, *The Master of Game* [1406], W., A. & F., Baillie-Grohman (London, 1904).

126   Edwardes, A.A.B., *A Girton Girl* [1890?].

127   Edwards, Sydenham, *Cynographia Britannica* [1800–5], (London, 1805).

128   Eliot, George, *Adam Bede* [1859]: from Vesey Fitzgerald, Brian, *The Book of the Dog*, Nicolson and Watson (London, 1948).

129   Elliot, G.F. Scott, *Prehistoric Man and his Story* [n.d.] Seeley, Service & Co. (London, n.d.).

130   Elliot, Rachel P., *Dogsteps* [1973] Howell Book House, Inc. (New York, 1973).

131   Ely, Scott, *Pit Bull* [1988] Penguin Books (London, 1990).

132   Emerson, R. Waldo (1856).

133   Farman, Edgar, *The Bulldog: A Monograph* [1899], Kennel Gazette (London, 1906).

134   Fiennes, Richard and Alice, *The Natural History of Dogs*, Weidenfeld & Nicholson (London, 1968).

135   Fiorone, Fiorenzo, *The Encyclopedia of Dogs* [1970], Fitzhenry and Whiteside (Toronto, 1973).

136   Fisher, J. *Cups at the Dog Show*: [n.d.] from Redlich, Anna (ed.), *A Golden Treasury of Dogs,* Skelton Robinson (London, n.d.).

137   Fitzpatrick, Sir Percy, *Jock of the Bushweld* [1907]: from Parker, Eric (ed.), *Game Pie* Country Life Books (London, 1977).

138   Flavianus, Arrianus, *Cynegetcus* [AD124], trans. George Dansey (London, 1831).

139   Fleming, Abraham, *Of Englishe Dogges* [1576], Denlinger (Washington DC, 1947).

140   Fortescue, Sir J.W., *My Native Devon* [1924]: Parker, Eric (ed.), *Game Pie* Country Life Books (London, 1977).

141   Fosbroke, T.D., *Encyclopaedia of Antiques*: from Redlich, Anna (ed.), *A Golden Treasury of Dogs*, Skelton Robinson (London, n.d.).

142   Franklyn, J.A., *Dictionary of Rhyming Slang*, Routledge (London, 1987).

143   Galsworthy, J., *Pitiful* [1911]: from D'Oyley, Elizabeth (ed.), *An Anthology for Animal Lovers*, William Collins Sons (London, 1927).

143a   Galsworthy, J., *The Forsyte Saga* (1920).

143b   Galsworthy, J., *The Patrician* (1911).

144   Gascoigne, George, *The Steele Glas* [1575]: from D'Oyley, Elizabeth (ed.), *An Anthology for Animal Lovers*, William Collins Sons (London, 1927).

145   Gay, John, *An Elegy on a Lapdog* [1726]: from Irving, William H. (ed.), *John Gay's London*, Archon Books, Hamden (Connecticut, 1968).

145a   Gay, John, *Rural Sports* [early 18th cent.]: from Irving, William H. (ed.), *John Gay's London*, Archon Books, Hamden (Connecticut, 1968).

145b   Gay, John, *Trivia* [1716]: from Irving, William H. (ed.), *John Gay's London*, Archon Books, Hamden (Connecticut, 1968).

145c   Gay, John, *The Art of walking the Streets of London* [1716]: from Irving, William H. (ed.), *John Gay's London*, Archon Books, Hamden (Connecticut, 1968)

145d   Gay, John, *The Birth of the Squire* [1720], *Selected Poems*, Fyfield Books (Manchester, 1979).

145e   Gay, John, *The Hound and the Huntsman* [1727]: from Irving, William H. (ed.), *John Gay's London*, Archon Books, Hamden (Connecticut, 1968).

145f   Gay, John, *The Mastiffs* [1727]: from Irving, William H. (ed.), *John Gay's London*, Archon Books, Hamden (Connecticut, 1968).

145g   Gay, John, *The Shepherd's Week* [1714]: from Irving, William H. (ed.), *John Gay's London*, Archon Books, Hamden (Connecticut, 1968).

146   Genders, Roy, *The Encyclopaedia of Greyhound Racing*, Pelham Books (London, 1981).

147   Gibbons, Stella, *Cold Comfort Farm* [1932], Penguin Books (London, 1983).

148   Gibson, A.C. *Keaty Curbison.*

149   Gilbert, John M., *Hunting and Hunting Reserves in Medieval Scotland*, John Macdonald (Edinburgh, 1979).

150   Glover, Harry, *A Standard Guide to Pure-Bred Dogs*, Macmillan (London, 1977).

151   Goldsmith, Oliver, *An Elegy on the Death of a Mad Dog* [1766], Frederick Warne (London, 1880?).

151a   Goldsmith, Oliver, *Animated Nature* [1766], Studio Editions (London, 1990).

151b   Goldsmith, Oliver, *The Deserted Village* [1766]: from Grigson, Geoffrey (ed.), *The Oxford Book of Satirical Verse,* Oxford University Press (Oxford, 1980).

151c   Goldsmith, Oliver, *The History of the Natural World* (1774).

152   Googe, Barnaby, *Foure Bookes of Husbandry* [1563]: from D'Oyley, Elizabeth (ed.), *An Anthology for Animal Lovers*, William Collins Sons (London, 1927).

153   Gough, Richard, *The History of Myddle* [1834], Penguin Books (London, 1982).

154   Grattius Faliscus, *Cynegetica*, [AD8], trans. Christopher Ware: from Jesse, George R., *History of the British Dog*, Robert Hardwicke (London, 1866).

155   Grave, J. *John Peel* [1832]: Mitchell, W.R., *The John Peel Story* Dalesman Pub. (1968).

156   Grayson, Peggy, *The History and Management of the Field Spaniel*, Scan Books (Brighton, 1984).

157   Grose, Francis, *Dictionary of the Vulgar Tongue* [1881], Macmillan (London, 1971).

158   H.H., *The Scientific Education of Dogs for the Gun* [1895], Sampson Low (Oxford, 1910).

159   Halliwell, James O., *Dictionary of Archaic Words* [1850], Bracken Books (London, 1989).

160   Hamilton-Wilkes, Monty and Cumming, David, *Kelpie and Cattle Dog* [1967], Angus and Robertson (London, 1982).

161   Hanger, Col. George, *To All Sportsmen* [1814]: from Parker, Eric (ed.), *Game Pie* Country Life Books (London, 1977).

162   Hare, K. *Sir Gawayne and the Green Knight* [14th cent.]: Looker, Samuel J. (ed.), *The Chase*, Daniel O'Connor (London, 1922).

163   Harington, Sir John, Letter to his wife for striking her dog [1596]: from Parson, Daniel (ed.), *In Praise of Dogs*, Country Life Books (London, 1936).

164   Hartwell, Dickson, *Dogs Against Darkness* [1944], Dodd Mead (New York, 1960).

165   Hawker, James, *A Victorian Poacher* [1961], Oxford University Press (Oxford, 1979).

166   Hawker, Lt.-Col. Peter, *Diary of a Sportsman* [1893]: Parker, Eric (ed.), *Game Pie*, Country Life Books (London, 1977).

166a   Hawker, Lt.-Col. Peter, *Instructions to Young Sportsmen* [1833], Ashford Press (Sheffield, 1986).

167   Henry IV of France, Letter to the Earl of Essex: from Jesse, George R., *History of the British Dog*, Robert Hardwicke (London, 1866).

168   Herbert, George, *Outlandish Proverbs* [1640]: from Browning, D.C. (ed.), *Everyman Dictionary of Quotations and Proverbs*, J.M. Dent & Sons (London, 1987).

169   Herrick, Robert, *Upon his Spaniell, Tracie*: from D'Oyley, Elizabeth (ed.), *An Anthology for Animal Lovers*, William Collins Sons (London, 1927).

170   Hesketh-Pritchard, H.V., *Sport in Wildest Britain* [1921]: Parker, Eric (ed.), *Game Pie* Country Life Books (London, 1977).

171   Heywood, J.A., *Dialogue containing the number and effect of all the Proverbs in the English Tongue* [1546]: from Browning, D.C. (ed.), *Everyman Dictionary of Quotations and Proverbs* J.M. Dent & Sons (London, 1987).

172   Hilliers, Ashton, *Demi-Royal*: from D'Oyley, Elizabeth (ed.), *An Anthology for Animal Lovers*, William Collins Sons (London, 1927).

173   Hogarth, M. and G. (eds.), *Collected Letters of Charles Dickens* (1882).

174   Hogg, James, *The Author's Address to his Auld Dog Hector* [1810]: from Parker, Eric and Croxton-Smith, A. (eds), *The Dog Lover's Weekend Book*, Seeley, Service & Co. (London, 1950).

175   Holdsworth, Jean, *Mango: The Life and Times of Squire John Mytton of Halston, 1796 to 1834*, Dobson Books (London, 1972).

176   Homan, Mike, *The Staffordshire Bull Terrier in History and Sport*, Nimrod Press (Hampshire, 1986).

177   Hood, Thomas, *Dog-grel verses, by a poor blind* [1826]: from Parson, Daniel (ed.), *In Praise of Dogs*, Country Life Books (London, 1936).

178   Horn, A., *The Ivory Coast in the Earlies* [1936?]: from Vesey Fitzgerald, Brian, *The Book of the Dog*, Nicholson & Watson (London, 1948).

179   Howard, Philip, *Weasel Words*, Hamish Hamilton (London, 1978).

180   Howitz, George, *The Alsatian*, Our Dogs (Manchester, 1923).

181   Hubbard, Clifford, L.B., *Dogs in Britain*, Macmillan & Co. (London, 1948).

181a   Hubbard, Clifford, L.B., *Working Dogs of the World* [1947], Sidgwick & Jackson (London, 1947).

182   Hudson, William, H., *A Shepherd's Life* (1910).

182a   Hudson, William, H., 'Dogs in London', in *The Book of a Naturalist* [1919], Wildwood House (London, 1980).

182b   Hudson, William, H. *The Book of a Naturalist* [1919] Wildwood House (London, 1980).

182c   Hudson, William, H., 'The Little Red Dog', in *The book of a Naturalist* [1919], Wildwood House (London, 1980).

183   Hume, David, *A Treatise of Human Nature* [1739]: from Thomas, Keith, *Man and the Natural World*, Penguin Books (London, 1984).

184   Hutchinson, Gen. W.N., *Dog Breaking: the Most Expeditious, Certain, and Easy Method*, John Murray (London, 1909).

185   Hutchinson, Walter (ed.), *Hutchinson's Popular & Illustrated Dog Encyclopaedia*, Hutchinson (London, 1935).

186   Idstone (Pearce, Thomas), *The Dog*, Cassell, Petter & Galpin (London, 1872).

187   Irving, Washington, *Abbotsford* [1820]: from Parson, Daniel (ed.), *In Praise of Dogs*, Country Life Books (London, 1936).

188   Jackson, Frank, *Crufts, the Official History*, Pelham Books (London, 1990).

188a   Jackson, Frank, *Dog Breeding, The Theory and the Practice*, The Crowood Press (Marlborough, 1994).

189   Jackson, Jean and Frank, *All About the Border Terrier*, Pelham Books (London, 1989).

189a   Jackson, Jean and Frank, *Parson Jack Russell Terriers*, The Crowood Press (Marlborough, 1990).

190   Jacob, G. *The Compleat Sportsman* [1718].

191   *Jamieson's Scottish Dictionary.*

192   Jaquet, Edward W., *The Kennel Club, A History and Record of its Work*, The Kennel Gazette (London, 1905).

193   Jefferies, Richard, *The Amateur Poacher* [1879], Longmans, Green & Co. (London, 1934).

194   Jerome, Jerome K., *Idle Thoughts of an Idle Fellow* [1889], Arrowsmith (Bristol, 1947).

194a   Jerome, Jerome K., *Second Thoughts of an Idle Fellow*, Hurst and Blackett (London, 1898).

194b   Jerome, Jerome K., *Three Men in a Boat* [1889], J.M. Dent & Sons (London, 1951).

195   Jesse, George R., *History of the British Dog*, Robert Hardwicke (London, 1866).

196   Johnson, Dr Samuel, *see* Boswell, James.

197   Johnston, George and Ericson, Maria, *Hounds of France*, Spur Publications (Hindhead, 1979).

198   Jones, E. Gwynne, *A Bibliography of the Dog*, The Library Assoc. (London, 1971).

199   Jonson, Ben, *English Grammar Made for the Benefit of Strangers* [1636]

199a   Jonson, Ben, *Every Man in his Humour* [1612]: from Parker, Eric and Croxton-Smith, A. (eds) *The Dog Lover's Weekend Book*, Seeley, Service & Co. (London, 1950).

200   Judy, Will, *The Chow Chow*, Judy (Chicago, 1934).

201   Kahn, Sammy, *You either got or you haven't got style.*

202   Kane, E.K., *The second Grimmel expedition in search of Sir John Franklin* [1885]: from Parson, Daniel (ed.), *In Praise of Dogs,* Country Life Books (London, 1963).

203   Kennel Club, The, *Breed Standards*, The Kennel Club (London, 1988).

203a   Kennel Club, The, *The Canine Code*, The Kennel Club (London, 1988).

204   Kelley, R.B., *Sheep Dogs: their breeding, maintenance and training* [1942], Angus & Robertson (Sydney, 1970).

205   Kelly, John, *Complete Collection of Scottish Proverbs* [1721]: from *The Everyman Dictionary of Quotations and Proverbs*, J.M. Dent & Sons (London, 1987).

206   Kerr, Eleanor, *Hunting Parson*, Herbert Jenkins (London, 1963).

207   Keyte-Perry, M. *The Samoyed*, Keyte-Perry (Woking, 1963).

208   Kingsley, Charles, *Hypatia or New Foes with Old Faces* [1853].

209   Kipling, Rudyard, *Action and Re-actions* [1903], *The Definitive Edition of Rudyard Kipling's Verse,* Macmillan (London, 1952).

209a   Kipling, Rudyard, *Just So Stories* [1902], Macmillan (London, 1952).

209b   Kipling, Rudyard, *The Hyaenas* [1903]: from Grigson, Geoffrey (ed.), *The Oxford Book of Satirical Verse,* Oxford University Press (Oxford, 1980).

209c   Kipling, Rudyard, *The Power of the Dog,* in *A Diversity of Creatures,* Macmillan (London, 1952).

210   Klein, Johann, *Textbook for Teaching the Blind* [1819]: *The Literary Dog,* Push Pin Press (New York, 1978).

211   Knight, E., *Lassie Come Home* [1938], Cassell (London, 1955).

212   Lacy, Richard, *The Modern Shooter* [1842]: from Parker, Eric (ed.), *Game Pie* Country Life Books (London, 1977).

213   Lamb, Charles, Letter to P.G. Patmore: from D'Oyley, Elizabeth (ed.), *An Anthology for Animal Lovers,* William Collins Sons (London, 1927).

214   Langland, William, *Piers Plowman* (1368).

215   Knight, Ruth A., *A Friend in the Dark,* Grosset & Dunlap (New York, 1937).

216   Landor, Walter S., *A Case at Sessions* [1824]: from Grigson, Geoffrey (ed.), *The Oxford Book of Satirical Verse,* Oxford University Press (Oxford, 1980).

216a   Landor, Walter S., *Bourbons* [1824]: from Grigson, Geoffrey (ed.), *The Oxford Book of Satirical Verse,* Oxford University Press (Oxford, 1980).

216b   Landor, Walter S., *The Scribblers* [1824]: from Grigson, Geoffrey (ed.), *The Oxford Book of Satirical Verse,* Oxford University Press (Oxford, 1980).

217   Lane, D.R., (Ed.), *Jones's Animal Nursing* [1966], Pergamon Press (Oxford, 1980).

218   Lavarack, Edward, *The Setter,* Longmans, Green & Co. (London, 1872).

219   Lawrence, D.H., *Rex,* in *The Dial,* Laurence Pollinger (London, 1921).

220   Lear, Edward, *More Nonsense Rhymes* (1871).

221   Lee, Rawdon B., *Modern Dogs,* Horace Cox (London, 1897).

222   Lehmann, Rudolph C., *Lady, a Sheep-dog* [1913]: from Menzies, Lucy (ed.), *The First Friend,* George Allen & Unwin (London, 1922).

222a   Lehmann, Rudolph C., *To Rufus, a Spaniel* [1913]: from Parson, Daniel (ed.), *In Praise of Dogs,* Country Life Books (London, 1936).

223   Leiber, Jerry and Stoller, Mike, *Hound Dog* [1956].

224   Leibling, A. Joseph, *The Honest Rainmaker* [1952], Fourth Estate (London, 1991).

225   Leighton, Robert, *Dogs and All About Them* [1910], Cassell (London, 1911).

225a   Leighton, Robert, *The Complete Book of the Dog* [1922] Cassell (London, 1932).

225b   Leighton, Robert, *The New Book of the Dog* [1906], Cassell (London, 1907).

226   Levy, Capt. R., *The Modern Shooter* [1842]: from Vesey Fitzgerald, Brian, *The Book of the Dog,* Nicholson & Watson (London, 1948).

227   Lilico, James, *Sheep Dog Memoirs* [New Zealand, 1880?]: from Kelley, R.B., *Sheep Dogs,* Angus and Robertson (Sydney 1970).

*227   Liné, Carl von [Carolus Linnaeus] *Systemae Naturae* (Amsterdam, 1735).

228   Lloyd, E., *The Methodist* [1776?].

229   Lloyd, Freeman, *The Whippet or Race-dog* (1776?), Upcott Gill (London, 1904).

230   Lloyd, H.S., *The Cocker Spaniel,* W & G Foyle (London, 1957).

231   Lloyd, Robert, *A Familiar Epistle to J.B. Esq.* (1764?).

232   Loisel, G. *Histoire des Manageries,* Doin et Fils (Paris, 1912).

233   *London Gazette* (1667).

234   Longfellow, William, *Golden Legend* (1851).

235   Lonsdale, Earl of and Parker, Eric, *Foxhunting,* Seeley, Service & Co. (London, 1930).

236   Lowe, Brian, *Hunting the Clean Boot,* Blandford Press (Dorset 1981).

237   Lucas, A., *E.V. Lucas, A portrait:* from Parker, Eric and Croxton-Smith, A. (ed.), *The Dog Lover's Weekend Book,* Seeley Service & Co. (London, 1950).

238   Lucas, Sir Jocelyn, *Hunt and Working Terriers,* Chapman & Hall (London, 1931).

238a   Lucas, Sir Jocelyn, *The Sealyham Terrier,* T.H. Crumbie (Leicester, 1922).

239   Lytton, The Hon. Mrs Neville, *Toy Dogs and their Ancestors,* Duckworth & Co. (London, 1911).

240   Macaulay, Thomas B., *History of England* (1849–61).

241   Mackenzie, Osgood, *A Hundred Years in the Highlands* [1921]): from Parker, Eric (ed.), *Game Pie,* Country Life Books (London, 1977).

242   Mackie, Sir Peter M., *The Keeper's Book* [1904], G.T. Foulis & Co. (London, 1924).

243   Malory, Sir Thomas, *Morte d'Arthur* [1478]: from Menzies, Lucy (ed.), *The First Friend*, George Allen & Unwin (London, 1922).

244   March, Earl of, *Records of the Old Charlton Hunt* [1910], quoting an anonymous poem [1737], Earl of March (1910).

245   Markham, Gervaise, *Hunger's Prevention or the Art of Fowling* [1615]: from Thomas, Keith, *Man and the Natural World*, Penguin Books (London, 1984).

245a   Markham, Gervaise, *Country Contentments* [1615]: from Thomas, Keith, *Man and the Natural World*, Penguin Books (London, 1984).

246   Markland, George, *Pteryplegia, or the Art of Shooting Flying* [1727]: from Parker, Eric (ed.), *Game Pie*, Country Life Books (London, 1977).

247   Marquis, Don, *certain maxims of archy* [1931], in *archy and mehitabel*, Faber and Faber (London, 1944).

247a   Marquis, Don, *the wail of archy* [1931], in *archy and mehitabel*, Faber and Faber (London, 1944).

248   Marston, John, *I was a Scholar* [1598]: from D'Oyley, Elizabeth (ed.), *An Anthology for Animal Lovers*, William Collins Sons (London, 1927).

249   Masefield, John, *Reynard the Fox* [1919], William Heinemann (London, 1926).

249a   Masefield, John, *The Ghost Heath Run* [1919], William Heinemann (London, 1926).

250   Mayhew, Henry, *London Labour and the London Poor* [1851], Spring Books (London, 1969).

251   McCausland, Hugh, *Old Sporting*, Batchworth Press (London, 1948).

252   McCulloch, J. Herries, *Sheepdogs and their Masters*, Robert Dinwiddie (Dumfries, 1938).

253   Middleton, Thomas, *The Roaring Girl* (1611).

254   Miller, M.B., *Guide to the Dissection of the Dog* [1947], Ithaca (New York, 1962).

255   Mitchell, A., *The Dobermann* (1980).

256   Mitchell, W.R., *The John Peel Story*, Dalesman Pub. Co. (Lancaster, 1968).

257   Moore, Daphne, *The Book of the Foxhound*, A. Allen & Co. (London, 1964).

258   Moore, Thomas, *Tory Pledges* [1852?]: from Grigson, Geoffrey (ed.), *The Oxford Book of Satirical Verse*, Oxford University Press (Oxford, 1980).

259   More, Sir Thomas, *Utopia* [1516]: from D'Oyley, Elizabeth (ed.), *An Anthology for Animal Lovers*, William Collins Sons (London, 1927).

260   Mortimer, Geoffrey, *The Field* (1901).

261   Munro, H.H. (Saki), *Beasts and Super Beasts* (1914).

262   Nash, Ogden, *The Private Dining Room* [1952], J.M. Dent & Sons (London, 1953).

263   Nash, T., *Pierce Penniless* (1552).

264   Newell, R.S., *The American Traveller*.

265   Niblock, Margaret, *The Afghan Hound: A Definitive Study*, K & R Classics (Horncastle, 1980).

266   Nimrod, *Hunting Reminiscences* [1843], John Lane, The Bodley Head (London, 1926).

266a   Nimrod, *Memoirs of the Life of the Late John Mytton, Esq.* [1837], Methuen & Co. (London, 1936).

266b   Nimrod, *The Life of a Sportsman* [1832], John Lehmann (London, 1948).

266c   Nimrod, *The Road*: from de Broke, Lord Willoughby (ed.), *The Sport of our Ancestors*, Constable and Co. (London, 1921).

267   Noakes, A., *Sportsmen in a Landscape* [1954]: from Parker, Eric (ed.), *Game Pie*, Country Life Books (London, 1977).

268   Nottingham, The Earl of, Letter to Robert Cecil [1598]; from Parson, Daniel, (ed.), *In Praise of Dogs*, Country Life Books (London, 1936).

269   North American Beauceron Club, *Breed Standard*, North American Beauceron Club (New York, 1992).

*269   Oakleigh Shooting Code [1833]: from Parker, Eric (ed.), *Game Pie*, Country Life Books (London, 1977).

270   O'Conor, Pierce, *Sporting Terriers*, Hutchinson & Co. (London, 1926).

271   O'Farrell, Valerie, *Manual of Canine Behaviour*, BSAVA (1986).
272   Ogilvie, Will H., *Alone with Hounds*, in *The Collected Sporting Verse of Will H. Ogilvie*, Constable & Co. (London, 1932).
272a Ogilvie, Will H., *A Moorland Signpost*, in *The Collected Sporting Verse of Will H. Ogilvie* Constable & Co. (London, 1932).
272b Ogilvie, Will H., *A Single Hound*, in *The Collected Sporting Verse of Will H. Ogilvie*, Constable & Co. (London, 1932).
272c Ogilvie, Will H., *Dandie Dinmonts*, in *The Collected Sporting Verse of Will H. Ogilvie*, Constable & Co. (London, 1932).
272d Ogilvie, Will H., *Nobody with Them*, in *The Collected Sporting Verse of Will H. Ogilvie*, Constable & Co. (London, 1932).
272e Ogilvie, Will H., *The First Whip*, in *The Collected Sporting Verse of Will H. Ogilvie*, Constable & Co. (London, 1932).
272f Ogilvie, Will H., *The Hill Men*, in *The Collected Sporting Verse of Will H. Ogilvie*, Constable & Co. (London, 1932).
272g Ogilvie, Will H., *The Moonraker*, in *The Collected Sporting Verse of Will H. Ogilvie*, Constable & Co. (London, 1932).
272h Ogilvie, Will H., *The Perfect Hat*, in *The Collected Sporting Verse of Will H. Ogilvie*, Constable & Co. (London, 1932).
272i Ogilvie, Will H., *The Right Sort*, in *The Collected Sporting Verse of Will H. Ogilvie*, Constable & Co. (London, 1932).
272j Ogilvie, Will H., *The White Hound* in *The Collected Sporting Verse of Will H. Ogilvie*, Constable & Co. (London, 1932).
272k Ogilvie, Will H., *To a Brace of Setters*, in *The Collected Sporting Verse of Will H. Ogilvie*, Constable & Co. (London, 1932).
272l Ogilvie, Will H., *'Ware Heel!*, in *The Collected Sporting Verse of Will H. Ogilvie*, Constable & Co. (London, 1932).
273   Oldham, John, *A satire addressed to a friend* [1683]: from Grigson, Geoffrey (ed.), *The Oxford Book of Satirical Verse,* Oxford University Press (Oxford, 1980).
274   Ollivant, Alfred, *Danny* [1903]: from Menzies, Lucy (ed.), *The First Friend*, George Allen & Unwin (London, 1922).
275   Onstott, Philip, *The New Art of Breeding Better Dogs* [1968].
276   Oppian [211BC]: from Ash, Edward, *Dogs: Their History and Development*, Ernest Benn (London, 1927).
*276 Ovid [Publius Ovidius Naso], *Metamorphoses* [42 BC–AD17], trans. Golding.
*276a Ovid [Publius Ovidius Naso], *Metamorphoses* [43 BC–AD17], trans. N. Tate (1682).
277   Paley, Sir William, *Evidences of Christianity* [1794]: from Thomas, Keith, *Man and the Natural World*, Penguin Books (London, 1984).
278   Parker, Dorothy, *Mr Durant* (1936).
279   Parker, Eric, *Best of Dogs*, Hutchinson & Co. (London, 1949).
279a Parker, Eric (ed.), *Game Pie*, Country Life Books (London, 1977).
280   Partridge, Eric, *A Dictionary of the Underworld* [1950], Wordsworth Editions (London, 1989).
281   Patmore, P.G., *Dash visits Charles Lamb*: from D'Oyley, Elizabeth (ed.), *An Anthology for Animal Lovers*, William Collins Sons (London, 1927).
282   Penn, William, *Some Fruits of Solitude in Reflections and Maxims Relating to the Conduct of Humane Life* [1669]: from Thomas, Keith, *Man and the Natural World*, Penguin Books (London, 1984).
283   Percy, Thomas, *Faery Pastoral* [1795]: from Halliwell, James O. (ed.), *Dictionary of Archaic Words* [1850], Bracken Books (London, 1989).
284   Philips, K., *The Irish Greyhound* [1664]: from Jesse, George R., *The History of the British Dog*, Robert Hardwicke (London, 1866).
285   Phillips, C.A. & Cane, R.C., *The Sporting Spaniel*, Our Dogs Pub. Co. (Manchester, 1906).
286   Pliny the Elder, *Natural History* [AD77]: from Parker, Eric and Croxton-Smith, A. (eds), *The Dog Lover's Weekend Book*, Seeley, Service & Co. (London, 1950).

287   Plutarch, *Life of Cato, the Censor* [AD98]: from Parker, Eric and Croxton-Smith, A. (eds), *The Dog Lover's Weekend Book*, Seeley, Service & Co. (London, 1950).

288   Pope, Alexander, *Sporus* [1728]: from Thomas, Keith, *Man and the Natural World*, Penguin Books (London, 1984).

288a   Pope, Alexander, *The Rape of the Lock* [1712]: from Grigson, Geoffrey (ed.). *The Oxford Book of Satirical Verse*, Oxford University Press (Oxford, 1980).

289   Puxley, W.L., *Collies and Sheep Dogs*, Williams & Norgate (1948).

290   Rabelais, François, *Gargantua and Pantagruel* [1534], World Classics, Penguin Books (London, 1934).

291   Raspe, Rudolph E., *The Travels and Surprising Adventures of Baron Munchausen* [1785], Dedalus (Sawtry, 1988).

292   Ray, J., *English Proverbs* [1670]: from Browning, D.C. (ed.), *The Everyman Dictionary of Quotations and Proverbs*, J.M. Dent & Sons (London, 1987).

293   Read, Joan, *The Norfolk Terrier*, Read (Livermore, 1989).

294   Reade, Charles, *The Cloister and the Hearth* [1861]: from D'Oyley, Elizabeth (ed.), *An Anthology for Animal Lovers*, William Collins Sons (London, 1927).

295   Redlich, Anna, *The Dogs of Ireland*, W. Tempest, Dundalgan Press (Dundalk, 1949).

296   Reid, Ed, *Canine Gladiators of Old and Modern Times*, Reid (London, 1980).

297   Renwick, W. Lewis, *The Whippet Handbook*, Nicholson & Watson (London, 1957).

298   Richardson, C., *Hunting in Many Countries*, The Field Press (London, 1922).

299   Riddle, Maxwell, *The Wild Dogs in Life and Legend*, Howell Book House Inc. (New York, 1979).

300   Rig-Veda, *Prayer to Yama* [2000BC]: from Ash, Edward, *Dogs: Their History and Development*, Ernest Benn (London, 1927).

301   Robinson, Roy, *Genetics for Dog Breeders*, Pergamon Press (Oxford, n.d.).

302   Rochester, Earl of, *Tunbridge Wells* (c1667).

303   Root, M.R., Kent, R.F., and Martin, J. (eds), *The Official Book of the Schipperke*, Howell Book House Inc. (New York, 1976).

304   Roper, H.T. (ed.), *Hitler's Table Talk*, Weidenfeld & Nicholson (London, 1973).

305   Rosten, Leo, *The Joys of Yiddish*.

*305   Rules of the National Coursing Club.

306   Runyon, Damon, *The Bloodhounds of Broadway*, in *Runyon on Broadway* [1937], Constable & Co. (London, 1950).

*306   Rutherford, James H., *History of the Linlithgow and Stirlingshire Hunt*, William Blackwood & Sons (Edinburgh, 1911).

307   Spottiswoode, J., *The Moorland Gamekeeper*, David and Charles (Newton Abbot, 1977).

308   Sandy-Winsch, Geoffrey, *The Dog Law Handbook*, Shaw and Sons (Crayford, 1993).

309   Sassoon, Siegfried, *Memoirs of a Foxhunting Man* [1928], Faber and Faber (London, 1930).

310   Savage R., *The Progress of a Divine* [1726]: from Grigson, Geoffrey (ed.), *The Oxford Book of Satirical Verse*, Oxford University Press (Oxford, 1980).

311   Saxe, J.G., *Ho-Ho of the Golden Belt* [1887]: from Silcock, Arnold (ed.), *Verse and Worse*, Faber & Faber (London, 1977).

312   Schneider-Leyer, Dr Erich, *Dogs of the World* [1960], Stanley Paul (London, 1964).

313   Scott, Capt. R., *Voyage of Discovery* [1906], John Murray (London).

314   Scott, Sir Walter, *Guy Mannering* [1815], Everyman's Library (London, 1968).

314a   Scott, Sir Walter, *Marmion* (1808).

314b   Scott, Sir Walter, *Rob Roy* [1817], Everyman's Library (London, 1966).

314c   Scott, Sir Walter, *The Lady of the Lake* (1810).

314d   Scott, Sir Walter, *The Lay of the Last Minstrel* (1805).

314e   Scott, Sir Walter, *The Talisman* [1826], Everyman's Library (London, 1973).

315   Scrope, William, *The Art of Deerstalking* [1838], John Murray (London, 1897).

316   Sentinel, *Hounds: their breeding and kennel management*, Horace Cox (London, 1905).

317   Serpell, James, *In the Company of Animals*, Basil Blackwell (Oxford, 1986).

318   Serrell, Alys F., *With Hound and Terrier in the Field*, William Blackwood (London, 1904).

319   Shakespeare, William, *As You Like It* [1599]: *The Complete Works of William Shakespeare*, Oxford University Press (Oxford, 1955).

319a   Shakespeare, William, *Comedy of Errors* [1592]: *The Complete Works of William Shakespeare*, Oxford University Press (Oxford, 1955).

319b   Shakespeare, William, *Coriolanus* [1607]: *The Complete Works of William Shakespeare*, Oxford University Press (Oxford, 1955).

319c   Shakespeare, William, *Hamlet* [1600]: *The Complete Works of William Shakespeare*, Oxford University Press (Oxford, 1955).

319d   Shakespeare, William, *Henry IV, Part I* [1597]: *The Complete Works of William Shakespeare*, Oxford University Press (Oxford, 1955).

319e   Shakespeare, William, *Julius Caesar* [1599]: *The Complete Works of William Shakespeare*, Oxford University Press (Oxford, 1955).

319f   Shakespeare, William, *King Henry V* [1599]: *The Complete Works of William Shakespeare*, Oxford University Press (Oxford, 1955).

319g   Shakespeare, William, *King Henry VI* [1590]: *The Complete Works of William Shakespeare*, Oxford University Press (Oxford, 1955).

319h   Shakespeare, William, *King Lear* [1605]: *The Complete Works of William Shakespeare*, Oxford University Press (Oxford, 1955).

319i   Shakespeare, William, *Macbeth* [1605]: *The Complete Works of William Shakespeare*, Oxford University Press (Oxford, 1955).

319j   Shakespeare, William, *Merry Wives of Windsor* [1602]: *The Complete Works of William Shakespeare*, Oxford University Press (Oxford, 1955).

319k   Shakespeare, William, *Midsummer Night's Dream* [1595]: *The Complete Works of William Shakespeare*, Oxford University Press (Oxford, 1955).

319l   Shakespeare, William, *Much Ado About Nothing* [1598]: *The Complete Works of William Shakespeare*, Oxford University Press (Oxford, 1955).

319m   Shakespeare, William, *Othello* [1622]: *The Complete Works of William Shakespeare*, Oxford University Press (Oxford, 1955).

319n   Shakespeare, William, *Richard III* [1592]: *The Complete Works of William Shakespeare*, Oxford University Press (Oxford, 1955).

319p   Shakespeare, William, *Romeo and Juliet* [1597]: *The Complete Works of William Shakespeare*, Oxford University Press (Oxford, 1955).

319q   Shakespeare, William, *Taming of the Shrew* [1593]: *The Complete Works of William Shakespeare*, Oxford University Press (Oxford, 1955).

319r   Shakespeare, William, *The Tempest* [1623]: *The Complete Works of William Shakespeare*, Oxford University Press (Oxford, 1955).

319s   Shakespeare, William, *Timon of Athens* [1623]: *The Complete Works of William Shakespeare*, Oxford University Press (Oxford, 1955).

319t   Shakespeare, William, *Titus Andronicus* [1594]: *The Complete Works of William Shakespeare*, Oxford University Press (Oxford, 1955).

319u   Shakespeare, William, *Troilus and Cressida* [1609]: *The Complete Works of William Shakespeare*, Oxford University Press (Oxford, 1955).

319v   Shakespeare, William, *Twelfth Night* [1623]: *The Complete Works of William Shakespeare*, Oxford University Press (Oxford, 1955).

319vv   Shakespeare, William, *The Rape of Lucrece* [1594]: *The Complete Works of William Shakespeare*, Oxford University Press (Oxford, 1955).

319w   Shakespeare, William, *Two Gentlemen of Verona* [1594]: *The Complete Works of William Shakespeare*, Oxford University Press (Oxford, 1955).

319x   Shakespeare, William, *Venus and Adonis* [1593]: *The Complete Works of William Shakespeare*, Oxford University Press (Oxford, 1955).

320   Shaw, Vero, *The Encyclopedia of the Kennel*, George Routledge (London, 1913).

320a   Shaw, Vero, *The Illustrated Book of the Dog*, Cassell, Petter, Galpin & Co. (London, 1890).

321   Shelley, Percy B., *Prometheus, The Mask of Anarchy* [1819]: from Grigson, Geoffrey (ed.), *The Oxford Book of Satirical Verse*, Oxford University Press (Oxford, 1980).

322   Sitwell, Sir Osbert, *The Gamekeeper* (1919).

323   Skelton, John, *At Elinor Rumming's Ale-house* [*c.*1529]: from *The Complete English Poems*, J. Scattergood, (London, 1983).

324   Skinner, J.S., *The Dog and the Sportsman*, Lea & Blanchard (Philadelphia, 1845).

325   Smart, C., *Praise of the Bulldog* [1760]: from Jesse, George R., *History of the British Dog*, Robert Hardwicke (London, 1866).

326   Smith, Sidney, *An Honest Creature* [1820?]: from Jackson, Frank and Jean (eds), *Dog Tales*, Richard Marples & Partners (Manchester, 1981).

*326   Smith, Thomas, *The Life of a Fox, as Written by Himself*.

327   Smollett, Tobias, *The Expedition of Humphrey Clinker* [1771], Folio Society (London, 1955).

328   Somervile, William, *The Chace* [1735], George Redway (London, 1896).

328a   Somervile, William, *Field Sports* (1742).

329   Somerville, E. OE, *An Appreciation* [1934]: from Brand, Gordon, *The Silver Horn*, Country Life Books (London, 1934).

329a   Somerville, E. OE & Ross, M., *Further Experiences of an Irish R.M.* [1902], Everyman's Library (London, 1983).

329b   Somerville, E. OE & Ross, M., *Some Experiences of an Irish R.M.* [1899], T. Nelson & Sons (London, n.d.).

330   Southey, Robert, *Letters from England* [1807], The Cresset Press (London, 1951).

331   Sparrow, Geoffrey, *The Terriers Vocation*, Corbridge Press (Hove, 1949).

332   Spencer, William R., *Beth Gelert or The Grave of the Greyhound* [1793]: from Menzies, Lucy (ed.), *The First Friend*, George Allen & Unwin (London, 1922).

333   Spenser, Edmund, *The Faerie Queen* [1590], Everyman's Library (London, 1964).

333a   Spenser, Edmund, *The Shepherd's Calendar* [1597]: from Ash, Edward, *Dogs: Their History and Development*, Ernest Benn (London, 1927).

334   Stagg, J., *New Year's Epistle*.

335   Steinbeck, John, *Travels with Charley in Search of America* [1962], from Covici, Pascal (ed.), *The Portable Steinbeck*, Penguin Books (London, 1979).

336   Stevenson, Robert Louis, *The Character of Dogs* [1885]: from Menzies, Lucy (ed.), *The First Friend*, George Allen & Unwin (London, 1922).

337   St John, C., *Wild Sports and Natural History of the Highlands* [1846], Macdonald Futura (London, 1981).

338   Stonehenge, *The Dog in Health and Disease* [1872], Longmans, Greens and Co. (London, 1887).

339   Strickland, A., *A Country Dog in Town*.

340   Stuart, Dorothy M., *A Book of Birds and Beasts*, Methuen & Co. (London, 1957).

341   Stuart-Wortley, Archibald, *The Partridge* [1893]: from Parker, Eric (ed.), *Game Pie*, Country Life Books (London, 1977).

342   Stubbes, J., *Anatomie of Abuses* (1583).

343   Summers, *Last Will and Testament*.

344   Surtees, Robert S., *Handley Cross* [1854], Methuen & Co. (London, 1903).

344a   Surtees, Robert S., *Hawbuck Grange*, The Folio Society (London, 1955).

344b   Surtees, Robert S., *Jorrocks's Jaunts and Jollities* [1838], Methuen & Co. (London, 1951).

344c   Surtees, Robert S., *Mr Facey Romford's Hounds* [1865], The Folio Society (London, 1952).

344d   Surtees, Robert S., *Mr Sponge's Sporting Tour*, Bradbury and Evans (London, 1853).

344e   Surtees, Robert S., *The Analysis of the Hunting Field* [1846], Edward Arnold (London, 1923).

345   Sutton, Catherine G., *Dog Shows and Show Dogs*, K.R. Books (Horncastle, 1980).

346   Swift, J., *On Poetry: A Rhapsody* [1733]: from Grigson, Geoffrey (ed.), *The Oxford Book of Satirical Verse*, Oxford University Press (Oxford, 1980).

346a   Swift, J., *On Rover, A Lady's Spaniel: instructions to a painter* [1733]: from Redlich, Anna (ed.), *A Golden Treasury of Dogs*, Skelton Robinson (London, n.d.).

346b   Swift, J., *A Description of a City Shower*.

347   Taber, Robert, *The War of the Flea*.
348   Taplin, William, *The Sportsman's Cabinet*, J. Cundee (London, 1803).
349   Tatham, Julie C., *World Book of Dogs*, World Publishing Co. (Cleveland, US, 1953).
350   Taylor, John, *The World Runnes on Wheeles* [1630]: from Redlich, Anna (ed.), *A Golden Treasury of Dogs*, Skelton Robinson (London, n.d.).
351   Tennyson, Alfred Lord, *Queen Mary* (1892?).
352   Thackeray, William M., *Vanity Fair* [1848], William Collins Sons? (London, n.d.).
353   *The Animal's Friend*.
354   Thomas, A., in *The Spectator* [1711], Everyman's Library (London, 1979).
355   Thomas, Dylan, *Under Milk Wood* [1954], J.M. Dent & Sons (London, 1954).
356   Thorne, C. (ed.), *The Waltham Book of Dog and Cat Care*, Pergamon Press (Oxford, 1992).
*356   *The Times*, 24 April 1845.
357   Todd, D.P., *The Terrier Song* [1980?]: from Jackson, Frank and Jean (eds), *Dog Tales*, Richard Marples & Partners (Manchester, 1981).
358   Tongue, Cornelius, *Records of the Chase*, George Routledge (London, 1854).
359   Topsell, William, *Historie of the Foure-Footed Beastes* [1607]: from Parson, Daniel (ed.), *In Praise of Dogs*, Country Life Books (London, 1936).
360   Tracy, J., *To the Author of the Chace*.
361   Triquet, R. and Wachtel, H., *Dreisprachiges Taschenwörterbuch der Kynologie*, Herausgegeben von der Hundeforschungsstelle des Osterreichischen Kynologenverbandes [Austrian Kennel Club] (1991).
362   Trollope, Anthony, *Last Chronicle of Barset* [1857], Macdonald & Co. (New York, 1978).
363   Turberville, George, *The Noble Art of Venerie or Hunting, translated and collected for the Use of all Noblemen and Gentlemen* [1576], Clarendon Press (London, 1908).
364   Turner, Trevor (ed.), *Veterinary Notes for Dog Owners*, Stanley Paul (London, 1990).
365   Twain, Mark, *Uncle Lem's Composite Dog* [1900?]: The Literary Dog, Pushpin Press (New York, 1978).
366   Twiti, Edward, *The Art of Hunting* [1328], trans. Sir Henry Dryden, Middle Hall Press (1843).
367   United Kennel Club *Breed Standards*, United Kennel Club (nd).
368   Vesey Fitzgerald, Brian, *The Book of the Dog*, Nicholson & Watson (London, 1948).
369   Vezins, Comte Élie de, *Hounds for a Pack* [1882], J.A. Allen (London, 1974).
370   Virgil, *Georgics* (37BC): from Vesey Fitzgerald, Brian, *The Book of the Dog*, Nicholson and Watson (London, 1948).
370a   Virgil, *The Art of Husbandry* (37BC).
371   Vyner, R.T., *Notitia Venatica* [1841], George Routledge (New York, 1910).
372   Wagner, R., *My Life* (1911).
374   Walpole, Sir Hugh, *Jeremy and Hamlet* (1930?): from Vesey Fitzgerald, Brian, *The Book of the Dog*, Nicholson & Watson (London, 1948).
374a   Walpole, Sir Hugh, *The Whistle* [1930?]: from Redlich, Anna (ed.), *A Golden Treasury of Dogs*, Skelton Robinson (London, n.d.).
375   Walsh, Edward, G., *Longdogs by Day*, Boydell Press (Suffolk, 1990).
375a   Walsh, Edward G., *Lurchers and Longdogs* [1977], Boydell Press (Suffolk 1990).
376   Walsh, J. Henry, *The Dogs of the British Isles* [1867], Horace Cox (London, 1872).
377   Walton, Isaac, *The Compleat Angler* [1653], Everyman's Library (London, 1974).
378   Waters, Bernard W., *Modern Training, Handling and Kennel Management*, Blakely Printing Co. (Chicago, 1889).
379   Watson, Frederick, *Hunting Pie*, H.F. & G. Witherby (London, 1931).
379a   Watson, Frederick, *In the Pink*, H.F. & G. Witherby (London, 1932).
380   Watson, James, *The Dog Book*, Heinemann (London, 1906).
381   Watson, John, *Poachers and Poaching*, Chapman and Hall (1891).
382   Waugh, Evelyn, *Decline and Fall* [1928], Penguin Books (London, 1951).
383   Wentworth Day, J., *The Dog in Sport*, Harrap (London, 1935).

*383   West, G. (ed.), *Black's Veterinary Dictionary* 13th edn, A & C Black (London, 1979).

384   Whitaker, John, *The History of Manchester* [1771]: from Jackson, Frank and Jean (eds), *Dog Tales*, Richard Marples & Partners (Manchester, 1981).

385   White, H.K., *Clifton Grove* (1803).

386   White, Rev. Gilbert, *Natural History and Antiquities of Selbourne* [1789], Harmonsworth Press (London, 1941).

387   White, Tim H., *England Have My Bones*, Collins (London, 1936).

387a   White, Tim H., *Dogs Have No Souls* [1939], in *A Joy Proposed*, Secker and Warburg (London, 1982).

387b   White, Tim H., *Once and Future King* [1958], Collins (London, 1961).

388   Whyte-Melville, G.J., *The Good Grey Mare* [1869]: from Looker, Samuel J. (ed.), *The Chase*, Daniel O'Connor (London, 1922).

388a   Whyte-Melville, G.J., *The King of the Kennel* [1869]: from Looker, Samuel J. (ed.), *The Chase*, Daniel O'Connor (London, 1922).

388b   Whyte-Melville, G.J., *Market Harborough* [1861], Country Life Books (London, 1933).

389   Wilcox, B. and Walkowicz, C., *The Atlas of Dog Breeds of the World*, TFH Publications Inc. (New Jersey, 1989).

390   Wilde, Oscar, *A Woman of No Importance* [1893].

391   Wilhelm, Andre, *The Dobermann*, Kaye and Ward (London, 1980).

392   Willett, A., *Hexapla in Leviticum.*

393   Williams, Charles, *Dogs and their Ways* [1865], George Routledge & Sons (London, 1865).

394   Williams, Sir R., *Actions in the Low Countries* [1618]: from Ash, Edward, *Dogs: Their History and Development*, Ernest Benn (London, 1927).

395   Willis, Malcolm B., *Practical Genetics for Dog Breeders*, Witherby (London, 1992).

396   Willoughby de Broke, Lord, *The Sport of our Ancestors*, Constable & Co. (London, 1921).

397   Wilmot, J., *Earl of Rochester, The Disabled Debauchee* [1675]: from Grigson, Geoffrey (ed.), *The Oxford Book of Satirical Verse*, Oxford University Press (Oxford, 1980).

398   Wilmot, Sir J.E., *The Reminiscences of a Foxhunter* [1880]: from Jackson, Jean and Frank, *Dog Tales*, Richard Marples & Partners (Manchester, 1981).

399   Witney, Leon F., *The Complete Book of Dog Care*, Howell Book House Inc. (New York, 1937).

400   Wodehouse, P.G., *Nothing Serious* [1936?], Herbert Jenkins (London, n.d.).

401   Wood, Frederick, *Sport and Nature in Sussex Downs*, Duckworth (London, 1928).

402   Wordsworth, William, *The Prelude* (1805).

403   Wynn, M.B., poem [n.d.]: from Redlich, Anna (ed.), *A Golden Treasury of Dogs*, Skelton Robinson (London, n.d.).

404   X, Malcolm.

405   Xenophon, *Cynegetica*: from Vesey Fitzgerald, Brian, *The Domestic Dog*, Routledge & Kegan Paul (London, 1957).

406   Youatt, William, *The Dog*, Longman, Brown, Green & Longmans (London, 1854).

407   Zend-Avesta, [18th cent.]: from Sloan A. and Farquar A., *A Dog and Man*, Hutchinson & Co. (London, 1925).